POLITICS ANI
MAKING IN 1

CU00324260

POLITICS AND POLICY MAKING IN THE UK

Paul Cairney and Sean Kippin

BRISTOL
UNIVERSITY
PRESS

First published in Great Britain in 2024 by

Bristol University Press
University of Bristol
1–9 Old Park Hill
Bristol
BS2 8BB
UK
t: +44 (0)117 374 6645
e: bup-info@bristol.ac.uk

Details of international sales and distribution partners are available at bristoluniversitypress.co.uk

© Bristol University Press 2024

British Library Cataloguing in Publication Data
A catalogue record for this book is available from the British Library

ISBN 978-1-5292-2234-0 hardcover
ISBN 978-1-5292-2235-7 paperback
ISBN 978-1-5292-2236-4 ePub
ISBN 978-1-5292-2237-1 ePdf

Cover design: Nicky Borowiec
Front cover image: Adobe Stock / wacomka
Bristol University Press uses environmentally responsible print partners.
Printed and bound in Great Britain by CPI Group (UK) Ltd, Croydon, CR0 4YY

FSC
www.fsc.org
MIX
Paper | Supporting
responsible forestry
FSC® C013604

Contents

List of Figures, Tables and Boxes

About the Authors

Paul Cairney is Professor of Politics and Public Policy, University of Stirling, UK (@Cairneypaul). His research includes comparisons of policy theories (*Understanding Public Policy*, 2020), co-authored accounts of international policy processes (*Global Tobacco Control*, 2012; *Public Policy to Reduce Inequalities*, 2022) and comparisons of UK and devolved policy making (*Why Isn't Government More Preventive?*, 2020). He uses these insights to explain the use of evidence in policy and policy making, in books (*The Politics of Policy Analysis*, 2021; *The Politics of Evidence-Based Policy Making*, 2016), articles and blog posts (https://paul cairney.wordpress.com/ebpm/).

Sean Kippin is Lecturer in Public Policy at the University of Stirling. He is the author of a number of publications covering British political and policy-making institutions, the UK Labour Party, and policy areas such as education and inequalities. He has a PhD in Politics and Public Policy from the University of the West of Scotland, where he also held a succession of teaching roles. Prior to this, he worked for the London School of Economics on the Democratic Audit UK and LSE Politics and Policy Blog projects.

Acknowledgements

We thank Zoe Forbes, Lloyd Langman, Stephen Wenham and two anonymous referees, who helped to commission, support and improve this book. We take full responsibility for any errors, but not for turning policymaker (and policymaking) into two words. The book uses the house style of 'policy maker' except when using the grammatically correct attributive noun 'policy-maker'. Both rules make sense independently but, when combined, you get this mix throughout the book. We invite you to see this outcome as a simple demonstration of what can happen when multiple rules, which make sense on their own terms, combine to produce something that seems wrong but endures nonetheless. If we get something so simple so wrong in the book, what hope is there for policy makers juggling many more rules?

Preface: How to Analyse UK Policy Making

It seems like there is never a good time to write a book on contemporary British politics (for example, Boris Johnson was Prime Minister when we began writing). Yet, if we can equip readers with key insights and analytical skills to examine these developments, it is always a good time to read about modern developments.

The first insight regards a sense of perspective in policy making: a focus on UK governments and ministers is not useful unless placed within a far wider context. Ministers matter, but they form part of a complex policy-making environment over which they have limited knowledge. By choice and necessity, they delegate the processing of most policy to other actors, including civil servants, other governments and public bodies. What happens next is beyond their control. Indeed, can you think of many policy outcomes that ministers wanted to happen? For example, is this what they meant by getting Brexit done? Did they really do all they could to minimise the fallout from COVID-19? Are they solving the climate crisis? Did they retreat victoriously from Afghanistan and Iraq? Is the economy working in the way they planned?

The second insight extends beyond British politics to inform a more general understanding of policy making: a focus on the 'centre' of policy making is not entirely useful. A traditional starting point is to see policy problems through the lens of policy analysis: identify the problem for your client, generate solutions, compare their political feasibility, predict their effects and make a recommendation. Yet, this approach identifies what policy actors *require* of policy making, not what happens. Therefore, our main focus is on how policy making actually works, and how we can use general insights to examine policy making in the UK. We do so through a critical lens: analysing who has the power to define and address policy problems, which social groups they favour and marginalise, and who wins and loses from policy outcomes. Analysis of the *overall* picture of British politics ignores the major inequalities that endure within the UK.

In that context, things are always changing but stay the same. New ministers emerge, but face the same constraints. New issues emerge, but inequalities endure. These insights help us to engage with the following phrase that often seems to sum up British politics.

No One Is in Control or Knows What They Are Doing

It is common to bemoan a lack of competence and trustworthiness of British policy makers. They don't know what they are doing, and few trust them to get the results they promise. This argument is common to simplistic popular accounts of British politics *and* more thoughtful stories in policy studies, but each approach provides very different conclusions.

In popular accounts, many claims are based on the idea that elected politicians are not up to the job. They connect to the lazy argument that all politicians are untrustworthy or incompetent, or the partisan argument that a change of government would bring in competent politicians with better ideas. The book is already written on the former (Clarke et al, 2018). The latter is misguided but important. It forms part of the *Westminster story* in which a small number of senior ministers are in control. This story asserts how British politics *should work*: if UK government ministers are in charge, we can hold them to account for policy. If they do badly, they can be replaced. It does not describe how British politics *actually works*.

Policy research provides a more useful story: the British state is too large to be controlled by a small number of powerful individuals, and the complexity of policy problems and processes ensures that they are beyond anyone's full understanding. The phrase *bounded rationality* describes the inability of policy makers to pay attention to, or understand, more than a tiny proportion of policy problems, while *policy making complexity* describes their inability to control the outcomes that emerge from the British political system. These limits apply to policy makers regardless of their competence, sincerity or trustworthiness, and we do a disservice to democracy if we ignore them in favour of simplistic stories of bad politicians.

That said, the Westminster story remains important and our alternative account – the *complex government story* – has its own problems. Therefore, throughout this book, we invite you to bear the following qualifications in mind.

First, UK government ministers might not be in control, but they remain very powerful and can still do damage (King and Crewe, 2014). One useful analogy is with people working with their natural environments: the environment constrains and facilitates their success when they try to *grow* crops or trees, but humans are much more powerful when it comes to their *destruction*.

Second, the Westminster story still underpins British political traditions and key functions of the British state (Duggett, 2009). Think of British politics as a confusing conflation of two different stories: of the concentration *and* diffusion of policy-making power. UK government ministers have to juggle these images to project an image of governing competence based on the sense that they are in control (how else would they win elections?) *and* that they share responsibility with many other policy makers (Hay, 2009).

Third, while no group can control policy outcomes, it would be wrong to ignore the regularity of patterns that emerge from social and political life. Some people win, many people lose, and these patterns result from unequal access to resources.

There is no escape from these confusing contradictions, but research can help us understand them. 'Policy studies' generate concepts, theories and research to understand policy processes (research *of* policy). This understanding is crucial to policy analysis – the identification of policy problems and possible solutions (research *for* policy) – where we use our knowledge of policy making to examine the feasibility of solutions to major problems. We seek the right balance between accepting policy-making complexity and the limits to policy-maker control *and* believing that well-designed policies, taken forward by key people and organisations, can improve people's lives. The cynical stoic is no better than the naïve optimist, but the stoical optimist might see some reward.

Further Resources

It is impossible to fit a comprehensive study of UK policy making into a book, and no one would appreciate the results if we tried. Instead, we provide two ways to introduce the subject and encourage wider reading.

First, we provide an initial way to think about policy making. We introduce a manageable number of concepts in this book, and provide further discussions in a suite of blog posts hosted by Cairney (https://paulcairney.wordpress.com/). Some focus on British policy making, as part of a university module. There is also a much larger set of resources on policy analysis, policy concepts and theories (pages called 500, 750 or 1000). Cairney consolidates the links in a dedicated page (https://paulcairney.wordpress.com/policymaking-in-the-uk/).

Second, we provide a manageable number of case studies of policy making. We asked ourselves what issues would be most relevant to people studying UK politics now. Many are impossible to ignore because they are part of daily lives, including: COVID-19, Brexit, climate change, economic crisis and 'austerity', race and racism, inequalities, and the role of the UK in armed conflict. We also provide two chapters to summarise the historical developments that remain central to modern developments. Overall, the case study chapters include developments from 1979.

These approaches provide a way to understand and investigate politics and policy making. The conceptual discussion examines how to relate case studies to *policy analysis*, to consider what policy change should look like, *policy studies*, to explain how policy change actually happens, and *critical policy analysis*, to consider who makes policy and why, and who wins and loses from their choices.

Introducing UK Politics and Policy Making

Chapter highlights

1. Describes the importance of policy and policy making to the study of UK politics.

2. Introduces three essential ways to research it, via policy analysis, policy studies and critical policy analysis.

3. Warns against equating UK politics with the Westminster story of power concentrated in the hands of government ministers.

4. Introduces an alternative complex government story, in which ministers can only influence a small proportion of their responsibilities.

5. Shows how to use these insights to analyse, explain and evaluate contemporary politics and policy making in the UK.

The purpose and approach of this book

There has never been a more important time to study UK politics and policy making. COVID-19 has prompted policy change at a size and speed only witnessed during wartime. Brexit has changed the UK's relationship with the European Union (EU) and wider world, and fuelled debates on who should control policy. 'Black Lives Matter' and other rallies raised attention to racism, and the lack of adequate policy to address it. The UK government faces pressure to address the existential threat of climate change. Its foreign and domestic policies have changed how we understand threats from war and terrorism. 'Austerity' measures from 2010 signalled reforms to reduce public spending and the role of the UK state. Any one example would justify the need to understand UK policy making. So too would new issues that have arisen since we drafted this book, including the UK's response to the Russian invasion of Ukraine and the cost of living crisis from 2022. Such issues show that policy is central to our understanding of UK politics. Yet, government policies do not solve social problems, and governments often exacerbate inequalities and crises.

We identify three ways to engage with these issues:

1. *Policy analysis*. What are the most important policy problems of our time, how do analysts and policy makers describe them, and what do they need to do to solve them?
2. *Policy studies*. What is their ability to understand and solve policy problems? How can we explain what actually happens in UK politics and policy making?
3. *Critical policy analysis*. Who decides how to understand policy problems, who makes policy, and who benefits or suffers from its outcomes? If the outcomes are unfair, how can we challenge them?

Values: beliefs about how people should behave and what principles they (and governments) should uphold.

Policy tool or **instrument**: a means to turn aims into action (for example, a regulation, tax, expenditure or organisation).

Stakeholders: policy actors with a 'stake' in policy processes and outcomes (including interest groups, public bodies and policy delivery organisations).

Frame: defines how an issue becomes a policy problem: smoking is an economic good or public health disaster; shale gas represents an economic boom, or fracking causes environmental catastrophe.

Actor: participant or player. An individual or organisation able to deliberate and make decisions.

Policy analysis involves the use of research to address policy problems. It lists the steps that analysts and policy makers take to define policy problems, identify feasible solutions, draw on their **values** to compare solutions, and make recommendations. *Policy design* describes how to create or select a mix of **policy tools** or **instruments** to address a policy problem. Contemporary studies focus on the extent to which this process is sufficiently 'evidence-based' or 'co-produced' with **stakeholders** and citizens (Cairney, 2021a).

Policy studies use research to understand how policy making works. They identify the limits to policy analysis and warn against equating what you think governments *should do* with what they *actually do*. This gap relates partly to contested politics: there is high disagreement on how to **frame** issues. There are many ways to think about a problem, prompting a competitive agenda-setting process where people try to draw attention to their preferred framing at the expense of others. Further, policy makers have a limited understanding and awareness of the problems they face, and tend to simplify and address only one aspect of multidimensional problems (Box 1.1). Policy makers also operate in a complex policy-making 'system' or 'environment' out of their control. Contemporary discussions focus on how to manage policy making when UK central governments share responsibility with other policy **actors**.

Box 1.1: The power to define problems and generate attention

Politics involves the power of actors to get what they want. It is not simply about visible conflicts where one wins and another loses. It involves influencing which issues we pay attention to and which conflicts arise. Attention lurches from one issue to another, and most issues are ignored. Some groups exercise power – in two main ways – to ensure that key issues do not receive attention, to preserve a status quo which benefits some and hurts others (Schattschneider, 1960; Bachrach and Baratz, 1970; Abbott et al, 2005: 35; summarised in Cairney, 2020a: Chapter 3).

First, to reinforce social attitudes. If public opinion is against government action, governments may not intervene. For example, if most people believe that poverty is the responsibility of individuals, they question the need for government intervention. Many battles are about which issues are *private*, with no role for government, or *public*, open to legitimate government action. Should governments intervene in disputes between businesses and workers, or disputes between a married couple? Should they stop people smoking in cars? Second, to keep 'safe' issues on the government agenda, causing less attention to policies that might address major imbalances of wealth and power within society.

Terms like **paradigms**, **ideology** or **norms** suggest that power is difficult to observe. It relates to the ability to influence how people think and what they believe: intentionally, as manipulation, or unintentionally, when they reinforce the beliefs they take for granted. Policy paradigms often endure for decades until challenged *gradually*, by actors who question dominant beliefs, or *radically*, by events that cause policy makers to rethink their beliefs after failure. Hall (1993) describes rapid change in UK economic policy following severe economic and political crisis. Rogers and Pilgrim (2001) and Studlar and Cairney (2014) describe gradual changes (over decades) to how governments addressed mental health and tobacco (see Chapters 4 and 5).

Paradigms: ways of thinking so ingrained that they are often taken for granted. Policy paradigms endure when the nature of problems is taken for granted.

Ideology: a broad set of political beliefs/values held by an individual, party or social group.

Norm: a rule or standard of behaviour considered to be normal and therefore acceptable.

Critical policy analysis focuses on identifying and challenging the unequal distribution of power that contributes to policies which exacerbate social and economic inequalities. For example, inequalities of power help determine whose knowledge or evidence counts in policy analysis, who is in a position of power to use it, and who wins or loses from policy (Bacchi, 2009; Doucet, 2019). Policy analysis and research is not an objective, technical process. The

Ministers: Members of Parliament (MPs) making policy in government departments. A Secretary of State (or the Treasury's Chancellor of the Exchequer) heads each department, aided by junior ministers.

Manifesto: a written public statement of policy aims (usually to seek election).

Civil servants: bureaucrats in government departments or agencies.

Whitehall: the home of key UK government departments.

Permanent Secretaries: the 'most senior civil servant[s] in a department', while the Cabinet Secretary is the 'Prime Minister's most senior policy adviser ... responsible for supporting all ministers in the running of government [and] providing professional leadership to the Civil Service' (HM Government, 2022e).

Liberal democracy: a general description of political systems that use regular elections to maintain the authority of governments, which (1) enforce the rule of law while protecting the rights and freedom of their citizens, and (2) maintain capitalism by regulating markets for goods and services.

production, interpretation and use of evidence for policy – *and how we research this process* – is a political act (for example, see UK **ministers** being 'guided by the science' in Chapter 6 and demonising critical race theory in Chapter 10).

These perspectives are crucial to: analyse contemporary policy problems, identify the willingness and ability of governments to solve them, and reflect on the unequal impacts of policy in society.

Comparing explanations of UK policy making

To explain how the UK political system works, we identify the contrast between two important ways to describe politics and policy making.

The Westminster model: a story of how policy should be made

The first story is that policy making relates to the wishes of the public: political parties engage in a battle of ideas, to attract the support of the voting public; the public votes in a general election; the winning party forms a government; the government turns its **manifesto** into policy; and, policy is delivered by **civil servants** (in **Whitehall** departments headed by **Permanent Secretaries**). In other words, in **liberal democracies**, there is a direct link between public preferences, the strategies and ideas of parties seeking votes, and the result.

We can adapt this general narrative to more specific ideas associated with the **Westminster model** and the UK's reputation as a **majoritarian democracy**. The UK has a plurality ('first past the post') voting system, which exaggerates support for, and tends to give a majority in Parliament to, the winning party. It has an adversarial style of politics and a 'winner takes all' mentality which tends to exclude opposition parties from government. The executive resides in the legislature, and power is concentrated in the **core executive**. Ministers head government departments and the Prime Minister heads (and determines the members of) **Cabinet**. The government is responsible for public policy and it uses its governing majority, combined with a party **whip**, to make sure that its legislation is passed by Parliament. There are many ways to tell this story (Chapter 3). However, the moral remains the same: power and responsibility go hand in hand. If you know who is in charge, you know who to reward or punish.

Complex government: a story of how policy is actually made

The second story suggests that the actions of ministers represent the tip of the iceberg. Most aspects of our lives are affected by the state, and the state is too large to be understood or managed fully. Most policy is processed, out of the public spotlight, by a large government and network of organisations (containing millions of public employees), with limited direction by ministers, and delivering a convoluted statute book which ministers do not understand. Consequently, regular changes of government do not cause wholesale shifts in policy. Further, governments do not really solve problems, which makes the term 'policy solutions' misleading. These factors help to explain the *necessity* of limited government powers, regardless of the *choice* to share powers with other 'centres' (such as the EU and devolved and local governments). They undermine the sense that there is a single powerful centre of government responsible for UK policy outcomes (Box 1.2).

Westminster model: the design of UK political institutions and practices (Chapter 3). Westminster is the home of the Houses of Parliament (Commons and Lords).

Majoritarian democracy: a political system using the plurality electoral system, which exaggerates a party's electoral victory and concentrates power at the centre of government.

Core executive: the centre of government, including the Prime Minister and Chancellor, and the administrative arrangements which support them (Dunleavy and Rhodes, 1990).

Cabinet: the government's formal policy-making body.

Whip: a system used to make sure that most MPs vote according to the 'party line'.

Box 1.2: Multi-centric policy making in the UK

UK central government shares policy-making responsibilities with many other 'centres', or venues for authoritative policy choice (Cairney et al, 2019a). Some sharing relates to *choice*. For example, until 2020 the UK was part of the EU. The UK government also shares powers with the devolved governments in Scotland, Wales and Northern Ireland (largely via Westminster legislation to establish devolved parliaments in 1999). It delegates policy making or delivery responsibilities to local authorities and other public bodies, and often supports 'localism' (Matthews, 2016). Some sharing relates to *necessity*, when policy makers:

- Can only pay attention to a tiny proportion of their responsibilities, and must ignore or delegate the rest.
- Operate in a policy-making environment containing many policy makers and influencers spread across many other levels or types of government, each with their own rules, networks, and ways of understanding and responding to policy problems. When there are multiple centres of authority, strong central government may be replaced by bargaining government (Kooiman, 1993; Rhodes, 1997; compare with Marsh, 2008).

There are many ways to describe this dynamic, including research on 'multi-level governance' in which there are blurry boundaries between those who make and influence policy across many levels of government (Bache and Flinders, 2004), and 'complex systems' in which policy outcomes seem to 'emerge' in the absence of central government control (Cairney, 2020a: 104–108). Either way, focusing only on UK central government does not give a full account of policy for the UK (Chapters 2 and 3).

This dynamic complicates policy analysis, when we are not sure who exactly is responsible for solving a problem or how much power they have to solve it. It complicates efforts to identify who makes policy and for whose benefit. We may also wonder how to hold policy makers to account effectively if so many actors are crucial to the fate of policy outcomes.

This focus on many policy-making centres is essential because it suggests that responsibility, and therefore accountability, is difficult to identify when ministers (1) share powers with others, *and* (2) have low knowledge and control of policy outcomes even if they are ostensibly in charge. It highlights a disconnect between popular understandings of UK politics and the complex government story, and highlights some important consequences of the latter:

- *The pragmatic and normative case for delegating policy attention.* Ministers can only manage a tiny proportion of their responsibilities, and they seek legitimate ways to pay attention to some and ignore most. Sometimes, it looks like ministers are passing the buck. However, there are often good reasons to place responsibility in the hands of others. Either way, there are blurry boundaries between the responsibilities of those who make, influence and deliver policy.
- *Multi-level policy and policy making.* What we call 'policy' is actually a collection of policy instruments produced in different levels of government (for example, from EU to local).
- *Fragmented policy making.* Policy making is 'fragmented' in the sense that UK government is broken down into departments and agencies. Most

policy problems cut across these departments, but it is difficult to 'join up' government.

- *Multi-level governance.* 'Governance' replaces 'government' when studies describe the diffusion of power from the core executive to other organisations, while 'multi-level governance' describes a web of relationships between actors with formal and informal sources of power at many levels of government (Box 1.2).
- *Policy inheritance.* Instead of seeing the election of each new government as turning a fresh page, think of it as adding new text to a remarkably long and full book.

Complex government and wicked problems

The Westminster model suggests that governments are in the problem-solving business. In contrast, policy research emphasises problem endurance. Descriptions such as 'wicked', 'messy' or 'complex' suggest that problems:

- are not amenable to technical or scientific policy analysis;
- endure despite many attempts to solve them (Rittell and Webber, 1973; McConnell, 2018; Turnbull and Hoppe, 2018; Head, 2019).

This endurance relates to three factors. First, the world is not conducive to human control. Humans adapt to their physical environments, which limit where and how they can live. Governments in liberal democracies seek to influence but not control patterns of social and economic behaviour, such as:

- Demographic structures, including the size of the working or school-age population and the number of older people receiving social security and care.
- Economic factors, including levels of employment, consumer spending, investment in industries and services, and the potential for taxation.
- Mass behaviour and attitudes, from healthy behaviour and education attainment, to levels of crime, racism and misogyny, or public attitudes to policies.

These factors represent a source of pressure on policy makers. Engagement with the physical environment prompts dilemmas on how to manage scarce resources such as clean air, water, food and fuel. The economic environment influences the ability of governments to finance policies, while changes to economic performance dominate the attention of governments (especially since most governments promise 'economic growth'), and crises prompt policy makers to reconsider their approach to economic policy. Demographic changes affect policy decisions, such as when a large retired population makes it expensive to maintain pensions, welfare and social care policies, or a baby boom influences demand for schools. Events, such as an extremely cold winter or epidemic, combined with a media and public reaction, prompt policy makers to make quick decisions on issues such as healthcare.

Second, differing values ensure that people disagree about:

- the nature of a problem, including its importance and cause;
- who should be responsible for solving it, such as individuals or governments; and
- which solutions are politically feasible.

For example, inequalities are often treated as 'wicked' problems because there is high and intense contestation to decide: which forms of inequality should receive most attention (including in relation to class, geography, gender or race); what causes poverty and economic inequalities and how to respond (as a structural problem to be solved by the state, or an individual problem to be solved with market forces); and if more state intervention – such as to tax income and wealth to redistribute resources – would be popular or lose the next election (Chapter 10; Cairney et al, 2022a).

Third, policy problems cross government departmental boundaries and require international cooperation between governments. For example, Levin et al (2012) describe climate change as a 'super wicked' problem because 'time is running out', policy makers partly cause the problem they seek to solve, there is no 'central authority' to solve a global problem, and people are not good at assigning importance to future events (Box 8.1).

Bringing both stories together

These insights do not completely undermine the Westminster story. Political parties still produce manifestos, and the party of government generally fulfils its manifesto commitments (Bara, 2005; McMillan, 2020). Further, it would be difficult for governments to justify the exercise of their powers without reference to the **legitimation** provided by elections and Parliament.

Legitimation: gaining public approval, such as via elections, referendums or Parliament.

Instead, policy studies prompt us to think about the bigger picture and shift our attention somewhat, from the high-profile and short-term nature of Westminster politics, to the long-term delivery of policy outcomes beyond the public spotlight. Ministers are *responsible* for this activity, and they can set the tone of many debates, but they cannot pay attention to everything. They promote some problems to the top of their agenda, often following an event or a successful pressure campaign. This activity *might* produce major policy change because ministerial attention encourages a wide range of people to get involved. However, greater attention to a problem does not guarantee a shift of approach. Further, the logical consequence of heightened attention to one issue is inattention to others. Business as usual prevails when so much policy making is delegated to people who deliver the existing statute book.

The approach of the book

We begin by describing three key perspectives: policy analysis focuses on how to define and solve problems; policy studies identify the policy-making environments that limit the impact of analysis and policy; and critical policy analysis asks who benefits disproportionately from analysis and policy. The comparison of perspectives helps to combine the empirical study of politics and policy making with normative research, to identify policy problems and think about how to understand the policies designed to address them. It allows us to compare different descriptions of 'good policy making', including the trade-offs between relatively centralised 'evidence-based' policy making and decentralised 'co-production' approaches to analysis. These comparisons help to inform evaluations of the 'government knows best' approach in the Westminster model and consider alternatives associated with complex government approaches.

We relate these general perspectives on policy making to developments in UK policy and policy making. We identify the transformation of the UK state: from the 'post-war consensus' on high state intervention and state responsibility for designing and delivering public services, to the **'neoliberal'** state characterised by reduced economic intervention and state ownership of industry, the use of private-sector methods to deliver services, and some shift from state to individual responsibility. Second, we use the three-perspectives approach to analyse contemporary case studies and explore the competition to define problems, seek solutions and decide who benefits from policy. The Westminster and complex government stories allow us to relate this contestation to a UK political system characterised – often misleadingly – as majoritarian and top-down.

> **Neoliberal**: broadly speaking, a preference to (1) encourage individual and market rather than state solutions, and (2) prioritise economic growth over other policy aims.

The structure of the book

Chapter 2 describes policy making in the UK from three key perspectives, to: analyse contemporary policy problems, identify the capacity of governments to solve them, and reflect on the unequal impacts of policy in society. It compares different reference points in policy studies, which identify: (1) what policy analysts need to do, and policy makers need to happen, to get what they want, versus (2) what actually happens. For example, studies of 'bounded rationality' describe how policy makers respond to their limited knowledge of policy and policy making, and most describe the absence of a straightforward and orderly 'policy cycle'. These studies of policy-making limitations inform our story of complex government.

Chapter 3 explores how policy is made in the UK. The *Westminster story* describes a concentration of power in a small number of people at the heart of central government. The *complex government story* describes a diffusion of power across many centres of government, with each developing its own ways of thinking, rules, networks and responses to socio-economic conditions and events. The Westminster model is an important reference point which influences how policy actors make and describe their choices. The complex government story may be more accurate, but it does not give policy makers a clear way to make and legitimise choices. Consequently, both approaches are necessary to explain UK policy making.

Chapter 4 identifies the major changes to have taken place in the post-war UK state. It highlights the choices of successive governments to 'roll back the state' and spread policy-making responsibilities across levels and types of government. They include changes to:

- Reduce state intervention in the management of the economy.
- Shift the balance between public and private provision by selling nationalised industries and social housing, charging for public services, reducing the role of local authorities in service delivery, and using non-governmental organisations to deliver services.
- Apply private-sector philosophies and methods to the public sector.
- Employment laws, to reduce trade union power and employee rights.
- Reduce or reform the welfare state.

Chapter 5 reflects on the implications of these changes for the study of policy making. UK state transformation prompted debates including:

- Did UK governments enforce major changes from the top down?
- Did they oversee incremental changes or bursts of radical change?
- Did they produce a 'lean' state more able to respond to issues, or a 'hollowed out' state unable to control key functions?

Each question helps to relate long-term trends to the *Westminster story*, emphasising central government control, and the *complex government story*, emphasising the limits on central government powers.

> **Globalisation**: the intensification of economic, social and political convergence made possible by advances in technology (and collective or coercive action).
>
> **Policy transfer**: the import/ export of knowledge, policy solutions or government programmes.

Chapter 5 also relates complex government to **globalisation**. It considers the extent to which the UK government is in control of domestic policy: must it share power with international organisations, and is it obliged to respond to the agendas of other governments (and corporations)? It highlights the global context in which domestic governments pursue an international 'neoliberal' policy agenda and engage in **policy transfer**.

Case studies in politics and policy making: responding to crisis?

We describe many **crises** in this book, including: *public health*, when COVID-19 prompted unprecedented policy changes; *economic*, when governments faced recession, banking collapses, huge debts and 'tough choices' about cuts to public services; *security*, in which governments responded to terrorist threats in their own countries and went to war with others; *energy*, when there are high prices and shortages of supply; *public service*, whenever a health, social care, police or education service was described as dysfunctional; *representative*, when elected politicians become embroiled in scandals about their conduct; and, *constitutional*, when the UK left the EU.

Crisis: a period of instability or major difficulty; a turning point requiring an important decision.

When we relate crisis only to choices in UK central government, it is tempting to think that the process is chaotic and characterised by 'blunders' (King and Crewe, 2014). However, this impression is self-fulfilling: we generate a sense of crisis by paying so much attention to few aspects of government while other government activity takes place with minimal media and public attention. The policy process is an odd collection of (1) very few issues which generate high levels of attention and involve many actors, and (2) many issues which are processed out of the public spotlight and involve very few. Or, some issues receive high attention at one point only to be ignored at another (Hogwood, 1987).

Chapter 6 shows that COVID-19 represents a way to understand policy-making crises and the social and economic dilemmas associated with public health. It prompted policy change in the UK at a speed and magnitude only seen during wartime. Major changes to state intervention, to limit social behaviour and fund economic inactivity, seemed inconceivable before 2020. These actions helped to address some, and exacerbate other, causes of unequal policy outcomes, such as in relation to income, gender, race and ethnicity, and disability, and the health inequalities that were apparent before and after the pandemic. This chapter examines COVID-19 policy through three lenses:

1. Policy analysis identifies how we can analyse COVID-19 as a policy problem: how the UK government could define it, consider the feasibility of solutions, apply value judgements to consider trade-offs (such as between state intervention to protect public health versus individual freedom), predict the effect of each solution, and make or accept recommendations.
2. Policy studies situate this analysis in the context of real-world developments, identifying the policy-making environment in which it made choices, and explaining key developments (including the major shift in policy from late March 2020, as the UK entered 'lockdown' for the first time).

3. Critical policy analysis identifies who benefited from action or lost out from inaction, in relation to factors such as: income/wealth and employment, gender, race and ethnicity, and age.

Chapter 7 shows that Brexit debates included constitutional issues (who should govern Britain?) and policy choices (who should win and lose from UK government policy?). Until COVID-19, UK withdrawal from the EU dominated political debate, and signalled potentially profound changes in policy and policy making. However, policy studies suggest that the oft-stated idea of the UK 'taking back control' of policy is highly misleading. Brexit will prompt many changes to policy making, but these are not summed up well by a simple shift of power from one venue to another. Brexit also kept wider constitutional change high on the agenda, such as by influencing the likelihood of a second referendum on Scottish independence. The Labour government of 1997–2010 had delivered different forms of devolution in Northern Ireland, Scotland and Wales, but did not succeed in settling their constitutional issues. This chapter examines post-Brexit policy through three lenses:

1. Policy analysis identifies how to treat constitutional change as many interconnected policy problems, including: what should be the relationship between the devolved and UK governments and the EU; what solutions exist to constitutional tensions and the need for intergovernmental cooperation; and, trade-offs between each option.
2. Policy studies situate this analysis in the context of real-world developments, including constitutional changes within the UK, the referendum on Brexit and its aftermath, and multi-centric policy making.
3. Critical policy analysis identifies who benefits or loses from these developments, in relation to factors such as: supporters and opponents of constitutional changes, the impact on immigration policies and EU citizens, and variations across broad sectors (such as economic and business policy) or subsectors (such as higher education).

Chapter 8 shows that climate change represents an existential crisis, requiring new ways for governments to collaborate – with each other, across policy sectors, and with non-governmental actors – to encourage major policy change. However, it enjoys only fleeting attention, producing policy change that appears to be insubstantial compared to the size of the problem. This chapter considers the rise of 'environmental policy' in the post-war period and its effect on more established policies on energy, transport and agriculture. Concern for the environment provided a new frame of reference to consider issues such as: the mix of fossil, nuclear and renewable energies; the environmental sustainability of food production; and, the mix between types of public and private transport. This chapter examines climate change policy through three lenses:

1. Policy analysis identifies how to treat climate change as a series of interconnected policy problems, including: what targets national governments and international organisations should adopt; what solutions exist to meet those targets; and what are the trade-offs between each option.
2. Policy studies identify real-world developments, including the lack of UK government control of energy systems, levels of public support for restrictive measures, and the spread of policy-making responsibility across levels and types of government.
3. Critical policy analysis identifies winners and losers, in relation to factors such as who bears the costs for policy changes, and debates on climate and energy justice.

Chapter 9 charts a long period of 'austerity' politics that followed the 2008 global economic crisis and Conservative-led UK governments from 2010. UK governments had contributed to a global trend towards neoliberalism, including state retrenchment in favour of market solutions and individual responsibility. This chapter examines these post-2008 developments, tracking Conservative government measures to address the economic deficit and its ideological agenda:

1. Policy analysis identifies how to treat economic policy as interconnected policy problems, including: what should be the level of economic growth and the size of the UK government deficit; what solutions exist to meet those targets; and how to consider trade-offs between each option.
2. Policy studies identify real-world developments, including the lack of UK government control of global economic activity, the government's framing of economic policy, and levels of public support for the shift to austerity.
3. Critical policy analysis identifies winners and losers, in relation to the balance of taxation from businesses and individuals, levels of support for businesses, families and individuals, and the unequal impact of austerity.

Chapter 10 shows that the UK is a highly unequal social and political system that privileges and marginalises populations in relation to class, race, ethnicity, gender, sexuality and disability. These issues rise and fall on the political agenda, often with minimal impact. One key example relates to race and racism. The UK was one of many countries to host Black Lives Matter protests in 2020, organised originally to protest police violence against people of colour (and Black men in particular) in the US. Protests are common in UK politics, but tend not to produce a direct impact on public policy. They include a series of protests and 'riots' in 2011 that were also fuelled by racial inequalities in relation to policing but characterised by the UK government as caused by bad parenting and 'troubled families'. A focus on protest highlights how governments try to solve some policy problems (such as unequal state spending on some families) and ignore or exacerbate others (such as poverty and racism). This chapter uses three lenses to connect protest and policy:

1. Policy analysis identifies how we can analyse race and racism as a series of problems, including: the evidence for institutional or systemic racism in the UK, what solutions exist to address racism, and which appear to be technically and politically feasible.
2. Policy studies identify real-world developments, including the tendency of the UK government to frame protests in relation to other policy agendas.
3. Critical policy analysis – and 'critical race theory' and theories of post-colonialism and decolonisation – highlight persistent inequalities and racism in the UK, and relate them to the UK's colonial history.

Chapter 11 examines UK foreign and defence policy. It suggests that the Labour government of 1997–2010 is remembered largely for its contribution to conflict in Afghanistan from 2001 and the Iraq War in 2003. Both were driven by UK government support for US intervention, connected rhetorically to the 'war on terror' prompted by the 9/11 attacks on the US. They prompted high public protest, related partly to scepticism about the US motives and UK evidence for Iraq's possession of 'weapons of mass destruction'. This chapter examines these developments using three lenses:

1. The well-established study of foreign policy analysis in theory and practice.
2. The Iraq Inquiry (2009–2011) and Chilcot Report (2016) help to identify foreign and defence policy and policy making in the UK (and its consequences).
3. Critical policy analysis identifies who wins and loses from these developments, including political benefits to governments, economic benefits to arms businesses, and the mortality of those involved.

Our conclusion uses recent developments – including the remarkably brief Truss government – to sum up the key insights explored in this book. First, we focus on policy analysis to identify (1) the overwhelming number of problems inherited by a new government, and (2) how they define them and set new priorities. Second, we show that UK government attempts to produce a top-down policy style following a well-established tradition of projecting strong government before making U-turns and compromises. Third, we identify the complex policy-making system that will inevitably cause a gap between stated ministerial intentions and actual outcomes. Finally, we sum up the theme of inequalities that runs throughout the book: while governments seem to take them seriously, they also examine them through a 'neoliberal' lens that individualises – and often exacerbates – the problem.

Perspectives on Policy and Policy Making

Introduction: The importance of many perspectives

This chapter describes policy and policy making from three perspectives, to analyse contemporary policy problems, the willingness and ability of governments to solve them, and the unequal impacts of policy.

Policy analysis is a research-informed activity to influence policy. Analysts treat policy makers as their audience, using steps including: defining the nature of a policy problem, seeking feasible solutions, using values and goals to identify trade-offs between solutions, and estimating their effects. Most guidebooks emphasise pragmatism, highlighting the limited time to produce analysis and the need to tailor analysis to the beliefs of your audience.

Policy studies are research to understand what policy is (Box 2.1) and how policy making works. They situate policy analysis in a wider context, to identify – for example – how a new policy solution would fit into the bigger picture (Box 2.1). There are many policy theories, but most identify two key issues: policy makers do not have the resources to understand problems comprehensively, and they operate in an environment that constrains their action.

Critical policy analysis combines research and advocacy to challenge how policy making works and support powerless or marginalised groups. It identifies the politics of policy analysis: actors exercise power to decide whose knowledge is relevant, whose values should inform choice, and who should benefit from policy. It highlights the politics of policy making: only some people influence policy and benefit from the outcomes. It reminds us that policy outcomes provide routine benefits to some groups and not others.

Box 2.1: What is public policy?

- 'Diverse activities by different bodies are drawn together into stable and predictable patterns of action which … come to be labelled "policy"' (Colebatch, 1998: x).
- 'Policy designs are observable phenomena found in statutes, administrative guidelines, court decrees, programs, and even the practices and procedures of street level bureaucrats' (Schneider and Ingram, 1997: 2).
- 'Whatever governments choose to do or not to do' (Dye, 1976).

There is no agreed-upon definition of public policy, but we can identify common themes. First, 'policy' describes one, or all, of: a statement of intent (we will solve this problem); specific proposals (such as a manifesto); proposals authorised by government and Parliament (such as legislation); proposals backed by resources such as funding and staffing ('outputs' or a policy programme); and outcomes of decisions (Hogwood and Gunn, 1984: 13–19). We could define public policy as 'the sum total of government action, from signals of intent to the final outcomes', but the outcomes differ from the stated intentions (Cairney, 2020a: 2). Some make promises they have no intention of fulfilling. Others see their policies go awry. Outputs such as more doctors do not cause outcomes such as healthier populations. Many outcomes result from old public-sector routines that are disconnected from new policy-maker choices.

Second, 'public' policy is made by governments and the organisations acting on their behalf. Most policy is carried out by bureaucracies and a range of – governmental, quasi-non-governmental and non-governmental – delivery organisations.

Third, policy may result from the interactions between policy makers and influencers (including interest groups and organisations delivering policy) (Rose, 1987: 267–268). It is difficult to know who is responsible, particularly when the issue is low on the agenda of elected officials (Colebatch, 1998: 18–22; 2006a: 1).

Fourth, policy is also about what governments *don't do*, and influence is often about ensuring that governments do *not* address problems (Box 1.1). To pay attention to one problem is to ignore many others.

Policy analysis: a five-step guide (and its limits)

There are many textbooks on how to do policy analysis (Mintrom, 2012; Dunn, 2017; Weimer and Vining, 2017; Meltzer and Schwartz, 2019; Bardach and Patashnik,

2020). They identify the analyst's **functional requirements** before reflecting on what analysts actually do and the gap between requirements and reality. We boil down their advice into five steps (Cairney, 2021a: 11–15).

> **Functional requirement**: what needs to happen to make something work.

1. Define a policy problem

Problem definition involves:

- framing an issue in relation to key properties (such as its size, severity and urgency);
- identifying its cause and amenability to solutions; and
- telling a persuasive story with a clear reason for a policy maker to intervene.

It is a political act tailored to the beliefs of your audience. For example, analysts can argue that poverty is the fault of individuals who deserve minimal state support, or the result of structural inequalities that can only be addressed by state intervention (Box 1.1).

2. Identify feasible solutions

Policy options should be technically feasible (they will work as intended if implemented) and politically feasible (they are acceptable to your policy-maker audience and the audiences they want to please). A solution can be rejected quickly if it is technically but not politically feasible. The politics may change following a crisis or election of a new government. Still, each government faces similar issues: **redistribution** is more controversial than **distribution**, and both are more costly to governments than **regulation** (Lowi, 1964; 1972: 299; Smith and Larimer, 2009: 36–41). Using technical and political criteria helps to create a manageable shortlist of solutions to research in enough depth to identify their costs and benefits.

> **Redistribution**: taking resources from one group and giving them to another.
>
> **Distribution**: giving out resources to benefit a group (without a clear sense that another group pays).
>
> **Regulation**: instructions backed by penalties for non-compliance.

3. Use value-based criteria and political goals to compare solutions

Common ways to evaluate solutions include reference to:

- *Efficiency*. Will it provide the most benefits in relation to the same costs?
- *Equity*. Will the outcomes be fair to the populations that policy makers care about?

- *Human rights* or *human dignity*.
- The impact on state intervention on *individual freedoms* (or a trade-off between freedom and security).
- The balance between individual, communal and state action.
- The impact of each policy on gender or racial equality or environmental sustainability.
- How the option was generated. For example, what evidence informed the analysis, and were stakeholders involved in deliberation?

These questions help policy makers think about trade-offs between their values and relate solutions to political goals (which option will be most supported?).

4. Predict the outcome of each feasible solution

It is not possible to *know* the outcomes of solutions, but there are techniques to estimate costs and benefits. Cost-benefit analysis aims to fit the results into a common currency to establish their value for money (and encourage ways to compensate people who lose out from policy). Cost-effectiveness analysis estimates the outputs to be gained for a certain cost (Meltzer and Schwartz, 2019: 141–155, 181–183). Models can generate best-case and worst-case scenarios to warn against basing policy on too-optimistic assumptions. Models allow policy makers to think further about trade-offs, such as how much of a bad service people might accept when cutting costs (Bardach and Patashnik, 2020). Another option is to monitor the impact of current choices to inform future decisions, while recognising that the evaluation of success or failure is highly contested (McConnell, 2010; Dunn, 2017: 250).

5. Make a recommendation to your client

It is *possible* to present aloof analysis with no recommendations, but the usual advice is to make recommendations consistent with your brief. Most advice is about *how* to make recommendations, emphasising the need to keep a written report simple, short and punchy, and include an executive summary (Smith, 2015).

While there are technical elements to producing competent policy analysis, most advice relates to politics: see the world through a policy maker's eyes; be efficient to meet tight deadlines; tell a persuasive story with data to grab audience attention (without *misleading* your audience); and minimise their 'cognitive load' to make the problem seem simple enough to solve (Cairney, 2021a: 16).

Only some encourage you to challenge to your audience. Mintrom (2012: 20–22) describes researching more radical options that they will not like immediately, and encouraging analysts to collaborate with stakeholders to widen their perspective. Meltzer and Schwarz (2019: 40–45, 66, 90–91) highlight the value of 'policy design' principles geared towards: generating 'empathy' with people affected by policy, 'co-creating' policy solutions with stakeholders, or thinking of solutions as 'prototypes' to be refined after testing. This focus on design helps us understand the meaning of 'policy instruments' (Box 2.2).

Box 2.2: Policy instruments: designing and measuring policy change

Policy tools or instruments are ways to turn policy aims into action. Hood and Margetts (2007: 5–6) describe four categories of tool:

1. *Nodality*. Providing a hub for information sharing.
2. *Authority*. Regulating individual, social or organisational behaviour.
3. *Treasure*. Collecting and distributing resources.
4. *Organisation*. Providing the resources (such as staff) for public services.

Policy analysts examine the design of instruments, including questions such as:

- *Taxation and tax expenditure*. How much should a government raise, and who or what should it tax (for example, on incomes, wealth, spending)? How 'progressive' should income tax be (for example, how much extra should higher earners pay)? Should a government use taxes to discourage some consumption (for example, petrol, cigarettes, sugar)?
- *Public expenditure*. What should be the balance between capital investment (for example, road versus public transport projects) and current spending? What should be the distribution across policy sectors (for example, defence versus social policy) and within them (for example, doctor and nurse pay)? How should spending be distributed among populations (for example, younger or older)? Should some spending (for example, income support) be conditional on behaviour (for example, seeking work)?
- *Regulation*. Should regulations be backed by enforcement with harsh legal sanctions? Or should governments focus on public education and encourage voluntary changes to (social or business) behaviour? Or use 'nudges' to influence choices by exploiting how people think (John, 2011; Lodge and Weigrich, 2012)?
- *Public services*. Should they be tax-funded, free and universal, or targeted and supported by charges? Should the state deliver and/or fund them?
- *How should governments design these instruments?* Prioritise commissioned research (Jordan and Turnpenny, 2015) or the 'co-production' of policy with citizens (Durose and Richardson, 2015)? Or some mix of both?

'New policy design' considers how policy instruments should be combined: what should be the combination of new instruments, how would they interact with current policy, and can they patch up the problems of old designs (Howlett et al, 2014: 297–300; Peters et al, 2018)? The mix can signal how serious a government is. For example, does it tax, spend and regulate to oblige social change, or rely on information and exhortation (Cairney and St Denny, 2020: 18)?

Policy studies focus on *measuring policy change*, using categories such as size, speed, direction and substance. This task is difficult because defining 'policy' is difficult (Box 2.1). Think of measurement as generating a narrative with empirical and normative elements. A narrative is based on: the timeframe, which government's instruments are important, how proportionate policy change is to the size of the problem, what motivates policy makers to act, and how to select and present data (Cairney, 2020a: 23–24).

This focus on instruments does not tell us about *outcomes*. The outcomes of complex mixes are not simply the sum of their parts: some reinforce each other (for example, to 'denormalise' smoking – Cairney, 2019a), while others can undermine them (in ways that are difficult to imagine). This problem is exacerbated by fragmented and multi-level policy making, with policy made by many different governments – and departments – at different times (Box 1.2).

What do policy analysts actually do?

These five steps tell analysts what they need to do, but what else needs to happen for analysis to make an impact? Studies of policy analysts compare old and new answers to that question. The old story describes the conditions that would be favourable to 'rational' policy analysis:

- Policy making is centralised and exclusive, providing a clear link between your analysis and a powerful audience.
- Participants agree that the role of analysis is to translate scientific knowledge into policy, using techniques such as cost-benefit analysis to find an optimal solution (Enserink et al, 2013: 17–34; Brans et al, 2017: 4–5; Radin, 2019; Cairney, 2021a: 35).

The new story treats the old story as the misguided aspirations of a bygone era. In the real world, conditions are not so favourable to the uptake of your analysis:

- Policy making is messy and competitive, involving many policy makers and influencers spread across political systems, and ruling out a direct link between analysis and a singularly powerful audience.
- The role of analysis is contested, involving a competition to frame problems, interpret evidence and negotiate solutions (Cairney, 2021a: 35).

Policy analysis training does not prepare you fully for a complex policy-making system. Radin (2019: 48) presents a list of skills that is too long for any individual, including to: conduct research; facilitate deliberation among many stakeholders in groups, organisations and networks; encourage cooperation inside and outside of government; and monitor the impact of a solution. Even the most skilled analyst could not know the full extent of the problem or the effect of potential solutions.

Policy studies: the ideal-type policy process

Ideal type: an abstract concept or scenario (not necessarily an ideal).

Our discussion of policy analysis highlights the difference between (1) what analysts need to happen, versus (2) what actually happens. This approach provides a useful connection to policy studies, where we use an **ideal type** to compare a simple vision of policy making (**comprehensive rationality**) with a more complex reality (**bounded rationality**). The concept of 'comprehensive rationality' helps to identify abstract elements of a simple model of policy making, explore why they are unrealistic, and identify the implications for policy making in the real world (Cairney, 2020a: 57–59).

First, policy makers do not have the means to translate their values and aims into policy unproblematically, to maximise the benefits to society. Essential elements are not met in the real world (Lindblom, 1959; Simon, 1976):

> **Comprehensive rationality**: an ideal type of policy making. It describes a single source of policy making. Policy makers at the centre translate their values and aims into policy following a comprehensive study of choices and their effects. This process takes place via linear stages (the 'policy cycle').
>
> **Bounded rationality**: describes the practical limits to processing information and making choices.

- *To gather all information about a policy problem and anticipate all effects of a solution.* Governments gather a sufficient amount of information to make and justify decisions.
- *To produce a coherent and consistent list of preferences to cover the full remit of government.* Policy makers focus on a small number of aims and ignore the rest. Their preferences are vaguely defined (for example, sustainable economic growth) and they only know their detailed preferences when choosing between them (for example, to minimise pollution and climate change or expand air and road capacity to encourage economic activity).
- *To completely separate facts and values.* Our values and beliefs influence how we gather and interpret information, and our selective attention to facts reflects and reinforces our values and priorities.
- *To maximise societal benefits from policy.* Policy makers 'satisfice', or seek an outcome that is 'good enough' (Simon, 1976: xxviii). There are always winners and losers from policy, with no obvious way to compensate the latter.

It would be a mistake to think that advances in science – or 'evidence-based policy making' – could overcome these problems (Botterill and Hindmoor, 2012: 367). Our greater ability to research the world does not remove uncertainty about complex problems, and evidence does not adjudicate between values or help policy makers bring order to their preferences (Cairney, 2016a; 2020a: 60). While our collective ability to generate information has risen, our individual ability to process it has not (you may be painfully aware of this problem while you read this book). Therefore, people combine cognition and emotion to simplify and make choices: 'People use short cuts to gather enough information to make decisions quickly: the "rational", by pursuing clear goals and prioritising certain kinds of information, and the "irrational", by drawing on emotions, gut feelings, values, beliefs, habits, and the familiar, to make decisions quickly' (Cairney and

Figure 2.1: The policy cycle

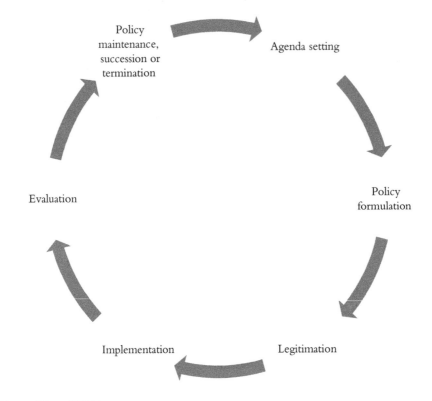

Source: Cairney (2017a)

Kwiatkowski, 2017: 2). We can describe these responses negatively ('cognitive biases') or positively ('fast and frugal heuristics') (Gigerenzer, 2001; Kahneman, 2012). Either way, our focus is on what happens when policy makers deal with bounded rationality.

A second requirement of comprehensive rationality is that the process is linear. It follows an ordered set of tasks, summed up by the stages of the 'policy cycle' (Figure 2.1):

- *Agenda setting.* Deciding which issues deserve attention, and defining the problem.
- *Policy formulation.* Identifying solutions, comparing their cost and benefits, and selecting policy instruments.
- *Legitimation.* Ensuring that policy solutions have support (for example, via legislative approval, consent through consultation with interest groups, referendums).
- *Implementation.* Assigning an implementing organisation, ensuring it has resources (for example, staff, money, legal authority) and that policy is carried out as planned.

- *Evaluation*. Assessing if the policy is implemented correctly, with the desired effect.
- *Policy maintenance, succession or termination*. Deciding if the policy should be continued, modified or discontinued (Cairney, 2020a: 26–27, drawing on Hogwood and Peters, 1983: 8; Hogwood and Gunn, 1984: 7–11).

However, real-world policy making does not work that way (Cairney, 2020a: 34–35). Rather, imagine a messy combination of multiple tasks and cycles taking place simultaneously across many levels and types of government (Sabatier, 2007: 7), to the extent that this image 'no longer gives us any guidance on what happens' (Cairney, 2021a: 54; also Cairney, 2017a). If so, *why does this image of a cycle remain so popular?*

First, some see this cycle as useful to describe policy making from the perspective of policy makers (Wu et al, 2017: 9). It may guide students and civil servants as a learning aid, and not necessarily 'to serve as "a foundation for good policy"' (Threlfall and Althaus, 2021: 39–41; also Althaus et al, 2013; 2015; Mercer, 2021: 55).

Second, it is difficult for a government to describe its policy process as chaotic and unmanageable! Policy makers tend not to describe the limits to their powers in public (Cairney, 2015a). An emphasis on rationality and order helps to present the 'public face' of policy making (McConnell, 2010: 222).

This image is particularly important in the UK, and shares many features with the Westminster model (Chapter 3). We find a simplified story of *agency* (Box 2.3), emphasising a small group of powerful policy makers at the heart of government, who make policy via a simple series of steps identifying their values and aims, making sure that those aims are carried out, and being held accountable for the outcomes through Parliament and general elections. UK government departments have long used cycles to describe their processes (Cabinet Office, 1999; Scottish Government, 2009), and the Treasury 'Green Book' still uses this terminology to tell the Westminster story (HM Treasury, 2020; Cairney, 2023a).

Stages as functional requirements, not part of a cycle

A focus on stages is useful if we see them as individual *functional requirements* in political systems. Policy studies identify how policy actors respond to such requirements:

- *Agenda setting* involves the power to draw attention to some issues, and ways to define the problem, at the expense of others (Box 1.1).
- *Policy formulation* involves the power to make sure that few solutions are considered, while most are ignored.
- *Legitimation* by Parliament is essential to the functioning of government, even though it seems peripheral to policy making (Russell and Cowley, 2016; Judge and Leston-Bandeira, 2021), and the more frequent activity in government

is civil service consultation with actors such as interest groups, delivery organisations and experts (Jordan and Richardson, 1982: 86).

- *Implementation* 'gaps' remain important when policy makers wonder why their decisions did not translate into expected outcomes. A 'top-down' perspective highlights things that could go wrong with a policy when it: is based on flawed evidence or logic; has unclear aims; is not backed by sufficient resources; is not implemented well by officials; does not receive enough support from key groups; and/or is undermined by socio-economic conditions (Hogwood and Gunn, 1984; Marsh and Rhodes, 1992; Cairney, 2020a: 28–30). A 'bottom-up' perspective focuses on the organisations or people responsible for delivery. Studies suggest that central governments provide only one of many influences on outcomes (Box 2.3; Chapter 3).
- *Evaluation* involves the power to declare a policy's success. It can be a technical process by analysts or a heated debate between parties. For ministers, success can relate to *politics* (for example, did it make me more popular?), *process* (was it managed and supported well?), or be *programmatic* (did it produce the desired outcomes?) (Box 5.3; McConnell, 2010; Compton and 't Hart, 2019).
- *Policy maintenance, succession or termination* reminds us that policies rarely begin on a blank screen.

Box 2.3: Agency and structure: how to describe policy-making context

'Agency' describes the ability 'to deliberate and act', emphasising 'intentional action based on an actor's thought process and ability to choose' (Cairney, 2020a: 10). However, it is difficult to know how people think and what motivates them to act. Further, agency is difficult to separate from its wider context. There are many metaphors to describe context, including agents interacting with:

- *Structures*, or a context that 'is relatively fixed and difficult but not impossible to break down' and 'influences the decisions that actors make' (2020a: 10). Social structures include the rules and norms of behaviour that seem impervious to change (2020a: 81).
- *Policy conditions*, including 'a political system's size, demographic structure, economy, and mass behaviour' (2020a: 95).
- *Environments*. Evolutionary metaphors note the 'sense that environmental influences on policy making often seem to be overwhelming or out of the control of individual policymakers' (2020a: 102). A focus on environments highlights: the large number of actors involved, making and influencing decisions in many venues; the institutions, or rules within different venues; the networks of actors who make and influence policy; the ideas which underpin policy debate; and, the conditions and events that influence policy-maker attention and limit their options.
- *Complex systems*. Studies emphasise 'the interdependence between a huge number of actors', and a tendency of systems to amplify or dampen the actions of policy makers (2020a: 104–105). They highlight: 'path dependence' when decisions made in the past

limit current options; 'strange attractors' which indicate regular patterns of policy making over long periods despite the ability of policy makers to intervene at any time; and, the 'emergence' of outcomes in the absence of central control (Cairney and Geyer, 2015).

Policy studies: how is policy *really* made?

Most studies of policy making identify what happens when policy makers deal with bounded rationality and the absence of a policy cycle. This field of study is difficult to navigate because it contains a diverse and unwieldy collection of approaches. To simplify, we describe:

- Examples of concepts and theories that describe policy-maker responses to bounded rationality.
- A simple representation of the policy-making environment, to generate a picture of 'complex government' to compare with the Westminster model in Chapter 3. This story of policy making in the real world highlights *the lack of centralised control* and a tendency for new governments to inherit and build on previous policy.

How could policy makers respond to bounded rationality?

Lindblom's (1959; 1979) classic account suggests that policy makers and governments tend towards 'incrementalism', which describes:

- *Policy analysis.* Limiting analysis to a small number of feasible solutions.
- *Policy making.* Policy change via a series of non-radical steps.

Lindblom (1959; 1979) described this approach as sensible and common: there is no point in using resources to investigate solutions that no one will select, and radical policy change is a shot in the dark. Trial and error helps monitor and change the effects of policy. Building on past policies makes sense when so much effort has been invested in an agreed position.

We examine the normative case for non-radical policy change in the next section. Here, we focus on many other ways to describe the cognitive and emotional responses to bounded rationality, including many that question the inevitability of incrementalism (see Cairney, 2020a). We summarise key concepts in what follows, and each has its own blog post in Cairney's 500- and 1,000-word series (https://paulcairney.wordpress.com/1000-words/).

Punctuated equilibrium theory (and policy communities)

Policy makers can only pay attention to a small number of problems at any one time. They pay disproportionately high attention to some and ignore or delegate the rest (Baumgartner and Jones, 2009). Consequently, most policy is processed through small and specialist 'policy communities' which manage issues at a level of government not particularly visible to the public (Richardson and Jordan, 1979; Jordan and Maloney, 1997; Jordan and Cairney, 2013: 238). The outcome is a small amount of major policy change (in issues receiving high senior policy-maker attention) and a huge amount of minor changes (in issues receiving minimal attention) (Baumgartner and Jones, 2009).

Power and ideas

Some beliefs about policy become taken-for-granted 'paradigms' that inhibit new ways of thinking and undermine policy change (Hall, 1993). Some groups monopolise how a policy is understood in government. Their dominance may be 'institutionalised' following the production of rules and norms used to guide policy making (Baumgartner and Jones, 2009). This dominance may prevent the discussion of new policy solutions (see Chapters 4 and 5 on the endurance then breakdown of paradigms).

Multiple streams analysis

Policy makers identify problems, solutions are produced, and choices are made, but these actions can happen in any order (Cohen et al, 1972: 1). Kingdon (1995) uses this insight to argue that major policy change may happen only when a 'window of opportunity' opens and three 'streams' come together: there is high attention to a policy problem (problem stream); a feasible solution already exists (policy stream); and, policy makers have the motive and opportunity to act (politics stream). This process is not linear, and defining a policy problem does not lead inevitably to the adoption of a solution.

Institutions and new institutionalism

Institutions are the formal and informal rules that policy makers use to simplify their choices, producing 'standard operating procedures' and norms of behaviour, rather than beginning from scratch each time (March and Olsen, 1984; Kenny, 2007; Ostrom, 2007).

Social construction and policy design

Policy makers make choices based on the quick and emotional – or strategic and cynical – use of social stereotypes. They assign benefits to 'deserving' groups and punishments to others. These choices become routine features of policy design, and send clear signals to citizens (Schneider and Ingram 1997, 2005; Box 3.6; Chapter 9).

Advocacy coalition framework

Policy actors enter politics to turn their beliefs into policy. They form coalitions with like-minded people, and compete with people who don't share their beliefs. Some issues are low salience, with scope for negotiation between coalitions. Others are high salience and controversial, prompting coalitions to romanticise their own cause and demonise their opponents (Weible et al, 2009; Weible and Ingold, 2018).

Narrative policy framework

Policy narratives help to simplify a complex world. Policy makers can be the audience, perhaps vulnerable to manipulation when they rely on simple stories from particular sources. Or, they can be the narrators, telling simple stories to persuade the public to see a policy problem and its solution through their eyes (Crow and Jones, 2018).

Policy learning

Policy learning is as much a political process (learning how to win, or dominate others) as the search for new information from experts or stakeholders (Dunlop and Radaelli, 2013; 2018).

In each concept, we find profound limits to 'rationality' which may contribute to: (1) policy-making inertia built on ignoring most evidence until there is a lurch of attention; (2) choices to favour some groups rather than societal benefits; and (3) learning for political gain rather than collecting evidence comprehensively. While some may seek goal-driven, evidence-informed policy, most theories describe why it will never be realised (Cairney, 2016a).

A simple representation of the policy-making environment

Cairney (2017a; 2023a) provides one way to visualise a complex policy process to seem as simple as the policy cycle (Figure 2.2). This image describes policy makers responding to bounded rationality (the 'psychology of choice') within an environment over which they have minimal control. The latter is summed up by five concepts which help to tell a story of policy making as follows (Cairney, 2020a: 232–234). There are many policy makers and influencers (*actors*), spread across many 'centres' of government (Box 1.2). Each centre has its own formal and informal rules (*institutions*), relationships between policy makers and influencers (*networks*), and dominant beliefs or ways to understand problems (*ideas*). As such, each centre is associated with a different policy-making *context* and responds more or less to different *events* (routine events include elections, while non-routine events include crises).

This image tells a story that contrasts with the ideal type of comprehensive rationality and the policy cycle. Instead of one powerful centre, there are many. Instead of producing 'rational', orderly and stable policy making, these centres combine to produce practices that can be stable or unstable, and outcomes that can lurch from continuity to change. A political system's 'central government' may be the most powerful centre, but it tends to be broken down into many smaller 'policy communities'. Senior policy makers could intervene in any issue at any time, but the logical consequence is to ignore most other issues.

We describe the UK variant of this story in Chapter 3. For present purposes, the point is that these dynamics should be taken into account when conducting policy analysis. For example, they help to warn against the idea that heroic individuals can overcome them (Box 2.4).

Box 2.4: Systems thinking and policy entrepreneurship

Concepts such as *complex systems* and *policy entrepreneurs* can be used to generate very different – agency or context-centred (Box 2.3) – messages about policy making (Cairney, 2021a).

In policy analysis, systems thinking is a useful antidote to simplistic policy analysis: identify the complexity of policy problems and the interdependence of the people solving them. However, many also describe their hope for disproportionate influence: 'if we engage in systems thinking effectively, we can understand systems well enough to control, manage, or influence them' (2021a: 130). This hope contrasts with policy studies messages: if policy tends to 'emerge' from complex systems in the absence of central control, accept policy-maker limitations and 'avoid the mechanistic language of "policy levers" which exaggerate human or government control' (2021a: 130).

In policy analysis, entrepreneurs can be the change agents with disproportionate influence on policy change. Analysts can learn how to emulate their success by generating similar *attributes* (for example, effective social skills and tenacity), *skills* (for example, in strategy, teamwork, persuasion), and *strategies* (for example, framing, building coalitions) (Mintrom, 2019: 308–320). In policy studies, the message is that most entrepreneurs fail, their success relates more to their environments than skills, and few actors have the opportunities to use them (Cairney, 2021a: 126–127).

Critical policy analysis: challenging how policy is made

Critical policy analysis helps us understand the wider *political context*, in which actors compete to determine whose evidence, values and aims matter, and *policy-making context*, in which there is no simple way to translate evidence and values into policy (Cairney, 2021a: 71–72; see also https://paulcairney.wordpress.com/policy-analysis-in-750-words/).

Figure 2.2: The policy process

Source: Cairney (2017a)

Stone's policy paradox

Stone (2012) examines the consequences of an absence of comprehensive rationality. First, there is no way to gather information comprehensively and objectively to produce a coherent list of preferences that maximise societal benefit. Rather, 'policy paradox' describes how the same policy makers (or publics) can understand the same issue in contradictory ways, and come to opposite conclusions in different contexts without changing their beliefs (2012: 2–3). Second, they cannot resolve this problem by generating more information to reduce *uncertainty*. Rather, problem definition is about resolving *ambiguity*. Ambiguity describes the ability to interpret problems in different ways, with reference to different values or different interpretations of the same values (for example, when deciding whose needs and freedoms matter) (2012: 14).

How do policy actors exercise power to resolve these problems in their favour? Stone (2012) describes their skilful use of persuasion strategies. They tell stories to draw attention to some issues over others and prioritise their preferred problem definitions and solutions. The aim is to: determine who should receive blame or sympathy when assessing the cause and consequence of the problem; make some solutions seem easier to understand and implement; identify which policy instruments to prioritise and which human rights to enforce; and, establish the role of governments. Storytellers are persuasive when they can exploit how people process information, employing:

- *Symbols*, to sum up an issue instantly.
- *Characters*, to determine who is to blame, and who deserves sympathy.
- *Narrative arcs*, to draw in an audience.
- *Synecdoche*, to equate the whole problem with one example.
- *Metaphor*, to associate a complex issue with something simple and relatable.
- *Numbers*, to simplify, and relate a story to expertise.
- *Ambiguity*, to encourage different people to support a policy for different reasons (Stone, 2012: 157–228).

Bacchi's *What's the Problem Represented to Be?*

How can we identify and respond to such stories? Bacchi (2009: 1–24) developed the six-step 'What's the Problem Represented to Be?' approach to highlight (1) how policy actors interpret policy problems as they define them, and (2) how to *challenge* these 'problematisations':

1. *What's the 'problem' represented to be?* Powerful actors make political choices to identify a problem's cause (for example, the poor behaviour of certain populations), the role of the state in solving it (for example, to regulate or not), and which part of the state is relevant (for example, is it a public health or crime issue?).
2. *What presuppositions or assumptions underlie this representation?* They draw on 'deep-seated cultural values' to identify which groups deserve support or punishment, what is normal versus deviant behaviour, and whether the state should be involved in individual or family life.
3. *How has this representation come about?* Explanations for a shift of attention include: new events or information, shifts in public attitudes, a change of government, or a technology that opens up new possibilities.
4. *Can the 'problem' be thought about differently?* Identify how powerful actors interpret the behaviour of others when assigning blame, and how else to interpret problems.
5. *What effects are produced by this representation?* Identify who wins and loses.
6. *How could it be questioned, disrupted and replaced?* Researchers have a responsibility to challenge the powerful actors who act to the detriment of powerless actors.

Policy analysis for marginalised groups

A wider community of researchers seeks to understand and challenge unfair policy outcomes resulting from unequal power in politics and society. This approach can be related to questions such as: whose knowledge and evidence matters, who decides what evidence to use, and who benefits from its use?

Decolonising research

L.T. Smith (2012: 10) highlights the political nature of the research used for policy analysis: 'Whose research is it? Who owns it? Whose interests does it serve? Who will benefit from it? Who has designed its questions and framed its scope? Who will carry it out? Who will write it up? How will its results be disseminated?' L.T. Smith (2012: 66–71) describes the enduring legacy of a narrow and damaging view of what counts as policy-relevant knowledge, developed by 'Western researchers' and supported by powerful colonising governments (such as the UK). It privileges the research methods used by highly trained scientists, who see themselves as objective, treat Indigenous communities as objects of research, and dismiss their claims to knowledge. The alternative is to recognise the inescapable link between power and knowledge and connect research explicitly to high-level political aims such as Indigenous community 'self-determination', 'survival' and 'recovery' (L.T. Smith, 2012: 121). This commitment to decolonising research would change key methods of policy analysis: working with marginalised communities to co-produce knowledge to inform problem definitions and solutions, rather than engaging in superficial consultation and aloof top-down policy making (L.T. Smith, 2012: 228–232: 13).

Critical race theory

Doucet (2019: 2–3) draws on 'critical race theory' (Chapter 10) to show that most research does not communicate well the 'experiences of marginalized groups', and policy makers have misused research to justify power inequalities, racism and unfair social outcomes. Doucet's (2019: 5–22) recommendations include to: challenge the idea that scientific research is objective and that researchers are 'beyond reproach'; recognise how research and analysis has been used and abused to 'reproduce the subordination of social groups'; respect 'experiential knowledge'; and, connect policy-relevant knowledge to a political commitment to 'social justice' which 'centres race' and helps to 'emancipate and empower marginalized groups'.

The implications for policy analysis and policy studies

Such insights help to identify important ways to interrogate policy making and its study.

Who should be involved in policy analysis and policy making?

Reject the idea that policy analysis can be conducted by a small number of experts using technical tools to produce optimal solutions. Analysis is a political act that should be accompanied by 'co-production' to share many sources of knowledge. Collaboration would involve the use of scientific evidence, but without assuming that scientific professions decide which forms of research produce the most useful knowledge (Mintrom, 2012; Meltzer and Schwartz, 2019). However, claims for 'co-production' should also be treated with caution, to reflect concern about its insincere use in policy making when major inequalities of power between participants remain, and the most powerful actors see problems primarily through their own eyes. Powerful actors may use the language of co-production – and a 'safe' vocabulary to describe the marginalisation of social groups – as a superficial alternative to substantive action (L.T. Smith, 2012; Ahmed, 2017: 103).

The perils of focusing on heroic individuals

As Boxes 2.3 and 2.4 describe, there is a tendency in policy analysis to focus on agency: analysts diagnosing problems; systems thinkers seeing the big picture; entrepreneurs selling solutions; and policy makers making things happen. Yet, these powers are distributed unequally, representing structural obstacles to policy change.

Challenging the status quo: should policy making be pragmatic and incremental?

Most texts recommend pragmatic action: focus on your client's aims and timetable, be efficient when collecting evidence, and favour politically feasible solutions (Cairney, 2021a: 88). They have a lot in common with incremental strategies: focus analysis on a few options, and do not depart radically from negotiated positions (Lindblom, 1959; 1979). Traditionally, this advice formed part of the 'art and craft' of analysis (Wildavsky, 1980), on the assumption of a pluralistic political system in which power is dispersed and there are widespread opportunities for influence. In contrast, critical policy analysis shows that cautious pragmatism protects the status quo which reproduces unequal social and political outcomes (Cairney, 2021a: 88). It reminds us that policy-making systems may be complex, but the outcomes still provide systematic benefits to some groups and punishments to others.

Bringing these three perspectives together

What would a combined focus on policy analysis, policy studies and critical policy analysis look like? Table 2.1 compares their insights by relating them to the five-step approach to analysis:

- Policy analysis steps help to define the problem for a client, identify feasible solutions, use values to compare them, predict their impact, and make a recommendation.
- Policy studies examine the extent to which policy makers understand the problems they face, relate new solutions to existing commitments, think systematically about the effect of policy mixes, and rely on many other centres to get things done.

Table 2.1: Three perspectives on five-step policy analysis

	Policy analysis texts	Policy process research	Critical policy analysis
Step 1	Define a policy problem identified by your client	Identify if a policy maker is willing and able to understand and address the problem	Challenge dominant ways to frame issues
Step 2	Identify technically and politically feasible solutions	Identify the mix of policy instruments already being used, and why	Use inclusive ways to generate knowledge and perspectives on solutions
Step 3	Use values and political goals to compare solutions	Identify how actors cooperate or compete to define and rank values	Co-produce the rules to produce and evaluate solutions
Step 4	Predict the outcome of each feasible solution	Emphasise uncertainty about the effect of your solution on the existing policy mix	Identify the impact on marginalised groups
Step 5	Make a recommendation to your client	Recommend how to adapt to policy-making systems. In the absence of centralisation, how can you deliver this instrument?	Co-produce your recommendations with stakeholders, and respect their reaction to your proposals

Source: adapted from Cairney (2021a)

- Critical policy analysis challenges dominant framings, fosters the co-production of solutions, and considers the unequal impacts of solutions.

This comparison helps to combine – in Chapters 6–11 – the empirical study of politics and policy making with normative research.

Conclusion

This focus on three perspectives provides different ways to understand politics and policy making. It equips you with critical skills to analyse policy processes. Five-step policy analysis emphasises the agency of key policy actors: what are their aims, and what do they need to do to achieve them? The study of policy analysts suggests that political systems do not meet their needs. Analytical and political skills are essential to policy making, but they do not ensure that policy makers can understand and solve the problems they face.

Policy studies highlight how difficult it is to know what policy is, measure the substance and impact of policy instruments, and identify who is responsible for the outcomes. It uses stories of ideal types to explore what happens in the real world. Policy makers face bounded rationality, which prompts them to use cognitive and emotional shortcuts to understand issues well enough to make choices. They engage in a policy-making environment over which they have limited knowledge and control. They pay attention to some issues but delegate responsibility for most. They take responsibility for overseeing policy making from the centre of government, but share responsibility with many other centres.

Each venue for policy choice has its own rules, networks, ideas, and ways to respond to events and issues. This perspective downplays agency in favour of context: the structures, environments, systems or conditions that limit their powers to understand and solve problems.

Critical policy analysis highlights what analysts and policy makers do, and how to challenge the results. Policy makers respond to bounded rationality and complexity by making goal- and emotion-driven choices. They describe their processes as objective, emphasising research and systematic techniques. They sell these choices with simple stories to assign praise and blame, benefits and punishments. They marginalise populations unfairly, diminishing their experiences, knowledge claims and campaigns for policy change.

What should we do next with these perspectives? Chapter 3 shows how they inform two very different stories of UK policy making. Chapters 6–11 use these insights to identify policy problems, examine how policy makers have sought to address them, and reflect on their unequal impacts.

Explaining UK Politics and Policy Making

Chapter highlights

1. Compares different stories of UK policy making.

   - The *Westminster story* describes the concentration of power in the hands of a few people at the heart of central government.

   - It remains an important reference point even when it provides an inaccurate account of policy making.

   - The *complex government story* describes the limits to central government control.

   - It is more accurate but less easy to understand and connect to UK political norms.

2. Explores what happens when policy makers draw on both stories for different reasons, even when they seem to contradict each other.

Introduction: Two ways to understand policy making in the UK

The UK political system is confusing. It is best understood by drawing on two different stories. One is the official story associated with the 'Westminster model'. It describes how the UK political system works *in principle*, based on its official rules and a claim about how politics *should* work. It helps to explain key functions such as its electoral system and the role of Parliament and government. The other is the unofficial story of complex government, representing a collection of insights generated from policy studies. It describes how policy making works *in practice*. It highlights the unwritten rules, and how policy makers deal with the unmanageable scale of government. It provides a more accurate account, and often contradicts the official story.

Why juggle these two stories if only one is accurate? One helps to explain the environment in which policy makers operate. The other helps to explain how they navigate that environment, using shortcuts and simple stories to turn complex government into manageable and effective-looking strategies. This dynamic influences how we draw conclusions from UK policy making: we demonstrate the importance of *and* limits to central government influence. Policy makers may try in vain to exert control over policy processes and outcomes.

However, they can still have a major impact, and often succeed in narrating their impact to maintain an image of governing competence.

The official story matters because people use it to describe how policy making works and who to praise or blame for the results. It guides how people act: voters during elections, parties competing for voters, ministers scrutinised by Parliament, media commentary, and civil servants delivering ministerial aims. Ministers and public servants may recognise the greater accuracy of the complex government story, but it does not give them a way to legitimise their activity (Cairney, 2015a). They often act according to one story, but tell another. Official stories are necessary, resistant to change, and have an effect on policy making and our perception of that process (Box 3.1).

We use these stories to describe essential features of UK politics and policy making. We begin with a focus on electing a powerful and decisive government in a Westminster system. We then describe the elements of complex government that limit the effects of that power. Finally, we ask: what happens when those stories collide? What if policy makers seek to balance (1) taking a pragmatic approach to complexity with (2) describing their activities in a way that the public can understand and support? Do they try to take less responsibility for policy outcomes, to reflect their limited role? Or, do they reassert central control, to try to be more influential since they will be held responsible? Successive governments have provided different answers to that question, but no attempt to centralise policy making has had the desired effect (Chapters 4 and 5). This conclusion informs every case study chapter (Chapters 6–11), including the 'take back control' narrative central to the Brexit debate (Chapter 7).

Box 3.1: The UK government minister as a modern-day King Canute

"I am meant to be in control … I'm the king who takes the decisions." (Alleged complaint by Boris Johnson about his lack of power while Prime Minister – Seldon and Newell, 2023)

There are several versions of the tale of King Canute and the sea, used to generate a moral story. He was *arrogant*, convinced that he could control the tides, *humble*, showing his courtiers that he could not, or, he *staged* the event to show the public the limits to monarchical powers in relation to God or the environment (Hay, 2009: 261). These tales help to explore different stories of UK government. First, what is the power of government ministers?

- Can they control their departments or policy outcomes?
- Do they *think* they are in control?
- Do they try to demonstrate to the public the limits to their influence on policy?

Second, if ministers fail to get the policy outcomes they want, does it reflect:

- Bad luck or judgement ('policy blunders' – King and Crewe, 2014)?
- Inevitable failure to control a policy-making environment?

Gathering evidence can address this question *partly*. However, we also bring our worldview to the interpretation (Hay, 2009: 263). If a minister has a minimal impact in one case, we can draw different conclusions:

- They had the policy levers at their disposal and failed to use them. The case study demonstrates incompetence or a lack of political will.
- They had limited resources (for example, attention, time, cognitive ability, access to policy instruments) to address a 'wicked' problem (Chapter 1). It is misleading to describe 'levers' or agency in an environment immune to control.

Third, what is the role of the protagonist in telling the story? Ministers influence how they – and their audience – interpret the problems they face and their ability to act competently to solve them. They use performance and rhetoric to portray their actions in a positive light, reminding us of the importance of the 'political skill and artistry of those who manipulate agenda(s)' (Riker, 1980: 445; Hay, 2009: 276–277). That said, we should not *assume* that ministers act strategically and skilfully, or influence their audience's reaction to their performance (Ball et al, 2021). Indeed, prime ministerial diaries and popular cultural references provide very different stories of their actions (compare Lynn and Jay, 1989; Iannucci et al, 2010; Dobbs, 2011 with Thatcher, 1993; Blair, 2010).

The Westminster model: a story of centralised power and control

The Westminster model helps to concentrate power at the centre of government (Rhodes, 1997; Bevir and Rhodes, 1999; Marsh et al, 2001; Richards and Smith, 2002: 3; Gains and Stoker, 2009; John, 2022; see Rhodes, 2011 on 'the Westminster story'). At its heart is a normative message about democratic accountability, based on concepts such as:

- *Representative democracy*. Most government accountability is to the public through elections (and parliamentary scrutiny).
- *Parliamentary sovereignty, and a fusion of executive and legislature*. Power is retained by a sovereign parliament which delegates power to the executive (His Majesty's Government, also known as UK central government).
- *Majority party control*. A plurality electoral system exaggerates a party's success. Parties can secure a minority of overall votes but a majority of MPs because each MP can win the seat with a plurality of votes (they receive more than any other candidate).
- *The UK as a unitary state*. The UK delegates responsibilities to other (devolved and local) governments but retains overall power and responsibility.
- *Cabinet government and individual ministerial responsibility*. The Prime Minister appoints the Cabinet. Secretaries of State are responsible for all that happens

in their departments, producing hierarchical structures in which civil servants deliver the wishes of ministers.

There are many ways to describe the Westminster model (King, 2015; Russell and Serban, 2021), but two elements are crucial. First, the moral of the story: power and responsibility go hand in hand since, if you know who is in charge, you know who to reward or punish in the next election. This arrangement reflects a 'British political tradition': the government is accountable to public, via Parliament, on the assumption that it is powerful and responsible. It takes responsibility for public policy and acts in a 'responsible' way, often making 'strong, decisive, necessary action, even when opposed by a majority of the population' (Blunkett and Richards, 2011). Second, the UK version of the Westminster model represents an archetype of a *majoritarian* democracy, in which the concentration of power in one party of government encourages a *winner takes all* mentality and top-down approach to government (Lijphart, 1999: 1–4; although see Box 3.2 on devolved governments).

Box 3.2: Majoritarian and consensus democracy in a devolved UK

Lijphart (1999: 3–4) describes a contrast between majoritarian and consensus democracy archetypes. The former has a plurality electoral system that exaggerates one party's majority of seats in Parliament, fosters single-party majority governments, and concentrates power in one executive. It encourages an 'exclusive, competitive and adversarial' political culture (1999: 3). The latter has a proportional electoral system that shares seats across multiple parties, fosters coalition governments, and encourages the executive to share power with the legislature and other centres of government. It encourages 'inclusiveness, bargaining and compromise' (1999: 2).

If we accept this account, we find that devolution has produced the potential for new forms of government since 1999 (Birrell, 2012). It includes a 'power sharing' model in Northern Ireland, obliging representation in government for parties representing Protestant and Catholic populations. It offers a mild shift towards consensus democracy in Wales and Scotland, with both using new electoral systems (mixed-member proportional). Flinders (2010: 176) identifies 'bi-constitutionality' following the promotion of consensus democracies within an overall majoritarian system (or the pursuit of 'new politics' as an antidote to 'old Westminster' – Cairney and McGarvey, 2013: 10–13).

Yet, one message of the complex government story is that the policy processes in the UK and devolved governments are not as different as they seem. The UK government's alleged tendency to make policy from the top down is exaggerated. Most policy is processed in relatively consensual 'policy communities' (Kriesi et al, 2006; Jordan and Cairney, 2013; Cairney, 2019b). Top-down and uncompromising policy making is 'politically expensive' and not the 'normal' policy-making style (Richardson et al, 1982: 10; see also Box 5.1).

The Westminster story taps into well-established ideas about how politics *should* work in the UK, sums up what people think they are voting for in general elections, and bolstered the 'take back control' Brexit message (Chapter 7). It dominates media and social media discussions even when it does not describe UK politics accurately (Jordan and Cairney, 2013). As such, it affects reality. It ensures that ministers have the means to pursue their policy agendas (Duggett, 2009). It gives them a frame of reference – with great power comes great responsibility – that they cannot ignore if they seek to win elections (Bevir and Rhodes, 2003; 2006; Lee et al, 2022). No one is running for election with the mere promise to try their best.

Disenchantment and the Westminster model

A belief in this image of UK politics underpins common ways to express disenchantment (see Clarke et al, 2018 on trends). Some of these concerns are discussed in the following sections.

Politics is too far removed from 'the people'

Politicians make decisions in isolation, with a 'top-down' mentality, causing 'one way traffic from those governing (the Government) to those being governed (society)' (Richards and Smith, 2002: 3). Policy making is a battle for election but not of ideas, since the main political parties present similar ideas and compete to demonstrate their governing competence (Green, 2007). Indeed, some politicians have exploited this idea of a political establishment to exercise power within parties (Box 3.3).

Box 3.3: How coherent are Britain's political parties?

British political parties are not hugely coherent, with Labour and the Conservatives hosting a wide variety of perspectives, priorities and agendas. Recent years have seen disagreements intensify with greater frequency (Kippin and Pyper, 2021; Chapter 7 on Brexit). Bale (2023) describes a fragmentation of the Conservative Party into competing camps of radical-right populists and market fundamentalists who battle with 'establishment' Conservatives for control of the party. Such labelling reflects long-standing groupings within the party, such as the (anti-EU) European Research Group, a hard-right 'Common Sense' faction, and a more ambiguous and moderate 'One Nation' tendency. Labour has similarly had divisions, with the period covering the late 1970s and early 1980s particularly fraught (Ward, 2022). From the 1990s, New Labour leaders deliberately and effectively marginalised the left of the party (Minkin, 2014), with the rise of the left-wing Jeremy Corbyn to the leadership in 2015 occurring despite opposition from most Labour MPs. The Liberal Democrats are divided into a 'social liberal' centre-left and 'orange book' (pro-market) centre-right (Marshall, 2012). Different party systems in Scotland and Wales have also created opportunities for intra-party conflict (A. Clark, 2018), while Northern Ireland has a largely separate system (Tonge, 2013).

The political class does not represent the public

The arrogant behaviour of the political class is exemplified by events such as an expenses scandal in 2009 (Pattie and Johnston, 2012; Vivyan et al, 2012). Policy making is elitist, carried out by a powerful political class that is too far removed from the public to know how best to govern (Stoker, 2006; Hay, 2007; Flinders, 2012; Allen and Cairney, 2017). Political systems privilege the recruitment and election of White, middle- or upper-class, elite-educated men at the expense of marginalised populations (Box 3.4, based on Butler et al, 2021; Cracknell and Tunnicliffe, 2022; see also Childs, 2004; Krook, 2006; Ashe et al, 2010; Durose et al, 2013; Evans, 2014; Campbell and Shorrocks, 2021; Kenny et al, 2022). This recruitment contributes to gendered, racialised and ableist practices in parliaments and government (Social Mobility Commission, 2021; Boswell et al, 2022; Evans and Reher, 2023; Scottish Parliament, 2023; Siow, 2023).

Box 3.4: The social background of MPs

MPs are generally unrepresentative of the social backgrounds of the UK public, but this problem is changing. There is growing representation according to gender, ethnicity and education, but also a tendency for MPs to be recruited directly from political roles (with diminishing experience in the occupations held by typical voters) (Butler et al, 2021):

- The number and proportion of men in Westminster was 430 MPs (66 per cent) in 2019 (Cracknell and Tunnicliffe, 2022: 6). Although high in relation to the UK population, this proportion is the lowest in Westminster history: falling from 97 per cent in 1979 (the first Thatcher government) and 82 per cent in 1997 (the first Blair government) (Cracknell and Tunnicliffe, 2022: 6). The rise in women MPs is fuelled primarily by Labour (51 per cent of its MPs in 2019 were women, compared to 24 per cent in the Conservatives) (Cracknell and Tunnicliffe, 2022: 7).
- An estimated 585 (90 per cent) MPs from a White background were elected in 2019 (Cracknell and Tunnicliffe, 2022: 14). The 65 MPs (10 per cent) 'from minority ethnic backgrounds' (compared to ten in 1997) was driven by Labour (41) (Cracknell and Tunnicliffe, 2022: 14).
- Twenty-nine per cent of MPs in 2019 had attended private/fee-paying schools, and 87 per cent were university graduates, including 22 per cent from Oxford or Cambridge (Cracknell and Tunnicliffe, 2022: 19). Although these figures are unrepresentative of the UK population (state school attendance is over 90 per cent), they represent positive trends. In 1979, 73 per cent of Conservative MPs had attended private schools and 49 per cent were Oxbridge graduates (Cracknell and Tunnicliffe, 2022: 20).

- Most of the 2019 intake held an occupation in a political role 'instrumental' to election, such as another elected position or working for the party (Cracknell and Tunnicliffe, 2022: 26; see also Cairney, 2007a; Butler et al, 2021).

While there were some hopes for improved representation in the Scottish Parliament and Senedd Cymru (the Welsh Parliament, formerly National Assembly for Wales), they were only met by the initially higher representation of women (less apparent since 2019) and attendees of state schools, but not in relation to minority ethnic representation, university education or occupation (Kenny and Mackay, 2014; Cairney et al, 2016; Keating et al, 2020).

Some leaders have addressed the issue, to some extent, when recruiting to Cabinet. Nicola Sturgeon's first Scottish Cabinet contained five women and five men (Brooks, 2014). Liz Truss's Cabinet marked the first time that a White man did not hold one of the four major roles (Prime Minister, Chancellor, Foreign Secretary, Home Secretary) (Pannett, 2022).

Politicians take power but not responsibility

Ministers are too likely to 'pass the buck' to other organisations. Too many decisions are being made by the 'unelected state' which consists of public bodies such as the Bank of England (central to monetary policies such as interest rates), **quangos** and non-governmental bodies such as 'third-sector' organisations (charities) delivering social services or private-sector companies building schools and hospitals (Flinders and Skelcher, 2012; Chapters 4 and 5).

> **Quangos**: quasi-non-governmental bodies, sponsored by government departments but operating at 'arm's length' from ministers. The less pejorative term is 'non-departmental public body'.

Complex government: a story of limited central control

The second story relates to complex policy-making systems and limited central government control. It draws on a general story derived from policy concepts and theories (Chapter 2). A focus on bounded rationality highlights the limits to policy makers' understanding of policy problems. A focus on context (Box 2.3) shows that policy makers operate in an environment over which they have limited understanding and even less control.

The UK variant of this story uses terms such as 'governance', 'multi-level governance', 'policy communities' or 'differentiated polity model' (Richardson and Jordan, 1979; Rhodes, 1997; Richards and Smith, 2002: 3; Bache and Flinders, 2004; Kerr and Kettell, 2006: 11). It challenges the notion that there is a core group of policy makers at the heart of the process, analysing and making policy from the 'top down'. Key elements are discussed in the following sections.

The pragmatic case for delegating policy attention

UK general elections often produce a new government, but changes of government do not cause wholesale shifts in policy because most decisions are beyond the reach of ministers. Ministers are ostensibly in charge of government departments, but can only pay attention to a tiny proportion of the issues for which they are responsible. They break policy making down into more manageable departments, and a large number of divisions within departments, dealing with issues that involve a small number of knowledgeable participants. Ministers rely on their officials for information and advice. For specialist issues, officials rely on specialist organisations. Organisations trade that information and advice (and other things, such as the ability to generate agreement among influential groups) for access to, and influence within, government (Richardson and Jordan, 1979; Jordan and Cairney, 2013). Consequently, there is a blurry boundary between formal responsibility and informal influence. Many actors are involved in the policy process, it is difficult to separate their effects, and policy outcomes are the product of collective action (Rose, 1987: 267–268).

Four concepts combine to describe these blurry boundaries between formal powers and informal influence. First, 'core executive':

> The innermost centre of British central government consists of a complex web of institutions, networks and practices surrounding the PM, Cabinet, cabinet committees and their official counterparts, less formalized ministerial 'clubs' or meetings, bilateral negotiations, and interdepartmental committees. It also includes some major coordinating departments – chiefly, the Cabinet Office, the Treasury, the Foreign Office, the law officers, and the security and intelligence services. (Dunleavy and Rhodes, 1990; see also Rhodes, 1995: 17; Rhodes, 2011: 213–219)

Pressure participants: actors attempting to influence public policy. They can be interest groups, businesses, public sector bodies, and other types of government (Jordan et al, 2004).

Second, 'policy communities' (or 'policy networks', the generic term) describes the relationships that develop between policy makers, actors who deliver policy, and the **pressure participants** who possess informal influence (see Cairney, 2020a: 152 for a summary of terms). Most policy is made in communities not particularly visible to the public or Parliament, and with minimal ministerial involvement.

Third, 'governance' often replaces 'government' when studies describe the diffusion of power from the core executive to other organisations, while 'multi-level governance' describes relationships between actors with formal and informal sources of power at many levels of government (Box 1.2).

Fourth, a collection of terms describe the idea that, to some extent, policy is made as it is implemented or delivered (Hill and Hupe, 2009). For example, 'street level bureaucrats' – such as in education, health, social work and criminal justice – turn an overwhelming number of government regulations into a routine response, and represent the face of government to service recipients (Lipsky, 1980). To some extent, these professionals can adopt 'entrepreneurial' strategies, such as to 'build relationships with the community' that they serve rather than simply adopt top-down measures (Durose, 2011; Arnold, 2021; see also Box 10.5).

The normative case for delegating key functions of government

There are often good reasons for 'hands-off' arrangements. A powerful example is when public bodies make sure that doctors and social workers act properly when they use the Mental Health Act to detain people for treatment against their will. There is also an important independent role for judicial bodies to interpret, uphold or challenge UK laws (in relation to wider principles or conventions on human rights). Or, advisory bodies need to project their independence from ministers to give credible advice. The outcome is that ministers cede some responsibility to other bodies, trusting that such bodies will act responsibly.

The multi-level nature of policy and policy making

What we call 'policy' is a collection of many policy instruments, made at many levels of government. For example, UK 'tobacco control policy' resulted from many instruments produced and delivered by the EU, UK, devolved governments and local authorities (Cairney et al, 2012; Cairney, 2019a). Further, 'gender mainstreaming' involves a large collection of policy instruments spread across all levels (Cairney et al, 2021a).

The fragmented nature of policy making

Policy making is 'fragmented' (Elliott et al, 2022) in two senses. First, a post-war rise in governmental responsibilities produced mutually reinforcing effects: more groups interested in government; and, a more stretched government, more reliant on outside advice (Jordan, 1981: 96–100). Second, the UK governmental structure is broken down into departments and agencies, and policy issues are managed in different sectors (such as agriculture) and subsectors (such as dairy farming). Departments share responsibilities for cross-cutting issues. For example, poverty and social inclusion may be addressed by departments responsible for employment, social security, taxation, and public services such as health, education and justice (see also Chapters 6 and 8). Some issues, such

> **Cross-cutting**: issues which defy simple department boundaries and require coordination across them.

> **Joined-up government**: the ability to address policy in a holistic manner (or ensure that policy in one department does not undermine policy in another).

as inequalities, defy attempts to introduce cross-departmental coordination (Cairney and St Denny, 2020). Governments set up units or 'mainstreaming' initiatives (to oblige each department to consider the effect of public policy on particular social groups) to encourage **joined-up government**, but often without backing them with sufficient political weight and staffing (Boswell et al, 2019).

Policy inheritance and the complexity of the statute book

Newly elected governments inherit the statute book and policies of their predecessors (Rose, 1990; Rose and Davies, 1994). The size and scope of the state is such that any 'new' policy is likely a revision of an old one (Hogwood and Peters, 1983). Parties might want to make serious changes, but are constrained by past decisions that produced organisations, regulations and employees which are difficult to remove. Innovations require policy terminations to reduce costs. Yet, complete termination may be opposed by groups associated with the policy, and undermined by organisations seeking to justify their existence (Geva-May, 2004). Policy making is about dealing with past decisions and their cumulative effect is profound. There are many Acts of Parliament (and Statutory Instruments) which are understood by few people, and it is 'extremely difficult to estimate how much legislation is in force at any one time' (Cabinet Office and Office of the Parliamentary Counsel, 2013).

How have policy makers responded to complex government?

Chapters 4 and 5 describe many examples of ministers trying to deal with the unmanageability of government, either to try to reassert central control or jettison the parts of government that most defy it. The list of reforms includes:

- *Privatisation*, including the sale of public assets.
- *Quasi-markets*, including subjecting schools and hospitals to competition.
- *Civil service reforms*, to make them more accountable to their publics.
- *Public sector reforms*, including 'contracting out' service delivery.

This process prompted academic debate about the extent to which the UK state became more able to focus on core tasks or exacerbated its own 'governance problem' (the gap between an appearance of central control and what central governments can actually do) (Cairney, 2009a). Many reforms were perhaps designed to reassert central government power, but actually reinforced a fragmented public sector and a sense that no one is in control (Chapters 4 and 5).

What happens when these two stories collide?

These stories collide when policy makers have to juggle their need to (1) appear to be in control, to defend their record in elections and to Parliament, and (2) be pragmatic and share policy-making responsibility to get things done.

The pragmatic response to complex government

There are good reasons for central governments to share power and responsibility with other actors. Civil servants have the capacity, knowledge and networks to research and make detailed policies. Quangos often need to be at 'arm's length' from ministers to achieve legitimacy in the eyes of their publics. Devolved governments have legitimate claims to some autonomy. Local governments have their own mandates, focus on the needs of local communities, and work in partnership with local stakeholders to produce local strategies. Stakeholders provide knowledge and advice on how to deliver policies in specialised areas. Service users have insights on the public services they receive. Overall, there are, *and should be*, many actors in public policy beyond a small group of people at the centre (Box 3.5). So, elected policy makers often try to share policy-making responsibility and encourage new mechanisms of accountability (Chapters 4 and 5).

Centralisation versus pragmatism

It is difficult to find a long-term and coherent plan to redraw the boundaries of the state and reform how we hold public bodies and government to account. Rather, there are many choices made with different motives. This juggling act reflects the difficulty of reconciling forms of accountability based on the centralisation versus diffusion of power. Further, it is difficult to know why policy makers pursue either aim:

- Do they centralise to ensure democratic accountability or power hoard for their own purposes?
- Do they delegate to ensure new forms of accountability or shirk responsibility for their actions?
- Do they try to do more than one thing, to combine the benefits of a consistent approach (such as power hoarding and accountability) or pursue contradictory aims (such as to power hoard and shirk responsibility)?

We may never know their motives when they need to tell different stories (Box 3.1). For example, during elections and parliamentary scrutiny, it is difficult for ministers to argue that they should only be held to account in a limited way. Consequently, they play the game of shared responsibility *and* democratic accountability. They try to construct an image of governing competence by making 'hard choices' and dominating the legislative process without expecting long-term results. They also focus on emotionally driven policies in which they express their *values* as much as strategies (Chapter 2 and Box 3.6). It may be possible to take responsibility for strategy and key choices, *and* blame public bodies for their inability to deliver. Or, ministers may be genuinely frustrated with their lack of progress, and seek to reform government to reassert power.

The enduring effect of the Westminster model of accountability

Governments may try to delegate responsibility to other organisations, such as to rely on the 'quango state' and private or third-sector bodies for the success of policy delivery (Flinders and Skelcher, 2012). However, the results become so convoluted that governments are prompted periodically to reform the public sector to reinject clarity (Richards and Smith, 2004). Either way, it is easier for Parliament to scrutinise ministers than government agencies (Cairney, 2009a: 359).

Overall, the Westminster model may be unrealistic, but its moral affects reality. 'Complex government' may undermine our ability to understand how central government works, but we still seek ways to hold it to account. Most recommendations associated with new ways to make policy do not mix well with the language of Westminster-style accountability (Box 3.5).

Box 3.5: Alternatives to power hoarding and centralised accountability

One problem with the complex governance story is that it does not come with a clear sense of how policy *should* be made. Further, many parts of that story are difficult to sell to policy makers and their audience. Cairney et al (2019a) relate these issues to the idea of multi-centric policy making (Box 1.2), which may:

- *Lack coherence* if many centres contribute without a clear sense of coordinated action.
- *Lack accountability* if many centres are responsible for only part of the problem.

However, these negative assessments relate to values associated with the Westminster model. Our argument may shift if we:

- *Challenge its normative value.* Lijphart (1999) argues that consensus democracies are more democratic and effective. Hooghe and Marks (2003: 233) argue that 'Centralized authority – command and control – has few advocates', and recommend multi-level systems that give citizens more ways to engage and are tailored to the problem at hand.
- *Challenge its lack of realism.* Maintaining the pretence of the Westminster story produces the worst of both worlds: no chance of achieving centralisation, and no opportunity to discuss properly how to manage policy in the real world.

A successful challenge could help to develop strategies for complex government. Common solutions include to:

- Reject central policy management in favour of delegating powers to actors to respond to events.
- Replace short-term performance measures based on the fiction of central control, in favour of longer-term and more flexible evaluation.
- Replace the language of policy failure with trial-and-error strategies focused on learning and adaptation (Geyer, 2012; Cairney et al, 2019a: 46–48).

Yet, it is difficult to see progress. Elected policy makers generally make reference to a Westminster story of success. They hope to tell a good story of governing competence to maintain their popularity.

Policy-making studies: examining key actors and their environments

These tensions inform how we describe UK government and policy making. The Westminster story helps us to compare an ideal type with reality, using an alternative story which better describes what happens. This task is essential, to (1) situate policy-maker agency within a wider context (Box 2.3), and (2) challenge assumptions about political systems and their reputations, such as that UK policy making is 'majoritarian' and therefore adversarial and top–down (Box 3.2).

That said, the official story still reminds us that the normative principles underpinning politics endure far longer than individual governments (Habermas, 1996). We should not lose sight of the enduring and cumulative role of governments. Policy makers, when competing for elected public office, articulate value judgements and make fundamental choices – about which social groups should be rewarded or punished – which have an enduring effect beyond the terms of single elections (Box 3.6).

Box 3.6: UK ministers and 'the social construction of target populations'

'Bounded rationality' describes the limits to policy-maker action, but the response to these limits still has a profound impact. The 'social construction and policy design' literature provides a three-step reminder of their potential effect (Schneider and Ingram, 1997; Pierce et al, 2014; Schneider et al, 2014; see Cairney and St Denny, 2020 on UK examples). First, they make quick and simple value judgements based on social stereotypes, to reward 'good' social groups with government support and punish 'bad' groups with sanctions (for example, 'strivers' and 'skivers' – O'Grady, 2022; see also Herd and Moynihan, 2018). These judgements may be emotional or strategic, or a combination of both. Second, they have a 'feed-forward' (also known as feedback) effect: they are reproduced in the institutions devoted to policy delivery, which become routine and questioned rarely in government.

Third, this outcome has an impact on citizens, who participate in politics according to how they are characterised by government. Demonised groups are alienated from politics, while romanticised groups engage routinely to reinforce their position. Social constructions are difficult to overcome when a sequence of previous policies, based on a particular framing of target populations, produces 'hegemony': the public, media and/or policy makers take these values for granted.

This account helps bring together our two stories of policy making. Its focus on emotionally driven policy making with a major impact fits well with the Westminster story of powerful ministers. Its focus on cumulative impact and hegemony links to many policy concepts – including path dependence, policy succession and inheritance before choice – which describe the enduring effects of institutions established, and policies made, in the past (Hogwood and Peters, 1983; Rose, 1990; Pierson, 2000).

Explaining the impact of key actors: ministers and the core executive

Our two stories help to interpret the role of actors such as ministers and concepts such as 'core executive':

- The *Westminster story* begins with one party winning an election and turning its manifesto into action. Ministers make key decisions as heads of government departments, departments are organised hierarchically, and civil servants look to ministers for direction. Ministers take responsibility for their choices.
- The *complex government story* highlights the limited extent to which ministers can pay attention to the issues for which they are responsible, and the tendency of most policy to be delivered on automatic pilot. New governments inherit the commitments of their predecessors, make decisions based on existing legislation, and spend most money on activities that continue by routine. New policy addresses the problems caused by the old. Ministers struggle to know what happens when actors carry out their choices.

In that context, we need to be careful about drawing conclusions from academic studies. It is not surprising to find case studies of ministerial influence when we study policy making from the 'top'. If we look for instances when they make decisions with a major impact, of course we will find them. It is not surprising to find case studies of limited or very indirect ministerial influence when we study policy making from the 'bottom', to track the many influences on actors in organisations far removed from central government. Each approach may be

> self-fulfilling: a focus on the bottom highlights a multiplicity of influences and distance from central government, but misses systematic patterns of adherence to targets set at the top; a focus at the top highlights central control and meeting targets that relate to a

small part of government business, ignoring the bulk of government responsibilities which are delivered out of the public spotlight. (Cairney, 2009a: 360)

The academic literature is full of attempts to accentuate one of these stories (for example, D. Marsh, 2011; Cairney and Jordan, 2015; Marsh and McCaffrie, 2015). If so, we should look for ways to juggle these accounts by (1) recognising that their initial perspectives and aims will influence their findings, and (2) being careful about pitting such approaches against each other when they may be reaching different answers because they ask different questions (Dowding, 2015).

Explaining the impact of key actors: parliaments

These accounts are also essential to the study of *parliamentary influence* since it relies, to a large extent, on the identification of *ministerial influence*. If ministers are at the heart of policy making, and parliaments have a direct influence on ministers, we can trace many policy outputs back to Parliament. If ministers represent one of many actors unable to control behaviour which 'emerges' from complex systems, the role of Parliament may seem negligible.

Russell and Cowley (2016) suggest that the latter story dominates (unfairly) the study of Parliament. Richardson and Jordan's (1979) phrase 'post-parliamentary democracy' remains influential. It relies on the timeless elements of the complex government story: ministers can only pay attention to a tiny proportion of their responsibilities; they delegate responsibility for most issues, and policy is processed at a low level of government, with minimal ministerial and parliamentary input (Jordan and Cairney, 2013: 236).

This finding can be qualified with reference to the Westminster story, since Parliament plays a central role in the wider system of representative democracy in which policy communities operate. Its importance is found in the 'process of representation and the legitimation of governmental outputs flowing from that process' (Judge, 1993: 2). Policy communities derive their legitimacy from the sense that they are overseen and approved by Parliament, and 'without this presumption of the ultimate authority of Parliament the outputs … would be far more difficult, if not impossible, to sustain as "authoritative" and "binding" policy' (Judge, 1993: 30). Civil servants seek to generate legitimacy for policies agreed in policy communities by feeding up to ministers and anticipating parliamentary scrutiny. Ministers and civil servants cannot ignore Parliament even if MPs and select committees can only pay attention to a tiny proportion of government business. Its influence can be found by observing the extent to which they make policy with Parliament in mind. We should recognise the importance of 'anticipated reactions' when, for example, a government tries to 'get a sense of what will and will not be acceptable' (Judge, 1990).

Such arguments contribute to the sense that Parliament is more powerful than you think *if you think it is completely unimportant* (Russell and Cowley, 2016; Russell et al, 2016; Connolly et al, 2022). Debates on Parliament may become circular, as people begin with different research questions and talk at cross purposes on the significance of their findings. For example, the 'policy communities' literature represented one way to reject the idea that policy making was captured well by 'the traditional model of Cabinet and parliamentary government' (Richardson and Jordan, 1979: 91), while new parliamentary studies often challenge the pervasiveness of accounts which treated Parliament as peripheral to the policy process (Russell and Cowley, 2016: 122; Russell and Gover, 2017). Their different conclusions often reflect very different reference points.

If we keep juggling both – Westminster and complex government – stories, we might conclude that actors like MPs only have the ability to pay attention to a tiny proportion of the issues processed by governments. So, they promote some to the top of their agenda and ignore the rest. Further, they do not have the resources to delegate scrutiny for all other issues to other bodies (like ministers delegating to civil servants) and, therefore, rely on government bodies to keep them informed of their progress. The aggregate outcome may be a limited effect by Parliament in most areas of policy, but a profound effect on some. For example, compare Chapter 7 on its pivotal role during Brexit negotiations from 2016 to 2020 with Chapter 6 on a more modest scrutiny role of COVID-19. Further, in 2022, its sustained attention to Prime Minister Boris Johnson's character and competence contributed somewhat to his resignation (see Box 12.4).

Conclusion

The Westminster story is a popular way to describe how policy making works and should work. It describes strong and responsible government generated by an electoral and political system that concentrates power in an executive. The government of the day makes policy from the top down, with little need to negotiate with Parliament, other types of government, or the stakeholders and publics affected by policy. Ministers head government departments and take responsibility for their outputs. People know whom to hold responsible. MPs and television, radio and print media focus their scrutiny on ministers, and the regularity of elections helps to hold powerful governments to account. Or, this story helps to articulate disenchantment with politics when policy makers are too aloof, grab power while dodging responsibility, or give up powers too readily to other governments. Either way, the story endures regardless of its accuracy.

The complex government story is an alternative way to describe how policy making works. It highlights bounded rationality and policy-making complexity. It suggests that policy makers have limited knowledge of policy problems and low control over their policy-making environments. Ministers are part of a powerful core executive, but need to delegate most policy to communities of civil servants, pressure participants and the organisations that deliver policy. They also delegate formal responsibility to devolved governments and, until recently, shared many responsibilities with the EU. As a result, policy making is multi-level, fragmented and out of anyone's full understanding. Ministers can make a difference, but in the context of a huge set of inherited commitments that are carried out routinely on their behalf. They share some powers by choice, but have limited powers by necessity.

The practical consequence is that policy makers juggle their responses to two different stories: ministers perform the role of powerful policy makers, responsible for making and defending hard choices, but also seek ways to get things done in a context where they rely on many others to succeed. They share responsibility with many other actors, but remain held to account for the overall results.

The consequence for research is the need to understand not only what happens but also how people interpret these outcomes. It is common to identify policy failure and pin the blame on central governments, when it may be more accurate to identify the ever-present limits to policy change.

This juggling act produces three key questions in UK policy and policy making:

1. *How can policy makers tell a coherent story of the Westminster narrative of democratic accountability?* If ministers are not in control of their departments, how can we hold them to account? How can they produce a model based on a pragmatic understanding of central government power, and new forms of accountability, that is sufficiently consistent with the Westminster model of democratic accountability? The answer is not clear. Instead, we have seen policy makers describe their task in very different ways.
2. *How have policy makers responded to the governance problem?* Instead of a grand, rational theme to ensure central government control, in Chapters 4 and 5 we identify a patchwork of reforms to respond to a lack of control, and the unintended consequences of reforms.
3. *How can we study this process empirically?* It is difficult to go beyond the same old phrases, such as that ministers are important but not the only important policy makers, that multi-level governance matters, that Parliament is more important than you think, and that policy dynamics vary from issue to issue. Yet, we should not be too dispirited by these routine messages. Life is full of wonderful contradictions and policy makers can act to produce good enough outcomes. Further, it is no mean feat to (1) study policy making across many policy areas and decades, (2) produce some simple and understandable concepts that help us sum up complex government in the UK, and (3) compare them meaningfully with policy making in many other countries. Indeed, this manageable understanding is crucial to critical policy analysis, since we can only use research to challenge inequity if we know how policy and policy processes perpetuate it.

The Transformation of the UK State

Chapter highlights

1. Describes the transformation of the UK state in the post-war period.

   - Transformation describes changes including the size of the UK state, its level of intervention in the market, and reforms to its policy-making and delivery functions.
   - There have been major changes in UK economic policy and ownership of industries.
   - UK governments have reformed public sector functions in health, education, housing and local government.

2. Relates state transformation to two reference points:

   - The post-war consensus story describing state ownership and intervention.
   - The neoliberal story describing a trend towards state retrenchment and privatisation in favour of market forces and individual responsibility.

3. Examines how parties make a difference in government.

   - In a few cases, a new party has become associated with a major change in the long-term direction of travel.
   - In most, a new party slows or accelerates the same trend.

4. Identifies the impact of devolution.

   - Devolution as a policy has accentuated UK state transformation.
   - However, devolved governments often opt out of the UK government policies associated with state transformation.

Introduction

This chapter describes four aspects of post-war state transformation. First, the UK state now has a less interventionist role in economic and social policy. Second, it reduced its ownership of industry. Third, it increased the use of private-sector methods to reform government and manage public services. Fourth, it increased the delegation of policy delivery. We recount a common story that the UK has (1) shifted from a high to low intervention state, but (2) in an inconsistent way and without reference to a coherent plan.

Table 4.1: Post-war governments and Prime Ministers

Election	Party	Prime Minister
1945	Labour	Clement Attlee
1951	Conservative	Winston Churchill
1955	Conservative	Anthony Eden (1955–1957), Harold Macmillan (1957–1959)
1959	Conservative	Harold Macmillan (1957–1963), Alec Douglas-Home (1959–1964)
1964	Labour	Harold Wilson
1966	Labour	Harold Wilson
1970	Conservative	Edward Heath
1974	Labour	Harold Wilson (1974–1976), James Callaghan (1976–1979)
1979	Conservative	Margaret Thatcher
1983	Conservative	Margaret Thatcher
1987	Conservative	Margaret Thatcher (1979–1990), John Major (1990–1992)
1992	Conservative	John Major
1997	Labour	Tony Blair
2001	Labour	Tony Blair
2005	Labour	Tony Blair (2005–2007), Gordon Brown (2007–2010)
2010	Coalition	PM David Cameron (Conservative), Deputy PM Nick Clegg (Liberal Democrat)
2015	Conservative	David Cameron (2015–2016), Theresa May (2016–2017)
2017	Conservative	Theresa May (2017–2019), Boris Johnson (2019)
2019	Conservative	Boris Johnson (2019–2022), Liz Truss (2022), Rishi Sunak (2022–)

We begin analysis from the mid-1940s to explore the fate of 'Keynesian' economic policies, state ownership of industry and the modern welfare state. Each became associated with the first post-war Labour government, encompassing state management of the economy, nationalised industries, and new or expanded provision in social security and public services. However, they were maintained by Labour and Conservative governments (Table 4.1), prompting the story of 'post-war consensus'.

This reference point underpins our analysis of developments from the 1970s, including the financial and political crises that prompted the search for new economic models, and the election of a Conservative government (1979–1997) committed to reducing the role of the state. It sought to reduce state management of the economy, privatise industries and introduce private-sector methods to public services. 'Neoliberal' sums up this policy direction, describing a preference for: (1) market forces over state intervention; (2) individual rather than state responsibility for welfare; and (3) economic growth over other policy aims.

This long period of Conservative government gave the Labour government (1997–2010) a reference point for its story of radical change, while Conservative-led governments from 2010 emphasised the need for reforms to address Labour's failures. Yet, both emphasised policy continuity, relating change to governing competence (elect us and we will do similar things better). Neither sought a return to the post-war consensus, and both accelerated neoliberal reforms. While the party of government makes a difference, we should not assume that a new party reverses the policies of its predecessors (Box 4.1).

In that context, the devolution of power in Northern Ireland, Scotland and Wales in 1999 had a mixed impact. Devolution *policy* marks further state transformation, with the UK government often responsible for health, education and local government for England only (Chapter 7). However, the devolved governments have been less likely (than the UK) to pursue neoliberal reforms as energetically.

Box 4.1: Did it matter which party was in government?

UK governments are led by the centre-right Conservative Party or centre-left Labour Party. In theory, each party could win an election every four–five years and reverse the policies of its predecessor. This possibility is a feature of Westminster stories (Box 3.2), and Finer (1975) used it to push for electoral reform.

In contrast, Rose (1984) described the sense that (1) electoral competitions exaggerate the difference between each party, (2) new governments inherit and keep most of their predecessor's policies, and (3) most policy is produced by 'the large agglomeration of complex bureaucracies that in practice carry out the work done in the name of Cabinet ministers' (Rose, 1984: 142). Parties 'make a difference in the way Britain is governed', but '[m]uch of a party's record in office will be stamped upon it by forces outside its control' (Rose, 1984: 142). Rose and Davies (1994) examined how post-1979 developments affected this analysis. The Thatcher government described itself as a source of radical change, but we need to analyse the evidence rather than rely on the rhetoric and reputations of politicians. When we do, we find evidence for the accumulation of 'Thatcherite' policy changes over a longer period, beginning before 1979, accelerating during the Conservative government until 1997 (although Thatcher resigned in 1990), inherited by the Labour government of 1997–2010, and accelerated by Conservative-led governments from 2010. We are often witnessing the same direction of travel, with new parties speeding up or slowing down rather than making U-turns.

What do we mean by UK state transformation?

State transformation involves profound changes to policy and policy making, to the extent that the role of the UK state in relation to the market and society has changed beyond recognition. The immediate post-war period is a common 'hook' for this analysis, allowing us to compare a gulf between two stories.

1. *The 'post-war consensus' story.* 'Consensus' refers to high societal and political party agreement on the central role of the state. It includes managing the

economy via fiscal and monetary measures, overseeing state-owned industries, and funding and delivering public services directly. This story often contains a moral dimension: the state *should* offer social protection to citizens in return for sacrifices during the Second World War.

2. *The modern 'neoliberal' story*. It emphasises state retrenchment in favour of 'market forces'. It was associated strongly with the Thatcher government from 1979, but has been maintained or accelerated ever since. UK central government no longer promises to ensure 'full employment' or control monetary policy directly, has privatised most industries, and has a reduced role in service delivery. The equivalent moral argument is that individuals should take responsibility for their own welfare (and the state is less efficient than the market). Opposition to this moral is generally a key feature of critical policy analysis (introduced in Chapter 2 and explored in Chapters 6–11).

These simple stories could give the misleading impression that they correspond to a coherent approach to policy making (Kerr, 2001). Rather, we use them to interpret post-war trends which could represent (1) a central government's grand plan linked to a coherent ideology, or (2) a collection of choices resulting from different causes and motivations. For example, motives for selling state industries can be ideological (to reduce state intervention), financial (to raise money and reduce state subsidies) and/or electoral (for example, if public share ownership is popular) (Rhodes et al, 2014: 3–5).

Economic policy: from Keynesianism to neoliberalism?

Economic policy is central to state transformation. Policy instruments include:

- Fiscal policies, to tax and spend.
- Monetary policies, to manage the supply of money and influence interest rates (the cost of borrowing) and currency exchange rates (the relative value of the UK pound sterling).
- Regulations on individual and business – 'market' – behaviour.
- Providing resources such as staffing (for example, in the Treasury).
- Collecting and sharing information to underpin public and private policies.

Successive UK governments *seem* to have used such policies to pursue contrasting approaches.

- *Pro-state intervention*. The belief – associated with John Maynard Keynes (and 'Keynesian' economists) – that state intervention is essential to a country's economy, since the 'free market' does not respond quickly enough to peaks and troughs of activity. For example, employment is driven by overall demand in the economy: individual (domestic) spending and investment, business exports to other countries, and government spending. During a recession, consumers are reluctant to spend, and businesses are reluctant to invest, prompting governments to spend (and invest in infrastructure) to maintain economic activity. During a boom, consumers and businesses spend too much and exacerbate inflation, prompting governments to spend less and tax more to reduce demand (Jahan et al, 2014).

• *Pro-market (or neoliberal)*. The belief – associated with Milton Friedman (and 'neoclassical' economists) – that state intervention disrupts more effective market mechanisms. 'Monetarism' describes an alternative to Keynesian measures to control inflation by ensuring that the 'growth rate of the money supply' matches the growth rate of the economy, via instruments such as issuing government bonds and changes to interest rates (the charge for borrowing) (Jahan and Papageorgiou, 2014). The 'natural rate of unemployment' describes the lowest level of unemployment that does not cause excessive inflation (allowing for some 'frictional unemployment' relating to business shifts and labour retraining). It suggests that too-high employment levels lead to inflationary wage demands, exacerbated by the negotiating power of trade unions and too-high unemployment benefits (reducing incentives to work for low pay) (Blanchard and Katz, 1997).

Government ministers tend not to be economics purists, so there is no direct connection from economic thought to government action (Chapter 5). Further, there have been periods when governments have adopted elements of both ideas, or used economic policy instruments that serve other purposes (such as to maintain popularity). Pro-market rhetoric does not guarantee a major reduction in state intervention. Still, a narrative of the embrace of Keynesianism in the 1940s, its late 1970s rejection, and its only partial resurgence from the late 1990s, helps us to describe a broad shift from the post-war consensus to neoliberalism.

The rise, fall and reinvention of Keynesianism

There was a major shift towards Keynesian state intervention in the 1940s, some challenges in the 1960s then a shift to its alternative by the late 1970s (Oliver and Pemberton, 2004).

1940s and 1950s: UK government policy changes consistent with Keynesian thought

The UK government prioritised fiscal policies to manage demand. It committed in 1944 to 'a high and stable level of employment', and state interventions to manage demand took place when unemployment had risen to 1.5 per cent in the 1950s (Oliver and Pemberton, 2004: 424). These measures marked the biggest break from the 'neoclassical' stronghold in the Treasury, which focused primarily on exports and monetary measures (such as interest rate changes and schemes to manage the value of sterling). Oliver and Pemberton (2004: 423) argue that experiences during the Second World War challenged 'laissez faire' (low state involvement) approaches, showing that state intervention boosted employment, and prompting the recruitment of Keynesian economists to manage the results (such as inflationary pressures).

1960s: making state intervention work by modifying a Keynesian approach

Oliver and Pemberton (2004: 425) describe successful battles to defend Keynesian approaches from neoclassical challengers in the Treasury (who sought to drop the commitment to full employment). These battles followed anomalies (such as unexpected inflation and interruptions to economic cycles) and the sense that UK economic policy was falling behind many other countries. 'Keynesian-plus' describes attempts to modify policies in ways not envisaged by Keynes, including state-led economic planning geared towards economic growth targets, and initiatives to manage wages and prices. They reflected a commitment to Keynesianism despite challenges such as a 'severe sterling crisis in 1966' (Oliver and Pemberton, 2004: 427).

1970s: a series of crises

In 1970, Heath's Conservative government promised to reduce taxes and state intervention. By 1972, 'the government quickly reverted to traditional Keynesian demand management' after a swift rise in unemployment (Oliver and Pemberton, 2004: 428). This shift did not have the desired effect, and 'the last thing Keynesian policy makers expected after reflating the economy was a simultaneous rise in unemployment and inflation, but this is what occurred' (Oliver and Pemberton, 2004: 429). The oil price crisis of 1973–1974 raised inflation *and* reduced business activity, which undermined government attempts to limit demand for wage increases and contributed to the 'three-day week' that ruined the Heath government (Oliver and Pemberton, 2004: 429).

The Labour government (1974–1979) faced greater policy problems, including rising inflation and unemployment, a reduction in the value of sterling, and the need to borrow to finance major spending deficits. It faced policy-making problems – including the failure of **tripartism** to limit

> **Tripartism**: policy making involving representatives of the government, business and unions. 'Corporatism' describes formalised tripartism (Grant and Marsh, 1977: 137–152).
>
> **Winter of Discontent**: many strikes organised by trade unions from 1978 to 1979, contributing to Labour's loss in the 1979 election, and used by the Thatcher government to push for curbs to union powers (López, 2014). Strikes in the UK in 2022 and 2023, to reflect the rejection of below-inflation pay offers, did not come close to this scale of activity (ONS, 2022f).

wage rises – that led to the '**Winter of Discontent**'. Each experience reduced faith in Keynesianism within the Treasury (Oliver and Pemberton, 2004: 429–430).

1979–1997: a rejection of Keynesianism?

By 1979–1980, in came the paradigm described as 'monetarist' (control inflation via the money supply) or 'neoliberal' (state intervention is an impediment to the market). Hall argued that:

> Macroeconomic efforts to reduce unemployment were rejected in favor of balanced budgets and direct tax reductions. Monetary policy replaced fiscal policy as the principal macroeconomic instrument, and it was reoriented toward fixed targets for the rate of monetary growth. Many regulatory instruments associated with state intervention, such as incomes policies, exchange controls, and quantitative limits on bank lending, were eliminated. (Hall, 1993: 284)

However, Oliver and Pemberton (2004: 433) suggest that the Conservative government had rejected Keynesianism in favour of monetarism *in theory*, but the 'government was struggling to balance theoretical monetarism with practical implementation'. Macroeconomic policy from 1985 exhibited 'some of the old tendencies of Keynesian demand management' (Oliver and Pemberton, 2004: 433). The result was a consistent focus on 'neoliberal' policy aims – to minimise inflation and avoid state intervention to manage demand – but inconsistent use of policy instruments.

1997 onwards: a mix of 'neoliberal' aims and 'new Keynesian' policies

The Labour government inherited these aims but modified policy instruments (Oliver and Pemberton, 2004: 434), often with reference to 'New Keynesian' ideas (Hodson and Mabbett, 2009: 1042; Clift, 2020). Labour promised to avoid a major departure from Conservative policies, describing:

- '*Fiscal prudence*', including the 'Golden Rule' (only borrow to invest in capital), and 'sustainable investment rule' (public sector net debt should not exceed 40 per cent of **gross domestic product**), to resist pressure for greater social policy spending and avoid criticism that spending would undermine economic growth (Hodson and Mabbett, 2009: 1047; Watson, 2009).

> **Gross domestic product (GDP)**: the annual total of goods and services produced in a country.

- '*Price stability*', and '*granting operational control of monetary policy to the Bank of England*' (Hodson and Mabbett, 2009: 1042). The Bank's approach reflected a 'New Keynesian consensus in macroeconomic theory': (1) linking inflation to 'wage–price dynamics' rather than the money supply; and (2) using interest rates rather than tax and spending to dampen or stimulate the economy (Hodson and Mabbett, 2009: 1042, 1045).

- '*Light-touch financial regulation*', via 'a single financial regulator, the Financial Services Authority (FSA)' to address the historic antipathy of 'the City' towards Labour governments (Hodson and Mabbett, 2009: 1042, 1049).

Quantitative easing: the central bank creates new money to buy government bonds to: (1) raise their price, reduce their attractiveness to investors, and encourage investors to lend instead to households and businesses, to (2) reduce the cost of borrowing and (3) help to reduce inflation.

All three measures came under pressure during the global economic crisis (2007–2008). The Bank of England used '**quantitative easing**' when interest rate changes were insufficient to minimise inflation and encourage spending. Further, high government borrowing – well beyond the fiscal prudence rules – replaced the more limited FSA compensation schemes for the creditors of financial institutions (such as when the government temporarily nationalised Northern Rock and the Royal Bank of Scotland) (Hodson and Mabbett, 2009: 1052). These moves prompted some to describe a return to Keynesianism, but the government focused primarily on supporting monetary policy during crisis rather than a return to tax and spending to manage demand (Hodson and Mabbett, 2009: 1053). Further, as Chapter 9 suggests, the election in 2010 of a coalition government, committed to 'austerity', ruled out greater support for state intervention.

Employment law reform and trade unions

A key part of the neoliberal 'natural rate' argument was that trade unions were too powerful, causing industrial unrest and too-high wage demands. It dovetailed with Thatcher's alleged loathing of unions, the Thatcher government's rejection of tripartism in favour of strong and decisive government, and its desire to shift the balance of power from unions to employers (Marsh, 1992: 35–36). The result was a sustained challenge to trade union powers – and worker rights – via Employment Acts in 1980, 1982, 1984, 1988 and 1990. These Acts were to challenge the 'closed shop' (obligatory union membership), make most 'secondary' strikes (by other unions, in support of the original strike) illegal, remove trade union immunity if a strike was unlawful, oblige a secret ballot and majority in favour of industrial action, and give greater rights to union members to work during a strike (Hanson, 1991: 18–19).

Employment reforms continued after Thatcher, including Acts under a Major government (for example, in 1993, to oblige a seven-day notice period for ballots, subject to independent scrutiny, and to make strike ballots postal) *and* a Blair-led Labour government (for example, in 2004 to address worker intimidation by employers and unions). Further, the Conservative Trade Union Act 2016 went further than any previous plan. It made strike action relatively difficult in general, by obliging an over 50 per cent response rate to the ballot. It added restrictions for those in 'important public services' (40 per cent of all eligible voters needed to vote to strike). It extended the notice period from seven to 14 days, and limited the start of strike action to within six months of the vote (Bogg, 2016; Institute of Employment Rights, 2021). The Conservative (2019) manifesto also promised legislation to oblige a minimum level of service during transport strikes (which the government then sought to relate to health service strikes in 2022). Overall, current employment laws are much more restrictive than Thatcher envisaged.

Privatisation and new public management

The first post-war UK government fostered a new model of state intervention, inspired partly by the **Beveridge Report** (Kelly and Pearce, 2023). The *welfare state* combined new entitlements to social security (including pension, unemployment and child benefits), access to free public services such as healthcare and education, and subsidised social housing. They were all 'linked by one overarching idea: that through rational and purposeful intervention, government can

Beveridge Report: William Beveridge's influential 1942 report for government ('Social Insurance and Allied Services') recommended 'cradle to the grave' services to improve employment, education, health, housing and social security (to tackle 'idleness, ignorance, disease, squalor and want').

remake society' (Renwick, 2017: back cover). The *industrial state* involved the nationalisation or control of public utilities and corporations.

Thatcher governments sought to reduce the latter via privatisation, which can include selling state assets, deregulating services, obliging the private delivery of public services, using private investment for capital projects, and reducing subsidies or increasing charges for services (Marsh, 1991: 462; Massey and Pyper, 2005: 111–126).

Thatcher governments also sought to reform government and public services by drawing on 'new public management' (NPM), defined generally as the application of private business methods to government. Hood (1991: 4) describes seven components:

1. Management reforms to ensure that a named individual is responsible for decisions.
2. Explicit standards and measures of performance.
3. Greater emphasis on results than outputs and procedures.
4. The disaggregation of large organisations to create 'manageable units'.

5. Greater competition in the public sector.
6. Private-sector management, moving from a 'military-style public service ethic' to a flexible system of hiring and rewards.
7. Doing more with less (Box 4.2).

Box 4.2: A government that worked better and cost less?

Hood and Dixon (2015) analyse the prediction that NPM measures would help governments reduce costs *and* improve services. In short, it proved to be false. After three decades of NPM reforms (1980–2010), the UK 'exhibited a striking increase in ... administrative costs in real terms, while levels of complaint and legal challenge also soared' (Hood and Dixon, 2015: 1). There are *some* examples of successful reforms, including an occasional reduction in the cost of collecting taxes (Hood and Dixon, 2015: 104–106). However, examples of a gulf between rhetoric and reality include:

- A reduction in the *number* of non-departmental public bodies (NDPBs, quangos) but a quadrupling of their *costs* (Hood and Dixon, 2015: 28).
- A rise in the 'running costs' of UK government departments during a period of 'cost cutting' rhetoric (Hood and Dixon, 2015: 74–75).
- Stable 'public spending relative to GDP' rather than major state retrenchment (Hood and Dixon, 2015: 35).
- No clear evidence – from surveys of citizens or measures of complaints – that government 'works better' (Hood and Dixon, 2015: 124–127).

It is tempting to conclude that NPM reforms make government *worse*. However, they were not implemented energetically, which (combined with limited data) makes it difficult to identify an NPM effect (Hood and Dixon, 2015: 181). This gap between NPM rhetoric and demonstrable outcomes is part of an international experience (Hood and Dixon, 2015: 152).

Selling nationalised industries

The post-war UK government controlled a remarkably large number of public utilities and corporations including water, coal, electricity, steel, gas, oil, rail, telecommunications and postal delivery. These industries employed around 2.3 million people, as part of a total of 5 million 'civilian public employees' in 1950 (Hogwood, 2008: 25). By 1980, while nationalised industry staff fell to 1.8 million, the civilian public workforce was over 7 million (Hogwood, 2008: 25).

Thatcher governments initiated a transformative shift from public to private ownership (House of Commons Library, 2014: 15):

- Thatcher's term (1979–1990) includes the sale of British Telecom (1984), Cable and Wireless, British Aerospace, Britoil (1985), British Gas (1986), British Airways, British Airports Authority, British Petroleum, Rolls Royce (1987), British Steel, Rover (1988), Water Authorities (1989) and regional electricity companies (England and Wales in 1990, Scotland 1991).
- John Major's term (1990–1997) includes British Telecom, National Power (1991), British Coal (1994), the rail franchise (from 1994), British Energy and Railtrack (1996).
- Labour did not reverse these sales, and sold the National Air Traffic Services (2001) and British Nuclear Fuels Ltd (2006).
- By the election of a coalition government, there were few companies left. The coalition government sold the Royal Mail in 2013.

Nationalised industry employees in the public sector fell from 1.8 million in 1980 to 0.24 million in 1997, while public employment overall fell from 7 million to 4.7 million (Hogwood, 2008: 25). Nationalised industries accounted for 9 per cent of GDP in 1979 and under 5 per cent by 1990 (Marsh, 1991: 463; Rhodes, 1994: 139). These sales raised £74 billion from 1979 to 1997 and £8 billion since then (House of Commons Library, 2014: 14; figures adjusted for 2020 prices using the GDP deflator).

The privatisation of housing

Post-war governments were committed to house building, albeit for different reasons. Labour governments emphasised a lack of accommodation for low-income groups, while Conservative governments focused on home ownership (Jones and Murie, 2006: 10–12).

The 1980 Housing Act (backed by legal action following local authority opposition) gave council house tenants the 'right to buy' (RTB) their home from their local authority at a highly discounted rate: two-thirds of its market value after living there for three years, plus a 1 per cent discount for every additional year (up to 50 per cent off) (Parker, 2009: 86). By 1983, 0.5 million homes were sold to tenants or development corporations, ensuring that: 'between 1979 and 1983 more public sector homes passed into private ownership than in all of the years since 1945' (Parker, 2009: 86). Subsequent Acts from 1984 to 1996 reduced the eligibility requirement to two years, raised the maximum discount to 60 per cent (70 per cent for flats), and allowed housing authorities to take over council provision (Jones and Murie, 2006: 38). These changes allowed Conservative governments to reduce housing expenditure dramatically (Jones and Murie, 2006: 36). They also accentuated a central government challenge to local authorities (Box 4.3). While the receipts went to local authorities, they did not fully fund additional house building, ensuring a rise in private homes and a reduction in social housing (and the most attractive houses were the quickest to sell).

From 1980 to 2003, 2.8 million homes had been sold. UK 'local authority rented' housing fell from 29 per cent in 1981 to 13 per cent in 2003, while home ownership rose from 58 per cent to 72 per cent and 'housing association' renting rose from 2.2 per cent to 7.4 per cent (Jones and Murie, 2006: 55). The success of the scheme – on its own terms – is reflected somewhat in Labour-era legislation. It continued the scheme in principle, and extended its reach to include purchases from housing associations. However, the Housing (Scotland) Act 2001 and the Housing Act 2004 (England) began to restrict RTB to address low social housing capacity in many areas (see Jones and Murie, 2006: 39–50 on differences between UK and devolved government policies).

Box 4.3: The poll tax: a policy disaster for Thatcher

Many Thatcherite policies reflected a lack of respect for local government, with ministers describing its wastefulness and lack of organisation (Rhodes, 1992; Stoker, 2001: 12). Examples of reforms include: obliging councils to sell their housing stock, the compulsory tendering of council services, using quangos to deliver public services, abolishing English metropolitan county councils and the Greater London Council, removing some powers over transport, centralising negotiations on teacher pay, and giving schools more autonomy from councils (John, 1991: 60–61; Massey and Pyper, 2005: 97–100). The highest-profile example of a frustration-driven and high-risk reform is the 'community charge' which came to be known as the 'poll tax' (McConnell, 1995; 2000). At face value, policy change related to technical and political problems with local government finance: 'Paying for local government is no easy option because it takes up about a third of public expenditure and not all of the finance can come from central government. Finding a tax which can raise enough revenue, be fair, and promote local accountability is almost impossible' (John, 1999: 49).

If we focus on the means of finance, options include: property taxes (on homes and/or business), local income tax, sales taxes or a 'poll tax' for each local resident (John, 1999: 49–50). However, the Thatcher government defined a dual problem: the need to (1) replace an increasingly unworkable property tax, and (2) curb local authority spending (Stoker, 2001: 180–185). It introduced the poll tax in 1989 (Scotland) and 1990 (England and Wales) (John, 1999: 52). As a *technical* solution, it had alleged benefits – to make people (1) highly aware of the charge, and (2) blame local authority extravagance for its too-high rate – but it was beset by administrative problems. As a *political* solution it was disastrous, seen as a highly unfair charge, contributing to Thatcher's resignation in 1990, and prompting her successor to replace it with a domestic property tax ('council tax') (John, 1999: 52–53; King and Crewe, 2014: 41–63).

Charging for public services (including university tuition fees)

Privatisation includes a reduction of public subsidy which prompts higher charges for a service, such as: museum fees, prescription charges, driver test and licence fees, council house rents, tolls for roads and bridges, and school meals fees (Heald, 1990: 233). Governments do not make it easy to identify the difference between taxes and charges, and exemptions for low-income (and other) groups reduces the scope of charges for prescriptions, dental and optical services. Still, Heald (1990: 239) finds an increase of fees from £8.6 billion in 1982–1983 to £13 billion in 1990–1991 (adjusted for 2020 prices, using the GDP deflator).

More recent reforms to university tuition fees overshadow these numbers (Box 9.2). The Thatcher government introduced full fees for international students in 1981, then sought to replace domestic student grants with loans for living expenses (in the name of widening participation – Grove, 2013). Then, tuition fees for undergraduate higher education began during a Labour government: at £1,000 per year in 1998, rising in England to £3,000 per year in 2003 and £9,000 per year in 2010 under the coalition government (£9,250 by 2023). UK universities generated £23.5 billion in higher education tuition fees in 2020/2021 (HESA, 2022).

Using non-governmental organisations to deliver services

The Thatcher government introduced 'compulsory competitive tendering' to oblige local authorities and the National Health Service (NHS) to put some services – such as waste management and catering – out to tender rather than automatically deliver them in-house (Greenwood et al, 2001: 37; Stoker, 2004). Labour's 'Best Value' policy obliged authorities to demonstrate that in-house delivery would be the most efficient option. It also signalled the expansion of public service delivery via third-sector organisations (Kelly, 2007). The National Audit Office (2013: 10) describes a major increase in 'contracting out' from a very small base in 1980 to 'around half of the £187 billion that the public sector spends on goods and services each year' by 2013. The UK government also spends £3 billion per year on 'public – private partnerships', paying the private companies who build and maintain capital projects such as hospitals, schools, roads and bridges (compared to £50 billion of direct government investment) (National Audit Office, 2018: 2).

Reforming public services: quasi-markets in health and education

Post-war governments remained committed to tax-funded public services free at the point of use. While no Conservative government sought to 'privatise' these services, NPM measures were a key feature of Thatcherite and subsequent reforms. Many reforms were of public services in England (see the final section on devolved government).

Reforming the National Health Service

The NHS was established in 1948. The government's need to negotiate with key professions resulted in concessions, to allow hospital consultants to also work privately, and for general practitioner (GP) and dental services to remain as independent contractors. Still, the NHS represented the consolidation of state intervention to fund healthcare (via taxes, not insurance) and deliver services (taking over hospitals from local authorities) (Ham, 2004: 5–16). Ham (2004: 16) describes the assumption in government that there was a fixed amount of ill health, suggesting that high NHS funding would improve population health and reduce demand for services. Instead, it exposed a continuous need for capital investment and to address the underinvestment in healthcare for marginalised groups (Ham, 2004: 16–24). Post-war governments pursued organisational reforms rather than spending cuts, and respected medical influence and unions such as the British Medical Association (Rhodes, 1988: 301–305).

By the 1980s, Conservative governments emphasised NHS reforms to make it more 'business-like' (Ferlie et al, 1996: 11–12; Cairney, 2002: 380; Ham, 2004: 30–34). Day and Klein (2000) suggest that Thatcherite reforms score highly on Hood's (1991) list of NPM activities and include: developing performance management measures (focusing more on services than staff); shifting NHS delivery to an agency (partly to shuffle off responsibility for what goes wrong); and, appointing key staff externally. They introduced 'quasi-markets', or internal competition, to demand or supply services, such as the purchaser/provider split in which GP fundholding bodies became purchasers and hospitals providers. They attempted to establish a clear line of hierarchical accountability by shifting powers from medical and other professions towards the NHS managers reporting to the health department (Ham, 2004: 51–52).

These reforms produced an image of continuous change often without a clear overall direction (see Pollitt, 2010: 84 on the 'sheer unrelenting dance of reforms', and Paton, 2016 on 'England's permanent revolution'). They continued in England under Labour, which described improving the Conservative policies that worked and removing the ones that didn't (Ham, 2004: 53–60). The former included: a greater focus on GP/primary care groups driving NHS choices via fundholding; market-style mechanisms such as 'patient choice' (describing patients as consumers of services) and 'Foundation' hospitals that could operate with greater autonomy if they met key performance targets; and, diminished opposition to working with the private sector to deliver services (Ham, 2004: 60–70). The coalition government accelerated measures – giving more powers to primary care organisations and more autonomy to Foundation hospitals – and furthered the delegation of policy delivery to the commissioning body NHS England (via the Health and Social Care Act 2010) (Tailby, 2012; Rivett, 2021). It also signalled that, while ministers were often unhappy with operational decisions by NHS England (such as to underfund mental health services), they would not intervene (Cairney and St Denny, 2020: 170–171).

The NHS remains tax-funded and free at the point of use, but the means to deliver healthcare has been reformed so much that it is difficult to know how it works. Successive ministers have sought to delegate responsibility and accountability to other actors, such as the chief executives of hospitals and NHS England, but largely in vain because the buck stops with ministers (Rivett, 2021).

Reforming education

Chitty (2014: 18–22) describes the 1944 Education Act as the 'cornerstone of the post-war Welfare State' and a vehicle for social reform. It raised the school leaving age from 14 to 15 (1947) then 16 (1972), established the modern primary/secondary distinction, and favoured administration by local rather than central government. Although ostensibly geared towards greater education equity, there remained high commitment to a mix of secondary schools according to estimated ability, including: 'grammar' schools for elite education (20 per cent of students, recruited via the 'eleven-plus' exam, and largely from the middle classes), 'secondary modern' for most other students (largely from the working classes) and a small number of 'technical' schools for vocational education. The government, local authority and teaching union relationship was generally 'characterized by consensus' (Rhodes, 1988: 270). There was limited movement towards 'comprehensive' schools (recruiting for all abilities) until the 1960s, followed by the 1976 Education Act to oblige local authorities to base school provision on the 'comprehensive principle' (Chitty, 2014: 20–32, 48).

Thatcherite reforms prompted a new direction – repealing the 1976 Act – but in a sector that was not uniformly comprehensive. The 1988 Education Act (for England and Wales) extended quasi-market mechanisms for school choice, centralised aspects of the curriculum and assessment, and sought to reduce local authority control by allowing schools to be funded directly by central government (Chitty, 2014: 51–52). Further, Chitty (2014: 101–102) suggests that Conservative governments fostered 'privatisation' by: reducing state spending to oblige greater parental contributions (for example, for school trips or materials); widening the performance gap so that parents would have a greater incentive to choose private schools; increasing spending on schemes to allow students to attend private schools; and, expanding schemes to allow private firms to build and lease schools.

While the Labour government (from 1997) placed more emphasis on equity via education, it did not mark a major shift of support back to the 'comprehensive principle' administered by local authorities. Rather, it oversaw reforms to encourage:

- A 'diverse' mix of schools, including 'Academy' schools free of local authority control (an alleged vehicle for improving low-performing schools in areas of high deprivation).
- A neoliberal idea of equity furthered by student testing and school league tables to raise standards via competition (Brehony and Deem, 2003; Chitty, 2014: 63–84).

The coalition government accelerated such measures, albeit for different reasons. Academies became a vehicle for high-performing schools to become autonomous from local government, and often to encourage the involvement of private-sector chains (Chitty, 2014: 94). It encouraged the creation of 'free schools', which could be set up by groups of parents, run by contractors and funded by the government. These moves prompted Hall and Gunter (2016) to describe England as a 'laboratory' for NPM in compulsory education. Overall, these reforms were not only consistent with the direction of travel under Thatcher, but also reflective of a neoliberal model of education equity that took off globally (Chapter 10).

Reforming the civil service, 'policy advisory systems' and delivery

UK government civil servants enter into a 'public service bargain': pledging their 'loyalty and competent service' to the government – *regardless of the party in power* – in exchange for 'job tenure' and the 'avoidance of public blame' (Hood, 2002: 320). They accept their part in a departmental hierarchy led by ministers, and try to deliver ministerial policies even when they doubt that they are sensible (Hood and Lodge, 2006: 119).

Many senior ministers provide a less positive image of civil servants, portraying bureaucracy much like the hilarious fictional book (and television series) *Yes Minister* (Lynn and Jay, 1989). A typical chapter would see senior civil servants agreeing to deliver policies while conspiring to block them. They controlled a minister's access to information and advice, and oversaw the huge bureaucracy that managed the policy process. That idea could be found in diaries of former ministers (for example, Crossman, 1979). Many sought to reform the civil service to make it more conducive to control, or to find ways to make policy while relying less on civil servants (Drewry, 1994; Foster, 2001).

The Conservative government's plan – under Thatcher then Major – was to reform the civil service as part of a general aim of 'rolling back the frontiers of the state' (O'Toole and Jordan, 1995: 3–4). Reforms included:

- Seeking to reduce the number of civil servants, and improve their efficiency.
- Influencing the appointment of Permanent Secretaries and appointing special advisors.

- Boosting the capacity of Policy Units overseen by Number 10 (Diamond, 2011: 147).
- 'De-layering' departments to allow access to civil servants in less senior grades.
- Giving control of policy delivery to Executive Agencies in government departments (Greer, 1994: 5, 23–31), or organisations outside of departments.

Executive Agencies were designed to accentuate a well-established but problematic distinction between:

- *Ministers responsible for policy and strategy*, supported by civil servants with experience of providing strategic advice (Dunleavy, 1991; 2019; Marsh et al, 2001). Ministers were to be free from the day-to-day responsibilities for administering policies. They fostered different kinds of accountability: *redirectory* (passing a query to a relevant agency), *reporting* (keeping Parliament informed), *explanatory* (explaining why something has gone wrong), *amendatory* (taking action as a result) or *sacrificial* (the rare cases of ministerial resignation) (Judge et al, 1997: 97).
- *Government agencies responsible for policy delivery*, via chief executives with experience of management and implementation. Agency heads were responsible for budgets and meeting targets, incentivised with performance-related pay, given more freedom from interference in delivery, and sometimes sacrificed following crises (Greer, 1994: 4; Massey, 2001: 21). In 2020, 51 per cent of civil service staff were listed as 'Operational Delivery' (part of 70 per cent with 'public-facing' jobs), and 7 per cent as 'Policy' (Cabinet Office, 2020: 18; Understanding the Civil Service, 2021).

Ministers also saw the quango as an alternative way to deliver public services, operating 'to a greater or lesser extent at arm's length from ministers ... NDPBs have different roles, including those that advise ministers and others which carry out executive or regulatory functions, and they work within a strategic framework set by ministers' (Cabinet Office, 2018).

Ministers often promise to reduce quango numbers to boost accountability, reduce bureaucracy and avoid criticisms that appointments are 'jobs for the boys'. However, NDPBs remain attractive to manage policy delivery from a distance while not giving the responsibility to local authorities (Greenwood et al, 2001: 152). The Conservative government's (1979–1997) use of such public bodies included Urban Development Corporations (local development and planning controls regarding regeneration), Housing Action trusts (to regenerate housing estates), further education colleges, grant-maintained schools, Training and Enterprise Councils, Careers Service pathfinders, and the Police Service (Greenwood et al, 2001: 157; Stoker, 2004: 32). They reduced the number of bodies described as NDPBs but boosted NDPB spending (Box 4.2; Hogwood, 1992: 177; Flinders, 2008: 78).

These negative stories of UK bureaucracy transcended party lines, as demonstrated by the Labour government's description of Thatcherite reforms: 'Before agencies were created, the Civil Service was a large monolith governed by a body of centrally laid down rules, even though it was too big and diverse to be managed as a single entity. This led to a culture more focused on avoiding errors than improving results' (Office of Public Services Reform, 2002). Labour built on Conservative reforms, to 'modernise' the civil service and seek alternatives to delivery via government departments (Flinders, 2008: 84). Labour added new bodies such as the Regional Development Agencies in England, described – in vain – as a precursor to elected regional assemblies (Greenwood et al, 2001: 153). It also boosted an overall sense of 'delegated governance' (Flinders, 2008: 79), which continued under Conservative-led governments.

At the same time, Labour and Conservative ministers sought to boost central capacity and control by reforming the bureaucracy. For example, Labour enlarged Policy Units to establish strategy and the Prime Minister's Delivery Unit to oversee its implementation (Diamond, 2011: 148). The coalition government sought further reforms, with Francis Maude (minister in the Cabinet Office) insisting that 'the civil service epitomised the inadequacies of statism' (Diamond, 2021: 5). Maude and colleagues sought to:

- Reduce the size of the civil service (by 35 per cent in many departments).
- Re-emphasise the hierarchy of departments, partly by trying to 'handpick' senior officials, recruit from outside the service, and recruit many more special advisors.
- Abolish the civil service 'monopoly' of policy advice (Diamond, 2020a), such as by contracting out strategic and policy advice to 'think-tanks, research institutes, non-governmental organizations, charities, community groups, management consultancies, and professional services companies' (Diamond, 2020b: 1; see also Craft and Henderson, 2023).
- Make departments and agencies operate more like business, while contracting out more delivery work to the private sector (Diamond, 2019b; 2021: 6–10).

The cumulative effect of decades of reforms is a general sense that UK government 'policy advisory systems' – and policy delivery – have changed profoundly. First, 'the provision of policy advice to central governments has been transformed by the deinstitutionalisation of policy making, which has engaged a diverse range of actors in the policy process' (Diamond, 2020b: 563). The civil service 'monopoly' over policy advice in government has ended (Diamond, 2021: 10). This dynamic extends to a wider process of agenda setting in which many interest groups and think tanks compete to draw attention to their ideas (Table 4.2).

Further, civil servants often feel that ministers do not play their part in the public service bargain, and this lack of respect for civil service staff, rules and principles came to a head under the Boris Johnson government, which prompted an 'unusual string of senior civil service departures' (Russell, 2022), although the 'permanent bureaucracy' remains 'remarkably resilient' (Diamond, 2019a: 256).

Second, their role in strategy and delivery is shared increasingly with non-governmental actors. The National Audit Office (2021) estimated that, by

Table 4.2: Prominent think tanks in the UK

Name of think tank	Political alignment
Adam Smith Institute	Centre-right, pro-Conservative
Bright Blue	Moderate right, pro-Conservative
British Future	Centre-left, non-aligned
Centre for Policy Studies	Centre-right, pro-Conservative
Centre for Social Justice	Social conservative, pro-Conservative
Chatham House	Non-aligned
Demos	Centre-left, pro-Labour
Fabian Society	Centre-left, affiliated to Labour Party
Institute for Economic Affairs	Right-wing libertarian, pro-Conservative
Institute for Fiscal Studies	Non-aligned
Institute for Public Policy Research	Centre-left, pro-Labour
Legatum Institute	Right, pro-Conservative
New Economics Foundation	Left, pro-Labour
New Local	Independent
Policy Exchange	Centre-right, pro-Conservative
Resolution Foundation	Centre/centre-left, non-aligned
Social Market Foundation	Centre, non-aligned

Source: author's assessment of general political alignment

2018–2019, arm's length bodies 'accounted for around £265 billion of public expenditure and employed just under 300,000 staff'. These reforms challenge the post-war assumption that civil servants are necessarily at the heart of UK government policy communities (Chapters 3 and 5).

Trends in spending and regulation: from state to personal responsibility?

Public expenditure and the regulation of behaviour are key indicators of state intervention. However, both are difficult to fit into a simple story of transformation. Public expenditure data is only useful if comparable over time, taking into account inflation when describing cash rises (to measure a 'real' spending rise), or identifying its proportion of economic activity (GDP) (Hogwood, 1992; Hood and Dixon, 2015: 44–64). Public expenditure qualifies the impact of Thatcherite attempts to 'roll back the state' and increase private spending: real spending rose continuously from 1979; and, while spending as a proportion of GDP fell from 54 per cent in 1982 to 45 per cent in 1988, the latter was higher than equivalent levels in the mid-1950s (Hogwood, 1992: 43; Mullard and Swaray, 2006: 498). Public expenditure then rose significantly under Labour (Mullard and Swaray, 2006: 503) before 'austerity' from 2010 (Chapter 9).

These trends hide differences across sectors (and countries, where UK public expenditure became much higher than the US but much lower than Nordic states – Hogwood, 1992: 59). For example, social security spending – including pensions and income support – demonstrates path dependence (the influence of choices made, and rules created, in the past). It rose from the equivalent of £22 billion in 1950 to £125 billion in 1990 (adjusted for 2020 prices), largely because each government inherited post-war commitments, there was a rise in entitlement for some groups (for example, single-parent families), and the abandonment of 'full employment' raised the cost of unemployment benefits (Hogwood, 1992: 46). Other sectors show party differences: Conservative governments (1979–1997) spent more on defence and criminal justice, while Labour spent more on health, education and housing (Mullard and Swaray, 2006: 503).

The role of the state in relation to individual and family health and welfare policies

Nudge: to encourage people to make other choices, such as by sending subtle signals, making information easier to understand, or changing what they see when making choices.

The Thatcher government maintained low levels of state intervention in population health: treating healthiness and wellbeing as an individual responsibility, and rejecting state intervention to address major inequalities in health (Cairney and St Denny, 2020: 140). A Labour government in 1997 marked a turning point in state activity, but with a mixed effect: tobacco control changed profoundly, but the wider public health agenda did not change to the same extent; it introduced more controls on 'anti-social behaviour' (Chapter 10); and, it experimented with ways to **nudge** rather than simply regulate behaviour (John, 2011). The coalition government flirted with the idea of using wellbeing as an alternative to GDP as a measure of prosperity (Box 9.4).

How did devolution influence state transformation?

The devolution of policy making in Northern Ireland, Scotland and Wales in 1999 represents another element of transformation towards multi-centric policy making (see also Pope et al, 2022 and Newman and Kenny, 2023 on – confusing – levels of devolution in England). These impacts vary since the Scottish Parliament enjoys more legislative powers than Senedd Cymru. Devolution in Northern Ireland was even more extensive (albeit without the legislative powers) but suspended by the UK government in 2000, 2002–2007 and 2017–2020, and in flux from 2022 (Torrance, 2022a; Chapter 7). Each devolved government has primary responsibility for health, education, local government and housing, plus shared powers in areas such as transport, while the Scottish Parliament has legislative responsibility for criminal justice and its powers have grown in areas such as energy and social security (see Birrell, 2012; Birrell et al, 2023; Chapter 8; Box 9.3).

Here we focus on the extent to which aspects of state transformation have diverged. The UK government makes policy largely for England (while producing spill-over effects for the others), while the devolved governments can form their own 'territorial policy communities' (Keating et al, 2009). We find some evidence that they reversed or opted out of reforms associated with UK state transformation.

Healthcare

The Scottish government reversed internal market policies in favour of central planning. The Welsh government discouraged the private sector and emphasised a shift from healthcare to public health. Northern Ireland changed little until the UK government introduced a new model of performance management (Greer, 2003: 198–199; Keating et al, 2012: 298). All three phased out prescription charges at different times, while the UK government focused on exemptions (Keating et al, 2012: 295; see also Chapter 10 on their public health policies).

Education

Scottish governments maintain a historically separate education system, delivered by local authorities and comprehensive schools (McPherson and Raab, 1988; Cairney, 2013a; Chitty, 2014: 132–136). Northern Ireland has a separate system, but is influenced more by UK government policy. Education 'continues to be academically selective and religiously segregated', as symbolised by republican party opposition to, and unionist party support for, the eleven-plus exam (Birrell, 2012: 58; Keating et al, 2012: 299; O'Neill, 2020). Welsh education was more tied to England, but also more in favour of comprehensive schools linked to local government (Keating et al, 2012: 296) and resistant to Conservative government reforms before 1999 (Farrell and Law, 1999). Scotland and Wales place 'less emphasis on testing', and all three governments abolished formal 'league tables' of school performance (Keating et al, 2012: 296–300; Andrews, 2014: 136–137). Still, all four governments produced similar school examinations crises in 2020 and 2021 (Box 6.5).

Local government

Devolution accentuated the role of local government as a major consultee and delivery partner in Wales, and central–local relations have been smoother in Scotland when compared to UK government (Cairney, 2008; 2009a; Connell et al, 2019; 2021). There is less of a tradition of local government in Northern Ireland, but devolution offered the chance for public sector reforms with their stronger role (Birrell, 2012: 185; Birrell et al, 2023).

Social housing

The Scottish government was quicker (than the UK) to address the lack of social housing caused by RTB: increasing the qualifying tenancy, reducing the discount and allowing RTB suspension in 'pressured' areas (Jones and Murie, 2006: 43; McKee, 2010).

Public expenditure

Devolved differences are funded by higher-per-head 'identifiable' public expenditure (that is, excluding spending for the UK that cannot be divided by territory). If the UK figure is 100, in 2019–2020 it was approximately 97 in England, 121 in Northern Ireland, 117 in Scotland and 110 in Wales (HM Treasury, 2021: 124). Supporters of the UK call Scottish spending the 'Union dividend', while supporters of Scottish independence argue that UK economic policies undermine the Scottish economy (Cairney and McGarvey, 2013: 225). Greater 'fiscal devolution' has allowed the Scottish government to raise taxes and spending modestly (Box 9.3; McIntyre et al, 2022).

Reforming government

There remains a UK civil service, but with distinctive administrative arrangements before and after political devolution (Rhodes, 1988: 143–152; Birrell, 2012: 131–137; Parry, 2016). Devolution offered an opportunity to reduce the role of Executive Agencies in favour of direct control of policy delivery (Birrell, 2012: 137–139), pursue distinctive approaches to civil service 'modernisation' (Parry, 2005), and seek 'joined-up' policy making in smaller, more manageable systems (Cairney and St Denny, 2020: 70–76). This potential has not produced any appreciable differences between UK and devolved government 'performance' (Hood and Dixon, 2015: 150–153).

Greer and Jarman (2008) identify differences in the 'policy tools' used by UK and devolved governments. UK government policy emphasised quasi-market mechanisms, regulation, audit and punishments for non-compliance, to reflect its 'low trust in providers' (Greer and Jarman, 2008: 172–173). Scottish and Welsh governments relied more on traditional service delivery to reflect 'a high degree of trust in the professionalism of providers' (Greer and Jarman, 2008: 178–183). The devolved governments have not produced profoundly different welfare state models, but smaller differences still matter.

Conclusion

There has been a transformation of the UK state. It moved away from a 'post-war consensus', built on the belief that governments *could* and *should* intervene to benefit the UK population by delivering employment, education, healthcare, housing and social security. It moved towards 'neoliberalism', built on the belief that state intervention undermines the market and that individuals should take responsibility for their welfare.

Compared to policies from the mid-1940s, the size of the UK state fell dramatically following the privatisation of industries and sales of social housing. The UK government is less committed to the 'old' Keynesian measures to tax and spend to manage demand in the economy. It has jettisoned a commitment to 'full employment', in favour of maintaining low inflation and using tools such as interest rates (set by an independent central bank). Tax-funded public services remain, but the state is much less likely to deliver them directly, while its reforms have changed how the civil service and policy advisory systems operate. Social security remains, but the framing of the problem changed: to reflect a reduced commitment to full employment, then to reduce the cost of unemployment benefits. Chapter 9 examines further 'austerity' reforms.

Parties made a difference to this transformation. Labour introduced the policies associated with the post-war consensus, and the Conservatives pursued a commitment to neoliberalism. Parties also inherited the commitments of their predecessors, accepting or accelerating policies of the past. Still, a long-term perspective allows us to get beyond the question of party differences at one point in time towards identifying an eventual transformation. A government story favouring state intervention, ownership, and welfare state and public service delivery has given way to policy consistent with the neoliberal story of state retrenchment and privatisation in favour of market forces and individual responsibility. This shift is profound no matter how we got there.

In that context, devolution has produced a mixed impact. When viewed through the lens of UK government, it is another policy to remove responsibility for policy making from a single centre (Chapter 7). When viewed as the chance for devolved governments to go their own way, we see examples of reversing or opting out of the UK government policies that we associate with the transformation towards a neoliberal state. These differences take place within a wider UK context that limits their autonomy. Most elements of state transformation are here to stay.

What Does State Transformation Tell Us about the UK Policy Process?

Introduction

This chapter relates UK state transformation to the Westminster and complex government stories. Long-term changes to policy (Chapter 4) are important in their own right. They also inform debates about how governments make and deliver policy, how policy changes, and the extent to which UK policy reflects wider international agendas rather than simply party ideology. We ask four key questions.

First, what was the style of policy making during transformation? 'Policy style' describes how governments make and deliver policy (Richardson et al, 1982). For example, as the Westminster story suggests, did governments push new policies from the top down? The complex government story warns against this assumption, situating governments within a wider policy-making environment over which they have limited control. Still, long-term transformation had an impact on policy making: the 'normal' policy style today is not the same as in previous decades.

Second, did policy change incrementally or in radical bursts? Chapter 4 describes policy continuity from the 1940s to 1970s, but major shifts associated with some periods (the mid–1940s and late 1970s). In some cases, a new government signalled an era-defining shift in direction. In many others, policy slowed down or accelerated. The Westminster story has *some* value, to describe periods of radical change directed from the centre, but only when situated in a wider context to identify the rarity of these changes. Further, these dynamics are not summed up well by 'incrementalism'. If we treat incrementalism as a strategy, we exaggerate the coherence of steps towards an endgame. If we treat it as a description of policy change, we struggle to explain key periods that do not fit the pattern.

Third, what was the impact of state transformation on central government? We describe ministers addressing the unmanageability of government, either to reassert central control or jettison the parts of government that defy it. Have these reforms reduced or exacerbated the limits to central control?

Fourth, how do these developments relate to the wider world? 'Globalisation' suggests that national governments do not simply manage their own affairs. Their high-profile aims – such as economic growth – depend on choices made by other governments, international organisations and non-governmental actors such as multinational corporations.

What was the UK policy style during state transformation?

Chapters 2 and 3 show that the UK policy style does not necessarily live up to its majoritarian reputation. Post-war governments recognised the benefits of processing policy in relatively consensual 'policy communities' (Richardson and Jordan, 1979; Jordan and Maloney, 1997). These benefits reflect the *choice* to avoid a 'politically expensive' top-down policy style that drains the resources of policy makers (Richardson et al, 1982: 10). They also reflect *necessity*: policy makers can only pay attention to a small number of issues, and must delegate responsibility for most. In turn, civil servants form relationships with the groups that they trust to give them information and advice, particularly when they represent an important population, profession or industry, and contribute to implementation (Maloney et al, 1994: 23). Civil servants base this relationship on:

- The 'logic of consultation', to encourage stakeholder 'ownership' of policy and gather knowledge of problems.
- The logic of 'bureaucratic accommodation', where civil servants lack the legitimacy and power of ministers and seek to cooperate with groups rather than impose decisions (Jordan and Richardson, 1982: 84–86; 1987: 29–30).

Many interest groups see the benefits of these arrangements, and follow informal 'rules of the game' to gain and maintain access to government. These rules can be summed up by the following statements. Support the government's right to define the policy problem. Keep discussions in-house and avoid public criticism of minsters. Present modest demands, and accept that things may not always go your way. Accepting short-term losses with grace will boost your reputation and potential for long-term gains (Grant, 1989: 21; Maloney et al, 1994: 34;

Jordan and Maloney, 1997; see also Rhodes, 1988: 91–93). Their status within government may be as:

- *core insiders*, seen as important in many sectors and able to bargain routinely with governments;
- *specialist insiders*, important in niche areas and engaged less regularly; or
- *peripheral insiders*, marginally important and more likely to be consulted cosmetically.

Other groups are *outsiders* because their beliefs and aims are too inconsistent with government policy and/or they are visible critics of government. Or, in some cases, groups are able to mix strategies (Maloney et al, 1994: 33–34; May and Nugent, 1982: 7; Mayne et al, 2018).

Did Thatcherism signal the end of policy communities?

The election of a Thatcher-led government seemed to prompt radical changes to policy and policy making:

- Reinforcing the majoritarian image where policy is made from the top down (Box 3.2).
- Emphasising state reforms to challenge the vested interests and cosy arrangements that they associated with government failure (for example, the 'Winter of Discontent', Chapter 4). They would make policy irrespective of opposition (Marsh and Rhodes, 1992: 8).
- Rejecting the need for consultation before radical action. Thatcher was 'determined not to waste time on internal arguments over policy making' (Marsh and Rhodes, 1992: 8).

Yet, the logic of policy communities arose largely from *necessity*: to pay attention to few issues and delegate responsibility for the rest; and, accept that most policy would be processed by civil servants cooperating with other actors. The Thatcher government clearly changed who would be consulted and what would be the agenda to discuss. However, the overall Thatcher effect was often overstated. Jordan and Richardson (1987: 30) were 'impressed with the sheer weight of consultation' in their interviews with civil servants, while Maloney et al (1994: 23) argue that 'the practice of consultation has been growing in importance over the last decade'. There was a major but inconsistent Thatcher effect, including:

- Variation by sector or profession. The effects were high in relation to trade unions.
- Variation by policy-making function. In some cases, ministers only rejected talks during policy formulation, but changed their approach during implementation.

Baggott's (1995: 489) survey of interest groups found that half perceived 'no change in the frequency or effectiveness of contacts with ministers and civil servants during the 1980s', while others complained that ministers were ruling out negotiation. Some also witnessed the displacement of consultation: ministers may attempt to internalise policy making, but depend on information and advice from civil servants, who depend on other actors. High-profile cases, such as National Health Service (NHS) reform, showed that ministers tried to internalise policy by using small review teams outside of government departments, but the process returned to its departmental home after initial plans lacked feasibility (Burch and Holliday, 1996: 233–234).

Do the early post-war communities resemble modern networks?

These limits refer to day-to-day policy making, but what about long-term and cumulative changes? Richardson (2018a: 223–229; 2018b: 29–48; 2023) highlights why modern policy communities do not resemble their pre-Thatcher equivalents:

- Many groups – such as trade unions – never returned to the privileged status that they enjoyed in previous eras.
- Many policies – such as new public management (NPM) reforms (Chapter 4) – were opposed vociferously then taken for granted.
- These reforms changed the role of the civil service, which became less central to policy making (Chapter 4). Richards and Smith (2016: 499) describe the minister–civil servant relationship as shifting from a 'symbiotic interdependent partnership' to 'a more universal command and control relationship'.
- Both parties have exploited multiple crises to make 'tough choices' backed by the 'government knows best' narrative. For example, the Blair government shifted styles to force changes to mental health policy (Box 5.1) and the Brown-led government became 'increasingly insular and inward looking' (Richards, 2011: 43).

Richardson (2018a: 227–229) suggests that the new normal policy style is to present policy solutions first, then consult on how to deliver. The old role of policy communities – to define and solve policy problems routinely within central government – has been eroded. The necessity of delegating policy making and the logic of consultation and bureaucratic accommodation still endure, but to produce a complicated mix of networks spread across the policy-making environment (Dorey, 2005a: 263–278; Cairney, 2019b).

Box 5.1: The mix of UK and Scottish policy styles for mental health

The UK government's policy style combines top-down *and* consensual practices: a small number of issues are non-negotiable, while many are processed routinely in policy communities (Jordan and Richardson, 1982: 98). This style was associated with Thatcherism, but continued under Blair-led governments: issues such as student testing in schools and NHS performance management were non-negotiable, but surrounded by routine talks between ministers or civil servants and unions (Cairney, 2008: 364–366). As such, a focus on high-profile top-down policy making exaggerates a difference in styles between UK and devolved governments (Box 3.2). Interest groups in Scotland and Wales may enjoy gratifying consultation, but they contrast this experience with what they *imagine* to be a less rewarding UK equivalent (Cairney, 2008: 369; 2019b).

Mental health policy exemplifies this mix of policy styles over decades. On the one hand, the UK Labour government exhibited the worst excesses of a top-down style from 1997, overseeing 'a ten-year stand-off between UK ministers and the vast majority of interest groups which united under the Mental Health Alliance (MHA) to oppose government legislation' (it passed in 2007, in a reduced form) (Cairney, 2009b: 672). In contrast, the Scottish government passed similar legislation in under four years (by 2003) after generating high consensus (Cairney, 2009b: 672). On the other hand, the UK experience represents a deviation from a long-term consensual process to reform mental health policy. Interest groups contrast it with:

- Their relationships with the UK government on almost any other issue during that time (for example, NHS reform and legislation on mental capacity).
- The 1959 and 1983 Acts which exhibited a 'long and proud history of modernisation' through policy styles comparable to those in devolved government (Cairney, 2009b: 686).

Post-war policy changes include deinstitutionalisation (from 150,000 NHS beds in 1954 to 20,000 in 2015), legislative reforms 'built increasingly on the need to protect human rights when depriving people of their liberty without trial', and attempts to increase the status of mental health services in the NHS and expand psychological therapies in the community (Rogers and Pilgrim, 2001: 55; Cairney and St Denny, 2020: 159). Governments also increased discussions with third-sector groups, many of which promoted the voices of service users.

In that context, Labour's approach was puzzling, reflecting a spill-over from its 'tough on crime' agenda. The Home Office introduced the category of 'Dangerous people with Severe Personality Disorder' to detain people if they were a risk to the public. It undermined a consensus focused on destigmatising mental health, emphasising support, patients' rights and minimising detention against someone's will (Cairney and St Denny, 2020: 159).

The coalition government closed the door on this episode, reviving group–government relations during policy work to secure parity between mental and physical health services. However, it opened another. It placed dispiriting limits on the extent to which disabled people were entitled to social security (during 'employability' reforms). This agenda spilled into mental health, with groups facing 'infrequent and "frosty" meetings with ministers' on this non-negotiable issue (Cairney and St Denny, 2020: 164–173).

Did policy change incrementally or in radical bursts?

Chapter 2 introduces the expectation that policy change is the combination of a small amount of major changes and a huge amount of minor changes. Two important contributions to policy studies identify 'punctuated equilibrium' or 'paradigm shift', to describe:

1. *Policy-making dynamics.* Long periods of policy-making stability followed by a burst of instability (or vice versa).
2. *Policy continuity and change.* Long periods of policy continuity followed by a shift in policy direction in relation to one problem. Or, an overall combination of many minor policy changes and a small number of major changes.

Punctuated equilibrium theory: policy change is a function of attention

Jones and Baumgartner (2005) show that policy change follows disproportionately high and low policy-maker attention, contributing to 'hyperincrementalism' in most cases but 'policy punctuations' in some. This emphasis may *seem* unimportant since most change is incremental, but it raises questions about the *cause* of these patterns: do they follow a fairly sensible and coherent approach to policy analysis and negotiation (incrementalism as an analytical and political strategy)? Or, do they follow dramatic lurches of attention (in the absence of a clear strategy)? Is the distribution of minor and major policy changes 'normal', or akin to the frequency of earthquakes?

Normal distribution: describes deviation from the mean: 68 per cent within one standard deviation (SD), and 95 per cent within two SDs. Data near the mean are far more frequent than data far from the mean.

Leptokurtic distribution: a distribution with a higher peak (more than 68 per cent of cases are within one SD) and longer tail (less than 95 per cent are within two). See True et al (2007) and Cairney (2017a) for a visualisation.

John and Margetts (2003) relate this question to changes in annual UK budgets from 1951 to 1996. They describe a tradition in budgetary analysis to relate changes to two different expectations: (1) incremental policy change, akin to a **normal distribution** (most changes are similar to the mean change, with very few outliers), or (2) punctuated change, which is **leptokurtic** (akin to very infrequent, unpredictable earthquakes) in which there are more 'hyperincremental' changes *and* outliers (John and Margetts, 2003: 415). They find a distribution of changes that matches the 'earthquake budget model' (John and Margetts, 2003: 422). This finding suggests that:

- Most policy changes *appear* to be incremental, reflecting policy inheritance and a reluctance to depart radically from the past.

- A small number of relatively unpredictable occurrences, of radical departures from the status quo, challenge the idea that budget changes result from incremental strategies.

Policy changes may be small for years or decades, then change radically and unpredictably and head in a different direction. The frequency of these 'punctuations' varies by sector, with defence and crime budgets more likely to fit the leptokurtic pattern than social security, housing and health (John and Margetts, 2003: 424). More recent work by John et al (2013) suggests that these changes do not *necessarily* reflect shifts of policy-maker attention. Defence budgets have diminished gradually, and crime budgets increased gradually, despite peaks and troughs of attention. There were periods of lower and higher healthcare and education spending, reflecting periodic attempts to make these sectors more efficient before major reinvestments from 1997 (John et al, 2013: 183–188; compare with Massey and Pyper, 2005: 66–70).

John et al (2013) also analyse these dynamics in relation to post-war policy statements and legislation. Some topics received disproportionately and consistently high attention (for example, macroeconomic policy, international affairs). Others saw bursts of attention (John et al, 2013: 98–102). When analysing **Queen's speeches,** they note multiple punctuations related to: a series of proposed 'social welfare' reforms in 1947 (to introduce a 'comprehensive system of assistance'), 1957 and 1996 (pension reforms), 1972 (the implications of EU membership for social policy) and 1998 (Labour's plan to expand provision); and, surges of attention to land use, house building and housing reforms in 1958, 1963 and 1970. When analysing legislative changes, they identify three categories of punctuation:

> **Queen's speech** (Speech from the Throne): the speech to open Parliament, used by the government's core executive to set out the highest priorities in its policy and legislative agenda.

1. *Procedural.* Many separate changes contribute to an overall change, including activity in the late 1960s to reform social work, provide milk for 'poor school children', and reform disability benefits.
2. *Low salience.* Major changes receive low media attention, including education reforms in the early 1970s.
3. *High salience.* Major changes receive high media attention. Examples include: late 1960s Labour government reforms to address poor industrial relations; early 1980s market reforms and privatisation; early 1990s environmental reforms connected to EU regulation; and, late 1990s constitutional reforms (John et al, 2013: 108–111).

High salience punctuations relate to periods of government described as major turning points. The Thatcher-led government in 1979 signalled a 'dramatic shift' in policy and policy making (John et al, 2013: 34–35). New Labour in 1997 prompted spending on social and public services, such as for health and education, and constitutional changes, including devolution in Northern Ireland, Scotland and Wales, and Bank of England independence (John et al, 2013: 34–35). New Labour's initial 'New Deal' rhetoric signalled a desire to correct some of the Thatcher government's worst excesses: 'to demonstrate the return of proactive state intervention and social conscience to politics after 17 years of neoliberal inspired marketisation under the conservatives' (Shaw and Docherty, 2008: 3, citing Giddens, 2000).

However, a sole focus on high-profile measures – major speeches and legislation – exaggerates the proportion of policy change that is signposted and visible. Major policy changes also take place out of the public spotlight, sometimes with no clear sense of direction, or with reference to technical adjustments of well-established aims (John et al, 2013: 111).

Hall's paradigm shift in economic policy: major change follows failure

This mix of routine minor policy changes and rare and unpredictable radical shifts is central to Hall's (1993) discussion of UK economic policy from 1970 to 1989. It exhibits different 'orders' of change:

1. *First order.* Frequent routine changes while maintaining policy goals. Civil servants adjust the settings of policy instruments (while consulting with insider advisers).

The early 1970s were characterised by first-order changes managed by the Treasury. Prime Ministers were unable or unwilling to take 'macroeconomic management out of the hands of their officials' since they lacked technical expertise (Hall, 1993: 280). Annual budgets afforded limited chances for group influence, even by the Confederation of British Industry and Trades Union Congress (Hall, 1993: 280).

2. *Second order.* Non-routine and less frequent changes, while maintaining policy goals. There may be new policy instruments or targets. More actors are involved, but civil servants maintain internally driven changes.

There were some instances of second-order changes advanced by Treasury officials. They included an early (failed) experiment to foster 'monetary control based primarily on interest rate changes' (1972–1973), a more effective way for the Treasury to limit public expenditure (1974–1977) and a new way to control monetary growth (1985) (Hall, 1993: 282). Each action related to learning and adapting to failing instruments, 'primarily in response to dissatisfaction with past policy rather than in response to new economic events alone' (Hall, 1993: 283).

3. *Third order.* Rare, radical shifts in policy, including changes to instrument settings, new policy instruments and *a reprioritisation of policy goals*. Far more external actors are involved, and civil servants are unable to manage existing networks.

Major changes from 1979 to 1980 reflect a 'radical shift from Keynesian to monetarist modes of macroeconomic regulation' (Hall, 1993: 279). The Conservative government heralded 'the most intense break' in policy when the 'hierarchy of goals and set of instruments employed to guide policy shifted radically' (Hall, 1993: 283–284). Monetary policy replaced fiscal policy, inflation and debt control became more important than unemployment, and state intervention reduced (Hall, 1993: 284).

Hall (1993: 284) uses the term 'policy paradigms' to explain this tendency towards inertia, punctuated rarely by radical change. A paradigm is a worldview. People adhere to, and often take for granted, a collection of beliefs about how the world works:

> Policymakers customarily work within a framework of ideas and standards that specifies not only the goals of policy and the kind of instruments that can be used to attain them, but also the very nature of the problems they are meant to be addressing … this framework is embedded in the very terminology through which policymakers communicate about their work, and it is influential precisely because so much of it is taken for granted and unamenable to scrutiny. (Hall, 1993: 279)

Paradigms can operate for long periods, subject to minimal challenge. Or, actors cooperate intensely when they share beliefs, and reject the ideas of actors operating in different paradigms (compare with advocacy coalitions in Chapter 2; Cairney and Weible, 2015).

In this case, one paradigm – Keynesianism – dominated policy for long periods, with policy change following routine learning from experience. First- and second-order changes are *standard operating procedures*. Radical policy change may only follow a rare crisis in which the application of a paradigm no longer solves a policy problem or explains why. Third-order change follows a rejection of that way of thinking. Hall (1993: 281) links it to policy failures that gather wide attention and undermine support for the current approach (and its advocates). It follows debate on 'first principles' which ends 'when the supporters of a new paradigm secure positions of authority over policy making and are able to rearrange the organization and standard operating procedures of the policy process so as to institutionalize the new paradigm' (Hall, 1993: 281). It involves a new government with new ways of thinking and/or the government rejecting current experts in favour of new ones.

In this case, gone was the 'Keynesian' paradigm when: (1) it could not explain why inflation *and* unemployment were growing (and the economy was not), (2) its adherents stretched its 'intellectual coherence' when attempting to shore up its appeal, and (3) these responses did not produced the desired effect. 'Cost of living agreements' in 1973 fuelled inflation. Corporate tax increases in 1974 exacerbated the impact of oil price rises on business. Poor estimates of public spending prompted larger public borrowing in 1975. Exchange rate policies in 1976 'precipitated a run on the pound that ended with recourse to the **IMF** and severe spending cuts in 1977'. Incomes policies (1972–1977) – involving 'tortuous negotiations with the unions' – undermined the Keynesian idea that governments could manage economies without 'intervening directly in the affairs of individual economic actors' (Hall, 1993: 285).

> **IMF** (International Monetary Fund): funded by countries to foster international cooperation on monetary and trade policies, and provide loans (with strict conditions) to countries in crisis. Not to be confused with the Impossible Missions Force.

While the new paradigm was associated with Conservative government, the Labour government's Prime Minister and Chancellor had already lost faith in the old by 1976, prompting many Treasury officials to leave (Hall, 1993: 286). The drop in Treasury influence went hand in hand with a rise in professional and media debate (the 'marketplace in economic ideas') and the expanded research and think tank capacity associated with a new paradigm (Hall, 1993: 286). Monetarism had 'political appeal', as a way for the Conservative Party to criticise the Labour government, narrate the failure of 'neo-corporatist' policy making (and trade unions in particular), *and* sell 'the long-standing Conservative position that public spending and the role of the state in the economy should be reduced' (Hall, 1993: 286). Thatcher appointed monetarists to Cabinet and as special advisors, and influenced the promotion of sympathetic civil servants (Hall, 1993: 287).

> **Ideas**: shared beliefs or ways of thinking. Examples include: (1) ideologies regarding how the world works and should work, (2) paradigms or world views (deeply held, taken-for-granted beliefs), (3) norms (rules or expectations of acceptable behaviour), or (4) policy solutions ('I have an idea') (Cairney, 2020a: 190–191).

Rapid paradigm shifts in economic policy are rare and incomplete

Hall describes a lurch of support from one **idea** to another, prompting the replacement of one policy programme with another (compare with Wood, 2015). Others are more sceptical about the arguments that governments adopt such ideas wholesale (Box 5.2).

Box 5.2: The unclear relationship between economic ideas and policy

A shift in government policy will never simply reflect a shift in adherence to economic (or NPM) ideas for the following reasons:

1. Abstract economic models are not easily translated into real-world policy (compare Dolowitz, 2004; Watson, 2004).
2. Economic thought is increasingly difficult to separate into different camps (Hodson and Mabbett, 2009: 1043).
3. Governments rarely label themselves as ideologically Keynesian or monetarist.
4. They seek to boost their electability by prioritising an image of governing competence (Hay and Watson, 2004) and portraying their policies as 'centrist' (Hindmoor, 2005).
5. Government reform ideas may result from 'fads' that do not come to much (Massey and Pyper, 2005: 44), or produce ill-considered choices (King and Crewe, 2014).
6. 'Much of government economic policy is a reaction to events, rather than an attempt to anticipate them' (Grant, 1993: 1). Policy makers' 'freedom of action' is illusory 'when in reality they are being driven by forces outside their control' (Klein, 1976: 402).
7. Ministers can be 'unwitting architects' of policy, stumbling across a new model 'serendipitously' (Hay, 2011: 244).
8. Historical analyses of economic policy gives government actions a 'unity in retrospect that they did not possess at the time' (Cairncross, 1985: 17; Peden, 2000: 362).
9. The phrase 'economic policy' is misleading, since policy is a collection of instruments associated with different purposes and pressures (Thompson, 1996).

A good example of points 8–9 is the UK government's timing when adopting the European Exchange Rate Mechanism in 1990 (Thompson, 1995). Going a decade sooner could have addressed an over-valued sterling and made domestic manufacturing exports more attractive. Going later (with low preparation) had no such benefits, left the government vulnerable to currency speculators when sterling was valued too highly, and ended in disaster – 'Black Wednesday' – in 1992 (Thompson, 1995: 248; King and Crewe, 2014: 95–110; Williams, 2022). The choice of timing reflected (1) *technical aims*, to smooth international trade and business planning by cooperating with other countries to manage the value of currencies, but also (2) *political aims*, to manage EU scepticism (Thompson, 1995: 249; Chapter 7).

Oliver and Pemberton (2004: 416) argue that policy change was less of a clean break. It was longer term and 'more intricate' than Hall describes because:

- The Heath government (1970–1974) was committed ideologically to rejecting Keynesianism, but reinstated a modified version after policy failures.
- The Labour government (1974–1979) was committed to its maintenance, but actually accelerated its demise, and introduced monetary growth targets in 1976 (Peden, 1991: 207–215; Oliver and Pemberton, 2004: 431; Hindmoor, 2019: 7–31).
- The Thatcher government struggled to 'balance theoretical monetarism with practical implementation', while macroeconomic policy from 1985 exhibited 'some of the old tendencies of Keynesian demand management' (Grant, 1993: 50–56; Oliver and Pemberton, 2004: 433). The governments' 'ideological language' of 'free market economics' and monetarism was 'only

rarely reflected in their policy decisions' (Thompson, 1996: 167). The aim to minimise inflation and avoid state intervention did not always match the use of policy instruments, and 'monetarist' policy under Thatcher was not coherent (Pemberton, 2000: 789; Massey and Pyper, 2005: 64–66).

Heclo and Wildavsky's (1981: ix–x; 14–21) study of 'village life' in Whitehall suggests that Hall exaggerated the ideology-driven exodus of Treasury staff. 'Treasury culture' remained 'part of the essence of British government', built more on trust in civil servants and distrust of outsiders than economic ideology (see also Rhodes, 2011: 211; Gamble, 2012; Berry, 2020).

Punctuated evolution: many terms describe 'non-punctuated change with profound long-term results' (Studlar and Cairney, 2014: 514). They include 'punctuated evolution' (Hay, 2002: 163), 'gradual change with transformative results' (Streeck and Thelen, 2005: 9) and 'gradual but profound' change (Palier, 2005: 129). Many refer to 'evolution' without clarifying what they mean (Cairney, 2013b).

In place of a story of rapid paradigm change in favour of *monetarism*, Oliver and Pemberton (2004: 433) describe a longer-term and less coherent process of '**punctuated evolution**' in favour of *neoliberalism*. This trend endured despite many 'quiet failures' of 'neoliberal economics' under Thatcher (Best, 2020; Clift, 2020). It continued under Major, who oversaw a growth model described as 'finance-led' or 'privatised Keynesianism', where debt-fuelled economic growth shifted from the state to the private sector. It became tied to assets such as homes, contributing (eventually) to the global economic crisis in 2007 (Hay, 2011: 246; Oren and Blyth, 2019: 606).

Labour (from 1997) inherited and supported this approach (Oliver and Pemberton, 2004: 434), with reference to 'fiscal prudence, price stability and a commitment to light-touch financial regulation' (Hodson and Mabbett, 2009: 1042). All three aims came under pressure during the global economic crisis. The crisis response prompted some commentators to describe state interventions, such as to nationalise failing banks, as a return to Keynesianism. However, 'new Keynesianism' focused on supporting monetary policy during crisis (Hodson and Mabbett, 2009: 1053; Kay, 2011: 150; see also Hay, 2011: 253 on Brown's 'interparadigm borrowing').

State transformation: trial and error, not a grand plan

Economic policy is not representative of policy overall. In other areas, we find paradigmatic policy change, but over several decades rather than years. Such change may follow the accumulation of many different policy instruments introduced to satisfy short-term aims rather than a coherent long-term plan. Or, we may witness trial and error rather than a 'big bang' (Studlar and Cairney, 2014: 513).

For example, while *privatisation* contributed to state transformation, there was no consistent plan based on a coherent Thatcherite ideology (such as to describe how asset sales and competition would boost industrial efficiency) (Dunn and Smith, 1990: 34–39; Marsh, 1991; Stevens, 2004; Massey and Pyper, 2005: 81–84). It became a signature policy *eventually*, but largely after 1983, following growing realisation that initial sales boosted public share ownership *and* the government's popularity among share owners, and deteriorating relations between the government and some nationalised industries. It also proved to be the most politically feasible way to meet promises on reducing the 'public sector borrowing requirement' (Marsh, 1991: 461–462). Further, post-Thatcher (Conservative and Labour) governments went much further than a 1979 government could. As Zahariadis (2003: 59) describes, we should treat privatisation overall as a key policy, but each sale as more or less feasible and requiring its own 'window of opportunity'. In particular, it took a decade to sell British Rail (Dudley and Richardson, 2000: 197–228; Zahariadis, 2003: 84). Further, charging over £9,000 per year for higher education tuition followed a series of steps by both parties (Chapter 4).

Similarly, although *employment law* became a signature policy, the Thatcherite challenge to trade unions began tentatively, based on uncertainty about compliance following the failure of the Heath-led Conservative government (Marsh, 1992: 33–36). Stronger measures were spaced out over a decade, and their impact on outcomes – such as levels of unionisation, the frequency of collective bargaining, strikes and wage levels – were not immediately obvious (Marsh, 1992: 40–44). Thatcher governments became emboldened to act when 'compliance was not a major problem' and the legislation boosted Thatcher's popularity and image of governing competence (Greenaway et al, 1992: 164–182; Marsh, 1992: 33–36).

More generally, there is no 'grand theme' to redraw the boundaries of the state and reform how people hold public bodies to account (Hogwood, 1997: 715). The reforms described in Chapter 4 were a mish-mash of policies explained by events and varying motivations, including the desire to reduce state intervention and raise money and government popularity through privatisation, introduce NPM (to encourage decentralised institutional accountability or reinforce central control), prompt public bodies to become more efficient or more responsive to the users of their services, raise revenue or reduce borrowing, and challenge totemic public bodies such as local authorities (Hood, 1995: 94; Common, 1998: 442; James, 2001; Dorey, 2005b; Goldfinch and Wallis, 2010). Further, examples such as the poll tax (Box 4.3) suggest that the implementation of an ideology-heavy plan can be disastrous and prompt a U-turn.

What is the impact of these changes on government? Did they foster a 'lean' or 'hollow' state?

There is considerable uncertainty – within academia and government – about the long-term impact of state transformation (Dunleavy, 2006; Burnham and

Pyper, 2008: 31–56). One interpretation is consistent with the Westminster story: reforms contributed to a 'rejuvenated' and 'lean' state, with ministers able to focus on core tasks without having to manage peripheral functions. They can make strategic decisions, create rules and regulations – backed by funding, inspection and performance management – to ensure that their aims are carried out by others, and minimise the powers of bodies (and local authorities in particular) with an alternative mandate (Hogwood, 1997; Holliday, 2000; Bache, 2003; Marinetto, 2003; Massey and Pyper, 2005: 140; Richards and Smith, 2006). Phrases such as 'asymmetric power model' and 'strong government, although increasingly challenged' suggest that these reforms did not diminish the relative power of UK central government (Taylor, 2000; Marsh et al, 2003: 308; Marsh, 2008: 255). Similarly, 'meta-governance' describes the government's ability to direct the design, goals, management and participants of networks of governmental and non-governmental organisations (Sørensen and Torfing, 2009: 236–237; Dommett and Flinders, 2015). See also Barber (2012) for a spin of Labour's record of policy delivery under Blair (compare with Rhodes, 2011: 25–29).

An alternative argument is that the UK government exacerbated its own 'governance problem', defined as the gap between a story of central control and what central governments can actually do (Cairney, 2009a). A collection of reforms fragmented the public landscape and exacerbated a sense that no one is in control. There is a never-ending and dispiriting cycle of such reforms, where a lack of central control prompts centralisation but produces the opposite (Bevir and Rhodes, 2003). For example, privatisation reduced the role of the state in important markets, while NPM reforms and outsourcing reduced the government's control of policy delivery and exacerbated unclear accountability (Rhodes, 1994: 139–142). Phrases like 'differentiated polity', 'hollowing out', 'fragmented government', departmental 'Balkanisation' and 'congested state' describe a government increasingly unable to address 'wicked' problems, 'join-up' policy, or influence policy outcomes without the aid of many other bodies (Rhodes, 1988: 3; 1994; 1997; Gray, 2000: 283–284; Skelcher, 2000; Bevir and Rhodes, 2003: 6; Exworthy and Powell, 2004; Massey and Pyper, 2005: 84–91; James, 2009). They reinforce the complex government story (Chapter 3) and concepts such as 'multi-level governance' (Chapter 1):

> Twenty years ago political institutions and political leaders were much more self-reliant and it was assumed – for good reasons – that the state governed Britain. Today, the role of government in the process of governance is much more contingent. Local, regional and national political elites alike seek to forge coalitions with private businesses, voluntary associations and other societal actors to mobilize resources across the public – private border in order to enhance their chances of guiding society towards politically defined goals. (Pierre and Stoker, 2000: 29)

How did governments react to the impact of these reforms?

Successive governments have bemoaned and exacerbated their governance problems by accepting or extending the policies of their Thatcherite predecessors (Richards and Smith, 2006). Labour pursued policy making designed to reassert central control *and* enhance the 'local autonomy' of delivery bodies, with no coherent links between aims (Richards and Smith, 2006). It fostered 'control freakery' in some areas but decentralised others (Wilson, 2003). This approach suggests that it entered government with concerns about:

> the perceived inability of elected governments to control and co-ordinate policy across and beyond Whitehall ... the policy arena had become a much more crowded environment, with numerous actors competing for political space. The net effect had been the curtailment of the government's ability to maintain some semblance of control by appealing to the traditional form of governing through state hierarchies. (Richards and Smith, 2004: 106)

From 1997, it responded by trying to recentralise to some extent, but seeking to manage policy networks rather than assert hierarchical relationships. It expanded the Prime Minister's policy unit, and pursued a *modernisation* programme, to address a lack of central strategic capability (Massey and Pyper, 2005: 57–58). It used central strategic powers to encourage 'joined-up government' and challenge 'departmentalism' (Kavanagh and Richards, 2001; Bogdanor, 2005). 'Public service agreements' set joint targets for departments. The Treasury's 'comprehensive spending review' prompted reforms to budget allocations to oblige departments to contribute to a joint agenda (Richards and Smith, 2004: 107–110). The list of cross-cutting projects includes:

- The *Sure Start* programme to foster 'early intervention' and combine pre-school and welfare provision.
- *Health Action Zones* to address inequalities via public service partnerships.
- The *New Deal for Communities* to foster regeneration and reduce unemployment.
- The *Social Exclusion Unit* to join up services to support families and address school exclusion, youth homelessness and teenage pregnancy (Taylor, 2000; Page and Jenkins, 2005: 87–90; Cairney and St Denny, 2020: 89–99).

By its second term (2001), Labour was frustrated by 'a lack of progress on joined-up government' (Cairney, 2009a: 359). It reverted to a top-down style, with public service agreement targets connected to funding and enforced by the Treasury (Richards and Smith, 2004: 106; Rhodes, 2011: 30–33, 211–212). However, it delegated public service delivery to non-departmental public bodies and non-governmental organisations (Chapter 4) and signalled support for some local government autonomy ('new localism' – Morphet, 2008: 108–111;

Davies, 2009). Flinders suggests that the lack of attention to this combination of approaches has exacerbated a sense that no one is in control:

> The British state is evolving in an ad hoc, arbitrary, and unprincipled manner which is evidence in three ways: (1) in the existence of widespread and fundamental confusion about the administrative structure of the state; (2) in confusion about the existence and utility of the control and accountability mechanisms surrounding delegated organizational forms; and (3) in the absence of any explicit logic or rationale that can explain the ambitions, consequences, or trajectory of this process. (Flinders, 2008: 1)

From 2010 to 2015, the coalition government attempted to localise *and* centralise policy making, with measures to encourage the 'co-production' of public services between local public bodies and service users, and government agencies to operate without ministerial interference. The coalition made a rhetorical commitment to reject its predecessor's centralisation (Matthews, 2016: 315). However, ministers were using decentralisation as a cover for reducing budgets (from 'targets and money' to 'no targets, no money'), intervening in local and agency business on an ad hoc basis (subjecting public bodies to 'special measures') and bypassing local authorities to establish a closer link between central government and schools (Matthews, 2016: 315–319). Governments let go *and* hold on, and try to conjure a coherent narrative of the contradictions (Matthews, 2016: 303; Box 5.3).

Box 5.3: Narrating policy success and avoiding blame

Success is in the eye of the beholder. Policy evaluation is a political process to determine whose goals, values, evidence and expectations we should use to declare success or failure (Bovens et al, 2001; Boyne, 2003; McConnell, 2010; Compton and 't Hart, 2019). Policy makers may refer to different questions when seeking success:

- *Political.* Will this policy boost my government's credibility and re-election chances?
- *Process.* Will it be straightforward to legitimise and maintain support for this policy?
- *Programmatic.* Will it achieve its stated objectives and produce beneficial outcomes if implemented (Page and Jenkins, 2005: 156–157; Marsh and McConnell, 2010: 571)?

These differences complicate assessment. For example, a measure could have exacerbated a loss of central control (programmatic failure) while being popular (political success). Governments may be ineffective in relation to central control, but effective when redirecting blame for crises (Hood, 2010; Boin et al, 2017). Some ministers seek policy change, but others are more akin to diplomats or managers of existing commitments, while some seek the perks of office (Headey, 1974; Marsh et al, 2001: 133; Richards and Smith, 2002: 212–220; Rhodes, 2011: 52–55, 62–69, 92–93). Most are not interested in, or too busy to oversee, government reform (Rhodes, 2011: 101–104). They may 'do nothing' even when state intervention is possible (Barber, 2017).

How did governments describe the impact of these reforms?

One reason to be uncertain is that we do not know what motivates ministers (Box 5.3). Are they frustrated with the lack of policy delivery, or focused on making popular strategic choices with limited follow-through? Do they seek central control or to shuffle off responsibility?

For example, the 'lean' government story connects to ministerial hopes that they would be held accountable for strategy, not delivery. Civil service reforms encouraged institutional accountability, to make civil servants more responsible for delivery (O'Toole and Jordan, 1995: 4; Judge et al, 1997: 97; Massey, 2001: 21). The delegation of authority to hospitals and schools, and introduction of league tables of performance, suggested that individual public bodies were responsible for their own success (Day and Klein, 2000: 238–240). Further, there are pragmatic – and legitimate – reasons for central governments to share responsibility with civil servants, quangos, local government, stakeholders and service users (Chapter 3). There are, *and should be*, many actors in public policy beyond a small group of people at the centre, and the 'digital era' facilitated new ways to consider that relationship (Box 5.4). Partly in recognition of the value of these actors and/or the necessity and inevitability of their involvement, elected policy makers may try to share policy-making responsibility and encourage new mechanisms of accountability that relate more closely to who is involved (Massey and Pyper, 2005: 148–165; Cairney, 2015b; Cairney et al, 2019a).

Still, we should avoid explaining policies as the most sensible or noble thing to do! We should not assign too much coherence to policy changes made for different reasons. There is also a major gulf between the *hopes* of ministers to be held less accountable for delivery and their *expectations* (Chapter 3). Many ministers have been genuinely frustrated with their lack of policy progress, seeking to reform government to reassert power (Hood, 2007).

Box 5.4: From new public management to 'digital era governance'?

State transformation coincided with technological transformation: new online technologies reshaped the day-to-day activities of politics, government, work and public services, and social media and online platforms became the primary means of communication. This shift had significant impacts on policy and policy making (Margetts, 2009).

First, new policy problems emerged, including crimes such as online fraud, the electronic distribution of illegal images of children, and cyber stalking, public health problems such as online gambling, and the collection of data by private businesses such as social media companies. Governments are also able to extract information from their citizens, such as social media contributions, public sector transactions, traffic volumes and hospital admissions. Such issues have triggered policy change, including through the EU's General Data Protection Regulation (GDPR), which aims to enhance individuals' control over their personal information while simplifying the regulatory environment for businesses.

Second, the rise in new problems was met by new digital solutions (Hood and Margetts, 2007; Margetts and Dunleavy, 2013), and the pursuit of algorithms and artificial intelligence (AI) to create new methods of addressing problems (Brown, 2016; Kippin and Cairney, 2022a). The availability of AI tools could help policy makers collate large amounts of data to inform problem definition, forecast the consequences of solutions, and monitor the success of a policy during implementation (Patel et al, 2021).

Third, online communication has changed the ability of citizens and pressure participants to engage in debates and access political institutions, and of researchers to produce new policy-relevant information. At the same time, it presented new issues of inequalities, such as to divide populations into those who could or could not live and work safely at home (Chapter 6), and exclude people without the resources or skills to access educational, economic and social benefits, as well as 'digital by default' public services (Weerakkody, 2021).

Dunleavy et al (2005) describe the rise of technology as contributing to a trend away from NPM towards envisaging new ways of working. While NPM encouraged the fragmentation of the state, 'digital era governance' encourages a shift towards reintegration via 'holistic' public service for citizens. However, we should not confuse the availability of new technology with the willingness and ability of policy makers to use it effectively.

UK transformation: part of a global neoliberal trend?

UK developments took place in a global context where many countries were defining and responding to problems in similar ways. Many faced similar crises of regulation that questioned the coordinative capacity of governments (Lodge and Weigrich, 2012: 27). Many have a similar concern that policy makers at the 'top' should, but do not, control implementation (Hill and Hupe, 2009: 29). All need to respond to global and domestic events and socio-economic conditions that constrain or facilitate action. Two concepts suggest that UK changes represent variations on global themes.

First, 'globalisation' suggests that national governments are not able to internalise the management of key policy aims. For example, economic policies relate to:

- international financial markets that influence the value of a country's currency;
- the technology that allows a global trade in goods and services;
- the power of multinational corporations, seeking the most favourable taxation, subsidy and regulatory systems from countries competing for their business;

- the migration of people seeking work in a country, or emigration of a business seeking to save labour costs;
- the power of international organisations such as the IMF to set strict conditions on a government's policies – to reduce state intervention and reform public services – in exchange for financial assistance (Wade, 2002; Stone, 2017: 59).

Second, many terms describe 'policy transfer', or the import or export of policy ideas (Dolowitz and Marsh, 1996). They include:

- *Lesson-drawing*, when policy makers seek to learn from their own experiences and those of other governments (Rose, 1993; 2005).
- *Policy diffusion*, when some governments innovate and others adopt very similar policy solutions (Walker, 1969; Busch and Jörgens, 2005).
- *Policy convergence*, when countries produce increasingly similar policies following emulation, the international exchange of ideas, the need to cooperate among interdependent states, or the pressure of some countries on others (Bennett, 1991).

Many countries pursued a similar transformation from high to low state intervention. The trend towards neoliberalism is global. It reflects the power of some countries and international organisations to set a global policy agenda, and of multi-nationals to oblige state reforms as a condition of doing business. 'Race to the bottom' describes the negative impact of these conditions: the diminished ability of governments to tax and regulate corporations undermines employee pay and conditions, the government's ability to fund welfare states, and environmental protections (Chapter 8). These dynamics emerge in different ways in each country, according to their existing commitments, the popularity of neoliberal policies, and the expectations of voters seeking lower taxes *and* higher spending (Hoberg, 2001: 128–130; Hay, 2006: 591). Indeed, changes to UK budgets and regulations have varied more than a race to the bottom would suggest (Hogwood, 1992: 43; Hindmoor, 2003: 208).

Further, many policy agendas in the UK have international equivalents (among left- *and* right-wing governments). Privatisation was a global phenomenon, with over 80 countries privatising over 8,500 entities from 1980 to 1992 (Kikeri et al, 1992). The UK was a trendsetter (Ikenberry, 1990: 88). NPM was popular among government reformers, with different variants reflecting how each country interprets the application of private-sector methods (Common, 1998: 442; Maor and Jones, 1999: 50; Larner and Walters, 2000).

Conclusion

Having once owned and delivered public services, the UK government now regulates, monitors and steers services. It has replaced state interventionism with neoliberalism. It has shifted from a unitary to a multi-level state, sharing power with international organisations, and devolved, regional and local governments. The UK government can set its policy agenda, but is influenced by major global trends, social and economic conditions, and events which capture attention and need a response. Its movement towards neoliberalism may reflect a level of competition or cooperation between countries, or the influence of international organisations and corporations, to set an international economic policy agenda that benefits some and puts immense pressure on others. In that context, UK state transformation represents a variation on an international theme.

What marks out the UK is how its policy makers responded to these issues with reference to the Westminster story of central control and responsibility. The UK experience of state transformation supports elements of the Westminster story if we modify its take-home messages. We have witnessed periods of government that made a major difference to the direction of travel. The post-war Labour government signalled a rise in state ownership, economic intervention and welfare state provision. Thatcher governments marked a shift in economic policy and a reduction in state ownership and the state's role in delivering public services. The party and ideology of government mattered, but in relation to a social and economic context that limited policy change, and a state too large and unwieldy to transform quickly. In most other cases, a change of party in government has made a difference, but to slow down or accelerate policy change rather than force a U-turn every four–five years.

The Westminster story helps to situate the UK government's policy style in the post-war period. The Thatcher government symbolised top-down policy making ('government knows best') but a tendency to replace imposition with negotiation over time. It paid unusually high attention to some issues, to impose an agenda and leave only the details of implementation to consultation. However, the flip-side of that coin is that it paid minimal attention to most other issues, which were processed by policy communities. This dynamic is a feature of post-Thatcher governments. High attention to a small number of non-negotiable issues – and periods of crisis used by the core executive to make 'tough choices' – exaggerates a top-down style (and a difference between UK and devolved government styles). Nevertheless, a long-term perspective demonstrates the cumulative impact of state transformation: reducing the status of groups such as trade unions in consultation, normalising neoliberal approaches that were once opposed vehemently, and reducing the role of central government civil servants once at the heart of policy communities. There may still be a 'normal' policy style processed by communities out of the public spotlight, but it does not mimic the normal style in the early post-war period.

The complex government story helps to make sense of the uneven path towards state transformation. Without it, we may be tempted to attach too much coherence to a large collection of policy changes made for different reasons. Even if someone had a grand plan for a neoliberal UK state, it is not reflected in the mess of UK government activity over the last five decades. Policy change consists of many tiny changes and some profound changes, and the latter do not necessarily follow from the manifesto commitments of new governments. The highest-profile shifts in economic policy (from the mid-1940s and late 1970s) followed a change of government and profound crises that limited their options. Parties also inherited the policies of their predecessors and responded to events with a mix of policy instruments that cannot be linked directly to blueprints from economic ideas. The history of privatisation, employment reform and NPM is of hesitant starts, bursts of activity and major compromises, all of which undermine the sense of a well-executed and coherent plan.

In other words, we may imagine (1) a powerful and strategic long-term thinker dedicated to state transformation at all costs or (2) a short-term operator, with limited powers or direction, seeking to remain in office and avoid major confrontations or obstacles to policy progress. Somewhere in between is the sense that UK post-war policy making has consisted of bursts of intense activity producing radical changes *and* periods of policy-making stability and policy continuity. There was no grand plan, and examples such as the poll tax (Box 4.3) show that plans can go disastrously wrong.

Did state transformation produce 'lean' government or a 'hollowed-out' state? A Westminster lens highlights dualism: policy makers need to consider how to take charge *and* let go, to take *and* share responsibility. If so, the lack of central capacity may be a big issue if governments seek to take charge and ensure meaningful policy change. Or, it may relate to presentation, to take responsibility for strategy and shuffle off the rest to delivery organisations.

State transformation has made a difference to these calculations. Governments no longer take the blame directly for the performance of private industries or many public services. However, they are expected to intervene in some cases, such as to manage an NHS crisis or regulate markets to ensure fair access to essentials such as water, fuel and online communication (in 2022 alone, the UK government faced pressure to solve the crisis of NHS and social care, the cost of living, petrol prices and soaring home energy bills). In such cases, contemporary debates focus on the extent to which governments can manage governance networks or rely on non-governmental organisations to share and deliver their aims. Post-war history suggests that governments have pursued central control – or joined-up government – in bursts of energy and optimism followed by fatigue and despair (Cairney and St Denny, 2020).

This longer-term focus is crucial to the interpretation of the case study chapters (6–11). One issue with focusing on the short term is that it is difficult to know if current events represent continuity or the beginning of major changes to policy and policy making. What may seem like rapid and radical change in year 1 may prove to be a blip by year 10. This perspective is important for many chapters. For example, Chapter 6's discussion of COVID-19 policies from 2020 suggest that many policy changes seem unprecedented and associated only with wartime crisis. Still, we do not know if they mark a new long-term trajectory – such as away from 'austerity' politics (Chapter 9) – or if governments seek to return to 'normal' as quickly as possible. Chapter 10 may generate different conclusions about race and racism over the short and long term. Does the latter offer hope that barriers to equity can be overcome eventually, or show that the link between high attention and policy change remains weak?

6

Crises and Policy Making: The UK Response to COVID-19

Chapter highlights

1. Studies of COVID-19 help to understand policy-making crises and the social and economic dilemmas associated with public health.

2. COVID-19 prompted rapid and radical UK policy change. State intervention, to limit behaviour and compensate for economic inactivity, seemed inconceivable before 2020. Yet, critics of the UK government identify a too-slow and ineffective response.

3. Three approaches highlight key perspectives on COVID-19 policy and policy making:

   • Policy analysis identifies how to address a profound existential crisis in public health. How *could* UK and devolved governments define and seek to solve this problem?

   • Policy studies identifies how governments address the problems and policy processes that they do not fully understand or control. How *did* governments respond?

   • Critical policy analysis identifies and challenges inequitable processes and outcomes. Whose knowledge mattered? Who won and lost from government action and inaction?

Introduction: How did policy makers address an existential crisis?

Although it looks like an extreme case, COVID-19 accentuates many key aspects of policy and policy making. It began as an urgent existential crisis that had to be addressed by governments before they knew its full extent or what solutions would be effective. It commanded unusually high policy-maker attention, turned some science advisors into household names, and prompted a dramatic shift in the solutions that governments considered to be feasible. COVID-19 accentuated the profound social and economic inequalities that contributed to unequal illness and death. The crisis also exposed how UK policy processes were unprepared to deal with this crisis, and it remains unclear if the UK government is prepared to address the next crisis more effectively. Each of these dynamics highlights the politics of policy making, or the contestation to determine: who the experts were on the problem, how much state intervention there should be, and whose lives matter the most. The UK government has also faced immense criticism about its lack of urgency or effective action in early 2020. While COVID-19 inquiries, commissioned by the UK and Scottish governments, will investigate such claims (see https://covid19.public-inquiry.uk/), the evaluation of policy success and failure will remain contested (Box 5.3). As such, this chapter uses COVID-19 policy and policy making to explain the governance of crises, protection or promotion of public health, and the politics of key choices.

Pandemic: the rapid spread of disease over a large area, such as in many countries or across the globe.

Lockdown: a vague term to describe state limits on behaviour (including 'stay-at-home' orders and public place closures). The aim is **social distancing**, to increase the physical distance between people to limit the spread of infection.

Our approach is to consider how the issue emerged in real time (rather than relying solely on the wisdom of hindsight). COVID-19 emerged in 2020 as an infectious disease with a worryingly high transmission and mortality rate and – initially – no vaccine or cure (WHO, 2020a; Cairney, 2021b). The World Health Organization (WHO) (2020b) declared a Public Health Emergency of International Concern in January and a **pandemic** in March. China was the first to respond to initial cases in January. The crisis hit Europe from February, prompting **lockdown** measures – to produce '**social distancing**' – in most European countries by March.

How did the UK government respond to COVID-19? Its early action (until March 2020) was largely *exhortation*, 'emphasising effective handwashing, to stay a safe distance from other people, and to stay at home if experiencing COVID-19 symptoms' (Cairney, 2021c: 100). From mid to late March 2020, it produced rapid and radical policy change, including:

- *State intervention to curb individual liberty*. It produced legislation to oblige people to stay at home, and close public places, rather than trusting people to behave as advised. The devolved governments produced similar measures (Box 6.1).
- *Government borrowing to expand public spending*. It borrowed heavily to fund public services (including the National Health Service [NHS]), increase social security benefits, fund employment 'furloughs', and subsidise and compensate businesses (Cairney, 2021c: 102).

These measures seem to be unprecedented and to contradict long-term trends against state intervention (Chapters 4 and 5). Further, the nature and speed of change was inconceivable before 2020, particularly under a Conservative UK government. Yet, the UK government was criticised frequently for not acting quickly enough to initiate a lockdown to prevent high numbers of illness and death (Cairney, 2021c: 90–91).

In that context, we examine COVID-19 policy through three lenses. First, we apply five-step policy analysis to address COVID-19: how could governments define the problem, what solutions seem feasible, how can they apply value judgements to consider trade-offs, can they predict the effect of each solution, and what should they do? For example, the most stark division of approaches was between actors seeking *maximal state intervention*, to seek 'zero COVID' until a vaccine or cure could be found, or *minimal state intervention*, to encourage '**herd immunity**'. Within this range are calls to minimise COVID-19 infection in the short term (emphasising state responsibility and maximal intervention) or manage for the long term (emphasising individual responsibility and moderate state intervention).

Herd immunity: high protection from disease, in a population, following previous infection (and/or vaccination if possible).

Second, we relate this analysis to real-world developments, exploring how UK policy makers addressed a policy problem out of their understanding or control. The UK government described an epidemic to be managed in the short term to ensure that a peak of infection did not overwhelm NHS capacity, while seeking to return to normal life when a vaccine became available (Cairney, 2021b: 252). Key aspects of policy change include measures to address COVID-19 directly (such as lockdown regulations) and the consequences of lockdowns (such as alternatives to school exams). The UK also led a 'four nations' approach with devolved governments (Box 6.1).

Third, we draw on critical policy analysis to identify who benefits from action or inaction. While UK ministers described everyone being in it together, the impact of COVID-19 has been unequal (Bambra et al, 2021; Cairney, 2021c: 107). The most visible inequality related to age, since older people were more likely to die from COVID-19. We also identify the social and economic factors – often described as the '**social determinants of health**' – that cause the unequal spread of **non-communicable diseases (NCDs)** and unequal impact of COVID-19 (Cairney et al, 2021b). These factors include *income, wealth and employment* (for example, the ability to live and work safely at home), *gender* (for example, the distribution of employment or caring responsibilities), *race and ethnicity* (for example, unequal exposure to infection at work) and *disability* (for example, the impact on social care).

Social determinants of health: the social and economic factors that influence population health and inequalities, such as income, wealth, education, housing, and safe physical and social environments.

Non-communicable diseases (NCDs): chronic diseases not passed from person to person, including heart and respiratory diseases, strokes, cancers and diabetes.

In the conclusion, we ask if COVID-19 prompted enduring changes to policy and policy making. The Conservative UK government emphasises state responsibility for public health, and its borrowing and spending was comparable to post-war Labour governments. However, it then signalled a return to pre-COVID-19 policies, reducing state public health and economic measures and appealing to individual responsibility more quickly than the devolved governments.

Box 6.1: Who is responsible for COVID-19 policies?

The UK and devolved governments each have responsibility whenever they class COVID-19 primarily as a public health problem. However, the UK government has a major influence on UK policy as a whole (Basta and Henderson, 2021):

Scientific Advisory Group for Emergencies (SAGE): expert group coordinating COVID-19 scientific advice to ministers.

PPE: personal protective equipment.

Leading a 'four nations' approach. The four governments coordinated responses (for example, school closures in March 2020) and drew on similar evidence (for example, from the **Scientific Advisory Group for Emergencies (SAGE)** and meetings of the four chief medical officers). The initial response was 'tightly choreographed', to coordinate health service responses, **personal protective equipment (PPE)** supply, testing capacity and food security (Paun et al, 2020b: 4). Policy for Northern Ireland tends to be close to policy for England. The Scottish and Welsh governments produced marginal divergences, such as by removing restrictions later or administering different schemes (Paun et al, 2020b: 5–6; compare with Colfer, 2020).

Making UK-wide policy. The UK government is responsible for borrowing and most taxes to fund additional spending. It allocates a share of UK spending to other territories (for example, the employment furlough scheme) or provides budgets 'consequential' on spending for England (for example, the devolved budget rises when NHS funding in England rises). Devolved governments could fund their own schemes, but have a limited budget to fund divergence. For example, they could have maintained longer lockdowns, but did not receive additional funding for the employee furlough scheme.

Legislating on behalf of devolved territories. The Coronavirus Act 2020 contains provisions that range in applicability, from England-only to UK-wide. It confers powers on devolved government ministers, such as to introduce regulations consistent with the Act. The Scottish Parliament also passed the Coronavirus (Scotland) Act 2020 to establish fines for lockdown non-compliance, prevent home evictions and reform court proceedings.

Each government oversees policy delivered by its public bodies, such as local or health authorities. The allocation of roles is contentious, such as when the UK government set up separate organisation rather than boosting local capacity (Diamond and Laffin, 2022).

Policy analysis: how to address the policy problem

Step 1: How could governments define COVID-19 as a policy problem?

COVID-19 is a physical problem and a policy problem. Policy problem framing combines evidence and persuasion to draw attention to one definition, which includes an account of: the problem's size (including severity and urgency), its cause, who it affects, and the role of the state (Chapter 2). Further, COVID-19 policies create additional problems, such as when lockdowns have knock-on effects for public services.

Both aspects of COVID-19 changed from 2020 to 2022. The physical problem was defined initially, by organisations such as the WHO, as a 'a virus and disease with a worryingly high transmission, incubation, and mortality rate and no known vaccine or cure' (Cairney, 2021b: 250). Then, effective treatments and vaccines emerged, boosting hopes of managing infections, particularly when new variants appeared to produce less severe illness among vaccinated populations.

These developments informed calculations regarding the benefits and costs of lockdown policies. They suggest that problem definition changed, from crisis in early 2020 to optimism in 2022. However, there is not one shared definition. Rather, any interpretation of developments relates to two competing grand narratives that connect a story of the physical problem to a role for the state.

1. The minimal intervention story

This story suggests that mass infection is inevitable, and most government restrictions delay an epidemic while adding burdens. It supports minimal state intervention, to (1) accept the inevitability of 'herd immunity' via the spread of disease among a healthy population, (2) isolate vulnerable populations, and (3) avoid overwhelming health service capacity (for example, The 'Great Barrington Declaration', https://gbdeclaration.org/; Kulldorff et al, 2020).

2. The maximal intervention story

This story suggests that rapid mass infection would cause massive population illness and death. **Non-pharmaceutical interventions (NPIs)** are essential until effective pharmaceutical interventions can be produced. This story supports

Non-pharmaceutical interventions (NPIs): policy instruments including stay-at-home orders, closing public places, mask mandates, and test–trace–isolate measures.

Precautionary principle: policy makers should act decisively when the problem is too urgent to ignore, and explain how policy relates to current evidence (Monaghan et al, 2012; Tosun, 2013; Cairney, 2023b). It can be invoked to prevent different things (for example, death, reduced wellbeing) and warn against action or inaction.

maximal intervention until a vaccine can be found (for example, the 'John Snow Memorandum' https://www.johnsnowmemo.com/; Alwan et al, 2020; Independent Sage, 2020). Use the **'precautionary principle'** to act decisively to prevent COVID-19 illness and death (Box 6.2; Cairney, 2021b: 254) and prevent 'social murder' (Abbasi, 2021).

Box 6.2: Key terms to describe the size and urgency of the policy problem

R: the reproduction number of a virus. The 'basic' number relates to a new population (R_0). The 'effective' number relates to a population with some immunity (R_e). An R of 3 means that one person would infect three people on average, with many infecting no one, and some infecting many (over, say, a five-day period). An R consistently below 1 means that the number of new cases would fall. Estimating R is difficult, with studies reporting a range of estimates and noting that the R_0 varies within and across countries because social contact varies (for example, avoid close proximity to unmasked people shouting in unventilated indoor areas). Liu and Rocklöv (2021: 1) estimated the R_0 of the original strain to be 2.8. Locatelli et al (2021: 1) estimated 2.2 in Western Europe, lower than estimates in China. The R_0 rose with each new variant. Alpha exhibited a '43 to 90% higher reproduction number' than previous strains (Davies et al, 2021: 1). Delta was estimated at 5 (Liu and Rocklöv, 2021) and Omicron 8 (Liu and Rocklöv, 2022).

Growth rate: the daily change in the number of infections.

Exponential growth: an increase in quantity, compounded in each time interval. If the R is 3 and new infections take five days: one person infects three (five days), three people infect nine (ten days), nine infect 27 (15 days), and so on, until (say) 1,594,323 infect 4,782,969 (70 days).

Doubling time: if we have 1,000 cases and a doubling time of three days, there would be 4,096,000 cases in 39 days.

Case fatality rate (CFR): the proportion of deaths resulting from infection. In early 2020 it appeared to be 1 per cent (40,960 deaths in our 39-day example).

Excess deaths: the estimated difference between usual/expected and actual deaths (to take into account the people who would have died regardless of COVID-19).

Asymptomatic: many people were infected and infectious without experiencing expected symptoms. Before tests were available, the initial symptoms for diagnosis were high temperature and persistent coughs. Subsequent symptom lists grew to include the loss of smell or taste, breathing difficulties, and fatigue.

QALY: The metric Quality Adjusted Life Year (one year of life in good health), used to compare the positive impact of medical interventions with the cost of treatment.

See Spiegelhalter and Masters (2021), McDonald (2022) and UK Health Security Agency (2022).

Figure 6.1: Deaths caused by COVID-19 per day in the UK, January 2020 to March 2023

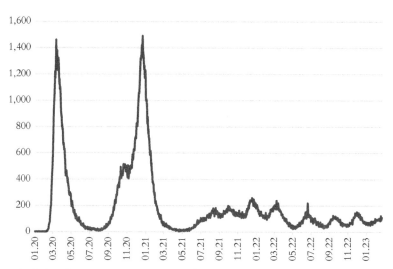

Source: author's chart from UK Government (2023) data. Describes 'Daily numbers of deaths of people whose death certificate mentioned COVID-19 as one of the causes' (see Table 6.1). The label describes month-end.

These competing approaches influence how to measure – and interpret – a remarkably complicated policy problem. Box 6.2 defines some technical terms that are unfamiliar to most people, while Table 6.1 summarises the key issues subject to interpretation. Examples include:

- *How to measure and explain urgency*. **Exponential growth** in cases, and a **doubling time** of a few days, was difficult to explain to policy makers and the public (Lammers et al, 2020). More familiar indicators include estimated numbers of infections, hospitalisations and deaths. For example, Figure 6.1 visualises recorded deaths per day in the UK to show *what we now know* to have happened. Knowledge about trends was unavailable (although the government could make reasonable estimates).
- *How to measure severity*. There was debate on what counts as a COVID-19-caused death (Tucker, 2022) and what is an unacceptable number of deaths. A focus on **excess deaths** shows that far more people were dying compared to five-year averages (Spiegelhalter and Masters, 2021: 102–103; McDonald, 2022).
- *How to identify the cause of the problem*. Initial advice on hygiene reflected an assumption that the main route for spreading was via droplets. Subsequent advice on face coverings reflected growing evidence on its airborne transmission (Greenhalgh et al, 2021). Scientific debates focused on *definitions* (what counts as aerosol transmission?), *the aim of mask wearing* (to protect the wearer or wider public?), *who should bear the burden of mask use*, and *how best*

Table 6.1: Measures of COVID-19, UK, by end of February 2022 (unless otherwise stated)

Category	Example	Example of issues with the measure or response
Recorded cases	18,886,701	Cases are concentrated in key periods (for example, July 2021 to February 2022) and vary by region. Cases in vulnerable groups provide a more useful measure of severity.
R	0.8 to 1.0	R tells us how many people one person will infect, not how quickly. The average hides concentrated rates in regions.
Growth rate, doubling time	2–3 days, initial Omicron spread	The UK government underestimated the doubling time of the first COVID-19 spread in March 2020.
Hospitalisations	730,973	A measure of severity after the fact.
People in intensive care	271 (peak of 4,077 on 24 January 2022)	In 2020 there were reasonable concerns that demand for intensive care would outstrip capacity.
Deaths	182,609* (A) (peak number recorded on one day, 1,364 on 19 January 2021)	'Deaths with COVID-19 on the death certificate' is A. 'Deaths within 28 days of positive test' (B) was 161,361. The second peak of infection caused far more deaths. 42,433 people (B) died in the first seven months (1 March to 30 September 2020). 85,616 (B) died in the next seven months (1 October to 30 April 2021). Over 70 per cent were of people 75+. Over 80 per cent were in people with at least one 'pre-existing condition' (ONS, 2022e).
Excess deaths	169,000 by end 2021	COVID-19 Excess Mortality Collaborators (2022: 11) estimated 169,000 by the end of 2021 (of 1.18 million in Western Europe and 18.2 million worldwide). The UK rate – 127 of every 100,000 – compared to a global 120 and Western Europe average of 140 (from effectively zero in Iceland to 227 in Italy) (COVID-19 Excess Mortality Collaborators, 2022: 1, 10).
Case fatality rate (or risk)	0.05–11.6 per cent (acc to age, 2nd wave, England)	Early SAGE estimates suggested a CFR of 1 per cent (one death in 100), but much higher among older unvaccinated people. The CFR dropped significantly when most people were vaccinated.
QALYs lost	Not measured	In theory, governments can use QALYs to compare the costs and benefits of NPIs, but few seem to do so.
Long COVID (self-reported)	1.8 million by 3 April 2022	It took time for governments to recognise it. Defined by the ONS (2022a) as 'symptoms persisting for more than four weeks after the first suspected coronavirus (COVID-19) infection that were not explained by something else'.
People vaccinated (age 12+, by dose)	1st: 53 million (91.5 per cent) 2nd: 49 million (85.2 per cent) 3rd: 38 million (66.4 per cent)	These proportions are higher among vulnerable groups. The UK and devolved government strategy was to prioritise by age and other causes of vulnerability.
People with antibodies	99 per cent	Combines people with antibodies following (1) infection and/or (2) vaccination. The proportion dropped in 2021 before the 'booster' programme (ONS, 2022b).
Health inequalities	Various measures	There are no equivalent 'dashboards' to treat inequalities as urgent indicators.

Sources: Harman et al (2021); Spiegelhalter and Masters (2021: 107); ONS (2022a; 2022b; 2022c); UK Health Security Agency (2022); UK Government (2022a).
Notes: * By 24 March 2023, deaths (A) were 223,738.

to gather and communicate relevant evidence (compare Greenhalgh et al, 2020; Greenhalgh, 2020 with Martin et al, 2020a; 2020b; Hanna et al, 2022; see also Escandón et al, 2021: 17–23). The WHO (and SAGE) shifted from discouraging mask use in April 2020 to greater encouragement from June 2020 (Martin et al, 2020b: 502; Cairney, 2021d: 10).

• *How to identify and interpret risk.* Key questions include: who is most at risk of infection and death (and why), which NPIs reduce the risk of infection, and how much do vaccinations reduce the risk of hospitalisation and death?

In each case, maximal and minimal approaches have provided very different interpretations. The former invites governments to treat COVID-19 infection as inevitable and not to over-react. The latter exhorts governments to treat COVID-19 as an urgent and profound public health crisis and warns about the mass deaths caused by under-reaction. Debates on lockdowns continue (for example, compare Hughes, 2022; Yates, 2022; see also Sridhar, 2020; 2022).

Step 2: Identifying feasible solutions

These debates inform assessments of solutions, focusing on: how to connect technical feasibility (a solution will work as intended if implemented) to political feasibility (acceptable to a policy-maker audience) (Chapter 2). For example, what if *maximal intervention* is the most technically feasible way to minimise COVID-19, but *minimal intervention* is the most acceptable to policy makers? Further, what if data on public attitudes to intervention is uncertain and contested? Analysts would draw on evidence and argumentation to narrate feasibility.

In early 2020, technically feasible solutions appeared be to (1) produce social distancing via strictly enforced regulations on behaviour, and (2) minimise spread via high-surveillance and high-coercion test, trace and isolate measures (Cairney, 2021c: 102). However, the most politically feasible options until March 2020 were to exhort and support behavioural change, via public education to encourage social distancing, handwashing and/or mask wearing. Lockdowns have adverse social and political consequences: school closures undermine learning and exam preparation, and the effect is unequal (Box 6.5); routine healthcare is restricted and crowded out by COVID-19 responses; care homes for older people become closed to visitors; people with disabilities have less access to state support; social distancing exacerbates isolation; and, many parts of the economy do not operate, which can exacerbate unemployment and poverty. Each example would prompt policy makers to hesitate before introducing or maintaining a lockdown.

Events and time influence this calculation of feasibility. First, by March 2020, the urgency and severity of COVID-19 quickly shifted policy-maker and public attitudes on the political feasibility of state intervention. Most people in the UK supported the first lockdown and would accept further restrictions in the spirit of social solidarity (Burkitt and Quigley, 2020; Gill, 2020b; Ibbetson, 2020; Jackson et al, 2020; Skleparis, 2020; Smith, 2020a; 2020b; Devine et al, 2021: 279; Foad et al, 2021; YouGov, 2022). Second, it was unclear how long people would accept the effects of restrictions (Oliver, 2020; Foad et al, 2021: 7). Consequently, it began to take 'a higher level of COVID-19 cases to elicit a similar response from national policymakers (in most contexts)' (Phillips et al, 2021: 4). Third, the mass roll-out of vaccines (from 2021) had a further impact on the political feasibility of lockdown measures, particularly when governments had described the need for lockdowns only until a vaccine was available.

Steps 3 and 4: Using values and goals to compare solutions and predicting the outcomes of solutions

Steps 3 and 4 were not a strong feature of initial COVID-19 policies or debates (Cairney, 2021b: 106; Pykett et al, 2022), and SAGE advice highlighted uncertainty about the impact of each NPI (Cairney, 2021d). Still, we can identify the key trade-offs between solutions as:

- State intervention for population *security* versus *individual freedoms* lost in lockdowns.
- *Efficiency* versus *resilience* in relation to (1) pandemic preparedness, when governments stockpile equipment, and (2) rapid responses, to produce high emergency capacity without knowing if it is required.
- Trading off *efficiency* for *equity*, such as when a focus on fair outcomes produces high spending on employment furloughs and social security.
- Actions to protect population *security* challenge *environmental sustainability*, such as the mass production of disposable PPE.
- One country's *resilience* may also cause global *inequity*, when richer countries hoard vaccines for multiple use.

There are also trade-offs associated with individual values such as equity or fairness. First, giving priority to the lives of COVID-19 patients may contribute to the deaths of others, when people avoid hospital (affecting older and poorer people disproportionately), or the lockdown exacerbates problems associated with 'poverty, unemployment and mental health problems' (Johnson, 2020a; 2020b). Second, lockdown highlighted 'distributional choices' since the effect on people facing gaps in education was starker in state than private schools, the loss in employment was higher among the under-25s and lowest-earning workers, and the employment furlough scheme prompted more women to stop work to look after children (Johnson, 2020a; 2020b). Third, when governments are releasing lockdowns, whose activities should return to normal first? For example, should governments open up schools first, to benefit children and their parents? Fourth, who should receive vaccinations and in what order?

Many of these trade-offs are contested, and there is debate about the alleged trade-off between health and the economy. Some argue that lockdowns in the name of public health exacerbate economic inactivity. Others argue that well-timed and well-designed NPIs (including stay-at-home measures) reduce COVID-19 spread and allow a quicker return to normal economic and social life (such as by minimising absences from work) (Casey, 2020).

What would a cost-benefit analysis look like?

Layard et al (2020: 1) related COVID-19 policy to a single metric: 'the number of Wellbeing-Years' (WELLBYs) gained or lost. They compared COVID-19 illness and deaths with the harm to 'incomes, unemployment, mental health, public confidence and many other factors' associated with lockdowns. The WELLBY is akin to the QALY measure, but focused on 'individuals' satisfaction with their lives' (Layard et al, 2020: 3). If 'average wellbeing in the UK' is 'approximately 7.5 measured on a scale of 0–10' then 'the loss of one year's life' is '7.5 WELLBYS lost' (Layard et al, 2020: 3). They sought a 'time to release the lockdown' (while maintaining social distancing and isolating vulnerable people) when the positives outweigh the negatives:

- Positives: 'increases people's incomes', 'reduces unemployment', 'improves mental health, suicide, domestic violence, addiction, and loneliness', 'maintains confidence in the government' (Box 6.3) and 'restores schooling' (Box 6.5).
- Negatives: 'increases the final number of deaths' from COVID-19 and the illnesses not treated by an overstretched NHS, and 'increases road deaths, commuting, CO2 emissions, and air pollution' (Layard et al, 2020: 2).

Their 'rough valuations' were to prompt the UK government to perform a more sophisticated analysis that calculates the unequal effects of lockdown and *the price of a life* (Layard et al, 2020: 8). The latter is routine for medicines policy: the **National Institute for Health and Care Excellence (NICE)** values a year of life at £25,000 when rationing medicines. Such valuations would suggest that no lockdown was necessary, suggesting that – in early 2020 – the UK government valued each life saved far more highly than usual (Layard et al, 2020: 16).

> **National Institute for Health and Care Excellence (NICE)**: gives advice on the effectiveness and value for money of technology (for example, medicines) and health and social care interventions.

Box 6.3: Public trust in government is essential

Cairney and Wellstead (2021: 1) define trust as 'belief in the reliability of other people, organizations, or processes'. They describe high stakes: 'people need to trust *experts* to help them understand and respond to the problem, *governments* to coordinate policy instruments and make choices about levels of coercion, and *citizens* as they cooperate to minimize infection' (emphasis in original). Drivers include:

- Individual factors, including (1) psychology, or a 'disposition to trust', (2) behaviour, to enhance a 'reputation for integrity, credibility, and/or competence', (3) a mutually valued reason to cooperate, such as shared beliefs, acceptance of authority and trustworthy reputations based on cooperation.
- The social and political rules to encourage cooperation and punish defection.
- The need for people to put their faith in strangers, to boost cooperation in political systems (Cairney and Wellstead, 2021: 4–5).

For example, citizens may trust governments based on their beliefs (trust relates to party preferences), a government's track record, or if policy makers follow their own rules (Cairney and Wellstead, 2021: 5). Or, a rise of mistrust occurs when policy makers flout their own rules.

One major let-down was in 2020 when Prime Minister Boris Johnson's special adviser Dominic Cummings was not sacked after being caught breaking lockdown rules (Boseley, 2020; Jackson et al, 2020). Trust in government was already falling during the patchy release of lockdown, then exacerbated by 'Cummings-gate' (Policy Institute, 2020). On 26 May 2020, Savanta ComRes (2020) described the 'government's approval rating ... at -2%, dropping 16 points in just one day, while the Prime Minister's own approval is now also below zero (-1%), having dropped 20 points since the end of last week'.

Another let-down was 'Partygate', in which many ministers and government staff flouted UK government rules at parties on the grounds of 10 Downing Street in 2020/2021, at a time when members of the public were prosecuted for similar activity. Intense attention to the scandal contributed to negative survey responses (trust in Johnson's 'competence and trustworthiness' reached 'new lows' – M. Smith, 2022), Johnson's resignation in July 2022, and investigations in government and parliament (Durrant, 2022; BBC News, 2023a).

Step 5: Making recommendations

Policy analysis texts advise that recommendations should be simple and punchy to make the problem seem solvable and the solution feasible. Yet, COVID-19 policy defied simple analysis. There was high contestation to define the problem. 'Lockdown' became the most technical solution, but its political feasibility was initially unclear and diminished, especially when vaccination offered governments a way out. There are numerous uncertainties about policy solutions, and governments seem unwilling to clarify their aims well enough to clarify the trade-offs. Further, the presence or absence of lockdown is only one part of the puzzle, since it contributes to problems relating to adapting public services – including health, social care, education, justice and social security – during crisis. COVID-19 policy involved continuous trial-and-error policy making during long periods of uncertainty. This approach is consistent with the complex government story, but not the Westminster story of centralised and authoritative government (Chapter 3; Cairney, 2021c: 108–109).

How did the UK and devolved governments respond to COVID-19?

Government responses have varied widely across the globe, and over time. It is difficult to describe any state intervention as minimal or maximal, although Sweden did not have coercive measures for social distancing (Pierre, 2020), while China had 'draconian quarantine and self-quarantine' measures (Shih, 2021: 67) and South Korea produced an interventionist test–trace–isolate system (Kim et al, 2020). The UK was more restrictive than Sweden, but ministers rejected the approaches of China and South Korea (Cairney, 2021d).

How did the UK government define the problem?

The UK government's definition varied over time, partly in relation to COVID-19 urgency and severity. Seven statements summed up its approach in early 2020 (informed by science advice – Box 6.4):

- COVID-19 can only be managed, not eliminated, until a vaccine is produced.
- We do not know if people will social distance voluntarily.
- Seek to suppress (not eliminate) COVID-19, using NPIs to manage R and the growth rate while shielding the most vulnerable. Aim to not overwhelm the NHS during a peak of cases (the UK government slogan was 'Stay Home, Protect the NHS, Save Lives').
- We don't know how long it will take suppression to work, or if there will be public support and compliance.
- Avoid enforcement that is too quick, since it may panic the public and reduce trust in government.
- Avoid too draconian measures, which may contribute to a more severe peak of infection when measures are relaxed.
- Transition from lockdown as soon as possible – to boost economic activity, education, and normal social life – while keeping R below 1 (Cairney, 2021b: 252).

This definition helps to explain initial hesitation to introduce a strict lockdown (until March), attempts to remove many lockdown measures (summer), and a shift to high restrictions only in places with the highest proportions of cases:

- Use targeted regional approaches to transition from lockdown measures, backed by a new system to test, trace and isolate infected populations.

The updated definition became necessary to explain the reimposing of some lockdown measures, from autumn 2020, when the R was too high and a second larger wave of infection was likely. Ministers related the latter to new variants (Box 6.2):

- New variants are more infectious, requiring temporary lockdown measures to protect NHS capacity during pressure periods (which peak during winter).

Finally, the mass roll-out of an effective vaccine allowed the UK government to modify its definition, emphasising the possibility of returning to minimal state intervention if mass immunity – or a massively reduced case fatality rate and well-functioning NHS – was achieved:

- High rates of vaccination offer a way to return to normal life, treating COVID-19 as a manageable problem that does not require drastic limits to individual freedoms.

Prime Minister Boris Johnson's speech in July 2021 trailed this shift. He noted that hospitalisations and deaths were rising, and key measures – including the test–trace–isolate system, and vaccine certification to travel abroad or attend some events – remained necessary, but high population immunity would allow a lessening of restrictions: 'there comes a point when restrictions no longer prevent hospitalisations and deaths, but simply delay the inevitable. And so we have to ask ourselves the question: if not now, when?' (Johnson, 2021). The UK government portrayed the UK's experience of the 'mild' Omicron variant (2021–2022 autumn and winter) as an indicator of the potential to remove restrictions further. Its 'Living with Covid' framing (February 2022) combined three statements: (1) vaccination as 'our first line of defence', (2) a commitment that 'restrictions would not stay in place a day longer than necessary', and (3) 'the UK is in the strongest possible position to learn how to live with Covid and end government regulation' (Prime Minister's Office, 2022).

Box 6.4: UK government ministers 'guided by the science'

UK ministers claimed to be 'guided by the science', which really meant 'our scientists':

- Senior government scientific advisors were the 'core insiders', consulted regularly on multiple aspects of the policy problem. They included the Chief Scientific Advisor (Sir Patrick Valance) and Chief Medical Officer (Professor Chris Whitty), both civil servants.
- Members of SAGE were the 'specialist insiders', treated as authoritative in their field, and consulted via the advisory group.
- Most others were 'peripheral insiders', consulted cosmetically.
- Some were 'outsiders' by *ideology* (their aims contrast with ministers) and/or *behaviour* (their criticism of ministers would rule out being consulted), including 'Independent SAGE' (Cairney, 2021d: 1–6).

Cairney (2021b: 253–254; 2021c: 6) identifies the 'strong influence of core and specialist advice' on the initial framing and 'the timing and substance of UK government policy'.

Analysis of 'limited action in January and February' and delayed lockdown in March 'shows that UK government policy was largely consistent with SAGE evidence and advice' (2021c: 6).

Ministers relied on a core group of advisors who adapted their advice to ministerial agendas and followed the 'rules of the game', such as to respect the right of ministers to make policy, present modest demands and keep discussions in-house (Cairney, 2021d: 4; Atkinson et al, 2022; Atkinson, 2023). This unusually high reliance on advisors diminished after the initial release of lockdown (House of Commons Health and Social Care and Science and Technology Committees, 2021: 5–9; Hodges et al, 2022; Cairney and Toth, 2023).

Did the devolved governments define the problem differently?

Throughout 2020–2022, we can detect devolved government differences in framing. They include greater attention to human rights frames, and distinctive ways to produce policy, in Scotland (Sinclair, 2022; Tisdall and Morrison, 2022: 3). Scottish and Welsh government ministers adopted more caution: focusing more on public health than individual choice, more reluctant to relax lockdown restrictions, and critical of the UK's communication of lockdown release (Kenny and Sheldon, 2020; Sheldon and Kenny, 2020). However, a four nations approach, combined with the UK government's disproportionate role (Box 6.1), suggests that they described variations on the same theme. Levels of ministerial, civil service and science advisor coordination were high during the March 2020 lockdown (Paun et al, 2020a). Further, the example of school closures demonstrates similar messaging and policies (Box 6.5).

Box 6.5: COVID-19 and the school examinations crises

The UK and devolved governments are responsible for their own school examinations systems. However, in 2020 and 2021, they sought a 'four nations' approach to coordinate choices, including to close schools on 18 March 2020, and learn from each other (Kippin and Cairney, 2022a; 2022b; Ozga et al, 2023). This approach did not prevent the fiascos that prompted them to reverse their policies within days of examinations results in 2020. These problems began when they closed schools for so long that it became infeasible to hold examinations (including Highers in Scotland and A levels in England, Northern Ireland and Wales). They had weeks to find a replacement to exams that would produce equivalent results in August and ensure that universities could admit students.

Kippin and Cairney (2022a) show that each government oversaw similar 'windows of opportunity' to select similar solutions. When defining the problem, they prioritised the 'credibility' of the exams system, using teacher-assessed grades (TAGs) but seeking to avoid teacher bias and 'grade inflation'. They described two options – TAGs alone, or using an algorithm to standardise their results – and they selected the latter while describing TAGs as unfair and unreliable. The exams-day results prompted media, public and parliamentary outcries, focused on unfairness when the standardisation process reduced more grades of students from schools in areas of relative deprivation. Each government defended their system briefly, then U-turned, embracing the TAGs that they had criticised.

Kippin and Cairney (2022b) show that each government focused on avoiding political crisis the following year. After cancelling exams, they sought ways to protect the integrity of exams without using an algorithm. Each oversaw a quality assurance process criticised as 'exams in all but name' since the coursework requirements placed a high burden on students and staff. The result was a process, and results, which did not receive the same levels of criticism, despite reproducing similar levels of 'grade inflation' and inequalities of attainment. This outcome reflects a tendency for one – 'neoliberal' – approach to dominate (Chapter 10). It prioritises equality of access to schools without substantive commitment to reducing inequalities of outcomes (Cairney and Kippin, 2021).

What policy solutions did the UK and devolved governments select?

We identify four main phases of policy change.

Phase 1: Government advice and voluntary behaviour (until mid-March 2020)

COBR or COBRA: 'Cabinet Office Briefing Room (A)' describes the UK government's Civil Contingencies Committee. It informs ministers of emergencies and fosters coordination. Meetings are chaired by the Prime Minister or senior minister. COVID-19 meetings include devolved government First Ministers (Paun et al, 2020b; Haddon, 2022).

There was relatively little government activity in January and February. SAGE and **COBRA** began to meet from late January. Early SAGE meetings described uncertainty about the likely spread and impact of COVID-19 in the UK, and the Prime Minister (and Scottish Government First Minister) did not attend initial COBRA meetings (Haddon, 2022).

The first half of March involved a UK government push to explain COVID-19 and how people could respond: wash your hands well, keep a safe distance from others, and isolate if experiencing symptoms (asymptomatic spread – Box 6.2 – was less well known). UK ministers and their advisors (Box 6.4) made regular media and parliamentary committee appearances to recommend behavioural changes and explain their definition of the problem (Kettell and Kerr, 2022; Allen et al, 2023).

An explicit policy aim was to 'flatten the curve' of population infection, containing the virus to make sure it: (1) *spreads at the right speed*, to allow most people to recover alone while the most ill are treated in the NHS, and (b) *peaks at the right time*, to coincide with the lowest NHS demand. Before lockdown, there was high uncertainty about which solutions would fulfil that aim. For example, if governments closed schools but not workplaces, would pupils go to their grandparents? If they banned attendance at large sporting events, would people gather in pubs? Further, SAGE described a ban on mass gatherings as low impact, and questioned the feasibility of international travel restrictions (Cairney, 2021d: 8).

Newspaper accounts (and SAGE meeting papers) suggest that the direct regulation of behaviour did not seem feasible to ministers, or their advisors, until mid-March (Calvert et al, 2020; Grey and MacAskill, 2020; Wickham, 2020). Their calculations changed when it seemed that – as in Italy in February – cases were rising too quickly for the NHS to cope (Imperial College COVID-19 Response Team, 2020: 16).

Phase 2: A rapid shift to enforced lockdown (late March to mid-May 2020)

The UK government combined new legislation and funding to produce one of the most rapid and substantive policy changes in the post-war era, including:

- A shift from voluntary to regulated behaviour change ('lockdown').
- A major rise in spending and borrowing.
- Organisation changes, to modify public services and establish new test–trace–isolate measures.

The UK and devolved governments closed public places from 18 March 2020, then announced stay-at-home orders from 23 March (Paun et al, 2020b: 14; Scott, 2020). The Prime Minister's speech describes combining restrictions on behaviour with police enforcement:

> People will only be allowed to leave their home for the following very limited purposes: shopping for basic necessities, as infrequently as possible; one form of exercise a day – for example a run, walk, or cycle – alone or with members of your household; any medical need, to provide care or to help a vulnerable person; and travelling to and from work, but only where this is absolutely necessary and cannot be done from home. ... If you don't follow the rules the police will have the powers to enforce them. (Johnson, 2020)

The Coronavirus Act 2020 (25 March) introduced many regulations, each of which represents major policy change, including to:

- *Regulate social behaviour.* It obliged people to stay at home and prohibited almost all gatherings of more than two people (unless in the same household).

It enabled police powers to enforce the measures through checks on public behaviour, and issue fines (or arrests) for non-compliance. It boosted national border security. It reduced the safeguards on detaining someone with reference to their mental illness.

- *Regulate business behaviour.* It obliged the closure of businesses and reserved the right to close schools and childcare services.
- *Boost public service recruitment.* It changed the rules to recruit and register more NHS and social work staff.
- *Modify healthcare rules,* on medical negligence, discharge, the registration of deaths, the disposal of bodies, inquests, and who can provide vaccinations to patients.
- *Modify judicial rules,* on judicial commission appointments, the retention of fingerprint and DNA data, online court proceedings, to postpone the completion of community service, and provide earlier prison release.
- *Foster food security,* giving ministers powers to compel companies to provide information on the food supply.
- *Postpone national and local elections.*
- *Postpone legal proceedings on property,* to protect people from eviction and businesses from lease forfeiture.

This Act's coverage ranged from England-only to UK-wide (the Scottish Parliament also passed a separate Coronavirus (Scotland) Act 2020), and included giving powers to devolved government ministers (Box 6.1). UK and devolved governments also produced or used new statutory instruments, or modified Acts of Parliament, to change arrangements during lockdown. For example, the UK Department of Health and Social Care (2020) introduced temporary measures to allow the abortion of a foetus under ten weeks (first using Mifepristone then Misoprostol tablets, coupled with a video medical appointment), and there were similar measures in Scotland and Wales (Goddard, 2020). Northern Ireland was an exception. While UK legislation decriminalised abortion by the end of March 2020: (1) pregnant women had to take Mifepristone in a healthcare setting, and (2) there are relatively few services available (Rough, 2022: 28).

The UK government introduced measures to deal with the economic fallout of lockdown. The novelty of the measures, and uncertainty about their duration, meant that the Office for Budget Responsibility could not estimate their impact accurately, with a first estimate of an additional £123 billion of additional spending rising substantially then falling to an estimate of £300 billion by November 2021 (OBR, 2020a; 2021). Its June estimates of £133 billion spending in 2020 (OBR, 2020b) included:

- A 'coronavirus job retention scheme' in which the government pays 80 per cent of the salary of 'furloughed' staff in the public and private sector (net £54 billion for eight months).
- The equivalent scheme for the self-employed (£15 billion).

- Tax reliefs, grants and loans to businesses (£33 billion).
- Additional spending on public services, charities and local authority schemes (£17.3 billion).
- Additional social security payments (£8 billion).
- Deferred Value Added Tax and self-assessed income tax (£3.1 billion).

Some changes grew as the size of the problem grew, including the employment furlough scheme which lasted longer than the first lockdown. Others related to public pressure, including a campaign by the high-profile footballer Marcus Rashford for the government to extend free school meal provision in England over the summer 2020 break (also producing budget 'consequentials' for devolved governments). There was also a commitment to increase spending to address a shortfall in PPE, introduce mass testing as part of a new test–trace–isolate system (allocated budget of £37 billion for England, 2020–2022 – Public Accounts Committee, 2021; Gill, 2020a), and fund vaccine research before placing large orders for vaccines. The National Audit Office (2022) estimates the total allocation of spending to UK and devolved government departments (of measures announced by the end of July 2021) as £370 billion (including £4.4 billion for vaccinations), with £261 billion spent by September 2021.

These changes were funded largely by government borrowing. Before COVID-19, the UK government's 'gross debt was £1,891.8 billion at the end of 2019, equivalent to 85.4% of gross domestic product' (ONS, 2020a). The estimate for March 2021 was £2,223.0 billion, or 103.7 per cent (ONS, 2022d; see also Figure 12.1). Emmerson and Stockton (2020) describe the initial £123 billion package as 'unprecedented' (albeit proportionately smaller than in Japan, the US, Canada and Germany), and the likely level of government borrowing in 2020 as 'the largest share of national income in peacetime'. The National Audit Office (2022) estimates that the Bank of England has provided loans or guarantees of £129 billion to fund COVID-19 measures.

Phase 3: Partial lockdown release, 'circuit breakers' and intermittent lockdowns (May 2020 to spring 2022)

This phase included regional differences in lockdown measures, intermittent lockdowns, brief periods described as exceptional (such as to relax some rules for Christmas), and some UK and devolved differences in the timing and substance of measures:

Reducing some restrictions on individual and business behaviour (May–October 2020)

Each government identified similar criteria to decide when to relax lockdown. They required that: infections are manageable and deaths are falling, NHS capacity is sufficient to manage infections and illness (including PPE and testing capacity), and relaxation would not cause a second peak of infection (Paun et al, 2020b: 10).

Then, they allowed similar relaxations at different dates, with the UK government tending to go earliest (Cameron-Blake et al, 2020: 11). Examples of UK government actions in May include reopening garden centres and removing strict limits on how far people could travel from home (Cameron-Blake et al, 2020: 11). Then, it encouraged business reopening during the summer – such as via the 'Eat Out to Help Out' scheme promoted by (then) Chancellor Rishi Sunak (costing £840 million – Hutton, 2020) – and encouraged summer holidays in the UK (Cameron-Blake et al, 2020: 12). At the same time, it required a 14-day home quarantine measure for people travelling from abroad, with a list of exempted countries (the Scottish government exempted fewer) (Cameron-Blake et al, 2020: 12). Schools opened more quickly in England, albeit with variation in relation to the willingness and ability of individual schools (Cameron-Blake et al, 2020: 12–13).

At the same time, each government changed its rules on face mask use: recommending their use in April (Scotland) and May (England); obliging their use in public transport from June; and, extending this obligation to shops and supermarkets from July, and most public places from August (both governments). This obligation began in September in Wales and October in Northern Ireland (Tatlow et al, 2021: 31).

Local or regional restrictions (summer to October 2020)

The UK government introduced a lockdown in Leicester in June 2020, based partly on data from new testing capacity in Public Health England (PHE) (Scott, 2020). UK and devolved governments sought a regional approach, introducing levels of restriction in relation to levels of infection. There were three – medium, high and very high – 'COVID alert levels' in England, and five (level 0 to 4) 'protection levels' in Scotland (Cameron-Blake et al, 2020: 13). The exception to an England-first approach related to care home visits for older people, with Northern Ireland and Scotland allowing some visits in October, and England and Wales partially reopening in November (Tatlow et al, 2021: 30).

Reimposing temporary lockdowns or 'circuit breakers' (autumn 2020 to spring 2021)

Very large rises in cases prompted all governments to reintroduce strong restrictions, including 'circuit breaker' measures (lockdowns for several weeks) in Wales and Northern Ireland, stay-at-home measures for 'very high' risk areas in England followed by a stay-at-home order during November, and similar restrictions in Scotland (particularly in Level 4 areas) without a specific circuit breaker (Cameron-Blake et al, 2020: 14–16; Tatlow et al, 2021: 22). There were exceptions made for Christmas (although strong advice not to travel or mix with other households), followed by stay-at-home orders across the UK from January 2021 (Tatlow et al, 2021: 29). All four produced their highest ever 'Stringency Index' scores in January 2021 – combining stay-at-home measures with international restrictions and other measures – to reflect a worryingly high rate of infection that would produce far more deaths than during the equivalent lockdown in 2020 (Tatlow et al, 2021: 2; Figure 6.1).

Lockdown releases (from late March/early April 2021)

The transition from lockdown prioritised school reopening across the UK, from March in England and Northern Ireland and February (primary school classes) and April (all classes) in Scotland and Wales (Tatlow et al, 2021: 26). Lockdown relaxations were similar to those in the summer of 2020, but now with mass vaccination.

Phase 4: Living with COVID-19 (from March 2022)

Johnson's 'Living with Covid' speech (February 2022) emphasised that mass vaccination was breaking the link between COVID-19 infection and major illness/death, thus allowing the removal of most restrictions (including mask use), and reducing state funding for testing, from March 2022 (Prime Minister's Office, 2022). The devolved governments struck a more cautious tone, but introduced similar policies, including removing mask use obligation in February (Northern Ireland), April (Scotland) and May (Wales).

What do these experiences tell us about Westminster and complex government stories?

Finlayson et al (2023) show that UK ministers presented a 'government knows best' approach during lockdown. However, COVID-19 also amplified limits to policy making: policy makers addressed a problem out of their understanding, and engaged in a policy-making environment over which they had limited control.

Bounded rationality: understanding and defining the policy problem

Early global responses to COVID-19 were characterised by low knowledge on what it was, how quickly it would spread, and how much of a problem it would become (Cairney, 2021d; Box 6.4). In the UK, this problem emerged in March 2020 when ministers acted too slowly to produce lockdown measures. Early commentaries highlighted a litany of mistakes, including that the UK government:

- Did not prepare well for a pandemic, with low capacity in emergency responses and PPE.
- Should have taken more preventive measures when information emerged from China and Italy.
- Acted more slowly than many other countries to close public places, issue stay-at-home orders, test–trace–isolate, and limit international travel.

- Treated COVID-19 like influenza (to downplay its importance) or measles (to emphasise 'herd immunity') (Cairney, 2021c: 90–91).

Many accounts identify ministerial 'blunders' (Gaskell et al, 2020). The House of Commons Health and Social Care and Science and Technology Committees (2021: 5–9) identified further explanations for poor UK government performance:

- *Insufficient initial action.* The UK response was based on fatalism. It assumed that infection spread was inevitable and that people would not tolerate lockdown. It should have intervened more quickly when there was no feasible alternative to lockdown.
- *Groupthink and an inability to learn from best practice.* The rejection of lessons from 'East and South East Asian countries' by policy makers and their scientific advisors reflects groupthink, where members of a small insulated group only respect ideas generated in that group (Box 11.5). This criticism can also relate to scientific specialism (for example, bias towards a 'bio-medical approach' – Cairney, 2021b: 5) or the social background of advisors (for example, most are men – J. Smith, 2022).
- *Limited capacity to test, trace and isolate.* The government gave up too early on community testing. Then, the establishment of *NHS Test and Trace* was chaotic.
- *Insufficient NHS capacity.* The government acted quickly to boost emergency hospital capacity, but without maintaining core services (for example, cancer treatment).
- *Failure to protect social care.* Policy makers were too late to recognise the impact of discharging people from hospitals to social care 'without adequate testing or rigorous isolation'.
- *Excessive ministerial optimism.* Ministers paid insufficient attention to scientific advice on the need for further lockdowns to address surges of infection in autumn 2020.

Our focus on how policy makers deal with bounded rationality (Chapter 2) is instructive: they use 'rational' ways to identify goals and trusted sources of information, and 'irrational' ways to make choices quickly (such as by drawing on gut instinct, emotions and deeply held beliefs). Combined, these responses show that uncertainty is not the sole explanation for these practices. Rather, ministerial responses were also based on their beliefs and values, which led them to prioritise the freedoms associated with liberal democracy rather than the minimisation of COVID-19 deaths. Their beliefs about the size of the problem, and values, prompted ministers to hesitate to lock down in March 2020 and – even when they had better information – to be sceptical about the need for a further lockdown in autumn 2020. The latter hesitation caused more deaths (Figure 6.1; Table 6.1), and shows that UK governments make mistakes even when better informed. Then, the benefits of mass vaccination reinforced the UK government's definition of the problem, to accentuate freedoms when there was less concern about the impact of COVID-19 on NHS capacity, and prioritise a return to 'normal' life for most people at the expense of the people most vulnerable to infection. The issue of mask wearing often exemplifies these dynamics: the *initial* lack of obligation to wear masks in 2020 reflected low knowledge about the airborne transmission of COVID-19 and an aversion to such obligations; the *subsequent* removal of obligations in 2022 reflected the prioritisation of individual freedoms over mask use to control infection.

Controlling the policy process and the outcomes of choices

COVID-19 exemplifies aspects of multi-centric policy making (Chapter 2). Some processes are by *choice*, when the UK government shared responsibility for health protection with the devolved governments, or delegated tasks to existing public bodies (including local authorities and the NHS), repurposed bodies (the UK Health Security Agency which replaced PHE) or set up new ones (NHS Test and Trace). Further, familiar issues arose: the UK and devolved government relationship has been unusually well coordinated at key moments (including mid-March 2020) but strained at others (Sheldon and Kenny, 2020); local authorities and public health organisations complained about the UK government's tendency to design new agencies; and the abolition of PHE was driven partly by ministerial blame games (Cairney, 2021d; Diamond and Laffin, 2022).

However, some aspects are by *necessity*, when UK government ministers can only pay attention to a small proportion of their responsibilities, and lack the ability to control outcomes. At times, there was an impressive amount of ministerial control, such as when the March 2020 lockdown had a major impact on behaviour. Still, it has been difficult to know exactly how many people followed government rules, and how long they would continue to do so. UK governments built this uncertainty into policy design: emphasising the temporary nature of restrictions, and signalling low desire to manage policy outcomes at that scale. Further, a series of crises have demonstrated that policy practices and outcomes related weakly to original intentions, including major shortages in NHS capacity (including PPE), unintended consequences of NHS discharges on care homes, schools examinations crises (Box 6.5), and waves of infections and deaths that no government would want to be responsible for (notwithstanding the rumours that Johnson was prepared to 'let the bodies pile high' – BBC News, 2021a). These examples help to portray the UK as an 'incoherent state' (Richards et al, 2022).

Critical policy analysis: whose lives matter to policy makers?

Critical policy analysis highlights the problem definitions and policy solutions that exacerbate the marginalisation of already vulnerable social groups (Chapter 2). In particular, a neoliberal belief in low state intervention, in favour of market forces and individual responsibility, reinforces low attention to social and economic inequalities and their impact on health. It contrasts with 'social determinants' approaches that relate profound health inequalities to inequalities in factors such as income, wealth, education and employment, causing unequal access to high-quality homes, water and nutrition, and safe and healthy environments (see Chapter 10).

The neoliberal approach has become increasingly dominant in UK government policies in the last 50 years, particularly when led by the Conservatives (Chapters 4 and 10). It has impacted public health:

- UK Conservative governments (1979–1997) downplayed health inequalities and emphasised personal responsibility to stay healthy.
- UK Labour governments (1997–2010), and the Scottish and Welsh governments, focused *initially* on the social and economic causes of health inequalities, before re-emphasising lifestyle choices.
- Conservative-led UK governments (2010 onwards) oversaw a period of 'austerity' that reduced funding for previous Labour measures (Harrington et al, 2009; Baggott, 2011; Cairney and St Denny, 2020: 87–88, 141–142).

There has been *some* commitment to reducing health inequalities as part of population health strategies and the work of public health agencies (Smith, 2013; Boswell et al, 2019; Cairney and St Denny, 2020: 137). It includes commitment to a 'Health in All Policies' (HiAP) strategy that treats health as a human right, focuses on the social determinants of health, and seeks ways to mainstream public health policies across government activity (Chapter 10; Cairney et al, 2021b). HiAP focuses primarily on NCDs and their unequal distribution. It can be fostered via strategies that encourage collaboration (Public Health England and Local Government Association, 2016) and/or the adoption of policy instruments to reduce unhealthy activity, including smoking, alcohol consumption, diet and exposure to pollution. For example, the UK and devolved governments have produced internationally high levels of tobacco control (Cairney, 2019a), and some restrictions on alcohol consumption (Butler et al, 2017), although the UK government is keener on voluntary business schemes to improve population diets (for example, to reduce salt in processed food) (Knai et al, 2015; Theis and White, 2021). Until 2020, NCDs appeared to be the main focus of UK and devolved public health agencies, with health protection – for example, to inoculate people with vaccines – less visible (and less contested).

A relatively individualistic approach to COVID-19 was clear during initial UK and devolved responses to COVID-19, which emphasised public health communication and personal responsibility to wash hands, socially distance and isolate. Then, a combination of lockdown measures and financial support signalled a – temporarily – radically different role for the state.

To what extent did UK COVID-19 policies address health inequalities?

COVID-19 reinforced the importance of social determinants. Bambra et al (2021: 8–9) describe how inequalities increase COVID-19: (1) 'vulnerability' and (2) 'susceptibility', since NCDs and 'long term exposures to adverse living and environmental conditions' make people more vulnerable to COVID-19 illness and death; (3) 'exposure', since lower-paid workers in service jobs are less able to work safely from home; and (4) 'transmission', since more deprived neighbourhoods have smaller homes shared by more people.

  UK policy makers *could* have defined the policy problem primarily as an inequalities problem (Chapter 10), relating to factors including (Cairney, 2021b: 255–256):

- *Age.* Older people are more vulnerable to COVID-19 illness and death. There were 43,256 deaths in care homes in England (2,367 in Wales) in two years from February 2020 (ONS, 2022e). Older people in care homes (many with dementia) were subject to prolonged periods of isolation during lockdown 'shielding'.
- *Income and wealth.* From 2020 to 2021, the COVID-19 death rate 'in the most deprived areas of England' was generally 'more than double that in the least deprived areas' (ONS, 2021b). Low-income households were more affected by COVID-19 and lockdown measures, contributing to a rise in demand for food banks (ONS, 2021b).
- *Gender.* Lockdowns and school closures have an unequal impact, with women more likely to take on more (unpaid) caring responsibilities, and women and girls more vulnerable to domestic violence and sexual assault (Home Affairs Select Committee, 2020; Bambra et al, 2021: 42–45; J. Smith, 2022).
- *Race and ethnicity.* The House of Commons Health and Social Care and Science and Technology Committees' (2021: 5–9) list of UK government failings includes a lack of appreciation that 'Black, Asian and Minority Ethnic communities' faced disproportionately (1) high rates of death and illness, (2) low access to PPE, and (3) low access to safe housing and working conditions. For example, from 2020 to 2021 in England, 'the rate of death involving COVID-19 was greatest for the Bangladeshi ethnic group: 5.0 and 4.1 times greater than White British men and women' (ONS, 2021b).
- *Disability.* People with disabilities are more vulnerable to COVID-19 illness and affected by the impact of lockdown on care services. For example, in England from 2020 to 2021, 'the rate of death involving COVID-19 was 3.0 times greater for more-disabled men and 3.5 times greater for more-disabled women' (ONS, 2021b). The House of Commons Health and Social Care and Science and Technology Committees (2021: 5–9) describe '[p]eople with learning disabilities and autistic people' who faced (1) higher mortality risk, exacerbated by inappropriate 'do not resuscitate' orders, (2) lower access to care services, and (3) diminished contact with family and carers.

- *Mental health and illness.* Mental illness 'is a major cause *and* indicator of health inequality', associated with lower life expectancy and more unhealthy behaviour (Cairney and St Denny, 2020: 156–157; emphasis in original). Long periods of isolation, or increased pressures associated with poverty, caring responsibilities, racial discrimination or domestic abuse, exacerbate mental ill health, while lockdown measures and NHS pressures reduce access to services (Bambra et al, 2021: 38–42; Flint et al, 2021).

However, COVID-19 accentuated a tendency for health inequalities rhetoric to be unmatched by delivery (Cairney et al, 2022b). COVID-19 'shone a spotlight on inequalities, and created an opportunity for change', but past experience does not suggest that this opportunity will be taken (Lewis et al, 2022). Further, spending to address poverty or low income was eclipsed by funding and tax reliefs for businesses. Overall, the impact of COVID-19, the governmental response and the cost of living crisis in 2022 combined to further marginalise already vulnerable populations (Marmot, 2022).

Conclusion: Did COVID-19 change UK policy for good?

In 2020, it seemed like UK politics and policy making had changed forever. COVID-19 prompted radical and rapid changes to UK and devolved government policy. Stay-at-home restrictions are highly unusual in liberal democracies, but they became the 'new normal' very quickly. The economic package was at a scale only seen during crises such as wars or major economic collapses, and it provided a level of social and employment security not usually associated with Conservative governments. Organisational reforms were rapid and expensive. Coordination between policy-making centres was unusually high. Policy and policy making changes created multiple windows of opportunity for long-lasting change.

However, by 2022, the UK largely returned to its old normal. The UK government signalled the end to most state intervention and the need to reduce spending. Organisations were reduced in scale (such as state funding for COVID-19 testing and monitoring), UK and devolved government coordination is less impressive, and public health funding is low (Finch and Vriend, 2023). Intense attention to COVID-19 in 2020–2021 has given way to two related issues. First, crisis in the NHS. It relates *partly* to the COVID-19 legacy (a backlog of care) and the additional impact of COVID-19 treatment on a stretched NHS during the winter of 2022–2023. Further, summer 2022 produced a high number of 'excess deaths' (McDonald, 2022). Second, the cost of living crisis, exacerbating energy and food poverty, and therefore unequal ill health. Although the UK government intervened, time will tell if it reverts to 'austerity' (Chapter 9).

Overall, the COVID-19 experience represents an extreme example of enduring aspects of policy making. First, it highlights how policy makers have dealt with bounded rationality: addressing a problem out of their understanding, responding quickly, then using their beliefs to chart a return to business as usual. Policy makers often exacerbated unequal negative outcomes over which they had limited understanding. Second, they engaged in a policy-making environment over which they had limited control. Policy-making coordination was unusually high, the UK government produced rapid organisational changes, and the state managed social behaviour in a way that we would not associate with liberal democracy. Yet, the results were not consistent with ministerial intentions. Rather, COVID-19 inquiries will identify how the UK and devolved governments can learn from their mistakes and plan more effectively for similar events.

7

Constitutional Policy: Brexit

Chapter highlights

1. In 2016, the '**Brexit**' campaign drew on the Westminster story to describe 'taking back control' of UK policy and policy making. In 2020, the UK left the EU.

2. The complex government story suggests that UK ministers have limited knowledge and control over policy processes. The Brexit process exposed those limitations, and changed only one of many drivers of fragmented and multi-level policy making.

3. Brexit created confusion about the new responsibilities of devolved governments, and amplified demands for a second referendum on Scottish independence.

4. Three approaches highlight key perspectives on these issues:

   • Policy analysis identifies how to address constitutional issues. For example, what case could people make to leave or remain in the **European Union**?

   • Policy studies identify how governments manage constitutional change. What was the consequence of Brexit on policy and policy making?

   • Critical policy analysis identifies and challenges inequitable processes and outcomes. Who won and lost from Brexit?

Introduction: Did the UK take back control?

Brexit is an extreme case that illuminates both of our stories of policy making. Its proponents drew – selectively – on the complex government story to complain that too much policy was made by the EU. They retold the Westminster story to demand that the UK 'takes back control' of policy making, to further the idea of an independent

Brexit: a portmanteau, combining *Britain* and *exit* from membership of the European Union. The referendum ballot wording was 'Should the United Kingdom remain a member of the European Union or leave the European Union?' and people could vote to 'Remain a member of the European Union' or 'Leave European Union'.

European Union: a multi- or supra-national confederation, to pool sovereignty and policy-making functions in pursuit of economic prosperity and peace (Ludlow, 2016). The UK joined in 1973. The EU includes the:

- European Council, consisting of national representatives of member countries (heads of government or relevant ministers). It makes the EU's high-level decisions.
- European Commission, the EU's executive and bureaucracy.
- European Parliament, which scrutinises Commission-initiated legislation.
- European Court of Justice, which ensures that European legislation is applied consistently across the Union and that EU institutions abide by EU law.

sovereign country able to reassert its borders, make policy for the UK in the UK, and play its own powerful role in the world. They argued that UK government control would allow it to limit migration from EU countries, and use the money it saved from its EU financial contribution to fund UK public services (Menon and Salter, 2016: 1305–1310). Control of policy making would allow Parliament and the public to hold the UK government directly to account, in contrast to a convoluted and distant EU process less subject to UK scrutiny. The 'Referendum on the United Kingdom's membership of the European Union' was held on 23 June 2016. 17.4 million people (52 per cent) voted for the UK to leave the EU (Menon and Salter, 2016: 1297), and the UK withdrew in 2020.

Post-referendum analysis has questioned this claim of control over policy, criticising the exaggerated and malicious claims about repatriating immigrants, and noting that the additional public spending did not materialise (partly because Brexit had a negative economic impact greater than the financial saving). There is also high uncertainty about Brexit's impact across policy sectors (including environmental policy, Chapter 8).

Claims about taking back control of policy making are also exaggerated, and build on an uncritical analysis of the Westminster story (Chapters 1–3; compare with Baldini et al, 2022a: Chapter 1; Bevir and Beech, 2022). The complex government story describes a different reality: the UK government operates in a multi-level policy-making system over which it has limited understanding, and policy outcomes appear to emerge despite attempts by the centre to control them. Brexit will prompt many changes to policy making, but not a simple shift of power from one venue to another. Nor does it remove the influence of EU and international organisations. The UK government now has the power to restrict activity (such as immigration) rather than create it (such as international trade).

To some extent, multi-level arrangements result from the *choice* to share responsibilities with other governments. For example, before 2016, EU membership reflected a choice to give some responsibilities to EU bodies and share others with devolved and local governments (albeit without full clarity on who does what – Box 7.1). Then, the UK government repatriated those powers and shared some with devolved governments. However, these arrangements also result from *necessity*, to reflect the inability of a single centre of government to control policy outcomes, and the fragmentation of responsibilities across many levels of government and types of organisations. Brexit did not resolve fragmented governance. Nor did it resolve constitutional crisis in the UK. Many still oppose Brexit, and Brexit amplified demands for a second referendum on independence in Scotland (where 62 per cent voted to remain – Electoral Commission, 2019).

Box 7.1: Before Brexit, who was responsible for what?

The European Commission's (2022) list of 'Areas of EU action' identify pre-Brexit powers. The EU controlled policies in relation to the 'four freedoms', or free movement of goods, persons, services and capital. It had 'exclusive competences' regarding customs (the movement of goods), competition policy (business practices), trade agreements and marine life (the 'Common Fisheries Policy').

For **Eurozone** countries, it controls monetary policy. The EU also had 'shared competences' with the UK. In some cases, the EU had a greater share of: EU citizen migration, 'single market', consumer protection, environmental, agricultural and fisheries policies, and to pool resources to foster 'economic, social and territorial cohesion'. It had narrower powers in relation to employment, transport, energy, justice and public health. The EU also 'helps' member states to foster policies for industry, culture, tourism, education and humanitarian action.

> **Eurozone**: the 19 countries that use the euro and accept the conditions of monetary union, including the authority of the European Central Bank (and the European Council to 'rescue the euro', Glencross, 2016).

In practice, the EU's role is difficult to piece together because most problems transcend jurisdictional boundaries. Therefore, we describe different roles in each case study chapter. Chapter 8 describes the EU's role as unusually important to environmental, agricultural and fisheries policies, and highly important to energy, by obliging or encouraging UK-wide action. In contrast, Chapter 6 (COVID-19 policy) barely mentions the EU because health *protection* was largely a UK and devolved government responsibility (although, without Brexit, the UK may have been part of an EU negotiation of vaccine supply). This story would be different if we described population health *promotion*. Responsibility for 'healthy behaviour' policy was shared across EU, UK, devolved and local government levels. Tobacco control measures helped the UK become a world leader in policy change (Cairney, 2019a). Alcohol controls were more mixed, such as when Scottish government policy was challenged in the EU (legislation to introduce a minimum unit price for alcohol had trade implications) and by local authorities (favouring 'night time economy' policies) (Holden and Hawkins, 2013; Fitzgerald and Cairney, 2022; Nicholls and Cairney, 2022; Hawkins and van Schalkwyk, 2023).

Further, note the importance of *perceptions* of the reach of EU policy, including 'the EU's expansion into policy areas traditionally the reserve of nation states' (Richardson and Rittberger, 2020: 658). It prompted outlandish claims about how much of UK law comes from multiple EU obligations (V. Miller, 2010: 5, identifies a range of 6–84 per cent!). The claim that there are few aspects of life *not* regulated by the EU underpins organised opposition to EU integration (Richardson and Rittberger, 2020: 657; Boxes 7.2 and 7.3).

This chapter examines these constitutional and governance issues through three lenses. First, policy analysis identifies how to connect the normative question 'who should govern the UK?' to a series of interconnected problems, asking:

- What was the general case for and against the EU (Box 7.2) and Brexit in 2016 (Box 7.3)? Is it like the case for Scottish independence (Box 7.4)?
- What form of Brexit was feasible during negotiations between the UK and EU?

Second, policy studies situate this analysis in the context of real-world developments:

- What forms of multi-level policy making are feasible (and fair) in theory and practice? Who should be responsible for what, and how should governments cooperate?
- What was the actual consequence of Brexit on policy and policy making?

Third, critical policy analysis identifies who benefits from these developments:

- Who wins and loses from Brexit?
- Did it help to reduce or exacerbate inequalities?

In the conclusion, we reflect on the extent to which Brexit, and its consequences, inform our Westminster and complex government stories.

Box 7.2: Europhile versus Eurosceptic views of the EU

Europhile approaches identify the following advantages of the EU:

- *Solving problems*. Pooling sovereignty addresses shared challenges across borders, with the UK able to lead agendas such as climate change (Heseltine, 1989; Blick, 2016; Hertner and Keith, 2017).
- *Boosting economic activity*. A single market reduces trade barriers. Free movement of people allows workers to relocate and businesses to recruit from a larger pool.
- *Boosting social protections*. The Social Chapter of the Maastricht Treaty introduced new rights for citizens and workers (Daniels, 1998; Busby and Zahn, 2013).

- *The peace dividend of membership.* The development of European institutions helps to overcome divisions and keep powerful countries in check (Birchfield et al, 2017).
- *The enhancement of cosmopolitan liberal democracy.* EU integration boosts cultural and social exchange and shared liberal democracy values (Robinson, 2020).

Eurosceptic accounts emphasise the incompatibility between UK and EU approaches to democracy (Schmidt, 2020), economic policy (Thompson, 2017a) or ways of life:

- *EU membership causes unfair competition that stifles UK business and free trade.* The UK 'gold plates' EU laws while other countries do not (Richardson and Rittberger, 2020: 655). Leaving the EU would cut 'red tape' and allow the UK to change its laws and fiscal rules to become more competitive (Thatcher, 1988; Gamble, 1994; Cash and Jenkin, 2013; Baker and Lavery, 2018; Rutter, 2020).
- *The 'creeping Europeanisation of British politics and government' stifles UK ways of life* (Gamble, 2018: 1224). EU policies place needless limits on social and business behaviour (Haller, 2019; Rankin and Waterson, 2019; Wing Chan et al, 2020; Zappettini, 2021).
- *Expansion and integration will keep getting worse, allowing uncontrollable immigration* (Dennison and Geddes, 2018). EU expansion allows mass migration from Eastern Europe. It puts unsustainable pressure on public services and diminishes British national identity (Virdee and McGeever, 2017).
- *The EU elite is eroding parliamentary sovereignty and taking power from the people.* Unelected EU bureaucrats and judges are not accountable to British voters even though they threaten a British way of life (Gamble, 2018: 1229; Iakhnis et al, 2018: 2; Marsh, 2018).
- *The 'democratic deficit' in the EU requires a radical solution* (Katz, 2001; Bond, 2011). It cannot be solved by trivial reforms to an EU governance system that few understand, or new low-profile elections (Gavin, 2002; Chalmers, 2017).
- *The EU is a capitalist project that undermines workers.* While Euroscepticism is associated with right-wing arguments, there is a left-wing case ('Lexit') based on the EU favouring big business at the expense of worker rights and social protection (Cini, 2011; Wellings and Baxendale, 2014; Guinan and Hanna, 2017; Worth, 2017). The free movement of people – willing to work for less – undermines the ability of British workers to secure fair conditions (Morris, 2006; Lewis, 2017).

Policy analysis: what exactly is the problem?

The Brexit debate is difficult to relate to five-step policy analysis (it was not as coherent as Box 7.2 suggests). The vote for Brexit may look decisive, but it became an unclear solution to a contested problem. To demonstrate, first we show that the Conservative Party leadership used a referendum to address party in-fighting whenever a new debate on EU integration would arise. Second, we identify the disconnect between vague hopes for Brexit and actual policy solutions. People were voting for something that the UK government did not support and could not deliver. Third, we show that more substantive analysis – by UK and EU policy makers – appeared after the vote. Finally, we use the five-step language to analyse the aftermath: what were the UK government's options during the process to leave the EU?

The Brexit referendum: a poor solution to an ill-defined political problem

The Conservative Party (2015) treated the referendum – 'to let the people decide' – as a solution to a long-term *political* problem (Blair, 2020). Conservative Party divisions over EU expansion and integration have existed for decades. Successive leaders tried to manage the problem in two ways. First, using rhetoric to express support for membership but opposition to EU overreach. Second, treating Euroscepticism – among a vocal minority of MPs, print media with high circulations (including *The Sun*, *Daily Mail*, *Daily Express* and *The Telegraph*) and public opinion – as a resource. They used it to negotiate exemptions from EU rules (such as the UK financial 'rebate' negotiated by Thatcher – Vernasca, 2016), or oppose further 'transfers of power' to the EU (Forster, 2002; Startin, 2015: 316; Bale, 2016):

Single European Act 1986: a 'major reform of the founding treaties of the three original European Communities' to foster integration, such as to increase the powers of the European Parliament, and establish European responsibilities for the 'single market', EU cohesion and environmental policy (Dinan, 2020).

Maastricht Treaty 1992 (to create the modern EU): 'One of the most important treaty changes in the history of European integration': creating the conditions for an 'Economic and Monetary Union' (including the Eurozone), further empowering the European Parliament, extending the use of 'Qualified Majority Voting' (reducing the veto powers of countries), and extending EU competences to social and other policies (Laursen and Vanhoonacker, 2019).

- Prime Minister Margaret Thatcher supported EU membership, and the **Single European Act 1986**, but her 'Bruges speech' in 1988 opposed further integration and 'became a rallying cry for UK Eurosceptics' (Startin, 2015: 314).
- John Major's premiership came under pressure from Eurosceptic Conservative MPs, particularly when seeking parliamentary support for more EU integration (Startin, 2015: 315; see also Box 5.2 on 'Black Wednesday'). In 1992, he could not prevent multiple MP rebellions in relation to the **Maastricht Treaty**, and – by 1995 – he initiated a party leadership contest to bolster his position (Cowley and Norton, 1999: 90). Further, the ratification process in other

countries normalised the idea that each state should hold a referendum to give consent for more EU integration (Startin, 2015: 315).

There followed 13 years of Labour government, generally supportive of EU integration and expansion, particularly when Blair could describe the UK's special place in EU affairs, highlight flexibility (for example, to maintain the UK 'rebate'), or portray UK leadership of agendas such as climate change (Daddow, 2013; Chapter 8). However, ministers were increasingly conscious of Eurosceptic newspaper coverage (Startin, 2015: 317) and public opinion in relation to EU immigration. During this time, the EU enlarged considerably: ten states joined in 2004 (Cyprus, Czech Republic, Estonia, Hungary, Latvia, Lithuania, Malta, Poland, Slovakia and Slovenia) and two in 2007 (Bulgaria, Romania). Labour had treated EU-to-UK migration as a boost to 'economic activity and tax receipts' on the assumption of modest activity (Sobolewska and Ford, 2020: 143). Further, unlike many Western EU members, the UK opted not to enforce transitional controls following enlargement in 2004 (Wright, 2010). Yet, migration from Central and Eastern Europe was much higher – and more spread across the UK – than expected. It prompted public 'concern about immigration' to reach an 'all-time high in 2007', and Labour to amend its rhetoric to appear less tolerant (Sobolewska and Ford, 2020: 144–147, 163). It was also concerned that a referendum on the **Constitutional Treaty** (2004) would have been lost (Cowley and Stuart, 2010: 134). The **Lisbon Treaty** (2007) was its more modest alternative. The Labour government rejected calls for a referendum on Lisbon, prompting Eurosceptic media criticism and some Labour MP rebellions (to support the Conservative Party's amendment of EU legislation) (Cowley and Stuart, 2010: 138).

> **Lisbon Treaty**: the original plan was to design a **Constitutional Treaty** (in 2004) that formalised EU status and roles/powers of its institutions. Referendums in France and the Netherlands (2005) prompted a retreat, in favour of the Lisbon Treaty (2007), to foster EU development but avoid the language of constitution development (Reh, 2009).

When the Conservatives re-entered government (from 2010, in coalition), there were multiple signs of Euroscepticism that were more difficult to manage:

- *The Daily Express*'s 'Britain out of Europe' campaign (2010), and other papers' routine criticism, helped to normalise Euroscepticism in public debate (Startin, 2015: 318).
- A vote in the House of Commons to hold a Brexit referendum (2011) was defeated 483 to 111, but 81 rebellions plus 14–19 abstentions helped to produce 'the largest Conservative rebellion of the 2010 Parliament to date, and one of the largest of the postwar era' (Cowley and Stuart, 2012: 402).
- EU freedom of movement undermined the Conservatives' anti-immigration reputation. The government created a 'hostile environment' for migrants

(under then Home Secretary Theresa May), but 'substantial EU migration continued' and the government failed to meet its immigration reduction targets (Sobolewska and Ford, 2020: 169–173).

- Smaller parties – the British National Party and UK Independence Party (UKIP) – succeeded in mobilising 'ethnocentric sentiments' against immigration to win votes (Sobolewska and Ford, 2020: 164). Then, UKIP (led by Nigel Farage, 2006–2009 and 2010–2016) became increasingly successful in combining 'a strong anti-migration stance with trenchant hostility to the EU' (Sobolewska and Ford, 2020: 175). It won a plurality of UK seats (24 of 73) in the European Parliament in 2014, and a small number of defections by Conservative MPs.

These developments put strong pressure on the party to produce a solution to its EU problem (Bale, 2022). By 2013, Prime Minister David Cameron promised that the UK would hold a referendum if the Conservatives won the next election (Jennings and Lodge, 2019; Bale, 2022: 3). Cameron had emphasised *inevitability*, since party pressure was becoming unmanageable (Bale, 2022: 3; see also Frosini and Gilbert, 2020), and *strategy*, in which Cameron chose to (1) use the threat of Brexit to renegotiate the UK's position in the EU, and (2) emulate previous referendum successes (to reject electoral reform in 2013 and Scottish independence in 2014 – Curtice, 2013; Box 7.4).

The first part of this strategy backfired, since Cameron did not secure the deal that he trailed (Bale, 2022: 30). Further, this referendum was not like the others. Compared to electoral reform, public interest was far higher and more emotionally driven (Bale, 2022: 17–26), and the Conservative Party was divided. Many UK government ministers – such as Michael Gove – campaigned energetically for Leave, while some – including Theresa May – gave minimal support to Remain (Bale, 2022: 26–27, 39–47). Compared to the Scottish referendum, 'Project Fear' – in which the UK government warned voters about the major economic costs of constitutional change – had less impact (Bale, 2022: 29–32). Cameron failed, and resigned on 24 June 2016 (Bale, 2022: 47–49).

The Brexit debate: a catch-all solution to too many problems

We use the Leave versus Remain campaigns to summarise the arguments made for and against Brexit. The Electoral Commission (2016) 'designated' the lead campaigns for each side: Vote Leave to support Brexit, and The In Campaign/ Britain Stronger in Europe to oppose it. Designation allowed each to spend up to £7 million and enjoy access to public and media space and leaflet distribution (the UK government also sent each voter a leaflet supporting membership). We summarise their arguments in Box 7.3 and Figure 7.1, which projects a simple word cloud from exemplars of speeches (see also Sobolewska and Ford, 2020: 224–249; Rone, 2022).

Box 7.3: The main arguments of Vote Leave and Britain Stronger in Europe

Vote Leave (2016: 1–15): 'Why should we Vote Leave on 23 June?'

- *EU membership has an excessive financial cost which could be better spent on public services.* 'The EU costs us over £350 million a week. Enough to build a brand new, full-staffed NHS hospital every week' (Boris Johnson campaigned with this message painted on a red bus – Menon and Salter, 2016: 1305–1310).
- *The EU controls UK immigration. Free movement undercuts UK workers and poor border control undermines the identification of terrorists.* 'We need to take back control of our borders so we decide who can come here – and who can't … the EU is a threat to our jobs and our security.'
- *The EU will expand, exacerbating financial costs and immigration problems.* 'The next countries set to join are' Albania, Macedonia, Montenegro, Serbia and Turkey (bordering Syria).
- *The UK has ceded too much control to the EU, with no say for UK voters or accountability for harmful legislation.* 'We should take back the power to kick out the people who make our laws … unelected EU bureaucrats in Brussels who we never voted for. The Eurozone has a permanent majority in the EU voting system – this means we're always outvoted.'
- *EU bureaucracy undermines UK business and limits trade.* 'Let's take back control over our economy and trade'; 'UK trade and jobs will thrive after we Vote Leave'.
- *The UK Prime Minister failed to renegotiate the UK's status, which will get worse after the referendum.* 'The European Court is still in charge of exactly the same things as it was before. … The EU is already planning its next power grab.'

Britain Stronger in Europe (2016: 1–8): 'Why Britain is Stronger in Europe'

- *EU membership improves the UK economy, trade and investment.* The EU has negotiated many trade deals, and companies invest in the UK to access the single market. 'Europe's single market facilitates greater trade and investment'; 'The EU accounts for 44% of the UK's exports, worth £229bn in 2014'; '200,000 British businesses trade with the EU'; 'Between 3 and 4 million jobs in Britain are linked to our trade with Europe'.
- *EU membership reduces the cost of living.* 'We all benefit from access to a wider range of goods and services, which leads to lower prices … each household on average benefits by £3,000 a year from EU membership' (including the cost of flights and mobile phone use).
- *EU membership improves security.* 'Britain is able to influence key decisions and work with our partners to ensure a coordinated response to international threats such as terrorism, organised crime or climate change' (such as the European Arrest Warrant).
- *EU membership protects workers.* It fosters 'minimum paid annual leave, protections against discrimination and harassment at work, and for statutory maternity and parental leave'.
- *EU membership helps to address climate change.* 'Britain benefits from EU environmental legislation and funding'; 'Britain is taking a lead in fighting climate change'.

- *All known alternatives to full membership are bad.* Some oblige the UK to follow EU rules without influence ('Norway model'), while paying into the EU budget ('Switzerland model'), or having no access to the single market for services ('Turkey model'). Or, the UK 'would subject UK–EU trade to new tariffs and increase costs for businesses and consumers'.

The government made a similar case for the value of EU membership ('stronger economy', lower cost of living, peace and security) and against a 'decade or more of uncertainty' as 'the UK unpicks our relationship with the EU'. It described its 'special status in the EU' after Cameron negotiated to maintain 'border controls', restrict 'access to our welfare system for new EU migrants' and avoid further EU integration (HM Government, 2016).

This comparison of campaigns is useful but incomplete. First, it helps to identify common points of debate, including how best to promote economic activity (trade, jobs, cost of living and doing business) and human security, and different agendas such as regarding immigration (Leave) or climate change (Remain). There is a similar language in keynote Leave/Remain speeches, but with greater emphasis by Leave on EU bureaucrats ('Brussels') and judges ('ECJ') (Figure 7.1).

Second, however, a binary campaign and vote exaggerates the coherence of each position. Simple campaigns encourage voters to invest their own beliefs in vague and aspirational policy solutions to their perception of the problem, without requiring a majority to define the problem clearly (or in the same way) before voting. There was no shortage of academic analyses warning against the economic costs of Brexit, but an evidence-informed comparison of trade-offs associated with Leave/Remain was not a feature of debate (Dunlop et al, 2020: 710–713).

Figure 7.1: Word cloud of speeches for Leave and Remain

Note: The left projects Leave speeches by Gove (2016), Johnson (2016b) and Farage (2016). The right projects Remain speeches by leaders of the three main British parties, Cameron (2016), Corbyn (2016) and Farron (2016).

Third, there were many actors presenting messages without being subject to the same scrutiny as the official campaigns (Cadwalladr, 2017 provides a famous account). Many drew on **populism**, pitting ordinary (or allegedly 'pure') people against the corrupt elites – in the EU and UK Remain establishment – making policies at their expense (Stanley, 2008; Mudde, 2009; Jennings et al, 2017; Werner-Muller, 2017; Richards et al, 2019). Many used misleading images. For example, Nigel Farage led a

> **Populism**: a political stance, appealing to 'the people' (ordinary people in general or specific ethnic groups) undermined by a corrupt 'elite' or 'establishment' (including elected politicians and unelected bureaucrats and judges).

campaign focused on whipping up opposition to EU-driven immigration with reference to images of unwanted immigrants fleeing war or persecution (pictured in Portes, 2022c). It was part of a wider discourse containing romanticised stories of a White British past, or concerns about a White working-class community 'left behind' by EU-fuelled globalisation, to suggest that Brexit would help 'to take our country back' (Bhambra, 2017; Shilliam, 2018: 135–163; Mondon and Winter, 2019; Spencer and Oppermann, 2020; Bale, 2022: 31–2; see also Hobolt, 2016).

While some organisations challenged Leave claims with reference to facts (for example, Full Fact, 2017), a sole focus on 'rational' ways to consider EU membership would miss the point. Brexit discourse was often driven by emotional appeals tapping into hopes and fears, deeply held beliefs and identity, which contributed to the mistrust of opponents (Richardson and Rittberger, 2020: 660–662; Bale, 2022: 29–32; Yates and MacRury, 2022). The debate also highlighted a specific English identity (Henderson et al, 2017). Identifying as Leave/Remain became far more important than traditional attachments to political parties (Sobolewska and Ford, 2020: 238). In that context, it is easier to appeal to these beliefs to encourage action – such as to vote – than to change them via campaigning (Sabatier et al, 1987; Jones and Crow, 2017). The Leave campaign was more able to exploit deeply held feelings around identity than the half-hearted Remain campaign focusing on aversion to the risk of change (Sobolewska and Ford, 2020: 228–229).

Analysing the vote for Brexit as a policy problem

The vote for Brexit did not solve a well-defined policy problem. Indeed, Baines et al (2020: 742) argue that it could not do so, because the Leave case focused only on *political* success (see Box 5.3). There was no possibility of *process* or *programmatic* success, because its case was 'baseless' and 'unfounded in any policy analysis' (Baines et al, 2020: 742). Further, it raised the prospect of new constitutional crises such as Scottish independence (Box 7.4).

Box 7.4: Comparing the case for Brexit and Scottish independence

The Scottish independence referendum was held on 14 September 2014. There are many overlaps between both debates. First, they relate somewhat to national identity, with a strong link between people who feel either 'Scottish, not British' and favour independence (Cairney and McGarvey, 2013: 248; Keating and McEwen, 2020), or 'English, not British' and see the EU as a 'Bad thing' (Henderson et al, 2017: 638). Second, the 'democratic deficit' features strongly, with the added argument in Scotland that most people voted historically for Labour or the Scottish National Party (SNP) in general elections but are governed by Conservatives (Cairney and McGarvey, 2013: 27). Third, they focused strongly on the economic consequences of constitutional change, with the Yes campaign emphasising the benefits of an economic plan tailored to Scotland, and Better Together (the official campaign for the Union) emphasising the multiple economic risks of independence, including lower tax revenues to support higher Scottish spending, less resilience to economic shocks, and no guaranteed ability to use sterling (Rioux, 2020: 9). Fourth, both campaigns had a negative focal point: for Yes, it was the Conservative UK government; for Leave, it was the EU. Finally, independence and Brexit represented all things to all people, with supporters expecting different things.

We can also identify key differences. First, the SNP-led Scottish government (2014) described specific plans for independence after a long period of consultation and debate (Keating and McEwen, 2020; Brown Swan, 2020). The UK government did not, because it opposed Brexit (then May used the 'Brexit means Brexit' slogan to discourage debate – Dunlop et al, 2020: 708). Second, the Yes campaign focused on 'civic nationalism' (emphasising country of residence over birth or ancestry), with no meaningful equivalent to Brexit's focus on immigration (Bennie and McAngus, 2020: 282; compare with Hill and Meer, 2020) or 'jingoistic' or 'populist' tone (Calhoun, 2017; Freeden, 2017; Inglehart and Norris, 2017).

Brexit helped to make the case for a second Scottish referendum (Cairney, 2017b). First, the SNP argued that Brexit represented a substantive change in political circumstances. In the 2019 general election it won 47 out of 59 seats (80 per cent, from 45 per cent of the vote in Scotland) 'on a platform committed to both independence and remaining in the EU' (Keating and McEwen, 2020: 672). Second, although the EU was not a major feature of the 2014 debate, the assumption was that (1) people voted to stay in the UK which would remain in the EU, and (2) Scotland's independence from the UK would make it problematic to rejoin the EU. Some voters will now prefer Scotland/EU to Scotland/UK. Third, the Brexit arithmetic reinforces the following 'democratic deficit' argument: we voted for X but got Y because we are outnumbered by voters in England (62 per cent voted Remain in Scotland). We have to accept governments and policies that we did not vote for (or challenge the outcome unsuccessfully in court – Kirkaldy, 2018; see also Sargeant, 2020; McEwen, 2021). Fourth, it undermined the idea that independence is parochial. Now, it is the cosmopolitan choice, rejecting a 'Little England' mentality. Finally, the UK government exacerbated tensions in UK-devolved relations: it did not pass on repatriated

CONSTITUTIONAL POLICY

responsibilities in a way expected by devolved governments (McHarg and Mitchell, 2017); and, it vetoed Scottish Parliament legislation for the first time in 2023 (the Gender Recognition Reform (Scotland) Bill – see Torrance and Pyper, 2023).

Yet, Brexit also bolstered the 'Better Together' case, since it shows that major constitutional change (1) is more difficult to achieve than advertised, and (2) has major short-term costs. The SNP also struggled to force the referendum issue, such as via the Scottish government's unsuccessful appeal to the UK Supreme Court (Torrance, 2022b). Then, the resignation of the unusually popular Nicola Sturgeon as First Minister in 2023, a divisive leadership campaign (won by Humza Yousaf), and a crisis in SNP finances, undermined the long-term argument that Scotland would be better independent since its government is more unified and competent than its UK counterpart. Yousaf also expressed the need to identify a 'clear majority' in favour of independence before making progress (Mason and Eardley, 2023).

This lack of a plan – and the fact that the referendum was advisory – gave some people the misguided hope that the UK government might not seek Brexit (Gordon, 2016; Morgan, 2017). Really, the problem was how to turn Brexit into more than a slogan. The search for a solution contributed to political crises in which the new Prime Minister, Theresa May (2016–2019), proved unable to secure a deal that suited the EU and a majority of Westminster MPs (Judge and Shephard, 2022). Boris Johnson's premiership (2019–2022) was built mostly on the 2019 general election slogan 'Get Brexit Done'. It helped to win that election by a large margin, and secure the UK's exit, but did not produce an outcome that could be meaningfully described as final. In that context, we use the five-step policy analysis categories to help make sense of the process.

Step 1: How could actors define the vote for Brexit as a policy problem?

The policy problem took years to resolve, and demonstrated that the choice to leave was not in the sole gift of the UK government. First, the process began with uncertainty about how and when the UK should trigger **Article 50** to give itself time to negotiate a feasible withdrawal agreement (see UK in a Changing Europe, 2021: 6–7). May had signalled that the UK government would trigger it by March 2017, and sought to establish that the government could act unilaterally. Then, the High Court ('Miller vs Secretary of State for Exiting the EU', 3 November 2016) ruled that Parliament had to approve this move, and the Supreme Court dismissed the

Article 50: The provision of the Lisbon Treaty that allows a member state to notify the European Council that it will withdraw from the EU (which triggers a maximum two-year timetable).

139

government's appeal (24 January 2017). The House of Commons vote (498 to 114) allowed it to go ahead, with formal notification sent on 29 March 2017. A subsequent Commons vote (309 to 305) established that the UK government could not make a final withdrawal agreement with the EU without a 'meaningful vote' in Parliament (UK in a Changing Europe, 2021: 11).

Second, UK and EU actors produced separate documents to describe different approaches and expectations (European Council, 2017; HM Government, 2017). They agreed the 'terms of reference' and what 'divorce issues' to prioritise ('citizens' rights, the financial settlement ... and a dialogue on the Ireland/ Northern Ireland border') in June 2017, but the EU rejected the UK proposal to discuss their 'future relationship' until they made progress on the withdrawal agreement (UK in a Changing Europe, 2021: 9). This process contrasted with referendum rhetoric (drawing on Westminster model images) suggesting that the UK would be in control of its exit.

Third, May sought a snap election (approved in Parliament on 9 June 2017) to give the Conservatives a larger majority and more authority during Brexit negotiations. However, the election produced a hung Parliament, with the Conservatives only able to maintain a majority when backed – in a 'confidence and supply agreement' – by the Democratic Unionist Party (DUP) (UK in a Changing Europe, 2021: 8–9). This agreement proved to be fragile when the DUP expressed opposition to initial plans on the Ireland/Northern Ireland border (UK in a Changing Europe, 2021: 10).

Step 2: Identifying feasible solutions

These issues help to explain a major gap between the technical and political feasibility of potential solutions: while many possible options could be described, few would secure enough support from EU and UK actors (McConnell and Tormey, 2020: 689–692).

Soft Brexit: remain a member of the economic, but not political, union

The UK could seek to join the European Free Trade Association bloc (Iceland, Liechtenstein, Norway and Switzerland). This 'rule-taker, not rule-maker' option would require the UK to meet a large proportion of EU rules regarding free trade (including environmental standards) without having a voice in EU political debates (Menon and Salter, 2016; Hepburn, 2019). The meaning of 'soft Brexit' was also unclear and contested, associated with different plans, including 'Norway Plus', 'Common Market 2.0' and a new customs union (Powell and Halfon, 2019; Wyatt, 2022). While supported by pragmatic Remain supporters, it held no appeal for Eurosceptics. For the latter, membership of the single market and customs union is too restrictive because it requires the UK to retain the 'four freedoms' of movement and accept the authority of EU bureaucratic and judicial actors (Box 7.1) (Ladrech, 2016; Menon and Fowler, 2016).

Hard Brexit: leave the economic union and seek a new trading agreement with the EU

This option is a decisive exit from all EU arrangements, focusing on negotiating a new relationship with the EU and the world (including a US led – until 2020 – by Brexit-supporting President Donald Trump – Wilson, 2017). Labels such as 'Canada Plus' described a desire to work with, but be separate from, the EU, and to tap into the UK's historic role as a leader of Commonwealth countries (O'Carroll, 2019). It had limited value for pragmatic UK negotiators seeking to appeal to a wide range of UK (and EU) stakeholders (Edwards, 2020). In particular, it threatened the spirit of the Good Friday Agreement (Box 7.5), since part of the 'hard border' between the UK and EU would be between Ireland and Northern Ireland (Muldoon et al, 2006; McCrudden, 2017; Doyle and Connolly, 2019; Halfon and Powell, 2019; Lagana, 2021; Kelly and Tannam, 2023).

Box 7.5: The Good Friday Agreement and Windsor Agreement

The Good Friday Agreement (Belfast Agreement) was signed on behalf of the UK and Ireland governments and supported by most political parties in Northern Ireland. It described the future governance of Northern Ireland, including: the principle of self-determination (such as to seek or oppose a united Ireland); plans to establish a Northern Ireland Assembly and Executive; regular meetings between actors representing North and South and between the UK/Ireland in the British-Irish Council; the decommissioning of weapons held by paramilitary organisations; the accelerated release of political prisoners; the reform of policing in Northern Ireland; and, a referendum to legitimise the agreement (Secretary of State for Northern Ireland, 1998).

A key aim of the Agreement had been to foster routine movement across a soft border (made easier by common EU membership), prompting Brexit negotiations to address how to deal with a necessarily 'harder' border. Initially, the Northern Ireland protocol (October 2019) made trade subject to greater restrictions moving between Northern Ireland and Great Britain than the EU. It was opposed by the Conservatives' European Research Group and the DUP (which had led the Northern Ireland Executive before it collapsed in 2017). Then, in February 2023, Prime Minister Rishi Sunak and European Commission President Ursula von der Leyen agreed the 'Windsor Framework'. It modified the Northern Ireland protocol to (for example) introduce a system of checks on goods moving between the EU, Northern Ireland and Britain, including 'green' and 'red' lanes depending on their final destination (UK Government, 2023b). An unusual feature was a mechanism for objecting to new European laws and regulations (the 'Stormont Brake'), whereby 30 members of the Northern Ireland Assembly can request that the UK government 'stop the application of amended or replacing provisions of EU law, that may have a significant and lasting impact specific to the everyday lives of communities in Northern Ireland' (European Commission, 2023). The 'Eurosceptic' European Research Group and the DUP opposed the agreement on the grounds that the Stormont Brake was likely to be ineffective (Breslin, 2023; Duparc-Portier and Figus, 2023; ITV News, 2023). Still, the Framework was approved in Parliament thanks to significant cross–party support.

No-Deal Brexit: go it alone, with no agreement possible

World Trade Organization (WTO): an international organisation that establishes and administers rules of trade between countries (in cooperation with other international organisations), monitors implementation and handles disputes. It has 164 members (98 per cent of global trade). Agreements are voluntary, but 'signed by the bulk of the world's trading nations … to ensure that trade flows as smoothly, predictably and freely as possible' (World Trade Organization, 2022).

This option is to exit the EU and rely on **World Trade Organization (WTO)** terms. It seemed like the 'nuclear' – lose-lose – option in 2016, and was not a feature of the Leave campaign. The UK would be required to manage import and export tariffs on goods and services, which would undermine its ability to engage economically with EU countries (firms in international supply chains would be subject to uncertainty and additional costs). The EU would be unable to establish the rights of EU citizens living in the UK.

However, it became more feasible each time the negotiations failed, and when the time to reach a deal began to run out. It found favour among Leave advocates including Nigel Farage (during a gap between leaving UKIP in 2016 and leading the Brexit Party from 2019 to 2021), Conservative MPs such as Steve Baker, and the lobby group Economists for Brexit (now Economists for Free Trade) led by Brexit-supporting economist Professor Patrick Minford. Its supporters called it a 'clean' Brexit, accompanied by a declaration of universal free trade and a guarantee that the UK would 'impose no tariffs of any kind of goods entering the UK market' (Gamble, 2018). They argued that the absence of EU constraints would allow the UK to become an 'offshore' hub for financial services and operate as a 'high innovation' and 'low tax' economy. This elite group used a romantic 'myth of no deal Brexit' to 're-mobilise support for their cause' (Kettell and Kerr, 2020: 1).

Hold a second referendum to check if people want this Brexit

This option would be to put the negotiated settlement to a public vote, largely to oppose Brexit. It drew on previous EU strategies, in which the response to the first unfavourable referendum was to reform and repackage the offer (as with the Lisbon Treaty). It also reflected the Remain argument that people were voting for something that Leave could not offer, and would reject Brexit when they could see its impact (Bellamy, 2019; see also Ellwood, 2022). The 'People's Vote' campaign sought to generate public enthusiasm. Its rally in 2018 contained several hundred thousand people in London, and its petition gained over one million signatures (Sabbagh, 2019). This idea had been suggested by the MP David Davis when standing for the leadership of the Conservative Party (Tempest, 2005), but rejected by Davis while Secretary of State for Exiting the EU (2016–2019).

Also note how these options are presented and ranked from an EU perspective. In December 2017, the European Commission Chief Negotiator Michel Barnier (2017) summed up the options in a 'staircase' of models, arguing that (1) EU membership was at the top, and no-deal/WTO rules were at the bottom, but (2) the UK's insistence of 'red lines' would push the result to the bottom.

Steps 3 and 4: Using values and goals to compare solutions, and predicting the outcomes of solutions

Chapter 6 suggests that steps 3 and 4 were not a strong feature of COVID-19 policy making: governments were not making explicit trade-offs based on competing values, or able to predict well the impact of solutions. The same is true of Brexit, with two added elements. First, there was a major gap between (1) the hopes for a Brexit deal expressed during the 2016 debate, and (2) political reality. Second, the UK central government is not the only audience for policy analysis. The Prime Minister sought a deal to be agreed by the EU and Parliament, while honouring (their perception of) what Leave voters wanted. Debates on solutions were chaotic (Dunlop et al, 2020), but the main trade-offs were clear:

• favour UK sovereignty and control over immigration and trade, versus
• adhere to EU rules, to give the UK access to the economic union and maintain a soft border between Ireland and Northern Ireland.

The prioritisation of 'taking back control' would lead to a hard or no-deal Brexit, producing a negative impact on the UK economy (Van Reenan, 2013; 2016; Erken et al, 2018) and crisis in Northern Ireland. Indeed, EU negotiators opposed any movement towards a 'hard border' if it would 'risk the peace' (Gormley-Heenan and Aughey, 2017; Stevenson, 2017).

In that context, it became commonplace for Remain actors to identify how Leave campaigners had made misleading claims. The term 'cakeism' – keeping your cake but eating it too – described the sense that Leave campaigners wanted access to the economic and trade benefits of EU membership without following EU rules, even though the EU ruled out this outcome (Musolff, 2020). Barnier and leaders such as (then) German Chancellor Angela Merkel stated that 'cherry picking' different parts of membership was not an option (European Economic and Social Committee, 2017; Enderlein, 2018). Initially, Leave campaigners – including UK ministers in key positions, like David Davis,

Liam Fox and Boris Johnson – argued that the UK 'held all the cards' in negotiations: needless trade obstacles would be opposed by EU businesses (who would complain directly to country leaders), and UK control of immigration would be a small price to pay for continued trade (Grey, 2017; BBC News, 2020b). Subsequently, they blamed EU negotiators and country leaders for failure, rather than admitting their misunderstanding of their counterparts' objectives (Figueira and Martill, 2020).

Step 5: Making recommendations

This contestation explains why the UK government failed to recommend a solution favourable to the EU and House of Commons (Schnapper, 2020), as well as the dysfunctional bargaining process (Dunlop et al, 2020: 715–718) and 'policy fiasco' that followed (McConnell and Tormey, 2020). First, when negotiating with the EU, May and senior ministers (including Davis, Fox and Johnson) did not support 'soft Brexit'. Their 'red lines' – including that the UK would leave the economic union and reject the jurisdiction of the European Court of Justice – ruled out that option (Richards et al, 2018). Second, the lack of a Conservative majority ruled out a 'hard Brexit' favourable to the UK and EU, since any vote would be undermined by Eurosceptic MPs insisting on a 'harder' deal or DUP MPs dissatisfied with the impact on Northern Ireland. Further, May's strategy to 'force party rebels to back down' did not work (Heinkelmann-Wild et al, 2020: 723).

Subsequently, May's 'Chequers Plan' (produced on 6 July 2018 and published as a White Paper on 17 July 2018) sought an 'attractive fudge' (Gallagher, 2018): to keep the UK *closely aligned* to EU regulations, to remain outside of the economic union but have access to EU markets and avoid a hard border. It suited neither side. Brexit-supporting ministers (Davis, Johnson and Baker) resigned following its publication, with Davis complaining that the UK was 'giving away too much and too easily' (8 July 2018), and Johnson scathing about the UK's 'status of a colony' (9 July 2022) (UK in a Changing Europe, 2021: 13). Then, Barnier (26 July 2018) and the European Council (20 September 2018) rejected the approach to customs as 'cherry picking' and damaging to the single market (UK in a Changing Europe, 2021: 14).

Any changes to the Chequers Plan would only suit one side. Negotiations with the EU (1) helped to produce (on 14 November 2018) a 'Withdrawal Agreement', an 'Outline of a Political Declaration for the future UK-EU relationship', a 'financial settlement', a deal on citizen rights, and a temporary agreement ('backstop') to prevent a hard customs border in Ireland, which were (2) endorsed by the European Council on 25 November 2018 (UK in a Changing Europe, 2021: 16; Cauvet, 2018). This agreement prompted further resignations from the UK government, and was never accepted in Parliament. Key events (summarised by UK in a Changing Europe, 2021: 17–25; see also Institute for Government, 2019; Kippin and Pyper, 2021) include:

- The government suffered multiple parliamentary defeats (4 December 2018) and delayed the 'meaningful vote' (10 December 2018) on a deal certain to be defeated.
- The deal was rejected during the first 'meaningful vote' (15 January 2019).
- The government amended its proposals on customs (the 'Malthouse Compromise', 3 February 2019), and secured EU assurances about the flexibility of their deal (11 March 2019), but the Commons rejected its proposals in the second meaningful vote (12 March 2019) (UK in a Changing Europe, 2021: 19).
- The Commons agreed that the UK should seek an extension of the Article 50 period, which the European Council endorsed on 21 March 2019 (then on 10 April 2019).
- There followed a remarkable series of Commons votes on various options but with no clear winner (27 March 2019 and 1 April 2019), a third rejection of May's deal (29 March 2019), and a vote to rule out EU withdrawal without a deal approved by Parliament (3 April 2019) (UK in a Changing Europe, 2021: 22).
- Talks between the government and Labour Party, 'aimed at breaking the Brexit impasse, end without an agreement' (17 May 2019).
- The Farage-led Brexit Party won a plurality of the 2019 European Parliament vote (30.9 per cent) (23 May 2019).
- Theresa May resigned as Prime Minister (7 June 2019).
- The government was rebuffed – in Parliament, then in the Supreme Court (24 September 2019) – to prevent the UK leaving the EU while Parliament was not sitting.

Boris Johnson became Prime Minister on 24 July 2019 and initially sought to renegotiate Brexit. The UK agreed a deal with the European Council (17 December 2019), replacing the 'backstop' with a plan to leave the EU customs union but assign special status to Northern Ireland, producing a 'differentiated Brexit' (Keating, 2022) that is 'bitterly opposed by unionists in Northern Ireland' (Murphy, 2022: 5). The new deal did not receive timely Commons support, not least because the debate had become 'toxic' and Johnson did not seem to be interested in cross–party compromise (Parry and Johnson, 2021). The delay necessitated a further extension of Article 50 or – as Johnson favoured (22 October 2019) – the abandonment of current legislation to 'accelerate plans for a no deal Brexit' (UK in a Changing Europe, 2021: 28). After initial opposition, Johnson secured enough support to call a new general election, giving the Conservatives a parliamentary majority (12 December 2019), allowing the government to pass the EU (Withdrawal Agreement) Bill (20 December 2019) and gain European Parliament approval (29 January 2020), allowing formal withdrawal from the EU (31 January 2020), followed by a 'transition period' until 31 December 2020 (UK in a Changing Europe, 2021: 31).

What forms of multi-level policy making are feasible (and fair)?

The Brexit process exposed long-standing debates about the feasibility and fairness of different ways to govern. Some focus on *technical feasibility*, to ask: can we identify an optimal division of policy-making functions? Optimality relates to problem-solving concerns, such as the efficiency of delivering services at different scales (for example, local or national), and the trade-offs between – say – the benefits of national or supranational uniformity (for example, if a programme works and should be rolled out) versus local flexibility (for example, if a programme is better tailored to each context) (Marks and Hooghe, 2000). It also relates to optimal ways to produce cooperation whenever multiple organisations are involved in policy delivery, such as to (1) avoid negative 'externalities', when the action of one has an unintended effect on another, and (2) maximise trust to minimise 'transactions costs' when designing and enforcing contracts (Swann and Kim, 2018).

Some focus on *political feasibility*, to ask: what are the competing demands to take or share control? They include UK calls to remove EU powers, territorial demands for devolved responsibilities or full independence, and local demands for greater autonomy. They relate partly to calls for government boundaries to match national, regional or local identity (Box 7.4). Further, there are regular tensions regarding which sectors or bodies should lead cross-cutting agendas (routine 'turf wars' can reflect professional or administrative tensions – Carey and Crammond, 2015).

These foci highlight two very different concerns: the *right to govern*, which often relates to demands for political autonomy, and, the *need to address policy problems*, which relates to functional requirements of policy making. Policy studies highlight a tendency to distribute policy-making functions in relation to political contestation, not the technical concerns of policy analysts. Indeed, the word 'technical' is often misleading, since 'optimality' is highly contested (Cairney et al, 2022a: 6).

Hooghe and Marks (2003: 233) combine these technical and political elements to argue that 'multi-level governance' should be defended: 'Centralized authority – command and control – has few advocates ... the dispersion of governance across multiple jurisdictions is both more efficient than, and normatively superior to, central state monopoly'. However, there are two different types (Hooghe and Marks, 2003: 236):

1. *Community or territorially focused.* The formal allocation of a collection of policy responsibilities to a small number of governments (for example, EU, UK, devolved), each with their own executive, legislative and judicial functions. The aim is a manageable number of authorities with clearly defined responsibilities.
2. *Task focused.* Many organisations cooperate to address the same problem. The aim is to generate positive responses to a problem from relevant organisations, emphasising flexibility, overlapping functions and collaboration.

In practice, we find combinations of both types. Regardless of the number of levels (for example, when removing the EU), we would still expect multi-level action to 'overlap continuously when governments produce different policy instruments to deal with the same problem' (Cairney, 2020a: 142). UK policy is made in the UK but not driven by one centre (John, 2018: 14). Further, contestation to define and address problems is a feature not only of national and regional policy making, but also intersectoral agendas within each jurisdiction (Cairney et al, 2022a: 6–7). For example, we find different intergovernmental relations in each case study chapter, from the strong 'four nations' approach to COVID-19 (Box 6.1) to unresolved tensions regarding who is responsible for energy policies (Box 8.2). It will also take time for many interest groups to identify which venues to lobby, following a bruising period in which policy changed against their wishes (Richardson, 2018b).

Insights from critical policy analysis prompt us to modify these questions to focus on inequalities in policy and policy making. First, can we identify the equivalent of an optimal division of policy making to reduce inequalities? Cairney et al (2022a: 38, 52, 70, 108, 153, 166) say no. Governments or policy designers may describe that aim in the abstract, but concrete discussions reveal routine contestation on who should do what and why. Further, 'even if there was an optimal level, it does not explain why competences are placed where they are ... their distribution is the outcome of political contestation in which claims to functional efficiency compete with interests, identities, and ideologies' (Cairney et al, 2022a: 6). Their case studies of multi-level policy making – to foster health, education, and gender equity agendas across the EU – identify many models, each producing modest impacts on inequalities.

Second, can we envisage more inclusive forms of policy making – such as collaborative governance between governments and stakeholders – dedicated to reducing inequalities? This language could be part of the Brexit story, in which a reallocation of policy-making functions kickstarts a fairer, more democratic and more prosperous UK (Davis, 2016; Johnson, 2016a; Spencer and Oppermann, 2020). It was used frequently when UK and devolved governments pursued 'preventive' policies to address the impact of social and economic inequalities on health and education (Cairney and St Denny, 2020). Most recently, this commitment is a feature of the vague UK government 'Levelling Up' agenda devoted to improving outcomes associated with 'left behind' populations and districts (Martin et al, 2022). Such aims tend not to lead to radical changes to policy; they do not come with a commitment to use tax and spending to redistribute resources (Bentley et al, 2010; Cocks, 2013; Pike et al, 2018; Jennings et al, 2021). Nor do they prompt policy-making reforms, such as greater 'localism', largely because the same governments also seek the benefits of Westminster-style centralisation (Chapter 3).

What was the actual consequence of Brexit on policy and policy making?

At the time of writing, the UK had experienced two years of non-EU membership, which makes it difficult to identify a substantive Brexit effect on

Table 7.1: Examples of policy changes following Brexit

Sector	Policy change
Immigration	A 'points based' system (with minimum-income requirements), initially to prioritise 'skilled' occupations then high-need sectors such as agriculture (following a mass exit of EU citizens – Wadsworth, 2018; Sumption and Kierans, 2021; Portes, 2022a; 2022b).
Trade	The EU–UK Trade and Cooperation Agreement (TCA) created new restrictions (reducing exports/imports by 7 per cent/14 per cent – Fusacchia et al, 2022). Several international trade agreements replicated agreements that the UK had enjoyed via the EU.
Financial services	UK financial institutions lost 'passporting rights' to do business in the EU. The UK government has yet to deregulate financial services to the extent proposed during Brexit debates (Hall and Heneghan, 2022).
Agriculture and fish (Chapter 8)	The UK government phased out the Common Agricultural Policy, replacing it with schemes to incentivise environmentally sustainable behaviours (Little and Lyon, 2022). The TCA replaces UK Common Fisheries Policy obligations, with a small increase in quotas in UK waters, but more onerous trade regulations (Connolly et al, 2020).
Climate change and energy (Chapter 8)	The Environment Act 2021 and other measures replace EU directives. The Act contradicts the idea that Brexit would remove environmental regulations seen as burdensome, costly and unnecessary (Burns, 2020; Jordan, 2022). Nor did the UK end VAT on energy bills or make new arrangements for nuclear materials (Watson and Drummond, 2022).
Crime and justice	The Human Rights Act remains in place (the European Convention on Human Rights is not an EU initiative). The draft Bill of Rights (2022) was designed to replace key elements (Reuters, 2022). Criminal law remains relatively untouched (Mitsilegas, 2020).
Health	Brexit's £350 million extra per week for the NHS did not materialise. Speculation that the government would encourage more private sector involvement in the health service was confirmed in August 2023 (Health Foundation, 2018; Dayan, 2021; Rogers, 2023).
Devolution and governance	The UK promised to send relevant repatriated powers to devolved governments, but the latter argue that this process did not happen (Torrance, 2020). Subnational institutions in England have some increased responsibilities (Hadfield and Turner, 2021).

policy as a whole (Table 7.1). There have been major changes in relation to salient issues, including the ending of the free movement of EU citizens, and new trading rules to replace the EU customs union and single market. Otherwise, policy change was modest, with no 'big bang' of 'major divergence from EU rules' (Reland et al, 2022: 4).

The more immediate impact was uncertainty during negotiation and transition, delaying plans for policy change and making life difficult for organisations seeking to adapt. For example, a new regime for trade regulations was onerous on small businesses, and the loss of EU schemes – in relation to regional economic investment, agriculture (Chapter 8), and university funding and student mobility schemes – necessitated a quick transition to new (and often less ambitious) arrangements (Swatridge, 2021; Brien, 2022: 15; Marshall and Mills-Sheehy,

2022). The future impact is less clear, even to the most vocal proponents of Brexit. For example, in June 2022, Jacob Rees-Mogg – when Minister of State for Brexit Opportunities and Government Efficiency – asked *Daily Express* readers for ideas to take advantage of Brexit. The response was calls to (for example) remove EU regulations on electrical products and vehicles (Maddox, 2022). Boris Johnson had also announced a plan to abolish hundreds of EU regulations in a 'bonfire', without providing details.

The impact on policy making is also uncertain, but early accounts identify a tendency of the UK government to seek centralisation. Ward (2021) and Ward and Ward (2021) describe the 'power hoarding' of the May and Johnson-led governments, while Baldini et al (2018; 2022b) suggest that Brexit has prompted some movement back to a 'majoritarian' UK system.

Critical policy analysis: who wins or loses from Brexit?

The UK government sought to describe Brexit as a 'success story' (Brusenbauch Meislová, 2023), but success and failure is contested and unequal. If we rely on Leave rhetoric, we would expect Brexit to have the biggest positive impact on the voters 'left behind' or damaged by EU integration, globalisation and deindustrialisation. They were concentrated in towns in the north and Midlands of England, in places like Sunderland and Stoke, 'as the emblematic sites of a "revolt" against the "establishment" and globalization; sometimes rendered as "Brexitland" in media and social media accounts' (Sykes, 2018: 148). This rhetoric builds on narratives of an English north/south divide which comes at the expense of a northern working class (McCann and Ortega-Argilés, 2021). Yet, Fetzer and Wang (2020) find that the immediate negative consequences of Brexit were felt more heavily in these areas, particularly in districts with lower levels of education. Increased restrictions on trade exacerbate the impact on manufacturing areas. Further, there has been a loss of EU investment in regions, with replacement funding – such as the Towns Fund – not as large as the amount lost (Arnold and Pendleton, 2019).

The worst Leave rhetoric suggests that the biggest negative impact should be for people who had sought the benefit of migration to the UK, or whose way of life challenges romantic stories of the British past. Further, populist rhetoric tends to contribute to the further marginalisation of less powerful groups, such as threatening women's, LGBTQIA+, and minority ethnic and immigrant rights (Bugaric and Kuhelj, 2018; Guerrina et al, 2018; Dustin et al, 2019; Kurylo, 2021; Rawad et al, 2021).

In that context, Hepburn (2020) identifies 137 negative 'social and equality' impacts to Brexit. Many resulted from the loss of EU legal rights, with no guarantee that they will be replicated by the UK. She identifies 'potential impacts across equalities groups, including the loss of legal rights, employment protections, funding opportunities, healthcare rights, and impacts on food, fuel, and medicines' as well as 'employment, housing, spending/consumer and wider community impacts' (Hepburn, 2019: 5). It highlights direct impacts on three social groups in particular:

1. Minority ethnic groups received a heightened amount of 'explicit racial, ethnic and religious intolerance' (UN Special Rapporteur on Racism, 2018; Nandi and Luthra, 2021). Many will lose protections from EU legislation, including employment rights which protect against discrimination, or lose direct support from European Structural and Investment Funds which assist minority ethnic populations (Hepburn, 2020). Further, the UK government is fostering a hostile immigration system to address asylum seeking to the UK via entry to the EU (Alexandre-Collier, 2022; Chapter 10).
2. Women lost economic and social rights, such as the Pregnant Worker's Directive and the Agency Worker's Directive (Hepburn, 2020: 30), while European Structural Funds provided support and training for women (Mott et al, 2018; Gupta, 2020).
3. Disabled people lost guarantees of rights (for example, related to non-discrimination) in the EU Charter of Fundamental Rights and the loss of recourse to the Court of Justice of the European Union, while one-fifth of the money allocated from European Structural Funds benefited disabled people (Sayce and Lawson, 2017; Hepburn, 2020; Whitmore, 2020). They could also suffer a loss of health and social services due to the consequences of tighter immigration rules on the EU.

Such reports also identify the impact of economic slowdown following Brexit (and COVID-19) (Francis-Devine et al, 2022). Minority ethnic populations are more likely to work in public sector roles vulnerable to service reductions, or low-paid jobs in the private sector (Runnymede Trust, 2018; Hepburn, 2020). UK government budget cuts have a disproportionately negative impact on women (Mott et al, 2018). Disabled people are more likely to live in poverty (due to the extra costs and barriers they face), while budget cuts hit services for disabled people (Hepburn, 2020; Whitmore, 2020). These issues reached crisis point in 2022, following a profound rise in the cost of living (Bell, 2022).

It is more difficult to identify genuine winners from Brexit. They may include some UK manufacturers (if they benefit from new UK rules on product specifications) and non-UK financial institutions (if they can exploit the loss of UK financial passports) (Scott, 2023). There is also growing demand for Brexit-related services, such as to advise on new customs rules, while many hedge funds and currency traders have been able to exploit crisis for financial gain (Fletcher and Martin, 2019; Jones, 2020; Thevoz, 2022). The people who have benefited most seem to enjoy close proximity to powerful policy makers, reflecting questionable public standards (Barrington, 2021). More generally, some groups 'win' because they are more able to weather the effects of slow economic growth and a cost of living crisis.

Conclusion: How does Brexit inform our Westminster and complex government stories?

The 'take back control' narrative is built on the Westminster story of UK policy making driven by a powerful centre of government in the UK, legitimised by a sovereign Parliament. While Brexit symbolises the success of that basic ambition, the Brexit *process* exposed the limits to UK central control. Ridiculous stories in 2016, of the likely ease of negotiations, gave way to the reality of major EU influence and an enduring legacy of UK membership of the EU (compare Zappettini and Krzyżanowski, 2019; Gstöhl and Phinnemore, 2021). Nor did the UK government get its way during the passage of EU withdrawal legislation through Parliament. The government endured years of delays and defeats, provoking multiple crises of leadership that threatened to derail Brexit or bring down the UK government. While these events demonstrated the power of Parliament, they also exposed the inability of the government and Parliament to function well enough to produce a clear resolution to an ostensibly simple policy problem (McConnell and Tormey, 2020: 695–697). These events also caused the shortened premierships of Cameron and May, which created a path for Johnson to produce a form of Brexit that suited Eurosceptic rhetoric but not their promises for improved policy and policy making. The overall effect is a UK political system with a damaged reputation and unclear future (more than seven years after the vote).

Brexit prompts us to change *somewhat* how we describe the complex government story. On the one hand, the removal of an important level of policy making reduces the need for multi-level cooperation and responsibility sharing. The *choice* to pursue Brexit is to simplify the formal division of powers in the UK (while maintaining the devolution or delegation of some powers). On the other hand, policy-making complexity is a *necessity*, reflecting bounded rationality and the inevitable delegation of policy making to a large number and wide range of actors across the UK political system. In that context, Chapter 8 is key to the consideration of a post-Brexit approach to existential issues such as climate change. Each case study helps to warn against the impression that one – albeit profound – change to the UK political system changes the ability to produce appropriate policy change in a complex policy-making system.

Brexit has also created the conditions to threaten the security, wellbeing and financial position of the most vulnerable groups in society. So far, we find strikingly few substantive winners from Brexit, and a great number of losers. We find a troubling drift towards populism in politics which may exacerbate regressive policies which remove safeguards from women, disabled people and minority ethnic people. The current economic stagnation, higher cost of living and punitive welfare system also produce highly unequal impacts. As Chapter 9 shows, recession and state retrenchment hit marginalised groups hard. Therefore, Brexit represents not just a policy fiasco as a process, but also real-world impacts to those who lack the resources and power to comfortably ride it out.

8

Environmental Policy: Climate Change and Sustainability

Chapter highlights

1. **Climate change** is an existential crisis requiring global and domestic cooperation to secure rapid and radical policy change.

2. There is a large gap between requirements and reality. Environmental issues receive fleeting attention, reforms have not produced the required outcomes, and other policies undermine their progress.

3. Three approaches highlight key perspectives on these issues:

   - Policy analysis identifies how to address environmental crises. For example, what policy instruments are technically and politically feasible?
   - Policy studies identify how governments address the impacts of climate change. Which policies have governments favoured, and what has been their impact? How coherent is their approach to climate change, energy, transport and food policies?
   - Critical policy analysis identifies and challenges inequitable processes and outcomes. Does policy address *climate justice* as well as climate change?

Introduction: Climate change as the ultimate 'wicked' problem

Climate change exhibits every known problem in policy and policy making. It is an existential crisis that has not been addressed adequately by current policies. It exemplifies the gap between what is required to address the problem and what actually happens. The requirement is for continuously high policy-maker attention and for governments to collaborate: *with each other*, to connect domestic and global policy agendas; *within government*, to join up policy

Climate change: 'long-term shifts in temperatures and weather patterns. ... Since the 1800s, human activities have been the main driver of climate change. ... Burning fossil fuels generates greenhouse gas emissions that act like a blanket wrapped around the Earth, trapping the sun's heat and raising temperatures. ... Clearing land and forests can also release carbon dioxide. Landfills for garbage are a major source of methane emissions. Energy, industry, transport, buildings, agriculture and land use are among the main emitters' (UN, 2022).

across many sectors; and, *with non-governmental actors*, to harness stakeholder ideas and connect government policy to the behaviour of businesses. Yet, the reality does not come close.

The rise of attention to environmental problems had *some* effect on policies on energy, transport and agriculture. Rising concern about climate change encouraged policy makers to reframe well-established policy aims, to:

- Transform energy systems from high to low carbon, such as by increasing renewable energy and energy efficiency, and reducing demand for fossil fuels.
- Encourage shifts in social and business behaviour, such as to use public transport and reduce car journeys and air flights.
- Encourage sustainable development in food production, including farming and fishing.

However, climate change enjoys only fleeting attention. It leads to policy change that is insubstantial compared to the size of the problem, especially when ambitious strategies lack follow-through. Globally, there is increasing evidence of coordinated activity, but without producing and enforcing substantive obligations. Domestically, there are frequent references to joining-up policy, and collaborative policy making inside and outside of government, but with limited effects. Multi-centric policy making results partly from the *choice* to share responsibilities, but also *necessity*, to reflect the inability of a single centre of government to control policy choices and outcomes, and the fragmentation of responsibilities across many levels of government and types of organisation. The end result may be 'tragedy' (Box 8.1).

This chapter examines these issues through three lenses. First, policy analysis identifies how to analyse environmental policy as a series of interconnected policy problems, including:

- What targets should governments and international organisations adopt to address climate change?
- What solutions would be technically and politically feasible?
- What are the trade-offs between each solution?

Second, policy studies situate this analysis in real-world developments, to note:

- The *eventual* shift from paying minimal to high attention to climate change.
- The multi-centric nature of policy making, with responsibilities spread across many centres, and outcomes driven by business and individual behaviour.
- A lack of coherent policy in energy, transport and food production.
- A tendency to prioritise economic growth over environmental concerns.

Third, critical policy analysis identifies who benefits or loses, and how to respond:

- Who bears most of the responsibility, and costs, of climate change?
- Who should bear the costs for policy changes towards sustainability?
- Can we envisage more inclusive *policy making*, including between governments and stakeholders, and *policy*, including climate and energy justice policies?

In the conclusion, we use the Westminster and complex government stories to reflect on the extent to which UK and other governments are likely to overcome the problems they face. These stories provide different ways to come to the same depressing conclusion.

Box 8.1: Climate change as a super wicked problem

Levin et al (2012: 124–126) identify a major gap between knowledge of the policy problem and current solution. There is a scientific consensus on the urgency of climate change, but it does not translate into a proportionate and effective response. They relate this gap to the 'super wicked' nature of climate change. Rittel and Webber (1973) had described 'wicked' problems to challenge too-simple approaches to policy analysis, when:

- The policy problem defies simple definition and understanding.
- The problem's definition and alleged cause is contested.
- The cause may be a symptom of another problem, or too complex to be compared to problems addressed in the past.
- It is impossible to know if all solutions have been identified, or if a problem is solved.
- Trial and error is difficult, since errors have major social consequences (Rittel and Webber, 1973: 161–167).

Super wicked problems have additional properties (Levin et al, 2012: 127–128):

1. 'Time is running out.' The problem becomes more acute when solutions are not found.
2. 'Those seeking to end the problem are also causing it.' Countries like the UK help to lead the climate change agenda, but are major contributors of emissions.
3. 'No central authority.' There are global policy agreements to tackle climate change, but each government is responsible for its own implementation.
4. 'Policies discount the future irrationally.' Actors place too little value on policies with long-term benefits and too much on short-term costs.

Levin et al (2012: 135–136) describe a likely 'tragedy' unless policy makers can make a *credible commitment*. They need to 'lock in' new behaviour via path dependence, in which the benefits of maintaining – and costs of reversing – policies increase over time (see also Auld et al, 2021).

Policy analysis: how to address the policy problem

Step 1: How could governments define climate change as a policy problem?

Greenhouse gases (GHGs): gases in the atmosphere – including 'water vapour, carbon dioxide, methane, and nitrous oxide' – that absorb solar energy and redistribute it as heat ('greenhouse effect'). Rising GHGs contribute to global warming (The Royal Society, 2022).

Global warming: the rising heat of the Earth's surface, contributing to climate change (see also **1.5°C and 2°C**).

Intergovernmental Panel on Climate Change (IPCC): described by the United Nations Framework Convention on Climate Change (UNFCCC, 2022a) as 'an independent body ... [which] assesses the scientific literature and provides vital scientific information to the climate change process ... [its reports] are widely recognized as the most credible sources of information on climate change'. IPCC supporters highlight the remarkably high extent to which scientific experts support its findings, with reference to its: 'rigorous selection process – they must be leading experts in their fields'; '721 scientists from 90 countries'; extensive peer review processes; and mechanisms to allow governments to describe the policy relevance of IPCC reviews without interfering in their production (Harris, 2021).

An environmental policy problem is not the same as a physical problem. Actors combine evidence and persuasion to draw attention to one problem definition, which includes an account of: the problem's size (including severity and urgency), its cause, who it affects, and the extent to which the state should intervene (Chapter 2).

First, they debate what to *call the problem*. Terms such as **greenhouse gases (GHGs)**, **global warming** and climate change represent an attempt to incorporate problem definition into the everyday language of politicians, media and the public.

Second, they debate who has the *authority to define the problem*. The assignment of scientific authority is highly politicised. The production of authoritative, policy-relevant reports require scientific rigour and political diplomacy (De Pryck, 2021). In countries like the US, climate change attracts intense partisan debate, fuelled by climate change experts and sceptics. Scientists can project their scientific authority in relation to professional rules that emphasise their objectivity and separation from party politics. Or, they might treat advocacy for policy change as part of their professional responsibilities. For example, Oreskes and Conway (2010: 2–7) describe the **Intergovernmental Panel on Climate Change (IPCC)** as 'the world's leading authority on climate issues', to:

- support most scientists who follow established rules (relating to research methods to produce evidence and peer review to validate it); and
- reject the claims to authority made by the bad faith actors – a 'handful' of scientists and many 'think tanks and private

corporations' – trying to create doubt about the quality of scientific evidence on the 'reality of global warming', its human cause, and the need for policy change to mitigate and adapt to the effects.

Partisan debates in the UK seem less polarised since the main political parties support policies to address climate change. Still, there is concern about the too-high influence of climate deniers in media coverage (see also van Eck and Feindt, 2022 on 'activist blogs'). The BBC accepted criticism that its format to ensure balanced debate – to interview someone for and against – created 'false balance' with actors who reject mainstream scientific findings (Fahy, 2017; Nerlich, 2017).

In that context, if we relied on the IPCC's findings, what would we discover about climate change? In a nutshell, it is caused by humans (not simply a natural occurrence) and represents an existential crisis:

> Human-induced climate change, including more frequent and intense extreme events, has caused widespread adverse impacts and related losses and damages to nature and people. ... The rise in weather and climate extremes has led to some irreversible impacts as natural and human systems are pushed beyond their ability to adapt. ... Widespread, pervasive impacts to ecosystems, people, settlements, and infrastructure have resulted from observed increases in the frequency and intensity of climate and weather extremes, including hot extremes on land and in the ocean, heavy precipitation events, drought and fire weather. (IPCC, 2022: 11)

The IPCC (2022: 7–13) describes worrying global trends in relation to extreme events, degrading ecosystems and natural resources, and the rising human costs of climate change. These trends will increase in line with global warming, to reduce biodiversity and produce crises in water availability and crop production, fire and flooding (IPCC, 2022: 15–19).

Step 2: Identifying feasible solutions

Policy analysis connects technical and political feasibility (Chapter 2). The IPCC (2022: 23) does it *to some extent*, by (1) describing technically feasible solutions, and (2) describing solutions vaguely to avoid undermining their political feasibility: 'Integrated, multi-sectoral solutions that address social inequities, differentiate responses based on climate risk and cut across systems, increase the feasibility and effectiveness of adaptation in multiple sectors'.

Negotiations to produce international agreements have also helped to manage political feasibility by setting broad, non-legally binding objectives. They allow countries to sign without overcommitting. In that context, the UNFCCC (2022b) described the **Paris Agreement** as a 'landmark' because, 'for the first time, a binding agreement brings all nations into a common cause

Paris Agreement: 'Legally binding international treaty on climate change ... adopted by 196 **Parties** at **COP** 21 in Paris' in 2015 (UNFCCC, 2022b).

Parties: the 197 organisations (usually country governments) developing and signing international agreements.

COP: Conference of the Parties. The 'supreme decision-making body' of the UNFCCC (2022c). Annual meetings began in 1995 (Kyoto was 3, Copenhagen 15, Paris 21).

UNFCCC: United Nations Framework Convention on Climate Change (from 1992).

1.5°C and 2°C: The Paris Agreement describes restricting global warming to 2°C (preferably 1.5°C) above 'pre-industrial levels'. The IPCC (2019: 4) estimates warming at 0.8–1.2°C, rising 0.1–0.3°C per decade, with 1.5°C to be reached between 2030 and 2052.

to undertake ambitious efforts to combat climate change and adapt to its effects'. It sets a target – a 'Long Term Global Goal' – for global warming 'to well below **2°C** above pre-industrial levels and to pursue efforts to limit the temperature increase to **1.5°C**' (UN, 2015: 3).

Setting a target would (1) encourage a peak of GHG emissions, (2) recognise that developed countries produce disproportionately high emissions, and (3) exhort them to provide financial support for developing countries when their climate actions undermine economic growth (although the definition of developed, and contributions, were contested – Dimitrov, 2016: 4–5; Schipani, 2017; Arlota, 2019).

The processes to determine technical and political feasibility are inseparable, such as when setting the Long Term Global Goal (Livingston and Rummukainen, 2020). Most negotiations took place in secret and the results were based on negotiations to minimise legally enforceable obligations on developed countries (Dimitrov, 2016: 6–7). The Paris Agreement's (UN, 2015) first two pages focus on political feasibility by listing a dozen reasons to qualify its ambitions. Article 6 accepts that some governments prefer not to regulate individual and business behaviour. Further, it does not define what 'pre-industrial levels' were (King et al, 2017), preferring to reach political agreement then ask the IPCC (2019) to coordinate further research. These moves reflect previous failures to mandate country action (during COP15), contributing to a shift towards recognising national autonomy and voluntary pledges (Falkner, 2016).

Steps 3 and 4: Using values and goals to compare solutions, and predicting the outcomes of solutions

There are many cost-benefit analyses of climate change policies, but their impact is questionable because few policy makers read them and many models do not incorporate political feasibility. In contrast, the **Stern Review** made a UK and international impact. It produced a cost-benefit case to address climate change: 'if we don't act, the overall costs and risks of climate change will be equivalent to losing at least 5% of global GDP each year, now and forever. ... In contrast, the costs of action ... can be limited to around 1% of global GDP each year' (Stern, 2006: vi; see also Markandya

> **Stern Review**: report in 2006 to HM Treasury on 'The Economics of Climate Change', chaired by Professor Nicholas Stern.

et al, 2018). Stern argued that insufficient action would lead to 2°C warming in a few decades, while a 5°C warming was likely in the longer term. Further, poorer countries would cause the least but suffer the most damage. It called for a reduction of emissions to 80 per cent of 1990 levels, via reduced demand, increased clean energy, and international cooperation to ration and trade emissions, foster innovation (including carbon capture schemes) and tackle deforestation (Stern, 2006: vi–ix).

Step 5: Making recommendations

Policy analysis texts advise that recommendations should be simple and punchy to make the problem seem solvable and the solution seem feasible. Yet, environmental policy defies simple analysis, and a list of technically and politically feasible solutions is generally absent from international agreements.

What exactly is UK environmental policy?

Defining 'environmental policy' is not straightforward since it covers so many areas. The Comparative Policy Agendas project (1) describes 'policies relating to water, waste disposal, air pollution, climate change, recycling, forest protection, land and coastal protection' as environmental, and (2) notes the connection to energy, agriculture and transport (John et al, 2013: 79). This definition raises three key points.

First, a broad range of activities, with blurry boundaries between them, makes it difficult to map the multi-level and multi-sectoral landscape (Box 1.2). For example, ecosystems policies focus on protecting the natural environment, such as to reduce air pollution, maintain a clean water supply, restrict sewage in rivers and seas, reduce waste going to landfill, protect fish stocks and minimise the damage of farming to land.

Policy-making responsibilities have long been multi-level by design. From the Single European Act 1986 until Brexit (Chapter 7), the EU took primary responsibility for environmental policies, and it already had responsibilities in agriculture and fish. It produced multiple changes (including **regulations** and **directives**) that obliged

> **Regulation**: a 'binding legislative act' that 'must be applied in its entirety across the EU'.
>
> **Directive**: a 'legislative act that sets out a goal that all EU

countries must achieve', with member state discretion to set their own laws.

Recommendation: non-binding legislation to encourage member states to improve policy (European Union, 2022).

Westminster legislation (and made many **recommendations**). The devolved governments took on responsibility for the administration of these obligations, with the UK responsible for monitoring their progress. Since 2020, the UK repatriated this responsibility (Maishman, 2022).

Second, if it is difficult to map responsibilities, it is harder to join up responsibilities to create a cross-cutting agenda – environmentally sustainable policies – and ensure that reforms are equitable. Governments set up dedicated departments or units to join up the activities of many departments (and governmental organisations), but they are often too small to direct others (Rayner and Jordan, 2016: 177; Sasse et al, 2020: 41).

Third, governments may try to 'mainstream' a policy aim into the work of other bodies via legislation or guidance. However, each potential contributor to a wider agenda has its own way to define and address problems. Policy makers in each sector may be also be addressing their own problems of policy incoherence (Alons, 2017: 1606). The classic example is the tension between policies to support environmental or economic policies. Our discussion of climate change shows that UK governments now pay attention, but seek to make solutions consistent with higher priority goals such as economic growth.

How did the UK and devolved governments respond to climate change?

Environmental issues remained low on the policy agenda until a dramatic rise in attention in the mid-2000s. John et al (2013: 79–80) describe:

- 'Little or no attention' in the 1950s and early 1960s.
- A brief 'spike in attention' from 1970 to 1971 to reflect late 1960s attention to pollution.

Chernobyl crisis: a disaster in 1986 at the Chernobyl nuclear plant (Ukraine, then in the USSR). It produced a major human and environmental toll, prompting governments to review the safety of nuclear power (International Chernobyl Project, 1991).

- Rising activity from the late 1980s following EU obligations. By 1991, environmental policy accounted for 15 per cent of Westminster legislation.
- The 'sudden prominence on the public agenda' in 1989 to coincide with growing public attention to ecological crises (and response to **Chernobyl**).
- 'Growing concern about climate change since 2005 ... with the issue now framed as an urgent societal risk' (John et al, 2013: 140).

How has the UK government defined the problem?

Policy-maker attention, and problem definition, changed markedly from the mid-2000s (Carter, 2014: 425). Multiple sources demonstrated that climate change 'would be much more severe than previously acknowledged', including authoritative IPCC reports, eye-catching films such as *An Inconvenient Truth*, and the Stern Review (Anderson et al, 2008; Carter, 2014: 426; Carter and Jacobs, 2014: 131). Stern signalled the need to reconcile environmental and economic aims (backed by Chancellor Gordon Brown and Prime Minister Tony Blair). Groups such as Friends of the Earth led high-profile campaigns to strengthen climate change policies (Carter and Childs, 2018; Carter and Little, 2021; Crawley et al, 2021). Climate change went from being the responsibility of a single department of the environment to multiple departments, including energy (Lovell et al, 2009: 91).

The push for policy change received high public and media attention, cross-party support, parliamentary weight (multiple committees had criticised government policy as insufficient), and limited vocal opposition by businesses, many of which followed Stern in proposing climate-friendly technologies to boost economic growth (Carter and Jacobs, 2014: 131–132, 135). There was a brief but strong 'competitive consensus', from 2006 to 2008, in which both leaders treated climate change as a **valence issue** (Carter and Clements, 2015: 205). The governing party (led by Blair) and opposition party (David Cameron) competed to establish their green credentials (Carter and Jacobs, 2014: 137; Lockwood, 2021: S32). This dynamic reinforced the motive and opportunity of Labour ministers to propose rapid and radical changes to policy (Carter and Jacobs, 2014: 134–136).

> **Valence issue**: when there is high public consensus (who would *not* want to address climate change?). If party positions are similar, they focus on governing competence.

What climate change commitments did UK governments introduce?

The UK went from 'laggard to leader' in relation to climate change commitments (Kern et al, 2014; Tangney and Howes, 2016). For most of the post-war period, it had a 'reputation for environmental policy neglect' (Tangney and Howes, 2016: 1120). Until 2006, the Labour government made promises but not major changes. Its environment department lacked the 'political clout' to make other departments 'prioritize climate change objectives' (Carter, 2014: 424). Brown was dissuaded from driving climate policies from the Treasury: in 1999, when businesses opposed a large 'Climate Change Levy', and, in 2000, when taxes on fuel contributed to the price rises and 'fuel protests led by hauliers and farmers' to bring 'the country to a virtual standstill' (Carter, 2014: 424). By 2006, the tax yield of 'fuel duties, air passenger duties, and the Climate Change

MtCO2e: million metric tons
of carbon dioxide equivalent
(to gauge GHG emissions).

**1990 levels (GHG
emissions)**: the UK
emitted 793.8 MtCO2e
in 1990, including carbon
dioxide (595.7), methane
(132.5), nitrous oxide (48.2),
hydrofluorocarbons (14.4),
perfluorocarbons (1.7) and
sulphur hexafluoride (1.3).
Emissions were 642.7 in
2008 and 451.5 by 2018
(Department for Business,
Energy & Industrial Strategy,
2020; I. Bolton, 2021).

Carbon budget: a maximum
of GHGs that the UK
can emit in a five-year
period. The Committee
on Climate Change makes
the recommendation to
government. The first cap was
3018 MtCO2e (for 2008–
2012), and the sixth agreed
cap is 965 (for 2033–2037)
(Department for Business,
Energy & Industrial Strategy,
2021). The first two targets (up
to 2017) were 'comfortably
met' (Lockwood, 2021: S26).

Levy' had *dropped* since 2000 (Carter, 2014: 424–425). The UK government's targets were modest – to reduce the UK's GHG emissions by 2–3 'million tonnes of carbon dioxide equivalent' (**MtCO2e**) per year – and without strong measures to achieve them (Carter and Jacobs, 2014: 125; Boswell and Rodrigues, 2016: 517–518).

After 2006, the Labour government produced 'radical policy change', with 'highly ambitious new policy objectives backed by a series of major policy initiatives' (Carter and Jacobs, 2014: 125). They included the 'pioneering' Climate Change Act 2008 to increase the government's emissions reduction targets and give them statutory weight, to coincide with UK government support for new EU targets (Carter and Jacobs, 2014: 125). The aim was to generate a 'credible commitment' to long-term change that would transcend changes of government (even though a UK Parliament cannot use legislation to bind its successors) (McHarg, 2011; Box 8.1). It legislated to set ambitious targets (by historic and international standards): a drop of 9 MtCO2e per year, culminating in a 34 per cent drop by 2020 and 80 per cent by 2050, compared to **1990 levels** (Carter and Jacobs, 2014: 125–126, 130). A focus on targets included setting a **carbon budget** every five years.

These targets would be met largely through 'much more interventionist energy policy' (Carter and Jacobs, 2014: 136), to manage:

- *supply*, by increasing the contribution of renewables to energy supply (15 per cent overall, 30 per cent in electricity) by 2020, and enabling new nuclear power stations (Carter and Jacobs, 2014: 130);
- *demand* and *efficiency*, such a via 'zero carbon homes' targets and smart energy meters, and subsidies for electric vehicles (Carter and Jacobs, 2014: 130).

The Labour government also pursued reforms to policy making. In 2006, it established the Office for Climate Change to coordinate policy across departments and lead the development of the Climate Change Bill (Carter and Jacobs, 2014: 135). In 2008, it created an independent Committee on Climate Change (CCC) to produce recommendations (for example, on the size of the carbon budget), and the new Department for Energy and Climate Change (DECC) to lead policies to meet targets (Carter and Jacobs, 2014: 136). Still, despite appearances, '[c]limate change was never a top priority for No 10 or the Treasury', leaving DECC to use statutory targets to keep climate change on the policy agenda and oblige other departments – such as in transport, trade, and industry – to act (Boswell and Rodrigues, 2016: 518).

Did climate change survive changes of UK government?

Carter (2014: 429) describes the breakdown of the 'competitive consensus'. The coalition government (2010–2015) was less committed to environmental policies. Climate change returned from a valence to a contested issue, with 'limited direct electoral benefits' (Carter and Clements, 2015: 205–209). The 'political sustainability' of the Climate Change Act has been in doubt ever since (Lockwood, 2013), albeit in the context of EU-obligated emissions reduction strategies (Lockwood, 2021: S28).

While Cameron had favoured state intervention, he faced opposition from the 'Conservative right', who described intervention as 'unwarranted', particularly when driven by the EU or in relation to hot topics such as onshore wind farms (Carter, 2014: 429; Carter and Clements, 2015: 216). Further, Chancellor George Osborne opposed cutting emissions more quickly than other EU states if it made the UK less economically competitive. He also 'made several moves that were inconsistent with a low carbon strategy', including economic support for offshore and onshore oil and gas (Lockwood, 2013: 1340; Carter, 2014: 430; Porter et al, 2015).

The Liberal Democrats led the 'green' agenda in the coalition, and their coalition agreement 'promised the "greenest government ever"', with commitments to: establish and give £3 billion funding to a Green Investment Bank (but delaying its ability to borrow), produce 'a Green Deal supporting household energy efficiency', set 'a minimum floor price for carbon', and oppose Heathrow airport expansion (Carter and Clements, 2015: 212; Carter and Little, 2021: 7). However, the Green Deal replaced a *government subsidy*, 'an obligation on energy utilities to supply energy saving measures funded by domestic energy bills', with a *household loan* 'fixed to the building and repaid through energy bills'; it 'was widely regarded as a policy failure' when few signed up (Carter and Clements, 2015: 212). Further, the coalition abolished advisory bodies as part of its 'cull of quangos' – including the Royal Commission for Environmental Pollution – and reduced funding to the Environment Agency and Natural England as part of austerity (Carter and Clements, 2015: 212–213; Chapter 9).

In the run-up to the 2015 election, the Conservatives, Labour and the Liberal Democrats produced a 'joint climate pledge' which – ultimately – 'did little to advance the climate agenda' (Carter and Little, 2021: 8). The Conservative government reduced support for renewable energy, sold the Green Investment Bank, dropped the 'zero-carbon home commitment', cut tax incentives for electric cars, supported Heathrow airport expansion, disbanded DECC, and moved climate change to the new (2016) Department for Business, Energy and Industrial Strategy (BEIS) (O'Neill and Gibbs, 2020; Carter and Little, 2021: 8; Lockwood, 2021: S26; BEIS was partly replaced by the Department for Energy Security and Net Zero in 2023). That said, it realised that meeting carbon targets was 'easier than feared', which kept 'the Conservative leadership engaged with the decarbonisation agenda' (Lockwood, 2021: S40).

The 'competitive consensus' returned somewhat during the 2019 election campaign. It was 'encouraged by the high-profile school climate strikes and Extinction Rebellion protests', which prompted the forthcoming Conservative government to produce a **net zero** emissions target by 2050, 'backed by rather vague ... commitments, including modest investments in energy efficiency, extensive tree planting, and working "with the market" to deliver 2 million green jobs' (Carter and Little, 2021: 8).

> **Net zero**: the amount of new GHGs entering the atmosphere is matched by the removal of GHGs.

Did the devolved governments define and address the problem differently?

The 2008 Act requires devolved governments to produce a five-yearly National Adaptation Programme report. It makes them accountable for the planning and delivery of policies to meet climate change targets, albeit in a multi-level context where (1) EU policies had set a baseline for emission reduction aims, and (2) the UK government retains responsibility for policy in key sectors (for example, energy). The UK and devolved political parties also have similar positions, but with a tendency for Scottish and Welsh governments to signal higher ambitions, and the potential for policy divergence to accelerate a 'race to the top' (McEwen and Bomberg, 2014: 64; Tangney and Howes, 2016: 1121; see also Nesom and MacKillop, 2021). For example, the Scottish and Welsh governments tied their sustainable economy ambitions to proposed expansions in renewable energy (Royles and McEwen, 2015: 1041–1043). Further, the three devolved governments have substantial powers to direct local authorities and public bodies.

The Scottish Parliament's Climate Change (Scotland) Act (2009) became, 'at the time, the world's most ambitious climate change legislation' because: (1) its interim target – reducing GHG emissions by 42 per cent by 2020 (1990 levels) – topped the UK target of 34 per cent (although both committed to 80 per cent by 2050); and (2) responsibility for progress rested with all Scottish government ministers (Nash, 2021: 1024–1025). It had international agenda-setting potential since it coincided with discussions on how to produce a 'global climate treaty replacing the expiring Kyoto Protocol' (Nash, 2021: 1030). During bill scrutiny, Scottish parties engaged in a 'bidding war', prompting a shift from the minority Scottish National Party (SNP) government's initial preference of 34 per cent (based on CCC recommendations) to cross-party agreement on 42 per cent (Nash, 2021: 1031–1032). It resulted from party politics, Scotland-specific lobbying by environmental groups, and the SNP tendency to use policies to signal divergence from the UK and demonstrate its potential to become a world leader (Cairney, 2011; McEwen and Bomberg, 2014: 75–79; Nash, 2021: 1032).

Senedd Cymru does not enjoy the same powers, and relied on Westminster to legislate (Royles and McEwen, 2015: 1035). However, since 2007, Welsh governments have made an equivalent commitment to climate change policies, and became the first to set targets 'to reduce carbon-equivalent emissions by 3% per year in areas of devolved competence from 2011' (Royles and McEwen, 2015: 1043). This strategy was equivalent to a 40 per cent reduction by 2020 (1990 levels). The Environment (Wales) Act 2016 set the 80 per cent by 2050 target and obliged Welsh ministers to set interim targets for each decade, plus five-year carbon budgets, guided by the Committee on Climate Change (2017: 8) recommendations.

The Northern Ireland Executive's National Adaptation Programme reports emphasise cooperation across government departments and partnerships with local stakeholders, to improve resilience to extreme events, regenerate waterways, reduce pollution and encourage environmental literacy (Department of Agriculture, Environment and Rural Affairs, 2019; Burns et al, 2022). Other existing policies are climate policy-relevant, including plans for marine resilience, sustainable agriculture and managing the historic estate (Climate Northern Ireland, 2021). The Climate Change Act (Northern Ireland) 2022 commits its Executive to the UK government's net zero by 2050 target, albeit with the Committee on Climate Change (2022a) warning that it 'is already playing catch-up with the rest of the UK'.

The growing storm: climate change aims versus outcomes

We should always expect *some* difference between ambitious government aims and their implementation (Pollitt, 2015: 184). However, early assessments of UK policy describe a *striking* contrast between hopeful reports of policy change in the mid-2000s and despairing accounts of outcomes by the mid-2010s. Governments signalled ambitious targets *in principle*, without demonstrating the changes they were prepared to make *in practice* (Somerville, 2021). Setting long-term targets allowed UK governments to:

- Present climate change as a 'tame' issue that can be addressed by technical measures (Willis, 2017) without the need for high public engagement (Shaw et al, 2018).
- Take the credit for easy choices to reduce emissions (Lorenzoni and Benson, 2014: 19).

- Delegate responsibility for targets to public bodies (Gillard, 2016: 32).
- Push back the harder choices to their successors.

More recent UK assessments still focus on the gap between political direction and delivery (Fankhauser et al, 2018: 3–5), albeit describing the durability of UK and devolved policy changes (Averchenkova et al, 2021; Lockwood, 2021; Nash, 2021: 1039). Hinde (2016: 90) presents a similar assessment of the Scottish government, praised for its ambitions, then failing to meet GHG emissions targets, partly because they are 'incompatible with current government practice', such as using tax powers to encourage regional aviation, opposing the closure of a coal-fired power station, and acting slowly on efficient homes and sustainable transport. The Committee on Climate Change (2022b) called for the Scottish government to produce a 'quantified' plan to meet its 2030 commitments and address a failure to meet milestones (for example, on 'energy efficiency in homes and peatland restoration'). Similarly, the CCC called for a 'step change' in Welsh policy delivery to ensure progress (Royles and McEwen, 2015: 1045).

Current concerns focus on limited progress towards net zero (Kuzemko, 2022). Sasse et al (2020: 5) contrast the government's concrete aim and vague plan for delivery, identifying:

- the resources needed for 'the biggest infrastructure transformation in 50 years';
- limited attempts 'to persuade people to accept and support big, intrusive changes';
- the lack of a 'coherent' analysis of how to secure emissions reductions across each sector in a fair way, without undermining economic aims;
- limited 'capacity to co-ordinate action across the whole of government and beyond';
- high uncertainty about the chances of multiple governments sustaining policy change 'over 30 years', and insufficient parliamentary scrutiny of progress (see also Committee on Climate Change, 2020: 13).

The UK government updated its strategy in 2021, but confirmed 'the government's market-oriented policy position', with minimal 'new public spending or state intervention' (Kuzemko et al, 2022: 8). The CCC (2022c: 14) then noted that, while 'the UK Government now has a solid Net Zero strategy in place', 'tangible progress is lagging the policy ambition'.

We use the case studies of sustainable energy, transport and food policies to explain this gap between ambition and progress. In each case, there is a growing focus on combining economic growth and environmental sustainability, but economic-focused policies are hard to overturn.

Case study 1: Who has the energy for sustainable policies?

Energy policy making is *multi-sectoral* and *multi-level*. Some sectors are obviously relevant to climate change – including domestic and industrial energy, and planning for buildings and land use (for example, to approve wind farms) – but many more play their part. Cox et al's (2016: 3–4) review highlights the importance of *13* non-energy sectors and cross-sectoral issues (including the regulation of markets). Large consumers of energy include trade and industry, agriculture, the military, transport, education, health and information/ communication technology.

Until Brexit, the EU, UK, and devolved and local governments enjoyed some responsibilities for energy policies. Cairney et al (2019b) identify those with a direct impact:

- EU: energy market rules, security of supply, regulating biofuels, and promoting renewable energy and energy efficiency.
- UK: the rights to extract fossil fuels, energy company licences, security of supply, energy taxation, energy efficiency subsidies/incentives.
- Devolved: promoting renewable energy and energy efficiency, some licences and consents for companies and extraction, administering fuel poverty schemes.

However, a list of direct responsibilities does not tell the full story. First, the 'Europeanisation' of policy included the generation of goals and targets, research, and relationships with international organisations (Kuzemko et al, 2022: 4). Second, there were many examples of *indirect responsibilities*, including rules on state aid, competition and free movement (EU), commercial, financial, health and safety, and environmental laws and regulations (UK), and rules on the use of property, transport and environmental emissions (often devolved). Local authorities also oversee land use planning and consent for new developments such as **fracking** and nuclear power stations (although devolved/UK governments could intervene) (Cairney et al, 2019b). Further, *informal influence* includes when one government encourages action from others or delegates responsibilities ('executive devolution'), or

> **Fracking/hydraulic fracturing**: the drilling process to seek oil and gas from shale. Describing 'fracking' often denotes opposition, while 'hydraulic fracturing' for 'shale oil and gas' would be used by supporters to emphasise energy security and economic benefits.

when another tests the boundaries of its authority or lobbies a higher-level government (Cairney et al, 2022a: Chapter 3).

These dynamics make it difficult to know who exactly does what, why and to what effect. Policy makers might seek a sense of central government control, or collaboration across levels, to ensure a coherent mix of policy instruments. However, they face 'the potential for *policy incoherence*, when many selected instruments undermine or contradict each other, and *policy conflict*, when one level of government challenges or subverts the policies of another' (Cairney et al, 2022a: Chapter 3; emphasis in original). Brexit does not solve these problems (Box 8.2).

Box 8.2: Does Brexit improve energy policy coherence?

Emissions Trading Scheme: an alternative to directly mandated business behaviour. The aim is to minimise the cost to business of reducing GHG emissions, 'through the buying and selling of a limited number of allowances on an emission market' (Nye and Owens, 2008: 2). The UK scheme (2002–2007) was voluntary, with businesses motivated by financial incentives, kudos and hope that the scheme would ward off legislation or taxation (Nye and Owens, 2008: 4–10). The UK entered the EU scheme in 2007 (while opposing a carbon-tax alternative) (Kuzemko et al, 2022: 8).

EU Internal Energy Market: EU Commission policy to replace state monopolies to supply electricity and gas (proposed 1989; agreed by 2008). The UK was a key supporter, and its reforms bolstered the Commission's case (McGowan, 2011: 200).

One argument for Brexit was that it allowed the repatriation of powers to the UK centre, better able to manage relations across the UK (Chapter 7). Is there evidence that this shift was successful? It is difficult to find a positive effect on 'sustainable energy policy', since UK and EU 'market liberalism' approaches are similar (Kuzemko et al, 2022: 7). The Brexit dividend is also absent because most policy-making attention was spent on redesigning UK schemes (the UK left the EU **Emissions Trading Scheme** and **Internal Energy Market**) and replacing EU with UK policy capacity (Kuzemko et al, 2022: 7–10). Kuzemko et al (2022: 16) argue that 'the UK has not achieved anything yet in sustainable energy that it could not do under EU membership', and changes have 'tended to be less-efficient mirrors of EU policies'.

It is also difficult to identify more fruitful intergovernmental relations (unlike Box 6.1). While Brexit 'spawned a significant intensification of formal intergovernmental relations', they relate largely to negotiations over devolved government autonomy (such as to maintain direct contact with the EU), compared to pre-Brexit, when policy meetings were useful before EU deliberations (McEwen, 2021: 1542).

We know what we want from energy systems, but not how to get there

There is a clear *need* for policy-making cooperation and policy coherence, but a tendency to produce a disjointed policy mix based on different rationales. UK governments seek a transition from high to low-carbon energy systems (minimising the burning of fossil fuels), but maintain energy security (relying heavily on fossil fuels) and independence (relying less on imported fuels).

The latter aims became high priorities following the Russian invasion of Ukraine in 2022, while the new energy strategy for Britain (HM Government, 2022b) was subtitled 'Secure, clean and affordable British energy for the long term'. The UK government highlighted the unaffordability and economic cost of a spike of fossil fuel prices, promising to (1) reduce long-term costs via energy efficiency and renewable energy programmes, but also (2) use new nuclear power projects to bolster energy security, and (3) support new oil and gas projects in the North Sea to bolster independence during global crises (HM Government, 2022b: 5–6). Government support for nuclear – for energy supply resilience – marks a shift in state intervention for Conservative governments compared to their predecessors (in the 1990s, they created an electricity market and demonstrated nuclear's 'poor economic performance' – Geels et al, 2016: 907). It also intervened, initially reluctantly, to subsidise the spiralling – domestic and non-domestic – cost of electricity and gas in 2022 (Mawhood et al, 2022, 2023; Department for Energy Security & Net Zero, 2023a; see Chapter 12).

This lack of policy coherence is a feature, not a bug, of political systems. First, it reflects the politics of policy change, prompting inevitable trade-offs, competing aims, and the possibility that some actors can win in some venues but lose in others. Second, it reflects policy-making complexity, to the extent that it is difficult to understand energy policy systems. This conceptual problem has two key elements.

1. Policy-making systems are complex systems, beyond the control of central government

Policy-making responsibilities are spread across levels and types of government, and policy sectors and subsectors. The fragmentation is beyond the full understanding of policy makers, who have limited capacity to coordinate from the centre. They inherit then add to a contradictory collection of policies and practices, without knowing the outcome. Research on *policy-making systems* suggests that outcomes seem to 'emerge' in the absence of central control (Box 1.2; Box 2.3; Chapter 3).

2. Energy systems are also complex systems, in which the role of government is unclear

Governments and researchers also describe *energy systems* to focus on social and business behaviour. An energy system consists of many actors who supply and demand energy. Policy is relevant, but not central, to understanding this system. Researchers struggle to use policy studies to understand the role of policy making in energy systems, and there are competing ways to describe the results (Box 8.3).

Box 8.3: What is an energy system, and how can it transform?

The aim is clear: transition from high-carbon to low-carbon energy systems. The means to achieve it is unclear. The technical side was once portrayed as simple (Hughes, 2004). Now, research identifies complexity beyond the knowledge of one discipline: we need social sciences to understand how humans interact with technology, humanities on what a fair system looks like, and policy sciences on how policy makers try to manage behaviour. The umbrella term is 'whole systems research', but Munro and Cairney (2020) identify very different approaches:

- *The multi-level perspective on socio-technical systems.* Geels (2004) and colleagues describe high-carbon systems as path-dependent but conducive to change through innovation. 'Macro-landscape' describes the social, economic and political cultures that endure for long periods and stifle change. 'Socio-technical regimes' are the rules and practices that favour some technologies (for example, to maintain fossil fuel use and undermine renewable development). However, 'niches' can encourage radical challenges to regimes. They provide initial protection for an innovation (for example, investing without seeking a short-term return): allowing it to grow as people learn how to develop the technology and secure social, political and economic support (Chilvers et al, 2017: 442). This insight helps to understand transformation, identifying (1) social and political obstacles, and how to form coalitions and exploit opportunities to challenge them, (2) the policies that could make the biggest difference, and (3) the need for public deliberation to generate ownership of a 'pathway' to systemic change (Rogge et al, 2020: 1).
- *Complex systems theories.* Our complex government story suggests that policy outcomes are not in the control of central governments. System dynamics can endure for long periods then change dramatically, but in ways not conducive to policy design. It is unrealistic to expect to (1) identify the levers to overcome inertia, (2) produce a policy mix with predictable consequences, or (3) generate a simple pathway to systemic change.
- *Social-ecological systems (and the institutional analysis and design framework).* Ostrom (1990; 2007; 2009; see also Orach and Schlüter, 2016) helps to understand how actors cooperate. Many 'centres' have authority, which requires voluntary collaboration inside and outside of government. They should learn from actors who cooperate successfully to design rules and maintain practices essential to resource management and environmental protection.

What is the combined take-home message? We know more about what is *required* (the transformation) than who gets us there, and how. There are many 'pathways' to transformation, driven by markets, states or civil society (Chilvers et al, 2017). Each would involve different short-term choices on technologies with long-term effects (Chilvers et al, 2017: 440; Jordan et al, 2022).

This conceptual problem contributes to a worrying practical problem: if we do not know what an energy system is, or how governments fit in, how can we know what to do? How can we design effective policy processes or anticipate the effect of new policies? When academics and policy makers try to answer this question, they respond by recommending 'whole systems thinking' but without agreeing what it is (Box 2.4; Nguyen et al, 2023)! They could be describing one of two contradictory propositions, to understand systems well enough to:

1. *Control them*. Address policy problems holistically, and project the sense that central governments are in the turning-chaos-to-order business. Find the right levers to make a disproportionate impact on outcomes.
2. *Give up on the idea of control*. Develop the humility to accept that we do not understand problems enough to address them holistically. Adapt to systems dynamics, accepting that outcomes emerge in ways beyond our understanding (Cairney, 2020b).

This problem extends to government strategies. The UK government uses the phrase 'energy system' frequently but vaguely, describing *the need* to transition not *its role* in that transition. The Scottish government describes 'whole systems' and 'systems thinking' to signal *the need* to consider how policies affect energy demand and supply, using simplistic metaphors to describe how systems work (Munro and Cairney, 2020: 3).

Is UK renewables policy a success story?

Renewable energy in the UK is a partial success story (see Box 5.3 on narrating success). *Programmatic success* relates to the aim to raise the proportion of electricity generated from renewable energy. It went from 2 per cent in 1991 to 15 per cent in 2013 then, '43% of our power coming from a mix of wind, solar, bioenergy and hydroelectric sources' in 2020 (National Grid, 2022). Coal has gone in the opposite direction, from 80 per cent in the early 1980s to 2 per cent by 2020 (Brauers et al, 2020: 241).

UK government policy contributed to both shifts. Its anti-coal policy began when the Thatcher-led Conservative government reduced subsidies, and pushed for plant closures, as a symbol of its challenge to trade unions (Chapters 4 and 5). It culminated in recent Conservative government efforts to (mostly) phase out coal to promote climate change policies (Brauers et al, 2020: 241).

Multi-level renewables policies from the late 2000s helped the UK go from 'laggard to leader' (Kern et al, 2014). EU policies included the European Renewable Energy Directive 2009, requiring the UK 'to supply 15% of its energy needs (disaggregated into electricity, heat and transport) from renewable sources by 2020' (Gillard and Lock, 2017: 645). The UK was already heading in this direction and, under Labour, pushed for more EU direction on targets (while opposing interference on which technologies to support) (Fitch-Roy and Fairbrass, 2018: 64, 92, 103; Rayner et al, 2020: 117–118). UK government initiatives included reforms to planning to limit blanket local opposition to renewables development, plus greater economic guarantees to support large volumes of renewable supply. The latter included: (1) ambitious **Renewables Obligation** targets (from 2002), (2) **feed-in tariff** schemes (2008–2019) for small renewable energy providers, and (3) **Renewable Heat Incentive** schemes (Toke, 2011: 528; Geels et al, 2016: 906–909; McGowan, 2020: 597–599; Box 8.4).

Box 8.4: Policy tools for renewable energy

Cairney and St Denny (2020: 18) draw on Hood and Margetts' (2007) categories of policy tools to describe different models of state intervention (Box 2.2; Chapter 10). 'Maximal' approaches would combine 'ambitious and specific' strategies focusing primarily on the environmental problem (*nodality*) with regulations to change social and business behaviour directly (*authority*), taxes and subsidies to change market behaviour (*treasure*), and strong departments to ensure policy delivery (*organisation*). Minimal approaches would produce vague strategies, backed weakly by other tools, and overshadowed by stronger tools for other aims (for example, prioritising economic growth).

In renewable energy, Labour and Conservative-led governments have made policy changes, but their effect is hard to follow, since new schemes (1) combine regulations and economic incentives, largely enforced and monitored by the regulator Ofgem (Office of Gas and Electricity Markets), (2) in different mixes, to signal more or less intervention. They include:

Renewables Obligation (RO): a statutory 'obligation on licensed electricity suppliers … to source a proportion of their supply to customers from eligible renewable sources' (Ofgem, 2022a). Suppliers buy ' "renewable obligation certificates" (ROCs) from accredited renewable energy generators' (Toke et al, 2013: 63). The original aim (2002) was to increase the obligation over time, but the scheme's closure by 2017 was announced in 2013 (Gillard and Lock, 2017: 647; Rayner et al, 2020: 103).

Contract for Difference (CfD): an auction/competitive tender to award a fixed number of subsidies to large electricity suppliers for the renewable energy they provide. CfD replaced the RO from the first auction in 2017. Successful companies receive 'a top-up payment between the market price' and a fixed price to guarantee their long-term income (and encourage them to invest) (Rayner et al, 2020: 104).

Feed-in tariff: a subsidy scheme to encourage the expansion of small-scale renewable energy production (especially solar and wind) by making a long-term commitment (say, 20–25 years) to pay producers for the energy they consume or feed in to the National Grid (Ofgem, 2022b).

Renewable Heat Incentive (RHI) (domestic or non-domestic): to encourage investment in renewable heating (for example, biomass boilers, solar, heat pumps) by guaranteeing payments according to how much heat is produced.

Labour's commitment to state intervention in the late 2000s replaced its predecessor's reliance on market mechanisms, then the coalition government argued that Labour had over-reacted (Rayner et al, 2020: 103). Its replacement of RO by CfD signalled limits to renewables obligations (Leiren et al, 2021: 40). A precise assessment of changes requires us to measure the size, rate, duration, and impact of subsidies (Rayner et al, 2020; Ofgem, 2022a; 2022b). However, a rough guide is that Labour allocated 'around £5 billion by 2010' to the RO scheme which the Conservatives did not match (Carter and Little, 2021: 6).

These changes to instruments only make sense when placed in the wider context of the UK electricity/energy markets, in which: (1) government energy policies reacted to technological change, and (2) six suppliers (the 'Big Six') dominated markets in the 2000s. Governments were not directly responsible for capital investment in renewables, and suppliers preferred to 'sweat' their assets than produce new capacity (Kuzemko, 2016: 116). Later, they were better placed to shoulder the risk of RO investments (smaller firms favoured feed-in tariffs) (Rayner et al, 2020: 108–112).

Renewable energy also highlights the potential for advocates to seek policy change in multiple venues, such as in Scotland and Wales (Gillard et al, 2017: 179; Kuzemko et al, 2022: 9). The Scottish government's ability to secure 'a larger policy role in relation to renewable energy than its legal capacity would indicate' reflected its contribution to the UK's EU renewables obligations (one-quarter of UK renewable energy generation) (Cairney et al, 2019b: 463; McEwen et al, 2019). This contribution followed the SNP's commitment, from its first election in 2007, to favour renewables and reject new nuclear power stations (largely through planning and land use choices). Its aim for Scottish renewables to produce the equivalent of 100 per cent of Scotland's electricity consumption by 2020 (from 37 per cent in 2011) was a major part of its (1) climate change commitments, (2) economic agenda, and (3) pursuit of political popularity to support its campaign for Scottish independence (Cairney, 2011: 181; Cairney and McGarvey, 2013: 182–183; Toke et al, 2013). The success of Scottish policy depended on UK government support for renewable energy. Still, Toke et al (2013: 64–65) argue that the SNP government 'gained three policy victories', securing: additional Treasury funding for renewables; the incorporation of its scheme ('extra incentives to wave and tidal stream' projects) into the RO; and, Ofgem's agreement to reduce charges on suppliers to send electricity to the rest of Britain. It nearly met its 2020 target (BBC News, 2021b).

On the other hand, the shift towards renewables is incomplete: 'fossil fuels still dominate the energy mix' and the UK is not on course to meet long-term GHG emissions targets (Kuzemko, 2016: 108; Kuzemko et al, 2022: 2). One explanation is path dependence and policy inheritance. Thatcher- and Major-led reforms had: shifted energy supply and capital investment from the state to the market (Chapters 4 and 5), encouraged market deregulation, created an energy regulator (Ofgem) that operated independently of government, and reduced energy policy capacity in government (Kuzemko, 2016: 111–114). The state role had gone 'from one of responsibility for national planning, infrastructure development and energy provision to neutral overseer and upholder of an agreed set of market rules and principles' (Kuzemko, 2016: 111, 117). Climate change was an energy markets problem (Lovell et al, 2009). State intervention rose under Labour from a low base. It took longer than countries like Germany 'to make any serious impact', learn from failures, and shake off the hope that markets plus government exhortation would produce necessary changes (Kuzemko, 2016: 116–119).

Another explanation is that long-term policy change is vulnerable to disruption, often by ministers seeking *political success* (Box 5.3; Gillard and Lock, 2017: 645–648). The coalition rejected calls to define a long-term target towards 'full decarbonisation' (Gillard and Lock, 2017: 646), argued that its predecessor had over-subsidised renewables, and blamed renewables for a rise in household bills (Gillard and Lock, 2017: 646). It accelerated the transition from high state intervention to moderate support for markets (Box 8.4): bringing forward the cut-off point for feed-in tariffs inclusion, and, replacing the RO with CfD (although the latter was supported by civil servants) (Kuzemko, 2016: 120; Gillard and Lock, 2017: 647; Leiren et al, 2021: 46).

It also signalled greater support for non-renewables. First, it agreed to subsidise a new nuclear project without the same conditions as renewables (Gillard and Lock, 2017: 648). Second, it sought greater fossil fuel supply, including fracking for shale oil and gas (albeit without ever making it feasible for businesses – UKOOG, 2022). Cameron declared 'we're going all out for shale', emphasised its economic and energy security benefits, announced tax expenditures to encourage companies to invest, and allowed local authorities to keep their local business rate income to encourage them to approve drill sites (Prime Minister's Office, 2014; Cairney et al, 2016; 2018). The Conservative government in 2015 went further, opposing onshore windfarm developments (for example, excluding them from CfD) and reducing subsidies for small-scale solar projects (Rayner et al, 2020: 115).

Finally, mixed support for bioenergy reminds us that there are more- or less-effective routes to climate aims. The IPCC (2022: 21) noted that 'poorly implemented bioenergy, with or without carbon capture and storage, can compound climate-related risks to biodiversity'. Further, groups like the Royal Society for the Protection of Birds highlight the negative impact of poorly planned biomass use on forests, wildlife and food production (B. Smith, 2022). Biomass also became associated with policy failure. First, a 'Non-Domestic Renewable Heat Incentive scheme' in Northern Ireland made it possible for companies to profit from heating empty buildings because the subsidy was greater than the cost. It contributed to a deficit of £140 million in the Executive's budget (RHI Inquiry, 2020) and a governance crisis (Northern Ireland Audit Office, 2022), highlighting the limited capacity to oversee a major change to complex energy systems (Lowes and Mitchell, 2021). Second, a BBC investigation (Crowley and Robinson, 2022) highlighted questionable wood-sourcing practices by the Drax power station in Yorkshire ('a converted coal plant, which now produces 12% of the UK's renewable electricity' and 'has already received £6bn in green energy subsidies').

Case study 2: The stop-start progress of sustainable transport policy

Transport produces one-quarter of GHG emissions in countries like the UK (Figure 8.1; Table 8.1; Shaw and Docherty, 2008: 4; Cooper-Searle et al, 2018; Marsden et al, 2020: 89).

Figure 8.1: Greenhouse gas emissions by sector

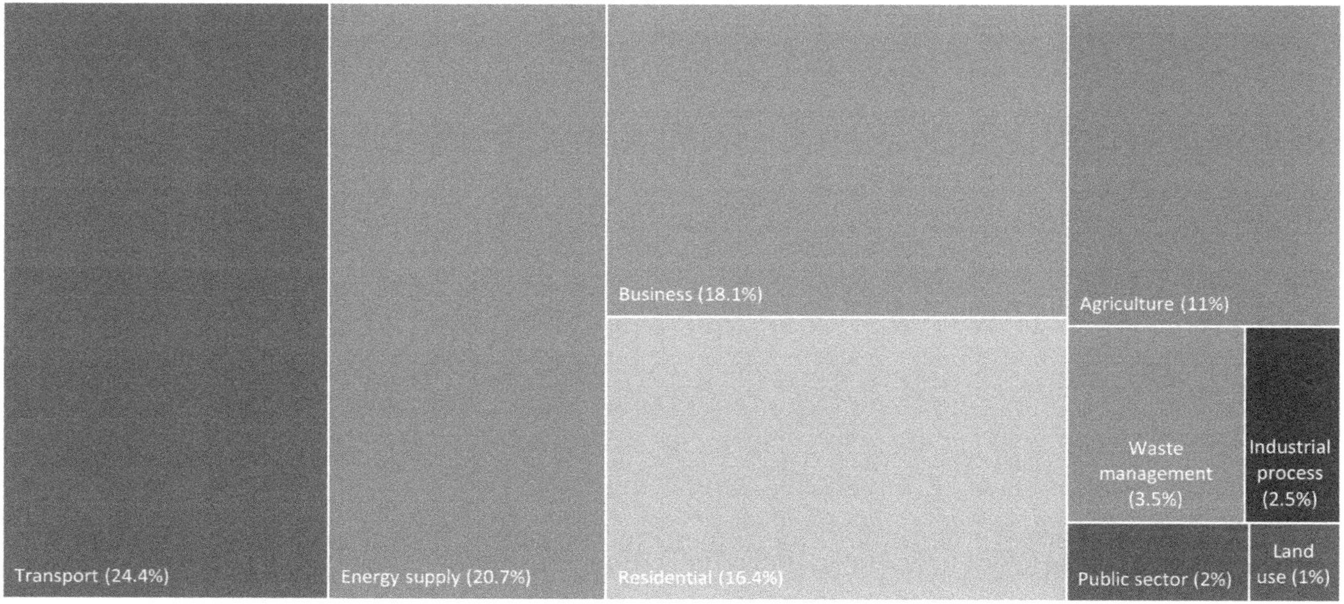

Sector	Percentage
Agriculture	(11%)
Industrial process	(2.5%)
Land use	(1%)
Waste management	(3.5%)
Public sector	(2%)
Business	(18.1%)
Residential	(16.4%)
Energy supply	(20.7%)
Transport	(24.4%)

Note: author's own, adapted from Department for Business, Energy & Industrial Strategy (2022)

Table 8.1: Greenhouse gas emissions by sector, 2020

Sector	Description of activities	Tonnes GHG (million)	% of total GHG
Transport	Road transport, domestic aviation, railways, domestic shipping and so on (includes public sector transport)	98.8	24.36
Energy supply	Electricity and other energy generation activities	84	20.71
Business	Emissions from the industrial and commercial sectors, including fuel combustion	73.4	18.1
Residential	Emissions from residential properties, primarily heating/cooking	66.3	16.35
Agricultural	Livestock, agricultural machinery and soils	44.8	11.04
Waste management	Treatment of solid and liquid waste (for example, landfill, incineration)	17.6	4.34
Industrial processes	Industrial processes (for example, chemical processing, cement production)	9.5	2.34
Public sector	Emissions from public sector institutions (for example, schools, hospitals)	7.4	1.82
Land use	Changes resulting from change in carbon stock in forest land	3.7	0.91
Total		405.5	100

Source: Department for Business, Energy & Industrial Strategy (2022)

If we designed a sustainable policy from scratch, prioritising the minimisation of energy use and pollution, we would favour pedestrian, cycling and public transport, and minimise car and air transport. The Labour government (1997) was *somewhat* committed to that idea (Box 8.5).

Box 8.5: Policy instruments for sustainable transport

The maximalist version of a sustainable transport plan would prioritise decarbonisation, replacing 'soft' measures (encouraging people to change behaviour) with 'hard' (obliging behavioural change). The latter may include: regulating business and social behaviour; using taxes to make road and air travel expensive, and subsidies to reduce rail fares; changing the value-for-money criteria underpinning capital investment to shift from road projects to walking/cycle paths and rail; and giving public bodies the powers to ensure delivery regardless of the electoral costs (Shaw and Docherty, 2019: 21).

However, Docherty and Shaw (2011: 225) suggest that Labour governments favoured measures associated with 'new realism', to combine (1) a reassessment of the role and effectiveness of transport policies and practices, with (2) reforms that could secure 'broad appeal'. Proposals included: planning measures to reduce journey lengths for cars and reduce urban lorry journeys; road pricing and traffic management regulation/enforcement to manage demand; investment in modern buses and bus lanes; infrastructure changes to make it easier to walk or cycle; and, subsidies to the cost of public transport (Docherty and Shaw, 2011: 228–229). Recent examples – including policies in London to reduce air pollution – show that a perceived lack of broad appeal can prompt parties to reconsider environmental measures (Furlong, 2022; Scott, 2023).

However, the following factors help to explain why this kind of policy design does not get off the ground.

1. Governments do not design policies on a blank page

There is a legacy of unsustainable transport policies with path-dependent effects. Dudley and Richardson (2000: 23–24) describe a post-war history of UK policies that used road transport to boost the economy (and government popularity) from the 1950s. Environmental concerns surfaced in the 1970s but, by then, the road lobby was powerful. The case for road building was 'destroyed' by environmental campaigners by the late 1990s, but the infrastructure was established. The prioritisation of roads combined with a focus on economic performance to undermine rail. Reforms in the 1960s focused on the commercial feasibility of train companies, while late-1980s agendas focused on their privatisation. Overall, there is major path and 'car dependence' (Docherty, 2003: 6). Investment in unsustainable physical infrastructure still commands resources for maintenance after governments have signalled a shift in policy (Reardon and Marsden, 2020: 233). Further, protests against new airport projects have enjoyed recent success, but in the context of decades of expansion (Nulman, 2015).

2. Reforms have immediate political costs and uncertain long-term gains

The attempt to produce major shifts in behaviour 'is a formidable endeavour that requires political bravery, risk taking and long-term planning … politicians perceive it could cost them an election' (Shaw and Docherty, 2008: 7). Shifts of state investment from road to trail, new charges to drive or park, and tax-driven fuel price hikes tend to be opposed by road lobbies, supermarkets and drivers, and are not attractive to 'risk-averse' civil servants or ministers (Dudley and Richardson, 2000; Shaw and Docherty, 2008: 10; Docherty and Shaw, 2011: 239). Further, not enough people care about transport, or perceive a crisis, to provide an electoral incentive to act (Shaw and Docherty, 2019: 4). Labour knew that their Conservative opposition would dub them 'anti-car' if they went too far (Carter and Little, 2021: 7).

Consequently, a Labour government that began with sincere reformist intentions: (1) settled for modest changes focusing on encouraging people and businesses to change, (2) removed the 'Fuel Duty Escalator' (a tax on fuel that rose by 3 per cent per year) after protests by farmers and truckers in 2000; and (3) backed off from plans to charge to use roads in 2007 (Shaw and Docherty, 2008: 10; Wolmar, 2008: viii; Shaw and Docherty, 2014: 6; 2019: 22; Reardon and Marsden, 2020: 231–232). Its successor coalition government treated transport as low priority during 'austerity' (with exceptions, such as some rail improvement and the high-speed rail project, HS2) (Shaw and Docherty, 2019: 13–14).

Aviation policy exhibited similar features. The Labour government relied on a 'freedom to fly' coalition of non-governmental actors (including airlines) to make the case for expansion during the 2000s (Howarth and Griggs, 2006). The coalition government paused further expansions in south-east England, but also argued that aviation expansion could be justified if done sustainably or efficiently (Griggs and Howarth, 2019). Overall, policy makers embody the 'pervading mindset that transport is "too difficult to change" substantively' because too many people would refuse to change behaviour or punish politicians for trying to make them (Marsden et al, 2020: 89).

3. Governments have multiple aims and environmentalism rarely wins the day

When governments emphasise the *dual aim* to use transport to boost economic activity and maintain environmental sustainability, the economy will trump the environment in the short term, even when governments recognise the long-term economic benefits of climate change policies. The Labour government's White Paper in 1998 described a road-driven economy as unsustainable (Docherty and Shaw, 2003: xviii). The Department of Transport (2007) sought to reduce car use and boost public transport. Still, the government was prioritising 'economic performance' and addressing 'business costs', while signalling that 'greener' transport would not come at a too-great economic cost (Department of Transport, 2007: 9).

4. Policy intention is not the same as delivery

Despite the Labour government's rhetoric, it oversaw major road building and increased air capacity without producing major expansions in rail and walking/cycle capacity, and without a high uptake of measures to discourage driving (such as 'congestion charges') (Docherty and Shaw, 2003: xviii).

5. Transport represents a classic case of unfulfilled policy integration across sectors

Even the meaning of 'integration' is unclear. It could mean cross-sectoral initiatives – to seek synergies between economic, environmental, energy, transport and other aims (such as to address health inequalities) – or transport-specific projects. The latter could mean better-integrated public transport to compete with roads (the 'radical' option), or make it easier to combine car and train travel (the 'stay popular' option) (Shaw and Docherty, 2008: 10–11).

6. The complex and multi-level nature of transport governance exacerbates a lack of coherence

Decentralised responsibilities could boost innovation or more coherent policies. For example, in London, there were innovations (such as 'congestion charging' fees) and successes relating to the well-funded and integrated Transport for London (Shaw and Docherty, 2019: 15). However, the 'multitude of governance networks ... makes it difficult to achieve integrated outcomes' across sectors and inside/outside of government (Marsden and Docherty, 2019: 3). Further, it is rare to connect networks of transport organisations to equivalent networks in other sectors (such as economic or environment). Or, when one cross-cutting agenda works in one area, it may contribute to 'misaligned boundaries' in others (Marsden and Docherty, 2019: 3–4).

Some of these policy-making problems relate to an 'accountability vacuum' (Bache et al, 2015: 65). The 'complex architecture of "fuzzy governance"' contributes to 'fuzzy accountability', in which many bodies are *theoretically* responsible for their contribution to sustainable transport, but without clear accountability measures to ensure progress. Further, if policy changes are unpopular, they have higher incentives to play 'blame games' than make tough choices (Bache et al, 2015: 65). While much governance uncertainty is unintentional (a routine feature of policy-making complexity), 'blame avoidance' is a strategic move (Bache et al, 2015: 66). For example, UK government policy delegation helped to shuffle off responsibility for unpopular measures, such as when the Labour government: (1) relied on an advisory body – the Commission for Integrated Transport – to make the case to avoid national targets on road-use reduction, and (2) got local authorities to manage schemes to charge people to drive or park at work (Reardon and Marsden, 2020: 231).

Other policy-making problems relate to poor connections between different reasons to devolve responsibilities. Territorial devolution is about meeting different demands for political autonomy rather than (1) designing a coherent package of devolved responsibilities (Mackinnon et al, 2010: 272–275), or (2) requiring close coordination between governments. There is some scope for innovation and learning, but devolved governments tended to follow the UK in avoiding controversial road charging while approving new road investment, and providing modest incentives to use public transport (for example, concessionary fares for older people) (Shaw et al, 2009: 560). A recent exception may be the Welsh government (Welsh Government, 2023) cancelling many major road projects to foster its climate change commitment.

Finally, in some cases, these problems combine. Both the UK and Scottish governments produced climate change legislation with ambitious targets. In both cases, 'how, exactly, targets will be assessed against performance and who would actually be held to account remains unclear' (Bache et al, 2015: 75). They delegated transport carbon reduction roles to local authorities, and encouraged them to co-produce policies with stakeholders, but the resultant 'lack of clarity over the carbon management framework amongst state and non-state actors was a major impediment' to implementation (Bache et al, 2015: 75). At the same time, both governments shifted their priorities to refocus on economic growth (while reducing local budgets), so local politicians knew that they would be blamed for not keeping the economy rolling in the short term but not be held accountable for 'intangible and long-term' aims like carbon management (Bache et al, 2015: 78).

Case study 3: Sustainable food system policies don't cut the mustard

The UK is part of a globalised food system that requires radical and rapid policy change. International organisations – such as the Food and Agriculture Organization of the United Nations (FAO) – seek 'integrated agricultural policies' to address climate change, foster biodiversity, and reduce land degradation, as part of the UN Sustainable Development Goals (compare with The Lancet Commission, 2019). The FAO (2023) describes the shift:

Common Agricultural Policy: established in 1962 to maintain food security by subsidising agricultural production (*direct income payments*). Now described by the European Commission (2022b) as 'a partnership between agriculture and society, and between Europe and its farmers', with the following aims: 'support farmers and improve agricultural productivity, ensuring a stable supply of affordable food; safeguard European Union farmers to make a reasonable living; help tackle climate change and the sustainable management of natural resources; maintain rural areas and landscapes across the EU; keep the rural economy alive by promoting jobs in farming, agri-food industries and associated sectors'.

- from prioritising food security, trade and economic growth (subsidising efficient production and global trade), to environmentally sustainable practices (policies for sustainable land management and regional trade), while
- recognising global inequalities (in income and access to safe water and healthy food) and the unequal impacts of policy changes.

It describes the policy-making problem as how to shift from exclusive agricultural policy communities (favouring farming organisations and unions) towards partnership working between multiple levels and types of government, and non-governmental actors, across sectors. We can deduce the lack of progress so far: stating the *requirement* to produce rapid and radical changes highlights their absence.

Until Brexit, environmental and food responsibilities were Europeanised (Burns and Carter, 2018; Burns et al, 2019) via the **Common Agricultural Policy** (CAP). CAP began as a means to support food production and security. There is substantive path dependence, and the impetus to change is not sufficiently strong. Alons (2017: 1604–1605) describes a rise in 'environmental discourse or rhetoric' and 'significant changes' to CAP. However, there were limited moves towards 'Environmental Policy Integration', 'due to low priority of environmental issues and a closed agricultural policy network'. There is limited commitment to a 'strong' form of Environmental Policy Integration, where environmental aims are more important than economics or food security (Alons, 2017: 1606–1608). Rather, most reforms were a by-product of economic considerations, such as taking land out of production (while still paying farms) to address over-production (Alons, 2017: 1612). It is hard to find a major shift of policy influence. The Commission's environmental directorate (DG ENVI) and environmental groups were peripheral to 1992 reforms. They were more involved in 2013, but unable to stop their proposals being 'watered down' (Alons, 2017: 1615). As a result, CAP reforms have not produced clear and 'significant environmental effects' (Alons, 2017: 1617). Similarly, Pe'er et al (2020) argue that CAP 'is failing with respect to biodiversity, climate, soil, land degradation as well as socio-economic challenges'.

The UK government could have gone further than EU requirements (as with 'organic agriculture', Greer, 2002; see also Keating, 2010 on Scotland). For example, since 2001, it connected environmental policies (biodiversity, forestry, land use, water and air quality) to food production (agriculture and fish) in one Department for Environment, Food and Rural Affairs (Defra). However, Defra performs a largely exhortative role, to share research with consumers and support industry and non-governmental organisations (Kerr and Foster, 2011: 422). There has been little direct intervention to, say, favour the small local farms willing to promote sustainable schemes but struggling to compete with global corporations focused on profit (Marsden, 2012: 141–142).

Brexit allows UK and devolved governments to replace CAP with more sustainable policies (Whitfield and Marshall, 2017; Antonopoulos et al, 2022). Each committed to the vague aim of sustainable agriculture, backed by legislation to link direct payments to environmental improvement (Downing and Coe, 2018; Hill, 2022). Early assessments suggest that the UK government's promise of a 'Green Brexit' contrasted with its plans to replicate CAP reforms and limit the discretion of devolved governments (Gravey, 2019). By 2020, it was unclear how the UK would replace CAP or how devolved governments could go their own way (Gravey, 2022: 97, 122). Gravey and Jordan (2023: 19) suggest that we may not witness major post-Brexit change for a decade. By 2023, there was evidence of a 'gradual disengagement from the EU environmental rule-book' (Gravey and Jordan, 2023: 1).

Critical policy analysis: who matters to policy makers?

The UK is in a group of economically developed and powerful countries that (1) produces a disproportionately high proportion of GHGs (in total and per person), but (2) faces a disproportionately low impact from climate change (Mott et al, 2021). **Climate justice** policy would involve areas such as:

- *foreign policy*, to negotiate more effective and equitable collective action;
- *international trade*, to negotiate the cost of importing climate damaging goods; and
- *international development*, to provide resources to countries damaged by UK actions.

Box 8.6: Defining climate justice, just transitions and equity

Climate justice. Produce policies to address climate change and fairness. Fairness relates to outcomes (who gets what?), processes (who decides?) and respect (whose knowledge and experiences count?) (IPCC, 2022: 9). There is no 'universalist philosophy of justice'; its meaning varies geographically and in academic or activist discourse (Santos, 2014; Newell et al, 2021: 2). Still, most research identifies injustice. Climate change is 'having the most severe effects on those with the least responsibility for causing it, and who, at the same time, are often excluded from decision-making processes' (Newell et al, 2021: 2). This problem relates to (1) current versus future generations (intergenerational injustice), and (2) more or less powerful actors (across or within countries), including the gendered impacts of climate change (Terry, 2009), 'racial justice' and 'intersectional' approaches (Newell et al, 2021: 6; Mattar et al, 2021: 1307; Tilley et al, 2022; Cairney et al, 2023).

Just transition. A fair process and outcome to ensure that the costs and benefits of transition towards sustainability are shared equitably (Heffron and McCauley, 2018: 74; Jenkins, 2018; IPCC, 2022: 29–30).

Equity. The avoidance of unfair inequalities. This term is contested, and cost-benefit exercises contain questionable assumptions about the trade-offs involved (Aldred, 2009). Issues include:

- *Assigning relative values to lives in different countries, and relating the value of deaths to inequalities.* Azar (1999: 250) relates (a) calculations of damage in the Global South caused by high emissions in the North, to (b) early studies to inform IPCC work. It placed a higher 'value of a statistical life (VOSL)' to populations in the 'industrialised world' than in 'low-income countries'. Tol (2001: 71) contrasts ways to translate climate equity concerns, from systems to (1) minimise GHG emissions but maintain existing global inequalities, or (2) ensure 'the higher the aversion to inequity, the higher optimal greenhouse gas emission reduction'.
- *How much value to place on costs and benefits in the future*: 'huge impacts in the distant future count for almost nothing in our current decision making' (Aldred, 2009: 475). Yang and Suh (2021) gauge what younger people gain from climate mitigation. They find greater benefits when they (1) reduce the 'discounting' of the value of costs/benefits in the future compared to today, and (2) increase the timescale to over 100 years (OECD, 2018; O'Mahony, 2021).

- *Contested comparisons.* The costs and benefits of new nuclear power stations relate to the stated alternative. Some relate them to fossil fuels (only comparing environmental costs), or renewables (also comparing value for money) (Kennedy, 2007).

These policies intersect with the aim of a **just transition**. First, economically developed countries – who have benefited from GHG-heavy economic growth – could compensate lower-income countries for the loss of equivalent growth and for their impact on the climate in those countries (Newell et al, 2021: 3–4). They have avoided being tied to specific commitments (Dimitrov, 2016: 4–5; Schipani, 2017), although HM Government (2021: 288) describes its commitment to 'mobilise' over $100 billion per year from public (12 per cent) and private sources. Second, the push towards new technologies has global distributional effects, when renewable energy production boosts the mining of copper and a shift from petrol to electric cars boosts demand for lithium. The result is unequal environmental impacts from mining and a highly (but unequally) contested market to secure scarce resources (Northey et al, 2013; Kaunda, 2020; Conway, 2022). Third, it is possible for some countries to address GHG targets by exporting the problem, directly (when exporting fossil fuels, waste or plastics) or indirectly (when importing GHG-intensive products made elsewhere) (Barnes, 2019; Chivers, 2022; Greenpeace, 2022). The UK net zero strategy recognises one aspect of this problem ('carbon leakage' – HM Government, 2021: 68).

Domestic climate justice

Similar ideas could apply to UK and devolved policies. Relevant distributional consequences of climate policies include those between worker and employer (Hampton, 2018) or energy company and consumer, since 'residential energy use is responsible for almost 30% of the UK's carbon emissions' (Mayne et al, 2017: 395). Further, issues such as **fuel poverty** highlight the intersection between climate, economic and equity aims (Box 8.7).

Fuel poverty: when 'people are unable to afford to heat their homes properly ... which can result in physical and mental health problems' (Mayne et al, 2017: 395).

Box 8.7: Fuel poverty measures across the UK

UK and devolved governments' express vague commitments to a *just transition to energy sustainability*. A just transition requires policies for (1) *sustainable* emissions, such as via the regulation and taxation of energy supply and demand, and (2) *affordable* energy, using (generally UK) social security and (generally devolved) housing energy efficiency measures.

The cost of living crisis in 2022 prompted intense attention to energy affordability, putting pressure on the UK government to reduce fuel duties for drivers (it announced a 5p per litre drop in March 2022), subsidise the rising cost of household energy bills, and address the contribution of fuel costs to rapidly rising inflation (BBC News, 2022a). However, fuel poverty is not new, and UK and devolved governments have never resolved the issue. Further, they define and address it differently (Liddell et al, 2012; Moore, 2012; Simcock et al, 2016).

UK government, for England (since 2021). A household (1) living in a property with an insufficient 'fuel poverty energy efficiency rating', which (2) when they 'spend the required amount to heat their home, they are left with a residual income below the official poverty line' (BEIS, 2022a). In 2020, this definition applied to three million households – 13.2 per cent – with a 'mean average fuel poverty gap' of £223 (BEIS, 2022b: 1). The Department for Energy Security & Net Zero (2023b) predicts a rise to 14.4 per cent and £443 in 2023. Its target (from 2014) is to ensure: 'as many fuel poor homes as is reasonably practicable achieve a minimum energy efficiency rating of Band C, by 2030' (HM Government, 2015: 12) (aka Low Income Low Energy Efficiency metric).

Scottish government (since 2019). If 'after housing costs have been deducted, more than 10% (20% for extreme fuel poverty) of their net income is required to pay for their reasonable fuel needs; and after further adjustments are made to deduct childcare costs and any benefits received for a disability or care need, their remaining income is insufficient to maintain an acceptable standard of living, defined as being at least 90% of the UK Minimum Income Standard' (Hinson and Boulton, 2022: 18). In 2019, this definition applied to 613,000 households (24.6 per cent) and the 'median fuel poverty gap' was £750 (Hinson and Boulton, 2022: 18). Its target (2019) is that, by 2030, 'no more than 15% of households in Scotland are in fuel poverty' (5 per cent 'extreme fuel poverty'), and the 'median fuel poverty gap of households' is 'no more than £350 [adjusted for inflation]' (Hinson and Boulton, 2022: 20).

Welsh government (since 2004). If a household 'would have to spend more than 10 per cent of their income on maintaining a satisfactory heating regime' (Hinson and Boulton, 2022: 20). In 2018, this definition applied to 155,000 households (12 per cent) (Hinson and Boulton, 2022: 20). Its target (2021) is that, by 2035, '[n]o households are estimated to be living in severe or persistent fuel poverty as far as reasonable practicable; Not more than 5% of households are estimated to be living in fuel poverty at any one time as far as reasonably practicable; The number of all households "at risk" of falling into fuel poverty will be more than halved based on the 2018 estimate' (Hinson and Boulton, 2022: 21).

Northern Ireland Executive. If 'to maintain a satisfactory level of heating (21°C in the main living room and 18°C in other occupied rooms), it is required to spend in excess of 10% of its household income on all fuel use' (Hinson and Boulton, 2022: 22). In 2018, this definition applied to 160,000 households (22 per cent) (Hinson and Boulton, 2022: 22). Its 2004 target 'to eradicate fuel poverty by 2016' was not met; its 2011 strategy describes it as a 'core goal' (Hinson and Boulton, 2022: 23).

These tensions will become increasingly important as the UK shifts from easy wins towards the net zero commitments that cause major disruptions to social and business behaviour (Sasse et al, 2020). Questions include:

- *Who is in greatest need during an energy transition?* The biggest government grants for retrofitting energy efficiency in homes (for example, Warm Front in England) related to proxy measures of need – those 'in receipt of specified benefits and credits, being disabled, aged over 60, or with a young family' – but 'this policy was unsuccessful in reaching those most in need' (Brooks and Davoudi, 2014: 105).
- *Should governments reward the most efficient, and oblige polluters to pay more?* Green Deal policies favoured higher-income households, more able to take on loans to invest in household efficiency or renewable energy, while running the risk that loans would not cover the full cost (Brooks and Davoudi, 2014: 106–107).
- *If the onus is on energy companies, how should they cover their costs?* The cost to insulate rural stone houses is disproportionately high, but companies recoup costs with price rises for all energy users (Brooks and Davoudi, 2014: 108).
- *Should energy policy instruments be targeted according to income?* UK VAT on domestic energy was 'the lowest within the EU … reflecting concern about the effect of higher prices on the poor' (Mayne et al, 2017: 395). Yet, the overall impact of policies regarding 'efficiency and renewables' is that 'the poorer will benefit less' (Mayne et al, 2017: 396).
- *What are the implications of international human rights principles?* 'Human rights based approaches' provide a lens to interpret energy justice policies (Aitken et al, 2016: 240). If humans have the right to be (1) healthy, and (2) 'protected from the impacts of climate change' and 'not harmed by mitigation', does it extend to the avoidance of 'cold homes' (Mayne et al, 2017: 398; Walker and Day, 2012)?
- *To what extent, and how, should the state be legally responsible for ensuring a just transition?* Aitken et al (2016: 238–239) compare 'pragmatic' approaches that fit climate justice policies into current practices, and 'transformative' approaches based on the argument that 'climate injustices are a product of current capitalist systems and that climate justice requires large, structural social and economic changes'.

It is difficult to identify how UK and devolved governments answer these questions, or what the distributional consequences might be. There are individual clues in pockets of activity, such as to relate climate change to public health strategies (Office for Health Improvement and Disparities, 2022) and the commitment to 'advance gender equity in climate action' (Foreign, Commonwealth & Development Office, 2021).

Conclusion

Both of our policy-making stories signal bad news for the environment. First, the Westminster story could, in *theory*, be harnessed to generate support for rapid and radical policy change, driven by a centralised focus on addressing an urgent problem. UK government activity from 2006, leading to the Climate Change Act 2008, symbolised that potential. In *practice*, parties respond inconsistently to electoral incentives and cycles, and contribute to slow or disrupted progress. Climate change policy requires continuously high government investment, bolstered by cross-party and public support, to secure 'policy stability', give people and businesses the confidence to change behaviour, and make it expensive to turn back (Rietig and Laing, 2017: 575). However, we have witnessed short bursts of party competition to seem the 'greenest' and long periods when climate change was low priority and overshadowed by economic concerns. Renewable energy shows how long-term plans are disrupted by short-term choices. Transport highlights a reluctance of ministers to challenge a car-based economy. Food exhibits slow progress to reform the agricultural practices that focused on maximising production. Overall, it is difficult to give governments credit for progress. Positive outcomes are often the 'fortuitous byproduct' of changes outside of government control (Rayner and Jordan, 2016: 173).

Second, environmental policy exhibits all of the elements of the complex government story, highlighting the absence of single central government control over policy outcomes. As energy policy shows, this absence of control has often resulted from *choice*. Governments from 1979 have sought to 'roll back' state intervention in favour of markets. This action included privatising major utilities (coal, gas, nuclear, and electricity suppliers), favouring light-touch regulation, and restricting its role to broad oversight (Kuzemko, 2016: 111–114). Further, the UK government has often avoided refereeing disputes between fossil fuel companies and environmental groups (Jordan, 2001).

The absence of control is also the result of policy-making complexity. As our discussion of energy systems transitions demonstrates, the *'super wicked' policy problem* comes with a *super-complexity policy-making problem*, to the extent that no one is quite sure how to describe it. Central governments exacerbate this confusion by fudging their role in energy systems. Ambiguity allows them to juggle both stories of policy making – we are in control (the Westminster story) *and* we are not in control (the complex government story) – to project a sense of governing competence but avoid full responsibility for policy outcomes. The result is that UK (and devolved) governments have described *maximally* their ambitions to deal with climate change, but *minimally* how they will achieve them.

9

Economic Policy: Austerity

Chapter highlights

1. The 2008 global economic crisis had a profound impact on the UK government, which borrowed extensively to support banks and deal with the cost of recession.

2. The 2010 coalition government sought to address the UK's **deficit** and **debt** problems by reducing public spending and reforming public services.

3. This emphasis on 'austerity' reinforced a longer-term trend towards neoliberalism, emphasising state retrenchment in favour of individual and communal activity.

4. Three approaches highlight key perspectives on these issues:

   • Policy analysis identifies how to address economic crises. For example, what is the size, urgency and cause of the problem? What solutions should governments adopt?

   • Policy studies identify how governments address the impacts of economic crisis. Which policies have governments favoured, and what has been their impact?

   • Critical policy analysis identifies and challenges inequitable processes and outcomes. We highlight choices to reduce social security spending, with a disproportionate impact on people with disabilities, women and minoritised populations.

Introduction: The shift to austerity politics

Chapters 4 and 5 identify the long-term trends in economic policy that contributed to state transformation. A 'post-war consensus' had favoured high state intervention to pursue 'Keynesian' economic policies, deliver public services directly and boost the welfare state. From the late 1970s, there was movement towards 'neoliberal' approaches that favoured state retrenchment in favour of 'market forces' and individual responsibility, relied less on taxing and spending to manage the economy, and preferred to contract out service delivery and limit social security entitlement. The election of a Conservative-led government in 2010, following the 2007–2008 global economic crisis (Box 9.1), contributed to a major acceleration of that agenda.

Deficit: the amount to borrow when annual government spending is higher than income.

Debt: the overall amount of government borrowing (from multiple deficits).

Recession: a sustained drop in economic activity. Often defined as a reduction in gross domestic product (GDP) over two successive financial quarters.

The economic crisis had three elements: financial crisis, followed by **recession** and high government debt. The Labour government borrowed extensively to deal with an urgent financial crisis, then to increase spending to address the longer-term cost of recession. This crisis helped to undermine Labour before the UK general election in 2010 (Kavanagh and Cowley, 2010: 19–44). The outcome was a Conservative-led coalition government (Kavanagh and Cowley, 2010: viii) committed to reducing public spending. The Conservative Prime Minister (David Cameron) and Chancellor of the Exchequer (George Osborne) led an agenda dubbed 'austerity', seeking to abolish the government deficit in five years.

'Austerity' is a modern example of Conservative-led governments describing action as *inescapable* or *natural* and in the national interest ('there is no alternative' – Robinson, 2013). Rather, UK policy was driven by *ideology* and *opportunism* (Blyth, 2013; Haynes, 2015). It was a response to crisis and an opportunity to reinforce a neoliberal narrative (Chapters 4–5; Hay, 2013; Bach, 2016). For example, the coalition prioritised reducing **welfare** spending – such as limiting entitlement to unemployment benefits and capping child benefits – while promoting '**Big Society**' initiatives.

Welfare: part of social security spending (which includes the state pension). It can be described positively or as a pejorative term.

Big Society: Cameron's (2010) way to encourage self-reliance and community support or charitable action as an alternative to public services.

The UK approach was not part of a uniform international response to crisis. Many pursued Keynesian approaches, boosting public spending to encourage economic growth (Haynes, 2015; Chapter 4). Nor did the UK deliver austerity policies consistently. Government spending dropped profoundly in some sectors, but grew in others, and often grew overall (Hindmoor, 2019: 242–243). This experience highlights a government's reliance on wider economic activity to deliver its promises: its policies did not produce the promised rise in economic growth, and the recession had knock-on effects for welfare spending (Hindmoor, 2019: 244).

This chapter examines these issues through three lenses. Policy analysis identifies how to analyse economic policy in relation to long-standing debates: what should be the role of the state in the economy, what size of government spending is appropriate, what size of deficit is feasible, how much tax should a government raise, and what taxes should it use (Chapter 4)? Approaches to these debates inform questions during economic crisis, including:

- What is the size, urgency, and cause of each – financial, recession and debt – problem?
- What solutions should governments adopt?
- If one solution is to reduce government spending, what should be cut?

Policy studies situate this analysis in real-world developments, exploring:

- If governments control their own economic policies in a global economy.
- If the government actually delivered 'austerity' as it planned.

Critical policy analysis identifies who benefits or loses, and how to respond:

- Who bears the costs of policy changes in the name of austerity?
- Can we envisage more inclusive *policy making*, including collaborative governance between governments and stakeholders, to encourage more equitable *policy*?

In the conclusion, we ask how these experiences inform Westminster and complex government stories. The coalition government used 'government knows best' to narrate its austerity agenda, but did it deliver? Did it face the same obstacles to reform that frustrate all governments (Chapters 4 and 5)?

Box 9.1: The cause of the global financial crisis

In 2008, the Chancellor of the Exchequer (Alistair Darling) asked Lord Adair Turner, chair of the UK's Financial Services Authority, to explain the cause of the crisis and recommend regulatory changes to make the banking system more resilient. The Turner Review (2009) describes 'what went wrong' as follows:

- 'Macro-imbalances' arise when some countries have major surpluses (for example, China, oil-exporting countries) and invest in countries with deficits (for example, UK, US) (Turner, 2009: 11–12).
- When they invest heavily in low-risk government bonds, the rate of return falls.
- It prompts financial actors to seek better returns via higher-risk investments.
- One 'innovation' was the expansion (from the 1980s) of 'corporate bonds'. Credit is ostensibly 'securitised' (for example, linked to an asset such as a house mortgage). However, the financial product's role in a chain of credit is unclear, creating a false sense of low-risk investment (Turner, 2009: 14–16).
- A rising proportion of defaulted loans exposed a lack of diversification. Some organisations issued too much credit, leveraged on loans that would not be repaid (for example, to low-income families to fund US home ownership) (Turner, 2009: 17–25).

- In 2007, this problem sparked a financial crisis, fuelled by a shift in investor thinking from 'irrational exuberance' (misplaced confidence in investments) to 'confidence collapse'. It prompted investors to seek their money from financial institutions, and many collapsed when they could not repay loans quickly.
- In 2008, governments intervened to prevent many bank collapses (Turner, 2009: 25–27).
- The experience undermines assumptions – of 'efficient and rational markets' – underpinning regulation. Regulators operated on the misguided assumption that (1) market prices reflect economic value, and (2) market discipline and competition manage risk and innovation well (Turner, 2009: 39).

UK financial actors were vulnerable to this problem via a global chain. Many contributed by incentivising and rewarding risky behaviour, including: reckless attempts to buy other companies, and, mortgage lending to people on low incomes on the assumption that rising house prices lowered risk (Turner, 2009: 31; Bell and Hindmoor, 2015: 199–234; Thompson, 2015).

Policy analysis: how to address the policy problem

Step 1: How could governments define economic crisis as a policy problem?

Problem framing includes an account of: the problem's size and cause, who it affects, and the extent to which the state should be responsible for intervention (Chapter 2). In this case, the crisis had three main elements (finance, recession and debt), and was exacerbated by urgency: events unfolded at an overwhelming speed, prompting rapid decisions between limited options (such as spend big to save a bank or face the consequences of its failure).

First, there was a *global financial crisis* from 2007: 'arguably the greatest crisis in the history of finance capitalism' (Turner, 2009: 5). The biggest problems arose in the US and Europe (the UK in particular). Some of the worst-hit banks described a temporary lack of liquidity: the inability to turn capital into available funds as quickly as required by investors. However, many did not have enough productive capital: their investments were not producing the required returns. For example, the Royal Bank of Scotland had engaged in 'risky securities trading', and Halifax Bank of Scotland overexposed itself to risky mortgage lending, sustaining 'crippling losses' to the extent that it 'had to be taken over by another bank or nationalized' (Bell and Hindmoor, 2015: 75). Without state intervention, this crisis could have knock-on effects, including the economic harm from a lack of confidence of banks and businesses in each other, and social harm and unrest if savers were unable to access their money or saw its value diminish (Kickert, 2012). This problem was acute in the UK because its financial sector represents a disproportionately large share of (1) global finance, and (2) UK economic activity. Further, UK governments – Conservative and Labour – had overseen 'light-touch' regulation (via the Financial Services Authority) (Hodson and Mabbett, 2009: 1042–1049; Chapter 5).

Second, there was a *crisis of economic growth* from 2008, following the near-collapse of UK organisations. The government introduced a modest fiscal stimulus to encourage spending, while the Bank of England used 'quantitative easing' and low interest rates to encourage spending (Chapter 5). Still, the UK recession lasted for five quarters (April 2008 to July 2009) and shrunk the economy by 6 per cent; it took five years to return to that level of GDP (ONS, 2018).

Third, there was a *debt crisis* from 2008. The UK government had 'committed £117 billion in cash to purchase shares in and lend money to UK banks at the peak of the 2008 crisis' *and* 'insured around £600 billion of financial assets and guaranteed £250 billion of wholesale bank borrowing' (Bell and Hindmoor, 2015: 198; compare with £300 billion devoted to COVID-19 policies, Chapter 6). UK government debt rose from 42 per cent to 85 per cent of GDP from 2007 to 2010, aided by major investors buying low-risk-low-return government bonds during crisis (Bell and Hindmoor, 2015: 67). This rise in debt had followed Labour's previous commitment to 'fiscal prudence' and to limit debt to 40 per cent of GDP (Hodson and Mabbett, 2009: 1047). It limited the government's ability to produce more ambitious fiscal stimulus measures.

What caused these crises to happen or get worse? What are the policy implications?

The cause and implications of crisis are contested relating to (1) the global financial system prompting crises outside of government control, or (2) government mismanagement. For some, the problem is systemic: the free market and capitalism, combined with state retrenchment, causes economic problems and inequalities (Bresser-Pereira, 2010). Further, UK policies helped banks and businesses to receive the rewards but not the penalties of risky investments. Therefore, if governments know that they will have to bail out banks, they should receive a greater share of rewards and/or make sure that their regulations are substantive, well enforced and effective enough to prevent crises. Such narratives highlight the role of corporate sector greed, governments 'captured' by financial elites, and misguided UK government policies. This was a crisis of 'neoliberalism', and a failure of the governing and financial elite, disproving the idea that 'light-touch' regulation was appropriate (Box 9.1).

The party political debate, during the 2010 election campaign, focused on the importance of competent government and the trade-off between prioritising fiscal stimulus or reducing deficits. Labour sought to avoid blame for the consequences of global events. It emphasised the catastrophic consequences if it had not intervened to support banks and address the recession (Darling, 2010). The Conservative Party blamed the government's mismanagement of the financial sector and economy, including its tendency to over-commit the state, overspend and not use boom years to reduce debt (Osborne, 2009; Conservative Party,

2010; Tailby, 2012; Gamble, 2012; 2015; NEF, 2013). It argued that, without quicker and deeper spending cuts, the UK would lose international economic credibility and its ability to service government debt (Osborne, 2009). It drew on think tanks – such as Policy Exchange and the Centre for Social Justice (Table 4.2) – to propose welfare state and public services retrenchment (Brien, 2009; Quarmby and Fazackerly, 2009; McKay, 2010; Pautz, 2018). There was little difference between political party deficit reduction policies overall, but plans to abolish the deficit in five (Conservative) rather than ten years (Labour) were significant (Elliott, 2010).

Step 2: Identifying feasible solutions – what should they prioritise?

Solving the financial crisis

There was some support for letting irresponsible banks fail (Rosas, 2009; Grossman and Woll, 2013). However, initial failures – such as of Lehman Brothers in the US – exposed the interconnectedness of financial markets and uncertainty about what would happen if more failed (Peston, 2009). Accounts by the Prime Minister, Chancellor and Governor of the Bank of England (Darling, 2011; King, 2016; Brown, 2017) highlight the infeasibility of letting banks fail (BBC News, 2009; Elliott, 2009). Financial collapse would be socially damaging and unpopular with voters. The 'contagion effect' of bankruptcy could be disastrous to the economy, and more costly than bailouts (Edmonds et al, 2011; Chwieroth and Walter, 2021).

In that context, the main focus was on how to save UK banks. The government nationalised Northern Rock (February 2008), bought the majority of shares of the Royal Bank of Scotland (initially over 60 per cent then over 80 per cent in 2009) and a minority of Lloyds (43 per cent in 2009), and provided insurance and loan guarantees to others (Sibert, 2009; Stacey and Goff, 2012; Bell and Hindmoor, 2015: 198). This bailout plan rested on 'a Bank Recapitalization Fund for £50 billion', a 'Credit Guarantee Scheme (a government loan guarantee for new debt issues between UK banks for up to £250 billion)' and 'short-term loans made available through a Special Liquidity Scheme operated by the Bank of England, for £200 billion' (Grossman and Woll, 2014: 590). Banking Acts in 2008 and 2009 also boosted government powers to intervene to address failing banks.

Solving the crisis of recession and low growth

Solving the crisis of low economic growth was another matter, and subject to debates between different versions of neo-Keynesian and neoliberal approaches (Chapters 4 and 5; Pettifor and McPherson, 2023). There were some calls to see the financial crisis as a sign that there should be a more interventionist state, including: greater public ownership of essential utilities and services; more stringent government regulation of business and finance; and more progressive – individual and business – taxation to redistribute wealth and fund spending for environmentally sustainable economic growth (Murray, 2009; White, 2013: 12).

While no major political party saw this state transformation as politically feasible, this reference point helps to separate the parties and signal a shift of policy from 2010. Labour favoured mildly Keynesian fiscal policies to prioritise economic recovery and growth (and poverty reduction), with deficit reduction as a lower-priority or longer-term aim (Darling, 2010; 2011). It aimed to use state spending to stimulate demand directly, and reduce some taxes to encourage consumer spending (although the growth in its debt limited fiscal measures to around £20 billion). Measures included a temporary reduction of VAT (17.5 per cent to 15 per cent), a £20 billion small enterprise loan scheme, and 'stamp duty holiday' for buyers of homes worth less than £175,000 (offset somewhat by measures including a new 50 per cent marginal tax rate on income above £150,000) (Kickert, 2012; IFS, 2017). In addition, the Bank of England – responsible for monetary policy – sought to minimise the cost of borrowing, improve bank liquidity, and maintain price stability to improve individual and business confidence (Deleidi and Mazzucato, 2018; Chapter 5).

Solving the debt crisis

The Conservative Party opposed Labour's fiscal stimulus since further deficits would exacerbate already large government debt (Grice, 2008). It proposed 'low taxes and sound money' (Milne, 2008). It defined the crisis as primarily of debt and deficits, caused by Labour mismanagement, rescue packages and lower tax revenues following recession (a simple austerity narrative that chimed with voters – Killick, 2018: 244). It also used the **Eurozone crisis** as a cautionary tale, to assert the urgency of reducing government debt to sustainable levels (Shaikh and Milliken, 2010; Blyth, 2013).

The 'cleaning up Labour's mess' rhetoric dominated the coalition's approach to economic crisis. It publicised a note, left by the outgoing Chief Secretary to the Treasury, declaring 'I am sorry, there is no money left' (Byrne, 2015). The new government argued that it symbolised a

Eurozone crisis (from 2009): some Eurozone countries raised government borrowing to high levels (for example, Greece's debt was 150 per cent of GDP), with interest payments undermining current spending and a realistic prospect of loan defaulting. To satisfy markets (and meet the conditions of EU, European Central Bank and International Monetary Fund [IMF] 'bailouts'), they cut public spending, which exacerbated recession (Exadaktylos and Zahariadis, 2014; Bell and Hindmoor, 2015: 68).

reckless 'gap between public expenditure and government revenues' which 'left the UK economy especially exposed to the effects of the global financial crisis'

(Hopkin and Rosamond, 2018: 647). A predilection for 'Big Government' caused this crisis, which could only be answered by the smarter management of a smaller state (Landale, 2013; Williams et al, 2014).

The coalition also related debt to the appropriate role of the state – in relation to welfare spending and public services – to highlight the need for 'public sector reform' rather than higher taxes (compare with Thatcherism in Chapter 4). Their preference was an 80:20 ratio of cuts and tax increases, geared towards a 'cyclically adjusted current deficit (the overall deficit less government investment) of zero' before the next election in 2015 (Wren-Lewis, 2015: R6). It would reduce government department budgets by £81 billion by 2015, 'with a quarter … from the welfare budget' (Tailby, 2012: 449).

Steps 3 and 4: Using values and goals to compare solutions, and predicting the outcomes of solutions

Chapters 6–8 suggest that Steps 3 and 4 were not a strong feature of policy debates. In comparison, partisan debates on austerity highlighted relatively explicit value-based trade-offs. Labour sought to stimulate the economy to take the UK out of recession, and use spending to address its unequal impacts. The Conservatives highlighted excessive spending and debt linked to a too-generous welfare state and too-large public services. The Conservatives also built (optimistic) expectations into state retrenchment plans, predicting that the private sector would drive higher economic growth when the state stopped 'crowding out' its activities (Gamble, 2012; Berry and Hunt, 2015).

Step 5: Making recommendations

Chapters 6 and 8 show that complex policy problems defy simple recommendations. Yet, the Conservatives presented a short and concise account of the policy problem and how to solve it: reject Labour's reckless spending and debt, in favour of a period of state retrenchment to abolish the deficit, then use the proceeds of growth to cut the debt.

Responding to crisis: is economic policy out of UK government control?

Chapters 4 and 5 chart the long-term trajectory of UK economic policy, contrasting post-war Keynesian policies with neoliberal policies from the mid-1970s, but also identifying neo-Keynesian policies that combined elements of both (see also Ludlam and Smith, 2000; Fielding, 2002; Jessop, 2003; Griffiths and Hickson, 2009; Berry, 2016). Governments still encouraged borrowing to spend, to boost demand and economic growth, but relied increasingly on private debt (and gave responsibility for monetary policy to the Bank of England).

In that context, key cases of economic crisis suggest that the content or impact of public policy was out of UK government control (plus currency fluctuations defy domestic control, even in the absence of crisis – Delis and Ioannidis, 2021). In other words, ministers lost their story of control when their policies made a demonstrable contribution to policy failure, resulting in immense pressure to change policy dramatically and/or face an electoral loss (Chapters 4 and 5). First, the initial neoliberal shift in the 1970s began with a crisis of UK economic performance and government borrowing, with organisations like the IMF prompting Labour to begin the reforms that became so associated with Thatcher governments. Second, the UK variant of neo-Keynesian policies (which began before Labour in 1997) contributed eventually to the financial crisis. Further, the 'Big Bang' of financial deregulation in 1986 symbolised a new tendency for both parties to favour 'light-touch' regulation (Crotty, 2009; Darling, 2011; Bellringer and Michie, 2014), while the accumulation of private-sector debt and risky bank activity fuelled global economic crisis (Hay, 2011: 246; Bach, 2016; Berry, 2016; Oren and Blyth, 2019: 606).

Controlling the crisis narrative

Governments may not control the events or conditions that influence their choices, but they often provide effective narratives of crises to signal the need for – otherwise highly unpopular – policy change (Boxes 3.1 and 5.3). Labour used a crisis frame to sell grave warnings about the economic and social cost of inaction (Darling, 2011; King, 2016; Brown, 2017). This narrative and response to economic crisis influenced other countries (Krugman, 2008). It bolstered **G20** efforts to coordinate national policy responses, urging "rapid effect" tax cuts, spending increases, and interest rate cuts' to avoid the recessionary effect of reduced spending (Krugman, 2008; Lawder and Jarry, 2008; MacLeavy, 2011).

> **G20**: Group of 20 (19 countries and the EU). An international organisation that seeks a 'strategic role in securing future global economic growth and prosperity'; it accounts for 80 per cent of global GDP (G20, 2022).

Then, the Conservative-led government's response to the 'debt crisis' used the opportunity to pursue 'an ideological commitment to neo-liberalism', which sat 'comfortably with the pursuit of austerity measures that it presents as necessary for pragmatic reasons' (Van Reenan, 2013; Mitton, 2016: 751). This commitment is shared by centre-right actors, including think tanks (such as Policy Exchange, Reform and the Institute for Economic Affairs – Table 4.2), business actors (including Conservative Party donors in the financial sector) and media outlets (such as the *Spectator* and *Daily Telegraph*), generating political support for austerity. Further, Osborne claimed 'that the situation he had inherited was much worse than he had expected', signalling that 'urgent action needed to be taken to bring the public finances under control' (Gamble, 2015). This argument represented one of seven parts of the austerity narrative described by the New Economics Foundation (NEF, 2013: 2):

1. Excessive debt is dangerous.
2. Britain is broke.
3. Austerity is a necessary evil.
4. Big government is bad government.
5. Welfare is like a drug, and government action should not encourage dependence.
6. Reform government to reward strivers and punish skivers.
7. We need to fix Labour's mess quickly.

The Conservative-led austerity narrative was a greater success than the policies it prompted, not least because each element is contested. First, UK debt levels were high but low interest rates made them affordable (Krugman, 2015; Skidelsky, 2017). Second, the 'broke' argument relies on a misleading household debt analogy (Blyth, 2013; Krugman, 2015). Third, the actions of other governments demonstrated that there were alternatives to austerity as a growth or deficit reduction strategy (Milmo, 2012). Fourth, the idea that too much public investment 'crowds out' private activity is contested (and not always followed by Conservative governments – Berry and Hunt, 2015). Fifth, 'welfare dependency' is an assertion rarely backed by evidence (Harkness et al, 2012; Wiggan, 2018). Finally, successive governments found that (for example) in-work poverty undermined their assertion that 'strivers' do not benefit from government support. Nevertheless, this rhetoric remained popular (NEF, 2013), and contributed to Conservative electoral success in 2015 (Gamble, 2015; Harrison, 2021).

Did the coalition government actually deliver 'austerity' reforms?

The coalition government drew on the Westminster story of central control, and 'government knows best' narrative, to promise a 'radical programme for a radical government' (Cairney, 2012: 231; Grimshaw and Rubery, 2012; Taylor-Gooby, 2012a; 2012b). 'Austerity' involved spending cuts, tax reforms, and public sector reforms, plus a surprising hike in university fees in England (Box 9.2). The UK government largely made these tax and spending changes across the UK, but with different effects in devolved territories (Box 9.3).

Box 9.2: The unexpected rise in higher education fees

The coalition government raised higher education fees – in England – to levels not foreseen by Thatcherite governments (Chapter 4). Universities in England now generate over £20 billion in 'tuition fees and education contracts' (HESA, 2022). The Labour government had increased fees for domestic students – to £1,000 per year in 1997 and – in England – £3,000 in 2003 (funded by low-interest loans) – to foster higher education expansion and widen participation while limiting costs (Thompson, 2012; Carasso and Gunn, 2015; Hillman, 2016). This move was opposed by the National Union of Students and many Labour MPs (and, initially, the Conservatives), prompting Labour's (2005: 40) manifesto promise not to raise fees further before 2010. It commissioned Lord Browne (CEO of British Petroleum) to lead a review of the sustainability of higher education (published after the 2010 election). The Browne report (2010: 4–5) identified six principles: greater higher education investment, student choice (where and what to study), reducing financial barriers, no up-front costs, deferring loan repayments until employment (with payments linked to income), and parity between part- and full-time students. It recommended allowing universities to 'charge different and higher fees provided that they can show improvements in the student experience and demonstrate progress in providing fair access' (Browne, 2010: 3).

The coalition government allowed universities in England to charge up to £9,000 per year, which they all did (on the condition of following schemes to widen access for low-income and under-represented groups – Dearden and Jin, 2014). The move was opposed by the National Union of Students and organisations promoting equity (Carasso and Gunn, 2015). It was also somewhat unexpected. The Coalition Agreement did not predict it (HM Government, 2010). The Conservative Party (2010) had been vague, but with the Minister for Universities and Science keen to reform (Carasso and Gunn, 2015) and the Chancellor keen to reduce the deficit. The Liberal Democrat manifesto (2010) had promised to 'Scrap unfair university tuition fees' and its leader – Nick Clegg – backed this pledge during the campaign (Clegg, 2016; Butler, 2021). However, the leadership saw it as a low priority, wanted to remove it, but accepted its inclusion because it had 'grass roots' support (Butler, 2021). Then, it agreed to policy change and followed Collective Cabinet Responsibility to support it publicly (Kippin and Pyper, 2021). Clegg eventually apologised for pretending to support fee cuts (Cutts and Russell, 2015; Atkins, 2018: 58–60). Labour took a similar journey in opposition: pledging to 'scrap' tuition fees under Corbyn in 2019, then removing this pledge in 2023 under Starmer (Zeffman and Woolcock, 2023).

The £3,000 then £9,000 fees in England contributed to divergence across the UK, but put pressure on devolved governments to converge (Gallagher and Raffe, 2012; Keating et al, 2012; Cairney et al, 2022a: 79). The Labour–Liberal Democrat Scottish government (in 2000) reduced the £1,000 fee and did not follow the £3,000 rise, and Scottish National Party government legislation (in 2008) abolished tuition fees for Scotland-domiciled students. The (Labour-led) Welsh government responded to the £3,000 per year fees by targeting fee reductions (around £2,000) for Welsh students at Welsh universities, then introduced £9,000 fees and means-tested grants. Policy in Northern Ireland largely converged with England by 2006, but the Executive froze or reduced fees for Northern Irish students studying in Northern Ireland (they are about half the fee in England). Each devolved system charges England-level fees for UK students outside their territory (but few Scottish universities charge for their fourth year).

The major reduction of public spending in some sectors

The coalition government turbo-boosted measures to reduce 'welfare state' funding, such as to make it more difficult to claim social security benefits, restrict entitlement or reduce spending per person (MacLeavy, 2011). It ramped up the 'welfare to work' reforms – to develop 'employability' – initiated by Labour (Cairney and St Denny, 2020: 172–173). They were built on the belief that: employment is key to mental health and wellbeing (and a way to reduce unemployment benefits); the social security system is too focused on demonstrating the inability to work; and, the jobs are there for people willing to work (Cairney and St Denny, 2020: 173). The Labour government had commissioned the Black Review which recommended that GPs stop issuing 'sick notes' in favour of 'fit notes' to describe how they can work and what would boost their employability (Black, 2008: 12). Labour also set up a contract with private company ATOS to pilot the Work Capability Assessment used by the Department for Work and Pensions to determine eligibility for disability-related benefits.

The coalition government repurposed this approach to prioritise austerity (rather than wellbeing), attaching strict conditions to the mandatory Work Capability Assessment process (Mattheys, 2015), and overseeing processes that alienated claimants (Grover, 2014). It increased sanctions for people who failed to meet the Jobcentre's requirements for job-seeking activity (often obliging people to take low-paid work – DWP, 2023a). Further, it sought to introduce 'Universal Credit', a consolidated benefits scheme to adjust more quickly to changing circumstances and reduce incentives to remain out of work (Beatty and Fothergill, 2014; Timmins, 2016). Other examples of reduced spending include:

- Reduced housing benefits to incentivise people to not have spare housing capacity became known as the 'bedroom tax' (Hopkinson and Robbins, 2013; Gibb, 2015; Mitton, 2016).
- A two-child limit for relevant benefits and tax credits, unless the claimant can demonstrate that another child 'is born as a result of non-consensual sexual intercourse', was often called the 'rape clause' (Machin, 2017).
- Local authority spending in England fell by 13 per cent between 2009/2010 and 2018/2019, largely due to a shrinking central government contribution (Johns, 2020: 3).
- A public sector wage freeze caused a real-terms cut in many sectors (Powell and Booth, 2021).
- Some departmental budgets were reduced significantly, including Justice (25 per cent) and aspects of Education (P. Bolton, 2014: 3; 2021).

Reforms to taxation

The government modified taxes without signalling radical reforms (Adam and Roantree, 2015). Revenue-raising changes included raising VAT from 17.5 per cent to 20 per cent and National Insurance by 1 per cent, and reducing tax expenditures on pensions, while tax cuts included increasing the income tax threshold, reducing corporation tax (28 per cent to 20 per cent, the lowest in the G20 – Maffini, 2015), and real-terms cuts to fuel duties. The net effect was £16 billion extra revenue per year by 2016 (£18–19 billion at 2020 prices).

Reforms to the public sector

Like Labour, the coalition government sought to 'modernise' the public sector (HM Government, 2010), drawing on new public management ideas to extend consumer/citizen choice and contract out the delivery of public services to private or third-sector organisations (Chapter 4; Levitas, 2012; National Audit Office, 2013; Raynor, 2020). It used 'payment by results' to incentivise the private companies paid to reduce the number of people who are long-term unemployed (Carter and Whitworth, 2015). It also experimented with contracting out some aspects of police services, while creating directly elected regional Police and Crime Commissioners to oversee each force (Raine and Keasey, 2012; White, 2015; 2020), and replaced Regional Development Agencies with private sector-led Local Enterprise Partnerships (Berry, 2020).

Unlike Labour, it favoured decentralisation, to replace centrally directed target-based approaches with localism (Cameron, 2011a; Williams et al, 2014: 2800). However, this rhetoric is misleading since the government also cut local authority budgets, to let them decide 'where the knife fell' (Eagle et al, 2017). They went from Labour's 'targets and money' to the coalition's 'no targets, no money' (Matthews, 2016: 315–318).

Box 9.3: Austerity and devolved government policy

From 1999, devolved governments had limited powers to raise money. They could influence local council taxes, business rates and the ability to charge for public services (the Scottish Parliament could also change UK income tax by 3p in the pound). Their budgets were largely provided by the UK government, but each settlement allowed for higher per person spending in Northern Ireland, then Scotland, then Wales, which was higher than in England overall (Birrell, 2012: 29; Brien, 2021). The 'Barnett Formula' provided routine annual changes to budgets, but not a successful way to 'depoliticise' funding (Birrell, 2012: 29–35). Pro-Union political parties in Scotland described higher funding as the 'Union dividend' (a view rejected by supporters of Scottish independence), Welsh politicians criticised its lower per capita settlement, and there was a 'growing perception in England that Scotland receives more than its fair share' (Cairney and McGarvey, 2013: 225, citing Wyn Jones et al, 2012).

Devolved governments had high autonomy to *spend* their own budgets and direct public services. Welsh and Scottish governments signalled policy divergence from the UK, in favour of state-led forms of service delivery (Chapter 4). Examples of more universalist provision in devolved territories (including fewer charges for National Health Services [NHS] prescriptions or university tuition) and Scotland-specific initiatives such as 'free personal care' for older people bolstered the idea of better-funded governments diverging from UK neoliberal policies (Keating et al, 2012).

These differences were already clear when all three governments in Britain were Labour-led, and when UK and devolved public expenditure had risen considerably in the first decade of devolution. They became starker when the Scottish National Party controlled the Scottish government from 2007, Labour left UK office from 2010, and UK and devolved budgets fell or remained static over the next decade. Devolved governments were critical of the coalition government's austerity, and/or explored how to mitigate its effects (Mac Flynn, 2015; Welsh Government, 2018; Coulter, 2019; Ifan and Sion, 2019; Scottish Government, 2019; Taylor-Collins and Downe, 2021). The Scottish government developed a nascent social security system, after the Scotland Act 2016 extended (1) its powers to provide disability and housing benefits, combined with (2) greater 'fiscal devolution' in income tax, some aspects of VAT, stamp duty, and potentially environmental taxes on airlines and aggregates (McIntyre et al, 2022).

Did the coalition government deliver austerity?

The coalition government was more successful at projecting austerity than achieving fundamental aims or outcomes. First, key aspects were not in their full control, or did not work as intended. Initial spending cuts were followed by recession in 2012, prompting even the IMF's Director to question the pace of cuts (Stewart, 2012; Elliott, 2013). The lack of growth had a negative knock-on effect for unemployment and social security spending (Hindmoor, 2019: 244; Chapter 4) and the shift to 'fit notes' did not boost employment (Dorrington et al, 2018). Then, the relaxation of austerity was followed by economic growth (Hindmoor, 2019: 242–243).

Second, the coalition avoided defunding in key areas: governments prefer to make the NHS more efficient and increase funding (Chapter 4), and not look like they are cutting pensions; and, demand for services or payments is driven heavily by demographic change. Still, the overall effect of austerity on government spending is substantive. We describe it in two different ways. Figure 9.1 shows that it oversaw modest rises – in real terms (adjusted for inflation, using the GDP deflator) – after higher annual rises under Labour. The modest rise in real spending under Conservative-led government is similar during the Thatcher and austerity years (then COVID-19 spending rose from 2020 – Chapter 6).

Figure 9.2 accentuates this effect of Conservative government. As with the early Thatcher years (Chapter 4), governments from 2010 oversaw annual drops in spending as a proportion of GDP. In other words, real spending rose modestly

Figure 9.1: Total managed expenditure, nominal and real terms, 1981–1982 to 2021–2022

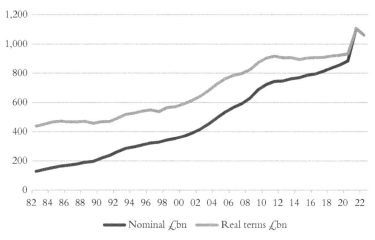

Source: author's own, generated from HM Treasury (2022: 71; Table 4.1). This source does not go beyond 1981–1982. Previous editions do not provide a consistent series.

Figure 9.2: Total managed expenditure as percentage of GDP, 1981–1982 to 2021–2022

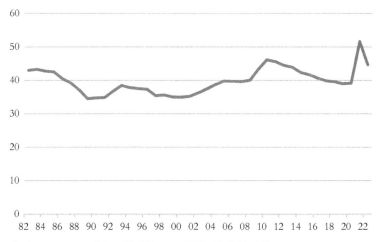

Source: author's own, generated from HM Treasury (2022; 71, Table 4.1)

and not as quickly as the economy (until the impact of COVID-19, prompting higher spending and lower growth).

Third, the government changed taxes but not the tax system:

> VAT has been increased but its base not broadened. Fuel duties have been cut but their increasing unsuitability for tackling congestion has not been addressed. Corporation tax has been cut but its base continues

to distort investment and financing decisions. Income tax and NICs [National Insurance Contributions] rates and thresholds have been changed but the two taxes have not been integrated. Business rates have been cut but made more unstable and continue to discourage property intensive production. Council tax has been cut but allowed to get ever more out of date. Inheritance tax has been increased but its loopholes untouched. Capital gains tax has been increased but with no clear strategy for dealing with the tension between minimising disincentives to save and minimising avoidance opportunities. (Adam and Roantree, 2015: 2)

Fourth, it is difficult to identify a clear effect of public sector reforms. The Big Society was vague and short-lived (Levitas, 2012). It fostered big ideas – 'decentralisation and community empowerment' (Williams et al, 2014; Jupp, 2021) – but Cameron lost interest. The initiative also boosted the formation of 'public service' mutuals, and a number of 'stakeholder mutual' Co-operative Schools, not envisaged by the Conservatives (Birchall, 2011; Woodin, 2019; Kippin, 2021). The Universal Credit reform began disastrously, albeit with the longer-term potential to work as intended (Norris and Rutter, 2016; Timmins, 2016). Police reforms did not come to much (White, 2015).

The coalition also followed a long tradition of promising to cut bureaucracy and unelected quangos but only engaging superficially. Gimmicks included the 'one in one out' rule for regulations, and the 'red tape challenge' (Cameron, 2011a). The government also cut the number of, but not spending on, quangos (Flinders and Skelcher, 2012: 328; Rutter et al, 2012; Hood and Dixon, 2015; Tonkiss and Skelcher, 2015; Pike et al, 2018; Box 4.2). The latter highlights the misleadingly selective categorisation of data by successive governments, which hinders a straightforward assessment of policy success. For example, the Thatcher government reduced unemployment on paper by (1) measuring only those claiming unemployment benefits successfully, and (2) expanding the use of 'sickness' benefits (Webster, 2002), thus helping to create the problems addressed by the coalition.

Critical policy analysis: who bears the cost of austerity?

Austerity produced intended and unintended consequences. Some are high salience, while others receive minimal attention. For example, the austerity narrative contains explicit statements about who should benefit from state intervention or retrenchment. As Box 3.6 describes, politicians assert value judgements based on social stereotypes, to reward 'good' social groups with government support and punish 'bad' groups with sanctions. These judgements inform policy design, including government regulations and targeted funding, and the actions of front-line delivery organisations (Chapter 3). Policy design and delivery sends encouraging or alienating signals to citizens, indirectly via media or directly when they seek government support. Schneider and Ingram (1993; 1997) identify four categories of groups, according to their social construction and resources to challenge or exploit it:

- *Advantaged* groups are treated positively and can act to enjoy the benefits (for example, small business groups).
- *Dependents* are treated positively but cannot act collectively to exploit this image (for example, 'strivers').
- *Contenders* are treated negatively but can negotiate benefits behind the scenes (for example, bankers).
- *Deviants* are treated negatively, and are unable to challenge negative government action.

Government portrayals of welfare claimants as 'skivers' drive them to the 'deviants' category (O'Grady, 2022). Coalition ministers (and their Labour predecessors) used negative images of the alleged lifestyle choices, laziness or fecklessness of benefit claimants to narrate welfare service reform (see Chapter 10 on 'troubled families'). These images undermine the idea of welfare states as symbols of social solidarity, in favour of individualism and divisiveness (Hamnett, 2014; Taylor-Gooby, 2016).

In that context, coalition success is subject to interpretation (Box 5.3). For example, the tendency for employability and disability assessments to alienate claimants represents failure in relation to stakeholder relations (Cairney and St Denny, 2020: 173) and population outcomes (Grover, 2014) but success in terms of Conservative aims to portray the party as intolerant of welfare spending (see also Gibb, 2015 on the 'bedroom tax'). Similarly, a tendency for 'welfare to work' organisations to devote most resources to the people easiest to employ ('creaming'), and not invest in people who face greater obstacles to work ('parking'), goes against stated policy intentions (Carter and Whitworth, 2015: 279–280) but still delivers political benefits.

In other cases, outcomes may relate to values expressed less explicitly or unintended consequences. For example, cuts and reforms often have disproportionate impacts on women, areas of higher socio-economic deprivation, people with disabilities, and minoritised populations, or have differential effects in relation to age.

The impact on disability benefits and services

The coalition government accelerated government policies to challenge disability-related unemployment benefits. It commissioned ATOS to oversee 'impersonal and mechanistic' processes that alienated claimants: assessing some (incorrectly) as capable to perform paid employment, prompting more successful appeals against their assessments (Grover, 2014: 1324–1325). The process and outcome contributed to an increase in 'suicides, self-reported mental health problems, and anti-depressant prescribing' (Barr et al, 2016). It exacerbated a 'public health crisis' (Stewart, 2022), 'mental health crisis' (Cummins, 2018; Stewart, 2019) and alleged 'deaths of despair' (Case and Deaton, 2020).

Reduced social care funding caused (1) 42 per cent of people with a learning disability to lose care and support, and therefore engage in fewer activities (Forrester-Jones et al, 2020), and (2) a 'sharp rise in families with disabled children going without the basics such as food, heating, and days out' (British Academy of Childhood Disability, 2014: 1). Following benefits and tax credit reductions, 'some families with disabilities are projected to lose £11,000 on average by 2021–2022, more than 30 per cent of their annual net income' (United Nations, 2019).

The impact of austerity on women

'**Gender status**': policies to 'empower all women as a group and counter the discrimination faced by women as women' (Sanders et al, 2019: 164). They include coalition policies to address 'violence against women and girls' (including to prosecute human traffickers, outlaw stalking, criminalise 'the possession of realistic depictions of rape and revenge pornography', forced marriage, female genital mutilation, and support domestic violence services) (Sanders et al, 2019: 164–168). The Equality Act 2010 combines status- and class-based policies by establishing a public sector duty to challenge discrimination in relation to 'age, disability, sex, gender reassignment, pregnancy and maternity, race, religion or belief and sexual orientation'. The Marriage (Same-Sex Couples) Act 2013 can 'be regarded as a status policy' since it challenges 'assumptions of heterosexuality' (Sanders et al, 2019: 164). See also Chapter 10 on gender mainstreaming.

The Women's Budget Group (2018: 1) describes a 'triple whammy' in relation to benefits, employment and services (see also Dalingwater, 2018). These impacts relate primarily to the 'class-based' policies that influence the 'sexual division of labour' (as distinct from '**gender status**') (Sanders et al, 2019: 164). In other words, coalition policies accentuated the tendency of UK policies to assume a traditional 'male breadwinner' in full-time employment (MacLeavy, 2011: 363), exacerbating an inequitable 'division of resources between men and women' (Sanders et al, 2019: 164, citing Htun and Weldon, 2010; see also Budgeon, 2019).

First, women make greater use of welfare benefits and were more affected by Universal Credit reforms, including benefit caps, the insistence 'on dividing a couple with children into a main earner and a main carer' (exacerbating unequal gender roles), providing less support to the lower earner (more likely to be a woman), reducing payments to lone parents under 25 and obliging Jobcentre staff to be inflexible in relation to availability to work (for example, outside of childcare or school hours), paying childcare too late in the month, the 'rape clause', and administrative obstacles to making legitimate claims (Garnham, 2018;

compare with Herd and Moynihan on 'administrative burden'). From 2010 to 2013, 79 per cent of welfare cuts were borne primarily by women (Busby and James, 2016; Sanders and Shorrocks, 2019).

Second, women form a higher proportion of the public sector labour force, so a public sector pay freeze and reduction in the workforce has a greater impact (Bell and Wilson, 2018; MacDonald, 2018). Third, women are more likely to provide unpaid labour to fill the gaps left by social and care services (Maassen and Zacchia, 2017). Issues include patchy services for older people, and reductions in England of the Sure Start centres that coordinate early years services (a UK Labour initiative, administered separately by devolved governments – Bate and Foster, 2017; Cairney and St Denny, 2020).

Austerity and minoritisation: race, religion and ethnicity

The United Nations Special Rapporteur described austerity measures as 'disproportionately detrimental to members of racial and ethnic minority communities, who are also the hardest hit by unemployment' and face a 'climate of national anxieties in which entire religious, racial and ethnic groups are presumed to be enemies' (Achiume, 2019: 9; see also Rafferty, 2014; Goodfellow, 2019; Qureshi et al, 2020).

These distributional impacts are not uniform. For example, the Joseph Rowntree Charitable Trust describes (on average) Indian and Chinese groups as financially more secure, but Black Caribbean, Pakistani and Bangladeshi groups in greater poverty than the 'White majority' (Fisher and Nandi, 2015). In that context, for example:

- From 2007/2008 to 2012/2013, 'absolute levels of deprivation did not change for the four poorest groups – Pakistani, Bangladeshi, Black Caribbean and Black African – but it worsened for all other groups, less so for the White majority' (Fisher and Nandi, 2015: 5).
- The UK's Equality and Human Rights Commission estimates that 'the racially disparate impact of austerity measures' will cause a disproportionately high loss in income for Black households (Achiume, 2019: 9).
- The Runnymede Trust and Women's Budget Group found that 'women and particularly those on low incomes and from a **BME** background were hardest

BME: abbreviates 'Black and minority ethnic populations'. BAME abbreviates 'black, Asian and minority ethnic populations' (often capitalising Black). These terms are problematic when used – primarily by White people – to mean *not White*, contributing to the sense of a homogenous minority experience, and highlighting only some groups. The UK government (HM Government, 2022b; Laux and Nissar, 2022) accepted a Commission on Race and Ethnic Disparities (2021) recommendation to '[s]top using aggregated and unhelpful terms such as "BAME", to better focus on understanding disparities and outcomes for specific ethnic groups'. Many broadcasters and organisations made that commitment (BBC News, 2021c).

Yet, people still seek terms to describe a shared experience of minoritisation and common ground for political participation (Linton, 2018: v; compare with LGBTQIA+ in Chapter 10). Variants of the term 'people of colour' (for example, women of colour) are often adopted respectfully in UK discourse, often to self-define 'in opposition to whiteness' (Linton, 2018: v).

hit by changes to benefits and gained the least from tax changes' (Hall et al, 2017: 21).

Age-related implications

A collection of policy changes helped older voters become relatively protected from austerity (and more likely to support the Conservative Party behind the reforms – Taylor-Gooby, 2016). Examples include:

• The pensions 'triple lock' (2010), ensuring that they would rise annually by whatever is highest: 2.5 per cent, price inflation or earnings growth (Portes, 2014; Emmerson, 2022).
• Retaining policies such as the Winter Fuel Allowance, free TV licences for over-75s, and subsidised travel passes for retirees.
• Protecting or boosting spending on the NHS, used primarily by the older people (Portes, 2014).

Meanwhile, younger people often lost out. Examples include:

• The cost of university tuition in England increased, and students graduated with an average of over £50,000 debt by 2017 (IFS, 2017; Hubble and Bolton, 2018).
• The Education Maintenance Allowance – to improve participation in post-16 education – was abolished, contributing to a 1.6 per cent reduction of participation (Weavers, 2021).
• The Child Trust Fund, to give children a £1,000 lump sum when turning 18, and encourage saving among low-income households, was scrapped (Zichawo et al, 2014).
• Housing benefit reductions, combined with new eviction powers to reduce squatting, affected younger people disproportionately, contributing to a major increase in homeless acceptances by English local authorities (Nowicki, 2017; Wilkinson and Ortega-Alcazar, 2017; Crisis, 2019; Borbely, 2020).

In this case, the distributional outcomes are contested, not least because services for older people may reflect their relative vulnerability and dependence on services, as well as National Insurance contributions to receive the state pension, while younger people are now more likely to attend university than previous generations (compare Ridge, 2013; Portes, 2014; Taylor-Gooby, 2016; Willetts, 2019).

Geographical impacts

The UK exhibits distinct regional disparities (Gonzalez, 2010). While often expressed as a north/south divide in England, patterns of poverty and inequality can be found within each area (including on-average affluent areas such as central London). Many coalition policies disadvantaged poorer areas, including:

- The Department for Communities and Local Government experienced the largest cut of any department, producing reductions in funding to Local Authorities in England. Cuts were 'particularly severe for municipal budgets' and cities with an 'older industrial base', while 'middle England' and south-central areas 'experienced the smallest spending cuts' (Gray and Barford, 2018: 558).
- Local and business leaders in the north-east were most likely to lament the abolition of Regional Development Agencies (Larkin, 2009; Pike et al, 2018; Shaw and Robinson, 2019).
- Funding cuts to charitable and voluntary organisations were distributed unequally, with (for example) organisations in Liverpool more affected than in Bristol (Jones et al, 2016; Dagdeviren et al, 2019).
- '£1 in every £7 cut from public health services has come from England's ten most deprived communities', meaning that 'absolute cuts in the poorest places have thus been six times larger than in the least deprived' (Thomas, 2019). Several studies attributed stalled increases in life expectancy to cuts in local government (Alexiou et al, 2021) and public services (Raleigh, 2022; see also Hiam et al, 2023; Scott, 2023 on unequally declining life expectancy).

Devolved analyses also highlighted unequal impacts. In Scotland, the Equality and Human Rights Commission (2019) found that large families, female lone-parent households, Black households, and severely disabled people would suffer relatively high losses of income due to the cumulative impact of UK government policy between 2010 and 2017. In Wales, budget cuts led to reductions in staffing in healthcare, local councils, the Welsh government, the Welsh NHS, police forces and the Fire and Rescue Services, and the closure of many libraries and youth centres (Mansour, 2019; Unison Wales, 2019). Austerity measures caused a 'significant negative impact on children and children's rights' and undermined the capacity of government to 'maintain essential services' (Hoffman, 2015: 3). In Northern Ireland, poorer households lost 'a higher proportion of their net incomes on average' than better-off households (Portes and Reed, 2018).

Can we envisage more inclusive forms of policy making?

Coalition rhetoric emphasised a desire to decentralise policy making in favour of localism and non-governmental action, and there was some support for other ways – than GDP growth – to measure progress (Box 9.4). This potential experimentation took place when other actors proposed more fundamental reforms (Dunleavy et al, 2018), such as to:

- Improve direct representation in the English regions, via an English Parliament, or regional assemblies taking on comparable powers to devolved parliaments (Kenny, 2016; Kippin and Campion, 2018).
- Set up a constitutional convention to reconsider how to share power across the UK (Garland and Palese, 2018), or 'crowd source' a new constitution (Landemore, 2014).
- Foster 'deliberative democracy', to 'bring together a broadly representative body of people', engaged in a process of finding common ground and reaching decisions (Wampler, 2008; Chwalisz, 2015; Involve, 2018).
- Foster the 'co-production' of policy between policy makers, stakeholders, service users and other citizens (Ostrom, 1996: 1079; Flinders et al, 2016; Sorrentino et al, 2018).

Frankly, few of these initiatives came to much. Case studies of co-production – largely in health and social policies – highlight *some* potential to extend their use, but as a small proportion of government business (see the Special Issue of *Social Policy and Administration* in 2019, Issue 2). Developments in Preston in England and North Ayrshire in Scotland demonstrate *some* potential for Community Wealth Building: to ensure that economic activity benefits the communities in which it takes place through the creation of community-owned cooperatives and placing immovable 'anchor institutions' at the centre of an economic ecosystem (Guinan and O'Neill, 2019). Proposals to distribute ownership and political power in society, to challenge iniquitous policy decisions (Mills et al, 2020), largely remind us of the lack of progress to that end. 'Prevention' measures, designed to intervene early in people's lives to mitigate the impact of inequalities, and coordinate policy making, also demonstrate high ambition but low progress (Box 9.4).

Box 9.4: Alternative measures of progress: GDP, doughnuts and wellbeing

GDP often seems to be a taken-for-granted way for governments to: (1) compare levels of economic activity over time and across countries, and (2) determine the prosperity of their countries. Indeed, a six-month reduction in GDP (recession) tends to prompt political crises and a major push to respond. Yet, GDP is a crude measure of economic activity, few people understand how it is calculated, and contested choices have a major impact on the calculation (Coyle, 2014).

Some calls to reject the primacy of GDP have captured international policy-maker attention, particularly 'in the context of economic crises and seemingly intractable social and environmental challenges' (Bache, 2019: 2). For example, Raworth's (2017: 25) 'doughnut economics' begins with a call to 'change the goal'. The 'fixation' with GDP 'has been used to justify extreme inequalities of income and wealth coupled with unprecedented destruction of the living world' (Raworth, 2017: 25), and should be replaced with more sustainable goals focused on human rights and environmental sustainability (Chapter 8).

This new idea chimes with long-standing attempts to shift governmental indicators of progress from economic growth to population 'wellbeing'. Traditionally, wellbeing has received low attention because it is a vague and hard-to-measure concept. Recently, there has been a major push – by international bodies such as the **Organisation for Economic Co-operation and Development (OECD)**, the EU and the UN – to foster better measures to compete with GDP (Bache, 2019: 2). Cameron announced in 2010 that Office for National Statistics measures of wellbeing 'would be used to guide public policies' (Bache and Reardon, 2013: 898; 2016).

> **Organisation for Economic Co-operation and Development (OECD)**: it has 38 country members (including the UK). It seeks to 'provide a unique forum and knowledge hub for data and analysis, exchange of experiences, best-practice sharing, and advice on public policies and international standard-setting' (OECD, 2022c).

However, such concepts have a marginal impact on public policy. The UK government struggles to turn vague agendas into concrete policies with a demonstrable impact. One small exception is funding to help identify 'what works' to foster wellbeing (in other words, using research of interventions to measure their positive impact – Bache, 2019: 3). Senedd Cymru passed 'unique and pioneering' legislation to connect Welsh policy to the UN Sustainable Development Goals, but 'the Act is vague, open-ended and aspirational' (Nesom and MacKillop, 2021: 432). The gap between vague aspiration and actual outcomes is a more general feature of policies – to reduce inequalities or public service costs – built on the idiom 'prevention is better than cure' (Cairney and St Denny, 2020).

Conclusion

The coalition government sought major public expenditure cuts to eliminate the UK deficit in five years, and 'austerity' became a slogan to describe its aims. It involved major cuts to state spending – and welfare state spending in particular – to foster state retrenchment in favour of economic markets and individual responsibility.

This experience exhibits elements of the Westminster story. First, the government produced a crisis narrative, emphasising the need for rapid and radical – centrally driven – action to deal with a debt crisis not of its making. This focus on debt crisis replaced Labour's emphasis on interventionist fiscal measures to promote economic recovery. It also used the 'government knows best' line: many of these reforms might be unpopular but they are definitely necessary. Second, the coalition was able to make many rapid and substantive changes to public policy, not least to reduce spending in intended areas and initiate public sector reforms. Third, the unequal impact of these reforms relates closely to its narrative about the social groups who are most deserving of government support or sanction.

Yet, the experience also undermines key aspects of that narrative: early policies did not have their intended effects on the economy, and there are clear instances in which it changed course. There was a 'spending pause' of high magnitude (Resolution Foundation, 2019; Keep, 2020) but low consistency, and with a modest impact on overall government debt (IFS, 2022; Keep, 2022). Further, public sector reforms exhibit the usual pattern of high superficial activity and low substantive impact (at least in the short term – see Chapter 4). The coalition government was engaging with a complex policy-making system over which it had limited understanding and control. Its austerity agenda was more useful as a dramatic story than a clear way to (1) control economic activity to promote a quick and positive impact on growth, or (2) reduce the deficit quickly. It also oversaw a tortuous process of reform to introduce Universal Credit.

In other words, it is possible for a government to deliver on most of its promises (for example, to cut spending in key areas) but not get what it wants (for example, reduced spending overall, or the economic benefits of state retrenchment). In this case, the coalition government ensured that public expenditure dropped in many parts of government, but only temporarily before a major hike during COVID-19 (Chapter 6). Further, its wider growth-boosting reforms are harder to spot, and were undermined by the uncertainty of Brexit (Chapter 7). Overall, the austerity period demonstrates the potential for government to make wide-ranging reforms to policy with an enduring impact, and control narratives of policy making, but also the fragility of such agendas when interrupted by events.

10

Social Policy: Inequalities, Racism and Protest

Chapter highlights

1. The UK contains a highly unequal social and political system.

2. Social and political attitudes to class, gender, race, migration, sexuality and disability are common causes. Unequal income, education and wellbeing are common effects.

3. There is sporadic government attention to inequalities, with limited impact on policy.

4. Protests against some causes of inequalities – such as racism – are a long-term feature of UK politics, but without producing a direct, substantive impact on policy.

5. Indeed, government responses to protest highlight a tendency to take some inequalities seriously while ignoring or exacerbating others.

6. The case study of London 'riots' shows how the UK government exploited crisis to accelerate its 'troubled families' agenda and reject criticism of policing.

7. Three approaches highlight key perspectives on these issues:

   • Policy analysis identifies how to address inequalities as a series of interconnected policy problems, including: what inequalities are the most severe and urgent, what is their cause, and which solutions are feasible?

   • Policy studies situate this analysis in real-world developments. The UK government maintains multiple, contradictory commitments to reducing inequalities.

   • Critical policy analysis encourages the use of 'critical race theory' to highlight and challenge persistent inequalities and racism.

Introduction: Contesting and protesting inequalities

'Social policy' describes a wide range of concerns, including policies and policy processes regarding ageing, children, families, education, crime, health, housing, social security, social services and social care (Hudson and Lowe, 2009; Baldock,

2012: 9–10). A key theme in the study of social policy is inequality. The UK contains a highly unequal social and political system that privileges or marginalises populations in relation to class, sex and gender, race and ethnicity, religion, sexuality, disability, and age. This unequal treatment has profoundly negative consequences, contributing to lower income, education attainment, health, wellbeing, life expectancy, and greater vulnerability to harm.

Policy action could help to address inequalities. Further, the urgent need for state intervention may seem self-evident to many: inequality is 'the defining challenge of our time' (Savage, 2021: vii) and the 'inequality question is back and is here to stay' (Fée and Kober-Smith, 2018: 1). Yet, there is minimal agreement on the definition, scale and cause of inequalities, and solutions are highly contested. There is intense debate on whose inequalities matter, or if inequality is the responsibility of individuals or governments (Cairney et al, 2022a). The need for greater state intervention is not self-evident to UK policy makers. Instead, these issues rise and fall on the policy agenda, often with minimal impact on policy or society.

Political protest may help to challenge inattention or policies and practices with inequitable outcomes. The UK has hosted many organised protests against the 'poll tax', austerity, violence against women, and racism. The latter includes Black Lives Matter (BLM) events across the UK in 2020 (BBC News, 2020a), organised originally in the US to protest police violence against people of colour, and Black people in particular, following the murder of George Floyd by a White police officer. They also include protests or 'riots' in 2011 following the police shooting of Mark Duggan in London.

We use the 2011 protests/riots to show how governments respond, and how their response translates into policy. While fuelled by racial inequalities in relation to policing, and perhaps even 'wider resistance to neoliberalism' (Murji, 2017: 174), UK ministers argued that they were caused by bad parenting and gang culture. Prime Minister David Cameron used the opportunity to promote and accelerate the 'Troubled Families' programme which aimed to 'turn around' the lives of a small proportion of families causing the most damage to society and the highest public service spending (Cairney, 2019c: 7). Such cases highlight the mediating role of governments when narrating events, even when events are initially out of their control. They show that governments decide how to define policy problems and use social stereotypes to describe the people who allegedly cause them (Box 3.6). They try to solve some policy problems (such as unequal spending on families) and ignore or exacerbate others (such as poverty and racism).

This chapter examines these issues through three lenses. First, policy analysis identifies how to analyse inequalities as interconnected policy problems, including:

- What kinds of inequalities and policies have prompted political protest?
- How should policy makers define inequalities, and which should they prioritise?
- What solutions to inequalities are technically and politically feasible?

Second, policy studies situate this analysis in real-world developments, exploring:

- The tendency for policy makers to pay fleeting attention to inequalities, then proposing solutions but not following through. Examples include initiatives to promote 'spatial justice', gender equality, and health and education equity.
- How UK governments frame protests in relation to their preferred policy agendas.

Third, critical policy analysis identifies who benefits or loses from these developments, and how to respond. For example, we examine the politicisation of 'critical race theory' by UK policy makers who appeared to be threatened by its implications.

In the conclusion, we reflect on the gap between policy expectations and outcomes. Drawing on the Westminster story, can we conclude that the government could tackle inequalities effectively, and that the persistence of inequalities reflects policy-maker choice or ambivalence? Drawing on the complex government story, can we conclude that even the most sincere policy makers would struggle to make fundamental changes?

What inequalities and policies have prompted political protest?

The poll tax (Box 4.3) prompted multiple large-scale protests, 'riots' and civil disobedience (including non-payment and protests against legal action to recover payment – Lavalette and Mooney, 1990). For example, in March 1990, '45,000 marched in Glasgow' and '200,000 demonstrated in London' (Lavalette and Mooney, 1990: 100).

Section 28. The Local Government Act 1988 Section 28 stated that '[a] local authority shall not (a) intentionally promote homosexuality or publish material with the intention of promoting homosexuality; (b) promote the teaching in any maintained school of the acceptability of homosexuality as a pretended family relationship'. Baker (2022) describes 'very British resistance' to such policies, because mass protests and organised debates were processed with regard to British rules of politeness. The contrast is with the 'Stonewall riots' in 1969 – 'when thousands of people protested in the streets in response to a police raid on a Greenwich Village [New York] gay bar' – which inspired international 'pride parades and protests' ever since (Stein, 2019). Kollman and Waites (2011) also relate the 'rather dramatic expansion of LGB rights in the UK since 1997' to a UK (and EU) political system that is more rewarding of quiet lobbying by interest group elites than outsider social movements. Examples include 'the equalisation of the age of consent, the creation of civil partnerships, the legalisation of adoption for same-sex couples, and the creation of a public sector "equality duty" by the Equality Act in 2010'. The Scottish Parliament voted to repeal the equivalent of Section 28 (Section 2A) in 2000, prompting protest and counter protest (opposition to repeal was largely funded by one millionaire, but also included the Scottish Conservatives and Catholic Church) (Milne, 2005). The UK Labour government repealed Section 28 in 2003 (Labour Party, 2018).

Austerity policies (Chapter 9) prompted multiple protests which 'emphasized the sharp contrast between the minority rich and the majority of British citizens whose conditions have dramatically worsened as a consequence of austerity measures' (Saunders et al, 2015: 171).

Tuition fee rises in England (Box 9.2) prompted 'a number of high profile, nationally and locally organised student protests' from 2010 to 2011, including the occupation of buildings and some damage to property (including the Conservative Party HQ) (Ibrahim, 2011: 425).

Women's marches. The 2016 election of Donald Trump as US President highlighted 'his reactionary policy platform that threatened to dismantle the fragile social citizenship gains of various marginalised groups' (Emejulu, 2018: 268). In the US, it prompted the Women's March ('5 million people across 550 cities') and solidarity marches in other countries ('2 million people across 161 cities'), including a Sister March in London of 100,000 people (Emejulu, 2018: 268).

Policing and violence against women. On 13 October 2021, there was a vigil in London for Sarah Everard, a woman raped and killed by a Metropolitan Police officer. Hundreds attended during the day (including the Duchess of Cambridge) and evening (BBC News, 2022b; Sisters Uncut, 2022). The police did not authorise it (it took place during COVID-19 restrictions), dispersed the crowd and arrested nine people (HMICFRS, 2021). Police action was criticised by politicians and challenged successfully in court (BBC News, 2022b). The event focused attention on police misogyny, low trust in officers to deal with sexual assault, and a culture of deprioritising violence against women (Dearden, 2020; Walker et al, 2020; Beighton, 2021; Halliday, 2021; see also the Casey review [2023] in Box 10.3).

Grenfell and 'social murder'. On 14 June 2017, a fire in Grenfell Tower in London killed 72 people (BBC News, 2019). Grenfell's cladding accelerated the fire's spread. It exemplified multiple policy failures, including to regulate or punish the companies providing dangerous cladding, and to protect marginalised residents, including refugees (Malik, 2017). Most residents were 'Black African and Caribbean, "other Asian" and "other"', with the latter including 'Muslims with North African backgrounds' (Shilliam, 2018: 170). Before the Grenfell fire, residents had been treated by governments as 'undeserving poor', occupying expensive real estate that should be demolished and re-used for profit (Shilliam, 2018: 168–171). Some linked Grenfell to Engels' concept of 'social murder': people who are exploited in capitalist systems, and receive insufficient state support, face ill health and premature death (Grover, 2019; Medvedyuk et al, 2021). Multiple protests in 2017 highlighted central and local government inaction (for example, to rehouse survivors locally), and provided the impetus for a public inquiry (Grierson and Gayle, 2017; Booth, 2022). These protests contrasted with government (and royal family) attempts to use Grenfell to emphasise a 'we are all in it together' narrative and downplay socio-economic inequalities and discrimination (Clancy, 2020).

BLM. BLM is 'a Black-centered political will and movement building project' to challenge racial discrimination and injustice (Black Lives Matter, 2022). High-profile US cases exemplify the killing of Black men without proportionate punishment, such as Trayvon Martin by private citizen George Zimmerman (acquitted of murder in 2013), and George Floyd by police officer Derek Chauvin in 2020 (unusually, he was found guilty of second-degree murder in 2021). There were many US and international BLM/Floyd protests in 2020. In the UK, protests reflected solidarity, but also a challenge to 'endemic racism in the United Kingdom', including racist practices in UK policing such as the disproportionate use of 'stop-and-search' powers (Joseph-Salisbury et al, 2021: 22; see also our case study discussion of Mark Duggan, and compare with the recent police killing of Chris Kaba – BBC News, 2022c; 2023b; Birchley, 2022 – and deaths of Black men in police or prison custody –Bhattacharyya, 1998: 19–20; Akhtar, 2022).

Such protests are important in their own right. They also contribute more widely to political activity that is not centred on representative democracy (or researched centring the Westminister Model – Akram, 2023), which allows us to identify several themes. First, there may be common messages, such as opposition to neoliberal reforms that individualise social problems, reduce state support and exacerbate inequalities. All examples that follow are of protests against Conservative-led government policies (see also Chapter 11 on the largest UK protest, against the Labour government's role in the Iraq War). Second, the *absence* of key messages may be notable. For example, 'minority women' may be affected disproportionately by taxes and fees, austerity, misogyny, police discrimination, xenophobia, and inadequate housing, without being as able to influence protest movements (Emejulu and Bassel, 2015: 86; Emejulu, 2018). One response may be 'women of colour's refusal politics', in which they embrace their marginalisation from 'dominant left activist spaces' and seek 'alternative ways of doing politics and being political' (Emejulu and van der Scheer, 2022: 9).

Third, the nature and impact of protest is contested. Their *proponents* describe them as essential, to challenge the systematic inequity that results from government policy or inaction (some narratives refer to an elite that protects its own). There is a long history of 'revolutionary grassroots action' that highlights the 'potential for sustained fundamental change of the economic and political landscape', pursued 'through an egalitarian, democratic process' that is 'transformative in rethinking and reshaping the parameters of what democracy can and should be' (Zaunseder et al, 2022: 2). Their *opponents* describe protests as socially and economically damaging 'riots', caused by criminals intent on looting, agent provocateurs intent on destruction, or outbursts of emotion. From 2019, the Conservative government used this framing to boost police powers to disperse protests, and punish new 'nuisance'-based offences (Joint Committee on Human Rights, 2022). Its ire focuses increasingly on environmental groups – for example, Extinction Rebellion and Just Stop Oil – which block roads (Gunningham,

2019), or anti-racist protests that damage or destroy statues of slave traders (Walker et al, 2020).

Policy analysis: how to address the policy problem

Step 1: How could governments define inequality as a policy problem?

Problem framing includes a contested account of: the problem's severity, urgency and cause, who it affects, and the extent to which the state should be responsible for intervention (Chapter 2). Further, inequality is often treated as 'wicked': the problem defies simple definition and understanding, its cause is contested, its complexity makes it impossible to know how solutions would work, and experimentation is difficult since errors have major social consequences (Rittel and Webber, 1973: 161–167; Box 8.1). There is intense debate on the following questions.

What inequalities are the most severe or urgent?

Policy makers describe a broad equity agenda but prioritise resources towards some social groups or policy problems. For example, the UK government 'Levelling Up' agenda became a high-profile but vague commitment to reducing inequalities in relation to social class and income and geography. Further, the *Equality Act 2010* underpins a very broad focus on anti-discrimination in relation to specific 'protected characteristics' ('age, disability, sex, gender reassignment, pregnancy and maternity, race, religion or belief and sexual orientation') but without signalling which types of enforcement are high priority (or, according to the EHRC, 2023, clarifying what sex means). There may be policies to foster **LGBTI** or **LGBT+** rights (Ayoub, 2019; 2022: 2; Turnbull-Dugarte and McMillan, 2022) or address 'the inequities faced by the **LGBTQ+** community' (Gregory and Matthews, 2022: 596), but without translating a general commitment into routine public service delivery (Gregory and Matthews, 2022: 606). There may be high state commitment to challenge 'discrimination' but strong reluctance to use 'affirmative action' to redress its effects (Abel et al, 2021: 63). Travelling communities experience some of the worst (and most openly tolerated) discrimination (Clark, 2018). There are legal protections for some (for example, Roma people), but they seem easy to subvert in practice

> **LGBTQ+**: lesbian, gay, bisexual, transgender, queer, and other identities. **LGBTI**: lesbian, gay, bisexual, trans, intersex. **LGB**: lesbian, gay, and bisexual. Different terms can reflect (1) innocuous shifts in description, or (2) political signals regarding which groups share the same experiences of marginalisation, policy aims, or reason to act collectively (compare with BAME usage in Chapter 9).

(Alexiadou, 2019: 425). Overall, the identification of so many possibilities in theory does not determine which issues take priority in practice.

What causes inequalities?

The cause of inequalities is highly contested (Cairney et al, 2022a: 1–2). Long-standing debates on poverty suggest that economic inequalities arise from (1) individual choices or lifestyles, merit or drive (requiring minimal state intervention), or (2) structural or systematic barriers to achievement in the market and society (requiring high intervention). Debates may focus on how to protect specific groups from discrimination, such as to assign rights, regulate behaviour and/or redistribute resources. Further, a state response to the *policy* problem also presents a *policy-making* problem: to make sure that a collection of responses to the same issue (the *policy mix*) produces a coherent and well-coordinated approach.

What are unfair or unjust inequalities?

Inequity describes *unfair* or *unjust* inequalities, but there is contestation to decide what is fair and if fairness should be a priority. For some, inequalities are fair if driven primarily by individual choices. It would be unfair for states to tax people and businesses highly to redistribute resources; it would undermine economic growth by limiting the incentive to earn high salaries or large profits. For some, inequalities are unfair reflections of factors that are outside of individual control. State intervention is a moral imperative (compare with Chapter 8 on 'just transitions'). Further, major inequalities can undermine growth, such as by skewing market behaviour or diminishing the expectation that investment in knowledge and skills will boost social mobility or earnings (OECD, 2014). There are similar arguments on fairness in relation to jurisdictions, such as for/against (1) the EU role in redistributing some member-state resources to EU regions, or (2) unequal funding for devolved territories or English regions.

It would be misleading to see the UK's main parties as emphasising state responsibility (Labour) or individualism (Conservative). Rather, the 'New Labour' government (from 1997) provoked a 'major ideological re-orientation', in which (1) redistributive efforts to foster more equal outcomes became 'neither feasible nor particularly desirable since it neglected the importance of rewarding effort and talent and fostering dynamism in the economy', and (2) the main focus was on alleviating poverty rather than addressing 'wider concerns with high levels of inequality' (Shaw, 2018: 150). Jeremy Corbyn's leadership of Labour (in opposition, 2015–2020) committed to 'a more equal society' but without producing politically feasible plans (Shaw, 2018: 162–163).

Contestation on inequalities includes how to identify the most useful measures. For example, the ONS (2022g) describes the Gini coefficient as the 'most widely used summary measure of inequality in the distribution of household income', and useful to measure long-term trends. In Figure 10.1, a score of 0

Figure 10.1: Gini coefficient, Great Britain, 1962–2021

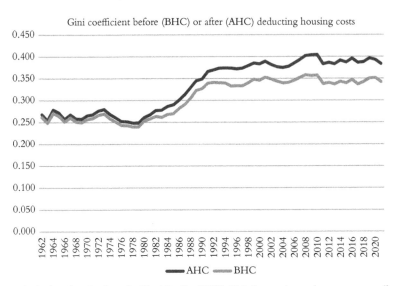

Source: author's chart from Institute for Fiscal Studies (2022). This dataset also tracks poverty: overall, or in relation to child, pensioner, or working age poverty.

represents complete equality and 1 complete inequality. It shows that inequality rose markedly during Thatcherism (1979–1990), followed by a more gradual shift towards greater inequality. The effect is more pronounced when we take housing costs into consideration, or when we compare the UK to other countries (for example, the OECD [2022a] lists the UK as the eighth most unequal of 41 countries). Other possible measures include in relation to absolute or relative poverty, or the measurement of income or household income inequality in relation to, say, race or ethnicity.

Step 2: Identifying feasible solutions: what should be the state's role?

Some argue that poverty relates to individual choices and seeks minimal state action (Box 1.1). Some identify structural causes, to seek interventions to redistribute resources, target service provision, and/or regulate individual and business behaviour. Approaches to discrimination may involve regulations to encourage a 'level playing field' for individuals, distributive measures to prioritise some social groups, or a challenge to 'austerity' policies that exacerbate inequalities (Chapter 9). There are also different solutions to policy-making problems: a government may set up units or departments focusing on a cross-cutting aim (for example, public health agencies to address inequalities of health – Boswell et al, 2019), or to **mainstream** a

Mainstream (verb): treat a problem or aim as crucial to all relevant activities, rather than a separate – and often marginalised – concern.

218

policy aim across government (Bell, 2009). For example, Cairney and St Denny (2020: 18) draw on Hood and Margetts' (2007) policy tool categories (Box 2.2; Box 8.4) to compare approaches:

- 'Maximal' approaches would combine 'ambitious and specific' strategies that prioritise the need to address inequalities (*nodality*) with strongly enforced regulations to change social and business behaviour (*authority*), taxes and subsidies to redistribute income and wealth or change market behaviour (*treasure*), and well-resourced departments to ensure policy delivery (*organisation*).
- 'Tentative' approaches would have similar strategies, but with regulations undermined by other priorities, modest redistribution and uneven delivery.
- 'Minimal' approaches would produce vague strategies, backed weakly by policy tools, and overshadowed by stronger tools for other aims (for example, prioritising economic growth).

These agendas play out in very different ways. While governments express the ambition to join up policies via intersectoral initiatives, we show there are many different initiatives relating to geography, gender and sectors such as health and education (Cairney et al, 2022a).

The pursuit of spatial justice

'Spatial justice' describes a challenge to 'uneven geographical development' (Weckroth and Moisio, 2018). It could involve measures to tax and spend to redistribute income and wealth, or strategy documents to describe general aspirations. Traditionally, the EU addresses uneven regional gross domestic product (GDP) via 'cohesion' policies, and 'structural funds' distribute revenue from member states to low-GDP regions (Weckroth and Moisio, 2020: 183–184). Recently, EU policy has focused on equal access to public services (Weckroth and Moisio, 2020: 183–184) and to give regions greater autonomy to decide what spatial justice means (Jones et al, 2020: 894–896).

At the same time, UK governments fostered geographically focused social and economic initiatives, such as regional development agencies (with equivalents in devolved territories) or policies to mitigate 'social exclusion' in relation to factors such as low income (Cairney and St Denny, 2020: 91–100, 180–181). In each case, governments have accepted the need to address the impacts of poverty and economic inequality (for example, Pickett and Wilkinson, 2009; Dorling, 2010) while rejecting claims that they are not doing enough (for example, Gordon Brown emphasised the successful reduction of child and pensioner poverty – Coates, 2008).

The most recent initiative is the vague idea of 'Levelling Up', turned (so far) into an incoherent and ineffective strategy (Jennings et al, 2021; Richards et al, 2022b; Westwood et al, 2022; see also UK in a Changing Europe, 2022).

Chapter 7 suggests that it harnesses the sense that Brexit would help to address White working-class populations 'left behind' by global change (compare with policies for 'community cohesion' – Jones, 2013; Kersten and Moreira de Souza, 2020). More recently, the government response to the Commission on Race and Ethnic Disparities connected it to the aspiration that 'everyone, from every community and in every corner of the UK, has opportunity. A person's race, social or ethnic background must not be a barrier to achieving their ambitions' (HM Government, 2022h). While 'Levelling Up' *could* refer to major intervention, using fiscal powers to redistribute income and wealth and invest in (for example, transport) infrastructure, it is overseen by a Conservative government seeking cuts to local government (Jennings et al, 2021: 7; Newman et al, 2023; Chapter 9).

UK decentralisation also allows devolved governments to pursue policies that could reduce inequalities in their territory but contribute to inequalities across the UK. Examples include:

- *Social care.* UK and devolved governments pursue their own policies to manage the costs of long-term social care for older and disabled people, focusing on who should deliver services and who should pay the costs for care home accommodation (for example, service users pay if they have capital or savings above a certain threshold). They seek equitable ways to subsidise services in each territory, but create different entitlements across the UK (Needham and Hall, 2022).
- *Free school meals* (FSM). UK-wide entitlement relates to the parent or guardian's receipt of social security benefits (for example, income support or child tax credits) and household income as a proxy of need. Further entitlement varies by territory (and over time): state schools provide FSM for children up to Year 2 (age up to 7) in England, Primary 5 (age 9) in Scotland, and all Primary (age 11) in Wales (by 2024). All four governments produced arrangements to provide meals or funding during COVID-19 school closures (Audit Wales, 2020; Department for Education, 2021; McClure and McNally, 2021; Morris, 2021; HM Government, 2022c; Northern Ireland Executive, 2022; Scottish Government, 2022a; Welsh Government, 2022).
- *English regions.* There is some experimentation to devolve key areas to some English regions, such as health service devolution in Greater Manchester (described by Britteon et al, 2022 as having a moderate positive impact on life expectancy in deprived areas).

Scottish and Welsh governments also seek distinctive-looking equalities agendas when responsibilities are shared with, or held by, the UK government. Examples include:

- From 2011 the Scottish government *obliged* 'all the bodies subjected to its pay policy' to pay the 'living wage', established the Living Wage Foundation (higher than the UK 'national living wage') and *encouraged* private-sector companies to follow its lead (Camp-Pietrain, 2018: 311–312). In 2022, First Minister Nicola Sturgeon (2022) described a rise in the 'Scottish Child Payment' (from £20 to £25 per week) as 'the most significant anti poverty measure in the UK'.

- The Welsh government does not have tax and social security powers to redistribute resources, so its 'anti-poverty strategies' are limited to measures such as a requirement on local authorities to produce 'a strategy to tackle child poverty' or to boost 'the capacity of families to deal with the effects of financial exclusion' (Davies and Parken, 2018: 330). Its Well-being of Future Generations Act 2015 encourages people to envisage how to foster a fair transition to sustainable ways of living (Davies and Parken, 2018: 334–335).

In Northern Ireland, the Good Friday Agreement (Chapter 7) includes a commitment 'to guarantee more equality among citizens in the field of general human rights and on economic, social and cultural issues', partly to address anti-Catholic discrimination in access to employment, housing and public services (Peyronel, 2018: 348).

Gender mainstreaming

Gender equality – or gender mainstreaming – policies can range from minimal to maximal in ambition and substance: 'minimalist anti-discrimination frameworks contrast with more expansive affirmative action policies designed to target particular groups to redress historically entrenched patterns of exclusion and unfairness' (Cairney et al, 2022a: 140). For example, EU policies have included 'hard' measures ('legally binding', with 'penalties for non-compliance') with a major impact on the UK, such as to enhance parental leave after childbirth, pension rights for mothers taking career breaks, and laws prohibiting sexual harassment (Cairney et al, 2022a: 147, citing Abbott and Snidal, 2003; MacRae, 2010: 160). Since the 1990s, EU policies have favoured 'soft' measures to set international benchmarks and encourage learning (Cairney et al, 2022a: 147–148).

UK gender equality policy is 'minimal' compared to the 'maximal' approach of Sweden (Cairney et al, 2022a: 163). UK policies focused on increasing the proportion of women in senior unelected positions (see also Box 3.4), increasing 'opportunities for input from women' in policy, and units or ministers responsible for women (Cairney et al, 2021a: 422, citing Childs and Whitey, 2004; Squires and Wickham-Jones, 2004; Daly, 2005; Durose and Gains, 2005; Lovenduski, 2005; Rees, 2005; Veitch, 2005; Miller, 2009; Hankivsky and Christoffersen, 2011; Campbell and Childs, 2015). These measures produced slow progress, and specialist units were as marginalised as the women they were designed to support. The Equality Act 2010 created a public sector duty to challenge discrimination, and symbolises important but patchy progress (Cairney et al, 2021a: 423). Scottish and Welsh governments (and parliaments) sought to go beyond UK efforts, to foster more meaningful mainstreaming, but in the context of a UK approach with limited scope for divergence (Conley and Page, 2017; Davies and Parken, 2018; Cairney et al, 2021a: 423).

In comparison, Sweden exhibits a 'system-wide commitment' to gender mainstreaming, combining a larger welfare state with 'high buy-in across different levels of government, including at the national, regional, and municipal levels' (Cairney et al, 2021a: 425–426; 2022a: 159). These differences relate to policies that are 'class based' (for example, challenging economic and other inequalities between women) *and* 'gender status' (for example, challenging violence against women and girls [VAWG]) (Htun and Weldon, 2010; Chapter 9).

First, Sweden's wider commitment to class-based policies informs the very different delivery of ostensibly similar policies, such as the 'early childhood' policies (0–8 years old) that have a disproportionate impact on women (including their relative ability to work). For example, from 1996, the Swedish, Scottish and UK (for England) governments 'moved responsibility for all early childhood education and care (ECEC) and school-age childcare (SACC) services from welfare into education' to foster policy and service integration (Cohen et al, 2021: 110; see Chapter 9 on Sure Start centres). However, the effect was markedly different: 'Sweden succeeded in achieving further integration and better access to services, while services in England and Scotland remained divided and fragmented' (Cohen et al, 2021: 110). The difference reflected a more favourable context in Sweden, with strong links between multiple policies, including:

- Wider redistributive measures, including higher taxes and benefits, 'significantly higher' ECEC spending (and 'indicators of child well-being') and 'significantly lower' child poverty (Cohen et al, 2021: 111–112).
- A longer history of meaningful support for a 'well-resourced, integrated system' of preschools and schools (open 'from around 7am to 6pm'); in the UK 'ECEC and SACC had long been neglected, poorly resourced, and fragmented' (Cohen et al, 2021: 112).
- Before 2003, the Swedish government introduced a 'a universal child-based right from 12 months to 10 years of age, independent of parental employment or student status' (Cohen et al, 2021: 113). In contrast, UK government policies had encouraged a market for separate and patchy pre-school provision largely provided and funded privately (Cohen et al, 2021: 113). From 2003, state-funded early years education in England rose from 12.5 to 15 hours per week (570 hours per year, plus more for means-tested parents) and extended from age 4 to 3/4 (or 2 when means-tested). Scotland was similar, with a higher proportion of care provided by local authorities. The SNP government (from 2007) raised entitlement from 475 to 600 hours (and more for means-tested parents), piloted 1,140 hours for 3/4-year-olds from 2016, and rolled out this policy from 2021 (Cohen et al, 2021: 115–117).

Second, Sweden's approach includes a '1998 law to criminalize the purchase of sexual services – designed to ban prostitution' and offer 'support to exit prostitution' (2021b: 425). Such approaches (the 'Nordic Model') are framed largely as part of a policy agenda to challenge VAWG or to argue that 'prostitution is a human rights violation against women and girls' (compare Bindel, 2017: vii with Hewer, 2021: 46–49). During this period, UK government policy has used frames regarding 'vulnerable' women, and legislation to criminalise buying sex 'if the individual from whom they bought sex was subject to exploitation', but unaccompanied by much support for women or prosecutions of men (Hewer, 2021: 26–27).

Contesting education equity policies

Gilead (2019: 439) identifies three ways to describe education equity aims, in relation to 'merit', 'thresholds' (everyone reaches a minimum level of attainment) or 'justice'. Advocates of 'justice' would criticise a focus on individual merit and motivation as producing 'severe inequalities and a neglect of the weakest members of society', while thresholds would improve 'the conditions of the least advantaged members of society' but allow others to 'preserve their relative advantages' (Gilead, 2019: 439). Contested ways to 'equate justice with equality' can focus on a geographically equal share of education resources, the equal opportunity to learn, more equal outcomes such as attainment (Gilead, 2019: 439), or aims such as 'the state should prohibit private schools' (Abel et al, 2021: 78; see also Knight et al, 2023 on UK and devolved 'inclusive education').

These debates contribute to a policy contest between *social justice* and *neoliberal* approaches to education equity (Cairney and Kippin, 2022). The former identifies state responsibility to deal with structural or systemic inequalities outside of an individual's control, with measures targeted at social groups supported by redistributive measures to secure fairer social and economic outcomes (the 'out of school' influences – such as poverty – on what happens in schools). The latter assumes individual responsibility, equating equity with the opportunity to access high-quality services (for example, schools or teachers), while equating the pursuit of equal attainment outcomes as damaging to the individuals thriving in existing systems.

In education equity research, academics identify the negative impact of the neoliberal approach, which emphasises the economic value of education rather than its social and emancipatory purpose (Rizvi and Lingard, 2010: 39–41; Rizvi, 2016: 5; Cairney and Kippin, 2022). Governments may also use 'social justice' rhetoric, but they prioritise individual merit and equal access to schools, and downplay 'out of school' causes of inequalities (Hajisoteriou and Angelides, 2020: 283; Kippin, 2023). They foster new public management solutions, including 'international benchmarking, the privatisation of education, importing management techniques from the corporate sector and other ideals such as choice, competition and decentralisation … school-based management, teachers' accountability, public–private partnerships and conditional fund-transfer schemes' (Hajisoteriou and Angelides, 2020: 277).

Chapters 4 and 5 show that UK government policies exhibit these neoliberal approaches while funding some social justice measures (including FSM and a 'pupil premium' to schools teaching students entitled to FSM – Beauvallet, 2018: 208–209). The UK government uses performance measures to encourage quality improvement via competition between schools and school inspections (Adnett and Davies, 2003; Power and Frandji, 2010: 394). Devolved governments diverge in key respects, with a greater commitment to comprehensive schools and less testing in Scotland and Wales. The 'history of Scottish education' includes 'a reduced emphasis on individualist/competitive cultures and instead focuses on social justice and equity' (Cairney, 2016b; Neary et al, 2022: 27). However, they also use devolved versions of neoliberal approaches to manage school practices (Chapman and Ainscow, 2019: 899, 909; Mowat, 2019: 67), accompanied by a social justice rhetoric with limited follow-through. For example, in 2015, Sturgeon promised in vain to 'close the attainment gap completely' (Cairney, 2016b; Seith, 2021; Hepburn, 2022).

Further, the UK and devolved experience of exam fiascos during COVID-19 highlighted major inequalities in (1) the ability to learn during lockdown (relating to school provision and family resources), and (2) exam outcomes, relating to teacher biases in relation to their unequal expectations for students, or standardised outcomes that reinforced inequalities in relation to deprivation (Box 6.5; Chadderton, 2022; Ozga et al, 2023).

Health in All Policies and the social determinants of health

Chapter 6 describes the 'social determinants of health' as the factors causing a major impact on population health and inequalities, such as income, wealth, education, housing, and safe physical and social environments (Whitehead and Dahlgren, 2006: 4; Solar and Urwin, 2010: 6; Marmot et al, 2020; Bambra et al, 2021; WHO, 2022). Health improvement (or promotion) researchers use this term to underpin a definition of the policy problem:

> [S]ignificant and persistent disparities in health outcomes caused by structural inequities in social and economic factors, including employment opportunities, the law and the justice systems, education, housing, neighborhood environments, and transportation. These elements are otherwise known as the social determinants of health. The opportunity or lack of opportunity to be healthy is too often associated with a person's socio-economic status, race, ethnicity, gender, religion, sexual identity, or disability. (Bliss et al, 2016: S88; see also Zeeman et al, 2019 on 'LGBTI health')

Health inequalities help us understand social and economic inequalities. For example, the 'ethnic and gender groups that suffer disproportionately from poorer health are also disadvantaged' in relation to 'insecure housing tenure', 'reduced labour participation', 'poorer educational outcomes' and 'residence in the most deprived neighbourhoods' (Bécares, 2015: 137–138). One cause of this is societal, governmental and 'structural' racism (Box 10.1).

Box 10.1: Societal, governmental and structural racism

Measures of societal racism can include:

- The recorded number of offences where racist hate crime is listed as a motivating factor (for example, 114,958 in England and Wales in 2021 – Allen and Zayed, 2021), as a proxy for a larger number of unreported crimes.
- Surveys in which White people describe themselves as harder workers than other ethnic groups (Heath and Richards, 2020).
- Racist media coverage (Sloane, 2021) defended as not racist (Waterson, 2021).
- Discrimination when seeking employment (Centre for Social Investigation, 2019).

Racism is an enduring feature of government policy, including:

- *Immigration policy*. A leaked Home Office report argued that from 1950 to 1981 'every single piece of immigration or citizenship legislation was designed at least in part to reduce the number of people with black or brown skin who were permitted to live and work in the UK' (Gentleman, 2022).
- *Deportation policy*. The Windrush Scandal saw hundreds of UK citizens deported or threatened with deportation to the Caribbean countries they left decades ago or had never lived in (Gentleman, 2019; Wardle and Obermuller, 2019; Goodfellow, 2019; Hewitt, 2020; Slaven, 2022).
- *Incarceration*. Black people in England and Wales are five times more likely to be imprisoned than White people (EHRC, 2010). Anti-terror legislation disproportionately targets Muslims (Choudhury and Fenwich, 2011).
- *Inequalities of treatment by public services*, including in health and education (Tereshchenko et al, 2020; Kapadia et al, 2022; Swiszczowski, 2022). For example, 'Black women were 3.7x more likely to die than white women (34 women per 100,000 giving birth)' (Knight et al, 2022: 5).
- Deliberate inattention to the unequal impact of austerity measures (Chapter 9).

'Structural racism' includes 'seemingly neutral policies and practices [that] can function in racist ways by disempowering communities of color and perpetuating unequal historic conditions' (Corburn et al, 2014: 628).

The impact of everyday racism on health can include: (1) the physical and psychological consequences of actual and feared racist violence or abuse; (2) knock-on effects, including 'coping mechanisms' such as smoking; and (3) lower access to rewarding jobs, high-quality schools, and safe and healthy accommodation and environments (Karlsen et al, 2019: 164–166; Swords and Sheni, 2022a; 2022b).

Public health responses include strategies such as 'Health in All Policies' (HiAP). HiAP suggests that governments: treat health as a human right, identify social determinants, identify 'upstream' or 'preventive' policy solutions (focusing the whole population rather than individualist approaches, and to prevent health inequalities rather than respond to them), promote intersectoral action (most policies for population health are not the responsibility of health departments), and maintain high political commitment to policy and policy-making changes (Cairney et al, 2022a: 88–90). We should not exaggerate the uniformity of HiAP approaches (McMahon, 2021; 2022). Nevertheless, they contrast with a neoliberal emphasis on individual healthy choices. The phrase 'unhealthy lifestyles' sums up the latter, to describe health inequalities that relate to smoking, drinking, unhealthy food consumption, or a lack of physical activity (Cairney and St Denny, 2020: 140; Cairney et al, 2022b).

Conservative governments have favoured relatively low state intervention for population health while boosting resources for healthcare. The Thatcher and Major governments treated population health as an individual responsibility, seeking modest regulations of behaviour in relation to smoking, drinking, eating and exercise (Chapter 4; Box 10.2 on sex and drugs). Labour's 1997 election made a clear difference (in the UK as a whole, or for England) in two main ways.

1. Tobacco control

Labour produced 'comprehensive' tobacco control policy by increasing taxes, restricting promotion, boosting warning labels, banning smoking in public places, increasing funding for health education and smoking cessation services, and raising the age for sales from 16 to 18 (Cairney, 2019b: 87–88; Cairney and St Denny, 2020: 149–153). State intervention has changed beyond recognition since the 1980s, and provides a model for alcohol and food (Cairney and Studlar, 2014; Studlar and Cairney, 2019). Its framing turned an old argument on its head (Cairney, 2007b: 62). Senior Labour figures (before and after 1997) had criticised tobacco policies as discriminating against working classes, since rates of smoking relate strongly to class and the costs would be borne unequally. Instead, the government argued that smoking is 'the single most significant causal factor for the socio-economic differences in the incidence of cancer and heart disease' (HM Treasury and Department of Health, 2002). Therefore, the most direct way to address health inequalities is to reduce inequalities in smoking (although the 'the inequality gap in smoking prevalence' remains – ONS, 2020b). While the Conservatives would not have emulated Labour, the coalition government kept then enhanced controls in 2015: introducing plain packaging for tobacco products, and banning smoking in cars with children present (Cairney, 2019a: 88). Subsequent Conservative governments have committed to address smoking as a cause of unequal health outcomes in relation to race and ethnicity (albeit while sending mixed messages – Campbell, 2022).

This comprehensive policy is present across the UK. The devolved governments were responsible for aspects of tobacco policy (including health education and smoking cessation services), and the Scottish Parliament was first to legislate to ban smoking in public places (Cairney, 2006; 2007b; 2007c; 2009c). UK government policy supports a 'four nations' approach, such as legislation to ban tobacco advertising and tax to reduce demand (Cairney, 2019a).

2. Health improvement/promotion

From 1997, Labour used a 'social determinants' lens to justify greater state intervention (Blackman et al, 2012: 49; Cairney and St Denny, 2020: 141). However, within five years, there was more 'enthusiasm for more concrete measures to regulate or encourage individual or lifestyle choices' (Harrington et al, 2009: 769; Baggott, 2011: 71–73, 391–395; Cairney and St Denny, 2020: 142). UK rhetorical commitment remained high, but its substantive commitment to a welfare state to support health equity was less impressive than in Nordic countries (Cairney et al, 2021b). Then, Conservative-led governments accelerated this shift towards individual responsibility and less state support (Chapter 9).

Devolved governments depend on the UK government to produce supportive policies on tax and social security, but can produce their own strategies (Cairney and St Denny, 2020). The Scottish and Welsh governments signalled a greater emphasis on social determinants from 1999, but struggled to produce meaningful policy change (Harrington et al, 2009: 769). They boosted healthcare spending, and faced a backlash when efforts to improve public health were portrayed as at the expense of National Health Service (NHS) performance (Keating et al, 2012: 297–298).

Box 10.2: Sex, sexuality, and drugs: abstention versus harm reduction policies

Governments are reluctant to invoke public health to prohibit legal behaviour. However, they intervene to influence behaviour that they deem to be deviant (for example, some sexual behaviour) or criminal (for example, some drug use) (see Larsen et al, 2012; Engeli et al, 2012 on 'morality policy').

The UK 'did not partially decriminalize sex between two men until 1967 in England and Wales, and the early 1980s in Scotland and Northern Ireland' (Kollman and Waites, 2011: 186). It had a legal age of consent at 21, reduced to 18 in 1994 and 16 in 2001 (UK Parliament, 2022). More recent reforms include: (1) anti-discrimination legislation (consolidated in the *Equality Act 2010*), to include 'sexual orientation' in a list of 'protected characteristics' and oblige public sector bodies to consider the impact of policy on inequalities; and (2) the Marriage (Same-Sex Couples) Act 2013 (and Marriage and Civil Partnership [Scotland] Act 2014) to legalise same-sex marriage. Still, policy delivery reinforces 'heteronormativity': heterosexuality is deemed normal and homosexuality is tolerated without informing policy design (Gregory and Matthews, 2022: 598; compare with Turnbull-Dugarte and McMillan, 2022: 3 on 'LGBT+ rights').

The UK government lists the drugs that are illegal to make, sell, share, possess or consume (devolved governments oversee policing and sentencing). They are classified in relation to the penalty for possession or production/supply (the latter is higher), including: Class A (for example, heroin, cocaine); B (for example, amphetamine, cannabis); C (for example, diazepam) (HM Government, 2022d).

HIV: Human Immunodeficiency Virus, generally spread via unprotected sex or the bloodstream. From the 1980s, until effective treatments became available, AIDS (Acquired Immune Deficiency Syndrome) was the usual term to describe 'late-stage or advanced HIV' before almost-inevitable death (Terrence Higgins Trust, 2022).

In the 1980s, **HIV** exposed the consequences of UK government policies, and prompted policy changes (Berridge, 1996). First, to challenge the belief that HIV was not a danger to heterosexuals. Early media coverage and surveys suggested that most people thought they would be unaffected since HIV originated in Africa and affected gay men via sex, haemophiliacs via blood infusions, and heroin users sharing needles (Kitzinger and Miller, 1992: 32). The UK government (1) funded a health education campaign in 1986–1987 ('Don't die of ignorance') to promote safer sex (for example, condom use), and (2) boosted HIV funding to address a predicted rise in population infection (Greenaway et al, 1992: 74). Campaigns to challenge 'gay plague' representations were largely successful, albeit while facing some critical press reaction (Wellings and Wadsworth, 1990: 114–115), and, while the NHS prohibited men who have sex with men from donating blood.

Second, to accept the value of 'harm reduction' drug policies, such as needle/syringe exchanges to minimise sharing (during a time when possession of drug paraphernalia was illegal, and needles had been confiscated by police) and oral methadone programmes to reduce needle use (Cairney, 2002). However, harm reduction was never embraced fully by UK governments – UK and devolved ministers tend to tolerate, not promote, it – despite regular calls by its advisory body, the Advisory Committee on the Misuse of Drugs. More punitive measures are implemented in a discriminatory way (for example, racial disparities in punishment) and do not address strong links between 'socio-economic deprivation' and the inequalities of drug harm and death (Stevens, 2019: 445; Cairney and St Denny, 2020: 210; see also Los, 2023).

In Scotland, high rates of HIV in heroin users prompted innovation in needle exchanges and methadone provision (Cairney, 2002). There is less innovation in relation to drug deaths. Scotland's 'drug misuse death rate in 2020 was 3.7 times the rate for the UK as a whole', and 'people in the most deprived areas were 15.3 times as likely to die from drug misuse as those in the least deprived areas' (National Records of Scotland, 2022: 19; 10). While it *might* be possible for the Scottish government to support 'drug consumption rooms' as a harm reduction measure, it is reluctant to find out (Cairney, 2022; Nicholls et al, 2022).

Steps 3–5: Comparing solutions, predicting outcomes and making recommendations

These discussions show that inequalities policies are plagued by ambiguity and contestation. There is the potential for high state intervention to address inequalities, but a tendency to favour modest intervention. As Chapter 9 (and Box 3.6) describes, politicians make explicit value judgements to identify who should benefit from government policies (and when to intervene or not). They engage with:

- Trade-offs between state and individual responsibility (such as to live healthily or work hard at school).
- Contestation to define human rights (for example, the right to be healthy versus the right to live free of state interference).
- Contestation to define equity in relation to efficiency. For example, the 'Heckman Curve' suggests that education equity and efficiency are both served best by early-years investment and worst by higher education spending (Heckman, 2022).

Policy makers also use implicit judgements about how far they are prepared to go to change social and economic outcomes. They make bold claims for policy changes in the name of equity, but have strong reasons to pursue policies that undermine them (Cairney and St Denny, 2020). Further, by accident or design, they may not know the equality impacts of policy reforms even though the Public Sector Equality Duty requires them to check (Khan, 2015; Clinks, 2017; Lammy Review, 2017; Roberts et al, 2018).

Overall, equity policies are difficult to sustain for three connected reasons (Cairney et al, 2022b: 5). First, policy makers make broad commitments without knowing what they mean. Second, when they make sense of these commitments, they find that new aims clash with more established and higher-salience policies. Third, few have, or are willing to use, the ability to challenge business-as-usual policy making, or make potentially unpopular choices, such as to:

- regulate social behaviour (as with smoking, drinking, and eating);
- shift money from highly visible front-line public services, which provide a clear and immediate benefit, to policies with a longer-term and less-visible effect;
- take resources from populations that they describe as hard-working and responsible, to give to populations that they describe as 'undeserving' (Shilliam, 2018).

Governments prefer to focus on policy-making reforms – to join up sectors or services to foster more equitable outcomes – without getting very far. As such, a rhetorical commitment to equity policies is not a good predictor of policy change, and a commitment to reforms is not a good predictor of policy-making change (Cairney et al, 2022a: 178–182).

Case study of the London 'riots' in 2011

The following case study shows how each aspect of inequalities policy analysis can be questioned. We know that, on 4 August 2011, Metropolitan Police officers shot and killed Mark Duggan, a 29-year-old British 'man of mixed-race origins' (Murji, 2017: 162) in Tottenham, North London. However, every other aspect is contested.

1. What caused this killing?

From the perspective of the police, they followed procedures to deal with a man they believed to be armed. From the perspective of their critics, they followed a pattern of racist or discriminatory behaviour in which young Black men are more likely to be stopped and searched, arrested, or subject to police violence (Bridges, 2012; Waddington, 2012).

2. What should we call what happened next?

We emphasise the competing frames used to narrate these events. Initial reactions began as isolated *protests* in Tottenham (or *'counter conduct'* – Blackwell, 2015; Sokhi-Bulley, 2016), followed by *riots* over several days in multiple English cities (Murji, 2017: 162) or 'one of the biggest *rebellions* that London has seen in a generation' (Mureithi, 2021; emphasis added). Over several nights, *violence* and *disorder* spread to other areas of London, then other places, including Salford, Nottingham and Birmingham. The disorder included *vandalism* and *looting*. At least five people died, and hundreds were injured. The police made 3,000 arrests. Hundreds of people had to leave their homes or businesses, and reported billions of pounds of *damage* (Newburn et al, 2012; Riots Communities and Victims Panel, 2012; Baudains et al, 2013). It took a high police presence, mass arrests and the deployment of the British Army to *restore order*.

3. What caused these events? Did the police exacerbate or solve the problem?

One explanation is that minoritised people respected a tradition of peaceful protest. Protest is fuelled by opposition to racial inequalities, systematic racism and racist policing (Box 10.3; Sutterlüty, 2014; Blackwell, 2015; Sokhi-Bulley, 2016; Sewell et al, 2021). The police have killed many people of colour before finding that their victims had not been a threat to their safety. Black people have a reasonable expectation of being treated relatively badly by the police, such as being more likely to appear in police gang databases, stopped and searched for weapons or drugs, or arrested after being tased (Lammy Review, 2017; Shiner et al, 2018; Goodfellow, 2018; Azfal, 2020; Joseph-Salisbury et al, 2021; Harris et al, 2022). Therefore, the local response reflects reasonable suspicion about (1) why the police killed Mark Duggan, and (2) the police's handling of protest. The poor policing of protest exacerbated the righteous anger of protesters, which caused protests to escalate.

Many accounts situate protests in the context of *economic crisis*, prompting higher unemployment, and *austerity*, prompting cuts to essential services (Chapter 9). For example:

- Most 'rioters' were unemployed and living in relatively deprived communities (Newburn et al, 2012: 3–6; 2015).
- Cuts to local authorities prompted reduced funding for essential youth projects and youth workers (Reicher and Stott, 2011; Bridges, 2012; Newburn et al, 2012; Thapar, 2021), and cuts to Education Maintenance Allowance reduced post-16 engagement with education (Weavers, 2021).
- Local governments favoured housing regeneration for profit rather than community investment, causing social and economic segregation and displacement via 'gentrification' (Dillon and Fanning, 2011).

The government response should be less spending on punitive policing, more on social security and public services (Chakelian, 2021), support for new building programmes to boost housing and economic growth (Hackney Citizen, 2011), and proper attention to racism and discrimination. Further, previous governments should not have rejected these recommendations in the past.

For example, Lord Scarman had been commissioned to explain the 'serious disorder' in Brixton (HC Deb, 10 December 1981) that was comparable to events in Tottenham in 2011. As well as focusing on policing (Box 10.3), to recommend better complaints procedures and community engagement, Scarman (1981: 135) highlighted racial 'discrimination' and 'disadvantage'. Lea and Hallsworth (2012) describe the latter as a 'toxic combination of unemployment, racism, a society which marginalised their political voice and which addressed the symptoms of urban decay with systematic over-policing' (see also Thomas, 2011). Scarman recommended state intervention to address barriers to employment, education and recreation. These recommendations went against a Thatcherite focus on personal responsibility (Gamble, 1994). They were 'out of key with the political temper of the times and triggered no significant political or policy response' (Hall, 1999: 190). In 2012, we saw a repeat of this process. The Riots Victims Panel made 60 recommendations, including improving numeracy and literacy standards, more targeted social care, revised police officer training, and to challenge discriminatory stop-and-search practices (Ball and Taylor, 2011; Newburn et al, 2012; 2015).

Box 10.3: Institutional racism and being 'woke'

The term *institutional racism* is ambiguous and a regular feature of debates on police culture (Lea, 2002; Hallsworth, 2006; BBC News, 2021d). Reviews of police officer conduct used it to argue that a *small minority of officers* are intentionally racist, but *the police force itself* is not (see Merriam-Webster, 2022 on the 'bad apple' metaphor). Police forces reinforce racist practices *unconsciously, unwittingly* and/or *unintentionally* (Ahmed, 2017 describes a similar 'unconscious bias' rhetoric by universities). This meaning differs from its original usage (in the US) emphasising *routine, everyday, taken-for-granted intentionality*: the 'acts by the total white community against the black community' that are less overt, but have the same destructive effect (Ture and Hamilton, 1967).

The shift of intended meaning is a regular feature of words coined by Black minorities then co-opted by White majorities. The latest is 'woke'. We can identify a similar initial usage (as Ture and Hamilton, 1967) in relation to racism: be awake to how the White majority will kill, harm and discriminate against you. It was co-opted by individuals to signal their left-wing politics, and organisations to aid marketing campaigns (Mirzai, 2019). Their right-wing critics used 'woke' pejoratively to portray left-wing actors as self-indulgent elitists (culminating in Home Secretary Suella Braverman's phrase '*Guardian*-reading, tofu-eating wokerati' – *The Guardian*, 2022).

The meaning shift of institutional racism also relates to the aim to criticise police practices while keeping officers on side (*The Guardian*, 1981; Scarman and Macpherson were commissioned by Home Secretaries). The Macpherson report (1999) used *institutional racism* to describe routine discrimination in the Metropolitan Police (Murji, 2017: 119–140). The police failed to investigate properly the racist murder of 18-year-old, Black British Stephen Lawrence. His parents argued that 'their colour, culture and ethnic origin, and that of their murdered son' influenced police attitudes, and Macpherson (1999: 41, 6.1) notes wide support for this position. However, Macpherson (1999: 41) denies that 'overt racism' is the problem. Rather, (1) the use of racist language to describe Black people reflects 'insensitivity and lack of training', (2) racial stereotyping is 'unconscious', and (3) the 'well intentioned' actions, that 'arise from racist stereotyping of black people as potential criminals or troublemakers', relate to a 'tightly knit [police] community' that reinforces rather than challenges its traditions (1999: 41–44). These *process* and *cultural* factors explain the lack of attention to racially motivated crime, and discriminatory behaviour (1999: 51). Macpherson (1999) quotes the Scarman report (1981: 11) which makes a similar case regarding *Britain* as an 'institutionally racist society': it does not 'knowingly' discriminate, but some 'practices' by 'public bodies' and 'private individuals' could be 'unwittingly discriminatory' against Black people. Similarly, the 'policies of the Metropolitan Police are not racist', but some officers may exhibit 'errors of judgment' based on stereotyping, while others exhibit 'ill considered immature and racially prejudiced actions' when engaging with Black residents (Scarman, 1981: 64).

The Casey review (2023: 6) continues this tradition of 'pro police' criticism of police forces, this time in relation to misogyny after Sarah Everard 'was abducted, raped and murdered by a serving Metropolitan Police Officer'. Casey (2023: 7–9) identifies 'institutional racism, sexism and homophobia in the Met' in a context where 'officers are 82% White and 71% male'. One aim of the review is to ensure that the police can 'earn our trust' (Casey, 2023: 8). It requires major changes to: better manage the Metropolitan Police and make it more accountable, increase officer integrity, tackle 'deep seated cultures' (fuelled by 'hubris', 'defensiveness and denial', 'looking the other way'), address low resourcing for VAWG, and tackle racist, sexist and homophobic bullying (Casey, 2023: 17). One key difference is the partial rejection of Macpherson's emphasis on 'unwitting' racism, to identify 'overt acts of homophobia, misogyny and racism by serving officers and staff in the Met', while noting that '[c]learly not everyone in the Met is racist, but there are racists and people with racist attitudes within the organisation' (Casey, 2023: 332).

The opposite explanation is that the riots were caused by criminality and family breakdown. First, Conservative leaders and some think tanks related social disorder to poor parenting. Cameron (2011b; see also Stratton, 2010) related 'broken society' to 'violent crime, teenage pregnancy, drug and alcohol addiction, family breakdown, debt, worklessness, inequality' and described Labour's large but ineffective state response. Iain Duncan Smith (Secretary of State for Work and Pensions, 2010–2016) blamed welfare dependency, the lack of 'role models except the violent and the criminal, like child soldiers of the third world' (Mulholland, 2011), and emphasised the rioters' 'lack of humanity' (Ball and Drury, 2012: 4). The Centre for Social Justice campaigned on issues related to nuclear family breakdown (Centre for Social Justice, 2010; Pautz, 2012) and worklessness (Walker, 2013). These characterisations received energetic support from right-wing papers such as the *Daily Mail* (Phillips, 2011). Further, the Labour MP for Tottenham, David Lammy, described a 'lack of male role models in young men's lives' and the Bishop of London asserted that the 'background to the riots is family breakdown and the absence of strong and positive role models' (The Christian Institute, 2011).

Second, the alleged problem is a 'feral underclass', operating outside of mainstream society, beset by anti-social behaviour and criminality (Clarke, 2011; Crossley, 2016a), including membership of criminal gangs (Home Office, 2011; Travis, 2011a; Densley et al, 2011; 2020; Densley, 2013). Duggan's gang links were emphasised by police, politicians and right-wing media (Ryder, 2014). Cameron told the House of Commons that the rioters were engaged in 'criminality, pure and simple' (Cameron, 2011c). In particular, 'territorial, hierarchical and incredibly violent … street gangs' were behind the violence. They are 'young boys' from 'dysfunctional homes', making money from theft and selling drugs, killing other gang members, and harming 'innocent bystanders', while 'bound together by an imposed loyalty to an authoritarian gang leader'

(Cameron, 2011c; Cottrell-Boyce, 2013). The response to these organisations should be punitive, requiring more policing (Travis, 2011b).

Cameron (2011b) also floated the idea of (non-military) national service as part of a 'fight back' narrative. Deputy Prime Minister Nick Clegg suggested that rioters should be made to apologise to those affected, and wear orange jumpsuits while making retribution (as in the US) (Total Politics, 2011), while the *Daily Express* (2011) ran a 'Reclaim Our Streets' campaign, and the Chief Constable of Greater Manchester Police talked of ramping up 'shock and awe' (Tiratelli, 2021). Ed Miliband, leader of the Labour Party, described rioters as 'yobs' (BBC News, 2011) and previous Labour governments had emphasised punitive measures for social disorder (Squires and Stephen, 2005).

What was the impact of protest and riots on government policy?

Our aim is not to resolve these debates. Rather, we show that the UK government response (largely to produce policy for England) reflected the criminality and broken family frames during a period of austerity (Chapter 9). Chapter 2 describes major policy change when a 'window of opportunity' opens: there is high attention to a problem; a feasible solution exists; and, policy makers have the motive and opportunity to act (Kingdon, 1995). This perspective helps to explore problem definition. The UK government did not ask: what is the evidence for systemic racism in the UK, what solutions exist, and which are feasible? Rather, ministers asked: how can we deal with broken families and criminal gangs? Further, it reminds us about the importance of feasibility. Ministers struggled to make one preferred solution politically feasible, because high state intervention and substantial spending on 'problem families' was (1) a Labour government agenda, and (2) not a fit with an austerity agenda sold as a response to Labour's failure (Chapter 9). They responded initially by describing the urgent need to intervene to protect the children of troubled families while punishing the deviant behaviour of adults (Cairney and St Denny, 2020: 190).

The 'Troubled Families' programme to fix a broken society

Cameron announced the acceleration of the 'Troubled Families' programme within a week of the riots (Crossley, 2015a). In two speeches, he drew on references to crime, immorality and family breakdown to put parenting policy on the top of the government's agenda:

> Now that the riots have happened I will make sure that we clear away the red tape and the bureaucratic wrangling, and put rocket boosters under this programme ... with a clear ambition that within the lifetime of this Parliament we will turn around the lives of the 120,000 most troubled families in the country. (Cameron, 2011b)

Officialdom might call them 'families with multiple disadvantages'. Some in the press might call them 'neighbours from hell'. Whatever you call them, we've known for years that a relatively small number of families are the source of a large proportion of the problems in society. Drug addiction. Alcohol abuse. Crime. A culture of disruption and irresponsibility that cascades through generations. (Cameron, 2011d)

How did the government deal with political feasibility? First, it described the problem as solvable (by limiting the problem to 120,000 families) and a way to save money overall: 'Last year the state spent an estimated £9 billion on just 120,000 families … that is around £75,000 per family' (2011b). Second, it sought cost management by increasing the 'Troubled Families' allocation to local authorities while cutting other local budgets. Third, it made sure that local authorities would declare policy success on behalf of the UK government, because:

> **Anti-social behaviour order (ASBO)**: introduced by UK and Scottish governments (Labour) as part of inclusive, punitive, then holistic phases of families policies. There was minimal use of ASBOs (and no equivalent to the Troubled Families programme) in Scotland (Cairney and St Denny, 2020: 181–184). Current UK government policies on 'drunken or threatening behaviour, vandalism and graffiti, playing loud music at night' are the 'Community Protection Notice (CPN) or Criminal Behaviour Order (CBO)' (HM Government, 2022f).

- *Local authorities would only receive full funding for success.* The UK government part-funded the cost (40 per cent of £10,000) to 'turn around' each family, using Payment By Results to pay for success when *self-declared* by local authorities.
- *The proxy for success was simplistic and easy to achieve without solving the alleged problem.* It defined a troubled family as meeting three criteria: at least one child is (1) engaging in anti-social or criminal behaviour (for example, subject to an **anti-social behaviour order [ASBO]**), and (2) failing at school (for example, excluded, suspended three times, or under 85 per cent attendance), and (3) at least one adult is receiving unemployment benefits. Turning around a family meant securing improvement in one of those criteria (Cairney and St Denny, 2020: 186–187).

This approach allowed the UK government to declare that the 'Troubled Families' programme was an effective response to the riots, then announce expansion to 400,000 families (without really following through). It was a classic case of political and process success (popular and easy to process) without programmatic success (it did not solve the problem it described – Box 5.3) (for a full account, see Cairney and St Denny, 2020: Chapter 9, drawing on Hayden and Jenkins,

2014; Levitas, 2014; Bond-Taylor, 2015; Crossley, 2015a; 2015b; 2016a; 2016b; Lambert and Crossley, 2017; see also Hodgkinson and Tilley, 2011; Cairney, 2019c; Loft, 2020; Barnes and Ross, 2021).

The criminal justice programme to punish the rioters

The Coalition government and Labour opposition supported a punitive response to the riots, which boosted the political feasibility of the following measures. First, *to reverse 'liberal' trends in policy* while expanding legal and judicial capacity to deal with those arrested. Measures included to relax an evidentiary threshold for public prosecution, allow under-18s to be tried for minor offences, recategorise theft as burglary, and treat more cases in crown courts (which can produce longer sentences) (Pina-Sànchez et al, 2016; Tiratelli, 2021). Second, *to halt proposed cuts to police numbers*, give them greater resources to disperse crowds (Newburn et al, 2012), and allow them to impose curfew zones (Travis, 2011b) or take a 'zero tolerance' approach to anti-social behaviour (Dodd, 2011). Third, to pursue the 'Ending Gang and Youth Violence' strategy (Home Office, 2011), including to compile data on alleged gang members, fund local anti-gang task forces, and try to punish gangs as a whole for individual crimes (Densley et al, 2020: 4).

Critical policy analysis at the heart of modern UK debates

Chapter 2 portrays critical policy analysis as a way to combine (1) research to highlight inequalities and marginalisation, and (2) advocacy to defend or support marginalised groups. Some accounts seek to 'decolonise' research and policy analysis, and some refer to 'critical race theory' (CRT) to show that policy makers have misused research to justify power inequalities, racism, and unfair social outcomes (Doucet, 2019: 2–3).

In other chapters, we suggest that critical analysis tends to raise important issues, but be ignored by most UK governments who favour neoliberal interpretations of policy problems. Here, we identify a recent tendency by right-wing politicians to describe CRT as a dangerous ideology to be resisted.

Critical race theory as a threatening set of ideas

Developments in the UK relate strongly to the US right-wing reaction to CRT. For CRT advocates, studies helped to document the profound difference between (1) the appearance of US equality, fostered by anti-discrimination laws or affirmative action policies, and (2) the endurance of White supremacy, racism, subjugation, and racialised outcomes in policy and society (Bell, 1992; Crenshaw et al, 1995; Warmington, 2020). This racism is overt and covert, and the latter 'acts by the total white community against the black community' are 'just as 'destructive of human life' (Ture and Hamilton, 1967; Box 10.3). CRT research monitors such activity in multiple sectors, such as law and education, to challenge a tendency to privilege individualist discourse at the expense of a focus on structural barriers or systemic discrimination (Mencke, 2010; Etmanski, 2012; Goodfellow, 2018; George, 2021). It also informs advocacy, such as to influence Black Lives Matter activism, anti-racist movements within the Democratic Party, or critical approaches to education policy (Bradbury, 2020; Mohdin et al, 2020; Laniyonu, 2021).

In that context, for its right-wing opponents, CRT represents a threat to US politics and society (Brewster, 2021). High-profile figures – including former President Trump – used a caricature of CRT to reject claims of US White supremacy, portray BLM activists as agent provocateurs (responsible for US riots), and stoke up support for their own ideological positions.

There is a UK version of this development. For example, race-conscious research is part of a tradition of critical research into the socio-economic impact of inequalities on outcomes such as education attainment (Gillborn et al, 2018; Warmington, 2020), and of studies of intersectional approaches to research and policy (Box 10.4). 'Decolonising' approaches highlight (for example) the damaging impact of the British Empire on colonised countries, the role of the slave trade in UK economic development (and funding of historic monuments), and the need to change how we narrate key historical figures (Kwoba et al, 2018; Nasar, 2020; Bourne, 2021). There are 'decolonising' initiatives in secondary and higher education (Bhambra et al, 2018; Begum and Saini, 2019; Shilliam, 2021; National Education Union, 2022). The BLM protests in the UK also focused attention on CRT ideas, such as to use the slogan 'defund the police' to foster more effective – and less discriminatory – ways to use public resources (for example, Seymour-Butler, 2019; Joseph-Salisbury et al, 2021). However, these ideas are not mainstream: organisational changes in their name (for example, decolonising universities) have generally been modest, and undermined by neoliberal policies (Bhopal, 2018), and more radical options are pursued rarely (Nurse, 2021).

Box 10.4: Intersectional approaches to research and policy

Crenshaw (1989: 139) coined 'intersectionality' to contrast: (1) the 'multidimensionality of Black women's experience' with (2) the 'single axis framework that is dominant in antidiscrimination law'. The latter 'erases Black women' by privileging the analysis of a privileged group in each social category. This focus 'marginalizes those who are multiply-burdened and obscures claims that cannot be understood as resulting from discrete sources of discrimination', such as if a court rejects a claim of discrimination if a company employs Black men and White women, but not Black women (Crenshaw, 1989: 140). Since 'the intersectional experience is greater than the sum of racism and sexism, any analysis that does not take intersectionality into account cannot sufficiently address the particular manner in which Black women are subordinated' (Crenshaw, 1989: 140). While focused originally on race and sex discrimination in US law, 'intersectional studies' now apply

Prevent: part of the UK government's domestic counter-terrorism strategy, which accompanied the US-led 'war on terror' after 9/11 (partly because wars in Afghanistan and Iraq responded to, and increased the likelihood of, domestic terrorism – Chapter 11). The elements are: Protect (security), Pursue (surveillance), Prepare (contingency planning) and Prevent (challenge the spread of an ideology that radicalises British citizens and fosters domestic terrorism). In theory, it applies to everyone. In practice, most people referred to the police, or deemed higher risk, are non-White and Muslim (O'Toole et al, 2012; Heath-Kelly, 2017; see also Heath-Kelly, 2023 on 'a specifically Scottish Prevent program').

generally to (1) research using an intersectional 'lens' to identify multiple, intersecting sources/objects of discrimination, and (2) challenges to discrimination (Cho et al, 2013: 785–786; see also Palència et al, 2014; Hankivsky and Jordan-Zachery, 2019).

Applications in the UK highlight ways to challenge the effects of discrimination, such as to support more universalist policies (Khan, 2015), or end austerity policies that 'negatively impacted women of colour the most', financial barriers to employment tribunals, the Home Office 'hostile environment' immigration policy, 'stop and search' and **'Prevent'** (Goodfellow, 2018: 152). They also connect to the social justice or social determinants approaches that we describe in relation to education and health equity, and to the need for thoughtful implementation of the Equality Act 2010 which lists separate 'protected characteristics' (compare Christoffersen, 2019 with Scottish Government, 2022c).

Two cautionary tales relate to governments making sense of useful concepts in unhelpful ways. First, intersectionality could represent another broad term to support the vague ambition to reduce policy-making silos, using buzz phrases like holistic government (Chapter 3). Second, policy makers can subvert (or 'whiten') this agenda with reference to 'generic intersectionality' (Christoffersen, 2022: 407–408). By stating that there are many intersecting sources of discrimination, a government can downplay the importance of each one. This perverse outcome is a feature of the 'colour blind' or 'equity for all' initiatives that replace a specific focus on racial inequalities with generic education equity aims (Cairney and Kippin, 2022).

Nevertheless, some right-wing politicians in the UK – including Nigel Farage (Chapter 7) – make similar claims about the danger of CRT, question its relevance in a UK that is allegedly tolerant and welcoming, and/or reject claims that the UK's history of imperialism was damaging to colonised countries (see El-Enany, 2020 on the connections between Brexit and 'nostalgia for empire'). Many subverted the term 'woke' to stoke 'culture wars' (Box 10.3; Pitts et al, 2021; Gill, 2022). This approach is part of Conservative government discourse. For example, Kemi Badenoch (then Minister for Equalities) told the Commons that the government stood 'unequivocally against' CRT, describing it as supporting the radical anti-capitalist BLM movement (Nelson, 2020).

The UK government alternative to critical race theory

BLM protests drew enough attention to racism to prompt the UK government to ask the Commission on Race and Ethnic Disparities to produce a report (2021). It emphasised the importance of building trust between police and communities and improving police training, encouraging greater opportunities for education and training, and investigating health and other disparities (HM Government, 2022h). It argued that 'the big challenge of our age is not overt racial prejudice, it is building on and advancing the progress won by the struggles of the past 50 years' (Goodhart, 2021).

Critics of the UK response argued that the Commission was set up to legitimise, rather than challenge, UK policy: most of its members reject social determinants approaches; it would be influenced by people in government who are unsympathetic to CRT (for example, Munira Mirza, then Director of the Number 10 Policy Unit); and, its language presents a benign framing of racialised outcomes (Gedalof, 2022). The report received similar criticism that it: dismissed the importance of systemic racism, and allowed for individualist interpretations of racialised outcomes (blaming marginalised populations – Kaur and Hague, 2021). As such, it continues a tradition in UK government to commission non-threatening reports that call for non-radical change (Box 10.3). The cumulative effect of paying lip service to policy problems is that many other policy actors become sceptical about any hopes for non-trivial policy change (Box 10.5).

Box 10.5: The stoicism and coping mechanisms of experienced policy actors

We began this chapter by showing that many people engage in protest to challenge the unfairness of unequal societal and policy outcomes. We end by noting that many others respond with: (1) stoicism, to find ways to cope when inequity persists, policy-making problems endure, and they may even reproduce the practices that they find so dispiriting; or, (2) fatalism, to suggest that nothing ever changes or will change. Three examples highlight this dynamic.

First, Tummers et al (2015, drawing on Lipsky, 1980) identify the 'coping mechanisms' that 'frontline workers, such as teachers and social workers' adopt when experiencing the stress of 'high workloads' and dispiriting exchanges with service users. For example, how do they get through the day when they must reconcile the difference between (1) their personal values and professional training, designed to support people when they are at their most vulnerable, and (2) social security or other systems that seem designed to stigmatise service users and make it hard to receive support? The range of answers includes compassionate responses and bending the rules to help clients, to cynical responses in which they become emotionally detached or question the motives of clients (Tummers et al, 2015: 4; see also Durose and Lowndes, 2023).

Second, Boswell and Corbett (2015: 1388) describe many public health policy actors as 'stoic democrats' who 'see little reward for their continual efforts', but some who are no longer willing to play the same old 'game' and seek to subvert the rules to get the outcomes they want.

Third, Bastow (2013) identifies the strong rationale to maintain a dysfunctional prison system (in England and Wales). Prison workers and prisoners would appreciate and benefit from reforms to make processes more efficient, but express little expectation that it will happen. Many actors could contribute to positive reforms collectively but, as individual actors, change is not in their gift. For example, changes to employment practices would provoke union concern and politicise the issue, which would undermine action by ministers who would perceive the rewards to be minimal (while reflecting on the costs of previous failed reforms). Perhaps ministers would act if they perceived profound policy failure, but prisons are able to continue to be chronically dysfunctional without prompting a sense of acute crisis.

Conclusion

How can we use the Westminster and complex government stories to reflect on inequalities policies? First, critics of the lack of policy progress often draw on the Westminster story to blame UK government ministers. Put simply, if ministers exhibited enough knowledge of the social determinants of policy problems, and the political will to address them, they could reduce inequalities in the UK. Instead, they ignore the issue, provide vague platitudes as a substitute for action, or make the problem worse by individualising social problems or producing discriminatory policies. For example, Conservative ministers made explicit value judgements regarding who should benefit from government policy, and implicit choices regarding the likely impact of austerity and other measures, to exacerbate social and economic inequalities across the UK. They also oversaw hostile policies to deter immigration and deport British citizens, and legitimised 'institutional racism' in public services such as police forces.

Second, the complex government story helps to explain the lack of progress to 'join up' policy and policy making to reduce inequalities. Modern UK governments put their faith in holistic policy making to take forward an ambitious rhetoric to address spatial, gendered or racialised outcomes in sectors such as health and education. As such, they have found (repeatedly) that these reforms never live up to their stated expectations, while many are undermined by more important agendas. Even the most sincere and energetic policy makers would struggle to translate ambitious plans into a genuinely more equitable British society; but, few ministers seem to try. Devolved government experiences exhibit fairly similar variations on this theme, albeit in a context where their ability to innovate is far more limited.

In that context, the case study of protests/riots in 2011 helps to focus attention on the UK government's engagement with race and racism in the UK. It is possible to produce a narrative that emphasises the wider social and economic context: (1) the police killing of Mark Duggan exemplified routine police discrimination, people had a right to protest, and also expected that the police would mishandle protest; and (2) these events took place when government policies were exacerbating inequalities in relation to unemployment, housing, and access to high-quality public services. However, the UK government chose the opposite narrative: (1) police forces act reasonably and do not discriminate deliberately, and their role was essential to restore order after riots; and (2) the solution to the problem is state intervention to turn around troubled families, punish criminality, and punish criminal gangs. This response in 2011 is typical. It builds on a long-standing tradition of criminalising protest against governmental and police treatment – particularly when instigated by Black people – and to support police forces even during a challenge to their practices.

Foreign Policy: The War on Terror

Introduction

The UK Labour government made a major contribution to international conflict in the name of the 'war on terror'. The terrorist attacks on the US on 9 September 2001 – 9/11 – prompted President George W. Bush to initiate the invasions of Afghanistan in 2001 and Iraq in 2003. The UK government, led by Prime Minister Tony Blair, supported intervention, providing political and military support. These interventions prompted unusually large public protests. Protests against the Iraq War took place in over 60 countries, and over one million people marched in the UK (BBC News, 2003). Protests related to limited UN support, scepticism about US motives for the invasion, and the UK's questionable evidence to support the invasion. Much criticism focused on the patchy and misleading **Iraq dossier** used by the UK government to identify

Iraq dossier: an **intelligence** briefing prepared for the UK government, used by Blair to narrate the case for invasion. Not to be confused with another report dubbed the 'dodgy dossier'.

Intelligence: information with strategic or military value (for example, of a foreign threat).

Weapon of mass destruction (WMD): a 'nuclear, radiological, chemical, biological, or other device that is intended to harm a large number of people' (Department of Homeland Security, 2023).

'weapons of mass destruction' **(WMDs)** in the hands of Iraq leader Saddam Hussein. These protests did not cause immediate UK government policy change. Rather, they prompted the eventual publication of inquiries – the Iraq Inquiry (2009–2011) and Chilcot Report (2016) – that criticised UK government action. Subsequently, Conservative-led governments played a different role in international conflict.

We use these examples to show how governments interpret and respond to international events. In particular, the Iraq War is a useful focal point, to help analyse the modern history of UK foreign and defence policy and relate it to contemporary developments. Chilcot provides a wealth of information on policy and policy making in relation to Iraq. This chapter examines these examples through three lenses:

1. Foreign policy analysis helps to deduce how policy actors define foreign policy problems and seek solutions.
2. Policy concepts and theories help to describe foreign policy in a comparable way to domestic policies. For example, one criticism of Blair's leadership was that it was too centralised, but it did not have central control over policy outcomes.
3. Critical policy analysis helps identify who wins and loses from these developments, including the perceived political benefits to foreign conflict, economic gains to arms businesses, and the harm to victims of wars.

In the conclusion, we reflect on the extent to which foreign policy accentuates the Westminster and complex government stories. Does the Westminster story help to explain Blair's 'presidential' style of policy making? Does the complex government story help to explain the continuous gap between policy expectations and outcomes in foreign *and* domestic policy.

Should we treat foreign policy as different from domestic policy?

The study of foreign policy is distinctive. It is generally pursued by International Relations (IR) scholars, with their own reference points and 'established theories', which are different from the mainstream policy theories we describe in Chapter 2 (McConnell, 2016: 668; McGlinchey et al, 2017; Brummer et al, 2019).

Nevertheless, to analyse foreign versus domestic policy completely separately is not sensible. First, in practice, the distinction seems artificial (Brummer et al,

2019: 3). For example, our domestic case study chapters identify (1) responses to non-military threats to national security, including a global COVID-19 pandemic, climate change and financial crisis, and (2) the UK's relationships with international organisations, including the UN and EU. Further, wars produce high opportunity costs (the value of something that a government could have funded instead), including an estimated £21.3 billion to fund the Afghanistan War and £8.2 billion for the Iraq invasion (2015 prices) (Ministry of Defence, 2015; compare with the savings associated with 'austerity' in Chapter 10). Foreign and defence departments also need to meet central targets and budgets (Hall, 2013).

Second, Morin and Paquin (2018) suggest that FPA shares the same reference points as policy studies, including:

- *What is policy?* It is difficult to know what foreign policy is. A key task is to analyse official and unofficial sources and deduce a government's goals (Morin and Paquin, 2018: 19–31). As with domestic affairs, it makes sense to describe foreign *policies*, to reflect the concentration of power in theory but distribution of responsibilities in practice (Williams, 2005).
- *Policy tools.* Most tools are broadly similar, from rhetoric/statements of intent and agenda setting, to investing in organisations, voluntary agreements and direct intervention to coerce behavioural change (although 'military intervention' has a different meaning in domestic and foreign affairs) (Morin and Paquin, 2018: 39–41).
- *Policy cycles.* The policy cycle does not sum up well a complex reality (Morin and Paquin, 2018: 41–45).
- *Evaluation.* The measurement of policy success is highly contested (Morin and Paquin, 2018: 46–51).
- *Bounded rationality and policy-maker psychology.* We need to understand how policy makers combine cognition and emotion to (1) understand policy problems, (2) estimate the impact of their choices, and (3) decide who to praise/blame or trust/distrust (Morin and Paquin, 2018: 69–91, 217–245).
- *Agency and structure.* There is a similar focus on how to conceptualise the relationships between actors and their policy-making context (Box 2.3) (Morin and Paquin, 2018: 317–333).
- *Rules and norms.* Institutions prompt regular patterns of policy making, including the formal rules of political systems (for example, parliamentary systems) and the formal and informal rules underpinning bureaucratic managerial 'styles' and standard operating procedures (Morin and Paquin, 2018: 127–151, 101–119; see also Ansell and Torfing, 2019; Scott and Gong, 2021). There is contestation to establish which international norms should prevail (Morin and Paquin, 2018: 262).
- *The unclear role of inconsistent public opinion.* Policy makers may respond to their perception of the 'national mood', but can influence public support (Morin and Paquin, 2018: 167–181). The phrase 'rally around the flag' helps to explain

support for war and the use of war metaphors to generate support for domestic policies (for example, Chapter 6 on COVID-19).

- *Key actors.* There is a similar focus on media influence, interest groups, and think tanks, and experts (Morin and Paquin, 2018: 182–199).
- *Gender.* There are similar discussions regarding how to mainstream gender in foreign policy (Morin and Paquin, 2018: 275–278) and what *feminist foreign policy* looks like (Aggestam et al, 2019; Scheyer and Kumskova, 2019; Thompson and Clement, 2019; Thomson, 2020). Foreign policy making and analysis is highly gendered, including (1) the marginalisation of women in policy making and analysis, and (2) the relative lack of attention to gendered violence – particularly sexual violence against women – during conflict (Haastrup et al, 2019).

Third, policy theories and concepts have much to offer the study of foreign policy (Chapters 2 and 3). They inform any analysis that does not rely solely on the idea of a single state actor or all-powerful centre of government (see Allison), or the personality of policy makers (Dyson, 2006: 290; Brummer et al, 2019: 2). This wider focus includes to map the networks of foreign policy making in multiple centres (Ansell and Torfig, 2019). Further, for example, Joly and Richter (2022) apply punctuated equilibrium theory to show that foreign policy exhibits the same patterns as domestic policy change ('many incremental and occasional dramatic changes'), such as in relation to 'troop deployments, foreign aid and international trade'. Similarly, the advocacy coalition framework has been applied to coalition building in Israel, policy learning during war, and changes to foreign policy in relation to Afghanistan and Iraq (Pierce and Hicks, 2019).

> **Cuban missile crisis** (1962): a potentially catastrophic dispute between two nuclear superpowers (US and USSR) about Soviet nuclear missiles in Cuba. Allison (1971: 253–254) used three conceptualisations to generate different perspectives to explain the crisis, as (1) a dispute between states acting in their own interests; (2) a consequence of the standard operating procedures of different bureaucracies in each state; and/or (3) a process of bargaining and compromise between key actors within each state.

Policy analysis: how to analyse foreign policy problems

In IR, FPA generally refers to what we call *policy studies*. Therefore, it is difficult to find a direct equivalent to the *how to do policy analysis guides* in Chapter 2. However, FPA shares with policy studies a focus on the ideal types of rationality and the policy cycle (albeit in different ways, for different purposes). FPA might treat key 'steps' of analysis or 'stages' of a policy cycle as follows.

Ideal type 1: Different kinds of rational actor

Allison (1969; 1971: 3–7, 257) describes three ways to conceptualise 'rationality' to explain the **Cuban missile crisis**:

1. *State rationality*. Drawing on 'neorealist' IR theories to treat states or their 'centrally coordinated' national governments as if they were 'purposive individuals'.
2. *Bounded rationality and organisations*. Drawing on policy studies to identify how organisations maintain 'standard operating procedures' to limit attention and process information selectively.
3. *Rational individuals*. Using **game theory** to make simple assumptions about individuals and consider the sum total of individual behaviour.

When exploring the first explanation, Allison (1971: 29–30) describes four requirements of 'rational action' among states seeking to maximise the gains from their choices:

1. *Defining goals and objectives*. The actor is able to articulate and rank their preferences.
2. *Selecting from alternatives*. They choose between different ways to meet their goals.
3. *Predicting the consequences*. They identify what outcome each choice will produce.
4. *Making a choice*. They make the choice most likely to produce the highest pay-off.

At first glance, it resembles a shorter version of five-step policy analysis (Chapter 2). However, it is actually Allison's (1971: 31) discussion of comprehensively rational policy makers, which serves a different purpose to our approach. We treat comprehensive rationality as an ideal type, to compare with real-world bounded rationality. Allison describes an approach more common to economics and IR: identify a 'rational actor' with the perfect ability to deliberate and make choices, model/predict would they would do in each context, and compare these 'optimal' outcomes with those in the real world (Farkas, 1996; Alden, 2017).

> **Game theory**: 'The use of simple mathematical models to compare how individuals interact with each other when faced with different incentives in different settings' (Cairney, 2020a: 111). In 'axiomatic' models, we assume that no one is subject to bounded rationality. Examples include: (1) the 'prisoner's dilemma', to show that people will not cooperate with each other even when they commit to do so; (2) the 'chicken game' where both sides face hefty penalties for non-cooperation; and (3) the 'assurance game', where cooperation is likely since at least one side has an incentive to cooperate (Hindmoor, 2006: 109–111).

Ideal type 2: The modified policy cycle

Morin and Paquin (2018: 42–44) modify the classic policy cycle (Figure 2.1) to identify notional stages of FPA:

- *Framing*. Identify and define a policy problem worthy of attention.
- *Agenda setting*. Find a way to put the problem high on a policy agenda.

- *Options*. Commission bureaucracies and experts to generate feasible solutions.
- *Decision*. Follow established procedures to choose between options.
- *Implementation*. Make sure that the preferred decision is carried out.
- *Evaluation*. Engage in contestation to declare policy success or failure.

As in Chapter 2, one reason to describe these stages is to compare them with theories that describe a far messier reality (Morin and Paquin, 2018: 44–45). In that context, we use our five-step policy analysis headings to identify how policy makers *could have* defined and sought to address key foreign policy problems, to help explain what they actually did.

Analysing the war on terror

We analyse the US-led 'war on terror' (Box 11.1) and the UK's response. The UK government gave military support to the invasion of Afghanistan in 2001 and Iraq in 2003, and played a highly visible international role in coalition and support building (for example, to seek UN support). We focus on Iraq in particular. While the US connected Afghanistan to punishing the people that facilitated 9/11, supporters of the Iraq invasion described a more disparate set of reasons.

Box 11.1: The global war on terror

On September 11, 2001, 19 militants associated with the Islamic extremist group al Qaeda hijacked four airplanes and carried out suicide attacks against targets in the United States. Two of the planes were flown into the twin towers of the World Trade Center in New York City, a third plane hit the Pentagon (the headquarters of the US Department of Defense) in Arlington, Virginia, just outside Washington, D.C., and the fourth plane crashed in a field in Shanksville, Pennsylvania. Almost 3,000 people were killed during the 9/11 terrorist attacks, which triggered major U.S. initiatives to combat terrorism and defined the presidency of George W. Bush. (History.com editors, 2022)

In the aftermath of 9/11, President Bush (2001) announced 'a war against all those who seek to export terror, and a war against those governments that support or shelter them'. The UK and others helped to forge an alliance against Al-Qaeda (Kampfner, 2004; Williams, 2005). They also described an opportunity to 'reshape alliances in the Middle East' (Kampfner, 2004: 120). In 2001, the US invaded Afghanistan to depose a theocratic Taliban regime which had provided training and support to Al-Qaeda (Council on Foreign Relations, 2021). In 2002, Bush described an 'Axis of Evil' encompassing Iraq, Iran and North Korea. In 2003, the US led an invasion of Iraq. The war on terror included smaller military actions in the Philippines, Northern Africa, Syria, Cameroon, Yemen, Kashmir, Libya (whose leader, Colonel Gaddafi shared with Saddam Hussain a reputation for being brutal, unpredictable, and possessing few foreign diplomacy skills). President Barack Obama made it official US administration policy to no longer use the phrase war on terror, but continued the US military presence in Afghanistan and Iraq (McCrisken, 2011), approved the operation to kill Al-Qaeda leader Osama bin Laden in 2011, and approved conflict in Iraq and Syria against militant Islamist groups from 2014.

Step 1: How could governments define foreign policy problems?

We identify two narratives – broadly 'for' and 'against' invasion and occupation – and US and UK variations on each theme. The 'for' case includes five main arguments.

1. Previous airstrikes and sanctions failed to change Saddam Hussein's behaviour

The Iraq War in 2003 represented unfinished business. It began with action led by President George Bush (George W's father) and including countries like the UK. Iraq's 1991 invasion of Kuwait prompted **Operation Desert Storm**, to halt Iraq's march on Kuwaiti oil fields (Finlan, 2003; Allison, 2012) rather than regime change (Zunes, 2001). A President Clinton-led US also oversaw political and economic sanctions on Iraq (Alnasrawi, 2001), and subsequent airstrikes in 1998 (Operation Desert Fox), to punish Saddam's violations of UN sanctions and reflect suspicions regarding his weapons programmes (Ritchie and Rogers, 2006). Before 9/11, President George W. Bush's policy was limited to modifying sanctions to make them more impactful on the regime, not the Iraqi population (CNN, 2001), and Bush had stated his opposition to US military forces being used for 'nation building' (quoted in P. Miller, 2010). After 9/11, the US deemed Saddam a threat that could no longer be managed by sanctions and periodic airstrikes.

> **Operation Desert Storm**: a military response to Iraq's invasion of Kuwait. The US led a multi-country diplomatic in August 1990. It led an 'air assault' on 16 January 1991 ('in line with UN Security Resolution 678 authorizing the use of force'), then a 'ground war' on 15 February, lasting 'one hundred hours' (Holland, 1999: 219).

2. Saddam's regime will use WMDs against his own people and his enemies

For decades, Saddam had established a reputation as a brutal dictator, using devastating weapons against his own people, particularly Iraq's Kurdish minority (Human Rights Watch, 1993; Gul, 2021). His regime deployed chemical and biological weapons – producing mass military and civilian deaths – during the war with Iran, 1980–1988 (McNaugher, 1990; Leigh and Hooper, 2003; Palkki and Rubin, 2021). The regime had attempted to develop nuclear weapons despite UN Security Council resolutions (NTI, 2022). Initially, the US and UK helped to arm Saddam's regime, preferring his secular Ba'athist regime to the theocratic Iranian Islamic Republic (Tarock, 1998; Phythian, 2005). Subsequently, US policy makers drew on government agency (Central Intelligence Agency and National Security Agency) intelligence to identify the enhancement of Saddam's WMDs which risked the security of the US and its allies.

3. A US value-oriented regime would provide strategic advantage in the region

The US had cultivated alliances with countries in the Middle East, but most were authoritarian regimes that did not share its liberal democratic values. It supported dictators for strategic reasons – such as to suppress communist movements (Bevins, 2020), and secure oil supplies – while narrating a mission to spread peace, liberty and democracy (T. Smith, 2012). Taking control of Iraq would go further, to reform its political and economic system (Reynolds, 2009).

4. Saddam is a dangerous foe of the US, and 9/11 could be the first of many attacks

Key figures in the US Presidency – including Vice President Dick Cheney, Defense Secretary Donald Rumsfeld and his deputy Paul Wolfowitz – joined with right-wing commentators to accuse Saddam of supporting Al-Qaeda and representing a threat to the US (with little evidence – Risen, 2004; see also Dizard, 2004: 1; Chulov and Pidd, 2011). They influenced Bush during a 9/11 trauma, prompting stories about terrorists plotting to destroy the US (Ricketts, 2002; De Goede, 2008; Updegraff et al, 2008).

5. Project American strength following 9/11

The US needs to strike back hard, to produce vivid and humiliating revenge, project military strength and restore the US role in global order. The Afghanistan invasion was not fulfilling those aims (Draper, 2020; Tharoor, 2021).

The US Presidency used these frames to generate domestic and international support for the Iraq invasion (Box 11.2). It expected allies to provide strong support (Kampfner, 2004; Jones, 2008). In particular, it expected US–UK action to reflect historic cooperation (during two world wars and ongoing conflict in Afghanistan – Porter, 2010).

Box 11.2: Seeking UN support for the invasion of Iraq (2002–2003)

Iraq raised the issue of the 'legality' of foreign invasion. As with Afghanistan, President Bush had considered unilateral action in Iraq. The former had some UN legitimacy in relation to its self-defence clause, but this case was harder to make for Iraq (Chinkin and Kaldor, 2017). Bush agreed to the 'UN route' to establish the war's legality and support.

Key countries – including Russia and China – expressed strong support for the US in relation to domestic terrorism, not foreign invasion (O'Loughlin et al, 2004). A first UN Security Council resolution – November 2002 (UNSCR 1441) – provided Saddam's regime with a 'final opportunity to comply with its disarmament obligations'. 15 members of the UN Security Council voted in favour, with no abstentions or votes against. It empowered weapons inspectors to seek evidence of WMD (after years of being denied access). They found minimal evidence of secret WMD capacity (but unable to 'prove an absence' – Thomas, 2017: 379). The US tabled a second UN Security Council resolution to gain authorisation for an invasion, but withdrew when it was apparent that the Council would not support it. As such, the war went ahead without clear authorisation.

In that context, the legality of the Iraq War is still contested. At the time, the US and its allies – including the UK Foreign Secretary Jack Straw – argued that previous UN resolutions (and 1441 in particular) provided a legal basis for invasion. The UK Attorney General Peter Goldsmith advised the UK Cabinet that the invasion was legal (Pidd and Mulholland, 2010; Chilcot, 2016, ES: par 458). Straw argued that the UN would be weakened without a strong response to Iraq (Atkins, 2013: 180). However, Chilcot (2016: 486) criticised the omission of 'conflicting arguments' during that process. Many allies – such as Germany and France – opposed the war (Schroeder, 2022), and General Secretary of the UN, Kofi Anann, argued that it was not legal (MacAskill and Borger, 2004). There was similar contestation to describe US-led action – or US foreign policy – in relation to the more subjective term 'legitimacy' (Scott and Ambler, 2007; Strong, 2017).

Opposition to the Afghanistan and Iraq Wars

Opponents of the Iraq War included the Senator and future President Obama (2009), former UK Foreign Secretary Robin Cook (2003), and 'figures from all three major opposition parties' in the House of Commons (Conservative, Liberal Democrat, Scottish National Party) (Knox, 2021: 174). Few would defend Saddam or reject claims about his use of chemical and biological weapons (Bloodworth, 2021). Rather, the 'against' case was based on a rejection of many 'for' claims:

- The link between Al-Qaeda and the Taliban (Afghanistan) or Saddam (Iraq) is not clear, and the US administration only sought evidence for what it 'believed to be true' (Kampfner, 2004: 168).
- Targeting a country for the crimes of a small number of people is disproportionate.
- Iraq is not a clear threat to the US or UK.
- It is not clear how an invasion of Iraq would fulfil US or UK aims (to use regime change to introduce liberal democracy).
- The US did not receive UN Security Council support, so its invasion would be illegal.

There were also more general forms of opposition. First, foreign invasion is costly in terms of military and civilian deaths, the costs of destruction and regeneration, and the ethnic or sectarian tensions that exacerbates. Second, it represents a new and damaging form of imperialism by a military superpower, willing to resort to violence to further its political and economic aims and protect its privileged position in the global order.

The latter informed organised opposition to the invasion of Afghanistan – such as via the Stop the War Coalition, associated with figures such as future UK Labour leader Jeremy Corbyn – as well as the use of **extraordinary rendition**, and prisons such as **Guantanamo Bay** and **Abu Ghraib** (Chan and Safran, 2006; Gillan et al, 2008; Phillips, 2008). Many protest marches were held against the war in Afghanistan, including 20,000 people in London in October 2001 (*The Guardian*, 2001). Iraq War protests were much larger, and coordinated on an international scale (February 2003). For example, in London, one million people marched against the imminent invasion, and popularised phrases such as 'no war for oil' and 'Bliar'.

> **Extraordinary rendition**: to transfer a detainee (for interrogation) to a foreign government.
>
> **Guantanamo Bay**: a US naval site in Cuba. One of several places to hold prisoners outside of the US for interrogation (before trying many for capital offences).
>
> Both measures are associated with detaining people while depriving them of human rights (such as to not be tortured or detained without trial) (Steyn, 2004; Sadat, 2005). These practices were also apparent in Iraq, such as in the **Abu Ghraib** prison.

What was the problem facing the UK government and the Labour Party?

Generally, when describing its role in foreign policy, the UK Labour government emphasised the need to foster collective action and lead international efforts, project strength, and be ready to engage in conflict, while meeting ethical foreign policy principles and prioritising humanitarian intervention (Gaskarth, 2013; Kettell, 2013; Kitchen and Vickers, 2013; Box 11.3).

Specifically, the UK was already committed to US alliance based on shared values and a strong response to Al-Qaeda (Blair, 2001; Williams, 2005). In the wake of 9/11, Blair described standing 'shoulder to shoulder with our American friends in this hour of tragedy and we, like them, will not rest until this evil is driven from our world' (BBC News, 2001). The UK had already joined the US-led (then NATO-led) coalition to invade Afghanistan (eventually contributing tens of thousands of troops over two decades) (Kampfner, 2004; Sundin et al, 2011). Opposition to the Afghanistan War was relatively muted (for example, the Conservative Party was supportive) and largely confined to perpetual opponents of US foreign policy (Benn,

2001), despite the long history of failed military interventions in Afghanistan (Hopkirk, 1992).

In that context, US action set the agenda for UK policy analysis in two main ways. First, to join the US in military action or not, rather than to help the US to decide if it should invade Iraq (for example, key figures like Rumsfeld were indifferent to UK participation – Dyson, 2006: 289). Second, to prompt UK policy makers to make a case for invasion, based largely on the US line: previous actions in Iraq have failed, Saddam aids terrorists, he will use WMDs on us and our allies, we need to project strength to our enemies, and our action in Iraq will have strategic benefits (compare with the UK portrayal of Iran during this period – Kitchen and Vickers, 2013). Further, the UK would need a strong case to counter domestic and international condemnation, since it would take place without UN Security Council approval (Box 11.2).

Step 2: What policy solutions were feasible?

The UK leadership sought to demonstrate the political feasibility of supporting the Iraq War, focusing on its relationship with the US, how to define Iraq's threat to the UK, the wider humanitarian consequences, and how to anticipate and counter political opposition.

UK support is essential to maintain US relations

Maintain the 'special relationship' with the US, as part of the UK's 'Atlanticist' orientation or ideology, as the best way to influence US policy (Williams, 2005: 54; Thornton, 2016). This relationship rests on 'shared security interests and interlinked global economic interests' and (for UK leaders) a story of British 'brains' and 'wise counsel' and American 'brawn' and 'youthful' idealism (Porter, 2010: 355–358). US norm enforcement could easily break this relationship, such as when US politicians (including Bush) criticised French opposition (Fisher, 2012). The Chilcot Report (2016: par 365) notes that the UK government was influenced by a '[c]oncern that vital areas of cooperation between the UK and the US could be damaged if the UK did not give the US its full support over Iraq' and a 'belief that the best way to influence US policy towards the direction preferred by the UK was to commit full and unqualified support, and seek to persuade from the inside'.

The Iraq War would stop a direct threat to the UK

Saddam's regime is a direct threat in relation to its possession of WMDs, which it could use quickly to harm neighbouring countries (for example, Israel) or supply to terrorist groups to attack the UK (Kampfner, 2004: 161). Much of the political feasibility of invasion rested on the urgency and scale of the problem. It was summed up in the Iraq dossier, made infamous when Blair relayed its vague but powerful claim that 'Iraq could use weapons of mass destruction within 45 minutes of an order' (BBC News, 2004). The UK government did not make it crystal clear, in its published case, that Iraq could not attack the UK with WMDs in 45 minutes (Intelligence and Security Committee, 2003: para 83; Betts and Phythian, 2020: 124).

Iraq intervention would produce positive humanitarian consequences

Military interventions are driven by humanitarian ends (Box 11.3). From 1998, Blair articulated a 'doctrine of international community' which set out the criteria for humanitarian intervention (Blair, 1999; Kampfner, 2004; Porter, 2018). Commentary related support for intervention to the need to oppose tyrannical or fascist regimes (Cohen, 2002; Aaronovich, 2003; Johnson, 2006). Blair's foreign policy, before and during Iraq, rested on 'activist, interventionist principles' (Dyson, 2006: 298).

Box 11.3: Combining humanitarian intervention and neoconservative ideas

Responsibility to Protect (R2P): an 'international security and human rights norm which seeks to enhance the state's ability to protect civilians from four mass atrocity crimes: genocide, crimes against humanity, ethnic cleansing and war crimes' (UN-A UK, 2022).

Humanitarian intervention describes the use of military force, against the wishes of a foreign state, to alleviate human suffering (compare with 'liberal interventionism' – Honeyman, 2017 – and the **Responsibility to Protect**). This idea grew in importance from the 1990s, following the failures of Western countries to prevent genocide in Rwanda and the former Yugoslavia (McCourt, 2013; International Criminal Tribunal for Rwanda, 2015; International Criminal Tribunal for the former Yugoslavia, 2017).

Blair (1999) described the 'doctrine of international community' to make a general case for multilateral humanitarian intervention. Then, when facing opposition to the Iraq War, he emphasised humanitarian intervention as a primary reason to act (Kettell, 2013: 269). At a similar time, US neoconservatives favoured ideas which centred American pre-eminence, espoused unilateral force and pre-emptive attacks, and sought a post-Cold War era in which there was only one superpower (for example, Bourgois, 2020). This idea underpinned military build-up and a sense of 'unfinished business' in Iraq. Proponents of each view regard the use of military force as inevitable and often desirable (although humanitarian narratives would favour joint action supported by the UN). The lead up to the war was fuelled by (1) neoconservative arguments, emphasising energy security, the need for a strategic outpost in the Arab-speaking world, and the post-9/11 projection of American power, and (2) humanitarian interventionist arguments, focused on Saddam's human rights abuses and WMDs.

In the UK, the legacy of the Iraq War was to undermine the use of *humanitarian intervention* alone to justify conflict. The coalition government sought to (1) draw on this principle, but also (2) distance itself from Blair's rhetoric and action, to (3) justify intervention in Libya then Syria as a response to the '**Arab Spring**' (Atkins, 2018: 109). Deputy Prime Minister Nick Clegg narrated the role for international cooperation in the context of: Liberal Democrat opposition to the Iraq War, the potential 'tragedy' if the 'mistakes of Iraq led to a retreat from the principle of liberal interventionism', and the 'lesson' from Iraq that intervention needs to 'be multilaterally sanctioned and driven by

> **Arab Spring**: a 'series of uprisings across North Africa and the Middle East' (Atkins, 2018: 109) by 'societies intent on overthrowing existing exclusionary and brutal orders' (Sadiki, 2015: xxxiv; Al-Agha, 2015).

humanitarian concerns' (quoted in Atkins, 2018: 112). While the Labour government was 'reckless', the coalition would be 'responsible' (Atkins, 2018: 112). In contrast to Iraq, Libyan intervention was: 'unambiguously legal', humanitarian, supported by Libya's neighbouring countries, 'focused on post-conflict stabilization and aid' and 'guided by clear objectives' (Atkins, 2018: 113). The Commons supported action by 557 to 13 in 2011 (Atkins, 2018: 118). In comparison, the rhetorical case for Syrian intervention was closer to Iraq (to address a brutal dictator using chemical weapons on his people), and similar problems emerged, including the absence of a UN Security Council resolution to invade. The Commons opposed action by 285 to 272 in 2013 (Atkins, 2018: 118).

Our political opponents do not have a good case against invasion

This focus on political feasibility was necessary to counter opposition to the Iraq War. First, opponents in the UK reframed the 'special relationship' argument to characterise Blair as Bush's 'lap dog' (Luce, 2007) and highlight the disastrous impact of previous uncritical UK support for US invasions (Danchev, 2007). Second, they highlighted the potential for humanitarian disaster and sectarian bloodshed following the end of military intervention (Cook, 2003). Third, they described the poor intelligence in the Iraq dossier (BASIC and Saferworld, 2003), dismissed the notion that Saddam posed a direct threat to the UK (HC Deb, 24 September 2002, c49), and recommended the UN-sanctioned push to inspect Iraq's weapons. This point became the biggest bone of contention, with some opponents accusing UK policy makers of selling the war misleadingly by exaggerating evidence of WMDs (Box 11.4).

These reasons to oppose the Iraq War informed public protest. The scale and intensity of protest (February 2003) prompted some – temporary – concerns in the UK government that it would undermine Blair's premiership and UK policy (Sinclair and Doherty, 2013). Still, the invasion began in March 2003, with the House of Commons ultimately agreeing (18 March) to contribute as the second largest member of the 'coalition of the willing' in spite of a sizeable rebellion (Kaarbo and Kenealy, 2016).

Steps 3 and 4: Comparing solutions and predicting their outcomes

In foreign policy, steps 3 and 4 identify the desired outcomes and likelihood of success (subject to high uncertainty). The coalition's desired outcomes – find the WMDs, create a democratic Iraq and gain strategic advantage – were accompanied by optimistic stories of success.

Depose Saddam and find and secure Iraq's weapons of mass destruction

The US and UK governments sought to disarm Saddam's regime, but their references to WMDs were vague. Chilcot noted the tendency to refer:

> only to Iraq's 'weapons of mass destruction' without addressing their nature (the type of warhead and whether they were battlefield or strategic weapons systems) or how they might be used (as a last resort against invading military forces or as a weapon of terror to threaten civilian populations in other countries). (Chilcot, 2016: ES, par 517)

They exaggerated the idea of 'a credible device capable of being delivered against a strategic city target' (Robin Cook resignation speech, HC, 17 Mar 2003, Column 727).

Create a democratic Iraq

The UK government avoided describing regime change as a legal justification for war (its Attorney General had ruled it out), which left three legal bases: self-defence, humanitarian intervention or UN Security Council authorisation (Betts and Phythian, 2020: 169). The US was less constrained, and the administration talked about replacing Saddam with an interim US-led coalition Provisional Authority (CPA) before transitioning to holding elections (likely producing majority Shiite rule) and prohibiting the Ba'ath Party (which had run Iraq for decades). The coalition described an aim to invade, occupy, replace the Iraqi regime, and leave the Iraqis to enjoy their newfound freedom.

Ensure that Iraq becomes a useful strategic outpost

The aim was a US-friendly regime which shared Western liberal democratic values and secured US security and economic interests (including access to Iraq's oil and government contracts – Halperin, 2011). A preference for democracy and freedom from state oppression (Bush, 2001) combined with a belief 'that people who are free and prosperous do not fly airplanes into skyscrapers' (Heinrich, 2015: 6).

Proponents argued that an ally in the Middle East could make it (1) easier to resolve the Israel–Palestine conflict, and (2) encourage other country reforms based on Iraq's experience (Indyk, 2003; *The Guardian*, 2005; *Jewish Chronicle*, 2016). These aspirations were shared by the UK government, arguing that 'a successful mission means winning the peace as well as the war' and an essential part of change would be a liberal, 'free market economy' (Thomas, 2017: 381).

The UK had additional objectives fuelled by optimistic expectations. First, to strengthen the 'special relationship' with overt support and covert action (Williams, 2004; Dunn, 2008; Porter, 2010; Gaskarth, 2013; Chilcot, 2016: ES para 372). Second, to influence US action: discouraging an emotional unilateral response to 9/11 in favour of rational international cooperation (Kampfner, 2004; Dyson, 2006; Porter, 2010: 360). Blair sought to translate a good personal relationship with Bush into UK influence (Kampfner, 2004: 128), and the US's pursuit of UN approval is one tangible example (perhaps the only one – Cook, 2004: 298). Chilcot (2016: 15) is less positive about Blair's influence. Other accounts described being sidelined or unable to navigate the US administration (Straw, 2013).

Step 5: Make a recommendation to maximise success

Foreign policy analysis compares the idea of maximising the benefits of choices versus actual outcomes: did the Iraq invasion achieve its aims? First, the US-led coalition succeeded in deposing Saddam after one month of initial conflict (Saddam was then caught by US forces in 2005 and executed after trial by the new Iraqi government), but not in finding WMDs (Beaumont et al, 2003; Wilson and Plesch, 2021). By April 2005, the Central Intelligence Agency stated that their search had 'gone as far as feasible' (Datta, 2005), while key sources eventually admitted the fabrication of evidence of WMDs (Chulov and Pidd, 2011).

Second, over months and years, the CPA and its successors faced violent insurgency, from Al-Qaeda then Islamic State in the Levant (ISIL, aka ISIS or Da'esh). Estimates of – mostly civilian – casualties range from 100,000 to over two million (Benjamin and Davies, 2018; Iraq Body Count, 2022). A key element was the CPA aim to achieve 'de-Baathification': to bar Iraqis who had ranked in the highest four tiers of the Ba'ath Party from government work, and disband the Iraqi Army and build a new one (Pfiffner, 2010). This approach enabled a stronger insurgency, able to recruit from a pool of trained soldiers and disaffected young people (Zinn, 2016).

Third, this conflict undermined the planned transition to a multi-party, multi-faith democracy and market economy (Constitution of Iraq, 2005; Abdullah et al, 2018). The new Iraqi government was a close ally of the West, but an ineffective government beset by corruption (Abdullah et al, 2018; Hencke, 2018; Hamilton, 2020; Hamourtziadou, 2021). This reputation would sow the seeds for ISIL, which would latterly control huge swathes of Iraq territory (Tucker-Jones, 2018).

Fourth, the special relationship remained strong. Fifth, Blair sought to use it to engage Bush in the Israel–Palestine peace process (Kampfner, 2004: 213).

However, the Blair–Bush relationship was temporary and its effect muted (Dunn, 2008; Henke, 2018). Then, Bush and Blair left office with damaged reputations (the reputations of intelligence services also suffered – Kippin, 2018; Dobson, 2019). For example, support for the US – associated with a 'global wave of sympathy ... after 9/11' (Hinnebusch, 2007: 26) – diminished, which undermined alliance building for future interventions (Burns, 2021). Bush's successor, President Obama, was elected on a promise of ending the Iraq War and withdrawing troops. Blair was replaced by Gordon Brown, who had supported the invasion but was keen to extricate the UK from a politically damaging situation. Iraq would be left as a country marked by internal displacement, widespread destruction and violence, and a government beset by corruption. It continued to host the radicalism that the invasion sought to prevent (Looney, 2008; Harrow, 2010).

Box 11.4: The politicisation of UK foreign intelligence

The 'politicisation' of intelligence refers to the contestation to (1) prioritise some forms of evidence over others, and (2) interpret or use valuable evidence selectively. It includes reinterpreting intelligence reports to support an existing preference (Bar-Joseph, 2013; Coletta, 2018; compare with 'policy based evidence' – Cairney, 2019c). For example, New Labour and Blair's team already had a reputation for news 'spin' (Mughan, 2000) and prioritising the 'presentation phase' of foreign policy (Williams, 2004: 929). Further, some commentators argued that UK policy makers and their special advisors (including Downing Street Director of Communications Alastair Campbell) manipulated the presentation of intelligence to exaggerate the threat of WMDs (Aldrich, 2005: 74). Most famously, BBC journalist Andrew Gilligan (29 May – *The Guardian*, 2003) described a source complaining that the Iraq dossier was 'transformed in the week before it was published to make it sexier'. Then, Dr David Kelly died (by suicide) on 17 July, after being identified by UK government actors as Gilligan's source. On 18 July, the Secretary of State for Constitutional Affairs commissioned Lord Hutton 'urgently to conduct an investigation into the circumstances surrounding the death of Dr Kelly' (Hutton, 2004: 1).

Formal inquiries did not uphold allegations regarding the *misrepresentation* or *manipulation* of evidence (Hutton, 2004: 319–320). There was a consensus among Western intelligence agencies that the Iraq regime probably had weapons in breach of UN Security Council resolutions (CNN, 2003). Rather, inquiries identify an attempt to *sell the war*, including narrating the evidence dramatically and simplistically to make 'the best possible case' and amplify the threat of WMDs (Aldrich, 2005: 74; Humphreys, 2005; Phythian, 2005: 129–130). The Butler Report (by a committee established by Blair on 3 February 2004 to 'review intelligence on weapons of mass destruction') criticised the government for downplaying the uncertainty and ambiguity in intelligence gathering, and for its contribution to the highly misleading '45 minute claim' (Butler, 2004: 125–127). The Chilcot Report (2016) criticised Blair's tendency to narrate intelligence rather than draw directly from reports (Thomas, 2017: 376; Betts and Pythian, 2020: 166).

Explaining foreign policy: relating the Iraq War to Westminster and complex government stories

Chilcot (2016) provides a detailed account of UK foreign policy making in relation to Iraq. It helps us to generate lessons and relate them to Westminster and complex government stories. In particular, foreign policy is characterised by unusually high centralisation, in which a small number of powerful actors make choices that are less subject to routine forms of collective decision making and accountability. It contributed to the charge that Blair sought a more 'presidential' form of policy making (Hennessy, 2005: 10). These accounts emphasise his tendency to take important decisions from Number 10 without the full consultation, agreement, or knowledge of key governmental individuals and organisations. Still, the complex government story helps to highlight the actors and factors that either pushed back against centralisation or caused a gap between the centre's expectations and actual outcomes.

The Westminster story and Blair's presidentialism

In a UK context, 'presidential' describes centralising power within the core executive, the marginalisation of Cabinet, and 'railroading' decisions through Parliament (Helms, 2005; Kettell, 2013). Several factors contributed to the idea that Blair sought this policy style:

- *Blair's perception of a personal mandate.* From 1997, Blair enjoyed landslide Labour victories in general elections, giving him a misleading sense of personal 'mandate' from the voting public. He also had high authority in the Labour Party (Fielding, 2002; Hennessy, 2005; Straw, 2013; Kippin, 2018), which had a parliamentary majority of 170 in 1997 and 167 in 2001 (falling to 66 in 2005).
- *Blair's self-confidence.* He projected a 'high belief in his ability to control events' and 'need for power' (Dyson, 2006: 290).
- *Blair's insular style in government.* His style was 'overly secretive, ad hoc, informal, and susceptible to groupthink' (Williams, 2004: 917).
- *Blair's love of spin.* His communications team sought to influence the media agenda, partly by making him the face of policy.
- *The absence of a Brown counterweight.* The equally powerful role of Chancellor Brown in domestic policy was not as relevant in foreign affairs.

The accumulation of power in 10 Downing Street

Blair concentrated power in Number 10 by appointing many advisors, establishing new policy units and a communications hub, and circumventing established patterns of policy making (Hennessy, 2005; Barber, 2008). Blair was the first Prime Minister to formally grant special advisors the authority to direct civil servants (Foley, 2008: 61). He appointed foreign policy advisors – such as David

Manning – who reported directly to him, were vested with greater trust and responsibility than their Foreign and Commonwealth Office (FCO) colleagues, and conducted unofficial diplomatic missions on Blair's behalf (Kampfner, 2004: 174). During the Iraq War, Alastair Campbell and Blair's Chief of Staff Jonathan Powell enjoyed highly significant roles in influencing policy and ensuring Blair's preferences were heard (Campbell, 2007; Chilcot, 2016). Blair's growing international profile emboldened him and his advisors to act with less reference to FCO rules (Kampfner, 2004: 117, 211), and he would 'make no apology for having a strong centre' when dealing with foreign crises (Kettell, 2013: 268).

The sidelining of Cabinet and other bodies

Blair was accused of diminishing the role of Cabinet as a deliberative body headed by the Prime Minister as 'first amongst equals' (Richards and Smith, 2009). He preferred short formal meetings preceded by informal agreements (Williams, 2004; Short, 2005; Dyson, 2006; compare with Gamble, 1994; Daddow, 2013: 115 on Thatcher and other leaders). UK policy making was often carried out by an 'inner inner circle' (Dyson, 2006: 301). Blair's approach was described as 'sofa government' (Williams, 2004: 916). It was characterised by 'informality and circumspection' and a reliance on ad hoc meetings of relevant ministers and advisors (Williams, 2004; Hennessy, 2005). Cabinet sub-committees – the traditional 'engine room' of British government – were used, but often informally (Aldrich, 2005).

These tendencies were particularly pronounced in foreign affairs, where (1) bilateral relationships between leaders or Foreign Ministers are common (Kampfner, 2004; Straw, 2013; Brummer et al, 2019), and (2) the 'involvement of Prime Ministers in international summitry' increased at the expense of traditional bureaucratic diplomatic relationships (Helms, 2005: 431). Bush and Blair held many bilateral meetings prior to the decision to invade (Kampfner, 2004). One meeting took place in Bush's ranch, where Blair gave a commitment that the UK would join the US invasion. Chilcot (2016: par 409) criticised Blair for not agreeing a position with Cabinet prior to this summit (Kampfner, 2004: 169–171). While Blair and senior colleagues narrated a strong role for Cabinet, Betts and Pythian (2020: 56) describe few opportunities for Cabinet to debate the issues; ministers were deferential to Blair (see also Straw, 2013; Thomas, 2017). The former Cabinet Secretary Lord Turner described Blair's way of working as 'I like to move fast. I don't want to spend a lot of time in kind of conflict resolution, and, therefore, I will get the people who will make this thing move quickly and efficiently' (Chilcot, 2016: ES, par 401).

Railroading Parliament

Labour's majority was so large that only a major rebellion (in combination with unified opposition) could produce a parliamentary defeat. Its leadership used

Parliament to rubber-stamp its aims. Traditionally, in foreign affairs, there was not a clear expectation that the government would seek parliamentary consent on troop deployments; the Prime Minister could use 'Royal Prerogative Powers' to declare war (Strong, 2015; Kaarbo and Kenealy, 2016; Mills, 2018). Indeed, prior to the Afghanistan invasion, 'there was no debate, or vote, on a substantive government motion relating to the deployment of British forces' (Mills, 2018: 15). There were only two Cabinet meetings held between 9/11 and Afghanistan deployment, and 'both were devoid of debate' (Kampfner, 2004: 129). However, in the case of Iraq, Parliament was granted a vote – and effective veto – over the decision to deploy troops (which set expectations for future conflicts). Indeed, Campbell's diaries confirm that a lost vote would have likely triggered a Prime Ministerial resignation (Sinclair and Doherty, 2013).

Blair and the Labour Party

The Labour Party fora for policy debate were often subsumed into Blair's leadership. The party was subject to a 'rolling managerial coup' (Minkin, 2014) which saw Blair's will permeate institutions such as the National Executive Committee, the National Policy Forum and the Labour Party conference (Schnapper, 2015: 11). Many MPs were loyal in exchange for ministerial positions, including the 'professional politicians' who were often former special advisors (Allen, 2013; Kippin, 2018).

These factors contribute to the sense that the decision of the UK government to invade Iraq is associated primarily with one man (Dyson, 2006: 289). Schnapper summarises this mainstream perception of Blair's leadership style:

> Important decisions were taken by him with a small group of people involving a few Ministers and advisers, rarely in the full Cabinet meetings. ... They were then 'sold' by the Prime Minister himself through a highly effective communications machine led by Alastair Campbell to both his party and the public at large. (Schnapper, 2015: 3)

Is presidentialism an accurate description?

That said, Blair was recommending action that 'enjoyed support or sympathy from within the Joint Intelligence Committee (JIC), the SIS, the Cabinet Office, the lion's share of print media, most of the government, and almost all of the Conservative opposition' (Porter, 2018: 41). We can produce a different narrative based on the involvement of other actors, including:

- Cross-party support ensured that Parliament voted to approve the Iraq invasion. While most non-'payroll vote' Labour MPs (that is, without a Ministerial or 'Parliamentary Private Secretary' position) voted against, Conservative Party MPs, under the 'hawkish' leadership of Iain Duncan Smith, expressed forthright support (Tempest, 2003).

- Downing Street and other staff made the presentational case, coordinated intelligence, and monitored combat and occupation phases.
- FCO staff engaged in intense negotiations with the US State Department.
- Ministry of Defence staff coordinated troop deployments with US counterparts.
- The powerful Chancellor and Treasury estimated the cost of war, and made no visible moves to block it (Neville, 2001; Cornish and Dorman, 2009; Brummer et al, 2020: 2).

They were joined by a sizeable proportion of the public who, for some time, gave the benefit of the doubt to the government's depiction of events and rationale for invasion (Strong, 2017). They were supported by an influential network of foreign policy activists, often with strong links to the US neoconservatives. Other UK political activists, commentators and bloggers supported the invasion for humanitarian reasons. In other words, the beliefs that underpinned the war were held far more widely than in 10 Downing Street. Roberts (2007: 385) describes a public feeling 'that it would be problematic to blame everything on one person when many people had been involved in the chain of events leading to war even when a particular misstep is associated strongly with one particular individual'.

The complex government story and policy failure

There is a big difference between a Prime Minister (1) trying to centralise the power to make key choices versus (2) enjoying a full understanding of the policy problem and control over wider processes and outcomes. Indeed, Bevir and Rhodes (2006: 97–98) show that '[e]ven as journalists, political scientists and practitioners tell tales of a Blair presidency, so they continue to recognize many limitations to Blair's ability to get his own way'. Rather than being a 'Napoleonic' figure, he faced routine problems of governance (Chapter 3) and was 'perpetually involved in negotiations and diplomacy with a host of other politicians, officials and citizens ... as just one actor among many interdependent ones in the networks that criss-cross Whitehall, Westminster and beyond' (Bevir and Rhodes, 2006: 98).

The Blair government's emphasis on 'joined-up government' recognises this reliance on others to make its policy work (Bevir and Rhodes, 2006: 107). Usually, this story identifies the countervailing power of Brown or other ministers (Bevir and Rhodes, 2006: 98–100). Further, they describe the fact that governments set strategy but rely on many other actors to (1) inform them about the nature of problems and likely impact of solutions, and (2) deliver their preferred policies (Bevir and Rhodes, 2006: 100–101). While many commentators draw on the Westminster model to narrate their story: 'The tales of presidentialism are a smoke screen that upholds Westminster fictions but behind which we find a widespread acceptance of the governance story' (Bevir and Rhodes, 2006: 105).

In the case of Iraq, Blair's limits include a failure to 'persuade international leaders on the case for war', or prevent ministerial resignations, MP rebellion and mass protest (Bevir and Rhodes, 2006: 101–102). Further, senior policy makers and intelligence agencies lacked full information on: Iraq's weapons programme; links between the Saddam regime and Al-Qaeda; and, the likely consequences of military action. Nor could it know Iraq's capabilities compared to potentially more powerful states such as 'Libya, North Korea, or Iran' (Betts and Pythian, 2020: 166).

Many of Chilcot's recommendations highlight this gap in understanding and influence. We can relate it to bounded rationality and policy-making complexity, which contributed to policy failure (Cairney, 2016c).

Recommendation: challenge groupthink based on sincere but unhelpful beliefs

Chilcot does not conclude that Blair's government acted cynically. Rather, it highlights the danger of **groupthink** and not subjecting beliefs – for example, 'that Saddam Hussein's regime retained chemical and biological warfare capabilities' – to proper scrutiny and debate (Chilcot, 2016: 55–61). There should

> **Groupthink**: when 'a group reaches a hasty or premature consensus and then becomes closed to outside ideas' (Houghton, 2008: 185).

be standard operating procedures to challenge beliefs (such as in Cabinet committees), consider evidence and legal advice properly, and put less pressure on key bodies to find evidence to justify action (see also Williams, 2004: 920; Aldrich, 2005: 76; Grube and Killick, 2021).

Recommendation: avoid action based on hubris or inflated expectations of influence

The lesson from the 'UN route' (Box 11.2) for UK Prime Ministers is that you might *think* that you can form a coalition to temper the actions of the US, but you may reinforce US action and not find a way out. Wider discussion with colleagues may have helped to anticipate this problem (Chilcot, 2016: 112; see also Lander, 2004: 486; Williams, 2005: 36; Mazarr, 2007; Daddow and Schnapper, 2013).

Recommendation: to avoid policy failure, ensure better planning for the long-term consequences of war

The US did not have a good plan for Iraq beyond regime change. Its Department of Defense disregarded State Department planning, partly on the expectation that the war would be quick and simple (O'Hanlon, 2005). The UK government was peripheral to its planning, and not well prepared when consulted. Then, when the war exacerbated problems in Iraq, there was little proper deliberation on how to respond, plus growing differences between US/UK strategy on providing more or fewer troops (Chilcot, 2016: 78–108; the Blair government rejected these arguments at the time – Kettell, 2013: 270).

Chilcot (2016: 109 onwards) identifies many policy failures according to different indicators. We can relate them to three categories of policy success (Box 5.3; Marsh and McConnell, 2010: 571):

1. *Political. Will this policy boost my re-election chances?* The Iraq War became unpopular in the UK: 'support for the missions is low, their perceived success is poor and there is evidence of cynicism regarding the motives in Iraq', producing 'doubts over the truthfulness of government sources' (Gribble et al, 2015: 141).
2. *Process. Will it be straightforward to legitimise and maintain support for this policy?* The decision to invade was controversial, failed to achieve direct UN authorisation, and was unpopular with several key allies. Public perceptions of the Iraq War undermined the UK government's ability to intervene in future conflicts (Gribble et al, 2015: 141).
3. *Programmatic. Will it achieve its stated objectives if implemented?* Saddam was deposed, and an elected Iraqi government established, but the invasion failed to live up to wider expectations. No WMDs were found. The huge death toll, prolonged occupation and regional instability suggest a serious miscalculation by policy makers.

Many commentators drew on the fiction of Blair's presidentialism to suggest that Chilcot was particularly damning of Blair. The range of commentary was remarkable, from identifying his mistakes in judgement to labelling him a war criminal. Rather, the general lesson from Chilcot is that government action is driven by value judgements, hope and unrealistic expectations based on an inflated idea of the power of UK Prime Ministers (Cairney, 2016c). While the lessons from Iraq came in a major report in 2016, the UK's chaotic withdrawal from Afghanistan in 2021 provided more vivid messages of failure (Box 11.5).

Box 11.5: The chaotic withdrawal from Afghanistan in 2021

UK combat operations in Afghanistan began in 2001 and ended in 2014, when the occupying coalition sought to transfer responsibility for security to the Afghan military. NATO forces maintained a strong presence while the deposed Taliban fought to regain control of the country.

A deal between the Taliban and the US was agreed in 2020, led by President Trump and inherited by President Biden. The US committed to reduce its troop presence 'from 13,000 to 8,600 and withdraw from five military bases within 135 days (with proportionate decreases in allied force levels) and withdraw all its forces by 1 May 2021' (Mills, 2021). The UK, under NATO, followed suit. In return, the Taliban stated that Afghan territory would not be used for terrorism or threaten the US and its allies. The deal also paved the way for (ill-fated) negotiations between the Taliban and Afghan government.

The troop withdrawal triggered Taliban advances. The final withdrawal of all UK forces, government employees, and other citizens was described by the Foreign Affairs Select Committee (2022) as a 'disaster and a betrayal of our allies that will damage the UK's interests for years'. It described a failure to (1) 'shape or respond to Washington's decision to withdraw', (2) 'predict the speed of the Taliban's takeover', or (3) produce a 'plan for evacuating Afghans who supported the UK mission … despite knowing 18 months before the collapse of Afghanistan that an evacuation might be necessary'. The evacuation was highly chaotic, with tens of thousands waiting too long to be processed and many 'abandoned' (West and Stewart-Smith, 2023). The Taliban quickly regained control of the country and reverted to pre-invasion policies (such as to place profound controls on the behaviour and education of women and girls). Overall, the UK government had low influence on US-led (and Taliban) policy and a limited ability to respond well to foreign events.

Critical policy analysis: who won and lost?

While it took one month to depose Saddam Hussain, US and UK troops were engaged in combat operations in Iraq for over six years (they ended officially in November 2009), followed by a far longer period of partial occupation, and a return to combat operations – against ISIL – that only ended in 2021 (with some troops remaining, to help Iraqi troops). As the war unfolded, it became clear that the US-led coalition's success would not be guaranteed, despite the triumphalist rhetoric (Cockburn, 2003). The initial phases saw relative calm, but the disbandment of the Iraqi Army and Ba'ath Party triggered mass violence (Zinn, 2016). This period was marked by rival Shia and Sunni sectarian violence, and saw US and UK forces fighting a rearguard action to retain control (Abdo, 2017). In 2007, the US administration sought to increase its control with a 'surge' of troops (Marsh, 2012) prior to large-scale withdrawal. The emergence of Al-Qaeda in Iraq prompted more prolonged involvement (Faulkner and Gray, 2014; Hassan, 2019). ISIL emerged in the years following the invasion, and latterly controlled large swathes of Iraqi territory, carrying out countless atrocities, prior to their evisceration by a military coalition including the UK (Wilson Centre, 2019).

Who suffered?

Key figures may be disproportionately responsible for these policy failures, but receive a disproportionately low share of the negative consequences. For example, Blair and Bush left office with damaged reputations, but their fate is almost insignificant compared to those of millions of people in Iraq. First, approximately 200,000 civilians died from direct war-related violence caused by the US, its allies, the Iraqi military and police, and opposition forces from the time of the invasion until October 2019 (Costs of War, 2021a). Second, the invasion 'displaced approximately 1 in 25 Iraqis from their homes, and fighting with ISIL contributed to additional displacement. As of 2020, 9.2 million Iraqis are internally displaced or refugees abroad' (Costs of War, 2021b). Third, the US and its allies led a systematic programme of detention and torture (Greenberg et al, 2005; Human Rights Watch, 2022), and the humiliation of prisoners by US troops became well known (for example, after the 'notorious' case of a photo from Abu Ghraib – Zalewski, 2010: 33).

Fourth, the high extent of 'rape and sexual exploitation in war' – primarily against women – is harder to document, partly because it has historically been:

- 'Systematically disregarded ... as war atrocities and crimes' (Hynes, 2004: 432).
- Tolerated (rape) or encouraged (sexual exploitation) by governments and army leaders (Hynes, 2004: 432), as well as private contractors stationed in Iraq (Farr, 2009: 13).
- Downplayed by invading governments, since sexual violence by 'the good guys' would undermine 'the official war story that the war on terror will liberate Afghan and Iraqi women' (Hunt, 2010: 120). The 'presumption of innocence' was a general feature of UK policy in relation to alleged war crimes (including unlawful killings, torture, and violence against children – Kettell, 2013: 272; Baldwin, 2020; Butchard, 2021).

Fifth, 179 UK armed service personnel were killed on duty, and many more were injured physically (Overton, 2020) and mentally (Mark et al, 2018; Stevelink et al, 2018).

Who benefited?

Most accounts of the 'winners' highlight the usual beneficiaries of war: large corporations, arms suppliers and dealers, and mercenaries (although see Gul, 2021 on high Kurdish support for the 'liberation' of Iraq, and treatment of Bush and Blair as heroes). First, the opportunity to access oil wealth was not the primary motive of governments (Meirang, 2016), but still allowed oil companies to profit. Indeed, the UK government lobbied its US counterparts to ensure 'a fair slice of the action for UK companies in a post-Saddam Iraq' (Bignell, 2011; see also Thompson, 2017b for a history of the role of oil in Western economies). Second, prior to the Iraq conflict, the UK government had committed itself to a new 'ethical foreign policy', including to reverse its policy to encourage the sale of arms from UK-based companies to regimes which were known to have breached human rights (Cook, 1997; Chandler, 2003; Kampfner, 2004). One such regime was Iraq under Saddam Hussein (Cook, 1995; Stothard, 2011), which meant that arms dealers benefited from sales to both sides of the conflict. Third, Overton (2018) reports that the UK government has spent 'approximately £50m annually' on mercenary companies, with the worldwide sector estimated to be worth up to £275 billion per year.

Conclusion

Foreign policy and policy making has distinctive elements, and is studied more through the lens of IR than policy theories. Yet, a strong distinction between foreign and domestic affairs would be artificial. Almost every problem analysed in this book has domestic and international elements, including the COVID-19 pandemic and extreme environmental events that pose a high threat to human health and security. Further, FPA is conducive to the analytical tools that we employ in other chapters, such as to ask: what is policy, what tools do governments prefer, how do they address high uncertainty and ambiguity, how do they deal with their limited control of policy making and their wider policy environment, and can we declare the outcome to be a success or failure? Many examples of foreign policy represent extreme cases of a general pattern of UK policy making. In particular, the long period of Blair-led Labour government accentuates key aspects of the Westminster and complex government stories.

The decision to play a key part in the Iraq War exemplifies Blair's pursuit of a 'presidential' style of policy making. Generally, he combined self-confidence with centralisation, informal and insular policy making, control over a high parliamentary majority, and media 'spin' to project high personal and government control over key choices. Specifically, he sought to boost and use his international status to play a key role in US-led conflict, with decisions made in bilateral discussions between country leaders. He maintained secrecy and restricted consultation to a small team, and narrated a secret intelligence-led case for Iraq invasion, to project a policy based on urgency, importance and his personal conviction regarding humanitarian intervention. That said, he failed to convince the UN, his own party's MPs, and a large proportion of the public of that case. Consequently, when the Iraq War looked like a political and policy failure, most commentary laid most blame at Blair's feet.

The Iraq War also accentuates the complex government story, to explain the continuous gap between policy expectations and outcomes in foreign policy. Prime Ministers may project a sense of control, but are subject to three main limitations. First, they are responding to events outside of their control, and their knowledge of the problem and the likely impact of their responses are limited. The Iraq War shows that the Blair government never really had an accurate picture of the strategic context. Second, they do not get what they want on their own. Rather, Blair relied on many government departments to coordinate intelligence gathering and policy cooperation with the US, cross-party cooperation to secure a vote in favour of invasion, and tabloid media support to help boost public confidence in his policy. Third, he had minimal control over key events and policy outcomes. This limitation began with a failure to convince enough UN actors of the case for invasion. It continued when it became clear that the WMD-fuelled case for invasion was misleading, the removal of Saddam solved one problem but exacerbated others, the invasion produced massive deaths, sexual assaults, displacement and turmoil for years, and the outcome was chaotic. Put simply, this outcome could not possibly be what a rational government leader would hope for when making the case for intervention.

The 'war on terror' also produced a longer UK foreign policy legacy. First, negative lessons informed subsequent discussions of the UK role in foreign conflict, to make an allegedly different case for intervention in Libya in 2011, fail to make the case to invade Syria in 2013, then play a 'non-lethal training and capacity building' role in 2015 before 'supplying defensive lethal weaponry' to help Ukraine defend itself from Russian invasion from 2021 (Mills, 2022). Second, the UK military has been more or less active in Afghanistan and Iraq until 2021, and its departure from Afghanistan was chaotic (Box 11.5). These experiences remind the UK government that it may control its foreign policy, but it is not in control of foreign affairs.

12

Conclusion

Chapter highlights

1. This chapter uses recent crises and dramatic experiences of UK government to reflect on more general and enduring aspects of UK politics and policy.

2. Policy analysis helps to identify the overwhelming number of problems facing a government at any one time, and how ministers define and prioritise problems.

3. Policy studies show how UK ministers draw – with modest success – on the Westminster story to portray strong, decisive government acting in the national interest.

4. Their experiences exemplify the limits associated with the complex government story, including the need to inherit problems and policies, and respond to multiple crises, while having a limited understanding of events and control over outcomes.

5. Critical policy analysis helps to show how policy makers, the media and public pay disproportionate and infrequent attention to inequality.

Introduction: A UK government facing polycrisis

There is never a good time to write a book keeping up with events in UK politics. When we began in summer 2021, Boris Johnson was the Prime Minister who had declared success on Brexit and was trying to steer UK policy towards 'normality' during the COVID-19 crisis (Chapters 6–7). By summer 2022, Johnson had resigned after

Polycrisis: when many connected crises happen at the same time (such as international conflict, economic, health and climate crises).

intense pressure to take responsibility for 'Partygate' during COVID-19 lockdown (Box 6.3). In October 2022, our draft conclusion noted that the new Prime Minster Liz Truss had only been in post for a month but had already replaced her Chancellor and was on the cusp of resigning after dramatic failures of economic policy (Worthy, 2022). By April 2023, Prime Minister Rishi Sunak had faced six months of economic difficulty, exacerbated by factors including COVID-19 and Russia's invasion of Ukraine, and Nicola Sturgeon resigned as Scotland's First

Minister in April 2023. By the time you read this book, the UK government may be led by a new party and a new Prime Minister, likely signalling a new dawn in British politics.

Yet, it is always a good time to draw on multiple conceptual lenses to examine contemporary developments. Policy analysis helps to identify the problem from the perspective of an analyst communicating with policy makers, to define a problem, generate and compare feasible solutions, and make a recommendation. Policy studies identify how policy making actually works. Critical policy analysis examines who has the power to define and address policy problems, which groups they favour and marginalise, and who wins and loses from policy. Our focus on the UK also helps to compare Westminster and complex government stories, to relate short-lived minister action to longer-term government.

Our concluding chapter uses examples of this dramatic period of government to reflect on more general and enduring aspects of UK politics and policy. First, we consider how governments analyse and frame the policy problems that they face. Other chapters zoom in on one (multi-faceted) problem to understand the competition to define and solve it. Here, we focus on how governments seek an overall narrative of all issues, to identify the overwhelming number of problems arising at any one time. In that context, what problems do they prioritise, how do they define them, what solutions seem feasible, and what are the main trade-offs?

Second, we examine how governments use the Westminster story to project strong and decisive government. They often signal the need for rapid and radical change from the past. Until recently, the Conservative story followed a return to government. Thatcherism narrated a break from Labour and the post-war consensus, describing economic, financial and public services crises to foster state transformation towards neoliberal approaches. Cameron's coalition government narrated a break from Labour following financial and debt crisis. Cameron used Thatcherite rhetoric to argue that 'austerity' had to follow the rise in government debt following Labour's failure. Yet, unlike Thatcher, recent Conservative Prime Ministers entered office after decades of state transformation. Unlike Cameron, they inherited crises *overseen by the Conservatives* (and most could not relate a new mandate to a decisive general election win). Theresa May and Boris Johnson became Prime Minister on the back of a promise to resolve Brexit (Chapter 7). Truss sought to harness Thatcherism to portray decisive action in the national interest, but largely to reject the economic approach of Chancellor Sunak. Prime Minister Sunak signalled a shift from the policies of a 49-day Truss government, and a Johnson government in which Sunak had served as Chancellor (Chapter 6). More generally, Prime Ministers alternate between narratives of conviction (to get things done) and consultation (to bring people with them). Our longer-term analysis of state transformation shows that approaches translate into bursts of reform ideas tempered by drivers of stability and continuity (Chapters 4 and 5). In contrast, the Truss government provided an extreme one-month example: an initial focus on conviction government was followed by 'listening' government, willing to U-turn when key measures – such as to abolish a **45p additional rate of income tax** – faced a backlash (Box 12.1).

Third, we show how policy makers navigate the limits associated with the complex government story (see Chapters 2–3 on bounded rationality and policy-making complexity). Ministers struggle to gain a full understanding of the problems they seek to solve, or the policy-making context and statute book that they inherit. They need to respond to multiple crises while navigating a policy-making environment out of their control. These problems include: the search for economic growth after the crisis of Brexit, and recovery from a COVID-19 crisis that saw inactivity rise and government debt grow; the profound impact of the Russian invasion of Ukraine; and, a cost of living crisis in relation to inflation, driven by a major rise in the cost of energy (fuel for buildings and vehicles), international rises in the cost of borrowing, and the falling value of the pound. These problems have prompted Conservative governments to signal a long-term desire to lower spending and taxes, but boost spending to respond to events.

Fourth, we use recent examples to highlight the politics of policies to address inequalities. The backlash to reducing taxes for high earners (Box 12.1) is one of a very small number where inequalities – temporarily – took centre stage (see also Box 6.5 on school exams). In most other examples, inequalities remain high while attention is fleeting, or unequal outcomes are sold as a consequence of policies pursued in the 'national interest' (Chapters 9 and 10).

45p additional rate of income tax: in 2022–2023, income tax bands were: 0 per cent up to £12,570, 20 per cent basic rate £12,571–50,270, 40 per cent higher rate £50,271–150,000, and 45 per cent additional rate over £150,000 (people pay 45 per cent on income above that amount) (HM Government, 2022a). The additional rate began in April 2010, starting at 50 per cent then cut to 45 per cent from April 2013 (OBR, 2012). The income-related National Insurance tax is 0 per cent up to £12,570, 13.25 per cent £12,571–50,270, and 3.25 per cent on additional income (HM Government, 2022g). Changing tax bands gathers higher attention than the 'stealthy and arbitrary' freezing of income tax bands to raise more revenue (Waters and Wernham, 2022). The Scottish government sets income tax (but not National Insurance): 0 per cent up to £12,571, 19 per cent starter rate £12,571–14,732, 20 per cent Scottish basic rate £14,733–25,688, 21 per cent intermediate rate £25,689–43,662, 41 per cent higher rate £43,663–150,000, and 46 per cent top rate above £150,000 (Scottish Government, 2022b).

Box 12.1: Narrating the unexpected: U-turns, blunders, trial and error

The Truss government signalled the need for centrally directed radical change to policy, to solve a cost of living crisis and foster economic growth. 'The markets' responded negatively to increased spending and uncosted tax cuts (prompting a decrease in the value of sterling). There was also a backlash to abolishing the 45p tax band, to favour high earners, while low earners were struggling to pay for energy. The subsequent U-turn shows that leaders pursue inflexible top-down policy making at their peril. It also connects to wider lessons from inconsistent government responses to crisis.

In Westminster politics, policy reversals damage political reputations. A conviction statement, and refusal to change course, makes U-turns particularly embarrassing. How can ministers respond? In theory, they could use the complex government story to emphasise trial and error: governments make choices, learn about their impact, then adapt and respond (Chapter 2; Box 3.5). In practice, this response is unlikely. The negative social consequences make the language of experimentation seem inappropriate (Box 8.1; Chapter 6). Further, ministers seek to project an image of governing competence based on the sense that they are in control, even while admitting that they get things wrong and share power with other actors (Box 3.1).

The Truss government tweaked the Westminster story to describe a 'listening government', willing to (1) modify measures while staying the course, and (2) consult with interest groups (for example, representing banks and business). Foreign Secretary James Cleverley emphasised decisive action in response to events (interview, Nick Robinson, *Radio 4 Today*, 5 May 2022, 8:16–8:17am). Robinson noted that 'the government has done a massive U-turn ... you changed approach and the markets responded'. Cleverly replied: '*That's what government is. Government is about responding, government is about deciding*'. Former Deputy Prime Minister Damien Green (*Radio 4 Today*, 17 October 2022, 8:19–8:20am) also described Truss as 'a pragmatist' who 'realised that the first budget ... didn't work in, spectacular fashion', and changed tack.

Error is not the same as 'failure' or 'blunders'. Actors use different criteria to declare success or failure: *political* (did it make us popular?), *process* (did we maintain legitimacy for the policy?) and/or *programmatic* (did it produce good outcomes?) (Box 5.3). In some cases:

- Failure is not up for debate, such as after the Grenfell disaster (Chapter 10).
- A dominant story of failure may emerge, such as after the Iraq War (Chapter 11).
- Some may declare *policy* to be a political success/failure but not the *process* to achieve it, or its impact on *outcomes* (Chapter 7).
- A new government comes in, declares that its predecessor failed, and signals radical and rapid change (Chapter 5 on Thatcher; Chapter 10 on Cameron).

A focus on 'blunders' emphasises the ministerial misjudgements causing failure. King and Crewe's (2014) examples include the poll tax (Box 4.3) and Black Wednesday (Box 5.3). Gaskell et al (2020) highlight COVID-19 failures (Chapter 6). The decision by Truss and Kwarteng to cut taxes and increase spending before showing how they would manage government debt would make this list (Flinders, 2022).

Policy analysis: what are the problems facing government?

Chapters 4–11 explore many issues that are important in their own right. They combine to produce a list of problems that could seem overwhelming to any new government and which are discussed in the following sections.

Economic crises and long-term problems with the economy

- Recessions, low growth, low productivity and low economic inactivity (Clift and McDaniel, 2022).
- A cost of living crisis.
- Continuous government deficits and historically high government debt.
- Trade-offs between encouraging immigration to aid business or discouraging it to satisfy some voters.
- How to foster more economic activity, such as among people not working but not classed as unemployed. For example, women with young children are more likely to not seek paid work because it would be overshadowed by the costs of childcare (Coleman et al, 2022; Chapters 9 and 10).

They combine with challenges to UK governing control, including:

- Global events outside of the government's control, including disruption to energy supplies following Russia's invasion of Ukraine.
- The reliance on markets and corporations to support economic policies (including their willingness to fund government borrowing by buying 'gilts' or government bonds).
- Changes to Bank of England monetary policy, such as to raise interest rates to address inflation and the low value of the pound (hindering people with loans/mortgages).
- The large number of private and public sector strikes (2022–2023) to seek pay rises in line with the cost of living, 'including many parts of the rail and bus networks, postal workers, civil servants, teaching staff and NHS staff' (King et al, 2023).

Dilemmas regarding spending commitments and cuts

- How to limit social security spending, given a long-standing commitment to protect the value of pensions (for example, by raising the state retirement age – DWP, 2023b).
- The pursuit of real-terms cuts ('efficiency savings') to government departments.

The ongoing impact of COVID-19

While the UK government downplays COVID-19 (Chapter 6), there remains uncertainty about its legacy and future impact, including:

- Concerns about further epidemics and the extent of 'long COVID' (Chapter 6).
- A National Health Service (NHS) under pressure, following high acute demand and deferred non-emergency treatment, exacerbated by problems in recruiting a sufficient workforce.
- The school exams crises that exposed education inequalities (Box 6.5).

Inequalities

- How to address social and economic inequalities in relation to factors such as geography, gender, race and ethnicity, disability, and sexuality (Chapter 10).

Climate change

- The lack of sustainable energy, transport and food systems, and limited progress towards the UK's 'net zero commitments' (Chapter 8).

Constitutional issues

- The impact of Brexit on trade (Chapter 7). The need to redesign policy instruments following withdrawal from EU schemes (for example, Chapter 8).
- Demands for greater territorial autonomy, including a Scottish National Party (SNP) government's call for a second Scottish independence referendum (Box 7.4).

How do new Prime Ministers define and prioritise problems? What solutions seemed feasible?

The radical rhetoric, U-turns and rapid end of the Truss government in 2022 gives the impression of an unusually short-lived battle of economic ideas – within the Conservative Party (Box 3.3) and government (Box 5.3) – that exposed the infeasibility of plans to radically reduce state intervention to foster economic growth (Macaskill and Piper, 2022). Key choices and consequences included:

Energy subsidies: UK government schemes (2022–2023) to subsidise domestic and non-domestic fuel bills. They included a £400 winter payment to households and a cap on electricity and gas prices ('energy price guarantee') (Mawhood et al, 2022; 2023).

- Kwarteng's 'mini-budget' (23 September 2022) included a commitment to tax cuts (including the 45p rate) and **energy subsidies**, but no reference to the estimated costs, usually provided by the Office for Budget Responsibility, or how they would be offset by spending cuts or revenue raising.

- A sense of budget loosening ('large and untargeted fiscal packages' – IMF, 2022), and the uncertainty surrounding overall government plans, contributed to a drop in the value of sterling, reduced demand for government bonds, and the downgrading of the UK's credit rating, prompting a major Bank of England intervention, to agree to buy government bonds to protect their value (an initial guarantee of £65 billion; compare with Chapters 5 and 9).
- This crisis prompted a partial U-turn on government policy (Box 12.1) and a greater commitment to respect policy processes, partly to ward off the sense that the Truss government was facing its 'Black Wednesday' (Box 5.3; Williams, 2022).
- Truss replaced Chancellor Kwarteng with Jeremy Hunt (14 October 2022). Hunt announced (17 October 2022) the reversal of the mini-budget (bar the – already legislated – cuts to stamp duty and removal of a proposed National Insurance levy to raise NHS funding) and that the energy subsidies would go from universal to targeted by April 2023 (HM Revenue and Customs, 2021; Foy, 2022).
- Sunak replaced Truss and kept Hunt as Chancellor, thus cementing a return to the policies that Sunak had proposed when competing with Truss to be Prime Minister.

However, the Truss fiasco also formed part of a longer-term experience of Conservative government, willing to change plans in response to events or experiences, while maintaining core ideas (Chapters 4 and 9). Further, Liz Truss' speech to the Conservative Party conference (Bloomberg, 2022) identified a set of priorities and proposals that would not be out of place in the speeches of her predecessors or successor. They include commitments to:

- Intervene to address crises, then seek state retrenchment (compare with Chapter 6). For example, Chakelian (2022) dubbed Truss' future plans as 'Austerity 2.0'.
- Limit state action to foster individual responsibility and incentives to work (Chapters 4, 5 and 9).
- Prioritise economic growth (unless it requires higher immigration) rather than redistribution or protecting the climate.
- Use growth to reduce deficits and fund priorities such as defence (Chapters 4 and 5). For example, the Truss government hoped that its policies would boost economic growth, but few organisations shared its optimism. PwC (2022) predicted over 3 per cent growth in 2022 to reflect some recovery from COVID-19, followed by stagnation or recession in 2023 and 2024 (see also OECD, 2022b). By 2023, actual and predicted UK gross domestic product (GDP) growth was lower than in the G7 and Eurozone (Harari, 2023).

- Strengthen UK borders, such as via boosting funding for border staff, expanding the 'Rwanda scheme', and resisting legal challenges to deportation (Box 12.2).

Box 12.2: UK government policy on asylum and immigration

Successive governments have sought to project strong UK borders in relation to immigration, with a clear spill-over to policies on asylum (Chapter 7). New Labour engaged in anti-immigration rhetoric (Maughan, 2010) and produced regulations to curtail support systems for asylum seekers (Schuster and Bloch, 2005: 4). Conservative-led governments ramped up this rhetoric for political gain (Consterdine, 2023), including Home Secretary Theresa May's (2010–2016) support for a 'hostile environment' for illegal immigrants and annual limits on legal migration (Boswell, 2019), and recent appointments of asylum hard-liners Priti Patel (under Johnson) and Suella Braverman (under Truss and Sunak). There were some exceptions during crises in Syria, Afghanistan and Ukraine, but often accompanied by the sense that UK efforts were relatively modest and slow (Box 11.5; although compare with Walsh, 2023).

Still, the UK has seen the arrival of tens of thousands of refugees and asylum seekers in recent years. Much is via unsafe sea routes, in the context of a lack of safe options for those seeking to exercise their legal right to claim asylum under international law (Syval, 2022). At least 166 people died or went missing between 2014 and 2022 (Home Affairs Select Committee, 2022). In March 2023, Sunak stood in front of a podium marked 'Stop the Boats', and announced an Illegal Immigration Bill to bar people who enter the UK 'illegally' from seeking asylum (Vohra, 2023). The government also signed an agreement with the Rwandan government to send asylum seekers for processing in Rwanda. The scheme provides a costly and ineffective deterrent, and legal challenges have minimised the numbers sent to Rwanda (Rosina and Kadhum, 2023). Refugee advocacy groups have strongly opposed such policies, and advocated for safe routes between countries (including the UK and France) (JCWI, 2022).

Braverman's comments on UK policy highlight elements of Westminster and complex government stories. Braverman emphasises the former when taking conviction politics to its extreme, and accepting that UK plans will push 'the boundaries of human rights law' (Hymas, 2023). Braverman also betrays elements of complexity when describing clear limits to policy progress, to describe the UK system as 'overwhelmed' by 'unprecedented' and 'unforeseen' levels of asylum seeking, and refuse to set a timeline for success (for example, the cessation of crossings, the rise in the numbers of people sent to Rwanda, or the reduction in the 'backlog' of people waiting in UK detention before a decision) (*Today* programme, 26 April 2023, 8:10–8:22am).

- Retain a strong UK role in relation to international security. For example, Johnson, Truss and Sunak governments signalled political support for Ukraine. Policies included 'an unprecedented package of sanctions to cut off funding for

Putin's war machine', providing military equipment and training to Ukraine soldiers (unilaterally or as part of NATO), and £400 million in 'humanitarian aid' (HM Government, 2023).

- Boost the UK's energy security – such as via fossil fuel extraction, renewables and nuclear – while (somehow) delivering the net zero commitment (Chapter 8).
- Maintain essential public services that improve everyday life, including policing, the NHS, education and social care (with less state intervention in areas such as housing).
- A vague commitment to 'Levelling Up' and addressing inequalities, but with limited state intervention (Chapter 10).

Each government has also sought to maximise the benefits of the UK exit from the EU (Chapter 7) while accepting devolution but resisting exit from the UK (Box 12.3). For example, each Conservative Prime Minister has rejected calls for a second referendum on Scottish independence while being less conciliatory than Cameron before the first (Box 7.4).

What are the main trade-offs, and the likely impact of their choices?

The rapid shift of UK government leadership from 2016 to 2022 – including Cameron, May, Johnson, Truss, then Sunak – exacerbated a tendency for ministers to engage sporadically with 'hard choices'. On the one hand, examples like austerity (Chapters 9 and 10), Brexit (Chapter 7), and the ill-fated Truss government reforms demonstrate high salience engagement with choices with clear distributional consequences. On the other, examples like COVID-19 (Chapter 6), climate change (Chapter 8) and the absence of 'fiscal responsibility' under Truss (the government did not announce how it would fund new policies) show that ministers do not seek routinely or systematically to identify the trade-offs between their choices (or estimate and monitor their effects). In particular, we find contradictory messages about a commitment to 'net zero' by 2050 but a high commitment to burning fossil fuels – to boost economic growth and energy security – in the meantime (Chapter 8; Horton, 2022). More generally, the list of government aims is too long to be described meaningfully as priorities (until we can look back to a record in government). There is often no real sense of which measures will command most resources, particularly when a new government promises more services but reduced budgets.

One stark difference in this calculation relates to trends in government debt (Figure 12.1). Unlike under Thatcher, there is minimal scope to privatise services (or increase public service charges) to raise revenue, government debt is much higher as a proportion of GDP (even after Cameron's 'austerity'), and the Institute for Fiscal Studies estimates that it will rise further (Adam et al, 2022). This trend helps to contextualise changing expectations over the years. For example, the Labour government had pledged to keep debt/GDP at 40 per cent or lower – in the name

Figure 12.1: UK government 'gross consolidated debt' as a percentage of GDP, 1992–1993 to 2021–2022

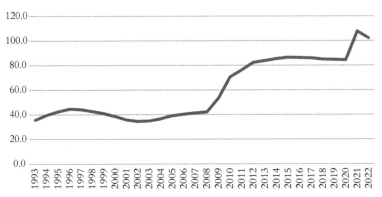

Source: authors' own chart from ONS (2023) data. '1993' describes data for financial year 1992–1993.

of 'fiscal prudence' – to compete with the Conservatives on an image of economic competence (Chapters 4 and 5). The financial crisis prompted it to borrow heavily to rescue banks and stimulate the economy, with debt/GDP at 76 per cent by 2011 (Chapter 9). Debt/GDP then rose under Conservative-led governments, including under the coalition government that sought to minimise the *deficit* by 2015 (Chapter 9), and remaining at around 85 per cent until the government borrowed heavily to finance COVID-19 management and recovery (Chapter 6).

In that context, further Conservative government deficits in response to crisis have contributed to a level of government debt/GDP that seemed unimaginable in the 1990s. Since then, both parties have sought – in vain – to minimise deficits and debt to project their prudential economic management (although in a context where the costs of 'servicing' debts are historically low – van Lerven, 2021). Most recently:

> The Government's costing of the Energy Price Guarantee for households and non-domestic consumers – £60 billion over the next six months – means that borrowing this year is now on course to climb to £190 billion. At 7.5% of national income this would make it the third-highest peak in borrowing since the Second World War, after the Global Financial Crisis and the COVID-19 pandemic. (Adam et al, 2022)

Box 12.3: Are the devolved governments addressing the same policy and policy-making problems?

The devolved governments are facing the same policy problems as the UK government, but only have the powers to address some. For example, they address very similar pressures on the NHS, exams crises and housing, while encouraging the UK government to address the costs of living via subsidies and spending commitments.

Devolved powers have changed somewhat since 1999, and the tendency to produce separate or four nations approaches varies considerably (for example, compare Chapters 6 and 8 on policy coordination). Chapter 4 also identifies examples of policy differences that began before 1999, including a tendency in Scotland and Wales to produce less radical reforms to the NHS and education (and reverse some after devolution), as part of distinctive policy styles that appear to be more consultative and put more faith in traditional modes of policy delivery led by local authorities (the picture in Northern Ireland was less clear, following periods of stasis then change often initiated by the UK government). In other words, devolved policy divergence has often resulted from jumping off the UK government reform train.

Could devolved governments also mitigate the effects of UK government policies? For example, we find different approaches to: energy (for example, renewables in Scotland and Wales – Chapter 8), inequalities (Chapter 10) and higher education tuition fees (Box 9.2); a varying ability to negotiate with unions directly (such as to offer different pay deals to nurses, local government or train staff); and, the increased Scottish government power to modify some taxes and social security benefits (Box 9.3). For example, before the UK government 45p U-turn, the Conservative Party criticised the SNP for having higher rates of income tax (it would have been 40 per cent versus 46 per cent over £150,000). The SNP's (2022) reply was that 'those with the broadest shoulders pay a bit more, while … [a]round 55% of taxpayers pay less income tax in Scotland than they would elsewhere in the UK' (then Deputy First Minister John Swinney also described the UK approach as 'menacing' – Radio Scotland, 3 November 2022, 8:16am).

This ability to diverge varies markedly, since Welsh and Northern Irish governments have fewer powers to go their own way on tax and spending. All three direct their allocated budgets, and rely on UK government policies to deal with security, energy and economic crises. In many cases, the most visible role of devolved ministers is to encourage their UK counterparts to change direction, or criticise the impact of policy for England on the rest of the UK. The same can be said of devolution within England, where there is a tendency to produce greater devolution in London (for example, to integrate transport), and experiment in some areas (for example, to devolve health services in Greater Manchester) or sectors (for example, Police and Crime Commissioners), while narrating overall central control (Diamond and Laffin, 2022).

Policy studies: how do policy makers use the Westminster story?

Successive UK ministers have used the Westminster story to project an image of governing competence (Chapter 3). As such, recent experiences exemplify – or take to extremes – that general approach. For example, Truss and Kwarteng expressed firm beliefs about how to solve policy problems, rejected criticisms of their plans, and argued that a lot of criticism would disappear when people saw policy working in the national interest. This approach included a rejection of advice from the 'usual suspects' and a determination to bypass standard operating procedures in government.

First, they portrayed routine sources of advice as part of the problem, particularly when rejecting the Treasury 'orthodoxy' (Davis, 2022; Richards et al, 2022). Kwarteng 'sacked his permanent secretary as his first act', while Truss 'sacked most of Boris Johnson's political advisers', replaced her 'National Security Adviser', and downgraded the status of others by moving them from 'Number 10' to the Cabinet Office (Rutter, 2022a). Sacking the Treasury Permanent Secretary was an 'immediate challenge to the constitutional norms around the civil service' and 'an attack on impartiality' (Rutter, 2022a).

Second, they rejected established (albeit non-binding) rules, such as to (1) respect the independence of the Bank of England, (2) ask the Office for Budget Responsibility to estimate the costs of their plans (Pope, 2022), or (3) ensure that special advisors are employed as civil servants who would be subject to 'civil service and special adviser codes of conduct' (Urban, 2022). This 'winner takes all' approach (Chapter 3) led to too many Yes people in Cabinet, too little parliamentary scrutiny, and too few attempts to gather information from experienced advisors.

Much of this approach backfired, prompting ministers to narrate U-turns and pay more respect to established procedures (Box 12.1). The experience suggests that the negative consequences of sidelining MPs, 'expert officials, and regulators' are 'a compelling advertisement for respecting ... constitutional checks and balances' (Russell, 2022). Respecting established processes is not only proper and pragmatic, but also a way to maintain 'market' confidence (White, 2022) and remain in charge.

Are we witnessing a break from the past, or the continuation of tradition?

The irony of this approach to policy making is that a new government (1) asserts that it represents a radical break from the past, while (2) using the same language and strategies as its predecessors, and (3) accepting the need for compromise and change. The Truss-led approach could have come straight from the Thatcher playbook, to project a major shift in policy making – using different ideas, and favouring central control over consultation and negotiation – to support radical changes to policy (Chapters 4 and 5). However, successive governments have used a similar playbook, which suggests that new governments contribute to accumulated changes to policy and policy making.

A new paradigm in economic policy?

The Thatcher government sought rapid and radical changes to economic policy and policy making (Chapter 4). Hall (1993) identifies 'third order' or paradigmatic change based on a rejection of Keynesian ideas and the embrace of monetarist approaches to economic policy. First, it replaced one source of advice with another: many Keynesian officials left the Treasury, and Thatcher appointed monetarists as special advisors and sought to promote civil servants sympathetic to policy change. Second, it set different priorities (reducing inflation and debt was more important than unemployment) and used different instruments (rejecting fiscal policies to manage economic supply and demand directly, in favour of monetary policies to manage inflation, and state retrenchment to foster greater market autonomy).

Chapter 5 shows that Hall's famous story has been qualified in both respects: the rapid exodus from the Treasury was exaggerated, and 'monetarism' was a short-lived experiment, applied rather inconsistently (using a mix of monetarist and Keynesian ideas). Yet, this debate focuses largely on the *speed* of personnel and policy change. In the longer term, Thatcher and successor governments oversaw a shift towards neoliberal approaches, where the state would seek less to manage demand or employment to foster economic growth, and more to stabilise inflation, while reducing regulation to encourage individual and business-led debt and growth. Thatcher and Major governments reduced financial regulation, and Blair and Brown governments inherited and enhanced that approach (while also granting independence to the Bank of England).

This approach contributed to the financial and economic crises of 2007–2008, associated with risky bank behaviour and overexposure to debt that would not be repaid, prompting government borrowing to bail out or support banks. However, crisis did not lead to another paradigm change. Rather, the election of a Cameron-led coalition government marked shifting priorities within that paradigm: (1) to oversee 'austerity' to reduce the government deficit much more quickly than Labour, and (2) to use austerity and state retrenchment to boost market autonomy and economic growth (Labour favoured modest debt-funded fiscal stimulus – Chapter 5). The austerity agenda reduced government spending as a proportion of GDP (although it rose in real terms, and debt rose as a proportion of GDP) until 2020. Then the Johnson government – with Sunak as Chancellor – borrowed heavily to fund COVID-19 policies (Figures 9.1, 9.2, 12.1) and sought to raise tax revenue substantially to avoid government deficits.

The Truss and Kwarteng story should be seen in that wider context: a vague rejection of the Treasury 'orthodoxy' regards debates within a paradigm (rather than a replacement with another), including how best to foster economic growth and how to fund deficit and debt reduction. Further, Sunak and Hunt's tax and spending plans do not seem particularly different to New Labour approaches: the 'tax burden' is 'at its highest sustained level since the 1950s' and Conservative governments borrowed heavily to deal with crisis (Adam et al, 2022).

A new policy style?

Chapters 2 and 3 show that UK government policy styles have generally not lived up to their 'majoritarian' reputations (Box 3.2). Commentators tend to pay attention to (1) the few cases where senior ministers identify priorities, reject debate, and face angry opposition from politicians and groups, at the expense of (2) most other issues that are less visibly contentious and exhibit more reasonable processes. A more consensual policy style results partly from choice. Governments recognise the limits to a top-down, uncompromising, insular style: it can be needlessly politically expensive and based on insufficient information on policy problems and solutions. It also results from necessity: ministers can only pay attention to a tiny proportion of their responsibilities, and delegate the rest to civil servants, who form policy communities with the actors giving them information and advice in exchange for access.

Successive governments have signalled a desire to challenge such policy communities, drawing on a version of the Westminster story to narrate their uncompromising and top-down style. While they may not get what they want in the short term, there is a substantial cumulative impact of reforms over decades.

In particular, Conservative governments since Thatcher have adopted variants of phrases – 'hard' or 'tough' choices, policies in the 'national interest', and 'there is no alternative' – to emphasise strong and decisive leadership that is good for the country even though it may be unpopular. Thatcherism became associated with two messages built on the Westminster story of central control and top-down imposition:

1. Our policy-making reforms will challenge the cosy arrangements between the civil servants who obstruct change and the vested interests that caused policy failure.
2. We will not waste time in debating our reform agenda before we implement.

Chapter 4 traces the cumulative impact of reforms to the civil service – and policy advisory systems – over five decades. First, to reduce public employment, largely by privatising nationalised industries and reducing the number of people employed directly as civil servants. Second, to distinguish between strategy and delivery, and give delivery responsibility to departmental Executive Agencies or quangos and non-governmental organisations (in the third or private sector). Third, to re-establish a departmental hierarchy, such as by influencing senior civil service appointments, making more political appointments (special advisors), and boosting policy units in Number 10. Fourth, to treat the civil service as only one source of policy advice, alongside reports from think tanks, consultants and other external researchers.

Chapter 5 shows that the Thatcher government rejected the need for consultation with interest groups before initiating radical action. Ministers sought to internalise policy making to set a strategic direction, with consultation restricted to questions of policy delivery. They also rejected tripartite negotiations and initiated a raft of legislation to present a profound challenge to trade union power in government and in relation to employers. This approach to policy making combined with reforms to government, driven by new public management tools to reduce the role of the state while making its core activities more business-like and amenable to central control. New public management tools included reforms to the civil service, contracting out service delivery, and introducing quasi-markets to foster internal competition in the NHS and education (with some potential for different administrative arrangements in territorial government departments). Again, successive Labour and Conservative governments inherited and accentuated these reforms.

Each new government has produced its own version of this drive towards reform and centralisation. Like Thatcher, Blair personalised UK policy making, and was often accused of being too 'presidential'. He encouraged a style of government that kept decisions within a small central team (albeit subject to the counterweight of Brown), and tried to 'spin' policy agendas while using evidence for policy selectively (Box 11.4). Like Thatcher, Blair was often accused of sidelining Cabinet and using the party whip to dominate parliamentary procedures. Similarly, the Brown-led government became 'increasingly insular and inward looking' (Richards, 2011: 43).

Since then, Conservative-led governments have been characterised by the projection of strength. The coalition government harnessed the national interest rhetoric to argue that there was no alternative to austerity (Chapter 9). The May and Johnson governments narrated their own versions of Prime Ministerial strength to translate the 2016 referendum vote into a plan for Brexit that protected the UK's interests. In particular, Johnson's lack of respect for checks and balances in government led to: many senior civil service resignations; continuous concerns about unethical conduct; and, 'repeated controversies over his government's handling of parliament', which included punishing Conservative MP dissent, minimising debate on key policy changes, and trying to bypass parliamentary consent (Russell, 2022; Box 12.4). In that context, the Truss government's decision to sack a permanent secretary, while sidelining other officials, reflects a growing tendency towards politicising the civil service to reassert ministerial control.

Recent experiences symbolise long-term changes

On the one hand, we need to note the difference between ministers *asserting* their uncompromising control and actually *being* in control, to the extent that they get the processes they want. Chapters 4 and 5 show that each Prime Minister's expectations have been tempered by experience, and they actually oversaw processes that were generally far more consultative. Or, their attempts to internalise policy making resulted in strategies that did not work, prompting them to rely on more established processes. Further, as leaders seeking re-election, they need to maintain popularity: using the Westminster story to project a strong sense of governing competence, while modifying policies following feedback to avoid damaging backlashes (and consulting widely to gather much-needed information). Government leaders have faced the need to juggle two different stories: to assert control to remain popular, and seek pragmatic solutions to reflect policy-making reality. For example, even in the extreme case of Blair's foreign policy and the Iraq War – where those centralising tendencies were amplified – we can find a story of the need to cooperate with, and gain the consent of, many other actors.

On the other hand, over many decades, these attempts to control policy making have produced a major cumulative impact on UK government policy styles (Chapter 5; Richardson, 2023). First, they undermined the traditional idea of policy made by policy communities of civil servants and interest groups, in favour of a far more complex and varied collection of processes across government. Second, they produced major change in government, including to shift from departments making and implementing policy towards setting strategies and expecting other bodies to carry them out. Third, they have prompted concerns about the fragility of minister and civil servant relations (Rutter, 2022b). Finally, they highlighted concerns about the standards regarding acceptable behaviour by senior ministers in government (Box 12.4).

Box 12.4: A decline in ministerial standards

'Standards' describes the conduct, ethics, integrity and financial dealings of political figures. Johnson's period as Prime Minister (2019–2022) put standards in the spotlight and contributed to his resignation. Accusations against Johnson include: promoting the business or other interests of friends while in power; failing to declare earnings, loans and gifts in the appropriate manner; mismanaging allegations related to the sexual and financial misconduct of senior Conservative MPs; and failing to adhere to his own government's COVID-19 guidance (Smout and Maclellan, 2022; Box 6.3 on Partygate).

Investigations into Partygate – including by the Parliamentary Commissioner for Standards, and the Parliamentary Committee for Privileges – contributed to Johnson's resignation (see House of Commons Committee of Privileges, 2023). However, the allegations as a whole highlight a lack of effective government and parliamentary enforcement of standards (Hine and Peele, 2016). For example, the Prime Minister's Independent Adviser for Ministerial Interests ('ethics watchdog') investigated Johnson (at his request) over the financing of refurbishments to the Prime Minister's official residence (Haddon, 2021). This 'watchdog' is unable to start investigations independently, and can only advise on whether the Prime Minister broke the Ministerial Code. Further, other investigations have been investigated by figures hand-selected by the Prime Minister. Kippin and Pyper (2023: 19) argue that the overall arrangements embody the 'weakest form' of accountability.

Many other recent developments have drawn attention to issues of standards and corruption in public life. They include accusations of cronyism in the awarding of COVID-19 government procurement contracts (Geoghan and Scott, 2020), bullying of civil servants by ministers (Diamond and Richards, 2023), and, former Chancellor Nadhim Zahawi's 'careless' tax affairs (Midgley, 2023). Debates about the integrity of public figures extend beyond Westminster, such as to allegations of corruption in English local government (Private Eye, 2023; Turley, 2023) and party finance mismanagement in the SNP (Box 7.4).

Policy studies: dealing with complex government

Our focus on policy styles shows that a new government's early experience – of Westminster storytelling, rapid policy change, backlash and U-turns – is relatively easy to relate to previous government experience. It is more difficult to gauge a new government's substantive impact on policy outputs and outcomes. Rather, we draw on policy concepts and theories to identify the general limits to that impact, and the case study chapters to draw parallels with previous attempts to set new policy directions.

Chapters 2 and 3 identify two foundational concepts in policy studies. First, bounded rationality describes the limits to a policy maker's understanding of policy and policy making, and how they respond. Ministers can only pay attention to a small proportion of their responsibilities, and only partially understand policy problems and the likely effect of solutions. So, they pay disproportionately high attention to some, and ignore – and effectively delegate responsibility for – the rest. They need to ignore most information to make choices efficiently, so they (1) identify realistic goals and decide which sources of information to trust, and (2) draw on gut instinct, emotions and firmly held beliefs to decide which social groups deserve support or punishment, and which policy actors are their allies and competitors. They may learn from previous policies (and policies in other countries), but learning about previous successes and failures is not a disinterested search for truth. Second, policy-making complexity describes a policy-making environment that defies the full understanding or control of any policy maker. Environments contain many important actors spread across multiple venues (or policy-making centres), each with their own formal and informal rules, networks, dominant ways to understand problems, and responses to events. These concepts underpin the complex government story of limited central control.

One response to these limits is to draw on the Westminster story to try to narrate control, while challenging the need to follow established rules or standard operating procedures. Another is for minsters to be pragmatic, to recognise their lack of control over outcomes, accept the value of delegating responsibility, and welcome information and advice from many relevant sources. In practice, they do both, although some ministers seem more frustrated with their lack of control than others, and have sought to reform government to try to make it more manageable. Consequently, successive governments have overseen reforms that have reduced or exaggerated the problem they began with. Over decades, the cumulative impact of these challenges has been a profound change to the relationship between ministers and civil servants during the production of strategy, and a new and more complex landscape of policy delivery. Each new government inherits not only a complex mix of policies with uncertain results, but also a fragmented and multi-level policy-making landscape that defies our full understanding.

These changes show that there is a big difference between reforming policy processes and controlling policy-making systems and outcomes. Governments have replaced relatively stable and predictable policy communities with a mess of diverse policy-making arrangements. A lack of direct control over policy communities has given way to a lack of understanding of policy delivery following decades of privatisation and contracting out services to non-governmental organisations. Chapters 4 and 5 describe a gulf between the rhetoric and reality of these government reforms, including Hood and Dixon's (2015) rejection of the idea that government is now more effective and efficient. Rather, governments have reduced the number of quangos while increasing their cost, overseen fairly consistent levels of public spending, and have not provided evidence from citizens that government is more responsive to their needs (Box 4.2). Others have noted that, while governments may project the idea of a long-term grand plan for state retrenchment and reform, they have produced a plethora of measures to respond to short-term needs. The end result is debatable. For some, we now see a 'lean state' that has shed the responsibilities that it struggled to control (for example, nationalised industries like coal and steel, rail transport, and utilities such as electricity and gas) in favour of more effective regulation of the market. For others, we see a fragmented state that has become even less amendable to control by central governments, as well as a multi-level system, in which many more elected governments take primary responsibility for key sectors.

The challenge of fragmented policy making seems most acute when a central government tries to 'join up' policy to deal with 'wicked' problems. These problems defy simple definition and understanding, their alleged cause is contested, their complexity makes it impossible to know how solutions would work, and experimentation is difficult since errors have major social consequences (Rittel and Webber, 1973: 161–167). Further, 'super wicked' problems arise when the matter is increasingly urgent but too few policy makers value the benefits of long-term action, governments are exacerbating the problem they seek to solve, and there is no 'central authority' (usually because the problem transcends country borders) (Levin et al, 2012; Box 8.1). Indeed, every case study chapter highlights this dynamic in different ways.

First, COVID-19 showed that a UK central government can oversee rapid and radical policy change to address an urgent public health crisis (Chapter 6). Yet, initial uncertainty exposed profound limits to policy makers' understanding of the problem and their ability to predict the impact of their solutions. They did not prepare well, respond quickly enough, or learn properly from their mistakes. Further, many attempts to reassert control, by establishing new units rather than coordinating existing capacity, produced needless costs and dubious benefits. It is difficult to look back on COVID-19 policy to declare that ministers expected or would have wanted these health, social and economic outcomes. Rather, they declared success by ignoring their enduring effects.

Second, Brexit exposes the difference between a vote to exit the EU and the power of the UK government to leave on its own terms (Chapter 7). From 2016, 'take back control' became an ironic reminder of the unfulfilled promises of the Leave campaign. The vote prompted one Prime Minister (Cameron) to resign, and another (May) to devote years to negotiations that failed to produce an agreement acceptable to the government, the EU and Parliament. Even today, the UK government is facing policy-making fragmentation as it struggles to establish new UK arrangements, and the negative consequences of Brexit on trade and the cost of doing business. It is difficult to declare that this is the Brexit that supporters wanted, or to interpret Johnson's promise to 'get Brexit done' as much more than a slogan.

Third, climate change highlights the growing size of a looming policy problem, the low attention of policy makers, their modest response, and the limited impact of their solutions. Our focus on plans for 'sustainable' energy, transport and food systems exposes governmental fragmentation and policy incoherence (Chapter 8). Initially, the lack of progress related to a history of low concern and unwillingness to produce environmental policies that harm economic growth. Subsequently, a rise in attention and action exposed the inability of the 'centre' to coordinate a profound shift from unsustainable to sustainable systems. Even when successive governments have taken the issue seriously, they have made limited progress that could be undermined by a change in government.

Fourth, the Brown-led government internalised policy making to respond to financial crisis that knocked its policy agenda off course. The crisis exposed the flaws of a long-term shift in government thinking, to encourage economic growth via private debt, with banking receiving light-touch oversight. The economic crisis exposed the lack of options for a government that borrowed heavily to bail out (and guarantee the existence of) banks, with limited ability to borrow further to stimulate growth. It was succeeded by a coalition government led by a Conservative Party committed to 'austerity' to remove the government deficit within five years. While the government did reduce spending as a proportion of GDP, and the government deficit (Figures 9.1, 9.2), its policies did not have the desired effect on economic growth, prompting it to change course to ward off further recession.

Fifth, the consequence of the Iraq War reminds us that there is a major difference between centralising some choices and having control over policy outcomes (Chapter 11). Prime Ministers are responding to conflicts outside of their control. While they might seek to centralise strategies, they do not get what they want on their own. Their intelligence on the problem is limited and there is high uncertainty about the likely impact of their responses. Indeed, wars of this magnitude highlight the yawning gulf between their stated expectations and the multiple failures of policy that resulted from their actions. The outcome could not possibly be what a rational government leader would hope for.

All of these examples accentuate a general image of complex government over which ministers have limited knowledge and even less control. They help to identify a stark contrast between the stated expectations of a new government, their likely limited impact on policy, and the inevitability of a raft of unintended consequences.

Critical policy analysis: who wins and loses?

In many of these case studies, ministers may be genuinely frustrated by the difference between their expectations and outcomes. In others, they have multiple and often contradictory aims, often (1) describing sincere intentions about (or paying lip service to) some issues, while (2) devoting more substantial resources to others. In particular, a long-term trend towards neoliberal approaches has had a major impact across multiple sectors. In this context, neoliberal describes a tendency to: treat economic growth as the top priority, seek state retrenchment in favour of market solutions, and relate problems to individual motivation and choice rather than social and economic structures (Chapter 4). It helps to explain, for example:

- An initial reluctance to intervene to address COVID-19, a desire to return to 'normal' to boost economic activity, and low attention to health inequalities (Chapter 6).
- A rhetorical commitment to address climate change but substantive commitment to policies that exacerbate it. Traditionally, governments have prioritised economic growth and sustainability policies if they do not undermine growth (Chapter 8).
- A shift from state-led to market-led economic growth, encouraging higher levels of private debt and bank risk, and contributing to financial crisis (Chapters 4 and 5).
- The reluctance of policy makers to relate public protests and 'riots' to an unequal social and economic context that marginalises and minoritises social groups, in favour of a focus on individual criminals, street gangs and dysfunctional families (Chapter 10).
- A tendency for governments to make little more than a rhetorical commitment to reduce inequalities (Chapter 10).

Successive governments have described their ambitions to reduce inequalities, but through a neoliberal lens that individualises the problem and relegates it to a low-priority issue. They have also described the sense that only some social groups deserve government support, such as the 'strivers' (not 'skivers') and the 'hard-working families' that are 'just getting by'. Their approach contrasts with intersectoral approaches that identify the social and economic determinants of inequalities that are outside of an individual's control:

- *Social determinants of health* describe the factors that have a major impact on population health and inequalities, such as inequalities regarding income, wealth, education, housing, and safe physical and social environments. The 'lack of opportunity to be healthy is too often associated with a person's socio-economic status, race, ethnicity, gender, religion, sexual identity, or disability' (Bliss et al, 2016: S88).

- *Out of school* describes the factors that influence educational attainment, including poverty and low income, and the school practices that minoritise some groups (such as by discrimination in relation to discipline or assessment, setting lower expectations, or limiting access to students whose parents have the resources to exploit opportunities).
- *Maximal versions of gender mainstreaming* emphasise the importance of redistributive taxation, a strong welfare state and spending – such as to subsidise childcare – that has a disproportionately positive impact on women (and addresses class-based differences).

Further, many have introduced policies that exacerbated the problems they sought to reduce. In particular, the coalition government's 'austerity' programme produced relatively high cuts to social security and limited access to benefits. The impact was disproportionately negative in relation to disability, women and minoritised social groups (Chapter 10).

This recent history helps to situate recent government policies in a context where we expect ministers to prioritise economic growth, mention inequalities but downplay their importance, and seek individualist solutions (perhaps while seeking to blame citizens for societal problems – Dowding, 2021). In some cases, this emphasis is front and centre of ministerial rhetoric and policy, such as when the Truss government sought to reduce taxes on incomes above £150,000 per year and to emphasise growing 'the pie' rather than distributing the pie more equally. Ministers also prioritised healthcare service performance over health inequalities, and an individualist narrative of gender-based inequalities. Further, Home Secretary Suella Braverman criticised police forces for focusing too much on inequality (or 'pandering to identity politics') rather than 'catching the bad guys', and signalled greater punishments for protestors (Lynch, 2022).

In other cases, the unequal impacts of policy choices are unearthed by groups critical of government policies (Chapter 10). For example, the Women's Budget Group (2022) noted that cuts to taxes on higher rates of income and corporation tax would give more benefit to men (as higher earners and 'the majority of business owners and shareholders'), while proposed reforms to social security would not address work-based obstacles for women (such as 'unaffordable childcare and social care'). The Resolution Foundation (2022) found that '[t]hose living in the South East or London will see over three times … the gains of those in the North East, Wales and Yorkshire'.

Conclusion

Recent experiences in government have been dramatic but not unusual. They highlighted key aspects of UK politics, policy and policy making. First, a focus on policy analysis shows that ministers inherit an overwhelming number of problems and policies from their predecessors. While their rhetoric focused on radical change from the past, they actually engaged in changing most policies at the margins while accentuating a small number of differences. The way that ministers narrate and prioritise problems matters, but does not provide a reliable guide to what happens next.

Second, a focus on policy styles shows that recent and older governments drew on the Westminster story to project an image of strong and decisive government – to change policy radically – in the national interest. For example, Truss sought to challenge senior civil servants, reject advice from the usual suspects and bypass standard operating procedures. Yet, Truss also reinforced an existing economic paradigm while seeking to modify key policy instruments and overseeing a rise in spending and borrowing that has become a feature of recent Conservative governments. Further, the ministerial treatment of the civil service, to reinforce ministerial power while diversifying their sources of policy advice (and delivery), is a long-term feature of government reforms over at least five decades. Whether or not it has the desired effect is a different matter, and the ministerial pivot to become a 'listening' government, willing to adapt to policy-making reality, reminds us of the difference between rhetoric and reality.

Third, a focus on the complex government story helps to situate recent experiences in a wider context. The examples from multiple case studies demonstrate that new governments can add to the pile of government reforms, but without producing a closer connection between (1) their stated aims and expectations, and (2) policy practices and outcomes. Such experiences reinforce the take-home message: ministers can narrate their own version of conviction politics all they want, but if they reject consultation and cooperation with other actors, and fail to appreciate the limits to their understanding and influence, they will not get what they want.

Finally, a focus on inequalities demonstrates that governments can still have a profound effect on the lives of the UK population. We describe a long-term post-war shift from high state intervention, focused partly on reducing inequalities (such as via tax and spending), towards state retrenchment in favour of market and individualist solutions. Governments make – often sincere – commitments to reducing inequalities, but also pursue an approach that guarantees their endurance.

References

Aaronovitch, D. (2003) 'Those weapons had better be there ...', *The Guardian*, 29 April, https://www.theguardian.com/g2/story/0,3604,945381,00.html (A: 07.10.22)

Abbasi, K. (2021) 'Covid-19: Social murder, they wrote – elected, unaccountable, and unrepentant', *British Medical Journal*, 372, 314, 1–3, http://dx.doi.org/10.1136/bmj.n314

Abbott, K.W. and Snidal, D. (2003) 'Hard and soft law in international governance', *International Organization*, 54, 3, 421–456, https://doi.org/10.1162/00208180055128

Abbott, P., Wallace, C. and Tyler, M. (2005) *Introduction to Sociology: Feminist Perspectives* (London: Routledge)

Abdo, G. (2017) *The New Sectarianism: The Arab Uprisings and the Rebirth of the Shi'a-Sunni Divide* (Oxford: Oxford University Press)

Abdullah, S., Gray, T. and Clough, E. (2018) 'Clientelism: Factionalism in the allocation of public resources in Iraq after 2003', *Middle Eastern Studies*, 54, 4, 664–682, https://doi.org/10.1080/00263206.2018.1444607

Abel, W., Kahn, E., Parr, T. and Walton, A. (2021) *Introducing Political Philosophy: A Policy-Driven Approach* (Oxford: Oxford University Press)

Achiume, T. (2019) 'Migration as decolonization', *Stanford Law Review*, 1509, https://papers.ssrn.com/sol3/papers.cfm?abstract_id=3330353 (A: 09.09.22)

Adam, S. and Roantree, B. (2015) *The Coalition Government's Record on Tax (Briefing Note BN167)* (London: Institute for Fiscal Studies), https://ifs.org.uk/sites/default/files/output_url_files/BN167170315.pdf (A: 04.03.22)

Adam, S., Delestre, I., Emmerson, C., Johnson, P., Joyce, R., Stockton, I., Waters, T., Xu, X. and Zaranko, B. (2022) 'Mini-budget response', *Institute for Fiscal Studies*, 23 September, https://ifs.org.uk/articles/mini-budget-response (A: 07.10.22)

Adnett, N. and Davies, P. (2003) 'Schooling reforms in England: From quasi-markets to co-opetition?' *Journal of Education Policy*, 18, 4, 393–406

Afzal, N. (2020) 'Black people dying in police custody should surprise no one', *The Guardian*, 11 June, https://www.theguardian.com/uk-news/2020/jun/11/black-deaths-in-police-custody-the-tip-of-an-iceberg-of-racist-treatment (A: 26.09.22)

Aggestam, K., Bergman Rosamond, A. and Kronsell, A. (2019) 'Theorising feminist foreign policy', *International Relations*, 33, 1, 23–39, https://doi.org/10.1177/00471178188118

Ahmed, S. (2017) *Living a Feminist Life* (London: Duke University Press)

Aitken, M., Christman, B., Bonaventura, M., van der Horst, D. and Holbrook, J. (2016) 'Climate justice begins at home: conceptual, pragmatic and transformative approaches to climate justice in Scotland', *Scottish Affairs*, 25, 2, 225–252, https://doi.org/10.3366/scot.2016.0128

Akhtar, S. (2022) 'Containment, activism and state racism: The Sheku Bayoh justice campaign', *Identities*, 29, 2, 164–185, https://doi.org/10.1080/10702 89X.2020.1813460

Akram, S. (2023) 'Dear British politics: Where is the race and racism?', *British Politics*, 1–24, https://doi.org/10.1057/s41293-023-00224-3

Al-Agha, M. (2015) 'Chronology' in Sadiki, L. (ed) *Routledge Handbook of the Arab Spring: Rethinking Democratization* (London: Routledge), xxiii–xxviii

Alden, C. (2017) 'Critiques of the rational actor model and foreign policy decision making' in Thompson, W.R. and Tereza, C. (eds) *Oxford Research Encyclopaedia of Politics* (Oxford: Oxford University Press)

Aldred, J. (2009) 'Ethics and climate change cost-benefit analysis: Stern and after', *New Political Economy*, 14, 4, 469–488, https://doi.org/10.1080/135634 60903288221

Aldrich, R.J. (2005) 'Whitehall and the Iraq War: The UK's four intelligence enquiries', *Irish Studies in International Affairs*, 16, 73–88

Alexandre-Collier, A. (2022) 'David Cameron, Boris Johnson and the "populist hypothesis" in the British Conservative Party', *Comparative European Politics*, https://doi.org/10.1057/s41295-022-00294-5

Alexiadou, N. (2019) 'Framing education policies and transitions of Roma students in Europe', *Comparative Education*, 55, 3, 422–442, https://doi.org/10.1080/03050068.2019.1619334

Alexiou, A., Mason, K., Fahy, K., Taylor-Robinson, D. and Barr, B. (2021) 'Assessing the impact of funding cuts to local housing services on drug and alcohol related mortality: a longitudinal study using area-level data in England', *International Journal of Housing Studies*, https://doi.org/10.1080/19491 247.2021.2002660

Allen, G. and Zayed, Y. (2021) 'Hate crime statistics', House of Commons Library, https://researchbriefings.files.parliament.uk/documents/CBP-8537/CBP-8537.pdf (A: 26.09.22)

Allen, P. (2013) 'Linking pre-parliamentary political experience and the career trajectories of the 1997 general election cohort', *Parliamentary Affairs*, 66, 4, 685–707

Allen, P. and Cairney, P. (2017) 'What do we mean when we talk about the "political class"?', *Political Studies Review*, 15, 1, 18–27

Allen, W., Bandola-Gill, J. and Grek, S. (2023) 'Next slide please: The politics of visualization during COVID-19 press briefings', *Journal of European Public Policy*, 1–28, https://doi.org/10.1080/13501763.2022.2160784

Allison, G. (1969) 'Conceptual models and the Cuban Missile Crisis', *American Political Science Review*, 63, 3, 689–718

Allison, G. (1971) *Essence of Decision: Explaining the Cuban Missile Crisis* (Boston: Little Brown)

Allison, W.T. (2012) *The Gulf War, 1990–92* (London: Bloomsbury)

Alnasrawi, A. (2001) 'Iraq: Economic sanctions and consequences, 1990–2000', *Third World Quarterly*, 22, 2, 205–218, https://doi.org/10.1080/0143659012 0037036

Alons, G. (2017) 'Environmental policy integration in the EU's common agricultural policy: Greening or greenwashing?', *Journal of European Public Policy*, 24, 11, 1604–1622, https://doi.org/10.1080/13501763.2017.1334085

Althaus, C., Bridgman, P. and Davis, G. (2013) *The Australian Policy Handbook: A Practical Guide to the Policy-Making Process*, 5th edn (Crows Nest: Allen & Unwin)

Althaus, C., Bridgman, P. and Davis, G. (2015) 'Learning about learning: Discovering the work of policy', *Australian Journal of Public Administration*, 74, 2, 112–113

Alwan, N.A., Burgess, R.A., Ashworth, S., Beale, R., Bhadelia, N., Bogaert, D., et al (2020) 'Scientific consensus on the COVID-19 pandemic: We need to act now', *The Lancet*, 396, 10260, e71–e72, https://doi.org/10.1016/S0140-6736(20)32153-X

Anderson, K., Bows, A. and Mander, S. (2008) 'From long-term targets to cumulative emission pathways: Reframing UK climate policy', *Energy Policy*, 36, 10, 3714–3722, https://doi.org/10.1016/j.enpol.2008.07.003

Andrews, L. (2014) *Ministering to Education* (Cardigan: Parthian Books)

Ansell, C. and Torfing, J. (2019) 'The network approach' in Brummer, K., Harnisch, S., Oppermann, K. and Panke, D. (eds) *Foreign Policy as Public Policy?* (Manchester: Manchester University Press), 139–170

Antonopoulos, I., Bell, M., Cavoski, A. and Petetin, L. (eds) (2022) *The Governance of Agriculture in Post-Brexit UK* (London: Routledge)

Arlota, C. (2019) 'Does the United States' withdrawal from the Paris Agreement on climate change pass the cost-benefit analysis test?', *UPenn Journal of International Law*, 41, 881–938

Arnold, G. (2021) 'Distinguishing the street-level policy entrepreneur', *Public Administration*, 99, 3, 439–453, https://doi.org/10.1111/padm.12703

Arnold, S. and Pendleton, A. (2019) 'Deprived towns fund is insignificant compared with staggering cuts', New Economics Foundation, https://newec onomics.org/2019/03/deprived-towns-fund-is-insignificant-compared-with-staggering-cuts (A: 08.09.22)

Ashe, J., Campbell, R., Childs, S. and Evans, E. (2010) '"Stand by your man": Women's political recruitment at the 2010 UK general election', *British Politics*, 5, 4, 455–480

Atkins, J. (2013) 'A renewed social democracy for an "Age of Internationalism": An interpretivist account of New Labour's foreign policy', *The British Journal of Politics and International Relations*, 15, 2, 175–191, https://doi.org/10.1111/j.1467-856X.2012.00536

Atkins, J. (2018) *Conflict, Co-operation, and the Rhetoric of Coalition Government* (London: Palgrave)

Atkinson, P. (2023) 'When should scientists rock the boat? Advising government in a pandemic', *Evidence and Policy blog*, 12 April, https://evidenceandpolicyb log.co.uk/2023/04/12/when-should-scientists-rock-the-boat-advising-gov ernment-in-a-pandemic/ (A: 13.04.23)

Atkinson, P., Mableson, H., Sheard, S., Martindale, A.M., Solomon, T., Borek, A. and Pilbeam, C. (2022) 'How did UK policy making in the COVID-19 response use science? Evidence from scientific advisers', *Evidence & Policy*, 18, 4, 633–650

Audit Wales (2020) *Providing Free School Meals During Lockdown* (Cardiff: Auditor General for Wales), https://www.audit.wales/sites/default/files/2020-11/FSM-portrait-eng.pdf (A: 05.07.22)

Auld, G., Bernstein, S., Cashore, B. and Levin, K. (2021) 'Managing pandemics as super wicked problems: Lessons from, and for, COVID-19 and the climate crisis', *Policy Sciences*, 54, 707–728, https://doi.org/10.1007/s11077-021-09442-2

Averchenkova, A., Fankhauser, S. and Finnegan, J. (2021) 'The impact of strategic climate legislation: Evidence from expert interviews on the UK Climate Change Act', *Climate Policy*, 21, 2, 251–263, https://doi.org/10.1080/14693062.2020.1819190

Ayoub, P.M. (2019) 'Tensions in rights: Navigating emerging contradictions in the LGBT rights revolution' in Brysk, A. and Shohl, M. (eds) *Contesting Human Rights: Norms, Institutions and Practice* (Cheltenham: Edward Elgar), 43–58

Ayoub, P.M. (2022) 'Not that niche: Making room for the study of LGBTIQ people in political science', *European Journal of Politics and Gender*, 5, 2, 154–172

Azar, C. (1999) 'Weight factors in cost-benefit analysis of climate change', *Environmental and Resource Economics*, 13, 3, 249–268, https://doi.org/10.1023/A:1008229225527

Bacchi, C. (2009) *Analysing Policy: What's the Problem Represented to Be?* (Frenchs Forest: Pearson)

Bach, S. (2016) 'Deprivileging the public sector workforce: Austerity, fragmentation and service withdrawal in Britain', *Economic and Labour Relations Review*, 27, 1, 11–28, https://doi.org/10.1177/1035304615627950

Bache, I. (2003) 'Governing through governance: Education policy control under New Labour', *Political Studies*, 51, 2, 300–314

Bache, I. (2019) *Evidence, Policy and Wellbeing* (London: Palgrave)

Bache, I. and Flinders, M. (2004) 'Multi-level governance and the study of the British state', *Public Policy and Administration*, 19, 1, 31–51

Bache, I. and Reardon, L. (2013) 'An idea whose time has come? Explaining the rise of well-being in British politics', *Political Studies*, 61, 4, 898–914

Bache, I. and Reardon, L. (2016) *The Politics and Policy of Wellbeing: Understanding the Rise and Significance of a New Agenda* (Cheltenham: Edward Elgar)

Bache, I., Bartle, I., Flinders, M. and Marsden, G. (2015) 'Blame games and climate change: Accountability, multi-level governance and carbon management', *The British Journal of Politics and International Relations*, 17, 1, 64–88, https://doi.org/10.1111/1467-856X.12040

Bachrach, P. and Baratz, M. (1970) *Power and Poverty* (New York: Oxford University Press)

Baggott, R. (1995) 'From confrontation to consultation? Pressure group relations from Thatcher to Major', *Parliamentary Affairs*, 48, 3, 484–502

Baggott, R. (2011) *Public Health Policy and Politics*, 2nd edn (Basingstoke: Palgrave)

Baines, D., Brewer, S. and Kay, A. (2020) 'Political, process and programme failures in the Brexit fiasco: Exploring the role of policy deception', *Journal of European Public Policy*, 27, 5, 742–760, https://doi.org/10.1080/13501763.2020.1722203

Baker, A. and Lavery, S. (2018) *Brexit and the Future Model of British Capitalism*, 1st edn (London: Routledge)

Baker, P. (2022) 'LGBT+ history: The bold, very British resistance to section 28', *The Conversation*, 11 February, https://theconversation.com/lgbt-history-the-bold-very-british-resistance-to-section-28-176851 (A: 12.09.22)

Baldini, G., Bressanelli, E. and Massetti, E. (2018) 'Who is in control? Brexit and the Westminster model', *The Political Quarterly*, 89, 4, 537–544, https://doi.org/10.1111/1467-923X.12596

Baldini, G., Bressanelli, E. and Massetti, E. (2022a) *The Brexit Effect* (London: Routledge)

Baldini, G., Bressanelli, E. and Massetti, E. (2022b) 'Back to the Westminster model? The Brexit process and the UK political system', *International Political Science Review*, 43, 3, 329–344, https://doi.org/10.1177/0192512120967375

Baldock, J. (2012) 'Social policy, social welfare, and the welfare state' in Baldock, J., Mitton, L., Manning, N. and Vickerstaff, S. (eds) *Social Policy*, 4th edn (Oxford: Oxford University Press), 5–30

Baldwin, C. (2020) 'UK war crime revelations in Afghanistan expose justice failings', *Human Rights Watch*, 5 August, https://www.hrw.org/news/2020/08/05/uk-war-crime-revelations-afghanistan-expose-justice-failings (A: 07.10.22)

Bale, T. (2016) *The Conservative Party: From Thatcher to Cameron*, 2nd edn (London: Wiley)

Bale, T. (2022) *Brexit: An Accident Waiting to Happen?* (London: Tim Bale Productions)

Bale, T. (2023) *The Conservative Party after Brexit: Turmoil and Transformation* (London: Polity Press)

Ball, J. and Taylor, M. (2011) 'Theresa May to review stop and search in wake of Reading the Riots study', *The Guardian*, 14 December, https://www.theguardian.com/uk/2011/dec/14/theresa-may-stop-search-review (A: 26.09.22)

Ball, R. and Drury, J. (2012) 'Representing the riots: The (mis)use of statistics to sustain ideological explanation', *Radical Statistics*, 106, 4–21, http://sro.sussex.ac.uk/id/eprint/41622/#:~:text=http%3A//www.radstats.org.uk/no106/BallDrury106.pdf (A: 14.07.22)

Ball, S., McConnell, A. and Stark, A. (2021) 'Dramaturgy and crisis management: A third act', *Public Administration*, 100, 3, 585–599, https://doi.org/10.1111/padm.12775

Bambra, C., Lynch, J. and Smith, K. (2021) *The Unequal Pandemic: COVID-19 and Health Inequalities* (Bristol: Policy Press)

Bara, J. (2005) 'A question of trust: Implementing party manifestos', *Parliamentary Affairs*, 58, 3, 585–599

Barber, M. (2008) *Instruction to Deliver: Fighting to Transform Britain's Public Services* (York: Methuen)

Barber, M. (2012) *Instruction to Deliver*, 2nd edn (London: Methuen)

Barber, S. (2017) *Westminster, Governance and the Politics of Policy Inaction: 'Do Nothing'* (London: Palgrave)

Bardach, E. and Patashnik, E. (2020) *A Practical Guide for Policy Analysis*, 6th edn (London: SAGE)

Bar-Joseph, U. (2013) 'The politicization of intelligence: A comparative study', *International Journal of Intelligence and CounterIntelligence*, 26, 2, 347–369, https://doi.org/10.1080/08850607.2013.758000

Barnes, M. and Ross, A. (2021) 'The problems with troubled families: Rethinking the analysis behind the 120,000 troubled families statistic', *Social Policy and Society*, 1–19, https://doi.org/10.1017/S1474746421000725

Barnes, S.J. (2019) 'Out of sight, out of mind: Plastic waste exports, psychological distance and consumer plastic purchasing', *Global Environmental Change*, 58, 101943, 1–9, https://doi.org/10.1016/j.gloenvcha.2019.101943

Barnier, M. (2017) 'Slide presented by Michel Barnier, European Commission Chief Negotiator, to the Heads of State and Government at the European Council (Article 50) on 15 December 2017', 19 December, https://ec.europa.eu/info/sites/default/files/slide_presented_by_barnier_at_euco_15-12-2017.pdf (A: 24.08.22)

Barr, B., Taylor-Robinson, D., Stuckler, D., Loopstra, R., Reeves, A. and Whitehead, M. (2016) '"First, do no harm": Are disability assessments associated with adverse trends in mental health? A longitudinal ecological study', *Journal of Epidemiology & Community Health*, 70, 339–345, http://dx.doi.org/10.1136/jech-2015-206209

Barrington, R. (2021) 'There is more corruption and corruption risk in and around this government than any British government since 1945', *LSE British Politics and Policy*, 25 November, https://blogs.lse.ac.uk/politicsandpolicy/government-corruption/ (A: 08.09.22)

BASIC and Saferworld (2003) 'Written evidence: Memorandum from BASIC and Saferworld', House of Commons Foreign Affairs Select Committee, https://publications.parliament.uk/pa/cm200203/cmselect/cmfaff/813/813we20.htm (A: 07.10.22)

Basta, K. and Henderson, A. (2021) 'Multinationalism, constitutional asymmetry and COVID: UK responses to the pandemic', *Nationalism and Ethnic Politics*, 27, 3, 293–310, https://doi.org/10.1080/13537113.2021.1954298

Bastow, S. (2013) *Governance, Performance, and Capacity Stress: The Chronic Case of Prison Crowding* (London: Palgrave)

Bate, A. and Foster, D. (2017) *Sure Start (England)* (Briefing Paper 7257) (London: House of Commons Library), https://researchbriefings.files.parliament.uk/documents/CBP-7257/CBP-7257.pdf (A: 23.05.22)

Baudains, P., Braithwaite, A. and Johnson, S.D. (2013) 'Target choice during extreme events: A discrete spatial choice model of the 2011 London riots', *Criminology*, 51, 2, 251–285, https://doi.org/10.1111/1745-9125.12004

Baumgartner, F. and Jones, B. (2009) *Agendas and Instability in American Politics*, 2nd edn (Chicago: Chicago University Press)

BBC News (2001) 'Blair's statement in full', 11 September, http://news.bbc.co.uk/1/hi/uk_politics/1538551.stm (A: 28.09.22)

BBC News (2003) '"Million" march against Iraq War', 16 February, http://news.bbc.co.uk/1/hi/uk/2765041.stm (A: 04.02.22)

BBC News (2004) 'Timeline: The 45-minute claim', 13 October, news.bbc.co.uk/1/hi/uk_politics/3466005.stm (A: 07.10.22)

BBC News (2009) 'Darling unveils borrowing gamble', 24 November, http://news.bbc.co.uk/1/hi/uk_politics/7745340.stm (A: 31.08.22)

BBC News (2011) 'Labour leader Ed Miliband visits riot-hit Manchester', 10 August, https://www.bbc.co.uk/news/uk-england-manchester-14480160 (A: 26.09.22)

BBC News (2019) 'Grenfell Tower: What happened', 29 October, https://www.bbc.co.uk/news/uk-40301289 (A: 06.09.22)

BBC News (2020a) 'Black Lives Matter protests held across England', 20 June, https://www.bbc.co.uk/news/uk-england-53120735 (A: 04.02.22)

BBC News (2020b) 'Brexit: UK "holds the cards" in EU talks – Gove', 18 October, https://www.bbc.co.uk/news/av/uk-politics-54590278 (A: 07.09.22)

BBC News (2021a) 'Covid: Boris Johnson's "bodies pile high" comments prompt criticism', 26 April, https://www.bbc.co.uk/news/uk-politics-56890714 (A: 07.04.22)

BBC News (2021b) 'Scotland's 100% renewables electricity target narrowly missed', 31 December, https://www.bbc.co.uk/news/uk-scotland-59837782 (A: 07.07.22)

BBC News (2021c) 'BAME acronym: UK broadcasters commit to avoiding catch-all term', 7 December, https://www.bbc.co.uk/news/entertainment-arts-59559834 (A: 03.09.22)

BBC News (2021d) 'Greater Manchester Police branded "institutionally racist"', 27 July, https://www.bbc.co.uk/news/uk-england-manchester-57982273 (A: 26.09.22)

BBC News (2022a) 'Fuel duty cut by 5p a litre to help motorists', 24 March, https://www.bbc.co.uk/news/business-60850217 (A: 04.07.22)

BBC News (2022b) 'Sarah Everard: New police challenge to vigil ruling', 29 April, https://www.bbc.co.uk/news/uk-england-london-61276743 (A: 14.10.22)

BBC News (2022c) 'Chris Kaba: Met suspends officer who shot dead unarmed man', 12 September, https://www.bbc.co.uk/news/uk-england-london-62878546 (A: 19.09.22)

BBC News (2023a) 'Partygate: A timeline of the lockdown parties', 21 March, https://www.bbc.co.uk/news/uk-politics-59952395 (A: 24.03.23)

BBC News (2023b) 'Chris Kaba: Met Police shooting case referred to CPS', 30 March, https://www.bbc.co.uk/news/uk-england-london-65123767 (A: 28.04.23)

Beatty, C. and Fothergill, S. (2014) 'The local and regional impact of the UK's welfare reforms', *Cambridge Journal of Regions, Economy and Society*, 7, 1, 63–79

Beaumont, P., Barnett, A. and Hinscliff, G. (2003) 'Iraqi mobile labs nothing to do with germ warfare, report finds', *The Guardian*, 15 June, https://www.theguardian.com/world/2003/jun/15/iraq (A: 07.10.22)

Beauvallet, A. (2018) 'Expanding opportunities at school level in England in the early 21st century: A government priority?' in Fée, D. and Kober-Smith, A. (eds) *Inequalities in the UK* (Bingley: Emerald), 205–215

Bécares, L. (2015) 'Which ethnic groups have the poorest health?' in Jivraj, S. and Simpson, L. (eds) *Ethnic Identity and Inequalities in Britain* (Bristol: Policy Press), 123–139

Begum, N. and Saini, R. (2019) 'Decolonising the curriculum', *Political Studies Review*, 17, 2, 196–201, https://doi.org/10.1177/14789299188084

Beighton, C. (2021) '(Un)trustworthy organisations? Implications of the Sarah Everard murder case', Canterbury Christ Church University, https://repository.canterbury.ac.uk/item/8z5xz/-un-trustworthy-organisations-implications-of-the-sarah-everard-murder-case#:~:text=https%3A//blogs.canterbury.ac.uk/expertcomment/untrustworthy%2Dorganisations%2Dimplications%2Dof%2Dthe%2Dsarah%2Deverard%2Dmurder%2Dcase/ (A: 26.09.22)

BEIS (Department for Business, Energy & Industrial Strategy) (2022a) 'Fuel poverty statistics', https://www.gov.uk/government/collections/fuel-poverty-statistics (A: 15.07.22)

BEIS (2022b) 'Annual fuel poverty statistics in England, 2022 (2020 data)', https://assets.publishing.service.gov.uk/government/uploads/system/uploads/attachment_data/file/1056777/annual-fuel-poverty-statistics-lilee-report-2022-2020-data.pdf (A: 15.7.22)

Bell, D. (1992) 'Racial realism', *Connecticut Law Review*, 24, 2, 363–380

Bell, D. and Wilson, T. (2018) 'Gender pay gap', Stirling Management School, https://archive2021.parliament.scot/S5_EconomyJobsFairWork/Inquiries/David_Bell_and_Tanya_Wilson.pdf (A: 09.09.22)

Bell, M. (2009) *Racism and Equality in the European Union* (Oxford: Oxford Academic), https://doi.org/10.1093/acprof:oso/9780199297849.001.0001

Bell, S. and Hindmoor, A. (2015) *Masters of the Universe, Slaves of the Market* (Cambridge, MA: Harvard University Press)

Bell, T. (2022) 'The cost of living crisis is going to hurt', *Resolution Foundation*, 3 May, https://www.resolutionfoundation.org/comment/the-cost-of-living-crisis-is-going-to-hurt/ (A: 08.09.22)

Bellamy, R. (2019) 'Was the Brexit referendum legitimate, and would a second one be so?', *European Political Science*, 18, 126–133, https://doi.org/10.1057/s41304-018-0155-x

Bellringer, C. and Michie, R. (2014) 'Big Bang in the City of London: An intentional revolution or an accident?', *Financial History Review*, 21, 2, 111–137, https://doi.org/10.1017/S0968565014000092

Benjamin, M. and Davies, N.J.S. (2018) 'The staggering death toll in Iraq', *Salon*, 19 March, https://www.salon.com/2018/03/19/the-staggering-death-toll-in-iraq_partner/ (A: 07.10.22)

Benn, T. (2001) 'Tackle terror at its roots', *The Guardian*, 12 November, https://www.theguardian.com/politics/2001/nov/12/britainand911.afghanistan (A: 07.10.22)

Bennett, C. (1991) 'What is policy convergence and what causes it?', *British Journal of Political Science*, 21, 2, 215–233

Bennie, L. and McAngus, C. (2020) 'The Scottish National Party' in Keating, M. (ed) *The Oxford Handbook of Scottish Politics* (Oxford: Oxford University Press), 278–300

Bentley, G., Bailey, D. and Shutt, J. (2010) 'From RDAs to LEPs: A new localism? Case examples of West Midlands and Yorkshire', *Local Economy*, 25, 7, 535–557, https://doi.org/10.1080/02690942.2010.532356

Berridge, V. (1996) *AIDS in the UK* (Oxford: Oxford University Press)

Berry, C. (2016) 'Austerity, ageing and the financialisation of pensions policy in the UK', *British Politics*, 11, 1, 2–25, https://doi.org/10.1057/bp.2014.19

Berry, C. (2020) 'From receding to reseeding: Industrial policy, governance strategies and neoliberal resilience in post-crisis Britain', *New Political Economy*, 25, 4, 607–625, https://doi.org/10.1080/13563467.2019.1625316

Berry, C. and Hunt, T. (2015) 'Austerity rests on a thesis the government doesn't believe in', *SPERI*, speri.dept.shef.ac.uk/2015/08/31/austerity-rests-thesis-government-doesnt/ (A: 09.09.22)

Best, J. (2020) 'The quiet failures of early neoliberalism: From rational expectations to Keynesianism in reverse', *Review of International Studies*, 46, 5, 594–612, doi:10.1017/S0260210520000169

Betts, J. and Phythian, M. (2020) *The Iraq War and Democratic Governance: Britain and Australia Go to War* (London: Palgrave)

Bevins, V. (2020) *The Jakarta Method: Washington's Anticommunist Crusade and the Mass Murder Program that Shaped Our World* (New York: Public Affairs)

Bevir, M. and Rhodes, R.A.W. (1999) 'Studying British government', *British Journal of Politics and International Relations*, 1, 2 (June), 215–239

Bevir, M. and Rhodes, R.A.W. (2003) *Interpreting British Governance* (London: Routledge)

Bevir, M. and Rhodes, R.A.W. (2006) *Governance Stories* (London: Routledge)

Bevir, M. and Beech, M. (eds) (2022) *Interpreting Brexit: Reimagining Political Traditions* (London: Palgrave)

Bhambra, G.K. (2017) 'Brexit, Trump, and "methodological whiteness": On the misrecognition of race and class', *The British Journal of Sociology*, 68, S214–S232, https://doi.org/10.1111/1468-4446.12317

Bhambra, G.K., Gebrial, D. and Nişancıoğlu, K. (eds) (2018) *Decolonising the University* (London: Pluto Press)

Bhattacharyya, G. (1998) *Tales of Dark Skinned Women: Race, Gender and Global Culture* (London: Routledge)

Bhopal, K. (2018) *White Privilege: The Myth of a Post-Racial Society* (Bristol: Policy Press)

Bignell, P. (2011) 'Secret memos expose link between oil firms and invasion of Iraq', *The Independent*, 19 April, https://www.independent.co.uk/news/uk/politics/secret-memos-expose-link-between-oil-firms-and-invasion-of-iraq-2269610.html (A: 07.10.22)

Bindel, J. (2017) *The Pimping of Prostitution* (London: Palgrave)

Birchall, J. (2011) 'The Big Society and the "mutualisation" of public services: A critical commentary', *Retrieving the Big Society*, 82, s1, 145–157, https://doi.org/10.1111/j.1467-923X.2011.02333.x

Birchfield, V.L., Krige, J. and Young, A.R. (2017) 'European integration as a peace project', *The British Journal of Politics and International Relations*, 19, 1, 3–12, https://journals.sagepub.com/doi/10.1177/1369148116685274

Birchley, E. (2022) '"Chris Kaba. Say his name!" Hundreds protest after black man is shot dead by police', *Sky News*, 17 September, https://news.sky.com/story/chris-kaba-say-his-name-hundreds-protest-after-black-man-is-shot-dead-by-police-12700018 (A: 19.09.22)

Birrell, D. (2012) *Comparing Devolved Governance* (Basingstoke: Palgrave)

Birrell, D., Carmichael, P. and Heenan, D. (2023) *Devolution in the UK* (London: Bloomsbury)

Black, C. (2008) *Working for a Healthier Tomorrow* (Dame Carol Black's review of the health of Britain's working age population) (London: The Stationery Office)

Black Lives Matter (2022) 'Herstory', https://blacklivesmatter.com/herstory/ (A: 06.09.22)

Blackman, T., Harrington, B., Elliott, E., Greene, A., Hunter, D.J., Marks, L., McKee, L. and Williams, G. (2012) 'Framing health inequalities for local intervention: Comparative case studies', *Sociology of Health & Illness*, 34, 1, 49–63

Blackwell, D. (2015) 'Reading the riots – London 2011: Local revolt and global protest', *Psychotherapy and Politics International*, 13, 2, 102–114, https://doi.org/10.1002/ppi.1354

Blair, A. (2020) 'The United Kingdom and the European Union', *Oxford Research Encyclopedia of Politics*, https://doi.org/10.1093/acrefore/9780190228637.013.157

Blair, T. (1999) 'Doctine of the international community', *British Political Speech*, www.britishpoliticalspeech.org/speech-archive.htm?speech=279 (A: 07.10.22)

Blair, T. (2001) 'Address at the Labour Party conference', *American Rhetoric Online Speech Bank*, https://www.americanrhetoric.com/speeches/tblair10-02-01.htm (A: 07.10.22)

Blair, T. (2010) *A Journey* (London: Hutchison)

Blanchard, R. and Katz, L. (1997) 'What we know and do not know about the natural rate of unemployment', *Journal of Economic Perspectives*, 11, 1, 51–72

Blick, A. (2016) 'Federalism: The UK's future?', *The Federal Trust*, https://fedtr ust.co.uk/wp-content/uploads/2016/05/FEDERALISM_THE_UKS_FUT URE.pdf (A: 07.09.22)

Bliss, D., Mishra, M., Ayers, J. and Lupi, M.V. (2016) 'Cross-sectoral collaboration: The state health official's role in elevating and promoting health equity in all policies in Minnesota', *Journal of Public Health Management and Practice*, 22, 1, s87–s93 http://doi.org/10.1097/PHH.0000000000000330

Bloodworth, J. (2021) 'George Galloway's disgraceful record shows he is no friend of progressives', *The New Statesman*, 22 June, https://www.newstatesman.com/comment/2021/06/george-galloway-s-disgraceful-record-shows-he-no-friend-progressives (A: 06.11.22)

Bloomberg (2022) 'Liz Truss's conference speech in full', 5 October, https://www.bloomberg.com/news/articles/2022-10-05/liz-truss-s-conference-speech-in-full (A: 04.10.22)

Blunkett, D. and Richards, D. (2011) 'Labour in and out of government: Political ideas, political practice and the British political tradition', *Political Studies Review*, 9, 2, 178–192

Blyth, M. (2013) *Austerity: The History of a Dangerous Idea* (Oxford: Oxford University Press)

Bogdanor, V. (2005) *Joined-Up Government* (Oxford: Oxford University Press)

Bogg, A. (2016) 'Beyond neo-liberalism: The Trade Union Act 2016 and the authoritarian state', *Industrial Law Journal*, 45, 3, 299–336, https://doi.org/10.1093/indlaw/dww023

Boin, A., 't Hart, P., Stern, E. and Sundelius, B. (2017) *The Politics of Crisis Management* (Cambridge: Cambridge University Press)

Bolton, I. (2021) 'UK and global emissions and temperature trends', *House of Commons Library*, 2 June, https://commonslibrary.parliament.uk/uk-and-global-emissions-and-temperature-trends/ (A: 14.07.22)

Bolton, P. (2014) 'Education spending in the UK', *House of Commons Library*, https://dera.ioe.ac.uk//22727/ (A: 09.09.22)

Bolton, P. (2021) 'Education spending in the UK', *House of Commons Library*, 17 November, https://researchbriefings.files.parliament.uk/documents/SN01 078/SN01078.pdf (A: 09.09.22)

Bond, J. (2011) 'The European Union's democratic deficit: How to fix it', *The Brown Journal of World Affairs*, 17, 2, 147–162, https://www.jstor.org/stable/24590804

Bond-Taylor, S. (2015) 'Dimensions of family empowerment in work with so-called "troubled" families', *Social Policy & Society*, 14, 3, 371–384, https://doi.org/10.1017/S1474746414000359

Booth, R. (2022) '"A merry-go-round of buck-passing": Inside the four-year Grenfell inquiry', *The Guardian*, 14 June, https://www.theguardian.com/uk-news/2022/jun/14/a-merry-go-round-of-buck-passing-inside-the-four-year-grenfell-inquiry (A: 06.09.22)

Borbely, D. (2020) 'The impact of housing subsidy cuts on the labour market outcomes of claimants: Evidence from England', *University of Strathclyde*, https://strathprints.strath.ac.uk/73441/ (A: 09.09.22)

Boseley, S. (2020) 'Cummings' actions show government cannot be trusted, says adviser', *The Guardian*, 25 May, https://www.theguardian.com/politics/2020/may/25/cummings-row-risks-breach-of-public-trust-says-psychology-expert (A: 13.07.20)

Boswell, C. (2019) *Manufacturing Political Trust: Targets and Performance Measurement in Public Policy* (Cambridge: Cambridge University Press)

Boswell, C. and Rodrigues, E. (2016) 'Policies, politics and organisational problems: Multiple streams and the implementation of targets in UK government', *Policy & Politics*, 44, 4, 507–524, https://doi.org/10.1332/03055 7315X14477577990650

Boswell, J. and Corbett, J. (2015) 'Stoic democrats? Anti-politics, élite cynicism and the policy process', *Journal of European Public Policy*, 22, 10, 1388–1405, http://dx.doi.org/10.1080/13501763.2015.1010561

Boswell, J., Cairney, P. and St Denny, E. (2019) 'The politics of institutionalizing preventative health', *Social Science and Medicine*, 228, May, 202–210, https://doi.org/10.1016/j.socscimed.2019.02.051

Boswell, J., Smith, J. and Devine, D. (2022) *Managing as a Minister* (London: IFG), https://www.instituteforgovernment.org.uk/publications/managing-minister (A: 11.08.22)

Botterill, L. and Hindmoor, A. (2012) 'Turtles all the way down: Bounded rationality in an evidence-based age', *Policy Studies*, 33, 5, 367–379

Bourgois, P. (2020) 'The PNAC (1997–2006) and the post-Cold War "neoconservative moment"', *E-International Relations*, https://www.e-ir.info/pdf/81246 (A: 13.07.23)

Bourne, J. (2021) 'Review: Green unpleasant land: Creative responses to rural England's colonial connections', *Race & Class*, 63, 1, 123–125, https://doi.org/10.1177/03063968211023370

Bovens, M., 't Hart, P. and Peters, B.G. (2001) 'The state of public governance' in Bovens, M., 't Hart, P. and Peters, B.G. (eds) *Success and Failure in Public Governance: A Comparative Analysis* (Cheltenham: Edward Elgar), 3–11

Boyne, G. (2003) 'What is public sector improvement?', *Public Administration*, 81, 2, 211–227

Bradbury, A. (2020) 'A critical race theory framework for education policy analysis: The case of bilingual learners and assessment policy in England', *Race Ethnicity and Education*, 2, 241–260, https://doi.org/10.1080/13613 324.2019.1599338

Brans, M., Geva-May, I. and Howlett, M. (2017) 'Policy analysis movement in comparative perspective: An introduction' in Brans, M., Geva-May, I. and Howlett, M. (eds) *Routledge Handbook of Comparative Policy Analysis* (London: Routledge), 1–24

Brauers, H., Oei, P.Y. and Walk, P. (2020) 'Comparing coal phase-out pathways: The United Kingdom's and Germany's diverging transitions', *Environmental Innovation and Societal Transitions*, 37, 238–253, https://doi.org/10.1016/j.eist.2020.09.001

Brehony, K. and Deem, R. (2003) 'Education policy' in Ellison, N. and Pierson, C. (eds) *Developments in British Social Policy 2* (London: Palgrave), 177–193

Breslin, J. (2023) 'DUP to vote against "Stormont Brake"', *The Irish News*, 20 March, https://www.irishnews.com/news/northernirelandnews/2023/03/20/news/dup_to_vote_against_stormont_brake_-3149986/ (A: 20.04.23)

Bresser-Pereira, L.C. (2010) 'The global financial crisis and a new capitalism?', *Journal of Post Keynesian Economics*, 32, 4, 499–534, https://www.jstor.org/stable/20798365

Brewster, J. (2021) 'Trump says critical race theory borders on "psychological abuse"', *Forbes*, 18 June, https://www.forbes.com/sites/jackbrewster/2021/06/18/trump-says-critical-race-theory-borders-on-psychological-abuse/?sh=732ab903450e (A: 26.09.22)

Bridges, L. (2012) 'Four days in August: The UK riots', *Race & Class*, 54, 1, 1–12, https://doi.org/10.1177/0306396812446564

Brien, N. (2021) *Public Spending by Country and Region* (London: House of Commons Library), https://researchbriefings.files.parliament.uk/documents/SN04033/SN04033.pdf (A: 01.07.22)

Brien, P. (2022) 'The UK shared prosperity fund', *House of Commons Library*, 26 April, https://researchbriefings.files.parliament.uk/documents/CBP-8527/CBP-8527.pdf (A: 08.09.22)

Brien, S. (ed) (2009) 'Breakthrough Britain: Dynamic benefits', *Centre for Social Justice*, https://www.centreforsocialjustice.org.uk/wp-content/uploads/2018/03/CSJ-dynamic-benefits.pdf (A: 09.09.22)

British Academy of Childhood Disability (2014) 'Impact of austerity measures on families with disabled children', https://documents.pub/document/impact-of-austerity-measures-on-families-with-to-get-a-different-perspective.html?page=1 (A: 09.09.22)

Britteon, P., Fatimah, A., Lau, Y.S., Anselmi, L., Turner, A.J., Gillibrand, S., Wilson, P., Checkland, K. and Sutton, M. (2022) 'The impact of devolution on health: A generalised synthetic control analysis of Greater Manchester in England', *The Lancet Public Health*, 7, 10, e844–e852, https://doi.org/10.1016/S2468-2667(22)00198-0

Brooks, E. and Davoudi, S. (2014) 'Climate justice and retrofitting for energy efficiency', *disP – The Planning Review*, 50, 3, 101–110, https://doi.org/10.1080/02513625.2014.979048

Brooks, L. (2014) 'Nicola Sturgeon announces Scottish cabinet with equal gender balance', *The Guardian*, 21 November, https://www.theguardian.com/politics/2014/nov/21/nicola-sturgeon-scottish-cabinet-equal-gender-balance (A: 07.09.22)

Brown, A. (2016) 'From the machines of today to the artificial intelligence of tomorrow', *Centre for Public Impact*, 18 May, https://www.centreforpublicimp act.org/insights/from-the-machines-of-today-to-the-machines-of-tomorrow (A: 11.10.22)

Brown, G. (2017) *My Life, Our Times* (London: Bodley Head)

Browne, J. (2010) *Securing a Sustainable Future for Higher Education* (Browne report) (London: Department for Business, Innovation and Skills), https://www.gov. uk/government/publications/the-browne-report-higher-education-funding-and-student-finance (A: 01.06.22)

Brown Swan, C. (2020) 'The independence question' in Keating, M. (ed) *The Oxford Handbook of Scottish Politics* (Oxford: Oxford University Press), 633–649

Brummer, K., Harnisch, S., Opperman, K. and Panke, D. (2019) *Foreign Policy as Public Policy? Promises and Pitfalls* (Manchester: Manchester University Press)

Brusenbauch Meislová, M. (2023) 'In quest for discursive legitimation of ongoing policy processes: Constructing Brexit as a success story', *JCMS: Journal of Common Market Studies*, 61, 3, 815–833, https://doi.org/10.1111/jcms.13427

Budgeon, S. (2019) 'The resonance of moderate feminism and the gendered relations of austerity', *Gender, Work and Organization*, 26, 8, 1138–1155, https://doi.org/10.1111/gwao.12315

Bugaric, B. and Kuhelj, A. (2018) 'Varieties of populism in Europe: Is the rule of law in danger?', *Hague Journal on the Rule of Law*, 10, 21–33, https://doi.org/10.1007/s40803-018-0075-4

Burch, M. and Holliday, I. (1996) *The British Cabinet System* (London: Prentice Hall/Harvester Wheatsheaf).

Burkitt, R. and Quigley, A. (2020) 'One month in: British public opinion on COVID-19', *IPSOS*, 29 April, https://www.ipsos.com/en-uk/one-month-brit ish-public-opinion-covid-19-coronavirus (A: 17.03.22)

Burnham, J. and Pyper, R. (2008) *Britain's Modernised Civil Service* (London: Palgrave)

Burns, C. (2020) 'Brexit's implications for environmental policy', *UK in a Changing Europe*, https://ukandeu.ac.uk/long-read/brexits-implications-for-environmen tal-policy/ (A: 08.09.22)

Burns, C. and Carter, N. (2018) 'Brexit and UK environmental policy and politics', *French Journal of British Studies*, 23, 3, 1–18, https://journals.openedit ion.org/rfcb/2385 (A: 12.08.22)

Burns, C., Gravey, V., Jordan, A. and Zito, A. (2019) 'De-Europeanising or disengaging? EU environmental policy and Brexit', *Environmental Politics*, 28, 2, 271–292, https://doi.org/10.1080/09644016.2019.1549774

Burns, C., Flood, S. and O'Dwyer, B. (2022) 'Mainstreaming climate change adaptation into planning and development: A case study in Northern Ireland' in Flood, S., Jerez Columbié, Y., Le Tissier, M. and O'Dwyer, B. (eds) *Creating Resilient Futures* (London: Springer), 129–147

Burns, N. (2021) 'Iraq War damaged US credibility', *Harvard Kennedy School*, 21 December, https://www.belfercenter.org/publication/iraq-war-damaged-us-credibility (A: 07.10.22)

Busby, N. and Zahn, R. (2013) 'European labour law in crisis: The demise of social rights', *Contemporary Issues in Law*, 12, 2, 173–192

Busby, N. and James, G. (2016) *Regulating Work and Care Relationships in a Time of Austerity: A Legal Perspective* (London: Routledge)

Busch, P. and Jörgens, H. (2005) 'The international sources of policy convergence: Explaining the spread of environmental policy innovations', *Journal of European Public Policy*, 12, 5, 860–884

Bush, G.W. (2001) 'Global war on terror', *George W. Bush Presidential Library*, https://www.georgewbushlibrary.gov/research/topic-guides/global-war-ter ror (A: 07.10.22)

Butchard, P. (2021) *UK War Crimes in Iraq: The ICC Prosecutor's Report* (London: House of Commons Library), https://commonslibrary.parliament. uk/uk-war-crimes-in-iraq-the-icc-prosecutors-report/ (A: 13.07.23)

Butler, C. (2021) 'When are governing parties more likely to respond to public opinion? The strange case of the Liberal Democrats and tuition fees', *British Politics*, 16, 336–354, https://doi.org/10.1057/s41293-020-00139-3

Butler, C., Campbell, R. and Hudson, J. (2021) 'Political recruitment under pressure, again: MPs and candidates in the 2019 general election' in Ford, R., Bale, T., Jennings, W. and Surridge, P. (eds) *The British General Election of 2019* (London: Palgrave), 387–420

Butler, R. (2004) *Review of Intelligence on Weapons of Mass Destruction: Report of a Committee of Privy Counsellors* (Butler Report), HC 898 (London: House of Commons), https://irp.fas.org/world/uk/butler071404.pdf (A: 01.09.22)

Butler, S., Elmeland, K., Nicholls, J. and Thom, B. (2017) *Alcohol, Power and Public Health: A Comparative Study of Alcohol Policy* (London: Routledge)

Byrne, L. (2015) ' "I'm afraid there is no money": The letter I will regret for ever', *The Guardian*, 9 May, https://www.theguardian.com/commentisfree/ 2015/may/09/liam-byrne-apology-letter-there-is-no-money-labour-general-election (A: 11.07.23)

Cabinet Office (2018) 'Public bodies', https://www.gov.uk/guidance/public-bod ies-reform (A: 22.09.21)

Cabinet Office (2020) 'Civil service statistics as at 31 March 2020', *Gov.uk*, https://assets.publishing.service.gov.uk/government/uploads/system/uploads/ attachment_data/file/940284/Statistical_bulletin_Civil_Service_Statistics_2020 _V2.pdf (A: 21.09.21)

Cabinet Office (Strategic Policy Making Team) (1999) *Professional Policy Making for the Twenty First Century*, https://dera.ioe.ac.uk/6320/1/profpolicy making. pdf (A: 19.08.21)

Cabinet Office and Office of the Parliamentary Counsel (2013) *When Laws Become too Complex*, http://www.gov.uk/government/publications/when-laws-bec ome-too-complex (A: 10.06.22)

Cadwalladr, C. (2017) 'The great British Brexit robbery: How our democracy was hijacked', *The Observer*, 7 May, https://www.theguardian.com/technology/2017/ may/07/the-great-british-brexit-robbery-hijacked-democracy (A: 19.08.22)

Cairncross, A. (1985) *Years of Recovery: British Economic Policy 1945–51* (London: Methuen)

Cairney, P. (2002) 'New public management and the Thatcher health care legacy', *British Journal of Politics and International Relations*, 4, 3, 375–398

Cairney, P. (2006) 'Venue shift following devolution: When reserved meets devolved in Scotland', *Regional and Federal Studies*, 16, 4, 429–445

Cairney, P. (2007a) 'The professionalisation of MPs: Refining the "politics-facilitating" explanation', *Parliamentary Affairs*, 60, 2, 212–233

Cairney, P. (2007b) 'A "multiple lenses" approach to policy change: The case of tobacco policy in the UK', *British Politics*, 2, 1, 45–68

Cairney, P. (2007c) 'Using devolution to set the agenda? Venue shift and the smoking ban in Scotland', *British Journal of Politics and International Relations*, 9, 73–89

Cairney, P. (2008) 'Has devolution changed the British policy style?', *British Politics*, 3, 3, 350–372

Cairney, P. (2009a) 'Implementation and the governance problem: A pressure participant perspective', *Public Policy and Administration*, 24, 4, 355–377

Cairney, P. (2009b) 'The "British policy style" and mental health: Beyond the headlines', *Journal of Social Policy*, 38, 4, 1–18

Cairney, P. (2009c) 'The role of ideas in policy transfer: The case of UK smoking bans since devolution', *Journal of European Public Policy*, 16, 3, 471–488

Cairney, P. (2011) *The Scottish Political System since Devolution: From New Politics to the New Scottish Government* (Exeter: Imprint Academic)

Cairney, P. (2012) '"Public administration in an age of austerity": Positive lessons from policy studies', *Public Policy and Administration*, 27, 3, 230–247, https://doi.org/10.1177/0952076712442212

Cairney, P. (2013a) 'Territorial policy communities and the Scottish policy style: The case of compulsory education', *Scottish Affairs*, 82, 10–34

Cairney, P. (2013b) 'What is evolutionary theory and how does it inform policy studies?', *Policy and Politics*, 41, 2, 279–298

Cairney, P. (2015a) 'How can policy theory have an impact on policy making?', *Teaching Public Administration*, 33, 1, 22–39

Cairney, P. (2015b) 'Scotland's future political system', *Political Quarterly*, 86, 2, 217–225

Cairney, P. (2016a) *The Politics of Evidence-Based Policy Making* (London: Palgrave Pivot)

Cairney, P. (2016b) 'The Scottish government's holistic education policy: A story of profound success or failure?', *Paul Cairney: Politics & Public Policy*, 13 December, https://paulcairney.wordpress.com/2016/12/13/the-scottish-governments-holistic-education-policy-a-story-of-profound-success-or-failure/ (A: 19.09.22)

Cairney, P. (2016c) 'Early thoughts on the Iraq Inquiry/Chilcot Report: Will anyone learn any lessons?', *Paul Cairney: Politics & Public Policy*, 6 July, https://paulcairney.wordpress.com/2016/07/06/early-thoughts-on-the-iraq-inquiry-chilcot-report-will-anyone-learn-any-lessons/ (A: 29.09.22)

Cairney, P. (2017a) '5 images of the policy process', *Paul Cairney: Politics & Public Policy*, 10 July, https://paulcairney.wordpress.com/2017/07/10/5-images-of-the-policy-process/ (A: 19.08.21)

Cairney, P. (2017b) 'Scottish politics in Brexit Britain: Is independence inevitable?', *Paul Cairney: Politics & Public Policy*, 14 March, https://paulcairney.wordpress.com/2017/03/14/scottish-politics-in-brexit-britain-is-independence-inevitable/ (A: 19.08.22)

Cairney, P. (2019a) 'The transformation of UK tobacco control' in Compton, M. and 't Hart, P. (eds) *Great Policy Successes* (Oxford: Oxford University Press), 84–104

Cairney, P. (2019b) 'Policy styles in the UK: Majoritarian UK versus devolved consensus democracies?' in Howlett, M. and Tosun, J. (eds) *Policy Styles and Policy-Making: Exploring the National Dimension* (London: Routledge), 25–44

Cairney, P. (2019c) 'The UK government's imaginative use of evidence to make policy', *British Politics*, 14, 1, 1–22, https://doi.org/10.1057/s41293-017-0068-2

Cairney, P. (2020a) *Understanding Public Policy* (London: Red Globe)

Cairney, P. (2020b) 'Policy analysis in 750 words: Complex systems and systems thinking', *Paul Cairney: Politics and Public Policy*, 23 December, https://paulcairney.wordpress.com/2019/12/23/policy-analysis-in-750-words-complex-systems-and-systems-thinking/ (A: 14.07.22)

Cairney, P. (2021a) *The Politics of Policy Analysis* (London: Palgrave)

Cairney, P. (2021b) 'Evidence-informed COVID-19 policy: What problem was the UK government trying to solve?' in Bryson, J. Andres, L., Ersoy, A. and Reardon, L. (eds) *Living with Pandemics: Places, People and Policy* (Cheltenham: Edward Elgar), 250–261

Cairney, P. (2021c) 'The UK government's COVID-19 policy: Assessing evidence-informed policy analysis in real time', *British Politics*, 16, 1, 90–116, https://doi.org/10.1057/s41293-020-00150-8

Cairney, P. (2021d) 'The UK government's COVID-19 policy: What does "guided by the science" mean in practice?', *Frontiers in Political Science*, 3, 1–14, doi: 10.3389/fpos.2021.624068

Cairney, P. (2022) 'Why is there high support for, but low likelihood of, drug consumption rooms in Scotland?', *Paul Cairney: Politics & Public Policy*, 31 May, https://paulcairney.wordpress.com/2022/05/31/why-is-there-high-support-for-but-low-likelihood-of-drug-consumption-rooms-in-scotland/ (A: 16.09.22)

Cairney, P. (2023a) 'What does policy making look like?', *Paul Cairney: Politics & Public Policy*, 13 February, https://paulcairney.wordpress.com/2023/02/13/what-does-policy making-look-like/ (A: 19.04.23)

Cairney, P. (2023b) 'Evidence-based policy making' in Tosun, J. and Graziano, P. (eds) *Encyclopedia of European Union Public Policy* (Cheltenham: Edward Elgar)

Cairney, P. and McGarvey, N. (2013) *Scottish Politics*, 2nd edn (London: Palgrave)

Cairney, P. and Studlar, D. (2014) 'Public health policy in the United Kingdom: After the war on tobacco, is a war on alcohol brewing?', *World Medical and Health Policy*, 6, 3, 308–323

Cairney, P. and Geyer, R. (2015) 'Introduction: A new direction in policy making theory and practice?' in Geyer, R. and Cairney, P. (eds) *Handbook on Complexity and Public Policy* (Cheltenham: Edward Elgar), 83–99

Cairney, P. and Jordan, G. (2015) 'Theories of the policy process: What is British and what is universal?', *British Politics*, 10, 4, 486–492, https://doi.org/10.1057/bp.2015.32

Cairney, P. and Weible, C. (2015) 'Comparing and contrasting Peter Hall's paradigms and ideas with the advocacy coalition framework' in Howlett, M. and Hogan, J. (eds) *Policy Paradigms in Theory and Practice* (Basingstoke: Palgrave), 83–89

Cairney, P. and Kwiatkowski, R. (2017) 'How to communicate effectively with policymakers: Combine insights from psychology and policy studies', *Palgrave Communications*, 3, 37, https://doi.org/10.1057/s41599-017-0046-8

Cairney, P. and St Denny, E. (2020) *Why Isn't Government Policy More Preventive?* (Oxford: Oxford University Press)

Cairney, P. and Wellstead, A. (2021) 'COVID-19: Effective policy making depends on trust in experts, politicians, and the public', *Policy Design and Practice*, 4, 1, 1–14, https://www.tandfonline.com/doi/full/10.1080/25741292.2020.1837466

Cairney, P. and Kippin, S. (2022) 'The future of education equity policy in a COVID-19 world: A qualitative systematic review of lessons from education policymaking', *Open Research Europe*, 1, 78, https://doi.org/10.12688/openreseurope.13834.2

Cairney, P. and Toth, F. (2023) 'The politics of COVID-19 experts: Comparing winners and losers in Italy and the UK', *Policy and Society*, 1–14, https://doi.org/10.1093/polsoc/puad011

Cairney, P., Studlar, D. and Mamudu, H. (2012) *Global Tobacco Control: Power, Policy, Governance and Transfer* (Basingstoke: Palgrave Macmillan)

Cairney, P., Fischer, M. and Ingold, K. (2016) 'Hydraulic fracturing policy in the UK: Coalition, cooperation and opposition in the face of uncertainty' in Weible, C., Heikkila, T., Ingold, K. and Fischer, M. (eds) *Comparing Coalition Politics: Policy Debates on Hydraulic Fracturing in North America and Western Europe* (London: Palgrave), 81–114

Cairney, P., Wilson, A. and Keating, M. (2016) 'Solving the problem of social background in the UK "political class": Do parties do things differently in Westminster, devolved, and European elections?', *British Politics*, 11, 2, 142–163

Cairney, P., Ingold, K. and Fischer, M. (2018) 'Fracking in the UK and Switzerland: Why differences in policy making systems don't always produce different outputs and outcomes', *Policy and Politics*, 46, 1, 125–147, http://dx.doi.org/10.1332/030557316X14793989976783

Cairney, P., Heikkila, T. and Wood, M. (2019a) *Making Policy in a Complex World* (Cambridge: Cambridge University Press)

Cairney, P., McHarg, A., McEwen, N. and Turner, K. (2019b) 'How to conceptualise energy law and policy for an interdisciplinary audience: The case of post-Brexit UK', *Energy Policy*, 129, 459–466, https://doi.org/10.1016/j.enpol.2019.02.022

Cairney, P., St Denny, E. and Kippin, S. (2021a) 'Policy learning to reduce inequalities: The search for a coherent Scottish gender mainstreaming policy in a multi-level UK', *Territory, Politics and Governance*, 9, 3, 412–433, https://doi.org/10.1080/21622671.2020.1837661

Cairney, P., St Denny, E. and Mitchell, H. (2021b) 'The future of public health policy making after COVID-19: A qualitative systematic review of lessons from health in all policies', *Open Research Europe*, 1, 23, https://doi.org/10.12688/openreseurope.13178.2

Cairney, P., Kippin, S., St Denny, E. and Mitchell, H. (2021c) 'Policy design for territorial equity in multi-level and multi-sectoral political systems: Comparing health and education strategies', *Regional Science, Policy and Practice*, 1–11, https://doi.org/10.1111/rsp3.12466

Cairney, P., Keating, M., Kippin, S. and St Denny, E. (2022a) *Public Policy to Reduce Inequalities across Europe: Hope versus Reality* (Oxford: Oxford University Press)

Cairney, P., St Denny, E. and Boswell, J. (2022b) 'Why is health improvement so difficult to secure?', *Open Research Europe*, 2, 76, https://doi.org/10.12688/openreseurope.14841.2

Cairney, P., Timonina, I. and Stephan, H. (2023) 'How can policy and policy making foster climate justice? A qualitative systematic review', *Open Research Europe*, https://open-research-europe.ec.europa.eu/articles/3-51

Calhoun, C. (2017) 'Populism, nationalism and Brexit' in Outhwaite, W. (ed) *Brexit: Sociological Responses* (London: Anthem Press), 57–76

Calvert, J., Arbuthnott, G. and Leake, J. (2020) 'Coronavirus: 38 days when Britain sleepwalked into disaster', *Sunday Times*, 18 April, https://www.thetimes.co.uk/edition/news/coronavirus-38-days-when-britain-sleepwalked-into-disaster-hq3b9tlgh (A: 07.05.20)

Cameron, D. (2010) 'Big Society speech', *Gov.uk*, 19 July, https://www.gov.uk/government/speeches/big-society-speech (A: 29.08.22)

Cameron, D. (2011a) 'Letter from the Prime Minister on cutting red tape', *HM Government*, 7 April, https://www.gov.uk/government/news/letter-from-the-prime-minister-on-cutting-red-tape (A: 09.09.22)

Cameron, D. (2011b) 'PM's speech on the fightback after the riots', *HM Government*, https://www.gov.uk/government/speeches/pms-speech-on-the-fightback-after-the-riots (A: 26.09.22)

Cameron, D. (2011c) 'David Cameron on the riots: "This is criminality pure and simple" – video', *The Guardian*, 9 August, https://www.theguardian.com/politics/video/2011/aug/09/david-cameron-riots-criminality-video (A: 26.09.22)

Cameron, D. (2011d) 'Troubled families speech', https://www.gov.uk/government/speeches/troubled-families-speech (A: 12.08.22)

Cameron, D. (2016) 'EU referendum: Full transcript of David Cameron's last-ditch plea for Britain to Remain', *The Independent*, 21 June, https://www.independent.co.uk/news/uk/politics/eu-referendum-brexit-latest-live-david-cameron-full-speech-remain-leave-a7093426.html (A: 02.09.22)

Cameron-Blake, E., Tatlow, H., Wood, A., Hale, T., Kira, B., Petherick, A. and Phillips, T. (2020) 'Variation in the response to COVID-19 across the four nations of the United Kingdom 1.0', *BSG Working Paper Series*, October, https://www.bsg.ox.ac.uk/research/research-projects/covid-19-government-response-tracker (A: 05.04.22)

Campbell, A. (2007) *The Blair Years: The Alastair Campbell Diaries* (London: Random House)

Campbell, D. (2022) 'Thérèse Coffey to drop smoking action plan, insiders say', *The Guardian*, 11 October, https://www.theguardian.com/society/2022/oct/11/therese-coffey-to-drop-smoking-action-plan-insiders-say (A: 11.10.22)

Campbell, R. and Childs, S. (2015) 'Conservatism, feminisation and the representation of women in UK politics', *British Politics*, 10, 2, 148–168, https://doi.org/10.1057/bp.2015.18

Campbell, R. and Shorrocks, R. (2021) 'Finally rising with the tide? Gender and the vote in the 2019 British elections', *Journal of Elections, Public Opinion and Parties*, 31, 4, 488–507, https://doi.org/10.1080/17457289.2021.1968412

Camp-Pietrain, E. (2018) 'Reducing inequalities in Scotland: Firm commitments, mixed results after 10 years of SNP governments' in Fée, D. and Kober-Smith, A. (eds) *Inequalities in the UK* (Bingley: Emerald), 305–321

Carasso, H. and Gunn, A. (2015) 'Fees, fairness and the National Scholarship Programme: Higher education policy in England and the coalition government', *London Review of Education*, 13, 2, 70–83

Carey, G. and Crammond, B. (2015) 'What works in joined-up government? An evidence synthesis', *International Journal of Public Administration*, 38, 13–14, 1020–1029, https://doi.org/10.1080/01900692.2014.982292

Carter, E. and Whitworth, A. (2015) 'Creaming and parking in quasi-marketised welfare to work schemes: Designed out of or designed in to the UK work programme?', *Journal of Social Policy*, 44, 2, 277–296, http://journals.cambridge.org/abstract_S0047279414000841 (A: 04.05.22)

Carter, N. (2014) 'The politics of climate change in the UK', *Wiley Interdisciplinary Reviews: Climate Change*, 5, 3, 423–433, https://doi.org/10.1002/wcc.274

Carter, N. and Jacobs, M. (2014) 'Explaining radical policy change: The case of climate change and energy policy under the British Labour government 2006–10', *Public Administration*, 92, 1, 125–141, https://doi.org/10.1111/padm.12046

Carter, N. and Clements, B. (2015) 'From "greenest government ever" to "get rid of all the green crap": David Cameron, the Conservatives and the environment', *British Politics*, 10, 2, 204–225, https://doi.org/10.1057/bp.2015.16

Carter, N. and Childs, M. (2018) 'Friends of the Earth as a policy entrepreneur: "The Big Ask" campaign for a UK Climate Change Act', *Environmental Politics*, 27, 6, 994–1013, https://doi.org/10.1080/09644016.2017.1368151

Carter, N. and Little, C. (2021) 'Party competition on climate policy: The roles of interest groups, ideology and challenger parties in the UK and Ireland', *International Political Science Review*, 42, 1, 16–32, https://doi.org/10.1177/0192512120972582

Case, A. and Deaton, A. (2020) *Deaths of Despair and the Future of Capitalism* (Princeton: Princeton University Press)

Casey, B. (2020) 'Covid-19: Is there a trade-off between economic damage and loss of life?', *LSE EUROPP*, 18 December, https://blogs.lse.ac.uk/europpblog/2020/12/18/covid-19-is-there-a-trade-off-between-economic-damage-and-loss-of-life/ (A: 16.08.22)

Casey, L. (2023) *Baroness Casey Review. Final Report. An Independent Review into the Standards of Behaviour and Internal Culture of the Metropolitan Police Service* (London: Metropolitan Police), https://www.met.police.uk/SysSiteAssets/media/downloads/met/about-us/baroness-casey-review/update-march-2023/baroness-casey-review-march-2023a.pdf (A: 03.05.22)

Cash, B. and Jenkin, B. (2013) 'The EU single market – is it worth it?', *ConservativeHome*, https://conservativehome.blogs.com/files/the-single-market-is-it-worth-it.pdf (A: 07.09.22)

Cauvet, P. (2018) 'Theresa May's government and the Northern Ireland issue: Brexit as the end of the consociational and postnational illusions', *Observatoire de la société britannique*, 21, 103–121, https://doi.org/10.4000/osb.2167

Centre for Social Investigation (2019) 'New CSI research reveals high levels of job discrimination faced by ethnic minorities in Britain', *Nuffield College Oxford*, csi.nuff.ox.ac.uk/?p=1299 (A: 26.09.22)

Centre for Social Justice (2010) *Green Paper on the Family*, https://www.bl.uk/collection-items/centre-for-social-justice-green-paper-on-the-family (A: 12.07.23)

Chadderton, C. (2022) 'Covid, schooling and race in England: A case of necropolitics', *Race, Ethnicity and Education*, 1–18, https://doi.org/10.1080/13613324.2022.2069736

Chakelian, A. (2021) 'A decade after the London riots, has anything actually changed?', *New Statesman*, 6 August, https://www.newstatesman.com/politics/2021/08/london-riots-2011-england-riots-police-ten-years-decade-anniversary-happen-again (A: 12.07.23)

Chakelian, A. (2022) 'Britain braces itself for the devastation of austerity 2.0', *New Statesman*, 6 October, https://www.newstatesman.com/politics/society/2022/10/uk-austerity-measures-meaning-devastation (A: 11.07.23)

Chalmers, D. (2017) 'Brexit and the renaissance of parliamentary authority', *The British Journal of Politics and International Relations*, 19, 4, 663–679, https://doi.org/10.1177/1369148117723460

Chan, S. and Safran, W. (2006) 'Public opinion as a constraint against war: Democracies' responses to Operation Iraqi Freedom', *Foreign Policy Analysis*, 2, 2, 137–156, https://www.jstor.org/stable/24907273

Chandler, D. (2003) 'Rhetoric without responsibility: The attraction of "ethical" foreign policy', *The British Journal of Politics and International Relations*, 5, 3, 295–316, https://doi.org/10.1111/1467-856X.00108

Chapman, C. and Ainscow, M. (2019) 'Using research to promote equity within education systems: Possibilities and barriers', *British Educational Research Journal*, 45, 5, 899–917, https://doi.org/10.1002/berj.3544

Chilcot, J. (2016) *The Report of the Iraq Inquiry* (London: Cabinet Office), https://www.gov.uk/government/publications/the-report-of-the-iraq-inqu iry (A: 13.07.23)

Childs, S. (2004) *New Labour's Women MPs: Women Representing Women* (London: Routledge)

Childs, S. and Whitey, J. (2004) 'Women representatives acting for women', *Political Studies*, 52, 3, 522–564, https://doi.org/10.1111/j.1467-9248.2004.00495.x

Chilvers, J., Foxon, T.J., Galloway, S., Hammond, G.P., Infield, D., Leach, M., Pearson, P.J., Strachan, N., Strbac, G. and Thomson, M. (2017) 'Realising transition pathways for a more electric, low-carbon energy system in the United Kingdom: Challenges, insights and opportunities', *Proceedings of the Institution of Mechanical Engineers, Part A: Journal of Power and Energy*, 231, 6, 440–477, https://doi.org/10.1177/0957650917695448

Chinkin, C. and Kaldor, M. (2017) *International Law and New Wars* (Cambridge: Cambridge University Press)

Chitty, C. (2014) *Education Policy in Britain*, 3rd edn (London: Palgrave)

Chivers, T. (2022) 'Want to save the oceans? Stop recycling plastic', *iNews*, 4 October, https://inews.co.uk/opinion/landfill-better-recycled-plastic-ends-up-sea-1891207 (A: 05.10.22)

Cho, S., Crenshaw, K.W. and McCall, L. (2013) 'Toward a field of intersectionality studies: Theory, applications, and praxis', *Signs: Journal of Women in Culture and Society*, 38, 4, 785–810, https://doi.org/10.1086/669608

Choudhury, T. and Fenwich, H. (2011) 'The impact of counter-terrorism measures on Muslim communities', *EHRC*, https://www.equalityhumanrig hts.com/sites/default/files/research-report-72-the-impact-of-counter-terror ism-measures-on-muslim-communities_0.doc (A: 26.09.22)

The Christian Institute (2011) 'Riots: Where are the fathers?', 12 August, https://www.christian.org.uk/news/riots-where-are-the-fathers/ (A: 26.09.22)

Christoffersen, A. (2019) 'Are we all "baskets of characteristics?" Intersectional slippages and the displacement of race in English and Scottish equality policy' in Hankivsky, O. and Jordan-Zachery, J. (eds) *The Palgrave Handbook of Intersectionality in Public Policy* (London: Palgrave), 705–732

Christoffersen, A. (2022) 'Is intersectional racial justice organizing possible? Confronting generic intersectionality', *Ethnic and Racial Studies*, 45, 3, 407–430, https://doi.org/10.1080/01419870.2021.1928254

Chulov, M. and Pidd, H. (2011) 'Curveball: How US was duped by Iraqi fantasist looking to topple Saddam', *The Guardian*, 15 February, https://www.theguard ian.com/world/2011/feb/15/curveball-iraqi-fantasist-cia-saddam (A: 07.10.22)

Chwalisz, C. (2015) *The Populist Signal: Why Politics and Democracy Need to Change* (London: Policy Network)

Chwieroth, J.M. and Walter, A. (2021) 'Neoliberalism and banking crisis bailouts: Distant enemies or warring neighbors?', *Public Administration*, https://doi.org/10.1111/padm.12774

Cini, M. (2011) 'The soft law approach: Commission rule-making in the EU's state aid regime', *Journal of European Public Policy*, 2, 192–207, https://doi.org/10.1080/13501760110041541

Clancy, L. (2020) '"This is a tale of friendship, a story of togetherness": The British monarchy, Grenfell Tower, and inequalities in the Royal Borough of Kensington and Chelsea', *Cultural Studies*, 1–23, https://doi.org/10.1080/09502386.2020.1863997

Clark, A. (2018) *Political Parties in the UK*, 2nd edn (London: Red Globe)

Clark, C. (2018) 'Sites, welfare and "barefoot begging": Roma and Gypsy/Traveller experiences of racism in Scotland' in Davidson, N., Liinpaa, M., McBridge, M. and Virdee, S. (eds) *No Problem Here* (Edinburgh: Luath Press), 145–161

Clarke, K. (2011) 'Punish the feral rioters, but address our social deficit too', *The Guardian*, 5 September, https://www.theguardian.com/commentisfree/2011/sep/05/punishment-rioters-help (A: 26.09.22)

Clarke, N., Jennings, W., Moss, J. and Stoker, G. (2018) *The Good Politician: Folk Theories, Political Interaction, and the Rise of Anti-Politics* (Cambridge: Cambridge University Press)

Clegg, N. (2016) *Politics: Between the Extremes* (London: Bodley Head)

Clift, B. (2020) 'The hollowing out of monetarism: The rise of rules-based monetary policy-making in the UK and USA and problems with the paradigm change framework', *Comparative European Politics*, 18, 3, 281–308

Clift, B. and McDaniel, S. (2022) 'The politics of the British model of capitalism's flatlining productivity and anaemic growth: Lessons for the growth models perspective', *British Journal of Politics and International Relations*, 24, 4, 631–648, https://doi.org/10.1177/13691481211044638

Climate Northern Ireland (2021) *Evidence for the Third UK Climate Change Risk Assessment (CCRA3): Summary for Northern Ireland* (Belfast: NICVA), https://www.ukclimaterisk.org/wp-content/uploads/2021/06/CCRA-Evidence-Report-Northern-Ireland-Summary-Final.pdf (A: 04.06.22)

Clinks (2017) 'Briefing on the final report of the Lammy Review', https://www.clinks.org/sites/default/files/2018-09/lammy_review_briefing_final.pdf (A: 26.09.22)

CNN (2001) 'Blair says meeting with Bush "productive"', 23 February, edition.cnn.com/2001/WORLD/europe/02/23/bush.blair.02/ (A: 07.10.22)

CNN (2003) 'Powell slams media on Iraq WMD reports', 9 June, edition.cnn.com/2003/WORLD/meast/06/08/sprj.irq.main/ (A: 13.07.23)

Coates, D. (2008) ' "Darling, it is entirely my fault!" Gordon Brown's legacy to Alistair and himself', *British Politics*, 3, 3–21, https://doi.org/10.1057/palgrave.bp.4200078

Cockburn, P. (2003) 'All this military triumphalism ignored the disastrous reality of post-war Iraq', *The Independent*, 30 May, https://www.independent.co.uk/voices/commentators/patrick-cockburn-all-this-military-triumphalism-ignored-the-disastrous-reality-of-postwar-iraq-106751.html (A: 07.10.22)

Cocks, M. (2013) 'Conceptualizing the role of key individuals in urban governance: Cases from the economic regeneration of Liverpool, UK', *European Planning Studies*, 21, 4, 575–595, https://doi.org/10.1080/09654 313.2012.722955

Cohen, B., Moss, P., Petrie, P. and Wallace, J. (2021) ' "A New Deal for Children?" – what happened next: A cross-national study of transferring early childhood services into education', *Early Years*, 41, 2–3, 110–127, https://doi.org/10.1080/09575146.2018.1504753

Cohen, M., March, J. and Olsen, J. (1972) 'A garbage can model of organizational choice', *Administrative Science Quarterly*, 17, 1, 1–25

Cohen, N. (2002) 'Who will save Iraq?', *The Guardian*, 11 August, https://www.theguardian.com/world/2002/aug/11/iraq (A: 07.10.22)

Colebatch, H. (1998) *Policy* (Buckingham: Open University Press)

Colebatch, H. (2006) 'Mapping the work of policy' in Colebatch, H. (ed) *Beyond the Policy Cycle: The Policy Process in Australia* (Crow's Nest: Allen & Unwin), 1–11

Coleman, L., Shorto, S. and Ben-Galim, D. (2022) *Coram Family and Childcare Survey 2022* (London: Coram), https://www.coram.org.uk/sites/default/files/resource_files/Coram%20Childcare%20Survey%20-%202022.pdf (A: 09.08.22)

Coletta, G. (2018) 'Politicising intelligence: What went wrong with the UK and US assessments on Iraqi WMD in 2002', *Journal of Intelligence History*, 17, 1, 65–78

Colfer, B. (2020) 'Herd-immunity across intangible borders: Public policy responses to COVID-19 in Ireland and the UK', *European Policy Analysis*, 6, 2, 203–225, https://doi.org/10.1002/epa2.1096

Commission on Race and Ethnic Disparities (2021) 'Independent report. Summary of recommendations', 28 April, https://www.gov.uk/government/publications/the-report-of-the-commission-on-race-and-ethnic-disparities/summary-of-recommendations (A: 03.09.22)

Committee on Climate Change (2017) *Building a Low-Carbon Economy in Wales* (London: CCC), https://www.theccc.org.uk/wp-content/uploads/2017/12/CCC-Building-a-low-carbon-economy-in-Wales-Setting-Welsh-climate-targ ets.pdf (A: 06.07.22)

Committee on Climate Change (2022a) 'Letter: Northern Ireland's Climate Change Bill', *CCC*, 25 March, https://www.theccc.org.uk/publication/let ter-northern-irelands-climate-change-bill/ (A: 14.07.22)

Committee on Climate Change (2022b) 'Scottish emission targets – first five-yearly review & progress in reducing emissions in Scotland – 2022 report to Parliament', 7 December, https://www.theccc.org.uk/publication/scottish-emission-targets-progress-in-reducing-emissions-in-scotland-2022-report-to-parliament/ (A: 26.04.23)

Committee on Climate Change (2022c) *Progress in Reducing Emissions: 2022 Report to Parliament* (London: CCC), https://www.theccc.org.uk/publication/2022-progress-report-to-parliament/#downloads (A: 11.07.23)

Common, R.K. (1998) 'Convergence and transfer: A review of the globalisation of new public management', *International Journal of Public Sector Management*, 11, 6, 440–450

Compton, M. and 't Hart, P. (2019) *Great Policy Successes: How Governments Get It Right in a Big Way at Least Some of the Time* (Oxford: Oxford University Press)

Conley, H. and Page, M. (2017) 'Revisiting Jewson and Mason: The politics of gender equality in UK local government in a cold climate', *Gender, Work and Organization*, 24, 1, 7–19, https://doi.org/10.1111/gwao.12135

Connell, A., Martin, S. and St Denny, E. (2019) 'Can meso-governments use metagovernance tools to tackle complex policy problems?', *Policy & Politics*, 47, 3, 437–454, https://doi.org/10.1332/030557319X15579230420072

Connell, A., St Denny, E. and Martin, S. (2021) 'How can subnational governments develop and deliver distinctive policy agendas?', *International Review of Administrative Sciences*, 88, 4, 1159–1175, https://doi.org/10.1177/00208523219964

Connolly, J., van der Zwet, A., Huggins, C. and McAngus, C. (2020) 'The governance capacities of Brexit from a Scottish perspective: The case of fisheries policy', *Public Policy and Administration*, 37, 3, 342–362, https://doi.org/10.1177/0952076720936328

Connolly, J., Flinders, M., Judge, D., Torrance, M. and Tudor, P. (2022) 'Institutions ignored: A history of select committee scrutiny in the House of Lords, 1968–2021', *Parliamentary History*, 41, 3, 463–490, https://doi.org/10.1111/1750-0206.12663

Conservative Party (2010) *Invitation to Join the Government of Britain* (Conservative Party Manifesto 2010) (London: Conservative Party), https://general-election-2010.co.uk/2010-general-election-manifestos/Conservative-Party-Manifesto-2010.pdf (A: 04.05.22)

Conservative Party (2015) *Strong Leadership. A Clear Economic Plan. A Brighter, More Secure Future* (Conservative Party Manifesto) (London: Conservative Party)

Conservative Party (2019) *Get Brexit Done. Unleash Britain's Potential* (Conservative Party Manifesto) (London: Conservative Party)

Consterdine, E. (2023) 'The UK's unworkable immigration plans allow the government to blame others for its failure', *The Conversation*, 31 March, https://theconversation.com/the-uks-unworkable-immigration-plans-allow-the-government-to-blame-others-for-its-failure-202207 (A: 20.04.23)

Constitution of Iraq (2005) constituteproject.org/constitution/Iraq_2005.pdf?lang=en (A: 07.10.22)

Conway, E. (2022) 'The inconvenient truth about climate change is that solving it will involve digging, blasting & leaching more minerals from the skin of this planet than ever before', Twitter, https://twitter.com/edconwaysky/status/1543219541337165824?s=21&t=TJSr_tUR1y1Ll9v3wWztiQ (A: 04.07.22)

Cook, R. (1997) 'Robin Cook's speech on the government's ethical foreign policy', *The Guardian*, 12 May, https://www.theguardian.com/world/1997/may/12/indonesia.ethicalforeignpolicy (A: 07.10.22)

Cook, R. (2003) 'Full text: Robin Cook speech', *CNN.com*, 18 March, edition. cnn.com/2003/WORLD/meast/03/18/sprj.irq.cook.speech/ (A: 13.07.23)

Cook, R. (2004) *Point of Departure: Diaries from the Front Bench* (London: Simon & Schuster)

Cooper-Searle, S., Livesey, F. and Allwood, J.M. (2018) 'Why are material efficiency solutions a limited part of the climate policy agenda? An application of the multiple streams framework to UK policy on CO_2 emissions from cars', *Environmental Policy and Governance*, 28, 1, 51–64, https://doi.org/10.1002/eet.1782

Corburn, J., Curl, S., Arredondo, G. and Malagon, J. (2014) 'Health in all urban policy, city services through the prism of health', *Journal of Urban Health: Bulletin of the New York Academy of Medicine*, 91, 4, 623–636, http://doi.org/10.1007/s11524-014-9886-3

Corbyn, J. (2016) 'My speech on the Labour case to vote remain in the EU in South Yorkshire', *Jeremycorbyn.com*, https://jeremycorbyn.org.uk/my-speech-on-the-labour-case-to-vote-remain-in-the-eu-in-south-yorkshire/ (A: 02.09.22)

Cornish, P. and Dorman, A. (2009) 'National defence in the age of austerity', *International Affairs*, 85, 4, 733–753, https://doi.org/10.1111/j.1468-2346.2009.00825.x

Costs of War (2021a) 'Iraqi civilians', https://watson.brown.edu/costsofwar/costs/human/civilians/iraqi (A: 07.10.22)

Costs of War (2021b) 'Iraqi refugees', https://watson.brown.edu/costsofwar/costs/human/refugees/iraqi#:~:text=Key%20Findings,internally%20displaced%20or%20refugees%20abroad (A: 07.10.22)

Cottrell-Boyce, J. (2013) 'Ending gang and youth violence: A critique', *Youth Justice*, 13, 3, 193–206, https://doi.org/10.1177/1473225413505382

Coulter, C. (2019) 'Northern Ireland's elusive peace dividend: Neoliberalism, austerity and the politics of class', *Capital & Class*, 43, 1, 123–138, https://doi.org/10.1177%2F0309816818818309

Council on Foreign Relations (2021) 'The Taliban', https://www.cfr.org/taliban/#!/ (A: 07.07.22)

COVID-19 Excess Mortality Collaborators (2022) 'Estimating excess mortality due to the COVID-19 pandemic: A systematic analysis of COVID-19-related mortality, 2020–21', *The Lancet*, 1–24, https://doi.org/10.1016/S0140-6736(21)02796-3

Cowley, P. and Norton, P. (1999) 'Rebels and rebellions: Conservative MPs in the 1992 Parliament', *The British Journal of Politics & International Relations*, 1, 1, 84–105, https://doi.org/10.1111/1467-856X.00005

Cowley, P. and Stuart, M. (2010) 'Where has all the trouble gone? British intra-party parliamentary divisions during the Lisbon ratification', *British Politics*, 5, 2, 133–148, https://doi.org/10.1057/bp.2010.1

Cowley, P. and Stuart, M. (2012) 'The cambusters: The conservative European Union referendum rebellion of October 2011', *The Political Quarterly*, 83, 2, 402–406, https://doi.org/10.1111/j.1467-923X.2012.02291.x

Cox, E., Royston, S. and Selby, J. (2016) *The Impacts of Non-Energy Policies on the Energy System: A Scoping Paper* (Sussex: UKERC), https://ukerc.ac.uk/publicati ons/impact-of-non-energy-policies-on-energy-systems/ (A: 06.05.22)

Coyle, D. (2014) *GDP: A Brief but Affectionate History* (Oxfordshire: Princeton University Press)

Cracknell, R. and Tunnicliffe, R. (2022) *Social Background of MPs 1979–2019* (London: House of Commons Library), https://researchbriefings.files.parliam ent.uk/documents/CBP-7483/CBP-7483.pdf (A: 14.05.22)

Craft, J. and Henderson, S. (2023) 'Policy staff and the evolving nature of policy analytical capacity in Australia, Britain, Canada, and New Zealand', *Policy Studies*, 1–25, https://doi.org/10.1080/01442872.2023.2233452

Crawley, S., Coffé, H. and Chapman, R. (2021) 'To what extent do interest group messages shape the public's climate change policy preferences?', *British Politics*, 16, 4, 436–455, https://doi.org/10.1057/s41293-020-00144-6

Crenshaw, K. (1989) 'Demarginalizing the intersection of race and sex: A Black feminist critique of antidiscrimination doctrine, feminist theory, and antiracist politics', *The University of Chicago Legal Forum*, 1, 139–167

Crenshaw, K., Gotanda, N., Peller, G. and Thomas, K. (1995) *Critical Race Theory: The Key Writings that Formed the Movement* (New York: The New Press)

Crisis (2019) 'Cover the cost: How gaps in Local Housing Allowance are impacting homelessness', https://www.crisis.org.uk/media/240377/cover_th e_cost_2019.pdf (A: 09.09.22)

Crossley, S. (2015a) '"Fast policy" in action: How the Troubled Families Programme expanded without any evaluation', *LSE British Politics and Policy*, 11 November, https://blogs.lse.ac.uk/politicsandpolicy/expansion-without-evaluat ion-the-troubled-families-programme-is-fast-policy-in-action/ (A: 19.09.22)

Crossley, S. (2015b) *The Troubled Families Programme: The Perfect Social Policy?* (London: Centre for Crime and Justice Studies), https://www.crimeandjust ice.org.uk/publications/troubled-families-programme-perfect-social-policy (A: 19.09.22)

Crossley, S. (2016a) 'Troubled Families: Well sold but morally compromised', *Centre for Crime and Criminal Justice Studies*, 3 March, https://www.crimeand justice.org.uk/resources/troubled-families-well-sold-morally-compromised (A: 19.09.22)

Crossley, S. (2016b) '"Realising the (troubled) family", "crafting the neoliberal state"', *Families, Relationships and Societies*, 5, 2, 263–279

Crossman, R. (1979) *The Crossman Diaries: Selections from the Diaries of a Cabinet Minister, 1964–1970* (London: Methuen)

Crotty, J. (2009) 'Structural causes of the global financial crisis: A critical assessment of the "new financial architecture"', *Cambridge Journal of Economics*, 33, 4, 563–580, https://doi.org/10.1093/cje/bep023

Crow, D. and Jones, M. (2018) 'Narratives as tools for influencing policy change', *Policy & Politics*, 46, 2, 217–234

Crowley, J. and Robinson, T. (2022) 'Drax: UK power station owner cuts down primary forests in Canada', *BBC News Panorama*, 3 October, https://www.bbc.co.uk/news/science-environment-63089348 (A: 04.10.22)

Cummins, I. (2018) 'The impact of austerity on mental health service provision: A UK perspective', *International Journal of Environmental Research and Public Health*, 15, 6, 1145, https://doi.org/10.3390/ijerph15061145

Curtice, J. (2013) 'Politicians, voters and democracy: The 2011 UK referendum on the Alternative Vote', *Electoral Studies*, 32, 2, 215–223, https://doi.org/10.1016/j.electstud.2012.10.010

Cutts, D. and Russell, A. (2015) 'From coalition to catastrophe: The electoral meltdown of the Liberal Democrats', *Parliamentary Affairs*, 68, 1, 70–87, https://doi.org/10.1093/pa/gsv028

Daddow, O. (2009) ' "Tony's war"? Blair, Kosovo and the interventionist impulse in British foreign policy', *International Affairs*, 85, 3, 547–560

Daddow, O. (2013) 'Margaret Thatcher, Tony Blair and the Eurosceptic tradition in Britain', *The British Journal of Politics and International Relations*, 15, 2, 210–227, https://doi.org/10.1111/j.1467-856X.2012.00534.x

Daddow, O. and Schnapper, P. (2013) 'Liberal intervention in the foreign policy thinking of Tony Blair and David Cameron', *Cambridge Review of International Affairs*, 26, 2, 330–349, https://doi.org/10.1080/09557571.2012.737763

Dagdeviren, H., Donoghue, M. and Wearmouth, A. (2019) 'When rhetoric does not translate to reality: Hardship, empowerment and the third sector in austerity localism', *Sociological Review*, 67, 1, 143–160, https://doi.org/10.1177/0038026118807631

Dalingwater, L. (2018) 'Gender inequalities in Britain: Bridging the gap in pay and prospects' in Fée, D. and Kober-Smith, A. (eds) *Inequalities in the UK* (Bingley: Emerald), 233–249

Daly, M.E. (2005) 'Gender mainstreaming in theory and practice', *Social Politics: International Studies in Gender, State & Society*, 12, 3, 433–450, https://doi.org/10.1093/sp/jxi023

Danchev, A. (2007) 'Tony Blair's Vietnam: The Iraq War and the "special relationship" in historical perspective', *Review of International Studies*, 33, 2, 189–203, https://doi.org/10.1017/S0260210507007462

Daniels, P. (1998) 'From hostility to "constructive engagement": The Europeanisation of the Labour Party', *West European Politics*, 21, 1, 72–96, https://doi.org/10.1080/01402389808425233

Darling, A. (2010) 'Budget 2010: Chancellor's statement in full', *The Guardian*, 24 March, https://www.theguardian.com/uk/2010/mar/24/budget-2010-chancellor-alistair-darling-speech-in-full (A: 09.09.22)

Darling, A. (2011) *Back from the Brink: 1000 Days at Number 11* (London: Atlantic Books)

Datta, A. (2005) 'CIA's final report: No WMD found in Iraq', *NBC News*, 26 April, https://www.nbcnews.com/id/wbna7634313 (A: 07.10.22)

Davies, J. (2009) 'Localism' in Flinders, M., Gamble, A., Hay, C. and Kenny, M. (eds) *The Oxford Handbook of British Politics* (Oxford: Oxford University Press), 404–422

Davies, N.G., Abbott, S., Barnard, R.C., Jarvis, C.I., Kucharski, A.J., Munday, J.D. et al (2021) 'Estimated transmissibility and impact of SARS-CoV-2 lineage B. 1.1. 7 in England', *Science*, 372, 6538, 1–9, https://doi.org/10.1126/science.abg3055

Davies, R. and Parken, A. (2018) 'Devolution, recession and the alleviation of inequality in Wales' in Fée, D. and Kober-Smith, A. (eds) *Inequalities in the UK* (Bingley: Emerald), 323–340

Davis, A. (2022) 'Time to take on the Treasury orthodoxy?', *UK in a Changing Europe*, 21 September, https://ukandeu.ac.uk/time-to-take-on-the-treasury-orthodoxy/ (A: 06.10.22)

Davis, D. (2016) 'David Davis gives a speech making the case for Brexit', *daviddavismp.com*, https://www.daviddavismp.com/david-davis-gives-a-speech-making-the-case-for-brexit/ (A: 08.09.22)

Day, P. and Klein, R. (2000) 'The politics of managing the health service' in Rhodes, R. (ed) *Transforming British Government*, vol 1 (London: Macmillan), 21–54

Dayan, M. (2021) 'The Brexit referendum five years on: What has it meant for the NHS?', *Nuffield Trust*, 23 June, https://www.nuffieldtrust.org.uk/news-item/the-brexit-referendum-five-years-on-what-has-it-meant-for-the-nhs (A: 08.09.22)

Dearden, L. (2020) 'Wembley murders: Six more police officers investigated over photos of dead sisters' bodies', *The Independent*, 25 August, https://www.independent.co.uk/news/uk/crime/wembley-murders-bibaa-henry-nicole-smallman-london-police-investigation-a9688146.html (A: 26.09.22)

Dearden, L. and Jin, W. (2014) 'The rise and demise of the National Scholarship Programme: Implications for university students', *Institute for Fiscal Studies*, 22 October, https://ifs.org.uk/articles/rise-and-demise-national-scholarship-programme-implications-university-students (A: 09.09.22)

De Goede, M. (2008) 'Beyond risk: Premediation and the post-9/11 security imagination', *Security Dialogue*, 39, 2–3, https://doi.org/10.1177/0967010608088773

Deleidi, M. and Mazzucato, M. (2018) 'The effectiveness and impact of post-2008 UK monetary policy', *Institute for Innovation and Public Purpose*, https://www.ucl.ac.uk/bartlett/public-purpose/sites/public-purpose/files/iipp-pb-03-qe-16-08-2018.pdf (A: 09.09.22)

Delis, A. and Ioannidis, C. (2021) 'Brexit: UK pound has not crashed yet, but here's why it will probably suffer in years to come', *The Conversation*, 13 January, https://theconversation.com/brexit-uk-pound-has-not-crashed-yet-but-heres-why-it-will-probably-suffer-in-years-to-come-152646 (A: 09.09.22)

Dennison, J. and Geddes, A. (2018) 'Brexit and the perils of "Europeanised" migration', *Journal of European Public Policy*, 25, 8, 1137–1153

Densley, J. (2011) 'Ganging up on gangs: Why the gang intervention industry needs an intervention', *The British Journal of Forensic Practice*, 13, 1, 12–23, https://doi.org/10.5042/bjfp.2011.0046

Densley, J. (2013) *How Gangs Work: An Ethnography of Youth Violence* (London: Springer)

Densley, J., Deuchar, R. and Harding, S. (2020) 'An introduction to gangs and serious youth violence in the United Kingdom', *Youth Justice*, 20, 1–2, 3–10, https://doi.org/10.1177/1473225420902848

Department of Agriculture, Environment and Rural Affairs (2019) *Northern Ireland Climate Change Adaptation Programme 2019–2024* (Belfast: DAERA), https://www.daera-ni.gov.uk/sites/default/files/publications/daera/Northern%20Irel and%20Climate%20Change%20Adaptation%20Programme%202019-2024%20 Final-Laid.PDF (A: 07.06.22)

Department for Business, Energy & Industrial Strategy (2020) '2018 UK greenhouse gas emissions: Final figures – data tables', *gov.uk*, 30 July, https://assets.publishing.service.gov.uk/government/uploads/system/uploads/atta chment_data/file/875508/final-greenhouse-gas-emissions-tables-2018.xlsx (A: 12.07.22)

Department for Business, Energy & Industrial Strategy (2021) 'Guidance: Carbon budgets', *gov.uk*, 13 July, https://www.gov.uk/guidance/carbon-budgets (A: 12.07.22)

Department for Business, Energy & Industrial Strategy (2022) '2020 green gas emissions, final figures', *gov.uk*, 1 February, https://assets.publishing.service. gov.uk/government/uploads/system/uploads/attachment_data/file/1051408/ 2020-final-greenhouse-gas-emissions-statistical-release.pdf (A: 06.09.22)

Department for Education (2021) 'Providing school meals during the coronavirus (COVID-19) outbreak', 5 October, https://www.gov.uk/government/publicati ons/covid-19-free-school-meals-guidance/covid-19-free-school-meals-guida nce-for-schools (A: 15.09.22)

Department for Energy Security & Net Zero (2023a) 'Guidance: Energy bills discount scheme', 9 January, https://www.gov.uk/guidance/energy-bills-disco unt-scheme (A: 26.04.23)

Department for Energy Security & Net Zero (2023b) 'Annual fuel poverty statistics in England, 2023 (2022 data)', 28 February, https://assets.publish ing.service.gov.uk/government/uploads/system/uploads/attachment_data/ file/1139133/annual-fuel-poverty-statistics-lilee-report-2023-2022-data.pdf (A: 27.04.23)

Department of Health and Social Care (2020) 'Temporary approval of home use for both stages of early medical abortion', 30 March, https://www.gov.uk/gov ernment/publications/temporary-approval-of-home-use-for-both-stages-of- early-medical-abortion--2 (A: 15.05.20)

Department of Transport (2007) *Towards a Sustainable Transport System* (Cm 7226) (London: Department of Transport)

Department of Homeland Security (United States) (2023) 'Countering Weapons of Mass Destruction Office (CWMD)', https://www.dhs.gov/employee-resources/countering-weapons-mass-destruction-office-cwmd#:~:text=A%20weapon%20of%20mass%20destruction%20is%20a%20nuclear%2C%20radiological%2C%20chemical,these%20weapons%20to%20harm%20Americans (A: 13.07.23)

De Pryck, K. (2021) 'Intergovernmental expert consensus in the making: The case of the Summary for Policy Makers of the IPCC 2014 Synthesis Report', *Global Environmental Politics*, 21, 1, 108–129, https://doi.org/10.1162/glep_a_00574

Devine, D., Gaskell, J., Jennings, W. and Stoker, G. (2021) 'Trust and the coronavirus pandemic: What are the consequences of and for trust? An early review of the literature', *Political Studies Review*, 19, 2, 274–285, https://doi.org/10.1177/1478929920948684

Diamond, P. (2011) 'Governing as New Labour: An inside account of the Blair and Brown years', *Political Studies Review*, 9, 2, 145–162, https://doi.org/10.1111/j.1478-9302.2011.00229.x

Diamond, P. (2019a) 'The Westminster system under the Cameron coalition: "Promiscuous partisanship" or institutional resilience?', *Public Policy and Administration*, 34, 3, 241–261, https://journals.sagepub.com/doi/10.1177/0952076717737595

Diamond, P. (2019b) *The End of Whitehall?* (London: Palgrave)

Diamond, P. (2020a) 'Externalization and politicization in policy advisory systems: A case study of contestable policy-making 2010–2015', *Public Money & Management*, 40, 1, 42–51, https://doi.org/10.1080/09540962.2019.1583890

Diamond, P. (2020b) 'Polycentric governance and policy advice: Lessons from Whitehall policy advisory systems', *Policy & Politics*, 48, 4, 563–581, https://doi.org/10.1332/030557320X15870482509817

Diamond, P. (2021) 'Core executive politics in the Cameron era, 2010–16: The dynamics of Whitehall reform', *Government and Opposition*, 1–19, https://doi.org/10.1017/gov.2021.47

Diamond, P. and Laffin, M. (2022) 'The United Kingdom and the pandemic: Problems of central control and coordination', *Local Government Studies*, 48, 2, 211–231, https://doi.org/10.1080/03003930.2021.1997744

Diamond, P. and Richards, D. (2023) 'What does Dominic Raab's resignation tell us about the current state of minister–civil servant relations?', *Mile End Institute*, 22 April, https://www.qmul.ac.uk/mei/news-and-opinion/items/what-does-dominic-raabs-resignation-tell-us-about-the-current-state-of-minister-civil-servant-relations.html (A: 02.05.23)

Dillon, D. and Fanning, B. (2011) *Lessons for the Big Society: Planning, Regeneration and the Politics of Community Participation* (Abingdon: Routledge)

Dimbleby, D. (2020) *The Fault Line*, Somethin' Else Productions, https://link.chtbl.com/CuMN_OQT (A: 07.10.22)

Dimitrov, R.S. (2016) 'The Paris agreement on climate change: Behind closed doors', *Global Environmental Politics*, 16, 3, 1–11, https://direct.mit.edu/glep/article/16/3/1/14984/The-Paris-Agreement-on-Climate-Change-Behind (A: 05.06.22)

Dinan, D. (2020) 'The Single European Act', *Oxford Research Encyclopedia of Politics*, https://doi.org/10.1093/acrefore/9780190228637.013.1053

Dizard, J. (2004) 'How Ahmed Chalabi conned the neocons', *Salon*, 4 May, https://samizdat.co/shelf/documents/2004/05.04-chalabi/chalabi.pdf (A: 07.10.22)

Dobbs, M. (2011) *House of Cards* (London: HarperCollins)

Dobson, M.J. (2019) 'The last forum of accountability? State secrecy, intelligence and freedom of information in the United Kingdom', *British Journal of Politics and International Relations*, 21, 2, 312–329, https://doi.org/10.1177/1369148118806125

Docherty, I. (2003) 'Policy, politics, and sustainable transport' in Docherty, I. and Shaw, J. (eds) *New Deal for Transport: The UK's Struggle with the Sustainable Transport Agenda* (Bristol: Policy Press), 1–15

Docherty, I. and Shaw, J. (2003) 'Preface' in Docherty, I. and Shaw, J. (eds) *New Deal for Transport: The UK's Struggle with the Sustainable Transport Agenda* (Bristol: Policy Press), i–iv

Docherty, I. and Shaw, J. (2011) 'The transformation of transport policy in Great Britain? "New Realism" and New Labour's decade of displacement activity', *Environment and Planning A*, 43, 1, 224–251, https://doi.org/10.1068/a43184

Dodd, V. (2011) 'Bratton in Britain: Can London learn lessons from former LAPD chief?', *The Guardian*, 14 August, https://www.theguardian.com/uk/2011/aug/14/bill-bratton-police-track-record (A: 26.09.22)

Dolowitz, D. (2004) 'Prosperity and fairness? Can New Labour bring fairness to the 21st century by following the dictates of endogenous growth?', *British Journal of Politics & International Relations*, 6, 2, 213–230

Dolowitz, D. and Marsh, D. (1996) 'Who learns what from whom: A review of the policy transfer literature', *Political Studies*, 44, 2, 343–357

Dommett, K. and Flinders, M. (2015) 'The centre strikes back: Meta-governance, delegation, and the core executive in the United Kingdom, 2010–14', *Public Administration*, 93, 1, 1–16

Dorey, P. (2005a) *Policy Making in Britain* (London: SAGE)

Dorey, P. (ed) (2005b) *Developments in British Public Policy* (London: SAGE)

Dorling, D. (2010) *Injustice: Why Social Inequality Still Persists* (Bristol: Policy Press)

Dorrington, S., Roberts, E., Mykletun, A., Hatch, S., Madan, I. and Hotopf, M. (2018) 'Systematic review of fit note use for workers in the UK', *Occupational and Environmental Medicine*, 75, 7, 530–539, https://doi.org/10.1136/oemed-2017-104730

Doucet, F. (2019) *Centering the Margins: (Re)defining Useful Research Evidence through Critical Perspectives* (New York: William T. Grant Foundation), https://wtgrantfoundation.org/library/uploads/2019/12/Fabienne-Doucet-2019-WTG-Digest.pdf (A: 05.05.22)

Dowding, K. (2015) *The Philosophy and Methods of Political Science* (London: Palgrave)

Dowding, K. (2021) *It's the Government, Stupid* (Bristol: Bristol University Press)

Downing, E. and Coe, S. (2018) *Brexit: Future UK Agriculture Policy* (Briefing Paper CBP 8218) (London: House of Commons Library), https://www.parliam ent.uk/globalassets/documents/commons-library/Brexit-UK-agriculture-pol icy-CBP-8218.pdf (A: 05.07.22)

Doyle, J. and Connolly, E. (2019) 'The effects of Brexit on the Good Friday Agreement and the Northern Ireland Peace Process' in Baciu, C.A. and Doyle, J. (eds) *Peace, Security and Defence Cooperation in Post-Brexit Europe* (Cham: Springer), 79–95

Draper, R. (2020) 'Colin Powell still wants answers', *The New York Times*, 16 July, https://www.nytimes.com/2020/07/16/magazine/colin-powell-iraq-war. html (A: 07.09.22)

Drewry, G. (1994) 'The civil service: From the 1940s to "next steps" and beyond', *Parliamentary Affairs*, 47, 4, 583–596

Dudley, G. and Richardson, J. (2000) *Why Does Policy Change? Lessons from British Transport Policy 1945–99* (London: Routledge)

Duggett, M. (2009) 'The return of the Westminster supermodel', *Public Money and Management*, 29, 1, 7–8

Dunleavy, P. (1991) *Democracy and Public Choice* (Hemel Hempstead: Harvester Wheatsheaf)

Dunleavy, P. (2006) 'The Westminster model and the distinctiveness of British politics' in Dunleavy, P., Heffernan, R., Cowley, P. and Hay, C. (eds) *Developments in British Politics 8* (London: Palgrave), 315–341

Dunleavy, P. (2019) '"The bureaucracy" as an interest group' in Congleton, R., Grofman, B. and Voigt, S. (eds) *The Oxford Handbook of Public Choice* (Oxford: Oxford University Press), 567–584

Dunleavy, P. and Rhodes, R. (1990) 'Core executive studies in Britain', *Public Administration*, 68, 1, 3–28

Dunleavy, P., Margetts, H., Bastow, S. and Tinkler, J. (2005) 'New public management is dead—long live digital-era governance', *Journal of Public Administration Research and Theory*, 16, 3, 467–494, https://doi.org/10.1093/ jopart/mui057

Dunleavy, P., Park, A. and Taylor, R. (2018) *The UK's Changing Democracy: The 2018 Democratic Audit* (London: LSE Press)

Dunlop, C. and Radaelli, C. (2013) 'Systematising policy learning: From monolith to dimensions', *Political Studies Review*, 61, 3, 599–619

Dunlop, C. and Radaelli, C. (2018) 'The lessons of policy learning: Types, triggers, hindrances and pathologies', *Policy & Politics*, 46, 2, 255–272

Dunlop, C., James, S. and Radaelli, C. (2020) 'Can't get no learning: The Brexit fiasco through the lens of policy learning', *Journal of European Public Policy*, 27, 5, 703–722, https://doi.org/10.1080/13501763.2019.1667415

Dunn, D.H. (2008) 'The double interregnum: UK–US relations beyond Blair and Bush', *International Affairs*, 84, 6, 1131–1143, https://doi.org/10.1111/ j.1468-2346.2008.00761.x

Dunn, M. and Smith, S. (1990) 'Economic policy and privatization' in Savage, S. and Robins, L. (eds) *Public Policy under Thatcher* (London: Macmillan), 77–95

Dunn, W. (2017) *Public Policy Analysis*, 6th edn (London: Routledge)

Duparc-Portier, G. and Figus, G. (2023) 'New Brexit deal will be better for Northern Ireland's economy than the protocol, research suggests', *The Conversation*, 3 March, https://theconversation.com/new-brexit-deal-will-be-better-for-northern-irelands-economy-than-the-protocol-research-sugge sts-200999 (A: 20.04.23)

Durose, C. (2011) 'Revisiting Lipsky: front-line work in UK local governance', *Political Studies*, 59, 4, 978–995

Durose, C. and Gains, F. (2005) 'Engendering the machinery of governance' in Annesley, C., Gains, F. and Rummery, K. (eds) *Women and New Labour* (Bristol: Policy Press), 93–114

Durose, C. and Richardson, L. (eds) (2015) *Designing Public Policy for Co-production* (Bristol: Policy Press)

Durose, C. and Lowndes, V. (2023) 'Gendering discretion: Why street-level bureaucracy needs a gendered lens', *Political Studies*, 1–24, https://doi.org/10.1177/00323217231178630

Durose, C., Richardson, L., Combs, R., Eason, C. and Gains, F. (2013) '"Acceptable difference": Diversity, representation and pathways to UK politics', *Parliamentary Affairs*, 66, 2, 246–267

Durrant, T. (2022) '"Partygate" investigations', 30 March, https://www.institu teforgovernment.org.uk/article/explainer/partygate-investigations (A: 24.03.23)

Dustin, M., Ferreira, N. and Millns, S. (2019) *Gender and Queer Perspectives on Brexit* (London: Palgrave)

DWP (Department for Work and Pensions) (2023a) *The Impact of Benefit Sanctions on Employment Outcomes* (released after an FOI request), https://www.gov.uk/government/publications/the-impact-of-benefit-sanctions-on-employment-outcomes-draft-report (A: 28.04.23)

DWP (2023b) 'State pension age review published', press release, https://www.gov.uk/government/news/state-pension-age-review-published#:~:text=The%20Government%20has%20confirmed%20the,following%20a%20rev iew%20published%20today (A: 02.05.23)

Dye, T. (1976) *Policy Analysis: What Governments Do, Why They Do It and What Difference It Makes* (Tuscaloosa: University of Alabama Press)

Dyson, S.B. (2006) 'Personality and foreign policy: Tony Blair's Iraq decisions', *Foreign Policy Analysis*, 2, 3, 289–306

Eagle, R., Jones, A. and Greig, A. (2017) 'Localism and the environment: A critical review of UK government localism strategy 2010–2015', *Local Economy*, 32, 1, 55–72, https://doi.org/10.1177/0269094216687710

Edmonds, T., Webb, D. and Long, R. (2011) 'The economic crisis: Policy responses', *House of Commons Library*, https://researchbriefings.files.parliament.uk/documents/SN04968/SN04968.pdf (A: 09.09.22)

Edwards, G. (2020) 'The UK's view of Brexit and its foreign policy implications' in Chaban, N., Niemann, A. and Speyer, J. (eds) *Changing Perceptions of the EU at Times of Brexit* (London: Routledge), 25–41

EHRC (Equality and Human Rights Commission) (2010) 'Equality, human rights and good relations in 2010', 1 March, https://www.equalityhumanrights.com/en/publication-download/how-fair-britain (A: 26.09.22)

EHRC (2023) 'Letter to Rt Hon Kemi Badenoch MP Secretary of State for Business, Energy and Industrial Strategy and Minister for Women and Equalities', 3 April, https://equalityhumanrights.com/en/file/43056/download (A: 28.04.23)

Electoral Commission (2016) 'Electoral Commission designates "Vote Leave Ltd" and "The In Campaign Ltd" as lead campaigners at EU Referendum', 13 April, https://www.electoralcommission.org.uk/electoral-commission-designates-vote-leave-ltd-and-campaign-ltd-lead-campaigners-eu-referendum (A: 17.08.22)

Electoral Commission (2019) 'EU referendum results by region: Scotland', https://www.electoralcommission.org.uk/who-we-are-and-what-we-do/elections-and-referendums/past-elections-and-referendums/eu-referendum/results-and-turnout-eu-referendum/eu-referendum-results-region-scotland (A: 27.01.22)

El-Enany, N. (2020) 'Europe's colonial embrace and the Brexit nostalgia for empire are two sides of the same coin', *LSE Brexit*, 29 April, https://blogs.lse.ac.uk/brexit/2020/04/29/europes-colonial-embrace-and-brexit-as-nostalgia-for-empire-are-part-of-the-same-story/ (A: 19.09.22)

Elliott, I.C., Bottom, K.A., Carmichael, P., Liddle, J., Martin, S. and Pyper, R. (2022) 'The fragmentation of public administration: Differentiated and decentered governance in the (dis)United Kingdom', *Public Administration*, 100, 1, 98–115

Elliott, L. (2009) 'We have to work our way through this crisis', *The Guardian*, 19 January, https://www.theguardian.com/business/video/2009/jan/19/banking-creditcrunch (A: 09.09.22)

Elliott, L. (2010) 'Alistair Darling: We will cut deeper than Margaret Thatcher', *The Guardian*, 25 March, https://www.theguardian.com/politics/2010/mar/25/alistair-darling-cut-deeper-margaret-thatcher (A: 11.07.23)

Elliott, L. (2013) 'George Osborne told by IMF chief: Rethink your austerity plan', *The Guardian*, 18 April, https://www.theguardian.com/politics/2013/apr/18/george-osborne-imf-austerity (A: 09.09.22)

Ellwood, T. (2022) 'We can upgrade Brexit and ease the cost of living by going back to the single market', *The House*, 1 June, https://www.politicshome.com/thehouse/article/we-can-upgrade-brexit-and-ease-the-cost-of-living-by-going-back-to-the-single-market (A: 07.09.22)

Emejulu, A. (2018) 'On the problems and possibilities of feminist solidarity: The Women's March one year on', *IPPR Progressive Review*, 24, 4, 267–273, https://doi.org/10.1111/newe.12064

Emejulu, A. and Bassel, L. (2015) 'Minority women, austerity and activism', *Race & Class*, 57, 2, 86–95, https://doi.org/10.1177/0306396815595913

Emejulu, A. and van der Scheer, I. (2022) 'Refusing politics as usual: Mapping women of colour's radical praxis in London and Amsterdam', *Identities*, 29, 1, 9–26, https://doi.org/10.1080/1070289X.2021.1914951

Emmerson, C. (2022) 'How to fix the pensions triple lock but still protect pensioners from high inflation', *The Conversation*, 12 August, https://theconve rsation.com/how-to-fix-the-pensions-triple-lock-but-still-protect-pensioners-from-high-inflation-186611#:~:text=The%20pensions%20triple%20lock%20 was,9.4%25)%20or%202.5%25 (A: 02.09.22)

Emmerson, C. and Stockton, I. (2020) 'How does the size of the UK's fiscal response to coronavirus compare with other countries'?', *Institute for Fiscal Studies*, 14 May, https://www.ifs.org.uk/publications/14845 (A: 14.05.20)

Enderlein, H. (2018) 'The four freedoms in the EU: Are they inseparable?', *Jacques Delors Institut*, https://institutdelors.eu/wp-content/uploads/2018/01/ 171024jdigrundfreiheitenenwebeinzelseitena4.pdf (A: 07.09.22)

Engeli, I., Green-Pedersen, C. and Larsen, L.T. (2012) 'How to study the two worlds of morality politics' in Engeli, I., Green-Pedersen, C. and Larsen, L.T. (eds) *Morality Politics in Western Europe* (London: Palgrave), 27–34

Enserink, B., Koppenjan, J. and Mayer, I. (2013) 'A policy sciences view on policy analysis' in Thissen, W. and Walker, W. (eds) *Public Policy Analysis* (London: Springer), 11–40

Equality and Human Rights Commission (2019) 'The cumulative impact of tax and welfare reforms – Country-specific appendix: Scotland', https://www.equa lityhumanrights.com/sites/default/files/cumulative-impact-assessment-report-scotland-appendix_0.pdf (A: 09.09.22)

Erken, H., Hayat, R., Prins, C., Heijmerikx, M. and de Vreede, I. (2018) 'Measuring the permanent costs of Brexit', *National Institute Economic Review*, 244, R46–R55, https://doi.org/10.1177/002795011824400114

Escandón, K., Rasmussen, A.L., Bogoch, I.I., Murray, E.J., Escandón, K., Popescu, S.V. and Kindrachuk, J. (2021) 'COVID-19 false dichotomies and a comprehensive review of the evidence regarding public health, COVID-19 symptomatology, SARS-CoV-2 transmission, mask wearing, and reinfection', *BMC Infectious Diseases*, 21, 1, 1–47, https://doi.org/10.1186/s12879-021-06357-4

Etmanski, C. (2012) 'A critical race and class analysis of learning in the organic farming movement', *Australian Journal of Adult Learning*, 52, 3, 485–506, https:// files.eric.ed.gov/fulltext/EJ1000191.pdf (A: 26.09.22)

European Commission (2022a) 'Areas of EU action', https://ec.europa.eu/info/ about-european-commission/what-european-commission-does/law/areas-eu-action_en (A: 17.08.22)

European Commission (2022b) 'The common agricultural policy at a glance', https://ec.europa.eu/info/food-farming-fisheries/key-policies/common-agric ultural-policy/cap-glance_en (A: 08.07.22)

European Commission (2023) 'Questions and answers: Political agreement in principle on the Windsor Framework, a new way forward for the Protocol on Ireland/Northern Ireland', https://ec.europa.eu/commission/presscorner/detail/en/qanda_23_1271 (A: 20.04.23)

European Council (2017) 'European Council (Art. 50) guidelines for Brexit negotiations', press release, 29 April, https://www.consilium.europa.eu/en/press/press-releases/2017/04/29/euco-brexit-guidelines/ (A: 23.08.22)

European Economic and Social Committee (2017) 'There is no cherry-picking on Brexit', 6 July, https://www.eesc.europa.eu/en/news-media/press-releases/there-no-cherry-picking-brexit (A: 07.09.22)

European Union (2022) 'Types of legislation', https://european-union.europa.eu/institutions-law-budget/law/types-legislation_en (A: 18.05.22)

Evans, E. (2014) *The Politics of Third Wave Feminisms* (London: Palgrave Macmillan)

Evans, E. and Reher, S. (2023) 'Gender, disability and political representation: understanding the experiences of disabled women', *European Journal of Politics and Gender*, 1–18, DOI: 10.1332/251510823X16779382116831

Exadaktylos, T. and Zahariadis, N. (2014) 'Quid pro quo: Political trust and policy implementation in Greece during the age of austerity', *Politics & Policy*, 42, 1, 160–183, https://doi.org/10.1111/polp.12058

Exworthy, M. and Powell, M. (2004) 'Big windows and little windows: Implementation in the "congested state"', *Public Administration*, 82, 2, 263–281

Fahy, D. (2017) 'Objectivity, false balance, and advocacy in news coverage of climate change', *Oxford Research Encyclopedia of Climate Science*, 29 March, https://doi.org/10.1093/acrefore/9780190228620.013.345 (A: 22.04.22)

Falkner, R. (2016) 'The Paris Agreement and the new logic of international climate politics', *International Affairs*, 92, 5, 1107–1125, https://doi.org/10.1111/1468-2346.12708

Fankhauser, S., Averchenkova, A. and Finnegan, J. (2018) *10 Years of the UK Climate Change Act* (London: CCCEP), https://www.researchgate.net/publication/325761231_10_years_of_the_UK_Climate_Change_Act (A: 18.06.22)

FAO (Food and Agriculture Organization) (2023) *Integrating Climate Change, Biodiversity, Environment and SDGs into Food and Agriculture Policies: A Sourcebook for Country Implementation* (Rome: FAO)

Farage, N. (2016) 'Nigel Farage: Why we must vote LEAVE in the EU referendum', *Daily Express*, 21 June, https://www.express.co.uk/comment/expresscomment/681776/nigel-farage-eu-referendum-brexit-vote-leave-independence-ukip (A: 02.09.22)

Farkas, A. (1996) 'Evolutionary models in foreign policy analysis', *International Studies Quarterly*, 40, 3, 343–361, https://doi.org/10.2307/2600715

Farr, K. (2009) 'Extreme war rape in today's civil-war-torn states: A contextual and comparative analysis', *Gender Issues*, 26, 1, 1–41, https://doi.org/10.1007/s12147-009-9068-x

Farrell, C. and Law, J. (1999) 'Changing forms of accountability in education?', *Public Administration*, 77, 2, 293–310

Farron, T. (2016) 'Tim Farron – 2016 speech on the EU', *UK Political Speeches Archive*, https://www.ukpol.co.uk/tim-farron-2016-speech-on-the-eu/ (A: 05.09.22)

Faulkner, C.M. and Gray, D.H. (2014) 'The emergence of Al Qaeda in the Arabian Peninsula (AQAP) and the effectiveness of US counterterrorism efforts', *Global Security Studies*, 5, 1, 1–16

Fée, D. and Kober-Smith, A. (2018) 'Introduction' in Fée, D. and Kober-Smith, A. (eds) *Inequalities in the UK: New Discourses, Evolutions and Actions* (Bingley: Emerald Publishing), 1–15

Ferlie, E., Ashburner, L., Fitzgerald, L. and Pettigrew, A. (1996) *The New Public Management in Action* (Oxford: Oxford University Press)

Fetzer, T. and Wang, S. (2020) 'Measuring the regional economic cost of Brexit: Evidence up to 2019', *CAGE*, https://warwick.ac.uk/fac/soc/econom ics/research/centres/cage/manage/publications/wp486.2020.pdf (A: 08.09.22)

Fielding, S. (2002) *The Labour Party: Continuity and Change in the Making of 'New' Labour* (London: Palgrave)

Figueira, F. and Martill, B. (2020) 'Bounded rationality and the Brexit negotiations: Why Britain failed to understand the EU', *Journal of European Public Policy*, 28, 12, 1871–1889, https://doi.org/10.1080/13501763.2020.1810103

Finch, D. and Vriend, M. (2023) 'Public health grant: What it is and why greater investment is needed', *The Health Foundation*, 17 March, https://www.health.org.uk/news-and-comment/charts-and-infographics/public-health-grant-what-it-is-and-why-greater-investment-is-needed (A: 25.04.23)

Finer, S. (1975) *Adversary Politics and Electoral Reform* (London: Wigram)

Finlan, A. (2003) *The Gulf War 1991* (London: Bloomsbury)

Finlayson, A., Jarvis, L. and Lister, M. (2023) 'COVID-19 and "the public": U.K. government, discourse and the British political tradition', *Contemporary Politics*, 1–18, https://doi.org/10.1080/13569775.2022.2162206

Fisher, M. (2012) 'Beyond freedom fries: The roots of American Francophobia', *The Atlantic*, 23 April, https://www.theatlantic.com/international/archive/2012/04/beyond-freedom-fries-the-roots-of-american-francophobia/256253/ (A: 07.10.22)

Fisher, P. and Nandi, A. (2015) 'Poverty across ethnic groups through recession and austerity', *Joseph Rowntree Foundation*, https://www.jrf.org.uk/report/pove rty-across-ethnic-groups-through-recession-and-austerity (A: 09.09.22)

Fitch-Roy, O. and Fairbrass, J. (2018) *Negotiating the EU's 2030 Climate and Energy Framework* (London: Palgrave)

Fitzgerald, N. and Cairney, P. (2022) 'National objectives, local policy making: Public health efforts to translate national legislation into local policy in Scottish alcohol licensing', *Evidence & Policy*, 1–21, https://doi.org/10.1332/174426421X16397418342227

Fletcher, L. and Martin, K. (2019) 'Odey homes in on UK assets ahead of key Brexit vote', *The Financial Times*, 11 January, https://www.ft.com/content/cc491f18-15bc-11e9-a581-4ff78404524e (A: 08.09.22)

Flinders, M. (2008) *Delegated Governance and the British State* (Oxford: Oxford University Press)

Flinders, M. (2010) *Democratic Drift* (Oxford: Oxford University Press)

Flinders, M. (2012) *Defending Politics: Why Democracy Matters in the 21st Century* (Oxford: Oxford University Press)

Flinders, M. (2022) 'Liz Truss resigns as prime minister: The five causes of her downfall explained', *The Conversation*, 20 October, https://theconversation.com/liz-truss-resigns-as-prime-minister-the-five-causes-of-her-downfall-explained-192979 (A: 01.05.22)

Flinders, M. and Skelcher, C. (2012) 'Shrinking the quango state', *Public Money & Management*, 32, 5, 327–334

Flinders, M., Wood, M. and Cunningham, M. (2016) 'The politics of co-production: Risks, limits and pollution', *Evidence & Policy*, 12, 2, 261–279, https://doi.org/10.1332/174426415X14412037949967

Flint, S.W., Brown, A., Sanders, G. and Tahrani, A.A. (2021) 'Exploring the awareness, attitudes, and actions (AAA) of UK adults at high risk of severe illness from COVID-19', *PloS One*, 16, 11, e0259376, https://doi.org/10.1371/journal.pone.0259376

Foad, C.M., Whitmarsh, L., Hanel, P.H. and Haddock, G. (2021) 'The limitations of polling data in understanding public support for COVID-19 lockdown policies', *Royal Society Open Science*, 8, 7, 210678, 1–11, https://doi.org/10.1098/rsos.210678

Foley, M. (2008) 'The presidential dynamics of leadership decline in contemporary British politics: The illustrative case of Tony Blair', *Contemporary Politics*, 14, 1, 53–69, https://doi.org/10.1080/13569770801913264

Foreign Affairs Committee (2022) 'Missing in action: UK leadership and the withdrawal from Afghanistan – report summary', *House of Commons*, https://publications.parliament.uk/pa/cm5803/cmselect/cmfaff/169/summary.html (A: 07.10.22)

Foreign, Commonwealth & Development Office (2021) 'UK boost to advance gender equality in climate action', https://www.gov.uk/government/news/uk-boost-to-advance-gender-equality-in-climate-action (A: 15.07.22)

Forrester-Jones, R., Murphy, G., Randall, A., Malli, M., Sams, L. and Harrison, R. (2020) 'Becoming less eligible? Intellectual disability services in the age of austerity', *NIHR*, https://www.sscr.nihr.ac.uk/wp-content/uploads/SSCR-research-findings_RF100.pdf (A: 09.09.22)

Forster, A. (2002) *Euroscepticism in Contemporary British Politics: Opposition to Europe in the British Conservative and Labour Parties since 1945* (London: Routledge)

Foster, C. (2001) 'The civil service under stress: The fall in civil service power and authority', *Public Administration*, 79, 3, 725–749

Foy, S. (2022) 'Key points: Jeremy Hunt's mini-Budget tax reversals', *The Telegraph*, 19 October, https://www.telegraph.co.uk/business/2022/10/18/key-points-jeremy-hunt-statement-mean-economy/ (A: 02.05.23)

Francis-Devine, B., Bolton, P., Keep, M. and Harari, D. (2022) 'Rising cost of living in the UK', *House of Commons Library*, 2 September, https://researchbr iefings.files.parliament.uk/documents/CBP-9428/CBP-9428.pdf (A: 08.09.22)

Freeden, M. (2017) 'After the Brexit referendum: Revisiting populism as an ideology', *Journal of Political Ideologies*, 1, 1–11, https://doi.org/10.1080/13569 317.2016.1260813

Frosini, J.O. and Gilbert, M.F. (2020) 'The Brexit car crash: Using E.H. Carr to explain Britain's choice to leave the European Union in 2016', *Journal of European Public Policy*, 27, 5, 761–778, https://doi.org/10.1080/13501763.2019.1676820

Full Fact (2017) '£350 million EU claim "a clear misuse of official statistics"', *Full Fact*, 19 September, https://fullfact.org/europe/350-million-week-boris-johnson-statistics-authority-misuse/ (A: 19.08.22)

Furlong, J. (2022) 'London air pollution: expanding the ULEZ is good but it won't work by itself', The Conversation, 9 December, https://theconversation. com/london-air-pollution-expanding-the-ulez-is-good-but-it-wont-work-by-itself-195587 (A: 7.8.23)

Fusacchia, I., Salvatici, L. and Winters, L.A. (2022) 'The consequences of the Trade and Cooperation Agreement for the UK's international trade', *Oxford Review of Economic Policy*, 38, 1, 27–49, https://doi.org/10.1093/oxrep/grab052

G20 (2022) 'About the G20', https://g20.org/about-the-g20/ (A: 01.09.22)

Gains, F. and Stoker, G. (2009) 'Delivering "public value": Implications for accountability and legitimacy', *Parliamentary Affairs*, 62, 3, 438–455

Gallagher, J. (2018) 'Chequers produces the best and most elaborate fudge available', *LSE Brexit Blog*, 9 July, eprints.lse.ac.uk/91009/ (A: 08.09.22)

Gallagher, J. and Raffe, D. (2012) 'Higher education policy in post-devolution UK: More convergence than divergence?', *Journal of Education Policy*, 27, 4, 467–490, https://doi.org/10.1080/02680939.2011.626080

Gamble, A. (1994) *The Free Economy and the Strong State: The Politics of Thatcherism*, 2nd edn (Basingstoke: Palgrave)

Gamble, A. (2012) 'Eurozone futures: The Conservatives' dilemma', *Public Policy Research*, 19, 2, 109–111, https://doi.org/10.1111/j.1744-540X.2012.00693.x

Gamble, A. (2015) 'The economy', *Parliamentary Affairs*, 68, 1, 154–167, https:// doi.org/10.1093/pa/gsv033

Gamble, A. (2018) 'Taking back control: The political implications of Brexit', *Journal of European Public Policy*, 25, 8, 1215–1232, https://doi.org/10.1080/ 13501763.2018.1467952

Garland, J. and Palese, M. (2019) *Westminster beyond Brexit: Ending the Politics of Division* (London: Electoral Reform Society), https://www.electoral-reform. org.uk/latest-news-and-research/publications/westminster-beyond-brexit-end ing-the-politics-of-division/ (A: 11.07.23)

Garnham, A. (2018) 'Something needs saying about Universal Credit and women – it is discrimination by design', *Child Poverty Action Group*, https:// cpag.org.uk/news-blogs/news-listings/something-needs-saying-about-univer sal-credit-and-women---it-discrimination (A: 08.09.22)

Gaskarth, J. (2013) 'Interpreting ethical foreign policy: Traditions and dilemmas for policymakers', *The British Journal of Politics and International Relations*, 15, 2, 192–209, https://doi.org/10.1111/j.1467-856X.2012.00535.x

Gaskell, J., Stoker, G., Jennings, W. and Devine, D. (2020) 'Covid-19 and the blunders of our governments', *Political Quarterly*, 91, 3, 523–533, https://doi.org/10.1111/1467-923X.12894

Gavin, N.T. (2002) 'Imagining Europe: Political identity and British television coverage of the European economy', *British Journal of Politics and International Relations*, 2, 3, 352–373, https://doi.org/10.1111/1467-856X.00041

Gedalof, I. (2022) 'Eviscerating equality: Normative whiteness and Conservative equality policy', *Critical Social Policy*, 43, 2, 257–276, https://doi.org/10.1177/02610183221093788

Geels, F. (2004) 'From sectoral systems of innovation to socio-technical systems: Insights about dynamics and change from sociology and institutional theory', *Research Policy*, 33, 6–7, 897–920, https://doi.org/10.1016/j.respol.2004.01.015

Geels, F.W., Kern, F., Fuchs, G., Hinderer, N., Kungl, G., Mylan, J., Neukirch, M. and Wassermann, S. (2016) 'The enactment of socio–technical transition pathways: A reformulated typology and a comparative multi-level analysis of the German and UK low-carbon electricity transitions (1990–2014)', *Research Policy*, 45, 4, 896–913, https://doi.org/10.1016/j.respol.2016.01.015

Gentleman, A. (2019) *The Windrush Betrayal: Exposing the Hostile Environment* (London: Faber)

Gentleman, A. (2022) 'Windrush scandal caused by "30 years of racist immigration laws" – report', *The Guardian*, 29 May, https://www.theguardian.com/uk-news/2022/may/29/windrush-scandal-caused-by-30-years-of-racist-immigration-laws-report (A: 26.09.22)

George, J. (2021) 'A lesson on critical race theory', *American Bar Association*, 11 January, https://www.americanbar.org/groups/crsj/publications/human_rights_magazine_home/civil-rights-reimagining-policing/a-lesson-on-critical-race-theory/ (A: 26.09.22)

Geoghan, P. and Scott, R. (2020) 'Government accused of "cronyism" after Tory councillor wins £156m COVID contract', *Open Democracy*, 9 October, https://www.opendemocracy.net/en/dark-money-investigations/government-accused-of-cronyism-after-tory-councillor-wins-156m-covid-contract/ (A: 11.07.23)

Geva-May, I. (2004) 'Riding the wave of opportunity: Termination in public policy', *Journal of Public Administration Research and Theory*, 14, 3, 309–333

Geyer, R. (2012) 'Can complexity move UK policy beyond "evidence-based policy making" and the "audit culture"? Applying a "complexity cascade" to education and health policy', *Political Studies*, 60, 1, 20–43

Gibb, K. (2015) 'The multiple policy failures of the UK bedroom tax', *International Journal of Housing Policy*, 15, 2, 148–166, https://doi.org/10.1080/14616718.2014.992681

Giddens, A. (2000) *The Third Way and Its Critics: Sequel to 'The Third Way'* (London: Polity)

Gigerenzer, G. (2001) 'The adaptive toolbox' in Gigerenzer, G. and Selton, R. (eds) *Bounded Rationality: The Adaptive Toolbox* (Cambridge, MA: MIT Press), 37–50

Gilead, T. (2019) 'Promoting distributive justice in education and the challenge of unpredictability', *Studies in Philosophy and Education*, 38, 439–451, https://doi.org/10.1007/s11217-019-09655-2

Gill, M. (2020a) 'Mass testing for covid-19 in the UK', *British Medical Journal*, 371, m4436, https://doi.org/10.1136/bmj.m4436

Gill, M. (2020b) 'Public trust and the public's health: Two sides of the same coin?', *BMJ Opinion*, 28 May, https://blogs.bmj.com/bmj/2020/05/28/public-trust-and-the-publics-health-two-sides-of-the-same-coin/ (A: 13.07.20)

Gill, M. (2022) 'Why the government's "war on woke" is failing', *The New Statesman*, 17 April, https://www.newstatesman.com/comment/2022/04/why-the-war-on-woke-is-imploding (A: 26.09.22)

Gillan, K., Pickerill, J. and Webster, F. (2008) *Anti-War Activism* (Basingstoke: Palgrave Macmillan)

Gillard, R. (2016) 'Unravelling the United Kingdom's climate policy consensus: The power of ideas, discourse and institutions', *Global Environmental Change*, 40, 26–36, https://doi.org/10.1016/j.gloenvcha.2016.06.012

Gillard, R. and Lock, K. (2017) 'Blowing policy bubbles: Rethinking emissions targets and low-carbon energy policies in the U.K.', *Journal of Environmental Policy & Planning*, 19, 6, 638–653, https://doi.org/10.1080/1523908X.2016.1266931

Gillard, R., Gouldson, A., Paavola, J. and Van Alstine, J. (2017) 'Can national policy blockages accelerate the development of polycentric governance? Evidence from climate change policy in the United Kingdom', *Global Environmental Change*, 45, 174–182, https://doi.org/10.1016/j.gloenvcha.2017.06.003

Gillborn, D., Dixson, A.D., Ladson-Billings, G., Parker, L., Rollock, N. and Warmington, P. (2018) *Critical Race Theory in Education* (London: Routledge)

Glencross, A. (2016) 'The European Council and the legitimacy paradox of new intergovernmentalism: Constitutional agency meets politicisation', *Journal of European Integration*, 38, 5, 497–509, https://doi.org/10.1080/07036337.2016.1178250

Goddard, T. (2020) 'Coronavirus and abortion law', *House of Lords Library*, 6 April, https://lordslibrary.parliament.uk/coronavirus-and-abortion-law/ (A: 30.03.22)

Goldfinch, S. and Wallis, J. (2010) 'Two myths of convergence in public management reform', *Public Administration*, 88, 4, 1099–1115

Gonzalez, S. (2010) 'The North/South divide in Italy and England: Discursive construction of regional inequality', *European Urban and Regional Studies*, 18, 1, 62–67, https://doi.org/10.1177%2F0969776410369044

Goodfellow, M. (2018) '"Race" and racism in the UK' in Macfarlane, L. (ed) *New Thinking for the British Economy* (London: Open Democracy), 150–159

Goodfellow, M. (2019) *Hostile Environment* (London: Verso)

Goodhart, D. (2021) 'The Sewell commission is a game-changer for how Britain talks about race', *Policy Exchange*, 31 March, https://policyexchange.org.uk/the-sewell-commission-is-a-game-changer-for-how-britain-talks-about-race/ (A: 26.09.22)

Gordon, M. (2016) 'The UK's sovereignty situation: Brexit, bewilderment and beyond', *King's Law Journal*, 27, 3, 333–343, https://doi.org/10.1080/09615 768.2016.1250465

Gormley-Heenan, C. and Aughey, A. (2017) 'Northern Ireland and Brexit: Three effects on "the border in the mind"', *The British Journal of Politics and International Relations*, 19, 3, 497–511, https://doi.org/10.1177%2F1369148117711060

Gove, M. (2016) 'The facts of life say leave: Why Britain and Europe will be better off after we vote Leave', *Voteleavetakecontrol.org*, http://www.voteleavetake control.org/assets-d3n8a8pro7vhmx.cloudfront.net/voteleave/pages/271/atta chments/original/1461057270/MGspeech194VERSION2.pdf (A: 02.09.22)

Grant, W. (1989) *Pressure Groups, Politics and Democracy in Britain*, 1st edn (Hemel Hempstead: Philip Allen)

Grant, W. (1993) *The Politics of Economic Policy* (Hemel Hempstead: Harvester)

Grant, W. and Marsh, D. (1977) *The CBI* (London: Hodder)

Gravey, V. (2019) 'Finally free to green agriculture policy? UK post-Brexit policy developments in the shadow of the CAP and devolution', *EuroChoices*, 18, 2, 11–16, https://doi.org/10.1111/1746-692X.12234

Gravey, V. (2022) 'Brexit and the Common Agricultural Policy: There and back again' in Antonopoulos, I., Bell, M., Cavoski, A. and Petetin, L. (eds) *The Governance of Agriculture in Post-Brexit UK* (London: Routledge), 1–27

Gravey, V. and Jordan, A. (2023) 'UK environmental policy and Brexit: Simultaneously de-Europeanising, disengaging and (re)-engaging?', *Journal of European Public Policy*, 1–23, https://doi.org/10.1080/13501763.2023.2201613

Gray, C. (2000) 'A "hollow state"?' in Pyper, R. and Robins, L. (eds) *United Kingdom Governance* (London: Macmillan), 283–299

Gray, M. and Barford, A. (2018) 'The depths of the cuts: The uneven geography of local government austerity', *Cambridge Journal of Regions, Economy and Society*, 11, 3, 541–563, https://doi.org/10.1093/cjres/rsy019

Green, J. (2007) 'When voters and parties agree: Valence issues and party competition', *Political Studies*, 55, 3, 629–655

Greenaway, J., Smith, S. and Street, J. (1992) *Deciding Factors in British Politics* (London: Routledge)

Greenberg, K.J., Dratel, J.L. and Lewis, A. (2005) *The Torture Papers: The Road to Abu Ghraib* (Cambridge: Cambridge University Press)

Greenhalgh, T. (2020) 'Face coverings for the public: Laying straw men to rest', *Journal of Evaluation in Clinical Practice*, 26, 4, 1070–1077, https://doi.org/ 10.1111/jep.13415

Greenhalgh, T., Schmid, M., Czypionka, T., Bassler, D. and Gruer, L. (2020) 'Face masks for the public during the covid-19 crisis', *British Medical Journal*, 369, 1–4, https://doi.org/10.1136/bmj.m1435

Greenhalgh, T., Jimenez, J.L., Prather, K.A., Tufekci, Z., Fisman, D. and Schooley, R. (2021) 'Ten scientific reasons in support of airborne transmission of SARS-CoV-2', *The Lancet*, 397(10285), 1603–1605, https://doi.org/10.1016/S0140-6736(21)00869-2

Greenpeace (2022) 'Plastic pollution', https://www.greenpeace.org.uk/challen ges/plastic-pollution/ (A: 15.07.22)

Greenwood, J., Pyper, R. and Wilson, D. (2001) *New Public Administration in Britain* (London: Routledge)

Greer, A. (2002) 'Policy networks and policy change in organic agriculture: A comparative analysis of the UK and Ireland', *Public Administration*, 80, 3, 453–474, https://doi.org/10.1111/1467-9299.00313

Greer, P. (1994) *Transforming Central Government: The Next Steps Initiative* (Milton Keynes: Open University Press)

Greer, S. (2003) 'Policy divergence: Will it change something in Greenock' in Hazell, R. (ed) *The State of the Nations 2003: The Third Year of Devolution in the United Kingdom* (London: The Constitution Unit), 100–120

Greer, S. and Jarman, H. (2008) 'Devolution and policy styles' in Trench, A. (ed) *The State of the Nations 2008* (Exeter: Imprint Academic), 167–197

Gregory, L. and Matthews, P. (2022) 'Social policy and queer lives: Coming out of the closet?', *Journal of Social Policy*, 51, 3, 596–610, https://doi.org/10.1017/S0047279422000198

Grey, C. (2017) 'The German car industry and Brexit', *Brexit & Beyond*, https://chrisgreybrexitblog.blogspot.com/2017/07/the-german-car-industry-and-bre xit.html (A: 07.09.22)

Grey, S. and MacAskill, A. (2020) 'Special report: Johnson listened to his scientists about coronavirus – but they were slow to sound the alarm', *Reuters*, 7 April, https://www.reuters.com/article/us-health-coronavirus-britain-path-speci/special-report-johnson-listened-to-his-scientists-about-coronavirus-but-they-were-slow-to-sound-the-alarm-idUSKBN21P1VF (A: 07.05.20)

Gribble, R., Wessley, S., Klein, S., Alexander, D.A., Dandeker, C. and Fear, N.T. (2015) 'British public opinion after a decade of war: Attitudes to Iraq and Afghanistan', *Politics*, 35, 2, 128–150

Grice, A. (2008) 'Tory back bench disagrees with Cameron over tax cuts', *The Independent*, 14 November, https://www.independent.co.uk/news/uk/polit ics/tory-back-bench-disagrees-with-cameron-over-tax-cuts-1032197.html (A: 09.09.22)

Grierson, J. and Gayle, D. (2017) '"We want justice": Grenfell Tower protests spill on to streets', *The Guardian*, 17 June, https://www.theguardian.com/uk-news/2017/jun/16/we-want-justice-grenfell-tower-protest-spills-into-town-hall (A: 08.08.22)

Griffiths, S. and Hickson, K. (eds) (2009) *British Party Politics and Ideology after New Labour* (Basingstoke: Palgrave Macmillan)

Griggs, S. and Howarth, D. (2019) 'Discourse, policy and the environment: Hegemony, statements and the analysis of U.K. airport expansion', *Journal of Environmental Policy & Planning*, 21, 5, 464–478, https://doi.org/10.1080/15239 08X.2016.1266930

Grimshaw, D. and Rubery, J. (2012) 'The end of the UK's liberal collectivist social model? The implications of the coalition government's policy during the austerity crisis', *Cambridge Journal of Economics*, 36, 1, 105–126, https://doi.org/10.1093/cje/ber033

Grossman, E. and Woll, C. (2014) 'Saving the banks: The political economy of bailouts', *Comparative Political Studies*, 47, 4, 574–600, https://doi.org/10.1177%2F0010414013488540

Grove, J. (2013) 'Thatcher had "immense impact" on higher education', *Times Higher Education*, 8 April, https://www.timeshighereducation.com/news/thatcher-had-immense-impact-on-higher-education/2003059.article (A: 05.10.21)

Grover, C. (2014) 'Atos Healthcare withdraws from the Work Capability Assessment: A comment', *Disability & Society*, 29, 8, 1324–1328, https://doi.org/10.1080/09687599.2014.948750

Grover, C. (2019) 'Violent proletarianisation: Social murder, the reserve army of labour and social security "austerity" in Britain', *Critical Social Policy*, 39, 3, 335–355, https://journals.sagepub.com/doi/10.1177/0261018318816932

Grube, D.C. and Killick, A. (2021) 'Groupthink, polythink and the challenges of decision-making in Cabinet government', *Parliamentary Affairs*, https://doi.org/10.1093/pa/gsab047

Gstöhl, S. and Phinnemore, D. (2021) 'The future EU–UK partnership: A historical institutionalist perspective', *Journal of European Integration*, 43, 1, 99–115, https://doi.org/10.1080/07036337.2020.1818074

The Guardian (1981) 'Verdict: Not a race riot, but a burst of anger', 26 November, https://uploads.guim.co.uk/2021/11/25/Scarman_26_Nov_1981.jpg (A: 26.09.22)

The Guardian (2001) '20,000 join anti-war protest', 13 October, https://www.theguardian.com/world/2001/oct/13/afghanistan.terrorism5 (A: 07.10.22)

The Guardian (2003) 'Full transcript of Gilligan's "sexed up" broadcast', 9 July, https://www.theguardian.com/media/2003/jul/09/Iraqandthemedia.bbc (A: 07.10.22)

The Guardian (2005) 'Beacon of hope fades', 24 August, https://www.theguardian.com/politics/2005/aug/24/iraq.iraq (A: 07.10.22)

The Guardian (2022) 'Suella Braverman blames "Guardian-reading, tofu-eating wokerati" for disruptive protests – video', 18 October, https://www.theguardian.com/politics/video/2022/oct/18/suella-braverman-blames-guardian-reading-tofu-eating-wokerati-for-disruptive-protests-video (A: 28.04.23)

Guerrina, R., Haastrup, T., Wright, K.A., Masselot, A., MacRae, H. and Cavaghan, R. (2018) 'Does European Union studies have a gender problem? Experiences from researching Brexit', *International Feminist Journal of Politics*, 20, 2, 252–257, https://doi.org/10.1080/14616742.2018.1457881

Guinan, J. and Hanna, T.H. (2017) 'Forbidden fruit: The neglected political economy of Lexit', *IPPR Progressive Review*, 24, 1, 14–24, https://doi.org/10.1111/newe.12032

Guinan, J. and O'Neill, M. (2019) *The Case for Community Wealth Building* (London: Wiley)

Gul, Z. (published as Gulmohamad) (2021) *The Making of Foreign Policy in Iraq: Political Factions and the Ruling Elite* (London: IB Tauris)

Gunningham, N. (2019) 'Averting climate catastrophe: Environmental activism, Extinction Rebellion and coalitions of influence', *King's Law Journal*, 2, 194–202, https://www.tandfonline.com/doi/abs/10.1080/09615768.2019.1645 424#:~:text=https%3A//doi.org/10.1080/09615768.2019.1645424

Gupta, A.H. (2020) 'With Brexit looming, experts worry women may be hit hardest', *New York Times*, 17 January, https://www.nytimes.com/2020/01/17/ world/europe/brexit-women-impact.html (A: 08.09.22)

Haastrup, T., Wright, K.A. and Guerrina, R. (2019) 'Bringing gender in? EU foreign and security policy after Brexit', *Politics and Governance*, 7, 3, 62–71, https://doi.org/10.17645/pag.v7i3.2153

Habermas, J. (1996) *Between Facts and Norms: Contributions to a Discourse Theory of Law and Democracy* (Cambridge, MA: MIT Press)

Hackney Citizen (2011) 'Ken Livingstone on riots, debt and the end of the world', 21 September, https://www.hackneycitizen.co.uk/2011/09/21/ken-livingst one-riots-debt-climate-change/ (A: 26.09.22)

Haddon, C. (2021) 'Investigations into the Downing Street flat refurbishment', *The Institute for Government*, 30 April, https://www.instituteforgovernment. org.uk/article/explainer/investigations-downing-street-flat-refurbishment (A: 20.04.23)

Haddon, C. (2022) 'COBR (COBRA)', *Institute for Government*, 19 January, https://www.instituteforgovernment.org.uk/explainers/cobr-cobra (A: 25.03.22)

Hadfield, A. and Turner, C. (2021) 'Risky business? Analysing the challenges and opportunities of Brexit on English local government', *Local Government Studies*, 47, 4, 657–678. https://doi.org/10.1080/03003930.2021.1895768

Hajisoteriou, C. and Angelides, P. (2020) 'Efficiency versus social justice? Teachers' roles in the epoch of globalisation', *Education, Citizenship and Social Justice*, 15, 3, 274–289, https://doi.org/10.1177%2F1746197919852564

Hall, D. and Gunter, H.M. (2016) 'Chapter 2: England – permanent instability in the European educational NPM "laboratory"' in Gunter, H.M., Grimaldi, E., Hall, D. and Serpieri, R. (eds) *New Public Management and the Reform of Education* (London: Routledge), 21–36

Hall, I. (2013) '"Building the global network?" The reform of the Foreign and Commonwealth Office under New Labour', *The British Journal of Politics and International Relations*, 15, 2, 228–245, https://doi.org/10.1111/j.1467-856X.2012.00533.x

Hall, P. (1993) 'Policy paradigms, social learning, and the state: The case of economic policy making in Britain', *Comparative Politics*, 25, 3, 275–296

Hall, S. (1999) 'From Scarman to Stephen Lawrence', *History Workshop Journal*, 48, 187–197

Hall, S. and Heneghan, M. (2022) 'Financial services' in Reland, J., Menon, A. and Rutter, J. (eds) *Doing Things Differently? Policy after Brexit* (UK in a Changing Europe), https://ukandeu.ac.uk/wp-content/uploads/2022/01/UKICE-Pol icy-Report_FINAL.pdf (A: 01.09.22)

Hall, S., McIntosh, K., Neitzert, E., Pottinger, L., Sandhu, K., Stephenson, M.A., Reed, H. and Taylor, L. (2017) 'Intersecting inequalities: The impact of austerity on Black and Minority Ethnic Women in the UK', *Women's Budget Group*, https://wbg.org.uk/wp-content/uploads/2018/08/Intersecting-Inequ alities-October-2017-Full-Report.pdf (A: 17.07.22)

Haller, M. (2019) 'The dream of the United States of Europe: An ambitious scenario challenged by the Brexit', *Österreichische Gesellschaft für Europapolitik*, https://www.oegfe.at/wp-content/uploads/2019/11/OEGfE_Policy_Brief-2019.22-2.pdf (A: 07.09.22)

Halliday, J. (2021) 'Sarah Everard murder: Police commissioner urged to resign over "streetwise" comment', *The Guardian*, 1 October, https://www.theguard ian.com/uk-news/2021/oct/01/sarah-everard-murder-police-commissioner-apologises-for-saying-women-should-be-more-streetwise (A: 26.09.22)

Hallsworth, S. (2006) 'Racial targeting and social control: Looking behind the police', *Critical Criminology*, 14, 293–311, https://doi.org/10.1007/s10612-006-9014-0

Halperin, S. (2011) 'The political economy of Anglo-American War: The case of Iraq', *International Politics*, 48, 2–3, 207–228, https://doi.org/10.1057/ip.2011.4

Ham, C. (2004) *Health Policy in Britain*, 5th edn (London: Palgrave)

Hamilton, A. (2020) 'The political economy of economic policy in Iraq', *London School of Economics and Political Science*, http://eprints.lse.ac.uk/104 086/4/Hamilton_political_economy_of_economic_policy_iraq_published. pdf (A: 07.10.22)

Hamnett, C. (2014) 'Shrinking the welfare state: The structure, geography and impact of British government benefit cuts', *Transactions of the Institute of British Geographers*, 39, 4, 490–503, https://doi.org/10.1111/tran.12049

Hamourtziadou, L. (2021) 'From invasion to failed state: Iraq's democratic disillusionment', *Open Democracy*, 23 July, https://www.opendemocracy.net/ en/north-africa-west-asia/from-invasion-to-failed-state-iraqs-democratic-disi llusionment/ (A: 07.10.22)

Hampton, P. (2018) 'Trade unions and climate politics: Prisoners of neoliberalism or swords of climate justice?', *Globalizations*, 15, 4, 470–486, https://doi.org/ 10.1080/14747731.2018.1454673

Hankivsky, O. and Christoffersen, A. (2011) 'Gender mainstreaming in the United Kingdom: Current issues and future challenges', *British Politics*, 6, 1, 30–51, https://doi.org/10.1057/bp.2011.1

Hankivsky, O. and Jordan-Zachery, J.S. (eds) (2019) *The Palgrave Handbook of Intersectionality in Public Policy* (London: Palgrave)

Hanna, E., Martin, G., Campbell, A., Connolly, P., Fearon, K. and Markham, S. (2022) 'Experiences of face mask use during the Covid-19 pandemic: A qualitative study', *Sociology of Health and Illness*, 1–19, https://doi.org/10.1111/1467-9566.13525

Hanson, C. (1991) *Taming the Trade Unions* (Basingstoke: Macmillan)

Harari, D. (2023) *GDP – International Comparisons: Key Economic Indicators* (House of Commons Research Briefing 02784), https://commonslibrary.parliament.uk/research-briefings/sn02784/ (A: 02.05.23)

Harkness, S., Gregg, P. and MacMillan, L. (2012) 'Poverty: The role of institutions, behaviours, and culture', *Joseph Rowntree Foundation*, https://www.jrf.org.uk/sites/default/files/jrf/migrated/files/poverty-culture-behaviour-full.pdf (A: 09.09.22)

Harman, K., Allen, H., Kall, M. and Dabrera, G. (2021) 'Interpretation of COVID-19 case fatality risk measures in England', *Journal of Epidemiology and Community Health*, 75, 415–416, http://dx.doi.org/10.1136/jech-2020-216140

Harrington, B., Smith, K., Hunter, D., Marks, L., Blackman, T., McKee, L., Greene, A., Elliott, E. and Williams, G. (2009) 'Health inequalities in England, Scotland and Wales: Stakeholders' accounts and policy compared', *Public Health*, 123, 1, e24–e28

Harris, R. (2021) 'Climate explained: How the IPCC reaches scientific consensus on climate change', *The Conversation*, 29 June, https://theconversation.com/climate-explained-how-the-ipcc-reaches-scientific-consensus-on-climate-change-162600 (A: 22.04.22)

Harris, S., Joseph-Salisbury, R. and White, L. (2022) 'Notes on policing, racism and the Covid-19 pandemic in the UK', *Race & Class*, 63, 3, 92–102, https://doi.org/10.1177/03063968211063436

Harrison, K. (2021) 'The futility of participation: Austerity and public reluctance to oppose it', *British Politics*, https://doi.org/10.1057/s41293-021-00174-8

Harrow, M. (2010) 'The effect of the Iraq war on Islamist terrorism in the West', *Cooperation and Conflict*, 45, 3, 274–293, https://www.jstor.org/stable/45084609

Hassan, H. (2019) 'The true origins of ISIS', *The Atlantic*, 30 November, https://www.theatlantic.com/ideas/archive/2018/11/isis-origins-anbari-zarqawi/577030/ (A: 07.10.22)

Hawkins, B. and van Schalkwyk, M. (2023) 'Politics and fantasy in UK alcohol policy', *Critical Policy Studies*, 1–21, https://doi.org/10.1080/19460171.2023.2188470

Hay, C. (2002) *Political Analysis* (London: Palgrave)

Hay, C. (2006) 'Globalization and public policy' in Moran, M., Rein, M. and Goodin, R. (eds) *The Oxford Handbook of Public Policy* (Oxford: Oxford University Press), 587–604

Hay, C. (2007) *Why We Hate Politics* (Cambridge: Polity Press)

Hay, C. (2009) 'King Canute and the "problem" of structure and agency: On times, tides and heresthetics', *Political Studies*, 57, 2, 260–279

Hay, C. (2011) 'Britain and the global financial crisis' in Heffernan, R., Cowley, P. and Hay, C. (eds) *Developments in British Politics* (London: Palgrave), 238–256

Hay, C. (2013) 'Treating the symptom not the condition: Crisis definition, deficit reduction and the search for a new British growth model', *The British Journal of Politics and International Relations*, 15, 1, 23–37, https://doi.org/10.1111/j.1467-856X.2012.00515.x

Hay, C. and Watson, M. (2004) 'Labour's economic policy: Studiously courting competence' in Taylor, G. (ed) *The Impact of New Labour* (London: Macmillan), 149–161

Hayden, C. and Jenkins, C. (2014) ' "Troubled Families" programme in England: "Wicked problems" and policy-based evidence', *Policy Studies*, 35, 6, 631–649, https://doi.org/10.1080/01442872.2014.971732

Haynes, R. (2015) 'The international financial crisis: The failure of a complex system' in Geyer, R. and Cairney, P. (eds) *Handbook on Complexity and Public Policy* (Cheltenham: Edward Elgar), 432–453

HC Deb, 10 December 1981, c1052, https://www.theyworkforyou.com/debates/?id=1981-12-10a.1052.0 (A: 12.07.23)

HC Deb, 24 September 2002, c49, https://www.theyworkforyou.com/debates/?id=2002-09-24.49.1 (A: 01.07.22)

Head, B. (2019) 'Forty years of wicked problems literature: Forging closer links to policy studies', *Policy and Society*, 38, 2, 180–197

Headey, B. (1974) *British Cabinet Ministers* (London: Allen & Unwin)

Heald, D. (1990) 'Charging by British government: Evidence from the public expenditure survey', *Financial Accountability & Management*, 6, 4, 229–261

Health Foundation (2018) *Policies for Healthy Lives: A Look Beyond Brexit* (London: The Health Foundation), https://www.health.org.uk/sites/default/files/Policies-healthy-lives_web.pdf (A: 08.09.22)

Heath, A. and Richards, L. (2020) 'How racist is Britain today? What the evidence tells us', *The Conversation*, 1 July, https://theconversation.com/how-racist-is-britain-today-what-the-evidence-tells-us-141657 (A: 26.09.22)

Heath-Kelly, C. (2017) 'The geography of pre-criminal space: Epidemiological imaginations of radicalisation risk in the UK Prevent Strategy, 2007–2017', *Critical Studies on Terrorism*, 10, 2, 297–319, https://doi.org/10.1080/17539153.2017.1327141

Heath-Kelly, C. (2023) 'Devolution and the Prevent strategy in Scotland: Constitutional politics and the path of Scottish P/CVE', *Parliamentary Affairs*, 1–21, https://doi.org/10.1093/pa/gsad007

Heckman, J. (2022) 'The Heckman Equation', https://heckmanequation.org/the-heckman-equation/ (A: 13.09.22)

Heclo, H. and Wildavsky, A. (1981) *The Private Government of Public Money* (London: Macmillan)

Heffron, R. and McCauley, D. (2018) 'What is the "just transition"?', *Geoforum*, 88, 74–77, https://doi.org/10.1016/j.geoforum.2017.11.016

Heinkelmann-Wild, T., Kriegmair, L., Rittberger, B. and Zangl, B. (2020) 'Divided they fail: The politics of wedge issues and Brexit', *Journal of European Public Policy*, 27, 5, 723–741, https://doi.org/10.1080/13501763.2019.1683058

Heinrich, M.N. (2015) 'One war, many reasons: The US invasion of Iraq', *E-International Relations*, https://www.e-ir.info/pdf/54555 (A: 07.10.22)

Helms, L. (2005) 'The presidentialisation of political leadership: British notions and German observations', *The Political Quarterly*, 76, 3, 430–438, https://doi.org/10.1111/j.1467-923X.2005.00702.x

Hencke, D. (2005) 'Blair strengthens power of advisers', *The Guardian*, 20 July, https://www.theguardian.com/politics/2005/jul/20/uk.Whitehall (A: 07.10.22)

Henderson, A., Jeffrey, C., Wincott, D. and Wyn-Jones, R. (2017) 'How Brexit was made in England', *The British Journal of Politics and International Relations*, 19, 4, 631–646, https://doi.org/10.1177/1369148117730542

Henke, M.E. (2018) 'Tony Blair's gamble: The Middle East Peace Process and British participation in the Iraq 2003 campaign', *British Journal of Politics and International Relations*, 20, 4, 773–789, https://doi.org/10.1177/136914811 8784708

Hennessy, P. (2005) 'Informality and circumscription: The Blair style of government in war and peace', *The Political Quarterly*, 76, 1, 3–11, https://doi.org/10.1111/j.1467-923X.2005.00651.x

Hepburn, E. (2019) 'Brexit scenarios: What might happen next?', *Centre on Constitutional Change*, 2 September, https://www.centreonconstitutionalcha nge.ac.uk/news-and-opinion/brexit-scenarios-what-might-happen-next (A: 08.09.22)

Hepburn, E. (2020) 'Brexit: social and equality impacts', The Scottish Government, https://www.gov.scot/binaries/content/documents/govscot/publications/research-and-analysis/2020/01/social-equality-impacts-brexit/documents/social-equality-impacts-brexit/social-equality-impacts-brexit/govs cot%3Adocument/social-equality-impacts-brexit.pdf (A: 07.09.22)

Hepburn, H. (2022) 'Where is ministers' energy and ambition for Scottish education?', *TES*, 6 May, https://www.tes.com/magazine/analysis/general/where-ministers-energy-and-ambition-scottish-education (A: 19.09.22)

Herd, P. and Moynihan, D. (2018) *Administrative Burden* (New York: Russell Sage)

Hertner, I. and Keith, D. (2017) 'Europhiles or Eurosceptics? Comparing the European policies of the Labour Party and the Liberal Democrats', *British Politics*, 12, 1, 63–89, https://doi.org/10.1057/bp.2016.4

HESA (Higher Education Statistics Agency) (2022) 'What is the income of HE providers?', https://www.hesa.ac.uk/data-and-analysis/finances/income#fees (A: 02.09.22)

Heseltine, M. (1989) *The Challenge of Europe: Through 1992 and Beyond*, 1st edn (London: Weidenfeld & Nicolson)

Hewer, R.M.F. (2021) *Sex-Work, Prostitution and Policy* (London: Palgrave)

Hewitt, G. (2020) 'The Windrush Scandal: An insider's reflection', *Caribbean Quarterly*, 66, 1, 108–128, https://doi.org/10.1080/00086495.2020.1722378

Hiam, L., Dorling, D. and McKee, M. (2023) 'Falling down the global ranks: Life expectancy in the UK, 1952–2021', *Journal of the Royal Society of Medicine*, 116, 3, 89–92, https://doi.org/10.1177/01410768231155637

Hill, B. (2022) 'Studies of the impact of Brexit on UK agriculture' in Antonopoulos, I., Bell, M., Cavoski, A. and Petetin, L. (eds) *The Governance of Agriculture in Post-Brexit UK* (London: Routledge), 1–27

Hill, E. and Meer, N. (2020) 'Ethnic minorities and political citizenship in Scotland' in Keating, M. (ed) *The Oxford Handbook of Scottish Politics* (Oxford: Oxford University Press), 336–353

Hill, M. and Hupe, P. (2009) *Implementing Public Policy*, 2nd edn (London: SAGE)

Hillman, N. (2016) 'The coalition's higher education reforms in England', *Oxford Review of Education*, 42, 3, 330–345, https://doi.org/10.1080/03054985.2016.1184870

Hinde, D. (2016) 'It's our environment: Two terms of SNP environmental policy', *Scottish Affairs*, 25, 1, 83–102, https://doi.org/10.3366/scot.2016.0112

Hindmoor, A. (2003) 'Public policy: The 2002 spending review and beyond', *Parliamentary Affairs*, 56, 2, 205–218

Hindmoor, A. (2005) *New Labour at the Centre* (Oxford: Oxford University Press)

Hindmoor, A. (2006) *Rational Choice* (Basingstoke: Palgrave)

Hindmoor, A. (2019) *12 Days That Made Modern Britain* (Oxford: Oxford University Press)

Hine, D. and Peele, G. (2016) *The Regulation of Standards in British Public Life: Doing the Right Thing?* (Manchester: Manchester University Press)

Hinnebusch, R. (2007) 'The American invasion of Iraq: Causes and consequences', *Perceptions: Journal of International Affairs*, 12, 1, 9–27

Hinson, S. and Boulton, P. (2022) *Fuel Poverty* (HC8730) (London: House of Commons Library), https://researchbriefings.files.parliament.uk/documents/CBP-8730/CBP-8730.pdf (A: 09.09.22)

History.com editors (2022) 'September 11 attacks', 1 September, https://www.history.com/topics/21st-century/9-11-attacks (A: 24.09.22)

HM Government (2010) 'The Coalition: Our programme for government', https://assets.publishing.service.gov.uk/government/uploads/system/uploads/attachment_data/file/78977/coalition_programme_for_government.pdf (A: 09.09.22)

HM Government (2015) *Cutting the Cost of Keeping Warm: A Fuel Poverty Strategy for England* (Cm9019) (London: HMSO), https://assets.publishing.service.gov.uk/government/uploads/system/uploads/attachment_data/file/408644/cutting_the_cost_of_keeping_warm.pdf (A: 07.09.22)

HM Government (2016) 'Why the government believes that voting to remain in the European Union is the best decision for the UK', 7 April, https://assets.publishing.service.gov.uk/government/uploads/system/uploads/attachment_data/file/515068/why-the-government-believes-that-voting-to-remain-in-the-european-union-is-the-best-decision-for-the-uk.pdf (A: 17.08.22)

HM Government (2017) *The United Kingdom's Exit from and New Partnership with the European Union White Paper* (Cm 9417) (London: HMSO), https://assets. publishing.service.gov.uk/government/uploads/system/uploads/attachment_ data/file/589191/The_United_Kingdoms_exit_from_and_partnership_with_ the_EU_Web.pdf (A: 05.08.22)

HM Government (2021) *Net Zero Strategy: Build Back Greener* (London: HMSO), https://assets.publishing.service.gov.uk/government/uploads/system/uploads/ attachment_data/file/1033990/net-zero-strategy-beis.pdf (A: 05.05.22)

HM Government (2022a) 'Income tax rates and personal allowances', https:// www.gov.uk/income-tax-rates (A: 04.10.22)

HM Government (2022b) *British Energy Security Strategy* (London: OGL), https:// assets.publishing.service.gov.uk/government/uploads/system/uploads/atta chment_data/file/1069973/british-energy-security-strategy-print-ready.pdf (A: 04.07.22)

HM Government (2022c) 'Apply for free school meals', https://www.gov.uk/ apply-free-school-meals (A: 15.09.22)

HM Government (2022d) 'Drugs penalties', https://www.gov.uk/penalties-drug- possession-dealing (A: 15.09.22)

HM Government (2022e) 'Our governance', https://www.gov.uk/government/ organisations/civil-service/about/our-governance (A: 06.10.22)

HM Government (2022f) 'Punishments for antisocial behaviour', https://www. gov.uk/civil-injunctions-criminal-behaviour-orders (A: 19.09.22)

HM Government (2022g) 'National Insurance: Introduction', https://www.gov. uk/national-insurance/how-much-you-pay (A: 04.10.22)

HM Government (2022h) 'Inclusive Britain: Government response to the Commission on Race and Ethnic Disparities', *Department for Levelling Up, Housing & Communities*, 17 March, https://www.gov.uk/government/publi cations/inclusive-britain-action-plan-government-response-to-the-commiss ion-on-race-and-ethnic-disparities/inclusive-britain-government-response-to- the-commission-on-race-and-ethnic-disparities (A: 26.09.22)

HM Government (2023) 'The UK government's response to the Russian invasion of Ukraine', https://www.gov.uk/government/topical-events/russian-invas ion-of-ukraine-uk-government-response/about (A: 02.05.23)

HMICFRS (Her Majesty's Inspectorate of Constabulary and Fire & Rescue Services) (2021) 'The Sarah Everard vigil – an inspection of the Metropolitan Police Service's policing of a vigil held in commemoration of Sarah Everard on Clapham Common on Saturday 13 March 2021', 30 March, https://www.justiceinspectorates.gov.uk/ hmicfrs/publication-html/inspection-metropolitan-police-services-policing-of- vigil-commemorating-sarah-everard-clapham-common/ (A: 06.09.22)

HM Revenue and Customs (2021) 'Health and Social Care Levy', 13 December, https://www.gov.uk/government/publications/health-and-social-care-levy/hea lth-and-social-care-levy (A: 12.08.22)

HM Treasury (2020) *The Green Book (2020)*, https://www.gov.uk/government/publications/the-green-book-appraisal-and-evaluation-in-central-governent/the-green-book-2020 (A: 19.08.21)

HM Treasury (2021) *Public Expenditure Statistical Analyses 2021* (London: HMSO), https://assets.publishing.service.gov.uk/government/uploads/system/uploads/attachment_data/file/1003755/CCS207_CCS0621818186-001_PESA_ARA_2021_Web_Accessible.pdfb (A: 23.07.22)

HM Treasury (2022) *Public Expenditure Statistical Analyses 2022 CP735* (London: HMSO), https://www.gov.uk/government/statistics/public-expenditure-statistical-analyses-2022 (A: 14.07.23)

HM Treasury and Department of Health (2002) *Tackling Health Inequalities: Summary of the 2002 Cross-Cutting Review* (London: Department of Health)

Hoberg, G. (2001) 'Globalization and policy convergence: Symposium overview', *Journal of Comparative Policy Analysis: Research and Practice*, 3, 127–132

Hobolt, S.B. (2016) 'The Brexit vote: A divided nation, a divided continent', *Journal of European Public Policy*, 23, 9, 1259–1277, https://doi.org/10.1080/13501763.2016.1225785

Hodges, R., Caperchione, E., Van Helden, J., Reichard, C. and Sorrentino, D. (2022) 'The role of scientific expertise in COVID-19 policy-making: Evidence from four European countries', *Public Organization Review*, 22, 2, 249–267

Hodgkinson, S. and Tilley, N. (2011) 'Tackling anti-social behaviour: Lessons from New Labour for the coalition government', *British Journal of Criminology*, 11, 4, 283–305, https://doi.org/10.1177/1748895811414594

Hodkinson, S. and Robbins, G. (2013) 'The return of class war conservatism? Housing under the UK coalition government', *Critical Social Policy*, 33, 1, 57–77, https://doi.org/10.1177/0261018312457871

Hodson, D. and Mabbett, D. (2009) 'UK economic policy and the global financial crisis: Paradigm lost?' *JCMS Journal of Common Market Studies*, 47, 5, 1041–1061

Hoffman, S. (2015) 'Championing children's rights in times of austerity: Local and regional authorities' responsibilities', *Congress of Local and Regional Authorities*, https://www.researchgate.net/publication/287199744_Championing_children%27s_rights_in_times_of_austerity_Local_and_regional_authorities%27_responsibilities (A: 09.09.22)

Hogwood, B. (1987) *From Crisis to Complacency* (Oxford: Oxford University Press)

Hogwood, B. (1992) *Trends in British Public Policy* (Buckingham: Open University Press)

Hogwood, B. (1997) 'The machinery of government 1979–97', *Political Studies*, 45, 704–715

Hogwood, B. (2008) 'Public employment in Britain: From working in to working for the public sector?' in Derlien, H. and Peters, B.G. (eds) *The State at Work, Volume 1: Public Sector Employment in Ten Western Countries* (Cheltenham: Elgar), 19–39

Hogwood, B. and Peters, B.G. (1983) *Policy Dynamics* (New York: St Martin's Press)

Hogwood, B. and Gunn, L. (1984) *Policy Analysis for the Real World* (Oxford: Oxford University Press)

Holden, C. and Hawkins, B. (2013) ' "Whisky gloss": The alcohol industry, devolution and policy communities in Scotland', *Public Policy and Administration*, 28, 3, 253–273, https://doi.org/10.1177/0952076712452290

Holland, L. (1999) 'The U.S. decision to launch Operation Desert Storm: A bureaucratic politics analysis', *Armed Forces and Society*, 25, 2, 219–242, https://doi.org/10.1177/0095327X9902500

Holliday, I. (2000) 'Is the British state hollowing out?', *The Political Quarterly*, 71, 2, 167–176

Home Affairs Select Committee (2020) *Home Office Preparedness for Covid-19 (Coronavirus): Domestic Abuse and Risks of Harm within the Home*, 27 April, https://publications.parliament.uk/pa/cm5801/cmselect/cmhaff/321/32102.htm (A: 13.05.20)

Home Affairs Select Committee (2022) 'Channel crossings, migration and asylum – First Report of Session 2022–23', https://publications.parliament.uk/pa/cm5803/cmselect/cmhaff/199/summary.html (A: 20.04.23)

Home Office (2011) *Ending Gang and Youth Violence: A Cross-Government Report*, https://assets.publishing.service.gov.uk/government/uploads/system/uploads/attachment_data/file/97861/gang-violence-summary.pdf (A: 12.07.23)

Honeyman, V. (2017) 'From liberal interventionism to liberal conservatism: The short road in foreign policy from Blair to Cameron', *British Politics*, 12, 42–62, https://doi.org/10.1057/bp.2015.46

Hood, C. (1991) 'A public management for all seasons', *Public Administration*, 69, 1, 3–19

Hood, C. (1995) 'The "new public management" in the 1980s: Variations on a theme', *Accounting, Organizations and Society*, 20, 2/3, 93–109

Hood, C. (2002) 'Control, bargains, and cheating: The politics of public-service reform', *Journal of Public Administration Research and Theory*, 12, 3, 309–332, https://doi.org/10.1093/oxfordjournals.jpart.a003536

Hood, C. (2007) 'Public service management by numbers', *Public Money and Management*, 27, 2, 95–102

Hood, C. (2010) *The Blame Game: Spin, Bureaucracy, and Self-Preservation in Government* (Princeton: Princeton University Press)

Hood, C. and Lodge, M. (2006) *The Politics of Public Service Bargains: Reward, Competency, Loyalty and Blame* (Oxford: Oxford University Press)

Hood, C. and Margetts, H. (2007) *The Tools of Government in the Digital Age* (London: Bloomsbury)

Hood, C. and Dixon, R. (2015) *A Government That Worked Better and Cost Less* (Oxford: Oxford University Press)

Hooghe, L. and Marks, G. (2003) 'Unraveling the central state, but how? Types of multi-level governance', *American Political Science Review*, 97, 2, 233–243

Hopkin, J. and Rosamond, B. (2018) 'Post-truth politics, bullshit and bad ideas: "Deficit fetishism" in the UK', *New Political Economy*, 23, 6, 631–655, https://www.tandfonline.com/doi/abs/10.1080/13563467.2017.1373757

Hopkirk, P. (1992) *The Great Game: The Struggle for Empire in Central Asia* (London: John Murray)

Horton, H. (2022) 'Rees-Mogg: "Britain must get every cubic inch of gas out of North Sea"', *The Guardian*, 23 September, https://www.theguardian.com/politics/2022/sep/23/rees-mogg-tells-staff-britain-must-get-every-cubic-inch-gas-out-of-north-sea (A: 07.10.22)

Houghton, D.P. (2008) 'Invading and occupying Iraq: Some insights from political psychology', *Peace and Conflict: Journal of Peace Psychology*, 14, 2, 169–192, https://doi.org/10.1080/10781910802017297

House of Commons Committee of Privileges (2023) *Matter Referred on 21 April 2022 (Conduct of Rt Hon Boris Johnson): Final Report (HC 564)* (London: House of Commons), https://committees.parliament.uk/publications/40412/documents/197897/default/ (A: 17.07.23)

House of Commons Foreign Affairs Committee (2022) *Missing in Action: UK Leadership and the Withdrawal from Afghanistan: First Report of Session 2022–23* (London: House of Commons), https://committees.parliament.uk/publications/22344/documents/165210/default/ (A: 13.07.23)

House of Commons Health and Social Care and Science and Technology Committees (2021) *Coronavirus: Lessons Learned to Date*, HC 92 (London: House of Commons), https:// committees.parliament.uk/ publications/7497/ documents/78688/default/ (A: 06.05.22)

Howarth, D. and Griggs, S. (2006) 'Metaphor, catachresis and equivalence: The rhetoric of freedom to fly in the struggle over aviation policy in the United Kingdom', *Policy and Society*, 25, 2, 23–46, https://doi.org/10.1016/S1449-4035(06)70073-X

Howlett, M., Mukherjee, I. and Woo, J.J. (2014) 'From tools to toolkits in policy design studies: The new design orientation towards policy formulation research', *Policy & Politics*, 43, 2, 291–311

Htun, M. and Weldon, S.L. (2010) 'When do governments promote women's rights? A framework for the comparative analysis of sex equality policy', *Perspectives on Politics*, 8, 1, 207–216, https://doi.org/10.1017/S1537592709992787

Hubble, S. and Bolton, P. (2018) 'Higher education tuition fees in England', *House of Commons Library*, https://researchbriefings.files.parliament.uk/documents/CBP-8151/CBP-8151.pdf (A: 09.09.22)

Hudson, J. and Lowe, S. (2009) *Understanding the Policy Process* (Bristol: Policy Press)

Hughes, R. (2022) 'Re: Was lockdown necessary? – Missing the point?', *British Medical Journal*, 23 March, 376, https://doi.org/10.1136/bmj.o776

Hughes, T. (2004) *Human Built World: How to Think about Technology and Culture* (Chicago: University of Chicago Press)

Human Rights Watch (1993) 'The Anfal campaign against the Kurds', hrw.org/reports/1993/iraqanfal/ANFALINT.htm (A: 07.10.22)

Human Rights Watch (2022) '20 years of US torture – and counting', 9 January, https://www.hrw.org/news/2022/01/09/20-years-us-torture-and-counting (A: 07.10.22)

Humphreys, J. (2005) 'The Iraq dossier and the meaning of spin', *Parliamentary Affairs*, 58, 1, 156–170, https://doi.org/10.1093/pa/gsi013

Hunt, K. (2010) 'The "ar on Tertrorism"' in Shepherd, J. (ed) *Global Matters in Global Politics: A Feminist Introduction to International Relations* (London: Routledge), 116–126

Hutton, B. (2004) *Report of the Inquiry into the Circumstances Surrounding the Death of Dr David Kelly C.M.G. by Lord Hutton* (Hutton Report), HC 247 (London: House of Commons), https://irp.fas.org/world/uk/huttonreport.pdf (A: 27.06.22)

Hutton, R. (2020) *Eat Out to Help Out Scheme* (Research Briefing CBP 8978) (London: House of Commons Library), https://researchbriefings.files.parliament.uk/documents/CBP-8978/CBP-8978.pdf (A: 23.05.22)

Hymas, C. (2023) 'Suella Braverman vows to "push boundaries of international law" to stop migrants', *The Telegraph*, 7 March, https://www.telegraph.co.uk/politics/2023/03/06/suella-braverman-vows-push-boundaries-international-law-stop/ (A: 20.04.23)

Hynes, H.P. (2004) 'On the battlefield of women's bodies: An overview of the harm of war to women', *Women's Studies International Forum*, 27, 5–6, 431–445, https://doi.org/10.1016/j.wsif.2004.09.001

Iakhnis, E., Rathbun, B., Reifler, J. and Scott, T.J. (2018) 'Populist referendum: Was "Brexit" an expression of nativist and anti-elitist sentiment?', *Research and Politics*, April–June, 1–7, https://doi.org/10.1177/2053168018773964

Iannucci, A., Armstrong, J., Blackwell, S. and Martin, I. (2010) *The Thick of It* (London: Faber & Faber)

Ibbetson, C. (2020) 'Do people approve of the new lockdown measures?', *YouGov*, 15 May, https://yougov.co.uk/topics/politics/articles-reports/2020/05/15/what-do-voters-make-new-lockdown-measures (A: 17.03.22)

Ibrahim, J. (2011) 'The new toll on higher education and the UK student revolts of 2010–2011', *Social Movement Studies*, 10, 4, 415–421, https://doi.org/10.1080/14742837.2011.614110

Ifan, G. and Sion, C. (2019) 'UK spending review 2019: The implications for Wales', *Wales Fiscal Analysis*, https://www.cardiff.ac.uk/__data/assets/pdf_file/0009/1699776/WFA-Spending-Round-2019-Briefing.pdf (A: 09.09.22)

IFS (Institute for Fiscal Studies) (2017) 'Fiscal response to the crisis', *Institute for Fiscal Studies*, https://web.archive.org/web/20210729175910/https://ifs.org.uk/tools_and_resources/fiscal_facts/fiscal-response-crisis (A: 09.09.22)

IFS (2022) 'UK public sector net debt since 1700', *Institute for Fiscal Studies*, https://ifs.org.uk/taxlab/taxlab-data-item/uk-public-sector-net-debt-1700 (A: 09.09.22)

Ikenberry, G.J. (1990) 'The international spread of privatization policies: Inducements, learning, and "policy bandwagoning" ' in Suleiman, E. and Waterbury, J. (eds) *The Political Economy of Public Sector Reform and Privatization* (London: Routledge), 88–110

IMF (International Monetary Fund) (2022) 'IMF statement on the UK', 27 September, https://www.imf.org/en/Countries/GBR (A: 07.10.22)

Imperial College COVID-19 Response Team (2020) 'Report 9 – Impact of non-pharmaceutical interventions (NPIs) to reduce COVID-19 mortality and healthcare demand', 16 March, https://www.imperial.ac.uk/mrc-global-inf ectious-disease-analysis/covid-19/report-9-impact-of-npis-on-covid-19/ (A: 07.04.20)

Independent Sage (2020) 'A better way to go: Towards to a zero COVID UK', https://www.independentsage.org/wp-content/uploads/2020/07/20200717-A-Better-Way-To-Go.pdf (A: 25.02.22)

Indyk, M.S. (2003) 'U.S. victory in Iraq opens possibility of Palestinian–Israeli settlement', Brookings Institute, 9 April, https://www.brookings.edu/on-the-record/u-s-victory-in-iraq-opens-possibility-of-palestinian-israeli-settlement/ (A: 07.10.22)

Inglehart, R. and Norris, P. (2017) 'Trump and the populist authoritarian parties: The silent revolution in reverse', *Perspectives on Politics*, 15, 2, 443–454, https://doi.org/10.1017/S1537592717000111

Institute of Employment Rights (2021) 'A chronology of labour law 1979–2017', *IER*, https://www.ier.org.uk/a-chronology-of-labour-law-1979-2017/ (A: 28.09.21)

Institute for Fiscal Studies (2022) 'IFS incomes, poverty, and inequality' (dataset tab 'Inequality'), https://ifs.org.uk/living-standards-poverty-and-inequality-uk (A: 22.09.22)

Institute for Government (2019) 'Cross-party cooperation on Brexit', 16 January, https://www.instituteforgovernment.org.uk/printpdf/5109 (A: 08.09.22)

Intelligence and Security Committee (2003) 'Iraqi weapons of mass destruction – intelligence and assessments', 10 September, https://isc.independent.gov.uk/wp-content/uploads/2021/01/200309_ISC_WMD_Report.pdf (A: 07.10.22)

International Chernobyl Project (1991) *The International Chernobyl Project: Technical Report* (Vienna: International Atomic Energy Agency)

International Criminal Tribunal for Rwanda (2015) 'The genocide', https://uni ctr.irmct.org/en/genocide (A: 28.09.22)

International Criminal Tribunal for the former Yugoslavia (2017) 'About the ICTY', https://www.icty.org/en/about (A: 28.09.22)

Involve (2018) 'Participatory budgeting', https://involve.org.uk/resources/meth ods/participatory-budgeting (A: 09.09.22)

IPCC (Intergovernmental Panel on Climate Change) (2019) *Summary for Policymakers (Global Warming of 1.5 °C)*, https://www.ipcc.ch/sr15/chapter/spm/ (A: 27.04.22)

IPCC (2022) *Summary for Policymakers*, https://www.ipcc.ch/report/ar6/wg2/downloads/report/IPCC_AR6_WGII_SummaryForPolicymakers.pdf (A: 20.04.22)

Iraq Body Count (2022) 'Homepage', https://www.iraqbodycount.org (A: 07.09.22)

ITV News (2023) 'Stormont Brake part of Windsor Protocol branded "practically useless" by group of Conservative MPs', 12 March, https://www.itv.com/news/utv/2023-03-21/stormont-brake-branded-practically-useless-by-mps (A: 20.04.23)

Jackson, J., Bradford, B., Yesberg, J., Hobson, Z., Kyprianides, A., Pósch, K. and Solymosi, R. (2020) 'Public compliance and COVID-19: Did Cummings damage the fight against the virus, or become a useful anti-role model?' *LSE British Politics and Policy*, 5 June, https://blogs.lse.ac.uk/politicsandpolicy/public-compliance-covid19-june/ (A: 13.07.20)

Jahan, S. and Papageorgiou, C. (2014) 'What is monetarism?', *Finance and Development*, 51, 1, 38–39, https://www.imf.org/external/pubs/ft/fandd/2014/03/basics.htm (A: 05.05.22)

Jahan, S., Mahmud, A.S. and Papageorgiou, C. (2014) 'What is Keynesian economics?' *Finance and Development*, 51, 3, 53–54, https://www.imf.org/external/pubs/ft/fandd/2014/09/basics.htm (A: 05.05.22)

James, O. (2001) 'Business models and the transfer of businesslike central government agencies', *Governance*, 14, 2, 233–252

James, O. (2009) 'Central state' in Flinders, M., Gamble, A., Hay, C. and Kenny, M. (eds) *The Oxford Handbook of British Politics* (Oxford: Oxford University Press), 342–364

JCWI (Joint Council on the Welfare of Immigrants) (2022) 'Joint statement on last week's deaths in the Channel / Communiqué commun sur les mort.e.s dans la Manche du 14 décembre 2022', https://www.jcwi.org.uk/joint-statement-on-last-weeks-deaths-in-the-channel (A: 20.04.23)

Jenkins, K. (2018) 'Setting energy justice apart from the crowd: Lessons from environmental and climate justice', *Energy Research & Social Science*, 39, May, 117–121, https://doi.org/10.1016/j.erss.2017.11.015

Jennings, W. and Lodge, M. (2019) 'Brexit, the tides and Canute: The fracturing politics of the British state', *Journal of European Public Policy*, 26, 5, 772–789

Jennings, W., Farrall, S., Gray, E. and Hay, C. (2017) 'Penal populism and the public thermostat: Crime, public punitiveness, and public policy', *Governance*, 30, 3, 463–481, https://onlinelibrary.wiley.com/doi/full/10.1111/gove.12214

Jennings, W., McKay, L. and Stoker, G. (2021) 'The politics of levelling up', *The Political Quarterly*, 92, 2, 302–311, https://doi.org/10.1111/1467-923X.13005

Jessop, R.D. (2003) 'From Thatcherism to New Labour: Neo-liberalism, workfarism, and labour market regulation' in Overbeek, H. (ed) *The Political Economy of European Employment: European Integration and the Transnationalization of the (Un)employment Question* (London: Routledge), 137–153

Jewish Chronicle (2016) 'For Blair, Iraq war was route to solving Israel–Palestine', 7 July, https://www.thejc.com/comment/analysis/for-blair-iraq-war-was-route-to-solving-israel-palestine-1.60261 (A: 07.10.22)

John, P. (1991) 'The restructuring of local government in England and Wales' in Batley, R. and Stoker, G. (eds) *Local Government in Europe* (London: Macmillan), 58–72

John, P. (1999) 'Ideas and interests; agendas and implementation: An evolutionary explanation of policy change in British local government finance', *British Journal of Politics and International Relations*, 1, 1, 39–62

John, P. (2011) *Making Policy Work* (London: Routledge)

John, P. (2018) 'Theories of British politics post-Brexit', SSRN, https://papers.ssrn.com/sol3/papers.cfm?abstract_id=3185193 (A: 08.09.22)

John, P. (2022) *British Politics* (Oxford: Oxford University Press)

John, P. and Margetts, H. (2003) 'Policy punctuations in the UK: Fluctuations and equilibria in central government expenditure since 1951', *Public Administration*, 81, 3, 411–432

John, P., Bertelli, A., Jennings, W. and Bevan, S. (2013) *Policy Agendas in British Politics* (London: Palgrave)

Johns, M. (2020) '10 years of austerity: Eroding resilience in the north', *IPPR North*, https://www.ippr.org/files/2020-06/10-years-of-austerity.pdf (A: 09.09.22)

Johnson, B. (2006) 'Saddam's trial – Iraq and post-war reconstruction', *Boris-Johnson.com*, https://www.boris-johnson.com/2006/09/28/saddams-trial-iraq-and-post-war-reconstruction/ (A: 07.10.22)

Johnson, B. (2016a) 'Of course our City fat cats love the EU – it's why they earn so much', *The Telegraph*, 15 May, https://www.telegraph.co.uk/news/2016/05/15/of-course-our-city-fat-cats-love-the-eu--its-why-they-earn-so-mu/ (A: 08.09.22)

Johnson, B. (2016b) 'Boris Johnson's speech on the EU referendum: Full text', *ConservativeHome.com*, https://conservativehome.com/2016/05/09/boris-johnsons-speech-on-the-eu-referendum-full-text/ (A: 02.09.22)

Johnson, B. (2020) 'PM address to the nation on coronavirus', 23 March, https://www.gov.uk/government/speeches/pm-address-to-the-nation-on-coronavirus-23-march-2020 (A: 07.04.20)

Johnson, B. (2021) 'PM statement at coronavirus press conference: 19 July 2021', *Gov.uk*, 19 July, https://www.gov.uk/government/speeches/pm-statement-at-coronavirus-press-conference-19-july-2021 (A: 24.03.22)

Johnson, P. (2020a) 'Huge ethical choices face those tasked with bringing the UK out of lockdown', *Institute for Fiscal Studies*, 13 April, https://www.ifs.org.uk/publications/14806 (A: 25.05.20)

Johnson, P. (2020b) 'We may be in this together, but that doesn't mean we are in this equally', *Institute for Fiscal Studies*, 27 April, https://www.ifs.org.uk/publi cations/14821 (A: 25.05.20)

Joint Committee on Human Rights (2022) 'Government creating hostile environment for peaceful protest, report finds', https://committees.parliam ent.uk/committee/93/human-rights-joint-committee/news/171503/governm ent-creating-hostile-environment-for-peaceful-protest-report (A: 26.09.22)

Joly, J. and Richter, F. (2022) 'The calm before the storm: A punctuated equilibrium theory of international politics', *Policy Studies Journal*, 51, 2, 265–282, https://doi.org/10.1111/psj.12478

Jones, B. (2020) *British Politics: The Basics* (London: Routledge)

Jones, B. and Baumgartner, F. (2005) *The Politics of Attention* (Chicago: University of Chicago Press)

Jones, C. and Murie, A. (2006) *The Right to Buy* (Oxford: Blackwell)

Jones, G., Meegan, R., Kennett, P. and Croft, J. (2016) 'The uneven impact of austerity on the voluntary and community sector: A tale of two cities', *Urban Studies*, 53, 10, 2064–2080, https://doi.org/10.1177/0042098015587240

Jones, H. (2013) *Negotiating Cohesion, Inequality and Change* (Bristol: Policy Press)

Jones, M. and Crow, D. (2017) 'How can we use the "science of stories" to produce persuasive scientific stories?', *Palgrave Communications*, 3, 53, https://doi.org/10.1057/s41599-017-0047-7

Jones, R., Goodwin-Hawkins, B. and Woods, M. (2020) 'From territorial cohesion to regional spatial justice: The Well-Being of Future Generations Act in Wales', *International Journal of Urban and Regional Research*, 44, 5, 894–912, https://doi.org/10.1111/1468-2427.12909

Jones, S.G. (2008) *Counterinsurgency in Afghanistan: RAND Counterinsurgency Study, Volume 4* (Washington, DC: Rand Corporation)

Jordan, A. (2022) 'Climate change' in Reland, J., Menon, A. and Rutter, J. (eds) *Doing Things Differently? Policy after Brexit* (UK in a Changing Europe), https://ukandeu.ac.uk/wp-content/uploads/2022/01/UKICE-Policy-Report_FINAL.pdf (A: 01.09.22)

Jordan, A. and Turnpenny, J. (eds) (2015) *The Tools of Policy Formulation* (Cheltenham: Edward Elgar)

Jordan, A., Lorenzoni, I., Tosun, J., Geese, L., Kenny, J., Saad, E.L., Moore, B. and Schaub, S.G. (2022) 'The political challenges of deep decarbonisation: Towards a more integrated agenda', *Climate Action*, 1, 1, 1–12, https://doi.org/10.1007/s44168-022-00004-7

Jordan, A.G. and Richardson, J.J. (1982) 'The British policy style or the logic of negotiation?' in Richardson, J.J. (ed) *Policy Styles in Western Europe* (London: Allen & Unwin), 199–264

Jordan, A.G. and Richardson, J.J. (1987) *Government and Pressure Groups in Britain* (Oxford: Clarendon Press)

Jordan, A.G. and Maloney, W.A. (1997) 'Accounting for subgovernments: Explaining the persistence of policy communities', *Administration and Society*, 29, 5, 557–583

Jordan, G. (1981) 'Iron triangles, woolly corporatism and elastic nets: Images of the policy process', *Journal of Public Policy*, 1, 1, 95–123

Jordan, G. (2001) *Shell, Greenpeace and Brent Spar* (London: Palgrave)

Jordan, G. and Cairney, P. (2013) 'What is the "dominant model" of British policy making? Comparing majoritarian and policy community ideas', *British Politics*, 8, 3, 233–259

Jordan, G., Halpin, D. and Maloney, W. (2004) 'Defining interests: Disambiguation and the need for new distinctions?' *British Journal of Politics and International Relations*, 6, 2, 195–212

Joseph-Salisbury, R., Connelly, L. and Wangari-Jones, P. (2021) ' "The UK is not innocent": Black Lives Matter, policing and abolition in the UK', *Equality, Diversity and Inclusion: An International Journal*, 40, 1, 21–28, https://www.emerald.com/insight/content/doi/10.1108/EDI-06-2020-0170/full/html (A: 17.08.22)

Judge, D. (1990) 'Parliament and interest representation' in Rush, M. (ed) *Parliament and Pressure Politics* (Oxford: Clarendon Press), 18–42

Judge, D. (1993) *The Parliamentary State* (London: SAGE)

Judge, D. and Leston-Bandeira, C. (2021) 'Why it matters to keep asking why legislatures matter', *The Journal of Legislative Studies*, 27, 2, 155–184, https://doi.org/10.1080/13572334.2020.1866836

Judge, D. and Shephard, M. (2022) 'Divining the UK's national interest: MPs' parliamentary discourse and the Brexit withdrawal process', *British Politics*, 1–24, https://doi.org/10.1057/s41293-022-00217-8

Judge, D., Hogwood, B. and McVicar, M. (1997) 'The "pondlife" of executive agencies: Parliament and "informatory" accountability', *Public Policy and Administration*, 12, 2, 95–115

Jupp, E. (2021) 'The time-spaces of austerity urbanism: Narratives of "localism" and UK neighbourhood policy', *Urban Studies*, 58, 5, 977–992, https://doi.org/10.1177/0042098020929503

Kaarbo, J. and Kenealy, D. (2016) 'No, prime minister: Explaining the House of Commons' vote on intervention in Syria', *European Security*, 25, 1, 28–48, https://doi.org/10.1080/09662839.2015.1067615

Kahneman, D. (2012) *Thinking Fast and Slow* (London: Penguin)

Kampfner, J. (2004) *Blair's Wars* (London: Simon & Schuster)

Kapadia, D., Zang, J., Salway, S., Nazroo, J., Booth, A., Villaroel-Williams, L., Becares, L. and Esmail, A. (2022) 'Ethnic inequalities in healthcare: A rapid evidence review', *NHS Race & Health Observatory*, https://www.nhsrho.org/wp-content/uploads/2022/02/RHO-Rapid-Review-Final-Report_Summary_v.4.pdf (A: 26.09.22)

Karlsen, S., Roth, M. and Bécares, L. (2019) 'Understanding the influence of ethnicity on health', in Chattoo, S., Atkin, K., Craig, G. and Flynn, R. (eds) *Understanding 'Race' and Ethnicity* (Bristol: Policy Press), 159–180

Katz, R.S. (2001) 'Models of democracy: Elite attitudes and the democratic deficit in the European Union', *European Union Politics*, 2, 1, 53–79, https://doi.org/10.1177/1465116501002001003

Kaunda, B. (2020) 'Potential environmental impacts of lithium mining', *Journal of Energy & Natural Resources Law*, 38, 3, 237–244, https://doi.org/10.1080/02646811.2020.1754596

Kaur, R. and Hague, G.M. (2021) 'Race commission report: The rights and wrongs', *The Conversation*, 1 April, https://theconversation.com/race-commiss ion-report-the-rights-and-wrongs-158316 (A: 26.09.22)

Kavanagh, D. and Richards, D. (2001) 'Departmentalism and joined-up government', *Parliamentary Affairs*, 54, 1, 1–18

Kavanagh, D. and Cowley, P. (2010) *The British General Election of 2010* (London: Palgrave)

Kay, A. (2011) 'UK monetary policy change during the financial crisis', *Journal of Public Policy*, 31, 2, 143–161

Keating, M. (2010) *The Government of Scotland*, 2nd edn (Edinburgh: Edinburgh University Press)

Keating, M. (2022) 'Taking back control? Brexit and the territorial constitution of the United Kingdom', *Journal of European Public Policy*, 29, 4, 491–509

Keating, M. and McEwen, N. (2020) 'The independence referendum of 2014' in Keating, M. (ed) *The Oxford Handbook of Scottish Politics* (Oxford: Oxford University Press), 650–674

Keating, M., Cairney, P. and Hepburn, E. (2009) 'Territorial policy communities and devolution in the United Kingdom', *Cambridge Journal of Regions, Economy and Society*, 2, 1, 51–66

Keating, M., Cairney, P. and Hepburn, E. (2012) 'Policy convergence, transfer and learning in the UK under devolution', *Regional and Federal Studies*, 22, 3, 289–307

Keating, M., Cairney, P. and Intropido, S. (2020) 'The political class in Scotland' in Keating, M. (ed) *The Oxford Handbook of Scottish Politics* (Oxford: Oxford University Press), 500–511

Keep, M. (2020) *Government Spending, Borrowing and Debt* (London: House of Commons Library)

Keep, M. (2022) *The Budget Deficit: A Short Guide* (London: House of Commons Library), https://commonslibrary.parliament.uk/research-briefings/sn06167/ (A: 17.08.23)

Kelly, C.J. and Tannam, E. (2023) 'The UK government's Northern Ireland policy after Brexit: A retreat to unilateralism and muscular unionism', *Journal of European Public Policy*, 1–28, https://doi.org/10.1080/13501763.2023.2210186

Kelly, G. and Pearce, N. (2023) 'Beveridge at eighty: Learning the right lessons', *Political Quarterly*, 94, 1, 8–15, https://doi.org/10.1111/1467-923X.13227

Kelly, J. (2007) 'Reforming public services in the UK: Bringing in the third sector', *Public Administration*, 85, 4, 1003–1022

Kennedy, D. (2007) 'New nuclear power generation in the UK: Cost benefit analysis', *Energy Policy*, 35, 7, 3701–3716, https://doi.org/10.1016/j.enpol.2007.01.010

Kenny, M. (2007) 'Gender, institutions and power: A critical review', *Politics*, 27, 2, 91–100

Kenny, M. (2016) *The Politics of English Nationhood* (Oxford: Oxford University Press)

Kenny, M. and Mackay, F. (2014) 'When is contagion not very contagious? Dynamics of women's political representation in Scotland', *Parliamentary Affairs*, 67, 4, 866–886

Kenny, M. and Sheldon, J. (2020) 'Territorial governance and the coronavirus crisis', *Centre on Constitutional Change*, 8 April, https://www.centreonconstitutionalchange.ac.uk/news-and-opinion/territorial-governance-and-coronavirus-crisis (A: 25.03.22)

Kenny, M., Bjarnegård, E., Lovenduski, J., Childs, S., Evans, E. and Verge, T. (2022) 'Reclaiming party politics research', *European Political Science*, 21, 274–291, https://doi.org/10.1057/s41304-022-00362-0

Kern, F., Smith, A., Shaw, C., Raven, R. and Verhees, B. (2014) 'From laggard to leader: Explaining offshore wind developments in the UK', *Energy Policy*, 69, 635–646, https://doi.org/10.1016/j.enpol.2014.02.031

Kerr, J. and Foster, L. (2011) 'Sustainable consumption: UK government activity', *Nutrition Bulletin*, 36, 4, 422–425, https://doi.org/10.1111/j.1467-3010.2011.01928.x

Kerr, P. (2001) *Postwar British Politics: From Conflict to Consensus* (London: Routledge)

Kerr, P. and Kettell, S. (2006) 'In defence of British politics: The past, present and future of the discipline', *British Politics*, 1, 1, 3–25

Kersten, J. and Moreira de Souza, T. (2020) 'Experiencing diversity in London' in Oosterlynck, S., Verschraegen, G. and van Kempen, R. (eds) *Divercities* (Bristol: Policy Press), 47–68

Kettell, S. (2013) 'Dilemmas of discourse: Legitimising Britain's war on terror', *The British Journal of Politics and International Relations*, 15, 2, 263–279, https://doi.org/10.1111/j.1467-856X.2012.00531.x

Kettell, S. and Kerr, P. (2020) 'From eating cake to crashing out: Constructing the myth of a no-deal Brexit', *Comparative European Politics*, 18, 4, 590–608, https://doi.org/10.1057/s41295-019-00200-6

Kettell, S. and Kerr, P. (2022) '"Guided by the science": (De)politicising the UK government's response to the coronavirus crisis", *British Journal of Politics and International Relations*, 24, 1, 11–30, https://doi.org/10.1177/13691481211054957

Khan, O. (2015) 'How the next government can reduce racial inequality', Runnymede Trust, https://www.runnymedetrust.org/blog/how-the-next-government-can-reduce-racial-inequality (A: 26.09.22)

Kickert, W. (2012) 'State responses to the fiscal crisis in Britain, Germany and the Netherlands', *Public Management Review*, 14, 3, 299–309, https://doi.org/10.1080/14719037.2011.637410

Kikeri, S., Nellis, J. and Shirley, M. (1992) *Privatization: The Lessons of Experience* (Washington, DC: The World Bank)

Killick, A. (2018) 'What do UK citizens understand about austerity' in Rhodes, R. (ed) *Narrative Policy Analysis* (London: Palgrave), 241–265

Kim, M., Cho, W., Choi, H. and Hur, J. (2020) 'Assessing the South Korean model of emergency management during the COVID-19 pandemic', *Asian Studies Review*, 44, 4, 567–578, https://doi.org/10.1080/10357823.2020.1779658

King, A. (2015) *Who Governs Britain?* (London: Pelican)

King, A. and Crewe, I. (2014) *The Blunders of Our Governments* (London: Simon & Schuster)

King, A., Henley, B. and Hawkins, E. (2017) 'What is a pre-industrial climate and why does it matter?', *The Conversation*, http://theconversation.com/what-is-apre-industrial-climate-and-why-does-it-matter-78601 (A: 27.04.22)

King, M. (2016) *The End of Alchemy: Money, Banking and the Future of the Global Economy* (Boston: Little, Brown Book Group)

King, S., Crees, M., Ball, C. and Gabriadze, M. (2023) 'The impact of strikes in the UK: June 2022 to February 2023', Office for National Statistics (ONS) briefing, 8 March, https://www.ons.gov.uk/employmentandlabourmarket/peopleinwork/workplacedisputesandworkingconditions/articles/theimpactofstrikesintheuk/june2022tofebruary2023 (A: 01.05.23)

Kingdon, J. (1995) *Agendas, Alternatives and Public Policies*, 2nd edn (New York: HarperCollins)

Kippin, S. (2018) 'Chapter 4.3: Accountability of the security and intelligence services' in Dunleavy, P., Parks, A. and Taylor, R. (eds) *The UK's Changing Democracy* (London: LSE Press), 173–181

Kippin, S. (2019) *A Fringe Concern? The Public Policy Influence of the Co-operative Party over New Labour (1997–2010)*, PhD thesis, University of the West of Scotland

Kippin, S. (2021) 'The Co-operative Party and New Labour: A study of policy entrepreneur influence', *British Politics*, https://doi.org/10.1057/s41293-021-00196-2

Kippin, S. (2023) 'Educational equity in England: the shortcomings of the UK Government's COVID-19 response [version 1; peer review: 1 approved]', *Routledge Open Research*, 2, 24, 1–14. https://doi.org/10.12688/routledgeopenres.17904.1]

Kippin, S. and Campion, S. (2018) 'Chapter 4.4: How undemocratic is the House of Lords?' in Dunleavy, P., Parks, A. and Taylor, R. (eds) *The UK's Changing Democracy* (London: LSE Press), 182–192.

Kippin, S. and Pyper, R. (2021) 'Collective ministerial responsibility in British government: The testing of a convention, 2010–2019', *The Political Quarterly*, 92, 3, 522–530, https://onlinelibrary.wiley.com/doi/10.1111/1467-923X.13012

Kippin, S. and Cairney, P. (2022a) 'The COVID-19 exams fiasco across the UK: Four nations and two windows of opportunity', *British Politics*, 17, 1, 1–22, https://doi.org/10.1057/s41293-021-00162-y

Kippin, S. and Cairney, P. (2022b) 'COVID-19 and the second exams fiasco across the UK: Four nations trying to avoid immediate policy failure', *British Politics*, https://doi.org/10.1057/s41293-022-00202-1

Kippin, S. and Pyper, R. (2023) 'Scrutiny of ministerial ethics and standards of conduct in the UK: Diluted accountability?', International Public Policy Conference, 27–29 June, Toronto

Kirkaldy, L. (2018) 'Legal challenge over Scottish Parliament Brexit bill to begin', *Holyrood*, 24 July, https://www.holyrood.com/news/view,legal-challenge-over-scottish-parliament-brexit-bill-to-begin_9024.htm (A: 07.09.22)

Kitchen, C. and Vickers, R. (2013) 'Labour traditions of international order and the dilemma of action towards Iran', *The British Journal of Politics and International Relations*, 15, 2, 299–316, https://doi.org/10.1111/j.1467-856X.2012.00529.x

Kitzinger, J. and Miller, D. (1992) '"African Aids": The media and audience beliefs' in Aggleton, P., Davies, P. and Hart, G. (eds) *AIDS: Rights, Risk and Reason* (London: The Falmer Press), 28–52

Klein, R. (1976) 'The politics of public expenditure: American theory and British practice', *British Journal of Political Science*, 6, 4, 401–432

Knai, C., Petticrew, M., Durand, M.A., Eastmure, E., James, L., Mehrotra, A., Scott, C. and Mays, N. (2015) 'Has a public–private partnership resulted in action on healthier diets in England? An analysis of the Public Health Responsibility Deal food pledges', *Food Policy*, 54, 1–10, https://doi.org/10.1016/j.foodpol.2015.04.002

Knight, C., Conn, C., Crick, T. and Brooks, S. (2023) 'Divergences in the framing of inclusive education across the UK: A four nations critical policy analysis', *Educational Review*, 1–17, https://doi.org/10.1080/00131911.2023.2222235

Knight, M., Bunch, K., Patel, R., Shakespeare, J., Kotnis, R., Kenyon, S. and Kurinczuk, J.J. (eds) on behalf of MBRRACE-UK (2022) *Saving Lives, Improving Mothers' Care Core Report* (Oxford: National Perinatal Epidemiology Unit, University of Oxford), https://www.npeu.ox.ac.uk/assets/downloads/mbrrace-uk/reports/maternal-report-2022/MBRRACE-UK_Maternal_MAIN_Report_2022_v10.pdf (A: 05.05.22)

Knox, R. (2021) 'International law, politics and opposition to the Iraq War', *London Review of International Law*, 9, 2, 169–195, https://doi.org/10.1093/lril/lrab014

Kollman, K. and Waites, M. (2011) 'United Kingdom: Changing political opportunity structures, policy success and continuing challenges for lesbian, gay and bisexual movements' in Tremblay, M., Paternotte, D. and Johnson, C. (eds) *The Lesbian and Gay Movement and the State: Comparative Insights into a Transformed Relationship* (Farnham: Ashgate), 181–196

Kooiman, J. (1993) 'Socio-political governance: Introduction' in Kooiman, J. (ed) *Modern Governance* (London: SAGE), 1–8

Kriesi, H., Adam, S. and Jochum, M. (2006) 'Comparative analysis of policy networks in Western Europe', *Journal of European Public Policy*, 13, 3, 341–361

Krook, M.L. (2006) 'Gender quotas, norms, and politics', *Politics & Gender*, 2, 1, 110–118

Krugman, P. (2008) 'Gordon does good', *The New York Times*, 12 October, https://www.nytimes.com/2008/10/13/opinion/13krugman.html (A: 09.09.22)

Krugman, P. (2015) 'The case for cuts was a lie. Why does Britain still believe it? The austerity delusion', *The Guardian*, 29 April, https://www.theguardian.com/business/ng-interactive/2015/apr/29/the-austerity-delusion (A: 09.09.22)

Kulldorff, M., Gupta, S. and Bhattacharya, J. (2020) 'Great Barrington Declaration', https://gbdeclaration.org (A: 14.06.22)

Kurylo, B. (2021) 'Counter-populist performances of (in)security: Feminist resistance in the face of right-wing populism in Poland', *Review of International Studies*, 48, 2, 262–281, https://doi.org/10.1017/S0260210521000620

Kuzemko, C. (2016) 'Energy depoliticisation in the UK: Destroying political capacity', *The British Journal of Politics and International Relations*, 18, 1, 107–124, https://doi.org/10.1111/1467-856X.12068

Kuzemko, C. (2022) 'Business, government and policy-making capacity: UK energy and net zero transitions', *Political Quarterly*, 93, 2, 235–243

Kuzemko, C., Blondeel, M. and Froggatt, A. (2022) 'Brexit implications for sustainable energy in the UK', *Policy & Politics*, 1–20, https://doi.org/10.1332/030557321X16510710991392

Kwoba, B., Chantiluke, R. and Nkopo, A. (eds) (2018) *Rhodes Must Fall: The Struggle to Decolonise the Racist Heart of Empire* (London: Bloomsbury)

Labour Party (2018) 'Here's what Section 28 was all about', *Labour*, 24 May, https://labour.org.uk/latest/heres-section-28/ (A: 12.09.22)

Ladrech, R. (2016) 'Explainer: What's the difference between "hard" and "soft" Brexit?', *The Conversation*, 6 October, https://theconversation.com/explainer-whats-the-difference-between-hard-and-soft-brexit-66524 (A: 11.07.23)

Lagana, G. (2021) *The European Union and the Northern Ireland Peace Process* (London: Palgrave Macmillan)

Lambert, M. and Crossley, S. (2017) '"Getting with the (troubled families) programme": A review', *Social Policy and Society*, 16, 1, 87–97, https://doi.org/10.1017/S1474746416000385

Lammers, J., Crusius, J. and Gast, A. (2020) 'Correcting misperceptions of exponential coronavirus growth increases support for social distancing', *Proceedings of the National Academy of Sciences*, 117, 28, 16264–16266

Lammy Review (2017) 'Lammy review: Final report', UK Government, 8 September, https://www.gov.uk/government/publications/lammy-review-final-report (A: 26.09.22)

Lancet Commission (2019) 'The global syndemic of obesity, undernutrition, and climate change: The Lancet Commission report', *The Lancet*, 393, 10173, 791–846, https://doi.org/10.1016/S0140-6736(18)32822-8

Landale, J. (2013) 'David Cameron: Labour's the point', *BBC News*, 2 October, https://www.bbc.co.uk/news/uk-politics-24371521 (A: 09.09.22)

Landemore, H. (2014) 'Inclusive constitution-making: The Icelandic experiment', *Political Philosophy*, 23, 2, 166–191, https://doi.org/10.1111/jopp.12032

Lander, S. (2004) 'International intelligence cooperation: An inside perspective', *Cambridge Review of International Affairs*, 3, 481–493, https://doi.org/10.1080/0955757042000296964

Laniyonu, A. (2021) 'Phantom pains: The effect of police killings of Black Americans on Black British attitudes', *British Journal of Political Science*, 1–17, https://doi.org/10.1017/S000712342100055

Larkin, K. (2009) 'Regional Development Agencies: The facts', 8 December, https://www.centreforcities.org/publication/regional-development-agencies-the-facts/ (A: 09.09.22)

Larner, W. and Walters, W. (2000) 'Privatisation, governance and identity: The United Kingdom and New Zealand compared', *Policy & Politics*, 28, 3, 361–377

Larsen, L.T., Studlar, D.T. and Green-Pedersen, C. (2012) 'Morality politics in the United Kingdom: Trapped between left and right' in Engeli, I., Green-Pedersen, C. and Larsen, L.T. (eds) *Morality Politics in Western Europe* (London: Palgrave), 114–136

Laursen, F. and Vanhoonacker, S. (2019) 'The Maastricht Treaty: Creating the European Union', *Oxford Research Encyclopedia of Politics*, https://doi.org/10.1093/acrefore/9780190228637.013.1067

Laux, R. and Nissar, S. (2022) 'Why we've stopped using the term "BAME" in government', *Civil Service Blog*, 19 May, https://civilservice.blog.gov.uk/2022/05/19/why-weve-stopped-using-the-term-bame-in-government/ (A: 03.09.22)

Lavalette, M. and Mooney, G. (1990) 'Undermining the "north–south divide"? Fighting the poll tax in Scotland, England and Wales', *Critical Social Policy*, 10, 29, 100–119, https://doi.org/10.1177/026101839001002908

Lawder, D. and Jarry, E. (2008) 'World leaders urge fast action on financial crisis', *Reuters*, 16 November, https://www.reuters.com/article/us-financial-summit1-idUSTRE4AD7AK20081116 (A: 09.09.22)

Layard, R., Clark, A., De Neve, J., Krekel, C., Fancourt, D., Hey, N. and O'Donnell, G. (2020) 'When to release the lockdown: A wellbeing framework for analysing costs and benefits', *Centre for Economic Performance Occasional Paper*, 49 (London: LSE), http://eprints.lse.ac.uk/104276/1/Layard_when_to_release_the_lockdown_published.pdf (A: 19.05.22)

Lea, J. (2002) 'The Macpherson Report and the question of institutional racism', *The Howard Journal of Crime and Justice*, 39, 3, 219–233, https://doi.org/10.1111/1468-2311.00165

Lea, J. and Hallsworth, S. (2012) 'Understanding the riots', *Criminal Justice Matters*, 87, https://www.crimeandjustice.org.uk/publications/cjm/article/understanding-riots (A: 26.09.22)

Lee, S., Ditko, S. and Kirby, J. (2022) *Amazing Spider-Man Epic Collection: Great Power* (US: Marvel)

Leigh, D. and Hooper, J. (2003) 'Britain's dirty secret', *The Guardian*, 6 March, https://www.theguardian.com/politics/2003/mar/06/uk.iraq (A: 07.10.22)

Leiren, M.D., Inderberg, T.H.J. and Rayner, T. (2021) 'Policy styles, opportunity structures and proportionality: Comparing renewable electricity policies in the UK', *International Political Science Review*, 42, 1, 33–47, https://doi.org/10.1177/0192512120907112

Levin, K., Cashore, B., Bernstein, S. and Auld, G. (2012) 'Overcoming the tragedy of super wicked problems: Constraining our future selves to ameliorate global climate change', *Policy Sciences*, 45, 2, 123–152

Levitas, R. (2012) 'The just's umbrella: Austerity and the Big Society in coalition policy and beyond', *Critical Social Policy*, 32, 3, 320–342, https://doi.org/10.1177/0261018312444408

Levitas, R. (2014) ' "Troubled families" in a spin', *Poverty and Social Exclusion*, 11 March, https://www.poverty.ac.uk/editorial/%E2%80%98troubled-families%E2%80%99-spin (A: 19.09.22)

Lewis, H. (2017) 'Jeremy Corbyn: "Wholesale" EU immigration has destroyed conditions for British workers', *The New Statesman*, 24 July, https://www.newstatesman.com/politics/2017/07/jeremy-corbyn-wholesale-eu-immigration-has-destroyed-conditions-british (A: 07.09.22)

Lewis, T., Buck, D. and Wenzel, L. (2022) 'Equity and endurance: How can we tackle health inequalities this time?', *The Kings Fund*, 16 March, https://www.kingsfund.org.uk/publications/how-can-we-tackle-health-inequalities (A: 08.04.22)

Liberal Democrat Party (2010) 'Liberal Democrat Manifesto 2010', https://www.markpack.org.uk/files/2015/01/Liberal-Democrat-manifesto-2010.pdf (A: 09.09.22)

Liddell, C., Morris, C., McKenzie, S.J.P. and Rae, G. (2012) 'Measuring and monitoring fuel poverty in the UK: National and regional perspectives', *Energy Policy*, 49, 27–32, https://doi.org/10.1016/j.enpol.2012.02.029

Lijphart, A. (1999) *Patterns of Democracy* (New Haven: Yale University Press)

Lindblom, C. (1959) 'The science of muddling through', *Public Administration Review*, 19, 79–88

Lindblom, C. (1979) 'Still muddling, not yet through', *Public Administration Review*, 39, 517–525

Linton, S. (2018) 'Editor's introduction' in Linton, S. and Walcott, R. (eds) *The Colour of Madness: Exploring BAME Mental Health in the UK* (Edinburgh: Skiddaw)

Lipsky, M. (1980) *Street-Level Bureaucracy* (New York: Russell Sage Foundation)

Little, R.A. and Lyon, J. (2022) 'Agriculture' in Reland, J., Menon, A. and Rutter, J. (eds) *Doing Things Differently? Policy after Brexit* (UK in a Changing Europe), https://ukandeu.ac.uk/wp-content/uploads/2022/01/UKICE-Policy-Report_FINAL.pdf (A: 01.09.22)

Liu, Y. and Rocklöv, J. (2021) 'The reproductive number of the Delta variant of SARS-CoV-2 is far higher compared to the ancestral SARS-CoV-2 virus', *Journal of Travel Medicine*, 28, 7, 1–3, https://doi.org/10.1093/jtm/taab124

Liu, Y. and Rocklöv, J. (2022) 'The effective reproduction number for the omicron SARS-CoV-2 variant of concern is several times higher than Delta', *Journal of Travel Medicine*, https://doi.org/10.1093/jtm/taac037

Livingston, J.E. and Rummukainen, M. (2020) 'Taking science by surprise: The knowledge politics of the IPCC Special Report on 1.5 degrees', *Environmental Science & Policy*, 112, 10–16, https://doi.org/10.1016/j.envsci.2020.05.020

Locatelli, I., Trachsel, B. and Rousson, V. (2021) 'Estimating the basic reproduction number for COVID-19 in Western Europe', *PLoS ONE*, 16, 3, e0248731, https://doi.org/10.1371/journal.pone.0248731

Lockwood, M. (2013) 'The political sustainability of climate policy: The case of the UK Climate Change Act', *Global Environmental Change*, 23, 5, 1339–1348, https://doi.org/10.1016/j.gloenvcha.2013.07.001

Lockwood, M. (2021) 'A hard act to follow? The evolution and performance of UK climate governance', *Environmental Politics*, 30, supp 1, 26–48, https://doi.org/10.1080/09644016.2021.1910434

Lodge, M. and Weigrich, K. (2012) *Managing Regulation: Regulatory Analysis, Politics and Policy* (Basingstoke: Palgrave)

Loft, P. (2020) 'The Troubled Families Programme (England)', *House of Commons Library*, https://researchbriefings.files.parliament.uk/documents/CBP-7585/CBP-7585.pdf (A: 22.09.22)

Looney, R.E. (2008) 'Reconstruction and peacebuilding under extreme adversity: The problem of pervasive corruption in Iraq', *International Peacekeeping*, 3, 424–440, https://doi.org/10.1080/13533310802059032

López, T.M. (2014) *The Winter of Discontent: Myth, Memory, and History*, vol 4 (Oxford: Oxford University Press)

Lorenzoni, I. and Benson, D. (2014) 'Radical institutional change in environmental governance: Explaining the origins of the UK Climate Change Act 2008 through discursive and streams perspectives', *Global Environmental Change*, 29, 10–21, https://doi.org/10.1016/j.gloenvcha.2014.07.011

Los, G. (2023) 'Critically explaining British policy responses to novel psychoactive substances using the policy constellations framework', *Drugs: Education, Prevention and Policy*, 1–9, https://doi.org/10.1080/09687637.2023.2218536

Lovell, H., Bulkeley, H. and Owens, S. (2009) 'Converging agendas? Energy and climate change policies in the UK', *Environment and Planning C: Government and Policy*, 27, 1, 90–109, https://doi.org/10.1068/c0797j

Lovenduski, J. (2005) 'Introduction' in Lovenduski, J. (ed) *State Feminism and Political Representation* (Cambridge: Cambridge University Press), 1–10

Lowes, R. and Mitchell, C. (2021) *Energy Governance for the Northern Ireland Energy Transition* (Exeter: Energy Policy Group), https://ore.exeter.ac.uk/repository/bitstream/handle/10871/125035/Energy%20governance%20for%20the%20Northern%20Ireland%20energy%20transition%20final%20published.pdf?sequence=1 (A: 10.09.22)

Lowi, T. (1964) 'An American business, public policy, case-studies, and political theory', *World Politics*, 16, 4, 677–715

Lowi, T. (1972) 'Four systems of policy, politics and choice', *Public Administration Review*, 32, 4, 298–310

Luce, E. (2007) 'Was Blair Bush's poodle?', *Financial Times*, 10 May, https://archive.ph/8N4qp#selection-1519.0-1600.0 (A: 07.10.22)

Ludlam, S. and Smith, M.J. (eds) (2000) *New Labour in Government* (London: Palgrave Macmillan)

Ludlow, N.P. (2016) 'The history of the EU: The European name game', *UK in a Changing Europe*, 20 April, https://ukandeu.ac.uk/explainers/the-european-name-game-2/ (A: 18.08.22)

Lynch, D. (2022) 'Police need to stop pandering to identity politics – Suella Braverman', *The Standard*, 5 October, https://www.standard.co.uk/news/politics/suella-braverman-home-secretary-police-conservative-party-sussex-police-b1030241.html (A: 11.10.22)

Lynn, J. and Jay, A. (1989) *The Complete Yes Prime Minister: The Diaries of the Right Hon. James Hacker* (London: BBC Books)

Maassen, L. and Zacchia, G. (2017) 'The effect of austerity on unpaid work and gender relations in Europe', *Exploring Economics*, https://www.exploring-economics.org/en/discover/austerity-unpaid-work/ (A: 09.09.22)

MacAskill, A. and Piper, E. (2022) 'Truss's demise ends the revival of Thatcher's libertarian economics', *Reuters*, 20 October, https://www.reuters.com/world/uk/trusss-demise-ends-revival-thatchers-libertarian-economics-2022-10-20/ (A: 01.05.23)

MacAskill, E. and Borger, J. (2004) 'Iraq war was illegal and breached UN charter, says Annan', *The Guardian*, 16 September, https://www.theguardian.com/world/2004/sep/16/iraq.iraq (A: 07.10.22)

MacDonald, E. (2018) 'The gendered impact of austerity: Cuts are widening the poverty gap between women and men', *LSE Politics and Policy*, 10 January, https://blogs.lse.ac.uk/politicsandpolicy/gendered-impacts-of-austerity-cuts/ (A: 09.09.22)

Mac Flynn, P. (2015) 'Austerity in Northern Ireland: Where are we and where are we going?', *Nevin Economic Research Institute*, https://www.nerinstitute.net/blog/austerity-northern-ireland-where-are-we-and-where-are-we-going (A: 09.09.22)

Machin, R. (2017) 'The professional and ethical dilemmas of the two-child limit for Child Tax Credit and Universal Credit', *Ethics and Social Welfare*, 11, 4, 404–411, https://doi.org/10.1080/17496535.2017.1386227

Mackinnon, D., Shaw, J. and Docherty, I. (2010) 'Devolution as process: Institutional structures, state personnel and transport policy in the United Kingdom', *Space and Polity*, 14, 3, 271–287, https://doi.org/10.1080/13562576.2010.532965

MacLeavy, J. (2011) 'A "new politics" of austerity, workfare and gender? The UK coalition government's welfare reform proposals', *Cambridge Journal of Regions, Economy and Society*, 4, 3, 355–367, https://doi.org/10.1093/cjres/rsr023

Macpherson, W. (1999) *The Stephen Lawrence Inquiry: Report of an Inquiry by Sir William Macpherson of Cluny* (London: HM Government), https://assets.publishing.service.gov.uk/government/uploads/system/uploads/attachment_data/file/277111/4262.pdf (A: 12.07.23)

MacRae, H. (2010) 'The EU as a gender equal polity: Myths and reality', *Journal of Common Market Studies*, 48, 1, 155–174, https://doi.org/10.1111/j.1468-5965.2009.02046.x

Maddox, D. (2022) 'Brexiteers give Boris 2,000 ideas to obliterate EU rules – and here are their suggestions', *The Daily Express*, 31 May, https://www.express.co.uk/news/politics/1618395/Brexit-news-Boris-Johnson-2000-ideas-Jacob-Rees-Mogg-suggestions-EU-rules-update (A: 08.09.22)

Maffini, G. (2015) 'Business taxation under the coalition government', Oxford University Centre for Business Taxation, https://oxfordtax.sbs.ox.ac.uk/business-taxation-under-coalition-government (A: 09.09.22)

Maishman, E. (2022) 'Sewage in sea: French appeal to EU over UK discharges of waste', *BBC News*, 25 August, https://www.bbc.co.uk/news/world-europe-62670623 (A: 26.08.22)

Malik, N. (2017) 'Grenfell shows just how Britain fails migrants', *The Guardian*, 16 June, https://www.theguardian.com/commentisfree/2017/jun/16/grenfell-britain-fails-migrants-north-kensington-london-refugee (A: 06.09.22)

Maloney, W., Jordan, G. and McLaughlin, A. (1994) 'Interest groups and public policy: The insider/outsider model revisited', *Journal of Public Policy*, 14, 1, 17–38

Mansour, N. (2019) 'What has austerity meant for Wales?', *Welsh TUC*, https://www.tuc.org.uk/blogs/what-has-austerity-meant-wales (A: 09.09.22)

Maor, M. and Jones, G.W. (1999) 'Varieties of administrative convergence', *International Journal of Public Sector Management*, 12, 1, 49–62

March, J. and Olsen, J. (1984) 'The new institutionalism: Organizational factors in political life', *The American Political Science Review*, 78, 3, 734–749

Margetts, H. (2009) 'The internet and public policy', *Policy & Internet*, 1, 1, 1–12, https://doi.org/10.2202/1944-2866.1029

Margetts, H. and Dunleavy, P. (2013) 'The second wave of digital-era governance: A quasi-paradigm for government on the web', *Philosophical Transactions of the Royal Society*, 371, 1987, https://doi.org/10.1098/rsta.2012.0382

Marinetto, M. (2003) 'Governing beyond the centre: A critique of the Anglo-governance school', *Political Studies*, 51, 592–608

Mark, K.M., Leightley, D. and Sharp, M. (2018) 'Increase in PTSD among UK veterans who served in Afghanistan and Iraq – new research', *The Conversation*, 8 October, https://theconversation.com/increase-in-ptsd-among-uk-veterans-who-served-in-afghanistan-and-iraq-new-research-104284 (A: 07.10.22)

Markandya, A., Sampedro, J., Smith, S.J., Van Dingenen, R., Pizarro-Irizar, C., Arto, I. and González-Eguino, M. (2018) 'Health co-benefits from air pollution and mitigation costs of the Paris Agreement: A modelling study', *The Lancet Planetary Health*, 2, 3, e126–e133, https://doi.org/10.1016/S2542-5196(18)30029-9

Marks, G. and Hooghe, L. (2000) 'Optimality and authority: A critique of neoclassical theory', *Journal of Common Market Studies*, 38, 5, 795–816

Marmot, M. (2022) 'Studying health inequalities has been my life's work: What's about to happen in the UK is unprecedented', *The Guardian*, 8 April, https://www.theguardian.com/commentisfree/2022/apr/08/health-inequalities-uk-poverty-life-death (A: 08.04.22)

Marmot, M., Allen, J., Goldblatt, P., Herd, E. and Morrison, J. (2020) *Build Back Fairer: The COVID-19 Marmot Review. The Pandemic, Socioeconomic and Health Inequalities in England* (London: Institute of Health Equity)

Marsden, G. and Docherty, I. (2019) *Governance of UK Transport Infrastructures* (London: Government Office for Science), https://www.gov.uk/government/publications/future-of-mobility-governance-of-uk-transport-infrastructures (A: 30.09.22)

Marsden, G., Anable, J., Chatterton, T., Docherty, I., Faulconbridge, J., Murray, L., Roby, H. and Shires, J. (2020) 'Studying disruptive events: Innovations in behaviour, opportunities for lower carbon transport policy?', *Transport Policy*, 94, 89–101, https://doi.org/10.1016/j.tranpol.2020.04.008

Marsden, T. (2012) 'Towards a real sustainable agri-food security and food policy: Beyond the ecological fallacies?', *The Political Quarterly*, 83, 1, 139–145, https://doi.org/10.1111/j.1467-923X.2012.02242.x

Marsh, D. (1991) 'Privatization under Mrs Thatcher: A review of the literature', *Public Administration*, 69, 4, 459–480

Marsh, D. (1992) 'Industrial relations' in Marsh, D. and Rhodes, R.A.W. (eds) *Implementing Thatcherite Policies* (Buckingham: Open University Press), 32–49

Marsh, D. (2008) 'Understanding British government: Analysing competing models', *British Journal of Politics and International Relations*, 10, 2, 251–269

Marsh, D. (2011) 'The new orthodoxy: The differentiated polity model', *Public Administration*, 89, 1, 32–48

Marsh, D. (2018) 'Brexit and the politics of truth', *British Politics*, 13, 79–89

Marsh, D. and Rhodes, R.A.W. (eds) (1992) *Implementing Thatcherite Policies* (Buckingham: Open University Press)

Marsh, D. and McConnell, A. (2010) 'Towards a framework for establishing policy success', *Public Administration*, 88, 2, 564, 583, https://doi.org/10.1111/j.1467-9299.2009.01803.x

Marsh, D. and McCaffrie, B. (2015) 'One cheer for Jordan and Cairney: Taking the governance literature seriously', *British Politics*, 10, 4, 475–485

Marsh, D., Richards, D. and Smith, M.J. (2001) *Changing Patterns of Governance in the United Kingdom* (London: Palgrave)

Marsh, D., Richards, D. and Smith, M.J. (2003) 'Unequal plurality: Towards an asymmetric power model of British politics', *Government and Opposition*, 38, 306–332

Marsh, K.P. (2012) 'The intersection of war and politics: The Iraq War troop surge and bureaucratic politics', *Armed Forces & Society*, 3, 413–437, https://doi.org/10.1177/0095327X11415492

Marshall, J. and Mills-Sheehy, J. (2022) 'Agricultural subsidies after Brexit', *Institute for Government*, 14 February, https://www.instituteforgovernment.org.uk/explainers/agriculture-subsidies-after-brexit (A: 08.09.22)

Marshall, P. (2012) 'The Orange Book, economic affairs, education and social mobility', *Economic Affairs*, 32, 2, 27–30

Martin, G.P., Hanna, E., McCartney, M. and Dingwall, R. (2020a) 'Urgency and uncertainty: Covid-19, face masks, and evidence informed policy', *British Medical Journal*, 369, https://doi.org/10.1136/bmj.m2017

Martin, G.P., Hanna, E., McCartney, M. and Dingwall, R. (2020b) 'Science, society, and policy in the face of uncertainty: Reflections on the debate around face coverings for the public during COVID-19', *Critical Public Health*, 30, 5, 501–508, https://doi.org/10.1080/09581596.2020.1797997

Martin, R., Pike, A., Sunley, P., Tyler, P. and Gardiner, B. (2022) '"Levelling up" the UK: Reinforcing the policy agenda', *Regional Studies, Regional Science*, 9, 1, 794–817, https://doi.org/10.1080/21681376.2022.2150562

Mason, C. and Eardley, N. (2023) 'SNP plays longer game in bid for Scottish independence', *BBC News*, 29 April, https://www.bbc.co.uk/news/uk-politics-65425495 (A: 02.05.23)

Massey, A. and Pyper, R. (2005) *Public Management and Modernisation in Britain* (London: Palgrave)

Massey, P. (2001) 'Policy, management and implementation' in Savage, S. and Atkinson, R. (eds) *Public Policy under Blair* (London: Palgrave), 20–40

Mattar, S., Jafry, T., Schröder, P. and Ahmad, Z. (2021) 'Climate justice: Priorities for equitable recovery from the pandemic', *Climate Policy*, 21, 10, 1307–1317, https://doi.org/10.1080/14693062.2021.1976095

Matthews, F. (2016) 'Letting go and holding on: The politics of performance management in the United Kingdom', *Public Policy and Administration*, 31, 4, 303–323

Mattheys, K. (2015) 'The coalition, austerity and mental health', *Disability & Society*, 30, 3, 475–478, https://doi.org/10.1080/09687599.2014.1000513

Maughan, B. (2010) 'Tony Blair's asylum policies: The narratives and conceptualisations at the heart of New Labour's restrictionism', *Refugee Studies Centre*, https://www.rsc.ox.ac.uk/files/files-1/wp69-tony-blairs-asylum-policies-2010.pdf (A: 20.04.23)

Mawhood, B., Bolton, P. and Stewart, I. (2022) 'Energy Bills Support Scheme: Government policy and FAQs' (House of Commons Library Research Briefing), 9 August, https://commonslibrary.parliament.uk/research-briefings/cbp-9461/ (A: 26.04.23)

Mawhood, B., Bolton, P. and Stewart, I. (2023) 'Constituency casework: Government support for energy bills' (House of Commons Library Research Briefing), 20 March, https://commonslibrary.parliament.uk/research-briefings/cbp-9685/ (A: 26.04.23)

May, T. and Nugent, T. (1982) 'Insiders, outsiders and thresholders: Corporatism and pressure group strategies in Britain', Political Studies Association Conference, University of Kent

Mayne, R., Fawcett, T. and Hyams, K. (2017) 'Climate justice and energy: Applying international principles to UK residential energy policy', *Local Environment*, 22, 4, 393–409, https://doi.org/10.1080/13549839.2016.1206515

Mayne, R., Green, D., Guijt, I., Walsh, M., English, R. and Cairney, P. (2018) 'Using evidence to influence policy: Oxfam's experience', *Palgrave Communications*, 4, 122, 1–10, DOI: 10.1057/s41599-018-0176-7

Mazarr, M.J. (2007) 'The Iraq War and agenda setting', *Foreign Policy Analysis*, 3, 1, 1–23, https://www.jstor.org/stable/24907218

McCann, P. and Ortega-Argilés, R. (2021) 'The UK "geography of discontent": Narratives, Brexit and inter-regional "levelling up"', *Cambridge Journal of Regions, Economy and Society*, 14, 3, 545–564, https://doi.org/10.1093/cjres/rsab017

McClure, H. and McNally, M. (2021) *School Meals in Northern Ireland 2020–21* (Belfast: NISRA), https://dera.ioe.ac.uk/37857/1/School%20Meals%20in%20Northern%20Ireland%202020-21%20statistical%20bulletin%20%28redacted%29.pdf (A: 09.08.22)

McConnell, A. (1995) *State Policy Formation and the Origins of the Poll Tax* (Aldershot: Dartmouth)

McConnell, A. (2000) 'Local taxation, policy formation and policy change: A reply to Peter John', *British Journal of Politics and International Relations*, 2, 1, 81–88

McConnell, A. (2010) *Understanding Policy Success: Rethinking Public Policy* (Basingstoke: Palgrave Macmillan)

McConnell, A. (2016) 'A public policy approach to understanding the nature and causes of foreign policy failure', *Journal of European Public Policy*, 23, 5, 667–684, https://doi.org/10.1080/13501763.2015.1127278

McConnell, A. (2018) 'Rethinking wicked problems as political problems and policy problems', *Policy & Politics*, 46, 1, 165–180

McConnell, A. and Tormey, S. (2020) 'Explanations for the Brexit policy fiasco: Near-impossible challenge, leadership failure or Westminster pathology?', *Journal of European Public Policy*, 27, 5, 685–702, https://doi.org/10.1080/13501763.2019.1657485

McCourt, D. (2013) 'Embracing humanitarian intervention: Atlanticism and the UK interventions in Bosnia and Kosovo', *The British Journal of Politics and International Relations*, 15, 2, 246–262, https://doi.org/10.1111/j.1467-856X.2012.00532.x

McCrisken, T. (2011) 'Ten years on: Obama's war on terrorism in rhetoric and practice', *International Affairs*, 87, 4, 781–801, http://dx.doi.org/10.1111/j.1468-2346.2011.01004.x

McCrisken, T. (2013) 'Obama's war on terrorism in rhetoric and practice' in Bentley, M. and Holland, J. (eds) *Obama's Foreign Policy* (London: Routledge)

McCrudden, C. (2017) 'The Good Friday Agreement, Brexit, and rights', *The British Academy*, https://www.thebritishacademy.ac.uk/documents/97/TheGoodFridayAgreementBrexitandRights_0.pdf (A: 07.09.22)

McDonald, S. (2022) 'Why have there been excess deaths this summer?', *UK in a Changing Europe*, 24 August, https://ukandeu.ac.uk/why-have-there-been-excess-deaths-this-summer/ (A: 24.08.22)

McEwen, N. (2021) 'Negotiating Brexit: Power dynamics in British intergovernmental relations', *Regional Studies*, 55, 9, 1538–1549, https://doi.org/10.1080/00343404.2020.1735000

McEwen, N. and Bomberg, E. (2014) 'Sub-state climate pioneers: The case of Scotland', *Regional & Federal Studies*, 24, 1, 63–85, https://doi.org/10.1080/13597566.2013.820182

McEwen, N., McHarg, A., Munro, F., Cairney, P., Turner, K. and Katris, A. (2019) *Brexit and Renewables in Scotland* (London: UKERC), https://strathprints.strath.ac.uk/72042/1/McEwan_etal_UKERC_2019_Brexit_and_renewables_in_Scotland.pdf (A: 14.08.22)

McGlinchey, S., Walters, R. and Scheinpflug, C. (2017) *International Relations Theory* (Bristol: E-IR), https://www.e-ir.info/publication/international-relations-theory/ (A: 14.09.22)

McGowan, F. (2011) 'The UK and EU energy policy' in Duffield, J.S. and Birchfield, V.L. (eds) *Toward a Common European Energy Policy* (London: Palgrave), 187–213

McGowan, F. (2020) 'Policy learning or politics as usual? Explaining the rise and retrenchment of renewable electricity support policies in Europe', *Environmental Politics*, 29, 4, 589–608, https://doi.org/10.1080/09644016.2020.1741114

McHarg, A. (2011) 'Climate change constitutionalism? Lessons from the United Kingdom', *Climate Law*, 2, 469–484, https://doi.org/10.1163/CL-2011-047

McHarg, A. and Mitchell, J. (2017) 'Brexit and Scotland', *The British Journal of Politics and International Relations*, 19, 3, 512–526, https://doi.org/10.1177/1369148117711674

McIntyre, S., Mitchell, J. and Roy, G. (2022) 'Fiscal devolution and the accountability gap: Budget scrutiny following tax devolution to Scotland', *Regional Studies*, 1–13, https://doi.org/10.1080/00343404.2022.2112166

McKay, L. (2010) 'Escaping the poverty trap: How to help people on benefits into work', *Policy Exchange*, https://policyexchange.org.uk/wp-content/uploads/2016/09/escaping-the-poverty-trap-mar-10.pdf (A: 09.09.22)

McKee, K. (2010) 'The end of the Right to Buy and the future of social housing in Scotland', *Local Economy*, 25, 4, 319–327

McMahon, N. (2021) 'Working "upstream" to reduce social inequalities in health: A qualitative study of how partners in an applied health research collaboration interpret the metaphor', *Critical Public Health*, 1–12, https://doi.org/10.1080/09581596.2021.1931663

McMahon, N. (2022) 'Framing action to reduce health inequalities: What is argued for through use of the "upstream–downstream" metaphor?', *Journal of Public Health*, 44, 3, 671–678, https://doi.org/10.1093/pubmed/fdab157

McMillan, F. (2020) 'Devolution, "new politics" and election pledge fulfilment in Scotland, 1999–2011', *British Politics*, 15, 251–269, https://doi.org/10.1057/s41293-019-00120-9

McNaugher, T.L. (1990) 'Ballistic missiles and chemical weapons: The legacy of the Iran–Iraq War', *International Security*, 15, 2, 5–34

McPherson, A.M. and Raab, C.D. (1988) *Governing Education: A Sociology of Policy since 1945* (Edinburgh: Edinburgh University Press)

McPherson, W. (1999) *The Stephen Lawrence Inquiry: Report of an Inquiry by Sir William McPherson of Cluny* (London: HM Government), https://assets.publishing.service.gov.uk/government/uploads/system/uploads/attachment_data/file/277111/4262.pdf

Medvedyuk, S., Govender, P. and Raphael, D. (2021) 'The reemergence of Engels' concept of social murder in response to growing social and health inequalities', *Social Science & Medicine*, 289, 114377, 1–13, https://doi.org/10.1016/j.socscimed.2021.114377

Meirang, E. (2016) 'Dismantling the oil wars myth', *Security Studies*, 25, 2, 258–288, https://doi.org/10.1080/09636412.2016.1171968

Meltzer, R. and Schwartz, A. (2019) *Policy Analysis as Problem Solving* (London: Routledge)

Mencke, B.C.B. (2010) *Education, Racism, and the Military: A Critical Race Theory Analysis of the GI Bill and Its Implications for African Americans in Higher Education*, PhD thesis, Washington State University, Pullman WA, https://eric.ed.gov/?id=ED527787 (A: 12.07.23)

Menon, A. and Fowler, B. (2016) 'Hard or soft? The politics of Brexit', *National Institute Economic Review*, 238, 1, R4–R12, https://doi.org/10.1177/002795011623800110

Menon, A. and Salter, J.P. (2016) 'Brexit: Initial reflections', *International Affairs*, 92, 6, 1297–1318

Mercer, T. (2021) 'What can policy theory offer busy practitioners?' in Mercer, T., Head, B. and Wanna, J. (eds) (Canberra: ANU Press), 49–81

Merriam-Webster (2022) 'One "bad apple" can spoil a metaphor: The history of a rogue phrase', https://www.merriam-webster.com/words-at-play/one-bad-apple-spoil-the-barrel-metaphor-phrase (A: 17.09.22)

Midgley, G. (2023) 'Nadhim Zahawi tax penalty: Accounting expert on what it means when HMRC fines you for being "careless"', *The Conversation*, 26 January, https://theconversation.com/nadhim-zahawi-tax-penalty-account ing-expert-on-what-it-means-when-hmrc-fines-you-for-being-careless-198 554 (A: 02.05.23)

Miller, K. (2009) 'Public policy dilemma – gender equality mainstreaming in UK policy formulation', *Public Money and Management*, 29, 1, 43–50, https://doi.org/10.1080/09540960802617350

Miller, P. (2010) 'Bush on nation building and Afghanistan', *Foreign Policy*, 17 November, https://foreignpolicy.com/2010/11/17/bush-on-nation-building-and-afghanistan/ (A: 07.10.22)

Miller, V. (2010) *How Much Legislation Comes from Europe?* (London: House of Commons Library), https://commonslibrary.parliament.uk/research-briefings/rp10-62/ (A: 11.06.22)

Mills, C. (2018) 'Parliamentary approval for military action', *House of Commons Library*, https://researchbriefings.files.parliament.uk/documents/CBP-7166/CBP-7166.pdf (A: 07.10.22)

Mills, C. (2021) 'Withdrawal of military forces in Afghanistan and its implications for peace', *House of Commons Library*, 17 August, https://commonslibrary.par liament.uk/research-briefings/cbp-9241/ (A: 07.10.22)

Mills, C. (2022) *Military Assistance to Ukraine 2014–2021* (SN07135) (London: House of Commons Library), https://researchbriefings.files.parliam ent.uk/documents/SN07135/SN07135.pdf (A: 05.03.22)

Mills, C., Kippin, S., Hunt, P. and Willetts, M. (2020) *Who Owns Europe?* (Brussels: Foundation for European Progressive Studies)

Milmo, D. (2012) 'Alternatives to austerity: 10 ideas from across the political spectrum', *The Guardian*, 19 October, https://www.theguardian.com/politics/2012/oct/19/alternatives-austerity-ideas-across-spectrum (A: 09.09.22)

Milne, K. (2005) *Manufacturing Dissent: Single-Issue Protest, the Public and the Press* (London: Demos), http://www.demos.co.uk/files/manufacturingdissent.pdf (A: 27.05.22)

Milne, S. (2008) 'The Tories have shown they are irrelevant to this crisis', *The Guardian*, 2 October, https://www.theguardian.com/commentisfree/2008/oct/02/davidcameron.conservatives (A: 11.07.23)

Ministry of Defence (2015) 'Response to Freedom of Information Request regarding the cost of the Iraq and Afghanistan wars', https://assets.publishing.serv ice.gov.uk/government/uploads/system/uploads/attachment_data/file/494526/FOI2015-08279-Cost_of_the_wars_in_Iraq_and_Afghanistan.pdf (A: 07.10.22)

Minkin, L. (2014) *The Blair Supremacy* (Manchester: Manchester University Press)

Mintrom, M. (2012) *Contemporary Policy Analysis* (Oxford: Oxford University Press)

Mintrom, M. (2019) 'So you want to be a policy entrepreneur?', *Policy Design and Practice*, 2, 4, 307–323

Mirzai, R. (2019) 'Where "woke" came from and why marketers should think twice before jumping on the social activism bandwagon', *The Conversation*, 8 September, https://theconversation.com/where-woke-came-from-and-why-marketers-should-think-twice-before-jumping-on-the-social-activism-bandwagon-122713 (A: 28.04.23)

Mitsilegas, V. (2020) 'Post Brexit challenges for criminal justice co-operation', *UK in a Changing Europe*, https://ukandeu.ac.uk/post-brexit-challenges-for-criminal-justice-co-operation/ (A: 08.09.22)

Mitton, L. (2016) 'The financial crisis as game changer for the UK welfare state' in Schubert, K., de Villota, P. and Kuhlmann, E. (eds) *Challenges to European Welfare Systems* (Cham: Springer), 743–765

Mohdin, A., Swann, G. and Bannock, C. (2020) 'How George Floyd's death sparked a wave of UK anti-racism protests', *The Guardian*, 29 July, https://www.theguardian.com/uk-news/2020/jul/29/george-floyd-death-fuelled-anti-racism-protests-britain (A: 26.09.22)

Monaghan, M., Pawson, R. and Wicker, K. (2012) 'The precautionary principle and evidence-based policy', *Evidence & Policy*, 8, 2, 171–191, http://dx.doi.org/10.1332/174426412X640072

Mondon, A. and Winter, A. (2019) 'Whiteness, populism and the racialisation of the working class in the United Kingdom and the United States', *Identities*, 26, 5, 510–528, https://doi.org/10.1080/1070289X.2018.1552440

Moore, R. (2012) 'Definitions of fuel poverty: Implications for policy', *Energy Policy*, 49, 19–26, https://doi.org/10.1016/j.enpol.2012.01.057

Morgan, G. (2017) 'Brexit and the elites: The elite versus the people or the fracturing of the British business elites', *Socio-economic Review*, 14, 4, 825–829, https://doi.org/10.1093/ser/mww043

Morin, J. and Paquin, J. (2018) *Foreign Policy Analysis* (London: Palgrave)

Morphet, J. (2008) *Modern Local Government* (London: SAGE)

Morris, N. (2006) 'Eastern Europeans take jobs Britons don't want', *The Independent*, 22 November, https://www.independent.co.uk/news/uk/this-britain/eastern-europeans-take-jobs-britons-don-t-want-425281.html (A: 07.09.22)

Morris, S. (2021) 'Rishi Sunak snubs Marcus Rashford's calls to continue free school holiday meals for the next three years', *Sky News*, 24 October, https://news.sky.com/story/rishi-sunak-snubs-marcus-rashfords-calls-to-continue-free-school-holiday-meals-for-the-next-three-years-12443248 (A: 15.09.22)

Mott, G., Razo, C. and Hamwey, R. (2021) 'Carbon emissions anywhere threaten development everywhere', *UN Conference on Trade and Development* (UNCTAD), 2 June, https://unctad.org/news/carbon-emissions-anywhere-threaten-development-everywhere (A: 14.07.22)

Mott, H., Fontana, M., Stephenson, M.A. and De Henau, J. (2018) 'Exploring the economic impact of Brexit on women', *Women's Budget Group*, https://wbg.org.uk/wp-content/uploads/2018/03/Economic-Impact-of-Brexit-on-women-briefing-FINAL-for-print.pdf (A: 08.09.22)

Mowat, J. (2019) ' "Closing the gap": Systems leadership is no leadership at all without a moral compass – a Scottish perspective', *School Leadership & Management*, 39, 1, 48–75, https://doi.org/10.1080/13632434.2018.1447457

Mudde, C. (2009) *Populist Radical Right Parties in Europe* (Cambridge: Cambridge University Press)

Mughan, A. (2000) *Media and the Presidentialization of Parliamentary Elections* (Basingstoke: Palgrave)

Muldoon, O.T., Trew, K., Todd, J., Rougier, N. and McLaughlin, K. (2006) 'Religious and national identity after the Belfast Good Friday Agreement', *Political Psychology*, 28, 1, 89–103, https://doi.org/10.1111/j.1467-9221.2007.00553.x

Mulholland, H. (2011) 'Duncan Smith blames riots on family breakdown and benefits system', *The Guardian*, 3 October, https://www.theguardian.com/politics/2011/oct/03/duncan-smith-riots-benefits-system (A: 26.09.22)

Mullard, M. and Swaray, R. (2006) 'The politics of public expenditure from Thatcher to Blair', *Policy & Politics*, 34, 3, 495–515

Munro, F. and Cairney, P. (2020) 'A systematic review of energy systems: The role of policy making in sustainable transitions', *Renewable & Sustainable Energy Reviews*, 119, 109598, 1–14, https://doi.org/10.1016/j.rser.2019.109598

Mureithi, A. (2021) 'Mark Duggan should have been the UK's George Floyd: Why didn't people let him be?', *Open Democracy*, 7 August, https://www.opendemocracy.net/en/opendemocracyuk/mark-duggan-should-have-been-the-uks-george-floyd-why-didnt-people-let-him-be/ (A: 16.09.21)

Murji, K. (2017) *Racism, Policy and Politics* (Bristol: Policy Press)

Murphy, M. (2022) 'The rise of the middle ground in Northern Ireland: What does it mean?' *The Political Quarterly*, 1–9, https://doi.org/10.1111/1467-923X.13175

Murray, R. (2009) 'Danger and opportunity: Crisis and the new social economy', *The Young Foundation*, https://www.bl.uk/britishlibrary/~/media/bl/global/social-welfare/pdfs/non-secure/d/a/n/danger-and-opportunity-crisis-and-the-new-social-economy.pdf (A: 09.09.22)

Musolff, A. (2020) 'Having cake and eating it: How a hyperbolic metaphor framed Brexit', *LSE Brexit Blog*, 13 February, https://blogs.lse.ac.uk/brexit/2020/02/13/having-cake-and-eating-it-how-a-hyperbolic-metaphor-framed-brexit/ (A: 01.09.22)

Musolff, A. (2021) 'Hyperbole and emotionalisation: Escalation of pragmatic effects of proverb and metaphor in the "Brexit" debate', *Russian Journal of Linguistics*, 25, 3, 628–644

Nandi, A. and Luthra, R.R. (2021) 'The EU referendum and experiences and fear of ethnic and racial harassment: Variation across individuals and communities in England', *Frontiers in Sociology*, https://doi.org/10.3389/fsoc.2021.660286

Nasar, S. (2020) 'Remembering Edward Colston: Histories of slavery, memory, and black globality', *Women's History Review*, 7, 1218–1225, https://doi.org/10.1080/09612025.2020.1812815

Nash, S.L. (2021) '"Anything Westminster can do we can do better": The Scottish climate change act and placing a sub-state nation on the international stage', *Environmental Politics*, 30, 6, 1024–1044, https://doi.org/10.1080/09644016.2020.1846957

National Audit Office (2013) *The Role of Major Contractors in the Delivery of Government Services* (London: NAO)

National Audit Office (2018) *PFI and PF2* (House of Commons, HC 718), https://www.nao.org.uk/wp-content/uploads/2018/01/PFI-and-PF2.pdf (A: 01.08.22)

National Audit Office (2021) *Central Oversight of Arm's-Length Bodies* (House of Commons, HC 297), https://www.nao.org.uk/wp-content/uploads/2021/06/Central-oversight-of-Arms-length-bodies.pdf (A: 01.08.22)

National Audit Office (2022) 'COVID-19 cost tracker', https://www.nao.org.uk/covid-19/cost-tracker/ (A: 06.04.22)

National Education Union (2022) 'Decolonising education', 25 February, https://neu.org.uk/advice/decolonising-education (A: 26.09.22)

National Grid (2022) 'How much of the UK's energy is renewable?', *National Grid*, https://www.nationalgrid.com/stories/energy-explained/how-much-uks-energy-renewable#:~:text=2020%20marked%20the%20first%20year,solar%2C%20bioenergy%20and%20hydroelectric%20sources (A: 04.07.22)

National Records of Scotland (2022) *Drug-Related Deaths in Scotland in 2021* (Edinburgh: NRS), https://www.nrscotland.gov.uk/files/statistics/drug-related-deaths/21/drug-related-deaths-21-report.pdf (A: 15.07.22)

Neary, J., Chapman, C., Hall, S. and Lowden, K. (2022) 'Local authorities and school-to-school collaboration in Scotland' in Armstrong, P.W. and Brown, C. (eds) *School-to-School Collaboration: Learning across International Contexts* (Bingley: Emerald), 27–41, https://doi.org/10.1108/978-1-80043-668-820221003

Needham, C. and Hall, P. (2022) 'Dealing with drift: Comparing social care reform in the four nations of the UK', *Social Policy & Administration*, 1–17, https://doi.org/10.1111/spol.12858

NEF (New Economics Foundation) (2013) 'Framing the economy: The austerity story', *New Economics Foundation*, https://neweconomics.org/uploads/files/framing-the-economy-1.pdf (A: 09.09.22)

Nelson, F. (2020) 'Kemi Badenoch: The problem with critical race theory', *The Spectator*, 24 October, https://www.spectator.co.uk/article/kemi-badenoch-the-problem-with-critical-race-theory (A: 26.09.22)

Nerlich, B. (2017) 'False balance', *University of Nottingham Making Science Public*, 15 August, https://blogs.nottingham.ac.uk/makingsciencepublic/2017/08/15/false-balance/ (A: 22.04.22)

Nesom, S. and MacKillop, E. (2021) 'What matters in the implementation of sustainable development policies? Findings from the Well-Being of Future Generations (Wales) Act, 2015', *Journal of Environmental Policy & Planning*, 23, 4, 432–445, https://doi.org/10.1080/1523908X.2020.1858768

Neville, P. (2001) 'Lord Vansittart, Sir Walford Selby and the debate about Treasury interference in the conduct of British foreign policy in the 1930s', *Journal of Contemporary History*, 36, 4, 623–633, https://doi.org/10.1177/002200940103600404

Newburn, T., Lewis, P., Taylor, M., McGillivary, C., Greenhill, A., Frayman, H. and Proctor, R. (2012) 'Reading the riots: Investigating England's summer of disorder', *The Guardian and the London School of Economics*, https://eprints.lse.ac.uk/46297/1/Reading%20the%20riots(published).pdf (A: 26.09.22)

Newburn, T., Cooper, K., Deacon, R. and Discki, R. (2015) 'Shopping for free? Looting, consumerism and the 2011 riots', *British Journal of Criminology*, 55, 5, 987–1004, https://doi.org/10.1093/bjc/azv007

Newell, P., Srivastava, S., Naess, L.O., Torres Contreras, G.A. and Price, R. (2021) 'Toward transformative climate justice: An emerging research agenda', *Wiley Interdisciplinary Reviews: Climate Change*, 12, 6, e733, https://doi.org/10.1002/wcc.733

Newman, J. and Kenny, M. (2023) *Devolving English Government* (London: IfG/Bennett Institute), https://www.instituteforgovernment.org.uk/publication/devolving-english-government (A: 06.04.23)

Newman, J., Collinson, S., Driffield, N., Gilbert, N. and Hoole, C. (2023) 'Mechanisms of metagovernance as structural challenges to levelling up in England', *Regional Studies*, 1–17, https://doi.org/10.1080/00343404.2023.2217215

Nguyen, L., Kumar, C., Bisaro Shah, M., Chilvers, A., Stevens, I., Hardy, R., Sarell, C. and Zimmermann, N. (2023) 'Civil servant and expert perspectives on drivers, values, challenges and successes in adopting systems thinking in policy making', *Systems*, 11, 4, 1–24

Nicholls, J. and Cairney, P. (2022) 'Using policy theories to interpret public health case studies: The example of a minimum unit price for alcohol', *Paul Cairney: Politics & Public Policy*, 14 April, https://paulcairney.wordpress.com/2022/04/14/using-policy-theories-to-interpret-public-health-case-studies-the-example-of-a-minimum-unit-price-for-alcohol/ (A: 17.08.22)

Nicholls, J., Livingston, W., Perkins, A., Cairns, B., Foster, R., Trayner, K., Sumnall, H.R., Price, T., Cairney, P., Dumbrell, J. and Parkes, T. (2022) 'Drug consumption rooms and public health policy: Perspectives of Scottish strategic decision-makers', *International Journal of Environmental Research and Public Health*, 19, 11, 6575, 1–13, https://doi.org/10.3390/ijerph19116575

Norris, E. and Rutter, J. (2016) *Learning the Lessons from Universal Credit* (London: Institute for Government), https://www.instituteforgovernment.org.uk/sites/default/files/publications/5087%20IFG%20-%20Universal%20Credit%20-%20Briefing%20Paper%20WEB%20AW_0.pdf (A: 14.07.22)

Northern Ireland Audit Office (2022) *Northern Ireland Non-Domestic Renewable Heat Incentive Scheme* (Belfast: NIAO), https://www.niauditoffice.gov.uk/files/niauditoffice/documents/2022-06/00269786_RHI%20Report_Combo_v3_Proof.pdf (A: 11.05.22)

Northern Ireland Executive (2022) 'Nutrition and school lunches', https://www.nidirect.gov.uk/articles/nutrition-and-school-lunches (A: 15.09.22)

Northey, S., Haque, N. and Mudd, G. (2013) 'Using sustainability reporting to assess the environmental footprint of copper mining', *Journal of Cleaner Production*, 40, 118–128, https://doi.org/10.1016/j.jclepro.2012.09.027

Nowicki, M. (2017) 'Domicide and the coalition: Austerity, citizenship and moralities of forced eviction in inner London' in Brickell, K., Fernandez Arrigoitia, M.F. and Vasudevan, A. (eds) *Geographies of Forced Eviction: Dispossession, Violence, Resistance* (London: Palgrave), 121–143

NTI (2022) 'Iraq', *Nuclear Threat Initiative*, https://www.nti.org/countries/iraq/ (A: 05.10.22)

Nulman, E. (2015) 'Dynamic interactions in contentious episodes: Social movements, industry, and political parties in the contention over Heathrow's third runway', *Environmental Politics*, 24, 5, 742–761, https://doi.org/10.1080/09644016.2015.1014657

Nurse, A. (2021) *Reparations and Anti-Black Racism* (Bristol: Bristol University Press)

Nye, M. and Owens, S. (2008) 'Creating the UK emission trading scheme: Motives and symbolic politics', *European Environment*, 18, 1, 1–15, https://doi.org/10.1002/eet.468

Obama, B. (2009) 'Transcript: Obama's speech against the Iraq War', *NPR*, 20 January, https://www.npr.org/templates/story/story.php?storyId=99591469#:~:text=Barack%20Obama%20delivered%20in%20Chicago,as%20poverty%20and%20health%20care (A: 13.07.23)

OBR (Office for Budget Responsibility) (2012) 'The additional rate of income tax', *OBR*, March, https://obr.uk/box/the-additional-rate-of-income-tax/ (A: 04.10.22)

OBR (2020a) 'Coronavirus analysis', *OBR*, 14 May, https://obr.uk/coronavirus-analysis/ [including the Coronavirus policy monitoring database – 14 May 2020, https://obr.uk/download/coronavirus-policy-monitoring-database-14-may-2020/] (A: 14.05.20)

OBR (2020b) 'Coronavirus analysis', 19 June, https://obr.uk/coronavirus-analysis/ [including the Coronavirus policy monitoring database – 14 May 2020, https://obr.uk/download/coronavirus-policy-monitoring-database-19-june-2020/] (A: 11.07.20)

OBR (2021) 'The rising cost of the coronavirus policy response', https://obr.uk/box/the-rising-cost-of-the-coronavirus-policy-response-2/ (A: 30.03.22)

O'Carroll, L. (2019) 'Can UK get "super Canada-plus" trade deal with EU by end of 2020?', *The Guardian*, 12 November, https://www.theguardian.com/politics/2019/nov/12/can-uk-get-brexit-super-canada-plus-trade-deal-with-eu-by-end-of-2020 (A: 07.09.22)

OECD (Organisation for Economic Co-operation and Development) (2014) 'Growth and inequality: A close relationship?', *Organisation for Economic Cooperation and Development*, https://www.oecd.org/economy/growth-and-inequality-close-relationship.htm (A: 14.09.22)

OECD (2018) *Cost-Benefit Analysis and the Environment* (Paris: OECD), https://doi.org/10.1787/9789264085169-en

OECD (2022a) 'Income inequality', https://data.oecd.org/inequality/income-inequality.htm (A: 22.09.22)

OECD (2022b) 'Economic survey of the United Kingdom (August 2022)', https://www.oecd.org/economy/united-kingdom-economic-snapshot/ (A: 07.10.22)

OECD (2022c) 'Who we are', https://www.oecd.org/about/ (A: 04.09.22)

Office for Health Improvement and Disparities (2022) *Climate and Health: Applying All Our Health* (London: OHID), https://www.gov.uk/government/publications/climate-change-applying-all-our-health/climate-and-health-applying-all-our-health (A: 02.03.23)

Office of Public Services Reform (2002) *Better Government Services* (London: HMSO)

Ofgem (2022a) 'Renewables Obligation (RO)', *Ofgem*, https://www.ofgem.gov.uk/environmental-and-social-schemes/renewables-obligation-ro/renewables-obligation-ro-energy-suppliers#:~:text=The%20Renewables%20Obligation%20(RO)%20places,and%20Industrial%20Strategy%20(BEIS) (A: 06.07.22)

Ofgem (2022b) 'Feed-in Tariffs (FIT)', *Ofgem*, https://www.ofgem.gov.uk/environmental-and-social-schemes/feed-tariffs-fit/tariffs-and-payments (A: 06.07.22)

O'Grady, T. (2022) *The Transformation of British Welfare Policy: Poltics, Discourse, and Public Opinion* (Oxford: Oxford University Press)

O'Hanlon, M.E. (2005) 'Iraq without a plan', *Brookings Institute*, 1 January, https://www.brookings.edu/articles/iraq-without-a-plan/ (A: 07.10.22)

Oliver, A. (2020) 'Separating behavioural science from the herd', *#LSEThinks*, 26 May, https://blogs.lse.ac.uk/covid19/2020/05/26/separating-behavioural-science-from-the-herd/ (A: 17.03.22)

Oliver, M. and Pemberton, H. (2004) 'Learning and change in 20th-century British economic policy', *Governance*, 17, 3, 415–444

O'Loughlin, J., Ó Tuathail, G. and Kolossov, V. (2004) 'A "risky westward turn"? Putin's 9–11 script and ordinary Russians', *Europe-Asia Studies*, 56, 1, 3–34, https://www.jstor.org/stable/4147436

O'Mahony, T. (2021) 'Cost-Benefit Analysis and the environment: The time horizon is of the essence', *Environmental Impact Assessment Review*, 89, 106587, 1–9, https://doi.org/10.1016/j.eiar.2021.106587

O'Neill, L. (2020) 'Decade after end of 11-plus, transfer tests popular as ever with parents', *Belfast Telegraph*, 24 January, https://www.belfasttelegraph.co.uk/news/education/decade-after-end-of-11-plus-transfer-tests-popular-as-ever-with-parents-38890320.html (A: 01.10.21)

ONS (Office for National Statistics) (2018) 'The 2008 recession 10 years on', 30 April, https://www.ons.gov.uk/economy/grossdomesticproductgdp/artic les/the2008recession10yearson/2018-04-30 (A: 31.08.22)

ONS (2020a) 'UK government debt and deficit: December 2019', *Office for National Statistics*, 17 April, https://www.ons.gov.uk/economy/governmentp ublicsectorandtaxes/publicspending/bulletins/ukgovernmentdebtanddeficitf oreurostatmaast/december2019 (A: 14.05.20)

ONS (2020b) 'Adult smoking habits in the UK: 2019', *Office for National Statistics*, 7 July, https://www.ons.gov.uk/peoplepopulationandcommunity/healthandsoc ialcare/healthandlifeexpectancies/bulletins/adultsmokinghabitsingreatbritain/ 2019 (A: 13.09.22)

ONS (2021a) 'Deaths involving COVID-19 by vaccination status, England: deaths occurring between 1 January and 31 October 2021', 20 December, https:// www.ons.gov.uk/peoplepopulationandcommunity/birthsdeathsandmarria ges/deaths/bulletins/deathsinvolvingcovid19byvaccinationstatusengland/ deathsoccurringbetween1januaryand31october2021 (A: 24.03.22)

ONS (2021b) 'Leaving no one behind – a review of who has been most affected by the coronavirus pandemic in the UK: December 2021', 3 December, https:// www.ons.gov.uk/economy/environmentalaccounts/articles/leavingnoone behindareviewofwhohasbeenmostaffectedbythecoronaviruspandemicintheuk/ december2021 (A: 08.04.22)

ONS (2022a) 'Prevalence of ongoing symptoms following coronavirus (COVID-19) infection in the UK: 6 May 2022', 6 May, https://www.ons.gov.uk/peoplepop ulationandcommunity/healthandsocialcare/conditionsanddiseases/bulletins/ prevalenceofongoingsymptomsfollowingcoronaviruscovid19infectionintheuk/ 6may2022 (A: 16.08.22)

ONS (2022b) 'Coronavirus (COVID-19) latest insights: Antibodies', 22 March, https://www.ons.gov.uk/peoplepopulationandcommunity/healthandsocialc are/conditionsanddiseases/articles/coronaviruscovid19latestinsights/antibod ies (A: 24.03.22)

ONS (2022c) 'Deaths involving COVID-19 by vaccination status, England: Deaths occurring between 1 January 2021 and 31 January 2022', 16 March, https:// www.ons.gov.uk/peoplepopulationandcommunity/birthsdeathsandmarria ges/deaths/bulletins/deathsinvolvingcovid19byvaccinationstatusengland/ deathsoccurringbetween1january2021and31january2022 (A: 24.03.22)

ONS (2022d) 'UK government debt and deficit: September 2021', 31 January, https://www.ons.gov.uk/economy/governmentpublicsectorandtaxes/publics pending/bulletins/ukgovernmentdebtanddeficitforeurostatmaast/september2 021 (A: 30.03.22)

ONS (2022e) 'Coronavirus (COVID-19) latest insights: Deaths', 7 April, https:// www.ons.gov.uk/peoplepopulationandcommunity/healthandsocialcare/condit ionsanddiseases/articles/coronaviruscovid19latestinsights/deaths (A: 08.04.22)

ONS (2022f) 'Labour disputes;UK;Sic 07;total working days lost;all inds. & services (000's)', 16 August, https://www.ons.gov.uk/employmentandlabou rmarket/peopleinwork/employmentandemployeetypes/timeseries/bbfw/lms (A: 24.08.22)

ONS (2022g) 'The Gini coefficient', 26 April, https://www.ons.gov.uk/peopl epopulationandcommunity/birthsdeathsandmarriages/families/methodologies/ theginicoefficient (A: 22.09.22)

ONS (2023) 'Dataset. Government debt and deficit' (Xls sheet 'rftm18tables'), https://www.ons.gov.uk/economy/governmentpublicsectorandtaxes/publicse ctorfinance/datasets/governmentdeficitanddebtreturn (A: 02.05.23)

Orach, K. and Schlüter, M. (2016) 'Uncovering the political dimension of social-ecological systems: Contributions from policy process frameworks', *Global Environmental Change*, 40, 13–25, https://doi.org/10.1016/j.gloenv cha.2016.06.002

Oren, T. and Blyth, M. (2019) 'From big bang to big crash: The early origins of the UK's finance-led growth model and the persistence of bad policy ideas', *New Political Economy*, 24, 5, 605–622, https://doi.org/10.1080/13563 467.2018.1473355

Oreskes, N. and Conway, E.M. (2010) *Merchants of Doubt: How a Handful of Scientists Obscured the Truth on Issues from Tobacco Smoke to Global Warming* (New York: Bloomsbury)

Osborne, G. (2009) 'Full text of George Osborne's speech', *The Guardian*, 15 September, https://www.theguardian.com/politics/2009/sep/15/george-osbo rne-speech-full-text (A: 09.09.22)

Ostrom, E. (1990) *Governing the Commons: The Evolution of Institutions for Collective Action* (Cambridge: Cambridge University Press)

Ostrom, E. (1996) 'Crossing the great divide: Coproduction, synergy, and development', *World Development*, 26, 6, 1073–1087, https://doi.org/10.1016/ 0305-750X(96)00023-X

Ostrom, E. (2007) 'Institutional rational choice' in Sabatier, P. (ed) *Theories of the Policy Process 2* (Cambridge, MA: Westview Press), 21–64

Ostrom, E. (2009) 'A general framework for analyzing sustainability of social-ecological systems', *Science*, 325, 5939, 419–422

O'Toole, B. and Jordan, A. (1995) *Next Steps* (Aldershot: Dartmouth)

O'Toole, T., Nilsson DeHanas, D. and Modood, T. (2012) 'Balancing tolerance, security and Muslim engagement in the United Kingdom: The impact of the "Prevent" agenda', *Critical Studies on Terrorism*, 5, 3, 373–389, https://doi.org/ 10.1080/17539153.2012.725570

Overton, I. (ed) (2020) 'For all was lost: Comparing UK and US military deaths in the War on Terror', *Action on Armed Violence*, https://aoav.org.uk/wp-cont ent/uploads/2020/11/For-all-was-Lost-latest.pdf (A: 07.10.22)

Ozga, J., Baird, J.A., Saville, L., Arnott, M. and Hell, N. (2023) 'Knowledge, expertise and policy in the examinations crisis in England', *Oxford Review of Education*, 1–19, https://doi.org/10.1080/03054985.2022.2158071

Page, E. and Jenkins, B. (2005) *Policy Bureaucracy: Government with a Cast of Thousands* (Oxford: Oxford University Press)

Palència, L., Malmusi, D. and Borrell, C. (2014) 'Incorporating intersectionality in evaluation of policy impacts on health equity', *Sophie*, www.sophie-project. eu/pdf/Guide_intersectionality_SOPHIE.pdf (A: 26.09.22)

Palier, B. (2005) 'Ambiguous agreement, cumulative change' in Streeck, W. and Thelen, K. (eds) *Beyond Continuity: Institutional Change in Advanced Political Economies* (Oxford: Oxford University Press), 127–144

Palkki, D.D. and Rubin, L. (2021) 'Saddam Hussein's role in the gassing of Halabja', *The Nonproliferation Review*, 28, 1–3, 115–129, https://doi.org/ 10.1080/10736700.2020.1795600

Pannett, R. (2022) 'Liz Truss's cabinet is the U.K.'s first without a White man in top office', *Washington Post*, 6 September, https://www.washingtonpost.com/ world/2022/09/06/uk-liz-truss-offices-of-state-women-poc/ (A: 07.09.22)

Parker, D. (2009) *The Official History of Privatization*, vol I (London: Routledge)

Parry, K. and Johnson, B. (2021) 'Humbug and outrage: A study of performance, gender and affective atmosphere in the mediation of a critical parliamentary moment', *British Journal of Politics and International Relations*, 1–18, https://doi. org/10.1177/13691481211062933

Parry, R. (2005) 'The civil service response to modernisation in the devolved administrations', *Financial Accountability & Management*, 21, 1, 57–74

Parry, R. (2016) 'Civil service and machinery of government' in McTavish, D. (ed) *Politics in Scotland* (London: Routledge), 123–129

Patel, J., Manetti, M., Mendelsohn, M., Mills, S., Felden, F., Littig, L. and Rocha, M. (2021) 'AI brings science to the art of policy making', *Boston Consulting Group*, 5 April, https://www.bcg.com/publications/2021/how-artificial-intel ligence-can-shape-policy-making (A: 20.05.23)

Paton, C. (2016) *The Politics of Health Policy Reform in the UK* (London: Palgrave)

Pattie, C. and Johnston, R. (2012) 'The electoral impact of the UK 2009 MPs' expenses scandal', *Political Studies*, 60, 4, 730–750

Paun, A., Shuttleworth, K., Nice, A. and Sargeant, J. (2020a) 'Coronavirus and devolution', *Institute for Government*, 1 July, https://www.instituteforgovernm ent.org.uk/explainers/coronavirus-and-devolution (A: 25.03.22)

Paun, A., Sargeant, J. and Nice, A. (2020b) 'A four-nation exit strategy', *Institute for Government*, https://www.instituteforgovernment.org.uk/sites/default/files/ publications/four-nation-exit-strategy-coronavirus.pdf (A: 29.03.22)

Pautz, H. (2012) 'The think tanks behind "Cameronism"', *The British Journal of Politics and International Relations*, 15, 3, 362–377, https://doi.org/10.1111/ j.1467-856X.2012.00518.x

Pautz, H. (2018) 'Think tanks, Tories and the austerity discourse coalition', *Policy and Society*, 37, 2, 155–169, https://doi.org/10.1080/14494035.2017.1397395

Peden, G. (1991) *British Economic and Social Policy*, 2nd edn (London: Philip Allan)

Peden, G. (2000) *The Treasury and British Public Policy, 1906–59* (Oxford: Oxford University Press)

Pe'er, G., Bonn, A., Bruelheide, H., Dieker, P., Eisenhauer, N., Feindt, P.H., Hagedorn, G., Hansjürgens, B., Herzon, I., Lomba, Â. and Marquard, E. (2020) 'Action needed for the EU Common Agricultural Policy to address sustainability challenges', *People and Nature*, 2, 2, 305–316, https://doi.org/10.1002/pan3.10080

Pemberton, H. (2000) 'Policy networks and policy learning UK economic policy in the 1960s and 1970s', *Public Administration*, 78, 4, 771–792

Peston, R. (2009) 'The Treasury hedge fund', *Peston's Picks* (BBC), https://www.bbc.co.uk/blogs/thereporters/robertpeston/2009/11/the_treasury_hedge_fund.html (A: 09.09.22)

Peters, B.G., Capano, G., Howlett, M., Mukherjee, I., Chou, M.H. and Ravinet, P. (2018) *Designing for Policy Effectiveness: Defining and Understanding a Concept* (Cambridge: Cambridge University Press)

Pettifor, A. and McPherson, N. (2023) 'Was austerity worth it?', *Prospect Magazine*, 5 April, https://www.prospectmagazine.co.uk/politics/austerity/60925/was-austerity-worth-it-we-asked-two-economic-heavyweights (A: 05.06.23)

Peyronel, V. (2018) 'Social inequalities in Northern Ireland' in Fée, D. and Kober-Smith, A. (eds) *Inequalities in the UK* (Bingley: Emerald), 341–356

Pfiffner, J.P. (2010) 'US blunders in Iraq: De-Baathification and disbanding the army', *Intelligence and National Security*, 25, 1, 76–85

Phillips, M. (2011) 'Britain's liberal intelligentsia has smashed virtually every social value', *The Daily Mail*, 11 August, https://www.dailymail.co.uk/debate/article-2024690/UK-riots-2011-Britains-liberal-intelligentsia-smashed-virtually-social-value.html (A: 26.09.22)

Phillips, R. (2008) 'Standing together: The Muslim Association of Britain and the anti-war movement', *Race & Class*, 50, 2, 101–113, https://doi.org/10.1177/0306396808096396

Phillips, T., Zhang, Y. and Petherick, A. (2021) 'A year of living distantly: Global trends in the use of stay-at-home orders over the first 12 months of the COVID-19 pandemic', *Interface Focus*, 11, 20210041, https://doi.org/10.1098/rsfs.2021.0041

Phythian, M. (2005) 'Hutton and Scott: A tale of two inquiries', *Parliamentary Affairs*, 58, 1, 124–137, https://doi.org/10.1093/pa/gsi011

Pickett, K. and Wilkinson, R.G. (2009) *The Spirit Level* (London: Penguin)

Pidd, H. and Mulholland, H. (2010) 'Lord Goldsmith changed legal view of Iraq war in two months, says adviser', *The Guardian*, 26 January, https://www.theguardian.com/uk/2010/jan/26/iraq-war-illegal-chilcot-inquiry (A: 07.10.22)

Pierce, J., Siddiki, S., Jones, M., Schumacher, K., Pattison, A. and Peterson, H. (2014) 'Social construction and policy design: A review of past applications', *Policy Studies Journal*, 42, 1, 1–29

Pierce, J. and Hicks, K.C. (2019) 'Foreign policy applications of the advocacy coalition framework' in Brummer, K., Harnisch, S., Oppermann, K. and Panke, D. (eds) *Foreign Policy as Public Policy?* (Manchester: Manchester University Press), 65–90

Pierre, J. (2020) 'Nudges against pandemics: Sweden's COVID-19 containment strategy in perspective', *Policy and Society*, 39, 3, 478–493, https://doi.org/10.1080/14494035.2020.1783787

Pierre, J. and Stoker, G. (2000) 'Towards multi-level governance' in Dunleavy, P., Drucker, H.M., Gamble, A, Holliday, I. and Peel, G. (eds) *Developments in British Politics 6* (London: Macmillan), 29–44

Pierson, P. (2000) 'Increasing returns, path dependence, and the study of politics', *The American Political Science Review*, 94, 2, 251–267

Pike, A., Coombes, M., O'Brien, P. and Tomaney, J. (2018) 'Austerity states, institutional dismantling and the governance of sub-national economic development: The demise of the regional development agencies in England', *Territory, Politics, Governance*, 6, 1, 118–144, https://doi.org/10.1080/21622671.2016.1228475

Pina-Sànchez, J., Lightowlers, C. and Roberts, J. (2016) 'Exploring the punitive surge: Crown Court sentencing practices before and after the 2011 English riots', *British Journal of Sociology*, 17, 3, 319–339, https://doi.org/10.1177/1748895816671167

Pitts, F.H., Thompson, P., Cruddas, J. and Ingold, J. (2021) 'Culture wars and class wars: Labour between post-Corbynism and Johnsonism', *Renewal: A Journal of Social Democracy*, https://research-information.bris.ac.uk/en/publications/culture-wars-and-class-wars-labour-between-post-corbynism-and-joh (A: 26.09.22)

Policy Institute (2020) 'Coronavirus: Growing divisions over the UK government's response', 26 May, https://www.kcl.ac.uk/policy-institute/assets/coronavirus-growing-divisions-over-uk-government-response.pdf (A: 13.07.20)

Pollitt, C. (2010) *Time, Policy, Management* (Oxford: Oxford University Press)

Pollitt, C. (2015) 'Wickedness will not wait: Climate change and public management research', *Public Money & Management*, 35, 3, 181–186, https://doi.org/10.1080/09540962.2015.1027490

Pope, T. (2022) 'Kwarteng and Truss show the perils of disregarding economic institutions', *Institute for Government*, 29 September, https://www.institutefo rgovernment.org.uk/blog/kwarteng-truss-economic-institutions (A: 06.10.22)

Pope, T., Dalton, G. and Coggins, M. (2022) *Subnational Government in England: An International Comparison* (London: Institute for Government), https://www.ins tituteforgovernment.org.uk/sites/default/files/2022-12/subnational-governm ent-in-england-international-comparison.pdf (A: 05.01.23)

Porter, J.J., Demeritt, D. and Dessai, S. (2015) 'The right stuff? Informing adaptation to climate change in British local government', *Global Environmental Change*, 35, 411–422, https://doi.org/10.1016/j.gloenvcha.2015.10.004

Porter, P. (2010) 'Why Britain doesn't do grand strategy', *RUSI Journal*, 155, 4, 6–12, https://doi.org/10.1080/03071847.2010.514098

Porter, P. (2018) *Blunder: Britain's War in Iraq* (Oxford: Oxford University Press)

Portes, J. (2014) 'Intergenerational and intragenerational equity', *National Institute Economic Review*, 227, 1, F4–F11, https://doi.org/10.1177%2F00279501142 2700110

Portes, J. (2022a) 'Immigration and the UK economy after Brexit', *Oxford Review of Economic Policy*, 38, 1, 82–96, https://doi.org/10.1093/oxrep/grab045

Portes, J. (2022b) 'A reply to O'Brien over immigration', *ConservativeHome*, 22 August, https://conservativehome.com/2022/08/22/jonathan-portes-a-reply-to-obrien-over-immigration/ (A: 26.08.22)

Portes, J. (2022c) 'The government's post-Brexit immigration policy is a rare success', *Byline Times*, 30 August, https://bylinetimes.com/2022/08/30/the-governments-post-brexit-immigration-policy-is-a-rare-success/ (A: 31.08.22)

Portes, J. and Reed, H. (2018) 'The cumulative impact of tax and welfare reforms', *Equality and Human Rights Commission*, https://www.equalityhumanrights.com/sites/default/files/cumulative-impact-assessment-report.pdf (A: 09.09.22)

Powell, A. and Booth, L. (2021) 'Public sector pay', *House of Commons Library*, 13 December, https://researchbriefings.files.parliament.uk/documents/CBP-8037/CBP-8037.pdf (A: 09.09.22)

Powell, L. and Halfon, R. (2019) 'Common market 2.0: Re-setting the UK – Europe relationship for the 21st century', *Norway Plus Group of MPs*, https://labourlist.org/wp-content/uploads/2019/01/Common-Market-2.0.pdf (A: 07.09.22)

Power, S. and Frandji, D. (2010) 'Education markets, the new politics of recognition and the increasing fatalism towards inequality', *Journal of Education Policy*, 25, 3, 385–396

Prime Minister's Office (2014) 'Local councils to receive millions in business rates from shale gas developments', *Gov.uk*, 13 January, https://www.gov.uk/government/news/local-councils-to-receive-millions-in-business-rates-from-shale-gas-developments (A: 06.07.22)

Prime Minister's Office (2022) 'Prime Minister sets out plan for living with COVID', *Gov.uk*, 21 February, https://www.gov.uk/government/news/prime-minister-sets-out-plan-for-living-with-covid (A: 24.03.22)

Private Eye (2023) 'Freeport latest: Asset-strip Tees', *Private Eye*, 19 April

Project for a New American Century (1997) 'Statement of principles', *University of Leeds*, https://universityofleeds.github.io/philtaylorpapers/vp012238.html (A: 07.09.22)

Public Accounts Committee (2021) ' "Unimaginable" cost of Test & Trace failed to deliver central promise of averting another lockdown', 10 March, https://committees.parliament.uk/committee/127/public-accounts-committee/news/150988/unimaginable-cost-of-test-trace-failed-to-deliver-central-promise-of-averting-another-lockdown/ (A: 06.04.22)

Public Health England and Local Government Association (2016) *Local Wellbeing, Local Growth* (London: PHE), https://assets.publishing.service.gov.uk/government/uploads/system/uploads/attachment_data/file/560593/Health_in_All_Policies_implementation_examples.pdf (A: 08.04.22)

PwC (PricewaterhouseCoopers) (2022) 'UK economic outlook September 2022', *PwC*, https://www.pwc.co.uk/services/economics/insights/uk-economic-outlook.html (A: 07.10.22)

Pykett, J., Ball, S., Dingwall, R., Lepenies, R., Sommer, T., Strassheim, H. and Wenzel, L. (2022) 'Ethical moments and institutional expertise in UK government COVID-19 pandemic policy responses: Where, when and how is ethical advice sought?', *Evidence & Policy*, 1–20, https://doi.org/10.1332/174426421X16596928051179

Quarmby, K. and Fazackerly, A. (2009) 'Building blocks? An investigation into building schools for the future', *Policy Exchange*, https://policyexchange.org.uk/wp-content/uploads/2016/09/building-blocks-jul-09.pdf (A: 09.09.22)

Qureshi, A., Morris, M. and Mort, L. (2020) 'Access denies: The human impact of the hostile environment', *IPPR*, https://apo.org.au/sites/default/files/resource-files/2020-09/apo-nid310869.pdf (A: 09.09.22)

Radin, B. (2019) *Policy Analysis in the Twenty-First Century* (London: Routledge)

Rafferty, A. (2014) 'Gender equality and the impact of recession and austerity in the UK', *Revue de l'OFCE*, 133, 2, 335–361, https://doi.org/10.3917/reof.133.0335.

Raine, J.W. and Keasey, P. (2012) 'From police authorities to police and crime commissioners: Might policing become more publicly accountable?', *International Journal of Emergency Services*, 1, 2, 122–134

Raleigh, V. (2022) 'What is happening to life expectancy in England?', *The King's Fund*, https://www.kingsfund.org.uk/publications/whats-happening-life-expectancy-england (A: 09.09.22)

Rankin, J. and Waterson, J. (2019) 'How Boris Johnson's Brussels-bashing stories shaped British politics', *The Guardian*, 14 July, https://www.theguardian.com/politics/2019/jul/14/boris-johnson-brussels-bashing-stories-shaped-politics (A: 07.09.22)

Rawad, J., Beland, D. and Pavolini, E. (2021) 'State of the art: "The people" and their social rights: What is distinctive about the populism–religion–social policy nexus?', *Social Policy and Society*, 20, 2, 267–281, http://doi.org/10.1017/S1474746420000664

Raworth, S. (2017) *Doughnut Economics: Seven Ways to Think Like a 21st Century Economist* (London: Random House)

Rayner, T. and Jordan, A. (2016) 'The United Kingdom: A record of leadership under threat' in Wurzel, R., Connelly, J. and Liefferink, D. (eds) *The European Union in International Climate Change Politics* (London: Routledge), 197–212

Rayner, T., Leiren, M.D. and Inderberg, T.H.J. (2020) 'The United Kingdom: From market-led policy towards technology steering' in Boasson, E.L., Leiren, M.D. and Wettestad, J. (eds) *Comparative Renewables Policy* (London: Routledge), 103–125, https://library.oapen.org/bitstream/handle/20.500.12657/41705/9780429584343.pdf?sequence=1#page=122 (A: 06.07.22)

Raynor, P. (2020) 'Probation for profit: Neoliberalism magical thinking and evidence refusal' in Bean, P. (ed) *Criminal Justice and Privatisation Key Issues and Debates* (London: Routledge), 18–31

Reardon, L. and Marsden, G. (2020) 'Exploring the role of the state in the depoliticisation of UK transport policy', *Policy & Politics*, 48, 2, 223–240, https://doi.org/10.1332/030557319X15707904263616

Rees, T. (2005) 'Reflections on the uneven development of gender mainstreaming in Europe', *International Feminist Journal of Politics*, 7, 4, 555–574, https://doi.org/10.1080/14616740500284532

Reh, C. (2009) 'Lisbon Treaty: De-constitutionalizing the European Union?', *JCMS: Journal of Common Market Studies*, 47, 3, 625–650, https://doi.org/10.1111/j.1468-5965.2009.01819.x

Reicher, S. and Stott, C. (2011) *Mad Mobs and Englishmen* (Oxford: Oxford University Press)

Reland, J., Menon, A. and Rutter, J. (eds) (2022) (eds) *Doing Things Differently? Policy after Brexit* (UK in a Changing Europe), https://ukandeu.ac.uk/wp-content/uploads/2022/01/UKICE-Policy-Report_FINAL.pdf (A: 01.09.22)

Renwick, C. (2017) *Bread for All* (London: Penguin)

Resolution Foundation (2019) 'The shape of things to come: Charting the changing size and shape of the UK state', https://www.resolutionfoundation.org/app/uploads/2019/11/The-shape-of-things-to-come.pdf#page=4 (A: 09.09.22)

Resolution Foundation (2022) 'Blowing the budget', 24 September, https://www.resolutionfoundation.org/publications/blowing-the-budget/ (A: 11.10.22)

Reuters (2022) 'Britain to shelve proposed Bill of Rights – The Sun', 7 September, https://www.reuters.com/world/uk/britain-scrap-proposed-bill-rights-sun-2022-09-07/ (A: 07.09.22)

Reynolds, D. (2009) *America, Empire of Liberty: A New History* (London: Penguin)

RHI Inquiry (2020) *The Report of the Independent Public Inquiry into the Non-domestic Renewable Heat Incentive (RHI) Scheme* (Belfast: Northern Ireland Department of Finance), https://cain.ulster.ac.uk/issues/politics/docs/rhi/2020-03-13_RHI-Inquiry_Report-V1.pdf (A: 04.07.22)

Rhodes, R. (1988) *Beyond Westminster and Whitehall* (London: Unwin Hyman)

Rhodes, R. (1992) 'Local government finance' in Marsh, D. and Rhodes, R.A.W. (eds) *Implementing Thatcherite Policies* (Buckingham: Open University Press), 50–64

Rhodes, R. (1994) 'The hollowing out of the state', *Political Quarterly*, 65, 138–151

Rhodes, R. (1995) 'From prime ministerial power to core executive' in Rhodes, R. and Dunleavy, P. (eds) *Prime Minister, Cabinet and Core Executive* (Basingstoke: Palgrave), 11–37

Rhodes, R. (1997) *Understanding Governance* (Milton Keynes: Open University Press)

Rhodes, R. (2011) *Everyday Life in British Government* (Oxford: Oxford University Press)

Rhodes, C., Hough, D., & Butcher, L. (2014). Privatisation (Research Paper 14/61) (London: House of Commons). https://researchbriefings.files.parliament.uk/documents/RP14-61/RP14-61.pdf (A: 24.05.22)

Richards, D. (2011) 'Changing patterns of executive governance' in Heffernan, R., Cowley, P. and Hay, C. (eds) *Developments in British Politics* (London: Palgrave), 29–50

Richards, D. and Smith, M. (2002) *Governance and Public Policy in the UK* (Oxford: Oxford University Press)

Richards, D. and Smith, M. (2004) 'The "hybrid state": Labour's response to the challenge of governance' in Ludlam, S. and Smith, M. (eds) *Governing as New Labour* (London: Palgrave), 106–125

Richards, D. and Smith, M. (2006) 'Central control and policy implementation in the UK: A case study of the Prime Minister's Delivery Unit', *Journal of Comparative Policy Analysis: Research and Practice*, 8, 4, 325–345, https://doi.org/10.1080/13876980600971151

Richards, D. and Smith, M. (2016) 'The Westminster model and the "indivisibility of the political and administrative elite": A convenient myth whose time is up?', *Governance*, 29, 4, 499–516

Richards, D., Diamond, P. and Wager, A. (2019) 'Westminster's Brexit paradox: The contingency of the "old" versus "new" politics', *The British Journal of Politics and International Relations*, 21, 2, 330–348, https://doi.org/10.1177/1369148119830009

Richards, D., Smith, M. and Warner, S. (2022a) 'Treasury orthodoxy and the short life and death of the Truss government', *Public Sector Focus*, September–October, 40–41, https://flickread.com/edition/html/63581ea15a325#43 (A: 06.01.23)

Richards, D., Warner, S., Smith, M.J. and Coyle, D. (2022b) 'Crisis and state transformation: Covid-19, levelling up and the UK's incoherent state', *Cambridge Journal of Regions, Economy and Society*, 1–18, https://doi.org/10.1093/cjres/rsac038

Richards, L., Heath, A. and Noah, C. (2018) 'Red lines and compromises: Mapping underlying complexities of Brexit preferences', *The Political Quarterly*, 89, 2, 280–290, https://doi.org/10.1111/1467-923X.12488

Richardson, J. (2018a) 'The changing British policy style: From governance to government?', *British Politics*, 13, 2, 215, https://doi.org/10.1057/s41293-017-0051-y

Richardson, J. (2018b) *British Policy-Making and the Need for a Post-Brexit Policy Style* (London: Palgrave)

Richardson, J. (2023) 'The study of policy style: Reflections on a simple idea' in Graziano, P. and Tosun, J. (eds) *Encyclopaedia of European Union Public Policy* (Cheltenham: Edward Elgar), 332–341

Richardson, J. and Jordan, G. (1979) *Governing under Pressure: The Policy Process in a Post-Parliamentary Democracy* (Oxford: Robertson)

Richardson, J. and Rittberger, B. (2020) 'Brexit: Simply an omnishambles or a major policy fiasco?', *Journal of European Public Policy*, 27, 5, 649–665, https://doi.org/10.1080/13501763.2020.1736131

Richardson, J., Gustafsson, G. and Jordan, G. (1982) 'The concept of policy style' in Richardson, J. (ed) *Policy Styles in Western Europe* (London: Allen & Unwin), 19–52

Richter, F. and Joly, J. (2019) '3: Punctuated equilibrium theory and foreign policy' in Brummer, K., Harnisch, S., Oppermann, K. and Panke, D. (eds) *Foreign Policy as Public Policy? Promises and Pitfalls* (Manchester: Manchester University Press), 41–64

Ricketts, P.F. (2002) 'Iraq: Advice for the prime minister', *UK National Archives*, https://webarchive.nationalarchives.gov.uk/ukgwa/20171123123237/http:/www.iraqinquiry.org.uk/media/211047/2002-03-22-minute-ricketts-to-sofs-fco-iraq-advice-for-the-prime-minister.pdf (A: 13.07.23)

Ridge, T. (2013) ' "We are all in this together"? The hidden costs of poverty, recession and austerity policies on Britain's poorest children', *Children & Society*, 27, 5, 406–417, https://doi.org/10.1111/chso.12055

Rietig, K. and Laing, T. (2017) 'Policy stability in climate governance: The case of the United Kingdom', *Environmental Policy and Governance*, 27, 6, 575–587, https://doi.org/10.1002/eet.1762

Riker, W. (1980) 'Implications from the disequilibrium of majority rule for the study of institutions', *American Political Science Review*, 74, 2, 432–446

Riots Communities and Victims Panel (2012) 'After the riots: The final report of the Riots Communities and Victims Panel', https://www.bl.uk/collection-items/after-the-riots-the-final-report-of-the-riots-communities-and-victims-panel (A: 26.09.22)

Rioux, X.H. (2020) 'Rival economic nationalisms: Brexit and the Scottish independence movement compared', *Canadian Foreign Policy Journal*, 26, 1, 8–24, https://doi.org/10.1080/11926422.2019.1617759

Risen, J. (2004) 'Threats and responses: The Czech connection; no evidence of meeting with Iraqi', *The New York Times*, 17 June, https://www.nytimes.com/2004/06/17/world/threats-and-responses-the-czech-connection-no-evidence-of-meeting-with-iraqi.html (A: 07.10.22)

Ritchie, N. and Rogers, P. (2006) *The Political Road to War with Iraq: Bush, 9/11 and the Drive to Overthrow Saddam* (London: Routledge)

Rittel, H. and Webber, M. (1973) 'Dilemmas in a general theory of planning', *Policy Sciences*, 4, 2, 155–169

Rivett, G. (2021) '2008–2017: An uncertain path ahead', *Nuffield Trust*, https://www.nuffieldtrust.org.uk/chapter/2008-2017-an-uncertain-path-ahead (A: 30.09.21)

Rizvi, F. (2016) 'Privatization in education: Trends and consequences', *Education Research and Foresight Series*, 18, 1–12 (Paris: UNESCO), https://en.unesco.org/node/262287 (A: 14.05.22)

Rizvi, F. and Lingard, B. (2010) *Globalizing Educational Policy* (London: Routledge)

Roberts, A. (2007) 'The UK and the use of force in Iraq: Academics and policy-makers', *Institute of International and Strategic Studies University of Peking*, https://web.archive.org/web/20210624211532/https://weblearn.ox.ac.uk/access/content/user/1044/China%20International%20Strategy%20Review%202016%20publ%20May-Jun%202018%20-%20AR%20on%20UK%20_%20Use%20of%20Force%20in%20Iraq.pdf (A: 07.10.22)

Roberts, S., Stafford, B. and Hill, K. (2018) 'Diluting substantive equality: Why the UK government doesn't know if its welfare reforms promote equality' in Fée, D. and Kober-Smith, A. (eds) *Inequalities in the UK* (Bingley: Emerald), 167–184

Robinson, E. (2020) 'Brexit and the cultural importance of Erasmus', *The New European*, 8 April, https://www.thenewfederalist.eu/brexit-and-the-cultural-importance-of-erasmus?lang=fr (A: 07.09.22)

Robinson, N. (2013) 'Economy: There is no alternative (TINA) is back', *BBC News*, 7 March, https://www.bbc.co.uk/news/uk-politics-21703018 (A: 29.08.22)

Rogers, A. (2023) 'Govt turns to private sector in attempt to cut NHS waiting lists', Sky News, 4 August. Available: https://news.sky.com/story/govt-turns-to-private-sector-in-attempt-to-cut-nhs-waiting-lists-12933175 (A: 07.08.23)

Rogers, A. and Pilgrim, D. (2001) *Mental Health Policy in Britain* (Basingstoke: Palgrave)

Rogge, K.S., Pfluger, B. and Geels, F.W. (2020) 'Transformative policy mixes in socio-technical scenarios: The case of the low-carbon transition of the German electricity system (2010–2050)', *Technological Forecasting and Social Change*, 151, 119259, 1–15, https://doi.org/10.1016/j.techfore.2018.04.002

Rone, J. (2022) 'Instrumentalising sovereignty claims in British pro- and anti-Brexit mobilisations', *British Journal of Politics and International Relations*, 1–18, https://doi.org/10.1177/13691481221089136

Rosas, G. (2009) *Curbing Bailouts: Bank Crises and Democratic Accountability in Comparative Perspective* (Ann Arbor: Michigan University Press)

Rose, R. (1984) *Do Parties Make a Difference?*, 2nd edn (London: Macmillan)

Rose, R. (1987) *Ministers and Ministries: A Functional Analysis* (Oxford: Clarendon Press)

Rose, R. (1990) 'Inheritance before choice in public policy', *Journal of Theoretical Politics*, 2, 3, 263–291

Rose, R. (1993) *Lesson-Drawing in Public Policy* (New York: Chatham House)

Rose, R. (2005) *Learning from Comparative Public Policy: A Practical Guide* (London: Routledge)

Rose, R. and Davies, P. (1994) *Inheritance in Public Policy: Change without Choice in Britain* (New Haven: Yale University Press)

Rosina, M. and Kadhum, O. (2023) 'Can the government's immigration bill succeed', *LSE British Politics and Policy*, 28 March, https://blogs.lse.ac.uk/politicsandpolicy/can-the-governments-immigration-bill-succeed/ (A: 20.04.23)

Rough, E. (2022) 'Abortion in Northern Ireland: recent changes to the legal framework', *House of Commons Library*, CBP 8909, https://researchbriefings.files.parliament.uk/documents/CBP-8909/CBP-8909.pdf (A: 30.03.22)

The Royal Society (2022) 'The basics of climate change', https://royalsociety.org/topics-policy/projects/climate-change-evidence-causes/basics-of-climate-change/?gclid=Cj0KCQjw3v6SBhCsARIsACyrRAk7Bmu3rAavFP_cZykmkLCzH5Hoa4-5LEXLD2utPyDh81eZBL9WsqkaAnddEALw_wcB (A: 20.04.22)

Royles, E. and McEwen, N. (2015) 'Empowered for action? Capacities and constraints in sub-state government climate action in Scotland and Wales', *Environmental Politics*, 24, 6, 1034–1054, https://doi.org/10.1080/09644 016.2015.1053726

Russell, M. (2022) 'The constitutional causes and consequences of the Truss–Kwarteng budget crisis', *The Constitution Unit*, 5 October, https://constitut ion-unit.com/2022/10/05/the-constitutional-causes-and-consequences-of-the-truss-kwarteng-budget-crisis/ (A: 06.10.22)

Russell, M. and Cowley, P. (2016) 'The policy power of the Westminster parliament: The "parliamentary state" and the empirical evidence', *Governance*, 29, 1, 121–137

Russell, M. and Gover, D. (2017) *Legislation at Westminster: Parliamentary Actors and Influence in the Making of British Law* (Oxford: Oxford University Press)

Russell, M. and Serban, R. (2021) 'The muddle of the "Westminster model": A concept stretched beyond repair', *Government and Opposition*, 56, 744–764

Russell, M., Gover, D. and Wollter, K. (2016) 'Does the executive dominate the Westminster legislative process? Six reasons for doubt', *Parliamentary Affairs*, 69, 2, 286–308

Rutter, J. (2020) 'Singapore on Thames is dead, long live Singapore on Thames', *UK in a Changing Europe*, 27 October, https://ukandeu.ac.uk/singapore-on-tha mes-is-dead-long-live-singapore-on-thames/ (A: 07.09.22)

Rutter, J. (2022a) 'Sacking Tom Scholar – a move that undermines the Treasury, the civil service and the government?', *UK in a Changing Europe*, 13 September, https://ukandeu.ac.uk/sacking-tom-scholar-a-move-that-undermines-the-treas ury-the-civil-service-and-the-government/ (A: 06.10.22)

Rutter, J. (2022b) 'Civil service–ministerial relations: Time for a reset', *Institute for Government*, 19 December, https://www.instituteforgovernment.org.uk/ publication/civil-service-ministerial-relations (A: 02.05.23)

Rutter, J., Malley, R., Noonan, A. and Knighton, W. (2012) 'It takes two: How to create effective relationships between government and arm's-length bodies', *Institute for Government*, https://www.instituteforgovernment.org.uk/sites/defa ult/files/publications/it_takes_two_final_0.pdf (A: 09.09.22)

Ryder, M. (2014) 'Why so many find the Mark Duggan verdict hard to accept', *The Guardian*, 19 January, https://www.theguardian.com/commentisfree/2014/ jan/19/mark-duggan-lawful-killing-inquest-verdict (A: 26.09.22)

Sabatier, P. (2007) 'The need for better theories' in P. Sabatier (ed) *Theories of the Policy Process 2* (Cambridge: Westview), 3–17

Sabatier, P., Hunter, S. and McLaughlin, S. (1987) 'The devil shift: Perceptions and misperceptions of opponents', *The Western Political Quarterly*, 40, 3, 449–476

Sabbagh, D. (2019) ' "There's no chance now": How the People's Vote movement died', *The Guardian*, 18 December, https://www.theguardian.com/politics/ 2019/dec/18/theres-no-chance-now-how-the-peoples-vote-movement-died (A: 07.09.22)

Sadat, L.N. (2005) 'Ghost prisoners and black sites: Extraordinary rendition under international law', *Case Western Reserve Journal of International Law*, 37, 2, 309–342, https://scholarlycommons.law.case.edu/jil/vol37/iss2/9 (A: 08.09.22)

Sadiki, L. (2015) 'Preface: The meme of the Arab Spring' in Sadiki, L. (ed) *Routledge Handbook of the Arab Spring: Rethinking Democratization* (London: Routledge), xxxii–xxxviii

Sanders, A. and Shorrocks, R. (2019) 'All in this together? Austerity and the gender-age gap in the 2015 and 2017 British general elections', *The British Journal of Politics and International Relations*, 21, 4, 667–688, https://doi.org/10.1177%2F1369148119864699

Sanders, A., Annesley, C. and Gains, F. (2019) 'What did the coalition government do for women? An analysis of gender equality policy agendas in the UK 2010–2015', *British Politics*, 14, 2, 162–180, https://doi.org/10.1057/s41293-018-00103-2

Santos, B. (2014) *Epistemologies of the South: Justice against Epistemicide* (London: Routledge)

Sargeant, J. (2020) 'The Sewel Convention has been broken by Brexit – reform is now urgent', *Institute for Government*, 21 January, https://www.instituteforgov ernment.org.uk/blog/sewel-convention-has-been-broken-brexit-reform-now-urgent (A: 07.09.22)

Sasse, T., Rutter, J., Shepheard, M. and Norris, E. (2020) *Net Zero: How Government Can Meet Its Climate Change Target* (London: Institute for Government), https://www.instituteforgovernment.org.uk/publications/net-zero (A: 12.07.22)

Saunders, C., Roth, S. and Olcese, C. (2015) 'Anti-cuts protests in the UK: Are we really all in this together?' in Giugni, M. and Grasso, M. (eds) *Austerity and Protest: Popular Contention in Times of Economic Crisis* (Ashgate: Farnham), 171–190

Savage, M. (2021) *The Return of Inequality* (London: Harvard University Press)

Savanta ComRes (2020) 'Coronavirus data tracker', 26 May, https://savanta.com/coronavirus-data-tracker/ (A: 26.05.20)

Sayce, L. and Lawson, A. (2017) 'The implications of Brexit for disability rights: Influencing future debate and policy', *Disability Rights UK*, https://www.disabilityrightsuk.org/news/2017/june/our-manifesto-disability-rights-post-eu-uk (A: 08.09.22)

Scarman, Lord (1981) *The Scarman Report* (London: HM Government)

Schattschneider, E.E. (1960) *The Semi-Sovereign People* (Fort Worth: Harcourt Brace, 1975 edition)

Scheyer, V. and Kumskova, M. (2019) 'Feminist foreign policy', *Journal of International Affairs*, 72, 2, 57–76, https://www.jstor.org/stable/26760832

Schipani, V. (2017) 'Trump on the Paris Agreement', *Factcheck.org*, 5 May, https://www.factcheck.org/2017/05/trump-paris-agreement/?gclid=Cj0KCQjw06OTBhC_ARIsAAU1yOW_9yFxbCA1EUfukiLE5I2RWFltxkbPpGD99_nPeFLI7t44o mvWPPsaArebEALw_wcB (A: 27.04.22)

Schmidt, S.K. (2020) 'No match made in heaven: Parliamentary sovereignty, EU over-constitutionalization and Brexit', *Journal of European Public Policy*, 27, 5, 779–794, https://doi.org/10.1080/13501763.2020.1733635

Schnapper, P. (2015) 'Tony Blair's leadership style in foreign policy: Hubris without constraints?' in Alexandre-Collier, A.A. and Chantal, F.V. (eds) *Leadership and Uncertainty Management in Politics* (London: Springer), 51–64

Schnapper, P. (2020) 'Theresa May, the Brexit negotiations and the two-level game, 2017–2019', *Journal of Contemporary European Studies*, 29, 3, 368–379, https://doi.org/10.1080/14782804.2020.1753665

Schneider, A. and Ingram, H. (1993) 'Social construction of target populations: Implications for politics and policy', *American Political Science Review*, 87, 2, 334–347

Schneider, A. and Ingram, H. (1997) *Policy Design for Democracy* (Lawrence: University Press of Kansas)

Schneider, A. and Ingram, H. (eds) (2005) *Deserving and Entitled: Social Construction and Public Policy* (Albany: State University of New York Press)

Schneider, A., Ingram, H. and deLeon, P. (2014) 'Democratic policy design: Social construction of target populations' in Sabatier, P. and Weible, C. (eds) *Theories of the Policy Process*, 3rd edn (Chicago: Westview), 105–149

Schroeder, G. (2022) 'Opposition to the Iraq War', *gerhard-schroeder.de*, https://gerhard-schroeder.de/en/war-peace/iraq-war/ (A: 07.10.22)

Schuster, L. and Bloch, A. (2005) 'Asylum policy under New Labour', *Benefits*, 13, 2, 115–118

Scott, E. (2020) 'Leicester lockdown: Changes since July 2020', *House of Lords Library*, https://lordslibrary.parliament.uk/leicester-lockdown-changes-since-july-2020/ (A: 06.04.22)

Scott, E. (2023) 'Mortality rates among men and women: impact of austerity', *House of Lords Library*, 6 January, https://lordslibrary.parliament.uk/mortality-rates-among-men-and-women-impact-of-austerity/ (A: 02.05.23)

Scott, I. and Gong, T. (2021) 'Coordinating government silos: Challenges and opportunities', *Global Public Policy and Governance*, 1, 12–38, https://doi.org/10.1007/s43508-021-00004-z

Scott, J. (2023) "Sir Keir Starmer calls for London mayor to 'reflect' on ULEZ after by-election loss as Sadiq Khan stands by policy", Sky News, 21 July, https://news.sky.com/story/london-mayor-stands-by-ulez-expansion-after-uxbridge-by-election-loss-12924859 (A: 7.8.23)

Scott, M. (2023) 'Brexit: Winners and losers', *Investopedia*, 28 June, https://www.investopedia.com/news/brexit-winners-and-losers/ (A: 11.07.23)

Scott, P. F. (2020) 'Responding to COVID-19 in Scots law', *Edinburgh Law Review*, 24, 3, 421–426, https://doi.org/10.3366/elr.2020.0657

Scott, S.V. and Ambler, O. (2007) 'Does legality *really* matter? Accounting for the decline in US foreign policy legitimacy following the 2003 invasion of Iraq', *European Journal of International Relations*, 13, 1, 67–87, https://doi.org/10.1177/13540661070742

Scottish Government (2009) *Review of Policy Making* (Edinburgh: Scottish Government)

Scottish Government (2019) 'Challenging UK austerity and uncertainty', https://www.gov.scot/news/challenging-uk-austerity-and-uncertainty/#:~:text="Austerity%20is%20a%20choice%20-%20and,as%20much%20certainty%20as%20possible (A: 09.09.22)

Scottish Government (2022a) 'School meals', https://www.mygov.scot/school-meals (A: 15.09.22)

Scottish Government (2022b) 'Income tax rates and personal allowances', 11 July, https://www.mygov.scot/income-tax-rates-and-personal-allowances (A: 04.10.22)

Scottish Government (2022c) 'Using intersectionality in policy making and analysis: summary findings', 9 March, https://www.gov.scot/publications/using-intersectionality-policy making-analysis-summary-findings/documents/ (A: 26.09.22)

Scottish Parliament (2023) *A Parliament for All: Report of the Parliament's Gender Sensitive Audit* (Edinburgh: Scottish Parliament), https://www.parliament.scot/-/media/files/spcb/gender-sensitive-audit.pdf (A: 13.07.23)

Secretary of State for Northern Ireland (1998) *The Belfast Agreement* (CM 3883) (London: HMSO), https://assets.publishing.service.gov.uk/government/uploads/system/uploads/attachment_data/file/1034123/The_Belfast_Agreement_An_Agreement_Reached_at_the_Multi-Party_Talks_on_Northern_Ireland.pdf (A: 28.05.23)

Seith, E. (2021) 'Why is it so hard to close the attainment gap?', *TES*, 26 March, https://www.tes.com/magazine/teaching-learning/general/why-it-so-hard-close-attainment-gap (A: 19.09.22)

Seldon, A. and Newell, R. (2023) *Johnson at 10: The Inside Story* (London: Atlantic)

Sewell, T., Aderin-Pocock, M., Chugtai, A., Fraser, F., Khalid, N., Moyo, D., Murocki, M., Oliver, M. and Shah, S. (2021) 'Commission on Race and Ethnic Disparities: The report', *Commission on Race and Ethnic Disparities* (London: HM Government), https://assets.publishing.service.gov.uk/government/uploads/system/uploads/attachment_data/file/974507/20210331_-_CRED_Report_-_FINAL_-_Web_Accessible.pdf (A: 08.07.23)

Seymour-Butler, A. (2019) 'Escaping the sunken place: Indefinite detention, asylum seekers and resistance in Yarl's Wood, IRC', *Denning Law Journal*, 31, 167–186

Shaikh, F. (2009) 'CBI says debt reduction a false political dividing line', *Reuters*, https://www.reuters.com/article/britain-cbi-idUKLNE5AJ00220091120 (A: 09.09.22)

Shaikh, F. and Milliken, D. (2010) 'Osborne says Greece is warning to UK', *Reuters*, 28 April, https://www.reuters.com/article/britain-election-osborne-idUKLNE63R06Y20100428 (A: 11.07.23)

Shaw, C., Hurth, V., Capstick, S. and Cox, E. (2018) 'Intermediaries' perspectives on the public's role in the energy transitions needed to deliver UK climate change policy goals', *Energy Policy*, 116, 267–276, https://doi.org/10.1016/j.enpol.2018.02.002

Shaw, E. (2018) 'The Labour party and the egalitarian project' in Fée, D. and Kober-Smith, A. (eds) *Inequalities in the UK* (Bingley: Emerald), 149–165

Shaw, J. and Docherty, I. (2008) 'New deal or no new deal? A decade of "sustainable transport" in the UK' in Shaw, I. and Docherty, I. (eds) *Traffic Jam* (Bristol: Policy Press), 3–28

Shaw, J. and Docherty, I. (2014) *The Transport Debate* (Bristol: Policy Press)

Shaw, J. and Docherty, I. (2019) 'Transport matters' in Docherty, I. and Shaw, J. (eds) *Transport Matters* (Bristol: Policy Press), 3–28

Shaw, J., MacKinnon, D. and Docherty, I. (2009) 'Divergence or convergence? Devolution and transport policy in the United Kingdom', *Environment and Planning C: Government and Policy*, 27, 3, 546–567, https://doi.org/10.1068/c0899r

Shaw, K. and Robinson, F. (2019) 'Whatever happened to the North East? Reflections on the end of regionalism in England', *Local Economy: The Journal of the Local Economy Policy Unit*, 33, 6, 842–861, https://doi.org/10.1177/0269094218819789

Sheldon, J. and Kenny, M. (2020) 'Why have the UK's governments diverged on easing lockdown?' *Centre on Constitutional Change*, 11 May, https://www.centreonconstitutionalchange.ac.uk/news-and-opinion/uks-governments-diverged-easing-lockdown (A: 15.05.20)

Shih, V. (2021) 'China's Leninist response to COVID-19 from information repression to total mobilization' in Greer, S., King, E., Massard de Fonseca, E. and Peralta-Santos, A. (eds) *Coronavirus Politics: The Comparative Politics and Policy of COVID-19* (Ann Arbor: University of Michigan), https://doi.org/10.3998/mpub.11927713

Shilliam, R. (2018) *Race and the Underserving Poor* (Newcastle: Agenda)

Shilliam, R. (2021) *Decolonizing Politics: An Introduction* (London: Polity)

Shiner, M., Carre, Z., Delsol, R. and Eastwood, N. (2018) 'The colour of injustice: 'Race', drugs and law enforcement in England and Wales', *Stopwatch, the London School of Economics,* and *Release*, https://www.lse.ac.uk/united-states/Assets/Documents/The-Colour-of-Injustice.pdf (A: 26.09.22)

Short, C. (2005) *An Honourable Deception? New Labour, Iraq, and the Misuse of Power* (London: Simon & Schuster)

Sibert, A. (2009) 'Assessment of the banking rescue packages of the member states: The case of the United Kingdom', *Birkbeck University and CEPR*, www.annesibert.co.uk/bankingpackages.pdf (A: 09.09.22)

Simcock, N., Walker, G. and Day, R. (2016) 'Fuel poverty in the UK: Beyond heating', *People, Place and Policy*, 10, 1, 25–41, https://doi.org/10.3351/ppp.0010.0001.0003

Simon, H. (1976) *Administrative Behavior*, 3rd edn (London: Macmillan)

Sinclair, I. and Doherty, A. (2013) 'Reconsidering the failure of the anti-Iraq War march', *Open Democracy*, 15 February, https://www.opendemocracy.net/en/opendemocracyuk/reconsidering-failure-of-anti-iraq-war-march/ (A: 27.09.22)

Sinclair, S. (2022) 'Challenges to the strategic state: Welfare reform lessons from a devolved polity', *Journal of Social Policy*, 1–18, https://doi.org/10.1017/S004727942200068X

Siow, O. (2023) 'Needles in a haystack: An intersectional analysis of the descriptive, constitutive and substantive representation of minoritised women', *European Journal of Politics and Gender*, 1–31, DOI: 10.1332/251510821X16739744241737

Sisters Uncut (2022) '"Police are the perpetrators": Sisters Uncut set to take action one year on from Clapham Common vigil', https://www.sistersuncut.org/2022/03/07/police-are-the-perpetrators-sisters-uncut-set-to-take-action-one-year-on-from-clapham-common-vigil/ (A: 28.09.22)

Skelcher, C. (2000) 'Changing images of the state: Overloaded, hollowed-out, congested', *Public Policy and Administration*, 15, 3, 3–19

Skidelsky, R. (2017) 'How would Keynes have analysed the Great Recession of 2008 and 2009?', https://robertskidelsky.com/2017/06/30/how-would-keynes-have-analysed-the-great-recession-of-2008-and-2009/ (A: 09.09.22)

Skleparis, D. (2020) '"All animals are equal": The relationship between the Cummings row and public trust in democracy', *LSE British Politics and Policy*, 3 June, https://blogs.lse.ac.uk/politicsandpolicy/trust-in-democracy-lockdown/ (A: 13.07.20)

Slaven, M. (2022) 'The Windrush Scandal and the individualization of postcolonial immigration control in Britain', *Ethnic and Racial Studies*, 45, 16, 49–71, https://doi.org/10.1080/01419870.2021.2001555

Sloane, W. (2021) 'Racism in the media', *London Metropolitan University*, https://www.londonmet.ac.uk/news/expert-commentary/2021/march/racism-in-the-media/ (A: 26.09.22)

Smith, B. (2022) 'Stop burning the world's forests for energy', *RSPB*, https://www.rspb.org.uk/about-the-rspb/about-us/media-centre/press-releases/bioenergy-report-may-2022/ (A: 04.07.22)

Smith, C. (2015) *Writing Public Policy* (Oxford: Oxford University Press)

Smith, J. (2022) 'Representation in times of crisis: Women's executive presence and gender-sensitive policy responses to crises', *Journal of European Public Policy*, 1–27, https://doi.org/10.1080/13501763.2022.2110142

Smith, K. (2013) *Beyond Evidence Based Policy in Public Health: The Interplay of Ideas* (London: Palgrave)

Smith, K. and Larimer, C. (2009) *The Public Policy Theory Primer* (Boulder: Westview Press)

Smith, L.T. (2012) *Decolonizing Methodologies*, 2nd edn (London: Zed Books)

Smith, M. (2020a) 'Public overwhelmingly backs the government's new measures to tackle coronavirus', *YouGov*, 24 March, https://yougov.co.uk/topics/health/articles-reports/2020/03/24/public-overwhelmingly-backs-governments-new-measur (A: 17.03.22)

Smith, M. (2020b) 'COVID-19: Four in ten Brits think we need a tougher lockdown', *YouGov*, 3 April, https://yougov.co.uk/topics/health/articles-reports/2020/04/03/covid-19-four-ten-brits-think-we-need-tougher-lock (A: 17.03.22)

Smith, M. (2022) 'Public opinion of Boris Johnson's competence and trustworthiness reach new lows', *YouGov*, 22 February, https://yougov.co.uk/topics/politics/articles-reports/2022/02/22/public-opinion-boris-johnsons-competence-and-trust (A: 23.03.22)

Smith, T. (2012) *America's Mission: The United States and the Worldwide Struggle for Democracy*, expanded edn (Princeton: Princeton University Press)

Smout, A. and Maclellan, K. (2022) 'Factbox: The many scandals of Boris Johnson's premiership', *Reuters*, 7 July, https://www.reuters.com/world/uk/many-scandals-boris-johnsons-premiership-2022-07-06/ (A: 20.04.23)

SNP (Scottish National Party) (2022) 'Scottish taxpayers get the best value in the UK', *SNP*, 6 April, https://www.snp.org/scottish-taxpayers-get-the-best-value-in-the-uk/ (A: 04.10.22)

Sobolewska, M. and Ford, R. (2020) *Brexitland* (Cambridge: Cambridge University Press)

Social Mobility Commission (2021) *Navigating the Labyrinth: Socio-economic Background and Career Progression within the Civil Service* (London: SMC)

Sokhi-Bulley, B. (2016) 'Re-reading the riots: Counter-conduct in London 2011', *Global Society*, 2, 320–339, https://doi.org/10.1080/13600826.2016.1143348

Solar, O. and Urwin, A. (2010) *A Conceptual Framework for Action on the Social Determinants of Health* (Geneva: WHO)

Somerville, P. (2021) 'The continuing failure of UK climate change mitigation policy', *Critical Social Policy*, 41, 4, 628–650, https://doi.org/10.1177/02610 18320961762

Sørensen, E. and Torfing, J. (2009) 'Making governance networks effective and democratic through metagovernance', *Public Administration*, 87, 2, 234–258

Sorrentino, M., Sicilia, M. and Howlett, M. (2018) 'Understanding co-production as a new public governance tool', *Policy and Society*, 37, 3, 277–293, https://doi.org/10.1080/14494035.2018.1521676

Spencer, A. and Oppermann, K. (2020) 'Narrative genres of Brexit: The Leave campaign and the success of romance', *Journal of European Public Policy*, 5, 666–684, https://doi.org/10.1080/13501763.2019.1662828

Spiegelhalter, D. and Masters, A. (2021) *Covid by Numbers: Making Sense of the Pandemic with Data* (London: Pelican)

Squires, J. and Wickham-Jones, M. (2004) 'New Labour, gender mainstreaming and the women and equality unit', *British Journal of Politics and International Relations*, 6, 1, 81–98, https://doi.org/10.1111/j.1467-856X.2004.00128.x

Squires, P. and Stephen, D. (2005) 'Rethinking ASBOs', *Critical Social Policy*, 25, 4, 517–528, https://doi.org/10.1177/0261018305057038

Sridhar, D. (2020) 'The pandemic is not over – we need to push now for a zero-coronavirus Britain', *The Guardian*, 22 June, https://www.theguardian.com/commentisfree/2020/jun/22/pandemic-zero-coronavirus-britain (A: 07.04.22)

Sridhar, D. (2022) 'Now that science has defanged Covid, it's time to get on with our lives', *The Guardian*, 19 January, https://www.theguardian.com/commentisfree/2022/jan/19/science-covid-ineradicable-disease-prevention (A: 07.04.22)

Stacey, K. and Goff, S. (2012) 'Darling considered full RBS nationalisation', *Financial Times*, 2 August, https://www.ft.com/content/65173a4c-dca6-11e1-bbdc-00144feab49a (A: 01.09.22)

Stanley, B. (2008) 'The thin ideology of populism', *Journal of Political Ideologies*, 1, 95–110, https://doi.org/10.1080/13569310701822289

Startin, N. (2015) 'Have we reached a tipping point? The mainstreaming of Euroscepticism in the UK', *International Political Science Review*, 36, 3, 311–323, https://doi.org/10.1177/0192512115574126

Stein, P. (2019) *The Stonewall Riots: A Documentary History* (New York: New York University Press)

Stern, N. (2006) *The Economics of Climate Change: The Stern Review* (London: HM Treasury), https://webarchive.nationalarchives.gov.uk/ukgwa/20100407172811/https:/www.hm-treasury.gov.uk/stern_review_report.htm (A: 14.08.22)

Stevelink, S., Jones, M., Hull, L., Pernet, D., MacCrimmon, S., Goodwin, L., MacManus, D., Murphy, D., Jones, N., Greenberg, N., Rona, R.J., Fear, N.T. and Wessely, S. (2018) 'Mental health outcomes at the end of the British involvement in the Iraq and Afghanistan conflicts: A cohort study', *The British Journal of Psychiatry: The Journal of Mental Science*, 213, 6, 690–697, https://doi.org/10.1192/bjp.2018.175

Stevens, A. (2019) ' "Being human" and the "moral sidestep" in drug policy: Explaining government inaction on opioid-related deaths in the UK', *Addictive Behaviors*, 90, 444–450

Stevens, R. (2004) 'The evolution of privatisation as an electoral policy, c.1970–90', *Contemporary British History*, 18, 2, 47–75

Stevenson, J. (2017) 'Does Brexit threaten peace in Northern Ireland?', *Survival: Global Politics and Strategy*, 69, 3, 111–128, https://doi.org/10.1080/00396338.2017.1325606

Stewart, H. (2012) 'George Osborne's austerity is costing UK an extra £76bn, says IMF', *The Guardian*, 13 October, https://www.theguardian.com/business/2012/oct/13/imf-george-osborne-austerity-76bn (A: 09.09.22)

Stewart, M. (2019) 'Preventable harm: Creating a mental health crisis', *Journal of Public Mental Health*, 18, 4, 224–230, https://doi.org/10.1108/JPMH-07-2019-0070

Stewart, M. (2022) 'The public health crisis created by UK social policy reforms', *Justice, Power and Resistance*, 1–12, https://doi.org/10.1332/GQDH4178

Steyn, J. (2004) 'Guantanamo Bay: The legal black hole', *International & Comparative Law Quarterly*, 53, 1, 1–15

Stoker, G. (2001) *The Politics of Local Government*, 2nd edn (London: Macmillan)

Stoker, G. (2004) *Transforming Local Governance: From Thatcherism to New Labour* (London: Palgrave)

Stoker, G. (2006) *Why Politics Matters: Making Democracy Work* (Basingstoke: Palgrave Macmillan)

Stone, D. (2012) *Policy Paradox*, 3rd edn (London: Norton)

Stone, D. (2017) 'Understanding the transfer of policy failure: Bricolage, experimentalism and translation', *Policy & Politics*, 45, 1, 55–70

Stothard, M. (2011) 'UK secretly supplied Saddam', *The Financial Times*, 30 December, https://archive.ph/dRqyu#selection-1615.0-1626.0 (A: 07.10.22)

Stratton, A. (2010) 'Edlington case is symptom of "broken society", says David Cameron', *The Guardian*, 22 January, https://www.theguardian.com/politics/2010/jan/22/david-cameron-edlington-broken-society (A: 26.09.22)

Straw, J. (2013) *Last Man Standing: Memoirs of a Political Survivor* (London: Pan Books)

Streeck, W. and Thelen, K. (2005) 'Introduction: Institutional change in advanced political economies' in Streeck, W. and Thelen, K. (eds) *Beyond Continuity: Institutional Change in Advanced Political Economies* (Oxford: Oxford University Press), 1–39

Strong, J. (2015) 'Why parliament now decides on war: Tracing the growth of the parliamentary prerogative through Syria, Libya and Iraq', *British Journal of Politics and International Relations*, 17, 4, 604–622, https://doi.org/10.1111/1467-856X.12055

Strong, J. (2017) *Public Opinion, Legitimacy and Tony Blair's War in Iraq* (London: Routledge)

Studlar, D. and Cairney, P. (2014) 'Conceptualizing punctuated and non-punctuated policy change: Tobacco control in comparative perspective', *International Review of Administrative Sciences*, 80, 3, 513–531, https://doi.org/10.1177/0020852313517997

Studlar, D. and Cairney, P. (2019) 'Multilevel governance, public health and the regulation of food: Is tobacco control policy a model?', *Journal of Public Health Policy*, 40, 2, 147–165

Sturgeon, N. (2022) 'Pleased to confirm today that the Scottish Child Payment – the most significant anti poverty measure in the UK – will rise to £25 per eligible child per week, and be extended to children up to age 16, from 14 November', *Twitter*, 6 September, https://twitter.com/NicolaSturgeon/status/1567061069742460928 (A: 14.09.22)

Sumption, M. and Kierans, D. (2021) 'Integration in the UK and the post-Brexit immigration system', *The Oxford Migration Observatory*, https://migrationobservatory.ox.ac.uk/wp-content/uploads/2021/03/COMPAS-Commentary-Integration-in-the-UK-and-the-Post-Brexit-immigration-system.pdf (A: 08.09.22)

Sundin, J., Forbes, H., Fear, N.T., Dandeker, C. and Wessley, S. (2011) 'The impact of the conflicts of Iraq and Afghanistan: A UK perspective', *International Review of Psychiatry*, 23, 2, 153–159, https://doi.org/10.3109/09540261.2011.561303

Sutterlüty, F. (2014) 'The hidden morale of the 2005 French and 2011 English riots', *Thesis Eleven*, 121, 1, 38–56, https://doi.org/10.1177/0725513614528784

Swann, W. and Kim, S. (2018) 'Practical prescriptions for governing fragmented governments', *Policy and Politics*, 46, 2, 273–292

Swatridge, C. (2021) 'Was Erasmus altogether too European?', *L'Europe Unie*, 16, 16–21, https://www.ceeol.com/search/article-detail?id=997686

Swiszczowski, L. (2022) 'We need to talk about racism in the UK education system', *Teach First*, 9 March, https://www.teachfirst.org.uk/blog/racism-uk-schools (A: 26.09.22)

Swords, B. and Sheni, R. (2022a) *Systemic Change Required. Black Lived Reality: Why We Need Systemic Change* (London: Black Equity Organisation and Clearview Research), https://blackequityorg.com/wp-content/uploads/2022/09/Systemic-change-required-V10.pdf (A: 17.09.22)

Swords, B. and Sheni, R. (2022b) *'Brick Wall after Brick Wall': The Lived Realities and Concerns of Black Communities in the UK* (London: Black Equity Organisation and Clearview Research), https://blackequityorg.com/black-voices-reports/ (A: 12.08.22)

Sykes, O. (2018) 'Post-geography worlds, new dominions, left behind regions, and "other" places: Unpacking some spatial imaginaries of the UK's "Brexit" debate', *Space and Polity*, 22, 2, 137–161

Syval, R. (2022) 'Calls for safe routes to UK as arrivals by small boat treble in a year', *The Guardian*, 4 January, https://www.theguardian.com/uk-news/2022/jan/04/calls-for-safe-routes-to-uk-as-arrivals-by-small-boat-treble-in-a-year (A: 20.04.23)

Tailby, S. (2012) 'Public service restructuring in the UK: The case of the English National Health Service', *Industrial Relations Journal*, 43, 5, 448–464

Tangney, P. and Howes, M. (2016) 'The politics of evidence-based policy: A comparative analysis of climate adaptation in Australia and the UK', *Environment and Planning C: Government and Policy*, 34, 6, 1115–1134, https://doi.org/10.1177/0263774X15602023

Tarock, A. (1998) *The Superpowers' Involvement in the Iran–Iraq War* (Hauppauge: Nova Science Publishers)

Tatlow, H., Cameron-Blake, E., Grewal, S., Hale, T., Phillips, T. and Wood, A. (2021) 'Variation in the response to COVID-19 across the four nations of the United Kingdom 2.0', *BSG Working Paper Series*, April, https://www.bsg.ox.ac.uk/research/research-projects/covid-19-government-response-tracker (A: 05.04.22)

Taylor, A. (2000) 'Hollowing out or filling in? Taskforces and the management of cross-cutting issues in British government', *British Journal of Politics and International Relations*, 2, 1, 46–71

Taylor-Collins, E. and Downe, J. (2021) 'The local government response to austerity in a small devolved country: The case of Wales', *Local Government Studies*, 1–23, https://doi.org/10.1080/03003930.2021.1996357

Taylor-Gooby, P. (2012a) 'Overview: Resisting welfare state restructuring in the UK', *Journal of Poverty and Social Justice*, 119–132, https://doi.org/10.1332/175982712X652023

Taylor-Gooby, P. (2012b) 'Root and branch restructuring to achieve major cuts: The social policy programme of the 2010 UK coalition government', *Social Policy and Administration*, 46, 1, 61–82, https://doi.org/10.1111/j.1467-9515.2011.00797.x

Taylor-Gooby, P. (2016) 'The divisive welfare state', *Social Policy and Administration*, 50, 6, 712–733, https://doi.org/10.1111/spol.12257

Tempest, M. (2003) 'Labour MPs revolt over Iraq', *The Guardian*, 26 February, https://www.theguardian.com/politics/2003/feb/26/foreignpolicy.uk2 (A: 07.10.22)

Tempest, M. (2005) 'Davis pledges two EU referendums', *The Guardian*, 2 November, https://www.theguardian.com/politics/2005/nov/02/toryleadership2005.conservatives (A: 07.09.22)

Tereshchenko, A., Mills, M. and Bradbury, A. (2020) *Making Progress? Employment and Retention of BAME Teachers in England* (London: UCL Institute of Education), https://discovery.ucl.ac.uk/id/eprint/10117331/ (A: 15.08.22)

Terrence Higgins Trust (2022) 'About HIV', https://www.tht.org.uk/hiv-and-sexual-health/about-hiv (A: 15.09.22)

Terry, G. (2009) 'No climate justice without gender justice: An overview of the issues', *Gender & Development*, 17, 1, 5–18, https://doi.org/10.1080/135520 70802696839

Thapar, C. (2021) *Cut Short: Why We're Failing Our Youth – and How to Fix It* (London: Penguin)

Tharoor, I. (2021) 'The world 9/11 created: What if the U.S. had not invaded Iraq?', *The Washington Post*, 9 September, https://www.washingtonpost.com/world/2021/09/09/911-us-invasion-iraq-counterfactual/ (A: 07.10.22)

Thatcher, M. (1988) 'Speech to the College of Europe ("The Bruges Speech")', *Margaret Thatcher Foundation*, https://www.margaretthatcher.org/document/107332 (A: 07.09.22)

Thatcher, M. (1993) *The Downing Street Years* (London: HarperCollins)

Theis, D.R. and White, M. (2021) 'Is obesity policy in England fit for purpose? Analysis of government strategies and policies, 1992–2020', *The Milbank Quarterly*, 99, 1, 126–170, https://doi.org/10.1111/1468-0009.12498

Thevoz, S. (2022) 'How Jacob Rees-Mogg's new Brexit post could make him richer', *Open Democracy*, 9 February, https://www.opendemocracy.net/en/opendemocracyuk/jacob-rees-moggs-new-brexit-post-make-him-richer/ (A: 08.09.22)

Thomas, C. (2019) 'Hitting the poorest worst? How public health cuts have been experienced in England's most deprived communities', *IPPR*, https://www.ippr.org/blog/public-health-cuts (A: 09.09.22)

Thomas, O.D. (2017) 'Good faith and (dis)honest mistakes? Learning from Britain's Iraq War Inquiry', *Politics*, 37, 4, 371–385, http://dx.doi.org/10.1177/0263395716688488

Thompson, D. (2012) 'Tuition fees: David Blunkett recalls introduction', *BBC News*, 2 March, https://www.bbc.co.uk/news/av/uk-politics-17223282 (A: 09.09.22)

Thompson, H. (1995) 'Joining the ERM: Analysing a core executive policy disaster' in Rhodes, R. and Dunleavy, P. (eds) *Prime Minister, Cabinet and Core Executive* (Basingstoke: Palgrave), 248–274

Thompson, H. (1996) 'Economic policy under Thatcher and Major' in Ludlam, S. and Smith, M. (eds) *Contemporary British Conservatism* (London: Macmillan), 166–184

Thompson, H. (2015) 'A crisis of the financial sector' in Richards, D., Smith, M. and Hay, C. (eds) *Institutional Crisis in 21st-Century Britain* (London: Palgrave), 181–197

Thompson, H. (2017a) 'Inevitability and contingency: The political economy of Brexit', *The British Journal of Politics and International Relations*, 19, 3, 434–449

Thompson, H. (2017b) *Oil and the Western Economic Crisis (Building a Sustainable Political Economy)* (Sheffield: SPERI Research & Policy)

Thompson, L. and Clement, R. (2019) 'Defining feminist foreign policy', *International Center for Research on Women*, 1–7, http://www.icrw.org/wp-cont ent/uploads/2019/03/Defining-Feminist-Foreign-Policy-Brief_web-version. pdf (A: 10.10.22)

Thomson, J. (2020) 'What's feminist about feminist foreign policy? Sweden's and Canada's foreign policy agendas', *International Studies Perspectives*, 21, 4, 424–437, https://doi.org/10.1093/isp/ekz032

Thornton, D. (2016) 'The UK in Iraq: A case study in policy failure?', *Institute for Government*, 13 July, https://www.instituteforgovernment.org.uk/blog/uk-iraq-case-study-policy-failure (A: 07.10.22)

Threlfall, D. and Althaus, C. (2021) 'A quixotic quest? Making theory speak to practice' in Mercer, T., Head, B. and Wanna, J. (eds) *Learning Policy, Doing Policy: How Do Theories about Policy Making Influence Practice?* (Canberra: ANU Press), 29–48

Tilley, L., Ranawana, A., Baldwin, A. and Tully, T. (2022) 'Race & climate change: Towards anti-racist ecologies', *Politics*, 1–12, https://doi.org/10.1177/02633957221127166

Timmins, N. (2016) *Universal Credit: From Disaster to Recovery* (London: Institute for Government), https://www.instituteforgovernment.org.uk/sites/default/files/publications/5064%20IFG%20-%20Universal%20Credit%20Publicat ion%20WEB%20AW.pdf (A: 05.04.22)

Tiratelli, M. (2021) 'Crowds, police and provocations: Temporal patterns of rioting in Britain, 1800–1939', *Sociology*, 56, 4, 749–765, https://doi.org/10.1177/00380385211058027

Tisdall, E.K.M. and Morrison, F. (2022) 'Children's human rights under COVID-19: Learning from children's rights impact assessments', *The International Journal of Human Rights*, https://doi.org/10.1080/13642987.2022.2036135

Toke, D. (2011) 'The UK offshore wind power programme: A sea-change in UK energy policy?', *Energy Policy*, 39, 2, 526–534

Toke, D., Sherry-Brennan, F., Cowell, R., Ellis, G. and Strachan, P. (2013) 'Scotland, renewable energy and the independence debate: Will head or heart rule the roost?', *The Political Quarterly*, 84, 1, 61–70, https://doi.org/10.1111/j.1467-923X.2013.02431.x

Tol, R.S. (2001) 'Equitable cost-benefit analysis of climate change policies', *Ecological Economics*, 36, 1, 71–85, https://doi.org/10.1016/S0921-8009(00)00204-4

Tonge, J. (2013) *Northern Ireland: Conflict and Change*, 2nd edn (London: Routledge)

Tonkiss, K. and Skelcher, C. (2015) 'Abolishing the Audit Commission: Framing, discourse coalitions and administrative reform', *Local Government Studies*, 41, 6, 861–880, https://doi.org/10.1080/03003930.2015.1050093

Torrance, D. (2020) *EU Powers after Brexit: 'Power Grab' or 'Power Surge'?* (London: House of Commons Library), https://commonslibrary.parliament.uk/eu-powers-after-brexit-power-grab-or-power-surge/ (A: 14.07.22)

Torrance, D. (2022a) *Devolution in Northern Ireland* (House of Commons Library Research Briefing CBP-8438), https://researchbriefings.files.parliament.uk/documents/CBP-8439/CBP-8439.pdf (A: 25.08.22)

Torrance, D. (2022b) 'Supreme Court judgment on Scottish independence referendum', *House of Commons Library*, 23 November, https://commonslibrary.parliament.uk/supreme-court-judgment-on-scottish-independence-referendum/ (A: 02.05.23)

Torrance, D. and Pyper, D. (2023) *The Secretary of State's Veto and the Gender Recognition Reform (Scotland) Bill* (House of Commons Library Research Briefing CBP-9705), https://researchbriefings.files.parliament.uk/documents/CBP-9705/CBP-9705.pdf (A: 17.05.23)

Tosun, J. (2013) 'How the EU handles uncertain risks: Understanding the role of the precautionary principle', *Journal of European Public Policy*, 2, 10, 1517–1528, https://doi.org/10.1080/13501763.2013.834549

Total Politics (2011) 'Nick Clegg's riot work programme', 16 August, https://www.totalpolitics.com/articles/news/nick-cleggs-riot-work-programme (A: 26.09.22)

Travis, A. (2011a) 'UK riots analysis reveals gangs did not play pivotal role', *The Guardian*, 24 October, https://www.theguardian.com/uk/2011/oct/24/riots-analysis-gangs-no-pivotal-role (A: 26.09.22)

Travis, A. (2011b) 'England riots: Theresa May under fire over proposed police curfew powers', *The Guardian*, 16 August, https://www.theguardian.com/uk/2011/aug/16/england-riots-may-police-curfew (A: 22.09.22)

True, J.L., Jones, B.D. and Baumgartner, F.R. (2007) 'Punctuated equilibrium theory' in Sabatier, P. (ed) *Theories of the Policy Process*, 2nd edn (Cambridge, MA: Westview Press), 155–187

Tucker, J. (2022) 'To say only 17,000 people have died from COVID-19 is highly misleading', *National Statistical, News and Insight from the Office for National Statistics*, 26 January, https://blog.ons.gov.uk/2022/01/26/to-say-only-17000-people-have-died-from-covid-19-is-highly-misleading/ (A: 28.02.22)

Tucker-Jones, A. (2018) *Daesh: Islamic State's Holy War* (Barnsley: Pen and Sword)

Tummers, L.L., Bekkers, V., Vink, E. and Musheno, M. (2015) 'Coping during public service delivery: A conceptualization and systematic review of the literature', *Journal of Public Administration Research and Theory*, 25, 4, 1099–1126

Ture, K. and Hamilton, C.V. (1967) *Black Power: The Politics of Liberation in America* (New York: Vintage Books)

Turley, A. (2023) Twitter, 20 April, https://twitter.com/annaturley/status/1648 663585260810241 (A: 20.04.23)

Turnbull, N. and Hoppe, R. (2018) 'Problematizing "wickedness": A critique of the wicked problems concept, from philosophy to practice', *Policy and Society*, 29, 1–23

Turnbull-Dugarte, S.J. and McMillan, F. (2022) ' "Protect the women!" Trans-exclusionary feminist issue framing and support for transgender rights', *Policy Studies Journal*, https://doi.org/10.1111/psj.12484

Turner, A. (2009) *The Turner Review: A Regulatory Response to the Global Banking Crisis* (London: FSA), http://www.actuaries.org/CTTEES_TFRISKCRISIS/Documents/turner_review.pdf (A: 01.08.22)

UK in a Changing Europe (2021) *Brexit Timeline (Version 3)* (London: UK in a Changing Europe), https://ukandeu.ac.uk/wp-content/uploads/2021/01/UKICE-Timeline-v3.pdf (A: 17.08.22)

UK in a Changing Europe (2022) 'Levelling up: What England thinks', 19 October, https://ukandeu.ac.uk/research-papers/levelling-up-what-england-thinks/ (A: 28.04.23)

UK Government (2022a) 'UK summary: The official UK government website for data and insights on coronavirus (COVID-19)', 28 February, https://coronavirus.data.gov.uk/ (A: 01.03.22)

UK Government (2022b) 'Writing about ethnicity', https://www.ethnicity-facts-figures.service.gov.uk/style-guide/writing-about-ethnicity (A: 03.09.22)

UK Government (2023a) 'Coronavirus (COVID-19) in the UK', https://coronavirus.data.gov.uk/details/deaths (A: 24.03.23)

UK Government (2023b) 'The Windsor Framework: A new way forward', https://assets.publishing.service.gov.uk/government/uploads/system/uploads/attachment_data/file/1138989/The_Windsor_Framework_a_new_way_forward.pdf (A: 20.04.23)

UK Health Security Agency (2022) 'The R value and growth rate', 25 February, https://www.gov.uk/guidance/the-r-value-and-growth-rate#about-r-and-growth-rate (A: 01.03.22)

UKOOG (United Kingdom Onshore Oil and Gas) (2022) 'UKOOG response to reintroduction of moratorium', press release, 28 October, https://www.ukoog.org.uk/about-ukoog/press-releases/260-ukoog-response-to-reintroduction-of-moratorium (A: 26.04.23)

UK Parliament (2022) 'Regulating sex and sexuality: The 20th century', https://www.parliament.uk/about/living-heritage/transformingsociety/private-lives/relationships/overview/sexuality20thcentury/ (A: 15.09.22)

UN (United Nations) (2015) *The Paris Agreement* (New York: UN), https://unfccc.int/sites/default/files/english_paris_agreement.pdf (A: 25.11.22)

UN (2019) 'Visit to the United Kingdom of Great Britain and Northern Ireland Report of the Special Rapporteur on extreme poverty and human rights', https://documents-dds-ny.un.org/doc/UNDOC/GEN/G19/112/13/PDF/G1911213.pdf?OpenElement (A: 09.09.22)

UN (2022) 'What is climate change?', https://www.un.org/en/climatechange/what-is-climate-change (A: 20.04.22)

UN Special Rapporteur on Racism (2018) 'End of mission statement of the special rapporteur on contemporary forms of racism, racial discrimination, xenophobia and related intolerance at the conclusion of her mission to the United Kingdom of Great Britain and Northern Ireland', United Nations Human Rights Office of the High Commissioner, https://www.ohchr.org/en/statements/2018/05/end-mission-statement-special-rapporteur-contemporary-forms-racism-racial (A: 08.09.22)

UN-A UK (2022) 'The Responsibility to Protect. In detail', https://una.org.uk/r2p-detail#:~:text=The%20Responsibility%20to%20Protect%20(R2P,ethnic%20cleansing%20and%20war%20crimes (A: 02.10.22)

Understanding the Civil Service (2021) 'The UK Civil Service – detailed stats', https://www.civilservant.org.uk/information-other_statistics.html (A: 21.09.21)

UNFCCC (United Nations Framework Convention on Climate Change) (2022a) 'Background – cooperation with the IPCC', https://unfccc.int/topics/science/workstreams/cooperation-with-the-ipcc/background-cooperation-with-the-ipcc (A: 20.04.22)

UNFCCC (2022b) 'The Paris Agreement', https://unfccc.int/process-and-meetings/the-paris-agreement/the-paris-agreement (A: 26.04.22)

UNFCCC (2022c) 'Conference of the Parties (COP)', https://unfccc.int/process/bodies/supreme-bodies/conference-of-the-parties-cop (A: 26.04.22)

Unison Wales (2019) 'Shocking picture of austerity cuts to services in Wales revealed by UNISON', https://cymru-wales.unison.org.uk/news/2019/12/shocking-picture-austerity-cuts-services-wales-revealed-unison/ (A: 09.09.22)

Updegraff, J.A., Silver, R.C. and Holman, E.A. (2008) 'Searching for and finding meaning in collective trauma: Results from a national longitudinal study of the 9/11 terrorist attacks', *Journal of Personality and Social Psychology*, 95, 3, 709–722, https://doi.org/10.1037/0022-3514.95.3.709

Urban, J. (2022) 'Mark Fullbrook's No10 arrangement exposes problems with special adviser recruitment', *Institute for Government*, 30 September, https://www.instituteforgovernment.org.uk/blog/mark-fullbrook-no10-arrangement-exposes-problems (A: 06.10.22)

van Eck, C.W. and Feindt, P.H. (2022) 'Parallel routes from Copenhagen to Paris: Climate discourse in climate sceptic and climate activist blogs', *Journal of Environmental Policy & Planning*, 24, 2, 194–209

van Lerven, F. (2021) 'Public debt – the untold story', *New Economics Foundation*, 26 May, https://neweconomics.org/2021/05/public-debt-the-untold-story (A: 02.05.23)

Van Reenan, J. (2013) 'The state of the UK economy: Diagnosis, prognosis and recommended treatment', *LSE Politics and Policy*, 29 December, https://blogs.lse.ac.uk/politicsandpolicy/the-state-of-the-uk-economy-diagnosis-prognosis-and-recommended-treatment/ (A: 09.09.22)

Van Reenan, J. (2016) 'Brexit's long-run effects on the U.K. economy', *Brookings Papers on Economic Activity*, 47, 2, 367–383

Veitch, J. (2005) 'Looking at gender mainstreaming in the UK government', *International Feminist Journal of Politics*, 7, 4, 600–606, https://doi.org/10.1080/14616740500284615

Vernasca, G. (2016) 'The UK's EU rebate – explained', *The Conversation*, 6 June, https://theconversation.com/the-uks-eu-rebate-explained-58019 (A: 09.09.22)

Virdee, S. and McGeever, B. (2017) 'Racism, crisis, Brexit', *Ethnic and Racial Studies*, 41, 10, https://doi.org/10.1080/01419870.2017.1361544

Vivyan, N., Wagner, M. and Tarlov, J. (2012) 'Representative misconduct, voter perceptions and accountability: Evidence from the 2009 House of Commons expenses scandal', *Electoral Studies*, 31, 4, 750–763

Vohra, A. (2023) 'Rishi Sunak's government is anti-asylum', *Foreign Policy*, 12 June, https://foreignpolicy.com/2023/06/12/uk-sunak-asylum-migration-boats/ (A: 11.07.23)

Vote Leave (2016) 'Briefing room', http://www.voteleavetakecontrol.org/briefing.html (A: 17.08.22)

Waddington, D. (2012) 'The law of moments: Understanding the flashpoint that ignited the riots', *Criminal Justice Matters*, 87, 1, 6–7, https://doi.org/10.1080/09627251.2012.670993

Wade, R.H. (2002) 'US hegemony and the World Bank: The fight over people and ideas', *Review of International Political Economy*, 9, 2, 215–243

Wadsworth, J. (2018) 'Off EU go? Brexit, the UK labour market and immigration', *Fiscal Studies: The Journal of Applied Public Economics*, 39, 4, 625–649, https://doi.org/10.1111/1475-5890.12177

Walker, B. (2013) *Up to the Job? How Reforming Jobcentre Plus Will Help Tackle Worklessness* (London: Centre for Social Justice), https://www.centreforsocialjustice.org.uk/wp-content/uploads/2013/08/Up-to-the-Job.pdf (A: 12.07.23)

Walker, J.L. (1969) 'The diffusion of innovations among the American states', *American Political Science Review*, 63, 3, 880–899

Walker, P., Topping, A. and Morris, S. (2020) 'Boris Johnson says removing statues is "to lie about our history" ', *The Guardian*, 12 June, https://www.theguardian.com/politics/2020/jun/12/boris-johnson-says-removing-statues-is-to-lie-about-our-history-george-floyd (A: 26.09.22)

Walker, G. and Day, R. (2012) 'Fuel poverty as injustice: Integrating distribution, recognition and procedure in the struggle for affordable warmth', *Energy Policy*, 49, 69–75, https://doi.org/10.1016/j.enpol.2012.01.044

Walker, T., Foster, A., Majeed-Ariss, R. and Horvath, M.A.H. (2020) 'The justice system is failing victims and survivors of sexual violence', *The Psychologist*, https://eprints.mdx.ac.uk/31570/6/Walker_Foster_Majeed-Ariss_Horvath_%282020%29_FINAL_Pre-Publication_version.pdf (A: 26.09.22)

Walsh, P. (2023) 'Asylum and refugee resettlement in the UK', *The Migration Observatory at the University of Oxford*, 27 January, https://migrationobservatory.ox.ac.uk/resources/briefings/migration-to-the-uk-asylum/#:~:text=Of%20all%20refugees%20resettled%20in,around%2070%25%20were%20Syrian%20citizens.&text=When%20compared%20against%20EU%2B%20countries,asylum%20seekers%20and%20resettled%20refugees (A: 02.05.23)

Wampler, B. (2008) 'When does participatory democracy deepen the quality of democracy? Lessons from Brazil', *Comparative Politics*, 41, 1, 61–81

Ward, B. (2022) 'Managing democracy in Corbyn's Labour Party: Faction-fighting or movement-building?', *British Politics*, 17, 353–365

Ward, J. (2021) 'Reasserting the centre: The Brexit doctrine and the imperative mandate in British politics', *Parliamentary Affairs*, 74, 4, 890–910, https://doi.org/10.1093/pa/gsaa015

Ward, J. and Ward, B. (2021) 'From Brexit to COVID-19: The Johnson government, executive centralisation and authoritarian populism', *Political Studies*, 1–19, https://doi.org/10.1177/00323217211037

Wardle, H. and Obermuller, L.J. (2019) '"Windrush generation" and "hostile environment": Symbols and lived experiences in Caribbean migration to the UK', *Migration and Society*, 2, 81–89, https://doi.org/10.3167/arms.2019.020108

Warmington, P. (2020) 'Critical race theory in England: Impact and opposition', *Identities*, 27, 1, 20–37, https://doi.org/10.1080/1070289X.2019.1587907

Waters, T. and Wernham, T. (2022) 'Reforms, roll-outs and freezes in the tax and benefit system', *Institute for Fiscal Studies*, 6 October, https://ifs.org.uk/publications/reforms-roll-outs-and-freezes-tax-and-benefit-system (A: 06.10.22)

Waterson, J. (2021) 'Society of Editors withdraws claim that UK media is not racist', *The Guardian*, 18 August, https://www.theguardian.com/media/2021/aug/18/society-of-editors-withdraws-claim-that-uk-media-is-not-racist (A: 26.09.22)

Watson, J. and Drummond, P. (2022) 'How has energy policy changed after Brexit?', *UCL Institute for Sustainable Resources*, https://www.ucl.ac.uk/bartlett/sustainable/news/2022/jan/how-has-energy-policy-changed-after-brexit (A: 08.09.22)

Watson, M. (2004) 'Endogenous growth theory: Explanation or post hoc rationalization for policy?', *British Journal of Politics & International Relations*, 6, 4, 543–551

Watson, M. (2009) 'The split personality of prudence in the unfolding political economy of New Labour', *Political Quarterly*, 79, 4, 578–589

Weavers, A. (2021) 'Education Maintenance Allowance (EMA)', *EDGE Foundation*, https://www.edge.co.uk/documents/194/Learning_from_the_past_Paper_No._4_EMA_Final.pdf (A: 09.09.22)

Webster, D. (2002) 'Unemployment: How official statistics distort analysis and policy, and why', *Radical Statistics Journal*, 79, http://www.radstats.org.uk/no079/webster.htm (A: 03.05.22)

Weckroth, M. and Moisio, S. (2018) *D1.2 Review of Discourses of Territorial Inequalities in EU Policies* (Brussels: ERC)

Weckroth, M. and Moisio, S. (2020) 'Territorial cohesion of what and why? The challenge of spatial justice for EU's cohesion policy', *Social Inclusion*, 8, 4, 183–193, http://dx.doi.org/10.17645/si.v8i4.3241

Weerakkody, V. (2021) 'Pandemic shows how "digital by default" government services exclude those who need them most', *The Conversation*, 4 March, https://theconversation.com/pandemic-shows-how-digital-by-default-government-services-exclude-those-who-need-them-most-154215 (A: 11.10.22)

Weible, C. and Ingold, K. (2018) 'Why advocacy coalitions matter and practical insights about them', *Policy & Politics*, 46, 2, 325–343

Weible, C., Sabatier, P. and McQueen, K. (2009) 'Themes and variations: Taking stock of the advocacy coalition framework', *Policy Studies Journal*, 37, 1, 121–141

Weimer, D. and Vining, A. (2017) *Policy Analysis*, 6th edn (London: Routledge)

Wellings, B. and Baxendale, H. (2014) 'Euroscepticism and the Anglosphere: Traditions and dilemmas in contemporary English nationalism', *Journal of Common Market Studies*, 53, 1, 123–139, https://doi.org/10.1111/jcms.12207

Wellings, K. and Wadsworth, J. (1990) 'AIDS and the moral climate' in Jowell, R., Witherspoon, S., Brook, L. and Taylor, B. (eds) *British Social Attitudes: The 7th Report* (Aldershot: Gower Press), 20–40

Welsh Government (2018) 'UK government must end austerity and provide the much-needed funding boost for public services and the economy – Mark Drakeford', https://gov.wales/uk-government-must-end-austerity-and-provide-much-needed-funding-boost-public-services-and-economy (A: 09.09.22)

Welsh Government (2022) 'Universal Primary Free School Meals (UPFSM)', https://gov.wales/universal-primary-free-school-meals-upfsm (A: 15.09.22)

Welsh Government (2023) 'Putting the brakes on carbon emissions, steering towards alternative solutions and driving towards net zero by 2050', press release, 14 February, https://www.gov.wales/putting-brakes-carbon-emissions-steering-towards-alternative-solutions-and-driving-towards-net-zero (A: 26.04.23)

Werner-Muller, J. (2017) *What Is Populism?* (London: Penguin)

West, K. and Stewart-Smith, M. (2023) 'Afghan teacher "abandoned by UK" fears for her life', *BBC News*, 11 January, https://www.bbc.co.uk/news/world-asia-64215445 (A: 29.04.23)

Westwood, A., Sensier, M. and Pike, N. (2022) 'The politics of levelling up: Devolution, institutions and productivity in England', *National Institute Economic Review*, 1–18, https://doi.org/10.1017/nie.2022.29

White, A. (2015) 'The politics of police "privatization": A multiple streams approach', *Criminology & Criminal Justice*, 15, 3, 283–299, https://doi.org/10.1177/1748895814549643

White, A. (2020) 'What is the privatization of policing?', *Policing: A Journal of Policy and Practice*, 14, 3, https://doi.org/10.1093/police/pay085

White, H. (2022) 'How Liz Truss lost trust', *Institute for Government*, 4 October, https://www.instituteforgovernment.org.uk/blog/how-liz-truss-lost-trust (A: 06.10.22)

White, J. (2013) 'Left and right in the economic crisis', *Journal of Political Ideologies*, 18, 2, 150–170, http://dx.doi.org/10.1080/13569317.2013.784006

Whitehead, M. and Dahlgren, G. (2006) 'Concepts and principles for tackling social inequities in health: Levelling up Part 1', *World Health Organization: Studies on Social and Economic Determinants of Population Health*, http://www.euro.who.int/__data/assets/pdf_file/0010/74737/E89383.pdf (A: 03.05.22)

Whitfield, S. and Marshall, A. (2017) 'Defining and delivering "sustainable" agriculture in the UK after Brexit', *International Journal of Agricultural Sustainability*, 15, 5, 501–513, https://doi.org/10.1080/14735903.2017.1337837

Whitmore, C. (2020) 'How Brexit will affect disabled people's lives and rights', *LSE Brexit Blog*, 13 January, https://blogs.lse.ac.uk/brexit/2020/01/13/how-brexit-will-affect-disabled-peoples-lives-and-rights/ (A: 08.09.22)

WHO (World Health Organization) (2020a) 'Coronavirus', https://www.who.int/health-topics/coronavirus (A: 06.04.20)

WHO (2020b) 'Rolling updates on coronavirus disease (COVID-19)', https://www.who.int/emergencies/diseases/novel-coronavirus-2019/events-as-they-happen (A: 18.01.22)

WHO (2022) *Social Determinants of Health* (Geneva: World Health Organization), https://www.who.int/health-topics/social-determinants-of-health#tab=tab_1 (A: 12.09.22)

Wickham, A. (2020) '10 days that changed Britain: "Heated" debate between scientists forced Boris Johnson to act on coronavirus', *Buzzfeed News*, 21 March, https://www.buzzfeed.com/alexwickham/10-days-that-changed-britains-coronavirus-approach (A: 13.05.20)

Wiggan, J. (2018) 'Policy boostering the social impact investment market in the UK', *Cambridge Law Journal*, 47, 4, 721–738, https://doi.org/10.1017/S0047279418000089

Wildavsky, A. (1980) *The Art and Craft of Policy Analysis* (London: Macmillan)

Wilkinson, E. and Ortega-Alcazar, I. (2017) 'A home of one's own? Housing welfare for "young adults" in times of austerity', *Critical Social Policy*, 37, 3, 329–347, https://doi.org/10.1177%2F0261018317699804

Willetts, D. (2019) *The Pinch* (London: Atlantic)

Williams, A., Goodwin, M. and Cloke, P. (2014) 'Neoliberalism, Big Society, and progressive localism', *Environment and Planning*, 46, 12, 2798–2815, https://doi.org/10.1068/a130119p

Williams, B. (2022) 'Black Wednesday: Thirty years on', *Political Insight*, 13, 3, 22–25, https://doi.org/10.1177/20419058221127468

Williams, P. (2004) 'Who's making UK foreign policy?', *International Affairs*, 80, 5, 911–929

Williams, P.D. (2005) *British Foreign Policy Under New Labour, 1997–2005* (London: Routledge), https://doi.org/10.1057/9780230514690

Willis, R. (2017) 'Taming the climate? Corpus analysis of politicians' speech on climate change', *Environmental Politics*, 26, 2, 212–231, https://doi.org/10.1080/09644016.2016.1274504

Wilson, D. (2003) 'Unravelling control freakery: Redefining central–local government relations', *The British Journal of Politics and International Relations*, 5, 3, 317–346

Wilson, G.K. (2017) 'Brexit, Trump and the special relationship', *The British Journal of Politics and International Relations*, 19, 3, 543–557, https://doi.org/10.1177%2F1369148117713719

Wilson, H. and Plesch, D. (2021) 'Three decades on, here's what we've learned about the effectiveness of UN weapons inspections in Iraq', *The Conversation*, 30 March, https://theconversation.com/three-decades-on-heres-what-weve-learned-about-the-effectiveness-of-un-weapons-inspections-in-iraq-156880 (A: 07.10.22)

Wilson Centre (2019) 'Timeline: The rise, spread, and fall of the Islamic State', 28 October, https://www.wilsoncenter.org/article/timeline-the-rise-spread-and-fall-the-islamic-state (A: 07.10.22)

Wing Chan, T., Henderson, M., Sironi, M. and Kawalerowicz, J. (2020) 'Understanding the social and cultural bases of Brexit', *British Journal of Sociology*, 71, 5, 830–851, https://doi.org/10.1111/1468-4446.12790

Wolmar, C. (2008) 'Foreword' in Shaw, I. and Docherty, I. (eds) *Traffic Jam* (Bristol: Policy Press), viii–x

Women's Budget Group (2018) 'Women, employment and earnings', https://wbg.org.uk/wp-content/uploads/2018/10/Employment-October-2018.pdf (A: 09.09.22)

Women's Budget Group (2022) 'An inequality budget unfit for a cost-of-living crisis', 29 September, https://wbg.org.uk/analysis/uk-budget-assessments/an-inequality-budget-unfit-for-a-cost-of-living-crisis/ (A: 11.10.22)

Wood, M. (2015) 'Puzzling and powering in policy paradigm shifts', *Critical Policy Studies*, 9, 1, 2–21, https://doi.org/10.1080/19460171.2014.926825

Woodin, T. (2019) 'Co-operative schools: Democratic values, networks and leadership', *International Journal of Inclusive Education*, 23, 11, 1164–1179, https://doi.org/10.1080/13603116.2019.1617359

World Trade Organization (2022) 'The WTO', https://www.wto.org/english/thewto_e/thewto_e.htm (A: 24.08.22)

Worth, O. (2017) 'Whither Lexit?', *Capital and Class*, 41, 2, 351–357, https://doi.org/10.1177/0309816817711558c

Worthy, B. (2022) 'Will Truss's time end in failure? Assessing the prospects of the latest "takeover" prime minister', *The Political Quarterly*, 93, 4, 717–722, https://doi.org/10.1111/1467-923X.13199

Wren-Lewis, S. (2015) 'The macroeconomic record of the coalition government', *National Institute Economic Review*, 231, 1, R5–R16, https://doi.org/10.1177/002795011523100102

Wright, C. (2010) 'The regulation of European labour mobility: National policy responses to the free movement of labour transition arrangements of recent EU enlargements', *SEER: Journal for Labour and Social Affairs in Eastern Europe*, 13, 2, 157–179 https://www.jstor.org/stable/43293356

Wu, X., Howlett, M., Ramesh, M. and Fritzen, S. (2017) *The Public Policy Primer*, 2nd edn (London: Routledge)

Wyatt, D. (2022) 'Why Keir Starmer has ruled out negotiating a soft Brexit', *LSE British Politics and Policy*, 22 April, https://blogs.lse.ac.uk/politicsandpolicy/why-keir-starmer-has-ruled-out-negotiating-a-soft-brexit/ (A: 07.09.22)

Wyn Jones, R., Lodge, G., Henderson, A. and Wincott, D. (2012) *The Dog that Finally Barked: England as an Emerging Political Community* (London: IPPR)

Yang, H. and Suh, S. (2021) 'Economic disparity among generations under the Paris Agreement', *Nature Communications*, 12, 1, 1–7, https://doi.org/10.1038/s41467-021-25520-8

Yates, C. and MacRury, I. (2022) 'Shameful and shameless: Projecting triumph and humiliation in the Brexit era; a psychosocial-group methodological approach' in Gerodimos, R. (ed) *Interdisciplinary Applications of Shame/Violence Theory* (London: Palgrave), 245–266

Yates, K. (2022) 'Was lockdown necessary?', *British Medical Journal*, 23 March, 376, https://doi.org/10.1136/bmj.o776

YouGov (2022) 'COVID-19: Level of support for actions governments could take' [a tracker with no fixed date], https://yougov.co.uk/topics/international/articles-reports/2020/03/17/level-support-actions-governments-could-take (A: 17.03.22)

Zahariadis, N. (2003) *Ambiguity and Choice in Public Policy* (Washington, DC: Georgetown University Press)

Zalewski, M. (2010) 'Feminist international relations: Making sense' in Shephard, L.J. (ed) *Gender Matters in Global Politics* (London: Routledge)

Zappettini, F. (2021) 'The tabloidization of the Brexit campaign: Power to the (British) people?', *Journal of Language and Politics*, 20, 2, 277–303, https://doi.org/10.1075/jlp.19103.zap

Zappettini, F. and Krzyżanowski, M. (2019) 'The critical juncture of Brexit in media & political discourses: From national-populist imaginary to cross-national social and political crisis', *Critical Discourse Studies*, 16, 4, 381–388, https://doi.org/10.1080/17405904.2019.1592767

Zaunseder, A., Woodman, S. and Emejulu, A. (2022) 'Introducing radical democratic citizenship: From practice to theory', *Identities*, 29, 1, 1–8, https://doi.org/10.1080/1070289X.2021.2013670

Zeeman, L., Sherriff, N., Browne, K., McGlynn, N., Mirandola, M., Gios, L., Davis, R., Sanchez-Lambert, J., Aujean, S., Pinto, N., Farinella, F., Donisi, V., Niedz´wiedzka-Stadnik, M., Rosin´ska, M., Pierson, A. and Amaddeo, F. (Health4LGBTI Network) (2019) 'A review of lesbian, gay, bisexual, trans and intersex (LGBTI) health and healthcare inequalities', *European Journal of Public Health*, 29, 5, 974–980, https://doi.org/10.1093/eurpub/cky226

Zeffman, H. and Woolcock, N. (2023) 'Sir Keir Starmer poised to ditch pledge on free university tuition', *The Times*, 2 May, https://www.thetimes.co.uk/article/sir-keir-starmer-poised-to-ditch-pledge-on-free-university-tuition-77h6s8t3n (A: 02.05.23)

Zichawo, W., Farber, C. and Mensah, L. (2014) 'Child trust funds: Renewing the debate for long-term savings policies', *Initiative on Financial Security at the Aspen Institute*, https://www.aspeninstitute.org/wp-content/uploads/files/content/docs/pubs/Child-Trust-Funds-Renewing-the-Debate-for-Long-Term-Savings.pdf (A: 09.09.22)

Zinn, C.M. (2016) 'Consequences of Iraqi De-Baathification', *Cornell International Affairs Review*, 9, 80–101

Zunes, S. (2001) 'Why the U.S. did not overthrow Saddam Hussein', *Foreign Policy in Focus*, https://fpif.org/why_the_us_did_not_overthrow_saddam_hussein/ (A: 07.10.22)

Index

References to figures appear in *italic* type; those in **bold** types refer to tables.